EDMUND S. MORGAN (BA and PhD, Harvard), Sterling Professor of History at Yale University, is a leading authority on the colonial and revolutionary eras. Several of his books and articles examine Puritan New England.

ROBERT G. POPE (BA, Marietta; PhD, Yale) teaches early American history at the State University of New York at Buffalo. His writings include *The Half-Way Covenant: Church Membership in Puritan New England* (Princeton, 1969).

DARRETT B. RUTMAN (BA, University of Illinois; PhD, University of Virginia) has written extensively on early New England and the Chesapeake colonies. He teaches in the history department at the University of New Hampshire.

DANIEL B. SHEA, JR. (BA, College of St. Thomas; PhD, Stanford) teaches English and American literature at Washington University, St. Louis. He is the author of *Spiritual Autobiography in Early America* (Princeton, 1968).

ANN STANFORD (BA, Stanford; PhD, University of California, Los Angeles) is in the English department at California State College, Northridge. She wrote *Anne Bradstreet: The Worldly Puritan. An Introduction to Her Poetry* (New York, 1974).

DAVID E. STANNARD (BA, San Francisco State University; PhD, Yale) teaches American studies and history at Yale. His publications include *The Puritan Way of Death* (New York, 1977).

ROBERT C. TWOMBLY (BA, Harvard; PhD, University of Wisconsin) specializes in American social and urban history at the City College of New York. He is the author of *Frank Lloyd Wright: An Interpretive Biography* (1973).

LAUREL THATCHER ULRICH (BA, University of Utah, MA, Simons) is studying and teaching at the University of New Hampshire. Her research interests are in early American social history, particularly the roles and perceptions of women in colonial New England.

RONALD G. VANDER MOLEN (BA, Calvin College; PhD, Michigan State) is in the history department at California State College, Stanislaus. He specializes in early modern European church history and the history of England.

ALDEN T. VAUGHAN (BA, Amherst; PhD, Columbia) teaches American colonial history at Columbia University. His research interests are in American Puritanism and early American ethnic and racial attitudes.

MICHAEL WALZER (BA, Brandeis; PhD, Harvard) is in the department of Political Science at Harvard University. He is especially concerned with the comparative study of revolutions, including the Puritan Revolution in seventeenth-century England.

PURITAN
NEW ENGLAND

Essays on Religion,
Society, and Culture

PURITAN
NEW ENGLAND

Essays on Religion,
Society, and Culture

Alden T. Vaughan and

Francis J. Bremer, editors

St. Martin's Press New York

EDITORS' PREFACE

Interest in American Puritanism is at an unprecedented high. Almost every year several new books add to the already impressive corpus on the early settlers of New England and their impact on American thought and culture. Equally important, but more elusive, is the proliferation of articles in scholarly journals. This anthology brings together some of the most recent and best of that periodical literature.

In compiling *Puritan New England*, the editors have sought to span the chronological and topical boundaries of the field, to present a range of methodologies, and to include many of the scholars who in the past two decades have brought the understanding of American Puritanism to its present sophistication. In trying to reconcile these criteria with the practical limits of length and cost, we have had to omit much that we admire. We especially regret the absence of writings by several of the early resuscitators of Puritan studies—such as Samuel Eliot Morison, Clifford Shipton, and Kenneth Murdock—who in the 1920s and 1930s helped Perry Miller rescue the Puritans from intellectual oblivion, and of several modern scholars—such as Philip Greven, David Hall, and Robert Middlekauff—who have contributed significantly to the current reassessment of early New England life and thought. We regret too that we could not include essays on every topic of importance—for example, on Baptist and Quaker dissent, on Puritan education, or on such major figures in early New England as John Cotton, Roger Williams, and the several illustrious Mathers. But it is the very abundance of Puritan scholarship that makes choice difficult and full coverage impossible. In our introductions we mention many works that will be of interest to readers who wish to enlarge their study, and still other works are of course cited in the footnotes within the essays.

We offer twenty-one essays, all originally published between 1961 and 1976 except the selection by Perry Miller, arranged to show the evolution of Puritan New England. Because we believe that monographs should be read in their entirety whenever possible, we have not wrenched chapters from books; rather, we have culled appropriate scholarly journals—in the fields of religion, literature, and history—to find essays which stand by themselves and analyze as well as describe the Puritan experience. Where space limitations forced us to shorten some of the selections, we have omitted material that is tangential to the author's thesis or overlaps with another selection; we have indicated minor deletions with the customary ellipses, longer deletions with centered dots. We have retained the original footnotes as integral parts of the author's presentation. (Where deletions in a selection have caused some notes to be omitted, the remaining notes.

have been renumbered to maintain a consecutive sequence.) Our editorial commentary places each article in its historiographical setting, and we have appended a chronology of major events in the history of English and American Puritanism to help readers unfamiliar with the era to see the broader context in which specific events occurred.

Puritan New England is designed to stand by itself as an introduction to American Puritanism, although we anticipate that it will prove a valuable supplement to our other efforts to broaden the general understanding of the subject: Alden T. Vaughan, ed., *The Puritan Tradition in America, 1620–1730* (New York: Harper and Row, 1972), a documentary history; and Francis J. Bremer, *The Puritan Experiment: New England Society from Bradford to Edwards* (New York: St. Martin's Press, 1976), a synthesis of modern scholarship. Whether by itself or in conjunction with other works, we hope that readers of *Puritan New England* will reach the judgment offered almost forty years ago by Perry Miller and Thomas Johnson that "without some understanding of Puritanism . . . there is no understanding of America."

A. T. V.
F. J. B.

CONTENTS

PART ONE |

THE ENGLISH BACKGROUND OF PURITAN NEW ENGLAND

To speak of the English Puritan is to invite a major historical dispute. Who were the Puritans? What did they believe? Why did men and women become Puritans? Historians have disagreed over these questions since the seventeenth century. There is general agreement that the term "puritan" can refer to those Christians—starting with St. Paul and continuing to the present day—who favor a plain form of worship and a strict adherence to rigid moral codes. But historians also use the word in a narrower sense (and usually with a capital "P") to identify and characterize a reform movement in Tudor and Stuart England and colonial America. However, this definition is complicated because the Puritans had no broad institutional organization and because their ideas were in constant flux.

Although most historians accept the existence of Puritanism, C. H. and Katherine George have argued in *The Protestant Mind of the English Reformation* (Princeton, 1955) that if such a movement existed its importance has been greatly exaggerated. Throughout their volume the Georges put the word "puritan" in quotes as if to question its legitimacy. They deny any significance to the theological divisions in the Church of England because even churchmen who were undoubtedly Anglican exhibited Calvinist tendencies similar to the so-called puritans'. And the Georges minimize the importance of ecclesiastical disputes by relegating individuals such as Thomas Cartwright and Walter Travers (who opposed the church establishment) to a radical fringe with few adherents.

Because of its startling assertions, *The Protestant Mind of the English Reformation* has influenced some historians, at least to the extent of making them more cautious of easy generalizations about the nature of the Anglican-Puritan split. But the Georges have been criticized for failing to deal with the Separatists or with those Puritans who migrated to New England and for failing to point out the diminishing importance of Calvinism within the Anglican establishment. John F. New's *Anglican and Puritan: The Basis of Their Opposition* (Stanford, 1964), a rejoinder to the Georges, probes the theological differences between the two sides and examines their opposing views on issues such as nature, grace, and the sacraments. While some scholars disagree with New's emphasis upon theological rather than ecclesiological distinctions, most historians recognize that the division between Anglican and Puritan was profound and of major significance in seventeenth-century English life.

1

1 | ANGLICAN AGAINST PURITAN: IDEOLOGICAL ORIGINS DURING THE MARIAN EXILE

RONALD J. VANDER MOLEN

An issue on which historians have tended to talk past one another rather than confronting each other's views deals with the origins of the Puritan movement. M. M. Knappen has traced the beginning of the Anglican-Puritan split as far back as William Tyndale's criticism of Henry VIII's reforms and Bishop John Hooper's opposition during the reign of Edward VI to the wearing of priestly vestments. Knappen's Tudor Puritanism *(Chicago, 1939) identifies the essence of Puritanism as the belief by some English Protestants that reform had not gone far enough, that the Church of England had not been sufficiently purified of Roman Catholic corruptions. Thus, in Knappen's study Puritanism is seen as the radical wing of English reform, visible from the very start of the Anglican phase of the Protestant Reformation.*

A widely accepted dating of the origins of Puritanism—as distinct from mainstream English Protestantism—considers the Marian exiles critical to the development of an ideological split within Anglicanism. The disputes among the English reformers who sought relief from the Catholic reaction of Queen Mary by fleeing to the continent are dealt with by Knappen but stressed more heavily in the following selection.

Traditionally, divisions among Protestant groups during the English Reformation have been examined as deep theological crises,[1] simply written off as manifestations of economic or political struggles,[2] or, more recently, treated as having roots in basic ideological commitments.[3] One of the most important Protestant divisions, that between Anglicans and Puritans, . . . [had its] roots and first appearance during the flight of Protestants from England after the reign of King Edward VI.[4] It is to the ideological and social factors which appeared in the congregation of English exiles at Frankfurt-am-Main in 1554-55 that I should like to draw attention, for it was in the "Troubles at Frankfurt" that the historical pattern of the Anglican-Puritan division assumed a form which was to have such a great impact on western society.[5]

THE TROUBLES AT FRANKFURT

Upon their arrival in June 1554, the Frankfurt exiles from England were offered the use of the same church used by the French Protestant exiles who were exiles for the second time: first from Catholic France, then from

Marian England. The French, under the leadership of Valaren Pullan, had recently arrived from Glastonbury, England, where they had found refuge during the reign of Edward VI. The one condition set down for the newly arrived Englishmen, however, was that they would not "dissent from the Frenchmen in doctrine or ceremonies lest they should thereby minister occasion of offense."[6] In conforming to that condition the English congregation used an order of worship which the Edwardian government had allowed to be used in immigrant churches only. In Frankfurt the English exiles did away with the congregational responses to the minister, the long-suspected surplice and "many other things".[7] In addition they created a creedal discipline; that is, new members were required to subscribe to doctrinal propositions. Thus "reformed", in August of 1554 the Frankfurt exiles sent out a general letter inviting the other English exiles on the Continent to join them "to the true setting forth of God's glory".[8] The English exiles at Strasbourg, however, saw the invitation both as an affront to English religious practices and to the dignity of the Strasbourg exiles as well.

The Strasbourgers' interpretation of the letter, much to the dismay of the Frankfurt congregation, was that Frankfurt really wanted pastors. They therefore offered the services of John Ponet, the late Bishop of Kent, John Scory, John Bale, Richard Cox or any two of them.[9] Rather than accept Strasbourg scholars, however, the Frankfurt congregation wanted to invite their own choices, of whom John Knox, ex-chaplain to King Edward VI and opponent of the Book of Common Prayer, was the most well known. With the consent of the leading lay exile, Richard Chambers,[10] the Frankfurt congregation refused the services offered by the other exiles and in October 1554 sent a letter to Strasbourg conveying their decision.[11] The letter was carried by Chambers, but he soon returned, this time with Edmund Grindal and a letter from the Strasbourg scholars. They demanded conformity to the English Prayer Book. Signed by sixteen residents, the Strasbourg reply indicated that the signers would come to Frankfurt in February 1555 to help establish the English book.[12] When they failed to arrive in February, the Frankfurt group, with Knox as minister, adopted the Genevan service book as the "most godly and farthest off from superstition".[13] A newly-arrived pastor, Thomas Lever, would not accept the Genevan service, however, and he constructed a compromise order of worship for temporary use. Meanwhile, the two major opponents of the English rites, Knox and William Whittingham, had appealed to John Calvin for his judgment on the English service book. They wrote a letter which described the Edwardian Book of Common Prayer in largely negative terms, and in January 1555 Calvin responded in kind by condemning the book and its proponents as having "delight in the Popish dregs".[14] Persuaded by Calvin's letter, the majority of the congregation voted to accept the Genevan order of worship; but since the decision on this course of action was not unanimous, another compromise service was proposed for use until the end of April 1555; and disagreements regarding it were to be resolved by a committee of five eminent Continental divines, Calvin, Wolfgang Musculus, Peter Martyr, Heinrich Bullinger and Pierre Viret.[15] This compromise service was not ac-

cepted by the Strasbourg leaders, and they responded by sending Richard
Cox to Frankfurt to force conformity with the English Prayer Book. Cox,
evidently accompanied by fellow scholars from Strasbourg, joined the
minority faction at Frankfurt, which had rejected both the French service
and the compromise service created by the Continental leaders. On March
13, 1555, Cox and his group proceeded to discredit the Frankfurt ministers
and disrupt the worship service.

Cox's method was direct, and victory for the Strasbourg viewpoint
came within sixteen days. He and his followers simply began using the
English liturgy by answering aloud during the service, and when the
church seniors inquired into this behavior Cox replied that he "would have
the face of an English church".[16] Knox reacted immediately. In a sermon
he resorted to the contemporary device of prophesying,[17] which, contrary
to its later meaning, did not involve predicting the future but meant the
application of biblical texts to specific contemporary situations. Rather
than "prophetical" it was actually "analogical". Knox's springboard for his
attack on the English order was the Genesis account of Noah's drunken-
ness and exposure, Knox's interpretation being that some things must be
kept secret and others should be revealed. The Prayer Book difficulties
were classified in the latter group, and Knox proceeded to attack the alleged sins of the English church: "slackness of religion", "want of
discipline", the Edwardian persecution of Bishop Hooper for his refusal to
wear vestments, "superstition" of the Prayer Book and the wealth of the
English clergy.[18]

The congregation resolved to deal with this flagellation of English Protestantism by holding a mid-week debate, and accorded Cox and his followers church membership so they could have an official voice in the
debate; however, once admitted, Cox simply "forbade Knox to meddle
anymore with the congregation".[19] Whittingham, Knox's ally and Cox's
former student at Christ Church College, immediately asked a Frankfurt
town senator, John Glauberg, to force the parties to compromise.[20] When
an attempt at compromise failed, the congregation successfully appealed
to the Frankfurt Senate, which on March 22 ordered the exiles to employ
the same French order of worship used on their initial arrival in the city.[21]
Though Cox is quoted as first accepting the Senate's order to comply with
the French form, his Prayer Book party did as Whittingham had done and
made their own special plea to the Frankfurt authorities.[22] This appeal,
however, was not theological. Cox's followers showed the Frankfurt
leaders a pamphlet which Knox had published for English Protestants, *A
Faithful Admonition unto the Professors of Gods Truth in England.* In the
pamphlet Knox had attacked England's Queen Mary, her husband Philip,
and Spaniards in general.[23] Unfortunately for Knox, Philip's father, the
Emperor Charles V, was attending the Imperial Diet in Augsburg at that
very time. The Imperial Diet thus had a major, though chance, impact on
English Protestantism, for the Frankfurt leaders were hardly ready to of-
fend Charles V by harboring a seditious theologian. On March 26, the
Frankfurt government sent Knox packing to Geneva. The same day,
Strasbourg scholars (three D.D.'s and thirteen B.D.'s) were presented to
the Frankfurt government as the new leaders of the church; and Whit-

tingham was ordered to refrain from making further trouble as well as being ordered not to join another church. In effect the town council was forcing the English Prayer Book upon English citizens, just as Edward VI had,
and in spite of the appeals of Anthony Gilby the government refused to intervene further as long as unity was maintained.[24]

Having achieved his victory in but two short weeks, Richard Cox proceeded to reorganize the government of the Frankfurt church. On March
28 he gathered "such as had been Priests and Ministers in England" for the
purpose of constructing the new organization. Though he proposed an
organization which included both clerical and lay leaders, he obviously
wanted a church governed by leadership provided by a learned clergy.
Only the clerics were allowed to nominate candidates for church offices.[25]
It was regarding this very fact that the second major Frankfurt "trouble"
first saw the light, for Christopher Goodman, a scholar who had come
from Strasbourg with Cox, proposed that the congregation itself should
vote on an order of worship and elect its own officers.[26] By contrast, Cox
clearly preferred clerical control as had been customary in England.

Though the struggle over the point raised by Goodman continued until
the end of August 1555, the opposition to Cox's party had been shattered
as soon as Knox's political views were publicized. Cox and his supporters
then turned to the task of getting Calvin's blessing and to creating a church
which would in the future resist any reappearance of the old difficulties.
The first goal was apparently achieved, for on April 5 Cox and his
followers wrote to Calvin and explained their behavior.[27] Because they
had restored peace and elected new officers, the Genevan leader responded
in a rather favorable way, though he did have some criticisms. Consistent
with his earlier dislike for English use of "Popish dregs", he stated that the
English followers of Cox were "more given and addicted to your country
than reason would".[28] Of greatest importance to Calvin, however, was the
fact that peace had been restored. Thus, in spite of a personal visit in April
by Whittingham to convince him to condemn Cox's Prayer Book party,
Calvin indicated in a letter written at the end of May that he would not in-
terfere with the Frankfurt church. Calvin then proceeded to suggest
guiding principles for the future. He maintained that the line between permissible ceremonies and those to be forbidden should be drawn at the use
of "lights and crossings or such like trifles", for those who used such
superstitions should "drink the dregs".[29] Secondly, he suggested that elections by the clergy should be effected "with common voices"; that is, he
did not want the votes of some clerics to outweigh the votes of others.[30]
Thirdly, Calvin condemned the treatment given John Knox, for he claimed
that the charges against Knox should have been made in England, not in a
foreign country. Despite such criticisms, however, Calvin still clearly considered Cox and his party to be acceptable Protestants; and it is further
clear that Coxians held Calvin in high regard. Calvin's parting wish was
that the Frankfurt episode "be buried in perpetual forgetfulness".[31]

Whittingham obviously did not forget, for he and his party again
asked for mediation of the differences. In April and May, during the exchange of letters between Cox and Calvin, Whittingham had gone to
both the Genevan leader and to Bullinger to urge them to oppose Cox.[32]

Having failed, he and his followers presented their position in August 1555 and again asked for compromise. Cox allowed a discussion between the parties, but the debate ended in failure: "certain warm words passed to and fro from the one to the other, and so in some heat [they] departed".[33] Whittingham's followers removed themselves to Geneva and Basel, and those who had come with Cox left also. Before leaving, the latter party set up a school and permitted some tolerance to the minority who still opposed the Book of Common Prayer. In a letter by Thomas Cole it was reported that the members of the Frankfurt church who did not accept all the English ceremonies were allowed to suit their own tastes.[34] Not much is known of the new school, but it could not have been too prosperous. Though lectureships were established in Greek, Hebrew and theology, troubles again shook the English at Frankfurt. The new difficulties resurrected the problem of discipline and church government, matters which caused so much bickering between Anglicans and Puritans during Queen Elizabeth's reign.

IDEOLOGICAL CONFLICT—ANGLICAN AGAINST PURITAN[35]

Bickering was not the only product of the troubles at Frankfurt. Rather, what was created was an ideological division which would recur as long as Englishmen took their religion seriously. The primary ideological problem which divided the parties was the proper character and necessary application of the concept of *adiaphora*. Cox was no stranger to this idea, and neither were the followers of Knox; but, though both sides accepted the principle that forms of worship were "indifferent matters", the Prayer Book party found it imperative to accept and enforce one form at the expense of all others. Hence, Cox pursued the establishment of the second Edwardian Book of Common Prayer until all opponents were defeated.[36] The first reason for loyalty to the Prayer Book was the very thing Cox's Anglicans were accused of ignoring, church discipline. Such discipline was precisely what Protestants had supported during the late rule of Edward VI, and the Anglican party was basically continuing that policy.[37] Though Knox's Puritans charged that Anglicans had no disciplinary principles, they were wrong. Instead, the real issue was precisely what kind of discipline should be adopted. The Anglican choice was based on the view that any principle which Christians wished to resurrect as the basis for discipline was of necessity historically conditioned. Anglicans were therefore willing to rely on national church traditions rather than return, as their opponents wanted, to what were thought to be first-century practices. Puritans saw no validity in historical church tradition, while Anglicans saw the Puritan ideal itself as being shaped by history. Strangely, the Puritans did not apply the same rigorous standards to their own as they did to Anglican practices.

The Anglican view was that Prayer Book unity was the only form of unity possible during the reign of Edward VI; for, instead of depending on formal creedal statements of doctrine, the English had chosen to write their doctrines into a liturgy. Those who became exiles, therefore, did have a positive statement around which they could rally in a unified way. More important, the exiles felt that they could not set aside a system of worship for which their former colleagues were being persecuted. In their letter of November 28, 1554, the Strasbourg exiles maintained that to give up the English service would amount to a desertion of their comrades who had remained in England, for many of those who remained had been members of committees which had written the Book of Common Prayer.[38] Changing the service, therefore, could be interpreted as admitting that the Prayer Book was corrupt. In short, it was argued that what some Englishmen were being martyred for should not be changed without impelling reasons. [39] Also, the Strasbourg exiles reasserted the theme that the Prayer Book promoted English unity in "one congregation, that with one mouth, one mind, and one spirit they might glorify God. . . ."[40] The Anglican party, though it accepted the relatives of the *adiaphora* idea, felt that unity was possible only when a common English form of worship was observed.

Another important factor in the early Anglican-Puritan difficulties is that Puritan ideology itself was experiencing dynamic change and was not as static as the Puritans themselves claimed. The documents contained in the *Troubles at Frankfort* do reveal changes in the Puritan stance. At the beginning of the struggle, the English exiles, the Puritans not excepted, seem to have accepted the French order of worship for a very practical reason: "lest they should . . . minister occasion of offence".[41] In such a statement no appeal is made to the ancient church or to biblically necessary forms of worship. The French, however, were not the only ones who served as models for the Puritans. In describing the order of worship of other reformed churches, Dutch, Italian, Spanish and Scottish Christians were held up as ideals.[42] Further, in defending the order adopted in Frankfurt, the author of the *Troubles* explained that many ceremonies had been omitted "for that in those reformed churches [Dutch, Italian, and so on] such things would seem more than strange".[43] He also claimed that the Frankfurt order was "framed according to the State and the times".[44] Though they adjusted their worship services to conform to local norms and values, the Puritans clearly thought of themselves as members of a worldwide rather than a parochial Reformation; but in their attempt to convince other English exiles that the new form of worship was pure, they adopted a rhetoric of perfection. They described their church as follows:

> being subject to no blemish, no, nor so much as the evil of suspicion (from the which few churches are free) we may preach, minister and use Discipline, to the true setting forth of God's glory and good example to others.[45]

It was only when such rhetoric was used that it became necessary to claim purity on the basis of scripture, and it was regarding this latter claim that opposition naturally arose among the Strasbourg intellectuals. As one of the intellectuals with humanist training, Cox had spent most of his life arguing against the idea that Christianity could be reduced to propositional forms.[46] Though his former opponents on that very issue were Roman Catholics, during the exile they were Puritan Protestants.

As the Puritans were called upon again and again to defend their position, they completely abandoned their earlier reliance on arguing from the principle of conformity when they confronted other reformed Christians. Instead, they progressively adopted terms such as "purely" and "truly" to describe their methods. They ultimately concluded that the Genevan order of worship which they had adopted was the "most godly and farthest off from superstition".[47] In a sense, therefore, one of the major principles of many Reformation theologians was allowed to die a rather unnatural death during the troubles at Frankfurt. The doctrine of *adiaphora*, which seemed a way to avoid radical differences, actually proved the basis for the Anglican party's solidification around the Book of Common Prayer, while the Puritans did the same regarding the Genevan order of worship. Of course, subsequent dialogue between the two parties did not build on the idea that the *adiaphora* had been abandoned. Rather, it was simply ignored, and each party went its own way to gather support for its particular position.

First, to gain support the leadership of each faction turned to its own followers within the Frankfurt congregation itself; however, there is confusion as to the social composition of each party. Antithetical concepts of the Christian community were developed, but the question remains whether clear material interests determined the ideological choices which were made. It has been customary for twentieth-century scholars, epitomized by Christian Garrett, simply to identify different sociological origins and material interests in each group of exiles and thus discount the ideological differences as mere rationalizations. Garrett accounts for the Frankfurt incident by claiming that the Strasbourg exiles, who were "notables" under Edwardian rule, were directed by the former bishop, John Ponet, to maintain control over the English of lower status at Frankfurt.[48] The major difficulty with this interpretation, aside from its uncritical acceptance of the views expressed by the Puritans themselves,[49] is that it reads seventeenth-century politics into sixteenth-century religious and ideological differences. Even the terminology of the later period is used: "Independency at Frankfurt, whiggery at Strassburgh, found each a fertile soil for growth in the freedom of exile".[50] In addition, Garrett's description of socially-determined conspiracy is questionable. Neither documents nor biographical information gives evidence of the social groupings identified by Garrett. Cox's followers were generally not members of any ecclesiastical or social hierarchy. According to Garrett's own description of those who signed Cox's first letter against Frankfurt practices, eight were simply "students". If there was a conspiracy, it surely failed, for five of these students were eventually won over to Whittingham's side.[51] By the same token, the anti-Prayer Book party was hardly a conglomeration of democratic individualists. All those identified as the core of the Frankfurt party are classified by Garrett herself as "Gentlemen".[52] In the subsequent history of the conflict the names of many additional members of the congregation appear, but as a group they defy definition. Rather than people with a unitary background, the Frankfurt congregation was made up of many types of individuals. In all probability the wealthy gentlemen held the real power, but they probably shared it with the man who gave the greatest amount of financial support to the exiles, the Duke of Württemburg. Virtually every exiled student who resided in Frankfurt or came with Cox and switched to the Puritan party received financial support from him.[53]

More important than material interests or social origins are the clearly defined ideologies which resulted from appeals to the Frankfurt congregation itself; for the exiles developed antithetical concepts of the institutional church. The Frankfurt exiles, aside from their desire to discipline the congregation according to creedal loyalty, had developed a concept of lay control of the church's policy.[54] By contrast, Cox's party favored control by intellectuals, a fact which contemporaries recognized but many historians have ignored. The author of the *Troubles* always referred to the Strasbourg immigrants as "the learned men of Strassburgh", and did not give a favorable connotation to that label.[55] In referring to the course of events after the Prayer Book troubles were concluded, the same author created the impression that the intellectuals acted as they wished in spite of the will of the congregations which had welcomed them:

> The learned men . . . returned again from whence they came, and some to other places, where they might have charges, and not to be either burdened or bound to the exercises of the congregation, so that, the exile which was to many a poor man full bitter grievous and painful, was (to some of the greatest persecutors of their poor brethren) as it were, a pleasant progress or recreation.[56]

The most apparent distinction, then, was between intellectuals and laymen, not between economically-determined classes. The ideological differences which this distinction promoted surely did foreshadow an important phase of the Elizabethan Anglican-Puritan split, namely, the proper use of knowledge. While Cox was willing to use his learning as a critical tool and as a means of suggesting solutions to problems, Knox's followers relied on learning to identify an ideal in the past and to work towards that ideal without wavering. Thus, in an important way Cox's brand of Anglicanism encouraged a kind of Christian humanism, for learning was a tool, and a relative one at that. Puritan learning, though rooted in scholarship produced by the same Christian humanism, became a tool for creating judgmental propositions and consequently was a death knell for humanistic scholarship. Thus, troubles at Frankfurt provided a living example of Protestant anti-intellectualism: the Frankfurt Knoxians refused to accept any leadership from the "learned men" led by Cox. As each faction looked to its own following in the Frankfurt congregation for support, each created a unique idea of who should have authority, laymen or intellectuals: Knoxian Puritans looked to the former, Coxian Anglicans relied on the latter.

A second source of authority for both groups of exiles was the Genevan reformer, Calvin. From the *Troubles at Frankfurt* one can deduce the fact that Calvin was the whole-hearted supporter of Knox and Whittingham, but that viewpoint is not entirely true. The Edwardian Prayer Book was initially described to Calvin in such prejudicial terms as "these follies who can suffer?" and "a certain kind of pity compelleth us to keep close [quiet]";[57] but Calvin's response was not entirely negative. Instead he encouraged unity, and though he did not like many of the ceremonies, he still indicated that he found "no manifest impiety".[58] Also, Cox's fellow Anglicans were not averse to using Calvin's method of discipline, that is, discipline administered by the clergy and leading laymen. The lay leaders later were called "elders" in the presbyterian system, but on the Continent they were referred to as "seniors"; and Cox was not at all opposed to relying on these men. For example, when Knox had been expelled, Cox proceeded to set up a church which included a head pastor, "Ministers, Seniors, and Deacons",[59] and in explaining their actions to Calvin the Prayer Book party made it clear to the Genevan leader that they had not altered the basic form of church government.[60] As Calvin relied on elders in Geneva for the administration of discipline, so Cox's followers were willing to use the same system when they gained control of the Frankfurt congregation. Calvin's main suggestion regarding this topic was that the English should allow an equal vote for all ministers, but beyond this he found nothing wrong with the church's organization. Further, he did not request that the Anglicans install a system of elected leaders as the Puritans had.[61] Calvin's own Geneva was more an example of clerical control than of lay leadership, and his view of polity was hardly the same as that of the followers of Knox and Whittingham. Calvin proved to be a source of authority for both Puritan and Anglican parties, and in an important way was relied upon more by Anglicans than by Puritans. As Puritans grew more confident of their biblical scholarship, they shed all appeal to the authority of other scholars, Calvin included.[62] Cox, on the other hand, was willing to use Calvinist ideas as well as Calvinist church discipline.[63]

In addition to the ideological differences created by their theological disputes, the warring factions at Frankfurt developed political ideologies which were to distinguish Anglicans from Puritans in subsequent reigns from Elizabeth to Charles I. The Coxian group, true to its leader's long history of political subservience under King Henry VIII, developed the Anglican view that political obedience was a Christian virtue. Knox's followers, on the other hand, refused such conformity and consequently some of them rejected continual submissiveness. Knox was willing to question the theory of obedience and to imply that active disobedience was necessary in some instances. It was because of these ideas that the Puritans were discredited before the Frankfurt magistrates,[64] just as they were in Elizabethan and Stuart England.

The origins of Knox's new political ideas lay in the instability of English and Scottish politics and in Knox's desire to create a Christian theoretical basis for resistance. In order to develop a new theory, in March 1554 Knox questioned Henry Bullinger regarding the right to revolt, and Bullinger forwarded Knox's questions and his own answers to Calvin for the latter's perusal.[65] Knox had advanced four questions. First, he queried whether a young ruler, "by reason of his tender age", deserved obedience by divine right. The reply cited the example of Edward

VI and indicated that obedience was necessary.[66] Secondly, Knox asked whether a woman could rule by divine right and transfer the same authority to her husband, an obvious reference to Queen Mary and her husband Philip. The answer was both vacillating and straightforward at the same time. Bullinger recognized that the divine right of a monarch and the rights of one's husband depended on the laws of the particular kingdom.[67] He also maintained that scripture demanded obedience: God demanded obedience and would "in his own time destroy unjust governments by his own people, to whom he will supply proper qualifications for this purpose".[68] Thirdly, the Scottish reformer touched on critical points in the Swiss reformers' political theory: the issues of the right of revolt allowed to lower magistrates and the right of passive disobedience. He asked whether obedience was due the ruler "who enforces idolatry and condemns true religion", and whether local political and military authorities had the right to "repel this ungodly violence".[69] Bullinger replied that martyrdom was better than obeying evil and that magistrates could revolt against "ungodly" rulers.[70] He was quick to add that each circumstance required a unique answer. Fourthly, Knox asked whom citizens were to follow in the case of "a religious Nobility resisting an idolatrous Sovereign".[71] The evasive answer must have been disappointing to Knox, for Bullinger simply encouraged piety and suggested letting the issue "be decided by the judgement of godly persons, who are well acquainted with the circumstances".[72]

Bullinger's views were apparently respected, for Knox's ensuing pamphlet to the English Protestants did not call for active political resistance. It is difficult to imagine, however, that the work inspired anything but discontent among Queen Mary's Protestant subjects.[73] All the epithets which could possibly condemn the English monarchy in the eyes of Protestants were brought against the government of Mary and Philip. Enforcement of the use of the Mass was condemned as idolatry.[74] The monarchy was classified as a tyranny rather than rightful government: "those bloody tyrants within the Realm of England doth kill, murder, destroy, and devour man and woman, as ravenous lions now loosed from bonds".[75] Queen Mary was compared unfavorably with "Jezebel, that cursed idolatrous woman"; for the queen was accused of hanging twice as many Englishmen as Jezebel had killed among the Israelites.[76] The people were exhorted to view their government as a Spanish one rather than English; the queen was referred to as one who "beareth a Spaniard's heart",[77] and Bishop Gardiner "and the rest of his pestilent sect" were asked, *in absentia*, of course, why they "would have a Spaniard to reign over England".[78] Knox's broadest condemnation of England's government, however, was that England was repeating the history of Israel. Throughout the pamphlet he continually applied Old Testament prophecies to contemporary English life and continually referred to Jewish heroes who had risen up as rebels to overthrow evil, idolatrous conquerors. The sum total of his condemnation was succinctly stated in a prayer: "Oh God! the Heathen are entered into thine inheritance: They have defiled thy holy temple and have profaned thy blessed ordinance."[79] Though Knox never invoked the cause of open rebellion, anyone who wished could easily have considered himself God's instrument for overthrowing evil. Knox ended his pamphlet with a prayer which could have produced little else but hatred for the monarchy: "Thou hast brought to ruin the palaces of tyrants; and therefore shall the afflicted magnify thee and the city of the tyranfull nations shall fear thee."[80]

It is easy to understand why Knox and his party were discredited in Frankfurt as seditious conspirators and why Knox's Puritan followers were later condemned by Queen Elizabeth. Knox's pamphlet obviously heroized Jewish rebels and condemned tyrants, including England's rulers. That most contemporary Calvinists subsequently were also labelled as seditious persons is one of the ironies of the period, for the political theories of the right to revolt against tyrants, the necessity of tyrannicide when the ruler is evil, and the belief in the political contract as the basis of the state, were actually not ideas derived from John Calvin himself. He, along with Bullinger, sanctioned revolt by magistrates only when they had the constitutional right to check the monarchy.[81] Also, Calvin consistently refused to alter his political conservatism, for he maintained that even though the Christian could refuse to do evil, he was always required by God to give strict, unalterable political obedience.[82] Cox's position in condemning Knox's political ideology was therefore more in line with Calvin's political ideas than were Knox's, Goodman's or Whittingham's.[83] Cox's experience at being submissive in politics was an old habit which had helped his survival and progress in the past, and he was not prepared to abandon it. The theme that the Puritans were seditious citizens became an idea around which Anglicans could unite, and already during the exile the Puritans were labelled as conspirators who were not to be trusted. Though conspiracy is not clearly demonstrable, the Puritans had attempted to expand their party. Whittingham wrote to Calvin that he was trying to recruit a following at Basel and that he wanted Calvin's counsel and aid.[84] In reacting to this move, the English leader at Basel, John Bale, did not hesitate to condemn the politics of Whittingham's followers. In reviewing their activities he completely denied their contention that the English service was "popish", and questioned the real motives of the Puritan party in rather strong words: "What then may be thought of our unnatural and bastardly brethren?"[85] He answered his question by further labelling the bastardly brethren" as "a seditious faction".[86] Both charges were oversimplifications, but it was true that some of the Puritan leaders had produced seditious pamphlets.

More important from the perspective of intellectual history is the fact that the different political theories implied a different ideological framework for each party. The Anglicans were willing to accept what history had given and to use their religion to account for their complete obedience to the state. The Puritans used their theology as a device for judgment and for returning to a point in history when Christianity was, in their opinion at least, "pure". When Anglican and Puritan political ideas are compared, it seems that Anglicans were much closer to Calvin than the Puritans. It is also apparent that the diversity of seventeenth century political views had clear ideological roots already planted by the mid-sixteenth century.

Before turning from this point, it should be indicated that Garrett's views on the exiles' political opinions seems faulty. Though she indicates that Anglican ideology emanated from a Strasbourg clique headed by John Ponet and that its ideology was spread among all Anglicans,[87] she has not taken into account the difference between the politics of Ponet and Cox. As author of *A Shorte Treatise of Politike Power*, Ponet clearly allied himself with the new politics of belief in social contract and the right of revolt.[88] As already demonstrated, Cox, whose political thought was close to that of Calvin and Bullinger, would have nothing to do with such ideas. In fact, by condemning such ideas and by identifying Knox as a devotee of them, he got Knox exiled from Frankfurt. Nor would many other Anglicans join a party which brought their political loyalty into question. The reaffirmation of Anglican political subservience was clearly expressed at the end of the exile period by John Aylmer. In a political tract he completely repudiated Knox's political ideas and in addition asserted a political theory opposed to Ponet's.[89] Aylmer's work condemned seditious people as being "among these ugly monsters and broods of the devil's brotherhood",[90] and upheld the principle that obedience was to be preserved at all costs.[91] By comparing Ponet's tract with Cox's actions and Aylmer's pamphlet, one can hardly come to the conclusion that Ponet was directing an Anglican conspiracy. If he was, he failed. The Anglicans reaffirmed their political loyalty to the crown, whatever its character was, and in addition protected the only device which had been successful in giving English Protestants some form of unity, the Book of Common Prayer. With these credentials they clearly demonstrated that they were ready to assume leadership at the accession of Queen Elizabeth.

That the period of exile was ideologically critical in English history is apparent, for the basic presuppositions behind Anglican and Puritan thought were clearly developed and given structure within the opposing religious parties. In addition, the Frankfurt episode exposed the Protestant divisions which were bound to result from the confusion surrounding the *adiaphora* idea. First, two different views of the church—Anglican and Puritan—emerged, but these church views were in turn based on different ideologies. Discipline, liturgy and church government may have been the points of reference, but the basic ideological character of each party came to the surface during the Frankfurt crisis. The doctrines originated in ideologies which neither party consciously recognized, but for which each was willing to fight. Secondly, the Frankfurt troubles revealed social views which were to divide Anglican and Puritan, the former resorting to complete obedience, the latter accepting theories of revolution. Thirdly, each theology rested on presuppositions and upon social and political differences which would be resurrected again and again for the next two centuries. Though sensational events in

Elizabethan and Stuart England reveal the deep gulf between Puritans and Anglicans, the troubles at Frankfurt demonstrate the ideological bases of those later struggles.

At issue between Knappen and Vander Molen is the essence of Puritanism. Knappen identifies a spirit or posture of reform as the distinguishing characteristic, whereas Vander Molen stresses the beginning of ideological differences within the reform movement. The same types of distinctions can be detected in the extensive literature that treats Puritanism in the reign of Queen Elizabeth. William Haller's Rise of Puritanism *(New York, 1938) focuses upon the key role of the clerical brotherhood in building a widespread demand for further reform. Avoiding a detailed treatment of theological or ecclesiastical disputes, Haller offers a masterly analysis of how the Puritan clergy functioned as "physicians of the soul" who ministered to the spiritual needs of the English populace. English scholar Patrick Collinson, on the other hand, is more concerned with ecclesiastical and political conflicts (*The Elizabethan Puritan Movement *[Los Angeles, 1967]).*

The purely theological issues at stake between Anglicans and Puritans are examined by George Yule in "Theological Developments in Elizabethan Puritanism" (Journal of Religious History, I [1960]). Yule focuses on the beliefs of the early Elizabethan reformers and the relation of those beliefs to the changing circumstances of the English church. He shows that Puritan theology evolved in new directions under the pressures of ecclesiastical opposition to the reform program.

Like Haller, and like Collinson in The Elizabethan Puritan Movement, *Yule examines the Puritan faction from the perspective of its leaders. But Collinson's "Towards a Better Understanding of the Early Dissenting Tradition" (in Robert Cole and Michael Moody, eds.,* The Dissenting Tradition *[Athens, Ohio, 1975]) stresses the importance of understanding the popular religious radicalism that helped shape ministerial positions from below. A similar point has been made by Christopher Hill. In a paper on "Lollards to Levellers: An Underground Tradition" (Folger Library Conference, 1976), Hill traced a number of radical Puritan ideas of the 1640s back through the Elizabethan period to the Lollard reformers in pre-Reformation England. Such studies of lower-class religious ferment allow new insights into the dynamic relationship between the clergy and church membership.*

NOTES

1. Allen Hinds, *The Making of the England of Elizabeth* (New York, 1895); H. J. Witherspoon, *The Second Prayer Book of Edward the Sixth and the Liturgy of Compromise* (London, 1905); Marshall M. Knappen, *Tudor Puritanism* (Chicago, 1965).

2. Christina Garrett, *The Marian Exiles* (Cambridge, 1938).

3. John New, *Anglican and Puritan: The Basis of Their Opposition* (Palo Alto, 1964).

4. On the Elizabethan period, see Patrick Collinson, *The Elizabethan Puritan Movement* (London, 1967); William Haller, *The Rise of Puritanism* (New York, 1939).

5. *A Brief Discourse of the Troubles Begun at Frankfort in Germany Anno Domini 1554* (England, 1575); cited below as *Troubles*. Though this is the main source for reconstructing the story of the Frankfort troubles, it is hardly unbiased. It is an anonymous, yet pro-Puritan tract and apparently was written to build Puritan loyalty and attack Anglicanism, especially the Anglicanism epitomized by Richard Cox, bishop of Ely. Though traditionally accredited to the Puritan William Whittingham, the pamphlet's authorship has been recently discussed by Patrick Collinson, "The Authorship of *A Brief Discourse*," *Journal of Ecclesiastical History*, 9, pp. 188-208.

6. *Troubles*, 6; for a discussion of the French order, see Henry Cowell, "The French Walloon Church at Glastonbury, 1550-53," *Proceedings of the Huguenot Society of London*, 13 (1923-29), pp. 502-503. Cowell points out that the French liturgy had its origin in John Calvin's religious service, which he created when in exile in Strasbourg.

7. *Troubles*, 6.

8. *Ibid.*, 7, 8.

9. *Ibid.*, 8.

10. Garrett, 111-114. Though there is confusion as to Chambers' exact identify, Garrett maintains that he was the exiles' contact, along with Robert Horne, with the English Protestant leaders. He and Horne apparently controlled the common purse, and thus their advice and consent was naturally cherished by the exiles.

11. Frankfurt Congregation to the Strasbourg Congregation, October, 1554, *Troubles*, 20.

12. Strasbourg Congregation to the Frankfurt Congregation, November, 1554, *Troubles*, 22, 24.

13. *Troubles*, 27.

14. John Calvin to the Frankfurt Congregation, January 2, 1555, *Troubles*, 35-36.

15. *Troubles*, 37. Musculus was a German reformer who had been influenced by Bucer. Viret was a disciple of Calvin. His influence on English religion is discussed by Robert Linder, "Pierre Viret and the Sixteenth-Century English Protestants," *Archiv fur Reformationsgeschichte*, 58 (1967), pp. 149-171.

16. *Troubles*, 38.

17. This method of preaching became a critical issue in the Elizabethan period. When Archbishop Grindal refused to discipline prophesiers, he was suspended by Queen Elizabeth.

18. John Knox, "Sermon", *Troubles*, 38, 39.

19. *Troubles*, 39.

20. *Ibid.*, 40. Glauberg was the intermediary between the exiles and Frankfurt's Senate, and is described as "one of the chiefest Senators" (*Troubles*, 6).

21. *Troubles*, 40-43.

22. *Ibid.*, 43, 49. This action opened Cox to charges of being "double-faced".

23. Knox accused Edward Isaac of giving the pamphlet to the authorities. John Knox, *Works* (Edinburgh, 1895), 4, pp. 46, 47.

24. *Troubles*, 45. Regarding Gilby, see Dan G. Danner, "Anthony Gilby: Puritan in Exile - A Biographical Approach," *Church History*, 40, 4 (December, 1971), 412-413.

25. *Troubles*, 46, 47. The clergy chose those "whom they thought most meant to be Bishops, Superintendent or Pastor with the rest of the officers, as Seniors, Ministers and Deacons".

26. *Ibid.*, 47. According to the author of the *Troubles*, Cox's "proceedings . . . were such as if there had been neither orders, officers, or church there, before their coming".

27. Richard Cox, *et al.* to John Calvin, April 5, 1555, *Original Letters Relative to the English Reformation*, Hastings Robinson, ed. (Cambridge, 1846), 2, pp. 755-56.

28. John Calvin to Richard Cox, *et al.*, *Troubles*, 51 ff.

29. *Ibid.*, 52.

30. *Ibid.*, 53.

31. *Ibid.*

32. *Troubles*, 50, 51. Bullinger apparently did not allow the use of surplices, wedding rings or private baptism; but neither would he intervene on Whittingham's side.

33. *Ibid.*, 53.

34. Thomas Cole, "Letter", n.d., *Troubles*, 59, 60.

35. The use of the labels "Puritan" and "Anglican" from this point on in the essay is based on the distinct ideology revealed by each exilic party, and admittedly not on contemporary usage. The writer of *The Troubles* viewed the distinction as one between "the learned men of Strasbourg" (Cox's followers) and those who were "most godly and farthest off from superstition" (Knox's followers). If one is to consider the parties' leadership, the correct labels are, as Patrick Collinson points out, "Coxian" and "Knoxian" (*Elizabethan Puritan Movement*, 13, 33). The Coxians wanted a church with an "English face", while Knoxians thought they could go "purely" and "truly" back to the New Testament model. Because each party relied on ideologies to give content to their charges and counter charges, they clearly revealed Puritan (Knoxian) and Anglican (Coxian) views which were later refined during the Tudor and Stuart eras. Also see Everett Emerson, *English Puritanism from John Hooper to John Milton* (Durham, N.C., 1968), 3-11; Leonard J. Trinterud, ed., *Elizabethan Puritanism* (New York, 1971), 3-10; and Knappen, *Tudor Puritanism*, 487-493.

36. D. Whitehead, *et al*, to John Calvin, September 20, 1555, *Original Letters*, 2, pp. 755ff. According to this letter, some changes were made in the Anglican order after Cox's party won its victory.

37. Objections to the book were maintained by Knox and the immigrant churches in England, but there is no evidence of widespread Protestant opposition.

38. Strasbourg exiles to the Frankfurt exiles, November 28, 1554, *Troubles*, 22.

39. *Ibid.*, 22.

40. *Ibid.*

41. *Ibid.*, 6.

42. "Description of the Worship Service," *Troubles*, 7.

43. *Ibid.*, 6.

44. *Ibid.*, 7.

45. Frankfurt exiles', "General Letter," November 28, 1554, *Troubles*, 8.

46. Cox had been educated in the New Learning at King's College, Cambridge. King's College was a center of radical thinking, from which Cardinal Wolsey recruited scholars, including Cox, for Cardinal's College, Oxford, in the 1520s. At Oxford, Cox had become associated with the Lutheran group and was put out of the University. Strangely, he returned to prominence almost immediately as head of Eton School, and (not so strangely) rose in the church and at the royal court during the 1530s. His views were solicited by Cranmer in the writing of the *Bishops' Book* and the *King's Book*, and he expressed Zwinglian theology quite forcefully; later, he was appointed tutor to Prince Edward. During the reign of King Edward VI, he was instrumental in writing the Edwardian Prayer Book, in reforming the canon law (a project which never was completed), and in bringing Protestants to Oxford. After the Marian exile he became Bishop of Ely, a very lucrative and powerful position. As bishop from 1559 to 1581, Cox carried on his attack against Puritans with considerable enthusiasm.

47. Frankfurt exiles to Strasbourg exiles, December 3, 1554, *Troubles*, 27, 29ff.

48. Garrett, 27, 329.

49. *Troubles*, 1. In the "Preface" the author alludes to a conspiratorial attempt to discredit the Puritans as frustrated office seekers.

50. Garrett, 329.

51. Biographical information is found in Garrett's work for the following men: Michael Reniger (269), Augustine Bradridge (96), Arthur Saule (284), Thomas Steward (299), Humphrey Alcoson (70), Thomas Lakin (216), John Huntington (194), and Thomas Crofton (137). Reniger, Bradridge, Saule, Steward and Crofton all left Cox's party eventually.

52. Garrett summarizes their lives: Edward Sutton (310), William Whittingham (327), Thomas Wood (343), William Williams (334), John Stanton (297), William Hammon (175) and Michael Gill (162).

53. This information is found in the biographies contained throughout Garrett's work on the exiles.

54. *Troubles*, 13, 61 ff. Whittingham's followers continually appealed to the belief that the congregation should select its own leaders and its own order of worship. The later troubles at Frankfurt were almost entirely devoted to the problem of lay control.

55. *Ibid.*, 12. Also see the letter written to Zurich and addressed to "The students of Zurich" (*Ibid.*, 20).

56. *Troubles*, 59.

57. Frankfurt congregation to John Calvin, *Troubles*, 33, 34.

58. John Calvin to the Frankfurt congregation, *Troubles*, 35.

59. Richard Cox, *et al.* to John Calvin, April 5, 1555, *Original Letters*, 2, pp. 753 ff; *Troubles*, 47.

60. *Original Letters*, 2, p. 753.

61. John Calvin to the Frankfurt exiles, May, 1555, *Troubles*, 53.

62. This was especially apparent in the later quarrels between Bishop Whitgift and Thomas Cartwright in the 1570s and 1580s. See P. Collinson, pp. 120 ff.

63. Appeals to Calvin by Anglicans were especially strong once the troubles passed. R. Whitead, Richard Cox, *et al.* to John Calvin, September 20, 1555, *Original Letters*, 2, pp. 755ff.

64. John Knox, *The First Blast of the Trumpet against the Monstrous Regiment of Women*, (Geneva, 1558).

65. Heinrich Bullinger to John Calvin, March 26, 1554, *Original Letters*, 2, pp. 543-547; Knox, *Works*, 3, pp. 216-226; cited below as "An Answer".

66. "An Answer," 22.

67. *Ibid.*, 223.

68. *Ibid.*, 223.

69. *Ibid.*, 223.

70. *Ibid.*, 224.

71. *Ibid.*, 225.

72. *Ibid.*, 226.

73. John Knox, *A Faithful Admonition*, *Works*, 3, pp. 257-330.

74. *Ibid.*, 261.

75. *Ibid.*, 286.

76. *Ibid.*, 294.

77. *Ibid.*, 296.

78. *Ibid.*, 297.

79. *Ibid.*, 327. It was the continued use of such prophecies that caused Queen Elizabeth to condemn Puritan prophesyings.

80. *Ibid.*, 329. This argument was invoked by French rebels in their *Vindiciae Contra Tyrannos* (London, 1924).

81. John Calvin, *Institutes of the Christian Religion*, H. Beveridge, trans. (Grand Rapids, 1962), Book 4, chapter 20.

82. *Ibid.*, b. 4, c. 20, p. 25. The debate concerning Calvin's political significance seems interminable, but is compactly discussed in Robert M. Kingdon and Robert Linder, eds., *Calvin and Calvinism, Sources of Democracy?* (New York, 1970), pp. vii-xii, 77-83. Further, the view of Calvin's impact on democracy is stressed in Herbert Foster, *Collected Papers of Herbert Foster* (privately printed, 1929), while Calvin's authoritarianism is emphasized in Jacob Mayer, *Political Thought* (New York, 1939). Modifications of Calvin's political thought by Frankfurt Puritans is discussed by Michael Walzer, *The Revolution of the Saints* (Cambridge, Mass., 1965), 93-113.

83. Christopher Goodman, *How Superior Powers Ought to be Obeyed* (Geneva, 1558). This pamphlet defended tyrannicide, and its preface was written by Whittingham, who injured his career by writing it, for he never rose above the position of Dean of Durham when he returned from the exile.

84. William Whittingham to John Calvin, *The Life of William Whittingham, from a MS of Anthony Wood*, Mary E. Green, ed., *Camden Miscellany*, 6 (London, 1870), p. 6.

85. John Bale to Thomas Ashley, John Strype, *Ecclesiastical Memories* (Oxford, 1824), 3, pp. ii, 314.

86. *Ibid.*, 315.

87. Garrett, 253 ff.

88. John Ponet, *A Short Treatise of Politike Power* (Strasbourg, 1556). If he was the head of an Anglican conspiracy, as Garrett contends, he held political ideas which were anathema to most Anglicans.

89. John Aylmer, *An Harborowe for the Faithful and true subjects against the late blown blast, concerning the government of women, where in he confuted all such reasons as a stranger of late made in that behalf with a brief exhortation to obedience* (Strasbourg, 1559).

90. *Ibid.*, A3.

91. *Ibid.*, B1.

2 | PURITANISM AS A REVOLUTIONARY IDEOLOGY

MICHAEL WALZER

Although the laity's influence in shaping the Puritan movement has only recently received attention from historians, the influence of Puritanism on lay behavior has long been of scholarly interest. Historians have tried to relate Puritanism to the changing economic climate, both internationally (as in Max Weber's The Protestant Ethic and the Spirit of Capitalism *[London, 1930] and R. H. Tawney's* Religion and the Rise of Capitalism *[New York, 1926]) and on the local level (as in George Homans, "The Puritans and the Clothing Industry in England,"* New England Quarterly, XII *[1940]). More recently, the relationship between Puritanism and the socioeconomic forces of the period has been skillfully examined by Christopher Hill in* Society and Puritanism in Pre-Revolutionary England *(New York, 1964); David Little in* Religion, Order, and Law *(New York, 1969); and by Michael Walzer in* The Revolution of the Saints: A Study in the Origins of Radical Politics *(Cambridge, Mass., 1965). Christopher Hill takes the broadest view of the subject, examining such topics as Sabbatarianism, the poor, the spiritualization of the household, attitudes toward labor, and individual discipline. David Little focuses upon the relationship between legal and religious concepts and the Puritans' repudiation of Anglican "traditionalism."*

Michael Walzer is a political scientist interested in the Marxist analysis of revolutions. In the selection reprinted below he brings the insights derived from that interest to his study of the character of the Puritans.

I

. . .

The purpose of this paper is to . . . explore in some detail the part played by ideas during a period of rapid social change and revolution. The startling spread of Puritanism in England during the late sixteenth and early seventeenth centuries will provide a case history and suggest in dramatic form the (often ugly) kinds of discipline and self-control which revolutionary ideology can develop in men and the strength of character it can inspire. And since Puritanism has already been the subject of so many explanations, the English example will provide the opportunity for a critique of several earlier views of the significance of the Calvinist faith, and of various methods of studying revolutionary ideology.

II

Puritanism has twice been assigned a unique and creative role in Western history. Neither of these assignments was made by a Marxist historian; it

19

was rather the Whigs and the Weberians who found modernity in the mind of the saints. . . .

Whig historians of the nineteenth and twentieth centuries saw in Protestantism in general, but more particularly in English Calvinism, the seed-bed of liberal politics. The purely individualistic relationship of the saint to his God, the emphasis upon voluntary association and mutual consent to church government among the saints themselves, the extraordinary reliance upon the printed word, with each man his own interpreter—all this, we have been told, trained and prepared the liberal mind.[1] And then the natural alliance of Puritans and parliamentarians created the liberal society. It is a clear implication of this view, though one not often expressed by Whig writers, that Puritanism *is* liberalism in theological garb, that is, in a primitive and somewhat confused form.[2]

Max Weber credited Puritanism with a rather different character and a different but related contribution to Western development. Writing in a more modern vein and free, up to a point, from Whig prejudices, he suggested that Calvin's ideas—again, especially in England—played a decisive part in the creation of the "spirit of capitalism". His views are so familiar that they need not be described in any detail here. But it should be said that they involve two rather distinct arguments, which will be considered separately below. Weber thought that Puritanism had sponsored a significant rationalization in behavior, especially in work: it had trained men to work in a sustained, systematic fashion, to pay attention to detail, to watch the clock. In this sense, the Calvinist ethic is related to that long-term process which culminates, but does not end, in a rational-legal (bureaucratic) society. Weber argued in addition to this that Puritanism had produced an extraordinary and apparently *irrational* impulse toward acquisition, which is more directly connected with the rise of a capitalist economy. The source of both impulses, toward rationalization and endless gain, lay in the anxiety induced by the theory of predestination—but the two are not the same and it is at least plausible to imagine the first without the second.[3]

A Marxist historian would obviously deny the views of historical causation expressed or implied by both Whigs and Weberians, but he would defend ardently the close connection of Puritanism with the liberal and capitalist worlds. So ardently, indeed, would he do so, that he would probably concede, for the sake of the connection, a kind of "interaction" between economics, politics and religion, and thus open the way for an eclectic amalgamation of the three different points of view. Thus, contemporary Marxist writers tend still to describe Puritanism as the reflection of a rising bourgeoisie, though not necessarily its direct reflection (and this point—suggested, for example, by Tawney's notion of a "magic mirror"—is none too clear). But they then go on to argue that the reflection reacts somehow upon the original subject, reinforcing latent, perhaps underdeveloped class characteristics, meeting psychic needs, and generally accelerating the progressive evolution.[4] This second argument is made in terms with which Whigs and Weberians would hardly disagree— especially since it constitutes a Marxist appropriation of their own insights. Such an eclecticism may incidentally make more sophisticated the history of all who adopt it; but it does not necessarily do so, for it provides no new insights and often involves the suspension of criticism for the sake of coherence. Giving up the hapless debate over whether Puritanism or capitalism came first would be, perhaps, no such loss. However, it would be a great loss indeed if no one called the union itself into question and sought to work out in a new way the historical experience of the saints.

. . .

A number of recent writers have gone so far as to describe the Puritan saints as traditionalists in both politics and economics, a description which has the virtue of standing the older theorists neatly on their heads, but which also makes the revolution incomprehensible.[5] This is not the view which will be argued here; it describes at best only the cautious conformity of Puritan preachers in dealing with such conventional topics as monarchy, rebellion, usury and charity. On the other hand, it is not diffiuclt to detect the sharply anti-traditionalist ideology of these same men working itself out in their attacks upon hierarchy, their new views of ecclesiastical organization, their treatises on family government, their almost Manichean warfare against Satan and his worldly allies, their nervous lust for systematic repression and control. The last two of these are obviously not compatible with liberal thinking (or with entrepreneurial activity). They point directly to the revolution, when the struggle against Anti-Christ would be acted out and, for a brief moment, the repressive Holy Commonwealth established. In the years before the actual revolution, the nature of Puritanism was best revealed in the endless discussions of church government and in the practices of such Puritan congregations as already existed. These practices can by no means be called liberal, even though they were founded upon consent. Precisely because of this foundation, however, they cannot be called traditionalist either. The experience of the saints suggests something very different.

III

It was, perhaps, not without a certain malice that the early Puritans were called "disciplinarians". But malice has its insights and this one is worth pursuing. The association of the brethren was voluntary indeed, but it gave rise to a collectivist discipline marked above all by a tense mutual "watchfulness". Puritan individualism never led to a respect for privacy. Tender conscience had its rights, but it was protected only against the interference of worldlings and not against "brotherly admonition". And the admonitions of the brethren were anxious, insistent, continuous. They felt themselves to be living in an age of chaos and crime and sought to train conscience to be permanently on guard against sin. The extent to which they would have carried the moral discipline can be seen in the following list of offenses which merited excommunication in one seventeenth-century congregation:[6]

—for unfaithfulness in his master's service.
—for admitting cardplaying in his house . . .
—for sloth in business.

—for being overtaken in beer.
—for borrowing a pillion and not returning it.
—for jumping for wagers . . .
—for dancing and other vanities.

Had the saints been successful in establishing their Holy Commonwealth, the enforcement of this discipline would have constituted the Puritan terror. In the congregation there was already a kind of local terrorism, maintained by the godly elders as the national discipline would have been by an elite of the saints. Thus, Richard Baxter reported that in his Kidderminster parish the enforcement of the new moral order was made possible "by the zeal and diligence of the godly people of the place who thirsted after the salvation of their neighbours and were in private my assistants".[7]

It was for this moral discipline that the saints fought most persistently, and it was over this issue that Baxter and his colleagues left the Established Church in 1662. Their failure to win from Charles II's bishops the congregational rights of admonition and excommunication finally forced them—as the political Restoration had not done—to acknowledge the failure of their revolutionary effort to turn "all England into a land of the saints". By that time, however, the effort had had a certain prosaic success—not at all of the sort which Puritan preachers once imagined.

The crucial feature of the Puritan discipline was its tendency to transform repression into self-control: worldlings might be forced to be godly, but saints voluntarily gave themselves to godliness. Liberalism also required such voluntary subjection and self-control but, in sharp contrast to Puritanism, its political and social theory were marked by an extraordinary confidence in the possibility of both a firm sense of human reasonableness and of the ease with which order might be attained. Liberal confidence made repression and the endless struggle against sin unnecessary; it also tended to make self-control invisible, to forget its painful history and naively assume its existence. The result was that liberalism did not create the self-control it required. The Lockeian state was not a disciplinary institution, as was the Calvinist Holy Commonwealth, but rather rested on the assumed political virtue—the "natural political virtue"[8]—of its citizens. It is one of the central arguments of this essay that Puritan repression has its place in the practical history, so to speak, of that strange assumption.

It is not possible, of course, to judge the effectiveness of this repression or the extent of the social need for it. For the moment it can only be said that Puritans knew about human sinfulness and that Locke did not need to know. This probably reflects not only different temperaments, but also different experiences. The very existence and spread of Puritanism in the years before the Revolution surely argue the presence in English society of an acute fear of disorder and "wickedness". The anxious tone of Tudor legislation—which Puritan leaders like William Perkins often vigorously seconded—is itself a parallel argument. On the other hand, the triumph of Lockeian ideas suggests the overcoming of that anxiety and fear, the appearance of men for whom sin is no longer a problem. In a sense, it might be said that liberalism is dependent upon the existence of "saints"—that is, of men whose good behavior can be relied upon. At the same time, the secular and genteel character of liberalism is determined by the fact that these are men whose goodness (sociability, self-discipline, moral decency, or mere respectability) is self-assured and relaxed, entirely free from the nervousness and fanaticism of Calvinist godliness.

This, then, is the relationship of Puritanism to the liberal world: it is perhaps one of historical preparation, but not at all of theoretical contribution. Indeed, there was much to be forgotten and much to be surrendered before the saint could become a liberal bourgeois. During the great creative period of English Puritanism, the faith of the saints and the tolerant reasonableness of the liberals had very little in common.

Roughly the same things can be said about the putative connection of Calvinism and capitalism. The moral discipline of the saints can be interpreted as the historical conditioning of the capitalist man; but the discipline was not itself capitalist. It can be argued that the faith of the brethren, with its emphasis upon methodical endeavor and self-control, was an admirable preparation for systematic work in shops, offices and factories. It trained men for the minute-to-minute attentiveness required in a modern economic system; it taught them to forego their afternoon naps—as they had but recently foregone their saints' day holidays—and to devote spare hours to bookkeeping and moral introspection. It somehow made the deprivation and repression inevitable in sustained labor bearable and even desirable for the saints. And by teaching self-control, it provided the basis for impersonal, contractual relationships among men, allowing workmanlike cooperation but not involving any exchange of affection or any of the risks of intimacy. All this, Calvinism did or helped to do. Whether it did so in a creative fashion or as the ideological reflection of new economic processes is not immediately relevant. The saints learned, as Weber has suggested, a kind of rational and worldly asceticism, and this was probably something more than the economic routine required. They sought in work itself what mere work can never give: a sense of vocation and discipline which would free them from sinfulness and the fear of disorder.[9]

But Weber has said more than this; he has argued that systematic acquisition as well as asceticism has a Calvinist origin. The psychological tension induced by the theory of predestination, working itself out in worldly activity, presumably drove men to seek success as a sign of salvation. The sheer willfulness of an inscrutable God produced in its turn, if Weber is correct, the willfulness of an anxious man, and set off the entrepreneurial pursuit of better business techniques and more and more profit. At this point his argument breaks down. If there is in fact a peculiar and irrational quality to the capitalists' lust for gain, its sources must be sought elsewhere than among the saints. For Puritanism was hardly an ideology which encouraged continuous or unrestrained accumulation. Instead, the saints tended to be narrow and conservative in their economic views, urging men to seek no more wealth than they needed for a modest life, or, alternatively, to use up their surplus in charitable giving. The anxiety of the Puritans led to a fearful demand for economic restriction (and political control) rather than to entrepreneurial activity as Weber has described it. Unremitting and relatively unremunerative work was the greatest help toward saintliness and virtue.[10]

The ideas of Puritan writers are here very close to those of such proto-Jacobins as Mably and Morelli in eighteenth-century France, who also watched the development of capitalist enterprise with unfriendly eyes, dreaming of a Spartan republic where bankers and great merchants would be unwelcome.[11] The collective discipline of the Puritans—their Christian Sparta—was equally incompatible with purely acquisitive activity. Virtue would almost certainly require economic regulation. This would be very different from the regulation of medieval corporatism, and perhaps it was the first sense of that difference which received the name *freedom*. It was accompanied by a keen economic realism: thus the Calvinist acknowledgement of the lawfulness of usury. But Calvinist realism was in the service of effective control and not of free activity or self-expression. Who can doubt that, had the Holy Commonwealth ever been firmly established, godly self-discipline and mutual surveillance would have been far more repressive than the corporate system? Once again, in the absence of a Puritan state the discipline was enforced through the congregation. The minutes of a seventeenth-century consistory provide a routine example: "The church was satisfied with Mrs. Carlton," they read, "as to the weight of her butter." Did Mrs. Carlton tremble, awaiting that verdict? Surely if the brethren were unwilling to grant liberty to the local butter- seller, they would hardly have granted it to the new capitalist. The ministerial literature, at least, is full of denunciations of enclosers, usurers, monopolists, and projectors—and occasionally even of wily merchants. Puritan casuistry, perhaps, left such men sufficient room in which to range, but it hardly offered them what Weber considers so essential—a good conscience. Only a sustained endeavor in hypocrisy, so crude as to astonish even the Marxist epigone, could have earned them that. The final judgment of the saints with regard to the pursuit of money is that of Bunyan's pilgrim, angry and ill-at-ease in the town of Vanity, disdainful of such companions as Mr. Money-love and Mr. Save-all.

The converse is equally true: to the triumphant bourgeois sainthood, with all its attendant enthusiasm and asceticism, would appear atavistic. And this is perhaps the clearest argument of all against the casual acceptance of the Whig or Weberian views of Puritanism. It suggests forcefully that the two views (and the Marxist also, for surprisingly similar reasons) are founded upon anachronism. Even if it is correct to argue that Calvinist faith and discipline played a part in that transformation of character which created the bourgeois—and too little is known about the historical development of character to say this without qualification—the anachronism remains. The historical present is hopelessly distorted unless the tension and repression so essential to the life of the saint are described and accounted for. Even more important, the effort to establish a holy commonwealth (to universalize the tension and repression) is rendered inexplicable once liberalism and capitalism are, so to speak, read into the Puritan experience. For then Puritanism is turned into a grand paradox: its radical voluntarism culminates in a rigid discipline; its saints watch their neighbors with brotherly love and suspicion; its ethic teaches sustained and systematic work but warns men against the lust for acquisition and gain. In fact, of course, these seeming contrasts are not paradoxical. The saints experienced a unity, common enough among men, of willfulness and repression, of fanatical *self-control*. Latter-day historians do the Puritans little honor when they search among the elements of the Puritan faith for something more liberal in its political implications or more economically rational. Indeed, the methods of that search invite in their turn the most searching criticism.

IV

. . .

It seems at times that Weber turns Puritanism into a virtual equivalent of the capitalist spirit. He argues, for example, that among the saints rational labor (conceived by Weber exclusively in economic terms) is a form of worship and worship itself a strenuous and systematic labor. The spirit of capitalism is *first embodied in a religious ideology*, and from this ideology it derives the moral force necessary to break through convention and routine. Without Puritanism, Weber believes, the capitalist spirit might never have taken a historically viable form. Calvinist theology was somehow the crystallizing agent, but at the same time, Puritanism was the crystallization. For nothing is added, according to Weber's account, by the subsequent secularization of capitalist endeavor; hence it must be said that the original form was complete. What existed at first exists still, more ugly, perhaps, as its theological meaning gradually is forgotten.[12] But this virtual confusion of the Puritan and capitalist spirits, which inevitably follows from Weber's work, points to a radical defect in his argument. Briefly put, the defect is this: Weber's explanation of acquisitive behavior—in terms of anxiety over salvation and the desperate need to win some conviction of grace—will serve as well to explain Puritan saintliness. Granted the connection, at best incomplete, the psychological mechanisms which shape the two seem identical. In history, the salvation panic, the concern and self-doubt which Weber describes, is quite common. It is the psychological crisis which culminates in conversion; out of it emerges the self-confident, austere and zealous saint. The saint's anxiety does not begin *after* his conversion, though it may in some manner be maintained by his new religious ideology—"a man at ease is a man lost", wrote the Puritan minister Thomas Taylor. And thus the saint does not become a capitalist through any subsequent psychological process; his acquisitiveness—given Weber's point—is only an aspect and in no historical sense a result of his saintliness. But it is not possible to explain capitalism in terms of Puritanism (that is, Puritanism can be neither a cause nor even a "decisive factor" in the development of capitalism) if both are generated by the same experience. Looked at in this light, Weber hardly raises the problem of causation, for he never asks what are obviously the crucial questions: Why did men become Puritans? Why did they make the experience of anxiety so central to their lives? Why were they open to the extraordinary character change which their new faith presumably effected?

The argument can be put differently. Weber assumes that the cause of anxiety is an anxiety-inducing ideology. He never concerns himself with the origins of Calvinist faith or with that "elective affinity" which its converts presumably experienced. Now ideologies are modes of perceiving the world, and one perceives, up to a point, what one needs to see. That is, ideologies organize and sharpen feelings and sensitivities which are already present. The future saint who "elects" Calvinism is not in utter ignorance of the salvation panic it may induce. He chooses Calvinism, and not some other religious ideology, precisely because it explains a world in which he is already anxious—worried, confused, neurotic or whatever—and it is this original anxiety which must be explained if his eventual conversion and salvation are, so to speak, to be anticipated.[13] The terms and character of the conversion are conditioned by Calvinist thought, but not explained by it. Indeed, a later generation of Puritans, without losing their beliefs, would find conversion enormously difficult.

All this is really a Marxist critique of Weber, but no Marxist has yet undertaken a description of the state of mind of the men who became Calvinist saints, or even of their historical experience. The reason undoubtedly is that the Marxist knows the beginning of Puritanism as well as Weber knew the end: at the beginning and the end is capitalism.

There is another defect in Weber's argument, and it also stems from a failure to ask historical questions about the saints. Neither Weber nor any of his followers have ever demonstrated that the men who actually became Puritans, for whatever reasons—who really believed in predestination and lived through the salvation panic—went on, presumably for the same reasons, to become capitalists. They have not immersed themselves in the history of the period. This by no means precludes all insight: Weber's discussion of the activity of the saint and the energizing effects of predestination—despite a logic which seems to lead to passivity and quiescence—is a triumph of psychological speculation. But his particular judgments are guesswork at best. There is, for example, considerable evidence to show that many of the most sensitive of the saints went on, after the crisis of their conversion, to become ministers, and very little evidence that many went on to become capitalist businessmen. Among lay Puritans, the weight of the diaries, letters and memoirs clearly suggests that the most significant expression of their new faith was cultural and political rather than economic. The saints were indeed activists and activists in a far more intense and "driven" fashion than the men who came after: Scottish peasants learned to read; English weavers worked with a book propped up over the loom; gentlemen attended to parliamentary affairs with a new assiduousness; godly mothers trained their sons to a constant concern with political life.[14] In their sermons, Puritan ministers urged many forms of activity, from methodical introspection to organized philanthropy to godly warfare. Addressing the gentry and their urban associates, the ministers spoke most often of *magistracy* and described a kind of political commitment and zeal which would have its effects in the revolution. Of business, apart from general injunctions to avoid idleness and work hard, they said very little.

But of business they are made to say a great deal through the anachronistic historiography not only of Weber but of the Marxists as well. Both, for example, place an emphasis on the Calvinist acceptance of usury which is totally unwarranted by the texts themselves.[15] Marxists understand this acceptance as a reflection of changing economic conditions. If so, it is a weak reflection indeed of such a common practice, and one which could hardly have brought much comfort to the new man staring hard and moodily into his ideological mirror. The difficulty with the theory of reflection is that one can see in the mirror only what one already sees in front of it. And here is an opening for the endless anachronistic errors into which Marxists fall. In front of the mirror-image of Puritanism they firmly set the capitalist man, a figure who has, for anyone familiar with the nineteenth century, the odd quality of being *déjà vu*. Inevitably, what results is a distortion—the mirror is "magic" indeed! Thus the extraordinary, intense, and pervasive seventeenth-century concern with personal salvation is hardly noticed by Marxist students of the mirror-image, and the scanty texts on usury are brought into the forefront of historical vision. The Puritan covenant is glimpsed in the mirror and all too quickly understood; the intentions and aspirations of the signers themselves are not studied, for real historical motives exist, so to speak, only on this side of the glass. The Puritan hatred of the economic vices, like laziness and profligacy, is sharply reflected, but the vast depths of sin and demonism are obscured. In the Marxist world of economic reason, beggars are duly whipped, witches untouched by the flame. It would be possible, of course, to put a different man in front of the mirror. But in order to know what man to choose, one would first have to look at the image—that is, to reverse the procedures of the usual Marxist methodology. This reversal will be taken up below.

Engels himself, aware up to a point of these difficulties, suggested a somewhat different epistemology in an effort to explain the Calvinist theory of predestination. This invocation of God's arbitrary willfulness, he wrote, was the "religious expression" of the functioning of a market economy, where a man's fate depends on impersonal forces over which he has no control. The method of the "expression" is analogical reasoning and not mere reflection. The particular analogical leap from market forces to divine decree is comprehensible, says Engels, given the general religious atmosphere.[16] This presumably explains the upward direction of the leap, but it is somewhat more of an explanation than is logically necessary. In fact the idea of analogy opens the way for a virtually indeterminate individual creativity. What are the limits of the analogical imagination? Men see shapes in clouds and inkblots and while the shapes they see undoubtedly tell us something about the men, the historian or the psychologist has extraordinary license in interpreting what that something is. And this is a license which works both ways: one may well wend one's way back from the theory of predestination and discover some material counterpart other than the market economy. The truth of the discovery cannot be judged formally; it will depend on how well the men who did the original thinking or imagining are known by the historian. At the very least the unraveling of such complex modes of thought as analogy or, in the seventeenth century, allegory, should not be prejudged. It is easy to see in Bunyan's *Pilgrim's Progress*, for example, a working out of such bourgeois themes as mobility, calculation and individualism, but not of accumulation, thrift or even sustained work in a calling. And it is never easy to say who are the Christians of this world.

V

. . .

The problem of the Puritan belief in witchcraft and demonology has already been suggested and may profitably be developed at greater length as an illustration of the above argument. One sees in the mirror (that is, in experience and thought) images which have no easy or readily explained connection with the supposed subject, middle-class man. Witchcraft indeed suggests a world altogether apart from the Marxist universe of interest. In his book *Navaho Witchcraft*, Clyde Kluckhohn has analyzed the psychological basis of the belief in terms of the concepts of hostility and anxiety and has sought to give these concepts some precision. He has discussed the possible ways in which historical events or particular social structures may generate those anxious or hostile feelings which presumably lead to the perception of witches (or of oneself as a witch) and to the responses of persecution and cruelty.[17] Now the history of the persecution of witches in England (also the history of the practice of witchcraft) directly parallels the career of the Puritans. The first enactments were produced by the returning Marian exiles; the persecution reached its height during the revolutionary period and in the centers of Puritan sentiment; interest in and fear of witches declined after the Restoration.[18] Perhaps Marxists have paid so little attention to witchcraft precisely because it had no future; it was neglected in that final process of selection which constituted the bourgeois world. The point here is that this piece of knowledge about Puritan feeling and behavior suggests certain possibilities in the "objective" environment to which Marxists have been singularly blind.

Anxiety seems to appear in acute form only among men who have experienced some great disorder or who are caught up in a process of rapid, incomprehensible change: the breakdown of some habitual system of conventions and routines, a departure to an unaccustomed world, the aftermath of epidemic or war. Events of this sort leave men without customary restraints upon their behavior and no longer responsible to revered authorities. The result often is that extraordinary panic which Erich Fromm has somewhat misleadingly called a "fear of freedom."[19] In human experience, this is more likely a dread of chaos, and one of its aspects is a sharp, if often delusory perception of danger and of dangerous men.

If Puritanism is studied with these ideas in mind, a new light is thrown on sixteenth- and seventeenth-century history. One searches more deeply in the life experience of the saints for those feelings of fearfulness which parallel the belief in witches—and for the sources of such fear. One searches for sudden changes in environment, habits, authorities. The result is a hypothesis which is in striking contradiction to that of the Marxists: Puritanism appears to be a response to disorder and fear, a way of organizing men to overcome the acute sense of chaos. With this hypothesis it becomes possible to understand, for example, the as yet fragmentary evidence which suggests that the Calvinist faith, especially in its more radical forms, appealed most of all to men newly come to London and not, as Marxists have always assumed, to experienced city dwellers.[20] For coming to the city was an event in a man's life which might well sharpen his sense of danger and even lead him to seek that discipline which has been described above as central to Puritan association. Thus, the sudden increase in London's population between roughly 1580 and 1625 takes on new significance: it may well be that London did not so much prepare men to become "saints" as that sainthood helped them, through the hard transition period, to become Londoners. Once they had become *urbane*, they were in fact unlikely to remain faithful to the original Calvinist creed; they became revisionists. Similarly, it is somewhat less of a paradox than Marxists might suppose that witchcraft should range more widely in the southeast of England, where economic development was most advanced. For it may be—and this, perhaps, can be investigated—that witchcraft helped solve, in the minds of the people, some of the problems raised by that very development and by its impact upon traditional ways of doing things. (This is, of course, only speculation, but it is speculation which begins at the right place: with a concern for the concerns of the Puritans themselves.)

It seems likely that certain modes of perception and response parallel certain basic historical experiences; if so, comparison is possible and one might arrive at general propositions. But the relationship between, for example, urbanization and some ideological response to urbanization (once again, it must be said that these are not distinct "spheres") must be understood in dynamic terms. Perhaps it would be best to figure to oneself an energetic man continually struggling to understand and cope with the surrounding world. Undoubtedly, energy and struggle are not universal in history: ways of thinking quickly become habitual, as does experience itself. But it is the creative moments which require explanation and at such moments ideology is never a mere habit or reflex, but a willful activity. For perhaps a hundred years after the original creative achievement of Calvin, the spread of Puritanism can still be described in the active tense: men, with their own problems and aspirations, continually rediscovered for themselves, with all the enthusiasm which must have attended the first discovery, the truths of the new faith. The historian who begins with these ideology-producing men may then work outward, so to speak, re-experiencing their world and only after this subjecting that world to such further analysis as will improve his own understanding of it.

The Puritan saints are such men, making their ideology, and making themselves. The sources and nature of this creativity must next be considered.

VI

The study of the Puritans is best begun with the idea of discipline, and all the tension and strain that underlies it, both in their writing and in what can be known of their experience. It is strange that theorists have had so little to say on this topic, especially since the rebellion against Puritan repression, or rather against its ugly remnants—devoid, as Weber's capitalism is, of theological reason—is still a part of our own experience. The persecution of witches, of course, was not a vital aspect of Puritan endeavor, but the active, fearful struggle against wickedness was. And the saints imagined wickedness as a creative and omnipresent demonic force, that is, as a continuous threat. Like Hobbes, they saw disorder and war as the natural state of fallen men, out of which they had been drawn by God's command and by the painful efforts of their own regenerate wills. But they lived always on the very brink of chaos, maintaining their position only through a constant vigilance and, indeed, a constant warfare against their own natural inclinations and against the devil and his worldlings.

The goal of this warfare was repression and its apparent cause was an extraordinary anxiety. It is by no means necessary to argue that these two constitute the "essence" of Puritanism, only that their full significance has not been realized. In Calvin's own work anxiety is presented as central to the experience of fallen man: this is anxiety of a special sort; it is not the fear of death and damnation, but rather the fear of sudden and violent death. Hobbes would recognize it as the dominant passion of man in his natural state. Thus Calvin:[21]

> Now, whithersoever you turn, all the objects around you are not only unworthy of your confidence, but almost openly menace you, and seem to threaten immediate death. Embark in a ship; there is but a single step between you and death. Mount a horse; the slipping of one foot endangers your life. Walk through the streets of a city; you are liable to as many dangers as there are tiles on the roofs. If there be a sharp weapon in your hand, or that of your friend, the mischief is manifest. All the ferocious animals you see are armed for your destruction. If you endeavor to shut yourself in a garden surrounded with a good fence, and exhibiting nothing but what is delightful, even there sometimes lurks a serpent. Your house, perpetually liable to fire, menaces you by day with poverty, and by night with falling on your head. Your land, exposed to hail, frost drought and various tempests, threatens you with sterility, and with its attendant, famine. I omit poison, treachery, robbery and open violence, which partly beset us at home and partly pursue us abroad . . . You will say that these things happen seldom, or certainly not always, nor to every man, [and] never all at once. I grant it; but we are admonished by the examples of others, that it is possible for them to happen to us. . . .

Among the saints such terrible fearfulness was overcome, and that was the great benefit of sainthood: it did not so much promise future ecstasy as present "tranquillity". "When the light of Divine Providence," wrote

Michael Walzer

Calvin, "has once shined on a pious man, he is relieved and delivered not only from the extreme anxiety and dread with which he was previously oppressed, but also from all care."[22] But relief was not rest in the Calvinist world; it was rather that security of mind which might well manifest itself as self-righteousness—or as fanaticism.

In Puritan literature this same fearfulness is made specific in social terms. . . . It is a fear which Hobbes would understand: the fear of disorder in society. It is apparent in the nervous hostility with which Puritan writers regarded carousal, vagabondage, idleness, all forms of individualistic extravagance (especially in clothing), country dances and urban crowds, the theater with its gay (undisciplined) audiences, gossip, witty talk, love-play, dawdling in taverns—the list could be extended.[23] The shrewdest among their contemporaries sensed that this pervasive hostility was a key to Puritanism—though they could hardly help but regard it as hypocritical. Ben Jonson's Zeal-of-the-land Busy is a caricature based, like all good caricatures, on a kernel of truth. Zeal-of-the-land is, for all his comical hypocrisy, insistently and anxiously concerned about the world he lives in—and the aim of his concern is supervision and repression.[24]

At times, Puritan preachers sounded very much like Hobbes: ". . . take sovereignty from the face of the earth," proclaimed Robert Bolton, "and you turn it into a cockpit. Men would become cut-throats and cannibals . . . Murder, adulteries, incests, rapes, robberies, perjuries, witchcrafts, blasphemies, all kinds of villainies, outrages and savage cruelty would overflow all countries."[25] But secular sovereignty was not their usual appeal. They looked rather to congregational discipline, as has been argued above. Thus Thomas Cartwright promised that the new discipline would restrain stealing, adultery and murder. Even more, it would "correct" sins "which the magistrate doth not commonly punish"—he listed lying, jesting, choleric speeches.[26] It need hardly be said that John Locke, a century later, was not terribly worried about such sins. Walsingham's spies reported in the 1580's and '90's that Puritan agitators were promising "that if discipline were planted, there should be no more vagabonds nor beggars". John Penry foresaw the "amendment" of idleness and hence, he thought, of poverty.[27] Now none of these concerns was unusual in Tudor or early Stuart England, but the intensity and extent of Puritan worry and the novelty of the proposed solution have no parallel among statesmen or traditional moralists. These latter groups also watched with apprehension the growth of London, the increasing geographic and social mobility, and the new forms of individualistic experimentation. It must be said, however, that the tone of their writings rarely reached a pitch of anxiety and fearfulness comparable to, for example, the diary of the Puritan minister Richard Rogers, endlessly worried about his own "unsettledness". Nostalgia was a more common theme, satire and mockery a more frequent defense among moralists like Thomas Dekker.[28] And the world they would have substituted for Renaissance England was an already romanticized version of medieval England. Not so the Puritans. Their discipline would have established dramatically new forms of association: the anxiety of the minister Rogers led him to join with his brethren in a solemn covenant—and these brethren were neither his immediate neighbors nor his kinfolk.[29]

What Rogers sought from his covenant was a bolstering of his faith, a steeling of his character. "The sixth of this month [December, 1587] we fasted betwixt ourselves," he reported in his diary,". . . to the stirring up of ourselves to greater godliness." The need for this "stirring up" is so pervasive among the Puritans that one might well imagine that what they feared so greatly was rather in themselves than in the society about them. In fact, what they feared was the image in themselves of the "unsettledness" of their world. Puritan fearfulness is best explained in terms of the actual experiences of exile, alienation, and social mobility about which the saints so often and insistently wrote.[30] Discipline and repression are responses to these experiences, responses which do not aim at a return to some former security, but rather at a vigorous control and a narrowing of energies—a bold effort to shape a personality amidst "chaos". Thus might be explained the extraordinarily regimented life recorded in Margaret Hoby's diary. Mrs. Hoby was a merchant's daughter, married to a gentleman (the son of the Elizabethan ambassador Sir Thomas Hoby, translator of Castiglione) and carried off to a country estate in Yorkshire where all her neighbors were Catholic and, in her eyes, rowdy and sinful men. There she spent her time in earnest conversations with her minister, reading and listening to sermons and laboriously copying them out in her notebook, adhering to a strict routine of public and private prayer, assiduous in her daily self-recrimination:[31]

> I talked of some things not so as I ought when I had considered of them, but I find what is in a man if the Lord's spirit do never so little hide itself . . . but this is my comfort, that my heart is settled to be more watchful hereafter. . . .

How many men have settled since for the same "comfort"!

Undoubtedly, Margaret Hoby's behavior might be differently explained, but not so as to account so well for the similar behavior of her brethren. These people felt themselves exceptionally open to the dangers about them and this must have been, in part, because they were cut off, as were the men who succumbed to chaos—beggars and vagabonds—from the old forms of order and routine. It is this sense of being cut off, alien, that is expressed in the endless descriptions of the saint as a stranger and pilgrim which are so important in Puritan writing.[32] Pilgrimage is, perhaps, one of the major themes in all Christian literature, but it achieves among the Puritans a unique power, a forcefulness and intensity in its popular expression which culminates finally in Bunyan's classic. Over and over again, with the detail which only experience or, perhaps, a continually engaged imagination can give, Puritans describe life as a journey (or, in the image which Hobbes later made famous, as a race) through alien country. And yet, at the same time, they write of the vagabond with venomous hatred: he is a dangerous man because he has not disciplined and prepared himself for his journey. "Wandering beggars and rogues," wrote William Perkins, "that pass from place to place, being under no certain magistracy or ministry, nor joining themselves to any set society in church or commonwealth, are plagues and banes of both, and are to be taken as main enemies of [the] ordinance of God . . .''[33] The bitterness of this passage suggests the self-hatred of the Puritan pilgrim, pitying and worrying about his own "unsettledness". When the famous preacher Richard Greenham told a Puritan audience "Paradise is our native country", some of his listeners surely must have winced to think: *not England*. "We dwell here as in Meshech and as in the tents of Kedar, and therefore we be glad to be at home." It was painful, but inevitable, that the saints should live in tents. Perkins himself wrote in the same vein, for all his hatred of the wanderer: "Alas, poor souls, we are no better than passengers in this world, our way it is in the middle of the sea."[34] For many Puritans, if not for Perkins himself, who grew old in Cambridge, these words must have had a meaning both literal and poignant. Since the days of Mary, exile had been a common experience for the saints. And a generation after Perkins wrote, the "middle of the sea" would become a path for tens of thousands.

The fanatical self-righteousness of that first Puritan John Knox, a Scottish peasant's son, set loose in Europe by war and revolution, is surely in some sense a function of his exile: righteousness was a consolation and a way of organizing the self for survival. The "unsettledness" of Richard Rogers was due in part to his devious struggles with the corporate church and its bishops; but Rogers, who remembered his Essex birthplace as a "dunghill", was ever an outsider, and Puritanism his way of stirring up his heart. When William Whitgift, the future archbishop, cruelly taunted the Puritan leader Thomas Cartwright for "eating at other men's tables", he was perhaps suggesting an important source of Cartwright's vision of congregational unity and holiness. Margaret Hoby's life would have been different indeed had she been raised in a traditional country family: there would, for example, have been dancing at her wedding, and her life thereafter would hardly have allowed for time-consuming religious exercises. Deprived of such a life, because of her social background (and the ideas which were part of it) or, perhaps, because of basic changes in rural life, she willfully sought new comforts.[35] Country gentlemen like John Winthrop and Oliver Cromwell, educated at Cambridge, knowledgeable in London, suddenly turned upon the traditional routine of English life as if it were actually vicious. Half in, half out of that routine, they anxiously sought a new certainty. "Oh, I lived in and loved darkness and hated light; I was a chief, the chief of sinners", wrote Cromwell of his seemingly ordinary and conventional life before conversion. But now, he went on, "my soul is with the congregation of the first born, my body rests in hope; and if here I may honor my God either by doing or by suffering, I shall be most glad."[36]

All this suggests once again the view of Puritanism as a response of particular men to particular experiences of confusion, change, alienation and exile. Now Calvinism obviously made men extremely sensitive to disorder in all its forms. It is more important, however, that it gave meaning to the experience of disorder and provided a way out, a return to certainty. It was an active response, and not a mere reflection of social confusion, for indeed other men responded differently. There is no rigid pattern in these responses. It seems probable that members of a rising middle class most sharply experienced that alienation from old England which drove men to the exercises of sainthood. On the other hand, there were both gentlemen and citizens who certainly enjoyed the new freedoms of mobility, extravagance, individuality and wit, and eagerly sought entrance to the Renaissance court, where freedom was cultivated. And from among these men undoubtedly came many future capitalists. It would not be easy to explain in particular cases why the court held such attractions for some men, while it was vicious and iniquitous in the eyes of others. No more is it readily comprehensible why some of the newcomers to the burgeoning city of London merged into the mob or explored the exciting underworld, while others hated the wickedness of the city and sought out virtuous brethren in the radical conventicles. What is important for the present is that Puritanism was a response to an experience which many men had; it provided one way of understanding the experience and of coping with it.

Coping with it meant being reborn as a new man, self-confident and free of worry, capable of vigorous, willful activity. The saints sometimes took new names to signify their rebirth. If alienation had made them anxious, depressed, unable to work, given to fantasies of demons, morbid introspection or fearful daydreams such as Calvin had suggested were common among fallen men, then sainthood was indeed a transformation.[37] Cromwell's pledge to honor his God "by doing" was no idle boast: he was obviously capable of just that. Perhaps this transformation gave businessmen the confidence necessary for innovation or freed them from the necessity of feeling guilty about routine connivance, usury, extortion. Thus argue Marxists and Weberians alike. But innovation was more likely due to the recklessness of the speculator than to the self-confidence of the saint; indeed, the saints hated the "projectors" who lived in and about the court, currying favor and waiting for opportunity. The congregational discipline, as has been seen, would have established controls hardly compatible with businesslike hard dealing. Cromwell's "doing" was obviously of a different order, and Cromwell was a representative man. His life suggests that the Puritan experience produced first of all a political activist.

The Puritan new man was active not so that success might reinforce his self-esteem, but in order to transform a world in which he saw his own ever-present wickedness writ large.[38] In a sense, his was a struggle to free himself from temptation by removing all alternatives to godliness, by organizing his own life as a continuous discipline and society as a regiment. His activity was political in that it was always concerned with government—though not only or, perhaps, not most importantly, at the level of the state. Puritans often imagined the congregation as a "little commonwealth", replacing the organic imagery of Anglicans and Catholics with expressions deliberately drawn from the world of coercion and sovereignty. Thus they made manifest their own pervasive concern with *control* rather than with harmony or love.[39] Their treatment of the family was similar: they saw it as a field for the exercise of discipline by a godly father usually described as a "governor". Puritan interest in the family parallels that of Jean Bodin (though, in contrast to Robert Filmer, also a Bodinian, the saints had little to say about paternal affection and benevolence) and probably has the same source. The insistence upon the absolute sovereignty of the father and upon the family as an institution for repressing and disciplining naturally wicked, licentious and rebellious children derives in both cases from an extraordinary fear of disorder and anarchy. Thus two Puritan preachers in a famous treatise on "family government":

> The young child which lieth in the cradle [is] both wayward and full of affections: and though his body be but small, yet he hath a great heart, and is altogether inclined to evil. . . . If this sparkle be suffered to increase, it will rage over and burn down the whole house. For we are changed and become good, not by birth, but by education. . . . Therefore parents must be wary and circumspect, that they never smile or laugh at any words or deeds of their children done lewdly . . . naughtily, wantonly . . . they must correct and sharply reprove their children for saying or doing ill. . . .[40]

The father was continually active, warily watching his children; the elders of the congregation were ever alert and vigilant, seeking out the devious paths of sin; so also the godly magistrate. "In you it is now to cleanse, to free your country of villainy," a Puritan minister told the judges of Norwich, ". . . consider your power to reform . . . if you be faithful, and God's power to revenge if you be faithless."[41] In Puritan writings, political activity was described as a form of work: it required systematic application, attention to detail, sustained interest and labor. Much that the godly magistrates undertook might be called, in Marxist terms, progressive; some of their activity, however, would clearly impede free economic activity. But description in these terms is valuable only if one seeks to understand those aspects of Puritan activity which, through a subsequent process of selection, became permanent features of the modern world. In the seventeenth century, Puritan politics obviously had an interest rather different from that suggested by the term "progress". Its immediate purpose was to regain control of a changing world; hence the great concern with method, discipline, and order, and the frequent uneasiness with novelty. When the saints spoke of reform, they meant first of all an overcoming of social instability and all its moral and intellectual concommitants. Godly magistracy was a bold effort to seize control of society, much as sainthood had been an effort to control and organize the self. And the first of these followed from the second: in this way did Puritanism produce revolutionaries. In much the same way, it may be suggested, did the Jacobin man of virtue become an *active citizen*, and the hardened and "steeled" Bolshevik first a *professional* revolutionary and then, in Lenin's words, a "leader", "manager", and "controller".[42]

These revolutionary men do not simply attach and transform the old order—as in the Marxist story. The old order is only a part, and often not the most important part, of their experience. They live much of their lives amidst the breakdown of that order, or in hiding or exile from it. And much of their rebellion is directed against the very "unsettledness" that they know best. The analogy with the Bolsheviks is worth pursuing. Lenin's diatribes against "slovenliness . . . carelessness, untidiness, unpunctuality, nervous haste, the inclination to substitute discussion for action, talk for work, the inclination to substitute discussion for action, talk for work, the inclination to undertake everything under the sun without finishing anything" were intended first of all as attacks upon his fellow exiles—whatever their value as descriptions of the "primitive" Russia he hated so much.[43] The first triumph of Bolshevism, as of Puritanism, was over the impulse toward "disorganization" in its own midst: here, so to speak, was Satan at work where he is ever most active—in the ranks of the godly. And it must be said that this triumph was also over the first impulses toward freedom. Thus the Puritans vigorously attacked Renaissance experimentation in dress and in all the arts of self-decoration and hated the free-wheeling vagabonds who "crowd into cities [and] boroughs . . . roll up and down from one lodging to another", never organizing themselves into families and congregations.[44] Similarly, the Jacobin leader Robespierre attacked the economic egotism of the new bourgeoisie and spitefully connected the radical free thought of the Enlightenment with anti-revolutionary conspiracy. Atheism, he declared, is aristocratic.[45] And again Lenin, preaching with all the energy of a secular Calvinist against free love: "Dissoluteness in sexual life is bourgeois, [it] is a phenomenon of decay. The proletariat is a rising class . . . It needs clarity, clarity and again clarity. And so, I repeat, no weakening, no waste, no destruction of forces."[46]

In fact, Lenin's morality had little to do with the proletariat, and the "dissoluteness" he attacked had little to do with the bourgeoisie. He might as well have talked of saints and worldlings as the Puritans did. The contrast he was getting at was between those men who had succumbed to (or taken advantage of!) the disorder of their time—speculators in philosophy, vagabonds in their sexual life, economic Don Juans—and those men who had somehow pulled themselves out of "unsettledness", organized their lives and regained control. The first group were the damned and the second the saved. The difference between them was not social but ideological.

Puritans, Jacobins and Bolsheviks did tend to come from the same social strata—that is, from the educated middle classes, preachers, lawyers, journalists, teachers, professional men of all sorts. But this is not because such men are representatives of larger social groups whose interests they defend. It has already been shown that the connection between Puritan theory and bourgeois interests is at best a difficult one, which is in no sense implicit in the theory, but is rather worked out later in a long process of corruption, selection and forgetting. Men like the godly ministers speak first of all for themselves: they record most sensitively the experience of "unsettledness" and respond to it most vigorously. For reasons which require further investigation, such men seem less integrated into their society—even in the most stable periods—and more available as it were, for alienation than are farmers or businessmen. This is not, of course, to reduce their moral discipline (or their radical politics) to the psychological therapy of alienated intellectuals. The alienation which John Knox or Richard Rogers experienced, with all its attendant fearfulness and enthusiasm, sometimes disfiguring and sometimes ennobling, was only a heightened form of the feelings of other men—in a sense, of all men, for ultimately the sociological range of the Puritan response was very wide.

But the historian must also record that "unsettledness" was not a permanent condition and that sainthood was only a temporary role. For men always seek and find not some tense and demanding discipline, but some new routine. The saints failed in their effort to establish a holy commonwealth and, in one way or another, their more recent counterparts have also failed. What this suggests is not that the holy commonwealth was an impractical dream, the program of muddled, unrealistic men. In fact, Puritan ministers and elders (and fathers!) had considerable political experience and the holy commonwealth was in a sense achieved, at least among those men who most needed holiness. Nor is it correct to argue from the failure of the saints that Puritanism in its revolutionary form represents only a temporary triumph of "ideas" over "interest", a momentary burst of enthusiasm.[47] For such moments have their histories, and what needs to be explained is why groups of men, over a fairly long span of time, acquired such an intense interest in ideas like predestination and holiness. Puritan ideology was a response to real experience, therefore a practical effort to cope with personal and social problems. The inability of the saints to establish and maintain their holy commonwealth suggests only that these problems were limited in time to the period of breakdown and psychic and political reconstruction. When men stopped being afraid, or became less afraid, then Puritanism was suddenly irrelevant. Particular elements in the Puritan system were transformed to fit the new routine—and other elements were forgotten. And only then did the saint become a man of "good behavior", cautious, respectable, calm, ready to participate in a Lockeian society.

VIII

The argument of the preceding section may now be concluded: Puritanism was not a revolutionary ideology in the Marxist sense, reflecting the interests of a rising class. Such interests are in the seventeenth century better represented by parliamentarians and common lawyers who had their own ideology. The faith of the saints was rather a peculiarly intense response to the experience of social change itself, an experience which, in one way or another, set groups of men outside the established order. It should be obvious that this may be the result of either "rising" or "falling" in economic terms; mobility itself is the key, especially if the old social order is traditionalist, dependent for its stability upon popular passivity. The Puritan response produced revolutionaries, that is, saints, godly magistrates, men already disciplined (before the revolution begins) for the strenuous work of transforming all society and all men in the image of their own salvation. Such men, narrow, fanatical, enthusiastic, committed to their "work", have little to contribute to the development of either liberalism or capitalism. To expect freedom from their hands is to invite disappointment. Their great achievement is what is known in the sociology of revolution as the *terror*, the effort to create a holy commonwealth and to force men to be godly.

The contribution of these men to the future is the destruction of the old order. Alienated from its conventions and routines—from its comforts—they feel no nostalgia as they watch its slow decay. They are capable not only of establishing, underground, an alternative system, but also of making a frontal assault upon the old order itself, in the case of the Puritans, upon hierarchy and patriarchy, the central principles of traditional government. Their extraordinary self-confidence, won at some cost, as has been seen, makes them capable finally of killing the king. Here Weber's analysis is undoubtedly closer to the truth than that of the Marxists: the saints are entrepreneurs indeed, but in politics rather than in economics. They ruthlessly (and anxiously) pursue not wealth or even individual power—never rely on great men, warned a Puritan preacher—but *collective control* of themselves, of each other, of all England.

. . .

Walzer's analysis, as set forth in the preceding essay and in Revolution of the Saints, *has been criticized for not going sufficiently beyond the problem of order. Also, in failing to account for the radical wing of the Puritan movement that would culminate in such figures as John Bunyan, John Milton, and George Fox, Walzer overlooks the movement's latent liberalizing effects. Still, his interpretation is valuable in highlighting the roots of the dynamic power behind Puritan reform and the relationship between Puritanism and the uncertainties of the age that gave it birth.*

Regional circumstances often influenced the Puritan movement's specific direction. We know that many of the figures Walzer examines found their situations intolerable enough in the 1640s to rebel against king and church. Others had departed England in the 1630s to build a more perfect society in America. The reasons some Puritans left England while others did not has been a subject discussed by colonial Puritans themselves (anxious to repudiate the charge of cowardice) and by historians after them. Studies of regional variations in religious administration and social changes under the Stuart monarchs, such as John Horton's "Two Bishops and the Holy Brood: A Fresh Look at a Familiar Fact" (New England Quarterly, XL [1967]) and Allan Everitt's Change in the Provinces: The Seventeenth Century *(Leicester, Eng., 1972), have shed new light on the growth of Puritan dissent. In the decades preceding the civil wars it appears that most Puritans were not sufficiently touched by the repressive arm of the Anglican establishment to either rebel or emigrate. By understanding regional differences in the Puritan experience we can better appreciate not only why certain areas such as East Anglia furnished a large share of the settlers of New England, but also the unique mixture of national and local concerns which led the émigrés to forsake their homeland.*

NOTES

1. A classic example of this argument is to be found in A. D. Lindsay, *The Modern Democratic State* (Oxford, 1943), 115-121; also G. P. Gooch, *English Democratic Ideas in the Seventeenth Century* (New York, 1959). The argument appears in a more sophisticated form in the introduction of A. S. P. Woodhouse's edition of the army debates, *Puritanism and Liberty* (London, 1951).

2. That ideas are merely "clothed" in religious fashion for convenience, out of force of habit, or because other clothing was somehow not available is, of course, a Marxist argument. See Perez Zagorin, *A History of Political Thought in the English Revolution* (London, 1954). It presupposes a very awkward theory of expression according to which content and form have little intrinsic connection.

3. Max Weber, *The Protestant Ethic and the Spirit of Capitalism*, trans. Talcott Parsons (New York, 1958), esp. 26-27, 53. When Herbert Marcuse analyzes Soviet Marxism, he discovers a "protestant ethic"—but this is clearly a rationalist ethic and not an acquisitive one; *Soviet Marxism: A Critical Analysis* (New York, 1961), 217, 222-23.

4. This view is most clearly argued by Christopher Hill, *Puritanism and Revolution* (London, 1958), esp. chapters 1 and 7; compare this with Hill's earlier pamphlet, *The English Revolution: 1640* (London, 1940).

5. See Perry Miller, *Orthodoxy in Massachusetts, 1630-1650* (Boston, 1959), chapter I; Charles H. and Katherine George, *The Protestant Mind of the English Reformation. 1570-1640* (Princeton, 1961), chapter 6; Richard Schlatter, *Richard Baxter and Puritan Politics* (New Brunswick, 1957), introduction.

6. Quoted in Horton Davies, *The Worship of the English Puritans* (Westminster, 1948), 235.

7. Richard Baxter, *Reliquiae Baxterianae*, ed. M. Sylvester (London, 1696), 87.

8. The term "natural political virtue" is that of Locke's latest editor; see Peter Laslett's edition of the *Two Treatises* (Cambridge, 1960), 108 f. The extraordinary difficulty with which self-control is learned is best described—that is, described with some sensitivity to human pain—by Nietzsche, in *The Genealogy of Morals*. He is writing of a very early period in human history, but his insights have some relevance to the sixteenth and seventeenth centuries. How free Locke was from any sense of the dangers of *uncontrolled* men is evident in his "Letter on Toleration". Compare his description there of voluntary association in religious matters with Jean Bodin's demand a century earlier for a strict moral discipline enforced by elders, *The Six Books of the Republic*, trans. M. J. Tooley (Oxford, n.d.), 184-85. On this point, as on many others, Bodin is very close to the Calvinists.

9. Weber's most recent critic, Kurt Samuelsson, hardly discusses the idea of rationalization which is so central to his argument; *Religion and Economic Action*, trans. E. G. French (Stockholm, 1961).

10. For a detailed criticism of Weber on these points, see George, *op. cit.*, chapters 2 and 3; also Samuelsson, *op. cit.*, esp. 27 ff. Samuelsson's first chapter discusses the men who have accepted or been significantly influenced by this aspect of Weber's argument; these are the men who are called "Weberians" in this essay. It should be said that Weber himself—if not always his followers—was very conscious of the savage repression which Calvinism sponsored; the question of why bourgeois men should accept such discipline is central to his book (*op. cit.*, 37). Nevertheless, the particular forms of repression and control described above are not considered in *The Protestant Ethic*.

11. The restrictionist attitudes of Mably and Morelli are discussed in J. L. Talmon, *The Origins of Totalitarian Democracy* (New York, 1960), 58 ff.

12. Weber, *op. cit.*, 180 ff.

13. This is not to suggest that anxiety about salvation—the fear of hellfire—was *really* anxiety about something else. It will be argued below that the Puritans *said* it was about something else.

14. On the last of these, see the fascinating (and moving) *Letters of Lady Brilliania Harley*, ed. T. T. Lewis (London, 1854).

15. Thus Christopher Hill: "[Calvin] abandoned the traditional absolute prohibition of usury (which theologians had whittled away by allowing exceptions) and permitted it in principle (though restricting it very stringently in a great many particular instances). So revolutions of thought are initiated. This slight shift of emphasis . . . was enough." (*op. cit.*, 219). One can only comment that intellectual revolutions of this sort are not revolutions. On the question of usury, see the interesting discussion in Samuelsson, *op. cit.*, 87 ff.

16. Marx and Engels, *Basic Writings on Politics and Philosophy*, ed. Lewis S. Feuer (New York, 1959), 55-56.

17. *Navaho Witchcraft* (Cambridge, Mass., 1944), esp. 50 ff and 64-66.

18. Wallace Notestein, *A History of Witchcraft in England from 1558 to 1718* (Washington, 1911), 14-15, 195 ff.

19. Much of the argument of this essay was first suggested by Erich Fromm's book, *Escape from Freedom* (New York, 1941), but the author cannot accept Fromm's easy distinction between two aspects of modern freedom: freedom *from*, which by itself leads to anxiety and the search for authority; and freedom *to*, which presumably is realized in a sense of dignity and a creative life. That the two are not distinct in history, that is, not always embodied in different people—Fromm clearly recognizes. He seems, however, to believe that their manifestations can be readily distinguished and judged. Thus, for example, he writes that the Puritans, when fighting against the old order, were expressing positive freedom ("strength and dignity of self"—*Escape*, 122). Since that fight involved an effort to establish the repressive holy commonwealth, this seems rather dubious.

20. On the growth of London, see the figures in F. P. Wilson *The Plague in Shakespeare's London* (Oxford, 1927), appendix. That members of Puritan conventicles were often newcomers to the city is suggested by the court records reprinted in Champlin Burrage, *The Early English Dissenters in the Light of Recent Research 1550-1641* (Cambridge, 1912), II.

21. *Institutes of the Christian Religion* (Allen translation), Book, I, chapter XVII, x.

22. *Ibid.*, xi.

23. Alfred Harbage has pointed out that Puritans objected more to the audience at the theaters than to the plays: see his *Shakespeare's Audience* (New York, 1951).

24. Jonson, *Bartholomew Fair*; see also his characterizations of two Puritans in *The Alchemist*.

25. Bolton, *Two Sermons* (London, 1635), I, 10. The passage is a curious one since it opens with a paraphrase of Hooker, *Ecclesiastical Polity*, I, iii, 2; but Hooker says nothing about the effects of disobedience *among men*, which is the Puritan writer's chief concern.

26. John Whitgift, *Works*, I, 21.

27. The report to Walsingham is quoted in Hill, *Puritanism and Revolution*, 234. John Penry, *An Humble Motion with Submission* (Edinburgh, 1590), 72.

28. The views of the moralists are described in L. C. Knights, *Drama and Society in the Age of Jonson* (London, 1937).

29. *Two Elizabethan Diaries*, ed. M. Knappen (Chicago, 1933), 69.

30. They wrote about more than these themes, of course, and even here described more than their own experience, for the outsider is an archetypal figure realized with especial force in Christian thought. The Puritans still lived within a cultural tradition which shaped their expression as it undoubtedly still shaped their experience. On the dangers of reductionism, see Leavis, *op. cit.*, 208-10.

31. *Diary of Lady Margaret Hoby, 1599-1605*, ed. D. M. Meads (London, 1930), 97.

32. See the comments of William Haller on Puritan wayfaring: *The Rise of Puritanism* (New York, 1957), 147 ff.

33. William Perkins, *Works* (London, 1616), III, 539; the passage is quoted in Hill, *op. cit.*, 228.

34. Greenham, *Works* (London, 1605), 645; Perkins, *op. cit.*, I, 398.

35. *Two Elizabethan Diaries*, 17; A. F. Scott-Pearson, *Thomas Cartwright and Elizabethan Puritanism* (Cambridge, 1925), 66; *Diary of Margaret Hoby*, 32—at their wedding, the Hoby's sought "only to please the beholders with a sermon and a dinner."

36. *Cromwell's Letters and Speeches*, ed. Carlyle (London, 1893), I, 79-80. On Winthrop see E. S. Morgan, *The Puritan Dilemma: The Story of John Winthrop* (Boston, 1958).

37. Indeed, Calvin thought that commercial competition, with its attendant anxiety, was an aspect of the life of *fallen* man; he pictured him nervously murmuring to himself: "I must use such a mean, I must practise such a feat. I must look into such a business, or otherwise I shall be behindhand in all things. I shall but pine away, I shall not get half my living, if I proceed not in this manner. . . ." *Sermons upon the Fifth Book of Moses* (London, 1583), 821. Presumably the saint would be free from such anxiety.

38. Most of the calls for activity in Puritan sermons are put in terms of the struggle against

social disorder; activity is rarely described as a way of overcoming the fear of damnation. The clear emphasis of the preachers is on the social effects of hard work, and not, as Weber thought, on success as a spiritual sign. See, for example, the discussion of work in Robert Cleaver and John Dod, *A Godly Form of Household Government* (London, 1621), Sig. P 6 and 7.

39. See Walter Travers, *A Full and Plain Declaration of Ecclesiastical Discipline out of the Word of God* (n. p., 1574).

40. Cleaver and Dod, *op. cit.*, Sig. S 8; Bodin, *op. cit.*, 9-13.

41. Thomas Reed, *Moses Old Square for Judges* (London, 1632), 98-99.

42. Lenin, *The Immediate Tasks of the Soviet Government* (1918) in *Selected Works* (New York, 1935-1937), VII, 332-33.

43. *How to Organize Competition* (1917, reprinted Moscow, 1951), 63; also see *Letters* trans. and ed. by Elizabeth Hill and Doris Mudie (New York, 1937), 161.

44. Henry Crosse, *Virtue's Commonwealth* (London, 1603), Sig. L₄ *vers*; Perkins, *Works*, III, 191.

45. Quoted in A. Aulard, *Christianity and the French Revolution* (Boston, 1927), 113.

46. Quoted in Klara Zetkin, "Reminiscences of Lenin", in *The Family in the U.S.S.R.*, ed. Rudolf Schlesinger (London, 1949), 78. It should be said that in all the revolutions discussed above, there were men who did not follow the Puritan saints or the vanguard Bolsheviks in their attacks upon human freedom. These men, radical sectarians, secularists, anarchists, libertarians of many sorts, were the products of the same society and the same experience which produced the others. They rarely made good revolutionaries, however, precisely because they never felt the intense need to yield to an organization and a discipline.

47. This is the view of revolutionary enthusiasm suggested in Crane Brinton's book on the French revolution, *Decade of Revolution* (New York, 1934) and again in his *Anatomy of Revolution* (New York, 1938). The analogy with religion argued in both books is, however, a very suggestive one.

PART TWO

THE NEW ENGLAND WAY: FAITH AND PRACTICE

The debate over the nature of Puritan theology is as heated as that dealing with the rise and influence of the movement. The course of the former debate was set primarily by Perry Miller. In *Orthodoxy in Massachusetts* (Cambridge, Mass., 1933), *The New England Mind: The Seventeenth Century* (New York, 1939), *The New England Mind: From Colony to Province* (Cambridge, Mass., 1953), and in essays collected in *Errand into the Wilderness* (Cambridge, Mass., 1956) and *Nature's Nation* (Cambridge, Mass., 1967), Miller presented a reconstruction of Puritan thought that remains one of the outstanding achievements of American intellectual history. Although he recognized an "Augustinian strain of piety" as vital to the Puritan movement, Miller chose instead to investigate the Puritan mind.

Before the publication of Miller's *New England Mind: The Seventeenth Century*, accounts of early America seldom gave serious attention to Puritan theology or philosophy; their primary concerns were with economic and political interests and institutions. Writers such as James Truslow Adams (*The Founding of New England* [Boston, 1921]) and Vernon Louis Parrington (*Main Currents in American Thought: The Colonial Mind, 1620–1800* [New York, 1927]) looked askance at Puritan rhetoric and assumed that it rarely meant what it said. Miller, on the other hand, took the Puritans largely, though not entirely, at their word. And he insisted that words—especially the words of clergymen in a theocentric society—mattered greatly because they revealed the society's fundamental ideas and aspirations. Thus Miller searched through vast numbers of sermons and religious tracts for insights into the Puritan mind.

Miller's explanations of early New England thought are not easy reading; he recognized the complexity of seventeenth-century religious ideology and respected its intellectual integrity. He attempted to reconstruct the New England mind, therefore, without reducing it to simplistic formulas or facile explanations. At times (we now know) Miller erred. But so far, no scholar has produced an adequate revision—in either magnitude or sophistication. What we know of the Puritan mind still depends heavily on Miller's analysis, augmented here and there by more recent scholarship.

3 | THE MARROW
OF PURITAN DIVINITY

PERRY MILLER

Central to Miller's synthesis was what he labeled "Federal Theology"—the Puritan reliance upon covenants. From their earliest days in New England, the Puritans, in Miller's view, used the covenant idiom extensively as they sought to make intelligible and to give order to relationships with one another and with God. Covenants dictated the organization of congregations (church covenants), communities (town covenants), and the state (social covenants). Covenantal imagery also defined the process of salvation (the covenant of works between God and Adam, the covenant of grace between God and fallen humanity) as well as the relationship between God and his new chosen people, the New England colonists (the national covenant). In their theological use of the concept, the Puritans created a hallmark of their uniqueness and demonstrated their distance from John Calvin. It was, in short, "The Marrow of Puritan Divinity," as Miller aptly refers to it in the title of the selection that follows.

We invariably think of the original settlers of New England as "Calvinists." So indeed they were, if we mean that in general terms they conceived of man and the universe much as did John Calvin. But when we call them Calvinists, we are apt to imply that they were so close in time and temperament to the author of the *Institutes* that they carried to America his thought and system inviolate, and to suppose that their intellectual life consisted only in reiterating this volume. Yet students of technical theology have long since realized that Calvinism was in the process of modification by the year 1630. There had come to be numerous departures from or developments within the pristine creed, and "Calvinism" in the seventeenth century covered almost as many shades of opinion as does "socialism" in the twentieth. The New England leaders did not stem directly from Calvin;[1] they learned the Calvinist theology only after it had been improved, embellished, and in many respects transformed by a host of hard-thinking expounders and critics. The system had been thoroughly gone over by Dutchmen and Scotchmen, and nothing ever left the hands of these shrewd peoples precisely as it came to them; furthermore, for seventy years or more English theologians had been mulling it over, tinkering and remodelling, rearranging emphases, and, in the course of adapting it to Anglo-Saxon requirements, generally blurring its Gallic clarity and incisiveness.

. . .

It is of the essence of this theology that God, the force, the power, the life of the universe, remains to men hidden, unknowable, unpredictable.

He is the ultimate secret, the awful mystery. God's nature "is capable properly of no definition," so that all that one can say is that "God is an incomprehensible, first, and absolute Being."[2] He cannot be approached directly; man cannot stand face to face with Him, "for in doing so, what do we else but draw neere to God, as the stubble or the waxe should draw neer to the fire? . . . He is a consuming fire to the sonnes of men, if they come to him immediately."[3] The English Puritans may be called Calvinists primarily because they held this central conception, though the thought is older in Christian history than Calvin, and they did not necessarily come to it only under Calvin's own tuition. "Now, sayth the Lord, my thoughts go beyond your thought as much as the distance is betweene heaven and earth."[4] William Ames, whose *Medulla Sacrae Theologiae* was the standard text-book of theology in New England, lays it down at the very beginning that "what God is, none can perfectly define, but that hath the Logicke of God himselfe,"[5] and argues that therefore our observance of His will can never be based upon God's "secret will," but only upon His explicitly revealed command.[6] William Perkins, from whom Ames and English Puritans in general drew a great share of their inspiration, asserted squarely once and for all that even the virtues of reasonableness or justice, as human beings conceive them, could not be predicated of God, for God's will "it selfe is an absolute rule both of iustice and reason"; and that nothing could therefore be reasonable and just intrinsically, "but it is first of all willed by God, and thereupon becomes reasonable and iust."[7] The glory of God no man or angel shall know, preached Thomas Shepard; "their cockle shell can never comprehend this sea"; we can only apprehend Him by knowing that we cannot comprehend Him at all, "as we admire the luster of the sun the more in that it is so great we can not behold it."

. . .

The history of theology in this period indicates that the process of development was accomplished in many guises. Learned doctors wrote gigantic tomes on the Trinity or the Incarnation, and soon were creating for Protestantism a literature of apologetics that rivalled the Scholastic, not only in bulk, but in subtlety, ingenuity, and logic-chopping. For our purposes it is possible to distinguish three important issues which particularly occupied the attention of Dutch and English Calvinists. These are not the only points of controversy or development, but they may be said to be the major preoccupations in the theology of early New England. Calvinism had already by 1630 been subjected to attack for what seemed to Catholic, Lutheran, and Anglican critics its tendency toward self-righteousness at the expense of morality; in spite of Calvin's insistence that the elect person must strive to subject himself to the moral law—"Away, then," he cried, "with such corrupt and sacrilegious perversions of the whole order of election"[9]— there was always the danger that the doctrine of predestination would lead in practice to the attitude: "If I am elected, I am elected, there is nothing I can do about it." If man must wait upon God for grace, and grace is irrespective of works, simple folk might very well ask, why worry about works at all? Calvinist preachers were often able to answer this question only with a mere assertion. Calvin simply brushed aside all objection and roundly declared: "Man, being taught that he has nothing good left in his possession, and being surrounded on every side with the most miserable necessity, should, nevertheless, be instructed to aspire to the good of which he is destitute."[10] Perkins taught that the will of man before it receives grace is impotent and in the reception is purely passive: "by it selfe it can neither beginne that conuersion, or any other inward and sound obedience due to Gods law";[11] he distinctly said that God's predestination is regardless of any quality or merit in the individual, and that man can achieve any sort of obedience only after being elected. Ames restated this doctrine; yet at whatever cost to consistency, he had to assert that though without faith man can do nothing acceptable to God, he still has to perform certain duties because the duties "are in themselves good."[12] The divines were acutely conscious that this was demanding what their own theory had made impossible, and they were struggling to find some possible grounds for proving the necessity of "works" without curtailing the absolute freedom of God to choose and reject regardless of man's achievement.

Along with this problem came another which Calvin had not completely resolved, that of individual assurance, of when and how a man might reach some working conviction that he was of the regenerate. The decrees of election and reprobation were, according to Calvin, inscrutable secrets locked deep in the fastness of the transcendent Will:

> Let them remember that when they inquire into predestination, they penetrate the inmost recesses of Divine wisdom, where the careless and confident intruder will obtain no satisfaction to his curiosity, but will enter a labyrinth from which he will find no way to depart. For it is unreasonable that man should scrutinize with impunity those things which the Lord has determined to be hidden in himself; and investigate, even from eternity, that sublimity of wisdom which God would have us to adore and not comprehend, to promote our admiration of his glory.[13]

This was sufficient for men of 1550, but men of 1600 wished to ascertain something more definite about their own predicament. The curve of religious intensity was beginning to droop, and preachers knew that a more precise form of stimulation had to be invoked to arrest the decline; men wished to know what there was in it for them; they could not forever be incited to faith or persuaded to obey if some tangible reward could not be placed before them. Yet to say roundly that all the elect would be immediately satisfied by God of their promotion was to say that God was bound to satisfy human curiosity. The theologians could only rest in another inconsistency that was becoming exceedingly glaring in the light of a more minute analysis. Assurance is sealed to all believers, said Ames, yet the perceiving of it "is not always present to all";[14] this uncertainty, he was forced to admit, is a detriment to "that consolation and peace which Christ hath left to believers."[15]

In both these discussions the attempt to arrive at bases for certainty led directly to the fundamental problem: no grounds for moral obligation or individual assurance could be devised as long as God was held to act in ways that utterly disregarded human necessities or human logic. In order to know that God will unquestionably save him under such and such circumstances, man must know that God is in reality the sort of being who would, or even who will have to, abide by these conditions, and none other. He must ascertain the whys and wherefores of the divine activity. In some fashion the transcendent God had to be chained, made less inscrutable, less mysterious, less unpredictable—He had to be made, again, understandable in human terms. If the sway of the moral law over men were to be maintained, men must know what part it played in their gaining assurance of salvation; if men were to know the conditions upon which they could found an assurance, they must be convinced that God would be bound by those conditions, that He would not at any moment ride roughshod over them, act suddenly from an abrupt whimsy or from caprice, that salvation was not the irrational bestowal of favor according to the passing mood of a lawless tyrant.

. . .

The Arminian movement in Holland (and the "Arminian" theology in the Church of England) represented one Calvinist attempt to supply a reasonable explanation of the relation of God to man. But Arminians went too far; they jeopardized the foundations of Calvinism, and were stigmatized as heretics at the Synod of Dort. In the seventeenth century Arminianism stood as a ghastly warning to all Calvinists. It was an admonition to stay well inside the structure of the creed, whatever redecorations they undertook. The orthodox soon perceived that the basic error in Arminianism was not any one of its "five points" formulated at Dort, but its exaltation of the human reason and consequently its reconstruction of God after the human image. William Ames said that grace, as conceived by the Arminians, "may be the effect of a good dinner sometimes";[16] and Thomas Shepard pointed out that by their putting into the unregenerate will and the natural reason an ability to undertake moral duties and to work out assurance without the impetus of grace, they became no better than heathen philosophers and Roman Stoics.

> . . . I heard an Arminian once say, If faith will not work it, then set reason a-work, and we know how men have been kings and lords over their own passions by improving reason, and from some experience of the power of nature men have come to write large volumes in defence of it; and . . . the Arminians, though they ascribe somewhat to grace, . . . yet, indeed, they lay the main stress of the work upon a man's own will, and the royalty and sovereignty of that liberty.[17]

The Arminians yielded too far to the pressure for construing theology in a more rational fashion and so succumbed to the temptation of smuggling too much human freedom into the ethics of predestination. A more promising, if less spectacular, mode of satisfying these importunities without falling into heresy was suggested in the work of the great Cambridge theologian, William Perkins, fellow of Christ College, who died in 1602. Anyone who reads much in the writings of early New Englanders learns that Perkins was a towering figure in Puritan eyes. Nor were

English and American divines alone in their veneration for him. His works were translated into many languages and circulated in all Reformed communities; he was one of the outstanding pulpit orators of the day, and the seventeenth century, Catholic as well as Protestant, ranked him with Calvin. He was one of the first to smell out the Arminian heresy[18]—"a new devised doctrine of Predestination," he called it—and his works were assailed by Arminius as being the very citadel of the doctrine he opposed. As I read Perkins today, it seems to me that the secret of his fame is primarily the fact that he was a superb popularizer. His books were eminently practical in character. He was typically English in that he was bored by too intricate speculation on a purely theoretical plane, and that he wanted results. Thomas Fuller hit him off with his customary facility when he said that Perkins "brought the schools into the pulpit, and, unshelling their controversies out of their hard school-terms, made thereof plain and wholesome meat for his people."[19] I cannot find that in making wholesome meat out of controversy Perkins added any new doctrines to theology; he is in every respect a meticulously sound and orthodox Calvinist. What he did contribute was an energetic evangelical emphasis; he set out to arouse and inflame his hearers. Consequently, one of his constant refrains was that the minutest, most microscopic element of faith in the soul is sufficient to be accounted the work of God's spirit. Man can start the labor of regeneration as soon as he begins to feel the merest desire to be saved. Instead of conceiving of grace as some cataclysmic, soul-transforming experience, he whittles it down almost, but not quite, to the vanishing point; he says that it is a tiney seed planted in the soul, that it is up to the soul to water and cultivate it, to nourish it into growth.[20]

This idea was palliative; it lessened the area of human inability and gave the preacher a prod for use on those already, though not too obviously, regenerate. In Perkins's works appear also the rudiments of another idea, which he did not stress particularly, but which in the hands of his students was to be enormously extended. He occasionally speaks of the relationship between God and man as resting on "the Covenant of Grace," and defines this as God's "contract with man, concerning the obtaining of life eternall, upon a certaine condition."[21] He uses the covenant to reinforce his doctrine of the duty that man owes to God of cultivating the slightest seed of grace that he may receive.

The most eminent of Perkins's many disciples was Dr. William Ames, who in 1610 was so prominent a Puritan that he found it advisable to flee to Holland, where he became professor of theology at the University of Franeker. He was the friend and often the master of many of the New England divines, and I have elsewhere claimed for him that he, more than any other one individual, is the father of the New England church polity.[22] Like Perkins, Ames was an orthodox Calvinist. His was a more logical and disciplined mind than that of his teacher, and his great works, the *Medulla Sacrae Theologiae* (1623) and *De Conscientia* (1630), became important text-books on the Continent, in England, and in New England because of their compact systematization of theology. There is very little difference between his thought and Perkins's, except that he accords much more space to the covenant. He sets forth its nature more elaborately, sharply distinguishes the Covenants of Works and of Grace, and provides an outline of the history of the Covenant of Grace from the time, not of Christ, but of Abraham.[23]

In 1622, John Preston became Master of Emmanuel College, Cambridge. Preston was the statesman, the politician among Puritan divines. He was that Puritan upon whom the Duke of Buckingham showered his favor while fondly endeavoring to delude the Puritans into rallying about his very un-Puritanical banner. Preston had been converted in 1611 by a sermon of John Cotton, and was a close friend of Cotton, Davenport, and Hooker; his works, like those of Perkins, were a mainstay of New England libraries. Like Perkins, he was a magnificent preacher, but he was so active a man that he published little before his death in 1628. His works were issued posthumously, one of the editors being John Davenport. Thomas Goodwin, later the great Independent leader, was another editor, and in the preface to one volume says that Preston spent his living thoughts and breath "in unfolding and applying, the most proper and peculiar Characters of Grace, which is Gods Image; whereby Beleevers came to be assured, that God is their God, and they in covenant with him."[24] This passage reveals the great contribution of Preston to the development of Calvinist thought, for in the elaborate exegesis which Preston devoted to unfolding and expounding the philosophy of the covenant, which he held to be "one of the main points in Divinitie,"[25] he contrived the seeming solution of the problems which then beset his colleagues. His greatest work on this subject (though all his many books deal with it to some extent) was entitled *The New Covenant, or The Saints Portion* (London, 1629). This work is prerequisite to an understanding of thought and theology in seventeenth-century New England.

Another friend of Preston, probably his closest, was Richard Sibbes, preacher at Gray's Inn from 1617 until his death in 1635, and Master of St. Catherine's Hall, Cambridge, from 1626. He, too, was an editor of Preston's work; it was to a sermon of his that John Cotton owed his own conversion, and Davenport and Goodwin edited many volumes of Sibbes's writings after 1635. Throughout these writings the covenant is expounded and all the theology reshaped in the light of this doctrine. One of the fascinating aspects of the history of this idea is the intimate connection that seems to exist among most of its exponents; they form a group bound together by personal ties, and the completed theology is the work of all rather than of any one man. Sibbes was associated with Gouge in the "feofees" scheme; he was the friend and correspondent of Bishop Ussher. He edited a work of John Ball, and one of his students at St. Catherine's was William Strong, who died in 1654, and whose treatise *Of the Covenant* was prepared for the press by Sibbes's friend Lady Elizabeth Rich in 1678. In the work of all these authors the covenant plays a conspicuous part. Furthermore, this group seems to coincide frequently with the coherent group who formulated the peculiar philosophy of Non-Separating Congregationalism.[26] They were students or friends of Ames, whose works they quote frequently. Sibbes owed his conversion to a sermon of Paul Baynes, and he edited Baynes's *Exposition of Ephesians*. There are many ascertainable relations of almost all the school with one or more of the New England divines; their works were read in New England, and Perkins, Ames, Preston, and Sibbes are clearly the most quoted, most respected, and most influential of contemporary authors in the writings and sermons of early Massachusetts. . . .

. . .

The theology of the Covenant of Grace, invested with such importance by these authors, proceeds upon a theory of history. It holds that man has not only been in relation to God as creature to creator, subject to lord, but more definitely through a succession of explicit agreements or contracts, as between two partners in a business enterprise. God entered into such a bond with man as soon as He created him. He stipulated that if Adam performed certain things He would pledge Himself to reward Adam and Adam's posterity with eternal life. In order that man might know what was required of him, Adam was given specific injunctions in the form of the moral law. In addition, the law was implanted in his heart, built into his very being, so that he might perform his duties naturally and instinctively. The original Covenant of Works, therefore, is the Law of Nature, that which uncorrupted man would naturally know and by which he would naturally regulate his life. Of course, Adam failed to keep this covenant, and by breaking the bond incurred the just penalties. But God did not rest there. Beginning with Abraham, He made a new covenant, and the seventeenth chapter of Genesis, which describes the new bargain, becomes thereby the basic text for the school. The new covenant is just as much an agreement as its predecessor, stipulating terms on both sides to which the contracting parties are bound.

> . . . these words containe the *Covenant* on both sides, sayth the *Lord*, this is the *Covenant* that I will make on my part, *I will be thy God* . . . you shall have all things in me that your hearts can desire: The *Covenant* againe, that I require on your part, is that you be *perfect with me*, that you be *upright*, that you be without *hypocrisie*. . . .[27]

The idea of a mutual obligation, of both sides bound and committed by the terms of the document, is fundamental to the whole thought.

> It has pleased the great God to enter into a treaty and covenant of agreement with us his poor creatures, the articles of which agreement are here comprised. God, for his part, undertakes to convey all that concerns our happiness, upon our receiving of them, by believing on him. Every one in particular that recites these articles from a spirit of faith makes good this condition.[28]

Furthermore, in form at least, a bargain between two persons with duties on both sides is an arrangement between equals.

> . . . he takes *Abraham* as a friend for ever, and *Abraham* takes God as his friend for ever; and this league of friendship implyes not only preservation of affection, but it requires a kinde of secret communication one to another, and a doing one for another.[24]

In the Covenant of Grace, God, observing the form, contracts with man as with a peer. But since the Fall man is actually unable to fulfil the law or to *do* anything on his own initiative. Therefore God demands of him now not a deed but a belief, a simple faith in Christ the mediator. And on His own side, God voluntarily undertakes, not only to save those who believe, but to supply the power of belief, to provide the grace that will make possible man's fulfilling the terms of this new and easier covenant. "In the Covenant of works a man is left to himselfe, to stand by his own strength; But in the Covenant of grace, God undertakes for us, to keep us through faith."[30] Man has only to pledge that, when it is given him, he will avail himself of the assistance which makes belief possible. If he can believe, he has fulfilled the compact; God then must redeem him and glorify him.

The covenant which God made with Abraham is the Covenant of Grace, the same in which we are now bound. The only difference is that Abraham was required to believe that Christ would come to be mediator for the covenant and compensate God for the failure of Adam; since Christ we have merely to believe that He has come and that He is the "surety" for the new covenant. But from Abraham to Peter Bulkley the covenant between God and man is one and the same. "We are the children of *Abraham*; and therefore we are under *Abrahams* covenant."[31] This arrangement between the two is not simply a promise on God's part, it is a definite commitment. These authors, in fact, practically do away with the conception of God as merely promising, and substitute a legal theory of God's delivering to man a signed and sealed bond. "It is impertinent to put a difference betweene the promise and the Covenant . . . The promise of God and his Covenant . . . are ordinarily put one for another."[32] The covenant therefore, is the only method by which God deals with man at all. Salvation is not conveyed by simple election, influence, promise, or choice; it comes only through the covenant and only to those who are in the covenant with God.

> God conveys his salvation by way of covenant, and he doth it to those onely that are in covenant with him . . . this covenant must every soule enter into, every particular soule must enter into a particular covenant with God; out of this way there is no life . . .[33]

This legalized version of Biblical history may at first sight seem to offer nothing toward a solution of the problems of Calvinism. It may even appear an unnecessarily complicated posing of the same issues, for the grace which gives salvation even in the covenant comes only from God and is at His disposing. But in the hands of these expert dialecticians the account leads to gratifying conclusions. In their view it succeeded in reconciling all contradictions, smoothing out all inconsistencies, securing a basis for moral obligation and for assurance of salvation while yet not subtracting from God's absolute power or imposing upon Him any limitations prescribed by merely human requirements.

. . .

The historical theory of the Covenant of Grace, its progressive unfolding from Abraham to the Christian era, permitted these theologians to add the final touches to their portrait of the divine character. God did not simply present the covenant point-blank to fallen man, but introduced it by degrees, unfolding it gradually as men could be educated up to it. The beginnings of this conception are to be found in Ames, and it was probably his chief contribution to the system. He said that though from the time of Abraham there has been one and the same covenant, "yet the manner . . . of administring this new Covenant, hath not alwayes beene one and the same, but divers according to the ages in which the Church hath been gathered."[34] While other writers in the school sometimes drew up charts of the stages different from Ames's,[35] all agreed that God has allowed the covenant to grow with time. He first administered it through conscience, then through the prophets and ceremonies, now through Christ, preaching of the Word, and the sacraments. He has done this, the writers agreed, out of solicitous consideration for man's limitations; had the whole thing been enunciated to Abraham, it would have put too great a strain upon his faith, already overburdened as it was in the effort to believe that Sarah would conceive. "Dr. *Ames* saith well," Bulkley wrote, "the Church was then considered . . . Partly as an heire, and partly as an infant. . . ."[36] By the long period of tuition in the covenant in its Old Testament form, the Church was educated up to grasping it clearly and distinctly.

> . . . the nature of man is so exceeding opposite to the doctrine of Christ and the Gospel, that if it had not been long framed by the tutoring of many hundred yeers by the Law, it had never been convinced of the necessitie of salvation by Christ, and the Gospel.[37]

The effect of this theory was to introduce an element of historical relativity into the absolute dogmatism of original Calvinism. God is seen deliberately refraining from putting His decisions fully into effect until man can cope with them and profit by them. He is not so much a mail-clad seigneur as a skillful teacher, and He contrives on every hand that men may be brought to truth, not by compulsion, but by conviction. For these reasons theologians of this complexion were eagerly disposed to prize knowledge, logic, metaphysics, and history. They were prepared to go as far as their age could go in the study of Biblical history and commentary, for truth to them resided in the history as well as in the doctrine. Preston confesses that intellectual persuasion and historical research are not in themselves sufficient for absolute faith in the Scriptures unless God also "infuseth an inward light by his Spirit to worke this faith." Yet even so he holds that sufficient testimonies exist in the Scriptures "to give evidence of themselves."[38] Knowledge is not to be despised because faith also is necessary: "Wisedome is the best of all vaine things under the Sunne."[39] Knowledge and faith must go hand in hand:

> I deny not but a man may have much knowledge, and want Grace; but, on the other side, looke how much Grace a man hath, so much knowledge he must have of necessity. . . . You cannot have more Grace than you have knowledge. . . .[40]

It is a significant indication of the bent of his mind that Preston argues for the reliability of Scripture because heathen histories corroborate Old Testament chronology.[41]

To describe this theology as "rationalism" would be very much to overstate the case; before the triumph of Newtonian science reason did not have the rigid connotation it was later to carry. Preston drew back from out-and-out mechanism, and he never doubted that even where God was steering events by the rudder of causation, He was charting the course according to His own pleasure. But in this way of thought appears an entering wedge of what must be called, if not rationalism, then reasonableness. It is a philosophy that put a high valuation upon intellect. Its tendency is invariably in the direction of harmonizing theology with natural, comprehensible processes. The authors were prepared to welcome the scientific advance of the century with open arms, until some of their successors in the next century were to realize too late that they had let the wooden horse of rationalism into the Trojan citadel of theology. But thus early there were few misgivings; the Puritans were so secure in their faith that they could with perfect serenity make it as understandable as possible.

. . .

The contract between God and man, once entered into, signed by both parties and sealed, as it were, in the presence of witnesses, is ever afterwards binding. This exceedingly legal basis furnishes the guarantee, not only for the assurance of the saints, but even for their perseverance. In the covenant, says Hooker, the soul "is inseparably knit to Christ";[42] though you falter in action and fall short of holiness, if you have once become a member of the covenant, the covenant "doth remain sure and firm," said John Cotton. "If we be hemm'd in within this Covenant, we cannot break out."[43]

Thus bound by His own commitment, God must live up to His word. If you do your part, He must, willy-nilly, do His. As Bulkley says, "He hath passed over those things by covenant, and he cannot be a covenant breaker"; hence, "we might have the more strong consolation, assuring ourselves of the fulfilling of his gracious promise towards us."[44] Pursuing this logic, these men broached one of their most daring ideas: if a man can prove that he has faith, he has then done his part and can hold God to account, hale Him into court and force Him to give what has become the man's just and legal due: "You may sue him of his own bond written and sealed, and he cannot deny it."[45]

> . . . when faith hath once gotten a promise, be sure that thou keepe thy hold, pleade hard with the *Lord*, and tell him it is a part of his Covenant, and it is impossible that he should deny thee . . . when thou art on a sure ground, take no denyall, though the *Lord* may defer long, yet he will doe it, he cannot chuse; for it is a part of his Covenant.[46]

We do not surrender ourselves to God without getting something in return: "we require this back againe of God, that as we give up our selves a sacrifice to him, so that the Lord Jesus Christ might be imputed unto us."[47] If we are in the covenant, "we are then out of danger, wee need not to fear."[48] Considering what the background of Protestant thought had been, what ruthless determination had been postulated behind the predestinating Divinity, one might well feel that Preston comments upon this conception of salvation with an understatement that is almost comic: "This is a very comfortable doctrine, if it be well considered."[49]

. . .

Thus the Federal theory, freeing man from the absolute moral impotence of the strict doctrine, first made possible an enlargement of his innate capacities. Secondly, it provided a logical device for immediately enlisting these capacities in the service of morality, even before they had been further invigorated by divine grace. It had been with these considerations in mind that God framed the covenant precisely as He did, and thereby demonstrated His cleverness by devising a scheme to insure the continuation of moral obligation even in a covenant of forgiveness. He did not discard the Covenant of Works after Adam's fall; He included it within the Covenant of Grace. "For the Morall Law, the Law of the ten Commandments, we are dead also to the covenant of that law, though not to the command of it."[50] But in this arrangement it exists no longer as a command, the literal fulfilment of which is required of man, but as a description of the goal of conduct toward which the saint incessantly strives. The Law, which no man can perfectly fulfil any more, exists as a "schoole-master"; it teaches us what we should do, whether we can or no, and as soon as we realize that we cannot, we flee to Christ for the assistance of grace. And since Christ has satisfied God by fulfilling the Law, there is no necessity that we do it also. It is only necessary that we attempt it. God's agreement in the second covenant is that if a man will believe, he will receive the grace enabling him to approximate a holy life, but his failure to reach perfection will not be held against him. "We ought not to thinke, because we are not exact in keeping all the Commandements of *God* . . . that therefore *God* rejects us. . . ."[51] The regeneration of any man, as long as he is in the body, will be imperfect at best. It will manifest itself in a perpetual struggle to an unattainable end, and according to the Covenant of Grace God will accept the intention and the effort for the deed.

> . . . there will bee impuritie in the heart wherein there is faith, but yet where there is faith, there is a continuall purging out of impuritie, as it manifesteth it selfe. You may conceive it by a similtude, if a pot be boyling upon the fire, there will a scum arise, but yet they that are good house-wives, and cleanly, and neat, they watch it, and as the scum riseth up, they take it off and throw it away, happily more scum will arise, but still as it riseth they scum it off.[52]

The demand made upon benighted human nature in the Covenant of Grace is not exorbitant, and demonstrates again how solicitous God appears as He is pictured by this school. It is indeed a little surprising to the modern student to find how large a part of Puritan sermons was devoted to proving to people that they need not be weighed down with too great a sense of sin. The ministers seem to have been fully aware that the stark predestination of early Calvinism was too often driving sincere Christians to distraction, and that it needed to be softened, humanized. Hence they said again and again that there need be very little difference between the performances of a saint and the acts of a sinner; the difference will be in the aims and aspirations of the saint and in the sincerity of his effort. The proof of election will be in the trying, not the achieving. "God accepts at our hands a willing minde, and of child-like indeavours; if we come with childe-like service, God will spare us; a father will accept the poor indeavours of his childe for the thing it selfe."[53]

Yet while our endeavors will be satisfactory though poor, they must still be real endeavors. Since the conception of grace in this theory is not so much that of rapture as of the reawakening of dormant powers, grace is by definition the beginning of a moral life. It is a strengthening of the remains of the Law that still exist in the natural heart, in unregenerate reason, and in conscience. Saints are not able to do all they should, "yet this they doe. . . . they carry a constant purpose of heart to doe it. . . . They never come to give over striving to doe it."[54] The regenerate, by the very fact of being regenerate, exert themselves to become sanctified:

> . . . by the same faith whereby we receive Christ to dwell in us, we receive the holy Spirit also, to work from Christ and through Christ, all that power of godlinesse which a Christian life holds forth, and from that day forward. . . .[55]

Conversely, it follows as night the day that sanctification is a very handy evidence of justification, and that we may even receive grace first in the form of a moral ability before we have any inward experience of regeneration.[56] God's predestination is of course absolute, He picks and chooses without regard to merit. But in the covenant He has consented to bestow His favor upon those who fulfil the conditions, and to guarantee to those who do so the assurance of their salvation. In this devious fashion the Puritans avoided the Arminian heresy of conditional election, but gained almost all that the Arminians sought by preaching a "conditional" covenant, which entailed the obligations of morality as thoroughly as did the erroneous doctrine, and yet did not bind the Lord to attend upon human performance.[57] "Though God's grace do all," said Sibbes, "yet we must give our consent,"[58] and Thomas Shepard wrote:

> God hath so linked together the blessing of the Covenant (which is his to give) with the duty and way of it (which is ours to walk in) that we cannot with comfort expect the one, but it will work in us a carefull endeavour of the other.[59]

Peter Bulkley reveals what the New England divines thought this version had gained over that of primitive Calvinism when he explains that if God simply predestined without imposing conditions, morality would fall to the ground, nothing would be required of men one way or another; but in the covenant our endeavors are made, not the cause, but the *sine qua non* of a heavenly future: "But hereby he would teach us, that when he makes with us a Covenant of Grace and mercy, he doth not then leave us at liberty to live as we list; but he binds us by Covenant to himselfe.

. . ."[60] The legalistic tone of the thought is illustrated by Cotton's comparison of the conditions attached to the covenant to those of becoming "a free man of a Corporation," which are, he says, apprenticeship or purchase. Into the corporation of the godly there is no admission by purchase, and consequently all who hope for grace must serve an apprenticeship in learning the trade of godliness.

> If we give our selves to be bound to this service, if we come to God, submit our selves to him in all things, to do with us as hee pleaseth, and as shall seem good in his sight, submitting our selves to be ruled and squared by him in all things, hee shall have our whole hearts to do with us what he will; here is the Covenant made up between God and a good Christian.[61]

Armed by this logic at every point, the theologians were prepared to concentrate their attack upon the question of passivity. They were equipped to counteract the danger of lassitude which threatened to result from the fatalistic doctrine of predestination. They could show that men are responsible for a great deal, even though God alone bestows grace, and in more ways than one they could prove that a sinner brings reprobation upon himself. All those who live within the hearing of Christian doctrine—particularly of covenant doctrine—are offered the opportunity of taking up the covenant, because to them its terms are made clear. An offer of the covenant from God includes also an offer of enabling grace, because God is under obligation to supply grace when He presents the contract to men. Therefore, when the covenant is presented, through the sermon of a minister, to a particular individual, and the individual does not then and there embrace it, or attempt to embrace it, then he must be resisting it. Though faith comes from God, yet because it is not forced upon any, but is presented through reasonable inducements, and is conveyed by "means," by sermons, and by sacraments, men have of themselves the power to turn their backs upon it, to refuse to be convinced by the most unanswerable demonstrations, to sneer at the minister, and to pay no attention to the sermon. Thereafter the onus is entirely on their own shoulders:

> Take heede of refusing the acceptable time . . . Beloved, there is a certaine acceptable time, when God offers Grace, and after that hee offers it no more . . . there are certaine secret times, that *God* reserves to himselfe, that none knowes but himselfe, and when that time is past over, he offers it no more.[62]

Consequently, men must be constantly in readiness to take up the covenant, so that they will not fail to respond when the acceptable time comes to them individually.

The covenant theory, then, was an extremely strategic device for the arousing of human activity: it permitted divine grace to be conceived as an opportunity to strike a bargain, a chance to make an important move, an occasion that comes at a specific moment in time through the agency of the ministry. If an individual does not close the deal when he has the chance, he certainly cannot blame God because it gets away from him. "The Lord is a suitor to many a man," said Shepard, "that never gives himself to him."[63] The heathen, indeed, might have some grounds for complaint, but not those who live under a ministry, because to them the preaching of the Word is *ipso facto* the presentation of the covenant.

> . . . they that live under such meanes, that are ever learning, and never come to the knowledge of the Truth, and so have brought a sottishnesse on themselves, they are inexcusable, because themselves are the cause of their not profiting, as a man that is drunke, though he is not able to understand the commands of his Master, yet because he was the first author of the drunkennesse, (which caused such sottishnesse), he is inexcuseable. . . . So . . . God requires no more of any man, than either he doth know, or might have knowne.[64]

Of course, God must give the faith; but by these agencies He is, as a matter of fact, giving it, and giving it thus out of respect for the intelligence of men. "Hee will not doe it without us, because wee are reasonable men and women, and God affords us meanes."[65] Consequently, the duty of any man in a Christian community is to use the means to the end for which they are intended:

> . . . howsoever God promiseth to enable his people to doe all he commandeth, yet this shutteth not out their endeavour. His promise of enabling them is upon this supposition, that they doe indeavour in the use of the meanes he shall appoint them. The Lord in promising doth not meane that they should be idle, and look that he should doe all; but his promising includeth their endeavouring, and upon their endeavouring in the use of the meanes that God hath appointed, he hath promised to enable them to doe what he hath commanded.[66]

Hooker says that if persons have lived under a "powerful ministry" a half-dozen years or so and have not profited therefrom, "It is no absolute conclusion, but . . . it is a shrewd suspicion, I say, that God will send them downe to hell."[67] Consequently, it behooves us all not to lie back until the Lord comes to us, but to exert ourselves at once in accordance with the instructions of our pastor.

On these grounds the school carried on Perkins's tendency to reduce the actual intrusion of grace to a very minute point. They not only insisted that the tiniest particle is sufficient to start a man on the road to salvation, they even argued that before any faith is generated, a man can at least "prepare" himself for it. He can put himself in an attitude of receptivity, can resolve with himself not to turn down the covenant when it seems to be offered to him.[68] God may decree, but a man must find out whether the decree applies to himself; "the kingdom of heaven is taken with violence."[69] "You must not thinke to goe to heaven on a feather-bed; if you will be Christs disciples, you must take up his crosse, and it will make you sweat."[70] If any man excuse himself by the sophistry that Christ must work for him and that he cannot under his own power "bring forth fruit to him," that man despises Christ's honor, and in that act rejects the Covenant of Grace.[71]

In this respect, as in others, the covenant doctrine did not intend to depart from essential Calvinism; it did not openly inculcate free-will. But by conceiving of grace as the readiness of God to join in covenant with any man who does not actively refuse Him, this theory declared in effect that God has taken the initiative, that man can have only himself to blame if he does not accede to the divine proposal. This was indeed a marvellous stratagem for getting around a thorny difficulty in theology, a hazard which Calvin had simply taken in stride by asserting roundly that though God elects or rejects according to His pleasure, the responsibility for damnation is man's own. The generation of Peter Bulkley could no longer accept so brusque or unsophisticated an account as this. They were under greater compulsion to clear God of the charge of arbitrary condemnation and to place the responsibility for success or failure squarely on human shoulders. . . .

The conclusion toward which the doctrine of the covenant shapes is always the practical one that activity is the essence of a Christian life, that deeds are not merely the concomitants of faith, but can even be in themselves the beginning of faith. Some kind of revision of Calvinism seemed absolutely inevitable if the doctrine of justification by faith were not to eventuate in a complete disregard of moral performance. The covenant theology was the form that that revision took among this particular group of thinkers. It was the preliminary to their proving that faith without performance is an impossibility, a contradiction in terms, and that that which must be performed is the moral law, the law which reason and common sense know to be good in itself. In dogmatic Calvinism morality could exist only as a series of divine commands. It had no other basis, and to Calvin it needed no other. The covenant theology is a recognition on the part of a subsequent generation that this basis was inadequate, that it reduced morality to an arbitrary fiat, that it presented no inducement to men other than the whip and lash of an angry God. Consequently, in New England morality was first of all the specific terms of a compact between God and man, and rested, therefore, not upon mere injunction but upon a mutual covenant in which man plays the positive rôle of a coöperator with the Lord. In the second place morality was also that which can be considered good and just.

This conception was of tremendous value to the leaders of Massachusetts, not only in the realm of faith and personal conduct, but just as much in the realm of politics and society. The sphere of moral conduct includes more than such matters as individual honesty or chastity; it includes participation in the corporate organization and the regulation of men in the body politic. The covenant theology becomes, therefore, the theoretical foundation both for metaphysics and for the State and the Church in New England. An exhaustive study of the social theory would lead too far afield for the purposes of this paper, but a brief indication of the connection between it and the theology will demonstrate that without understanding this background we shall misread even such a familiar classic as Winthrop's speech of 1645 on liberty. That address is not what it is most often described as being—an expression of pure Calvinism. All that strictly Calvinistic political theory needs to contain is in the fourth book of the *Institutes*. It amounts in effect to the mandate that men must submit to magistrates because God orders them to submit, to the assertion that the power of the governor is of God, never of the people. But Winthrop outlines a much more subtle conception in his account, and by invoking the covenant theory secures the sway of morality in the State in precisely the same fashion in which the theologians secured it in the religious life. He distinguishes between the liberty all men have in the state of nature, the liberty to do anything they wish, which generally means something bad, and the liberty men exercise in society:

> The other kind of liberty I call civil or federal, it may also be termed moral, in reference to the covenant between God and man, in the moral law, and the politic covenants and constitutions, amongst men themselves. This liberty is the proper end and object of authority, and cannot subsist without it; and it is a liberty to that only which is good, just, and honest.[72]

I do not believe that the real connotation of Winthrop's words has been altogether recognized in modern accounts. He is saying that just as the covenant between God and man is a coming to terms, and as the validity of that which is by its nature good, just, and honest rests not upon its intrinsic quality but upon its being agreed to by the contractors, so also in the State, the rule of law rests upon a similar agreement among the participants. The covenant theory cannot claim for that which is inherently good the force of a cosmic law, because the universe and man are corrupted; it cannot identify the good completely with the thought of God, because God transcends all systematic formulations. But being arrived at by compact, the good then acquires the power to compel obedience from those who have covenanted to observe it, be they gods or men. The personal covenant of the soul with God is impaled on the same axis as the social, like a small circle within a larger. Before entering into both the personal and social covenants men have a liberty to go their own gait; afterwards they have renounced their liberty to do anything but that which has been agreed upon. The mutual consenting involved in a covenant, says Hooker, is the "sement" which solders together all societies, political or ecclesiastical; "for there is no man constrained to enter into such a condition, unlesse he will: and he that will enter, must also willingly binde and ingage himself to each member of that society to promote the good of the whole, or else a member actually he is not."[73] . . .

The covenant upon which a Congregational church was founded was viewed by the theologians in the same light as the political compact. It was held to be a miniature edition of the divine covenant. The saints come together and formally agree to carry out in ecclesiastical life the obligations to which they stand individually bound by their covenant with God. The duties and requirements are those determined in the Covenant of Grace. The church compact is the agreement of the people in a body to constitute an institution which will facilitate the achievement of these ends. "The rule bindes such to the duties of their places and relations, yet it is certain, it requires that they should *first freely ingage* themselves in such covenants, and *then* be carefull to fulfill such duties."[74] The creation of a church by the saints is necessary, furthermore, because the church makes possible the machinery of "means." The argument from the covenant, therefore, clinched the theoretical justification for the existence of a formal ecclesiastical order, for the dispensing of sacraments, and for the application of such regulatory measures as censure and excommunication, while at the same time protecting the liberty of God to enter into covenant with anyone He chose, inside or outside the church. Yet as long as it seemed that God would normally work through the regular means, He would therefore generally dispense grace through the ordinances of the church. Consequently the children of the saints should be baptized as a means toward their conversion, and should be taken into the church covenant:

> The Covenant of Grace is to be considered, either according to the benefits of saving grace given in it, or according to the means of grace offered. . . . [The church covenant] is not the Covenant of the Gospel in the first sense; but it is within the verge, and contained within the compasse of the Covenant in the second sense.[75]

In this distinction between the covenant as faith and the covenant as the provision of means for the engendering of faith were contained the seeds of the difficulties which later produced the Half-Way Covenant. But in the first decades of New England history no difficulties were anticipated because the theologians were so supremely confident that grace would almost inevitably accompany the means. "God delights in us, when we are in his Covenant, his Covenant reacheth to his Church, and wee being members of that Church: Hence it comes to passe, that we partake of all the pleasant springs of Gods love."[76]

Thus the sign of true faith is not only a desire on the part of the regenerate individual to fulfil the moral law, but it is also a determination to join in the setting up of the one and only polity which Christ has outlined in Scripture. For this reason New England was settled: "When faith is stirring, it longs and desires much after the strongest, purest, and liveliest Ministery, and every Ordinance in the greatest purity."[77]

. . .

The achievement of this theology was that it did everything that could be done to confine the unconfinable God in human terms. It transformed the revealed Word from an exaction arbitrarily imposed by a conqueror into a treaty of mutual obligation. But it never forgot that at the long last God is not to be fathomed, understood, or described with absolute certainty. Such certainty as we do have is temporary, the result of an agreement, of God's having consented to be bound in the main by such and such conditions, of His condescending for the moment to speak the language of men. There is no absolute guarantee that all His manifestations will appear within the scope of the covenant. The essence of Calvinism and the essence of Puritanism is the hidden God, the unknowable, the unpredictable. In this sense the Puritans were indeed Calvinists. They hedged the undiscoverable Essence about with a much more elaborate frame than did Calvin. They muffled it and cloaked it (to borrow Cotton's phrase), they cabined it and circumscribed it up to a point; and though the point was far beyond anything Calvin would have allowed, there was still a limit beyond which even the Federal theologians could not go. They could not say that natural law was immutable and eternal, though they might say it was generally reliable.

They might say that God's justice was for all intents and purposes the same as human justice, but they could not say that it was invariably the same. Always they had to leave a loophole, they had to be wary and circumspect; for behind the panorama of the world, behind the covenant and behind the Scriptures there loomed an inconceivable being about whom no man could confidently predict anything, who might day in and day out deal with man in stated forms and then suddenly strike without warning and scatter the world into bits. There was no telling with unqualified certitude what He might do; there was only the rule of thumb, the working agreement that by and large He would save and reject according to reason and justice as we understand the words. For ordinary purposes this was enough; we could feel fairly secure, we need not be too distraught. But the Puritan, as long as he remained a Puritan, could never banish entirely from his mind the sense of something mysterious and terrible, of something that leaped when least expected, something that upset all regularizations and defied all logic, something behind appearances that could not be tamed and brought to heel by men. The covenant thought kept this divine liberty at several removes, placed it on a theoretical plane, robbed it of much of its terror, but it could not do away with it entirely.

. . .

In the years since Miller first advanced his views on Federal Theology, numerous historians have explored the same subject and have modified some of Miller's views. One such revisionist, Norman Petit, deals with the Puritan doctrine of preparation, which Miller discusses tangentially in the "Marrow of Puritan Divinity" and more elaborately in "Preparation for Salvation in Seventeenth-Century Massachusetts" (reprinted in his collection, Nature's Nation, *cited above). Petit's approach to the subject (*The Heart Prepared: Grace and Conversion in Puritan Spiritual Life *[New Haven, 1966]) is primarily theological and concerned with doctrinal development and nuances, in contrast to Miller's emphasis on function, especially on the doctrine's social implications. Petit examines the scriptural basis of the concept, the treatment of the doctrine by continental reformers, and the thought of English Puritan theologians such as Richard Greenham, Richard Rogers, and Arthur Hildersham before dealing with the American exponents of preparation. He differs from Miller in denying that the Puritans viewed the covenant as giving men and women an opportunity to strike a bargain with God and argues that Miller's emphasis on the intellectual component of Puritan faith obscures the importance of Puritan spirituality.*

*Others have taken issue with Miller's contention that the Federal Theology began with seventeenth-century Puritans such as William Perkins. Leonard Trinterud, in "The Origins of Puritanism" (*Church History, *XX [1951]), accepts the importance of the covenant for the Puritans but denies the origins of the doctrine in the period after Calvin. Instead he demonstrates the existence of the covenant theme* *in the writings of Huldreych Zwingli, Heinrich Bullinger, Martin Bucer, and other reformers from the Rhineland and northern Switzerland whose thought was known in England before the rise of Calvin.* Richard Greaves, in *"John Bunyan and Covenant Thought in the Seventeenth Century"* (Church History, XXXVI [1967]), *distinguishes three types of covenant thought, two of which he argues were clearly derived from Calvin's teachings. And Jens Møller ("The Beginnings of Puritan Covenant Theology,"* Journal of Ecclesiastical History, XIV [1963]) *also criticizes Miller's superficial understanding of Calvin, and emphasizes the compatability of covenant thought with Calvinist doctrine. Møller offers two different ways to understand the covenant: "One is represented in England by Tyndale—in the line of Zurich. The other by systematic Puritan theologians—in the line of Geneva. Tyndale underlines the ethical sides of the covenant idea, Calvinists the aspect of grace."*

Those who have written about the covenant since Miller have not so much reversed his conclusions as they have added to our knowledge of the doctrine's complexities and its many roots. They have also underlined the importance of studying Puritanism in the broad context of the European Protestant Reformation (a plea most forcefully made by David Hall in "Understanding the Puritans," published in Herbert Bass, ed., The State of American History *[Chicago, 1970]). Another criticism of Miller's works is that he failed to deal with the experiential piety of the Puritans and thus presented an overintellectualized picture of them. Alan Simpson concentrates on the emotional drive of the Puritans in* Puritanism in Old and New England *(Chicago, 1955), as do Geoffrey Nuttall in* The Holy Spirit in Puritan Faith and Experience *(London, 1946), Gerald Brauer in "Puritan Mysticism and the Development of Liberalism"* (Church History, XIX [1950]), *and James Fulton Maclear in "'The Heart of New England Rent': The Mystical Element in Early Puritan History"* (Mississippi Valley Historical Review, XLII [1956]). *Robert Middlekauff's "Piety and Intellect in Puritanism"* (William and Mary Quarterly, series 3, XXII [1965]) *tries to bring the intellectual and emotional strands together by analyzing their interaction in the lives of Puritans such as Samuel Sewall and Cotton Mather.*

NOTES

1. They did not even consider him the fountainhead of their thought, but regarded him as one among many "judicious" divines. To an English correspondent who asked if Calvin had not definitely settled a certain point, Thomas Shepard replied: "I have forgot what he hath wrote and myself have read long since out of him" (*Works*, John Albro, editor, Boston 1853, I. 326). Thomas Hooker did not hesitate to point out in a sermon that Calvin "casts a different construction" upon some words of Scripture, and to insist upon his own interpretation (*A Comment Upon Christs Last Prayer in the Seventeenth of John*, London, 1656, p. 157).

2. John Preston, *Life Eternall, or A Treatise of the Knowledge of the Divine Essence and Attributes* (London, 1631), p. 94.

3. John Preston, *The New Covenant, or the Saints Portion* (London, 1629), p. 503.

4. *Id.*, p. 111.

5. *The Marrow of Sacred Divinity* (London, 1643), p. 11.

6. *Id.*, p. 191.

7. *Works* (Cambridge, 1626), p. 278.

8. *Works*, I. 14.

9. *Institutes*, III. xxiii, 12.

10. *Id.*, II. ii, 1.

11. *Works*, p. 21

12. *Marrow*, p. 198.

13. *Institutes*, III. xxi, 1.

14. *Marrow*, p. 131.

15. *Id.*, p. 118.

16. Shepard, *Works*, I. 329.

17. Shepard, *Works*, II. 283.

18. *Works*, pp. 107-112.

19. *The Holy State*, Bk. II, Chap. x.

20. Cf. "A Graine of Mustard Seed," *Works*, pp. 637 ff.; "A Treatise Tending unto a Declaration Whether a man be in the estate of damnation," *id.*, 356 ff.; "A Case of Conscience," *id.*, pp. 423 ff.

21. *Works*, p. 32.

22. *Orthodoxy in Massachusetts* (Cambridge, Mass., 1933), chap. vi.

23. *Marrow*, pp. 101-103.

24. *Life Eternall*, p. A6 recto.

25. *New Covenant*, p. 317.

26. Miller, *Orthodoxy in Massachusetts*, pp. 73-102.

27. *New Covenant*, p. 38; the innovation of this theology upon the theology of Calvin becomes apparent when its interpretation of Biblical texts is compared with his. Calvin, for instance, finds no such proposal of terms in Genesis, xvii, but only a statement of the permanence of God's promises (*Institutes*, II. viii, 21; x, 9) or the institution of the sacraments of circumcision and baptism (*id.*, IV. xvi, 3; xvii, 21-22).

28. Richard Sibbes, *Works* (Alexander B. Grossart, ed.; Edinburgh, 1802), I. civ.

29. John Cotton, *Christ the Fountaine of Life* (London, 1651), p. 35.

30. Peter Bulkley, *The Gospel-Covenant*, (2 ed., London, 1951), p. 86.

31. *Id.*, p. 133 (cf. *id.*, pp. 38, 112-113, 120); Preston, *New Covenant*, pp. 352-353, 357; Hooker, *The Saintes Dignitie* (London, 1651), p. 104; Cotton, *The Grounds and Ends of the Baptisme of the Children of the Faithfull* (London, 1647), p. 38; Shepard, *Works*, III. 521.

32. Cotton, *Grounds and Ends*, p. 32.

33. Bulkley, *Gospel-Covenant*, p. 47; cf. p. 28.

34. *Marrow*, p. 170; probably as a result of his teaching, Cocceius particularly stressed the evolutionary theory, and in Holland more energies were devoted to this aspect of the doctrine than in New England.

35. *Id.*, pp. 38-42, 170 ff.; cf. Sibbes, *Works*, VI. 4.

36. *Gospel-Covenant*, p. 118.

37. Hooker, *Saintes Dignitie*, p. 105.

38. *Life Eternall*, p. 57.

39. *New Covenant*, p. 155.

40. *Id.*, p. 446.

41. *Life Eternall*, p. 55; he instances Alexander Polyhistor, Josephus, Cyril, "Chaldee Historians," Diodorus Siculus, Strabo, Xenophon, "The Tables of Ptolomy, lately found." Cf. George Phillips, *A Reply to a Confutation* (London, 1645): "The Argument from humane authority is as easily rejected as propounded, though otherwise much good use may be made of their writing" (p. 119).

42. Hooker, *The Soules Exaltation* (London, 1638), p. 8.

43. *The Covenant of Gods Free Grace* (London, 1645), p. 18.

44. *Gospel-Covenant*, p. 321.

45. Preston, *The New Creature* (London, 1633), p. 23.

46. Preston, *New Covenant*, p. 477.

47. Cotton, *Christ the Fountaine*, p. 32.

48. Cotton, *The Covenant of Gods Free Grace* (London, 1645), p. 18.

49. *New Creature*, p. 23.

50. Cotton, *The Way of Life* (London, 1641), p. 229.

51. Preston, *New Covenant*, p. 102.

52. Hooker, *Saintes Dignitie*, pp. 4-5.

53. Cotton, *Covenant of Gods Free Grace*, p. 12.

54. Preston, *A Sermon Preached at A Generall Fast Before the Commons-House of Parliament* (London, 1633), p. 281.

55. Cotton, *Way of Life*, pp. 347-348.

56. Shepard, *Works*, III. 128. It was in the tangle of this argument that Mrs. Hutchinson tripped and fell, and consequently denounced the law and works and called upon the regenerate to live by grace alone. And it was by the doctrine of the covenant that she was found in error and excommunicated by the Church of Boston: "If any therefore accuse the Doctrine of the Covenant of free grace, of Antinomianisme. . . . and if they commit any sin, they plead they are not bound unto the Law . . . The children of the Covenant of grace will only tell you, that they are free from the Covenant of the Law, but not from the Commandment of it" (Cotton, *The New Covenant*, pp. 134-135).

57. How strained the reasoning became at this point to distinguish the conditional covenant from Arminianism is illustrated by the argument of Peter Bulkley:
"The grace of the Covenant is free notwithstanding the condition, because we doe not put any condition as antecedent to the Covenant on Gods part, whereby to induce and move the Lord to enter in Covenant with us, as if there were any thing supposed in us, which might invite and draw him to take us into Covenant with himselfe; but onely we suppose a condition antecedent to the promise of life, which condition we are to observe and walke in; and in the observation thereof to expect the blessing of life which the Covenant promiseth" (*Gospel-Covenant*, p. 383).
The difference between the Federal theory and Arminianism, therefore, hinges upon the fact that in the covenant theory good works are not the cause, but the accompaniment of salvation. In the twentieth century, when theology has become a wearisome desert, this difference may seem to be a mere quibble over words, but to the first generation in New England it involved the fundamental problems of philosophy and of life: "Where we finde the promise of life made unto good workes, wee must not looke at them as workes of the Law, but as workes and fruits of Faith . . . These kind of promises . . . are . . . not casuall, but declarative, making manifest who be those true believers . . . . In these promises workes are not set as the causes of our salvation, but as evidences and signes of those that do believe unto life" (*id.*, p. 384).

58.. *Works*, VI. 8.

59. Preface to Bulkley, *Gospel-Covenant*, p. A₂ verso.

60. Bulkley, *Gospel-Covenant*, p. 315.

61. Cotton, *Covenant of Gods Free Grace*, pp. 19-20.

62. Preston, *New Covenant*, pp. 434-435.

63. *Works*, II. 31.

64. Preston, *The Saints Qualification* (London, 1633), p. 223.

65. Hooker, "The Poore Doubting Christian," in *The Saints Cordials* (London, 1629), p. 361.

66. Hooker, *Saintes Dignitie*, pp. 82-83.

67. *The Soules Implantation* (London, 1637), p. 77.

68. In many passages describing the extent to which an unregenerate man may go in the work of preparation, some of these writers passed beyond any limits that could be reconciled with Calvinism. In New England clearly the most extreme was Thomas Hooker, who with

great eloquence magnified the possibilities of a man's producing in himself the receptive frame of mind, bringing himself to be "willingly content that Jesus Christ should come into it" (*Soules Implantation*, p. 34), and dared to assert that he who could force himself to the point of readiness would certainly receive grace in time. . . .

69. Shepard, *Works*, II. 57.

70. Hooker, *The Christians Two Chiefe Lessons* (London, 1640), p. 64.

71. Shepard, *Works*, II. 224.

72. John Winthrop, *Winthrop's Journal "History of New England"* (James Kendall Hosmer, ed.; 2 vols., New York, 1908), II. 239.

73. *A Survey of the Summe of Church-Discipline* (London, 1648), pt. i, p. 50.

74. *Id.*, p. 69.

75. *Id.*, p. 78.

76. Cotton, *Covenant of Gods Free Grace*, p. 22.

77. Cotton, *Way of Life*, p. 357.

4 | NEW ENGLAND AND THE FIFTH MONARCHY: THE QUEST FOR THE MILLENNIUM IN EARLY AMERICAN PURITANISM

JAMES F. MACLEAR

One of the most important expressions of the Puritans' zeal was their desire to create new Jerusalems. Miller's "Errand into the Wilderness" (reprinted in the collection of the same title cited above) traces the importance of the Puritans' sense of election in prompting the Great Migration to New England. In the past twenty years scholars such as Peter Toon (Puritans, the Millennium, and the Future of Israel: Puritan Eschatology 1600 to 1660 [Cambridge, Eng., 1970]), John F. Wilson ("Comment on 'Two Roads to the Millennium,'" Church History, XXXII [1963]), *and* Sacvan Bercovitch ("Horologicals to Chronometricals: The Rhetoric of the Jeremiad," Literary Monographs, III [Madison, 1970]) *have discovered and analyzed the development of eschatological thought among English and American Puritans. The following article investigates the apocalyptic visions of the colonists and the interaction between English and American millenarianism in the first half-century of New England's existence.*

In all that has been written about the settlement of New England one curious omission stands out: historians have not yet given adequate weight to the Puritan scheme of apocalyptic history and its impact on early New England thought and institutions. Yet long before the "chiliasm" of Increase and Cotton Mather eschatological convictions supplied a profound dimension to Puritan life. They filled sermons and commentaries, colored diaries, martyrologies, and even poetry, and sometimes determined life decisions at the most personal level. While some wove this anticipation of the Last Things into the routine pattern of their lives and quietly expressed it in their piety, others watched for a dramatic alteration in history and prepared for a new political order. Like Edward Johnson, they expected to see Christ "Skipping over and trampling down the great Mountaines of the Earth" in order to set up his universal government. To such extremists world history, periodized conventionally in the four great empires foretold in Daniel 7, would soon be transcended by Christ's own rule "when not onely the Assyrian, Babilonian, Persian, Grecian and Roman Monarchies shall subject themselves unto him, but also all other new upstart Kingdomes."[1] In the three decades after 1630 many in New as well as Old England eagerly awaited the rise of the Fifth Monarchy, the monarchy of Christ.

Yet historians who have noted English Puritan interest in the Fifth

Monarchy have slighted this enthusiasm in New England. Reasons are not difficult to assign. Apocalyptic radicalism was indeed less pervasive in conservative Massachusetts than in revolutionary English religion. Moreover, since American Puritanism did not generate a party agitation for Christ's reign or its controlled printing press a controversial literature, interest in eschatological politics among the New England planters has been difficult to find. Neglect has also been the easier because generations of earlier scholars regarded eschatology as an alien complex of ideas, while later intellectual historians, brilliantly dominated by Perry Miller, often found reason to view it as a secondary concern.

. . .

Faith in the coming Christ and his promised government, seedbed for later Fifth Monarchy speculation, was held with peculiar intensity among Puritans of the migration age. Its basis lay in the developed Puritan "science" of eschatology that in turn rested on the usual Protestant historicist exegisis of prophetic scriptures, especially Daniel and Revelation. Identifying the sequential states through which the world must pass before the Last Judgment and observing contemporary turmoil, commentators commonly located their own age near the end of world history and, while expecting more tribulation and persecution, they also confidently awaited final divine judgments on oppressors of the church—notably the "Romish Antichrist" and the Turks.[2] These beliefs were not unusual—they were held by most Protestant Englishmen—but in three respects Puritans by 1630 had made a unique appropriation of this common Reformation heritage whereby they laid foundations for the later quest for Christ's monarchy in both Old and New England.

First, Puritans differed from many English and Continental Protestants in their tendency to view eschatology not primarily as a formal theological scheme explaining God's remote plans for the world and man, but as a description of the cosmic environment in which the regenerate soldier of Christ was now to do battle against the power of sin. As such it was closely related to the great personal doctrines of sanctification and assurance and even to the conversion experience itself that supplied the dynamic for striving in that vast theater of spiritual conflict which eschatology surveyed. The English political situation under Charles I ministered to the same sense of crisis. Because they were themselves engaged in a worsening battle against the bishops, Puritans perceived a new and terrible urgency in their times and a critical role for themselves in defending the gospel. To them the cosmic struggles of the Apocalypse were not so much a matter of study as of participation. This personal enlistment inevitably led to an activism that could ultimately regard victory and not mere faithful combat as its proper object. In such militancy lay the psychological roots of the famous apocalyptic morale of Oliver Cromwell's troopers or the ferocious thunderings against Antichrist of Edward Johnson's *Wonder-Working Providence*.[3]

Joined with this sense of crisis and struggle was a new and optimistic strain in Puritan prophetic commentary, a growing conviction that before the Judgment there would be within history an age of spiritual blessings for Christ's people and triumphant authority for his church.

The development was complex and closely related to the rise of millennialism in Anglican and Continental Reformed thought, but for Puritans the seminal influence was Thomas Brightman's. In commentaries on Revelation, Daniel, and Canticles published between 1609 and 1616, Brightman proved the imminence of a joyous New Age, thereby ministering to the later rise of widespread Puritan faith in a "latter-day glory" of worldwide religious revival before the Second Advent. Furthermore, Brightman greatly advanced specific millennial ideas in Puritanism by suggesting the transfer of the "millennium" of Revelation 20 from past to future. For while he accepted the traditional teaching of the binding of Satan between 300 and 1300 A.D., he also argued for a second and future millennium as the recovery of the gospel, begun by John Wyclif and the Reformers, increasingly gained sway in the world.[4] Thus the enthusiastic vision of a thousand-year reign of the saints, which had been anciently discarded by patristic tradition and more recently disgraced by Anabaptist heresy, was cautiously rehabilitated by Brightman—a rehabilitation that received fresh support from scholars such as the German encyclopedist, Johann Heinrich Alsted, and Joseph Mede of Cambridge. Among Puritans all three interpreters were immensely popular and frequently quoted, for their commentaries seemed to rationalize an entire prophetic system and relate the Fifth Monarchy of Daniel to the coming "glory" of Revelation. In scarcely more than a quarter-century this exegetical tradition culminated in the ardent Independent millennialism of the 1640s, made famous in sermons of Thomas Goodwin and John Owen.[5] But before these Dutch and English pronouncements were published John Cotton was building on Brightman to preach the New Age in the Massachusetts wilderness.

Lastly, many Puritans gave unusual schematic importance to the Jews in the divine providential plan. God's old people, now alienated and rebellious, were yet destined to submit to Christ and return to Zion. Expectations of Jewish conversion, absent from Martin Luther and John Calvin but expounded by Theodore Beza, had entered Puritanism through the Geneva Bible's gloss on Romans 11:26 and the enthusiastic advocacy of the Elizabethan theologian, William Perkins. By 1630 the Jew's convincement was widely regarded as one of the most reliable of apocalyptic signs. Furthermore, since they conceived of Christ's reign in mingled religious and political terms, Puritans turned in fascination to Old Testament accounts of Jewish law and government.[6] In ancient Israel they found the only example of God's perfect rule among his chosen people. Here were laws and precepts that might again be imposed when the Fifth Monarchy succeeded the worldly states now ascendant.

By the 1630s these themes were shaping a fervent millennial ideology in the English Puritan community, and there is reason to suppose that those Puritans who crossed the sea to Massachusetts held this faith in an especially vital form. The explanation lies partly in the colonists' predominant congregationalism, which sustained an eschatological dimension frequently overlooked. The "New England way" was not merely a polity. By its purity and faithfulness to God's word it was itself a sign of the approach of the millennium. The very gathering of the elect in objective holy communities anticipated the coming era when the saints would reign with the Lord. The forthright claim ascribed to the Arnhem church "that Independency is a beginning of Christs temporal kingdom here on earth" was repeated in more tempered form by Goodwin, Thomas Hooker, and others.[7] Significant too may be evidence that eschatology itself became a relentless pressure driving some men to New England. Few themes are more prevalent in migration literature than that of Old England's impending "desolation," a dread sentence that moved orthodox and heterodox alike, Richard Mather and Hooker as well as Anne Hutchinson, to seek overseas refuge. The poet Thomas Tillam struck a more positive note: the come-again Christ would reward his servants who had left English comforts for the wilderness:

> prepare to heare your sentence thus expressed
> Come yee my servants of my father Blessed.[8]

In either case preoccupation with the Last Things seems to have been a selective factor drawing many eschatologically sensitive Puritans to the New World. Finally, in America Independency exchanged a defensive for a constructive role. By spreading Christ's message in a barbarous land and preparing a bastion against Antichrist, the colonists were already advancing history toward the day of Armageddon. Most important of all, in this free environment Puritans were perfecting and actualizing the pure church and gospel hitherto only partially perceived in England and Holland.[9] Such work of building must also have urged some men to seek the social and political order that would be appropriate when Christ's reign came at last.

Consequently, it is not surprising to find New England's first planters dwelling on prophetic scriptures or scanning world horizons for clues to present and future meaning. Nor is it unexpected that the most important expressions of this mood, at once scholarly and enthusiastic, should be found in the preaching of New England's greatest theologian, John Cotton.

Cotton had already delivered his St. Botolph's lectures with their apocalyptic exegesis of the Song of Songs when he came to America in 1633. Late in the 1630s he began his Thursday lectures at the Boston church, expounding Revelation in systematic detail. There can be no doubt that Cotton's handling of these texts touched a deep emotional chord in the religious life of the infant colony. Thomas Allen, the minister of Charlestown, made the journey into Boston every week during the winter of 1639-1640 in order that he might have benefit of Cotton's teaching. Governor John Winthrop thought a 1641 comment from the Thursday lecture important enough to include in the *History of New England*. Edward Johnson, anticipating at mid-century the impending fall of Antichrist, recalled that "that holy man of God Mr. John Cotton . . . hath diligently searched for the Lords mind herein, and hath declared some sudden blow to be given to this blood-thirsty monster." Even Thomas Lechford, hostile to Cotton's apocalyptic views, stressed his preeminence in describing Massachusetts's lecture system in *Plain Dealing*.[10] We cannot now recapture the effect with which this teaching was delivered, but contemporaries were agreed that the pulpit style was compelling. "Mr. Cotton Preaches," asserted John Wilson, Cotton's ministerial colleague at Boston, "with such Authority, Demonstration, and Life that, methinks, when he preaches out of any Prophet or Apostle I hear not him; I hear that very Prophet and Apostle; yea, I hear the Lord Jesus Christ speaking in my Heart." Such sincerity may account for the assurance of grace won by troubled Capt. Roger Clap while listening to Cotton expound the Apocalypse.[11]

The text of Cotton's Massachusetts teaching we now have in only three published works, *An Exposition upon the Thirteenth Chapter of the Revelation; The Powring Out of the Seven Vials*, a commentary on Revelation 16; and *The Churches Resurrection*, a glowing sermon on the great millennial promise of Revelation 20. The first two works identify the final stages of terrestrial history and place the contemporary scene within them; the last is Cotton's anxious welcome to the dawning glory.[12] Significantly, all were composed in the critical years between 1639 and 1641 when the Puritan mood in England lifted from despair to soaring optimism. Cotton's general system as revealed by these works was consistent with the Independents' development of Brightman's ideas and was paralleled in the famous millennial sermons that Goodwin was contemporaneously delivering in Holland. Cotton identifies the seven-headed Beast of Revelation 13:1 with the Catholic church that is nearing destruction through the power of increasing evangelical preaching since the days of Wyclif. After the fall of the papacy, identified with the Second Beast of Revelation 13:11, Cotton expects Spirit-filled ministers to preach with such overpowering effect that Satan will suffer his prophesied bondage for a thousand years. Unlike Brightman, Cotton allows for only one future millennium. It will emerge in history not by Christ's personal presence, but by the ordinary means of faithfully propagating his gospel. In this era an unprecedented and sustained religious revival will occur, convincing repentant Jews and establishing Christ's kingship in both church and state through unchallenged worldwide rule by his saints. In accordance with prophecy, at the end of the thousand years Satan will be released. Then wicked men will triumph for a season, Catholicism will revive, persecution will flourish. But Christ's coming will soon follow, and with it the resurrection of the dead and the Last Judgment.[13]

To Cotton's Boston flock this formal eschatological doctrine, absorbing though it was, must have been far eclipsed by the preacher's specific references to their own age and condition. For Cotton clearly believed that the great transition to saintly power was even then about to appear! Interpreting the Beast's allotted time as twelve hundred and sixty years and calculating the pope's tyranny from 395 A.D., Cotton announced a cautious but wildly exciting conclusion: "I will not be two [sic] confident, because I am not a Prophet, nor the Son of a Prophet to foretell things to come, but so far as God helps by Scripture light, about the time 1655. there will be then such a blow given to this beast . . . as that we shall see a further gradual accomplishment and fulfilling of this Prophecy here." This exhilarating prediction, pronounced no later than early 1640, was matched in the following year by Cotton's identification of the bishops' current calamities with the pouring of the fifth vial of God's wrath in Revelation 16. Soon the remaining two vials would be emptied, God's enemies would be overwhelmed at Armageddon, and the "new light," already glimpsed in the purity of New England gospel and church order, would blaze forth.[14] Cotton's mounting excitement was most evident in his 1641 sermon, *The Churches Resurrection*. Here he cautioned that although the expected millennium had not yet begun, Scotland and England were travailing in reformation, New England's "faire preparation" led the world, and the blessed time could not be far off when "those that were branded before for Huguenots, and Lollards, and Hereticks, they shall be thought the only men to be fit to have Crownes upon their heads and independent Government committed to them . . . for a thousand years together." The work of the day was to persuade New England to grasp the present opportunity for the Lord's reign or risk a millennium of deadness: "If we do not now strike a fast covenant with our God to be his people, . . . then we and ours will be of this dead hearted frame a thousand years."[15]

Cotton's millennial teaching must have continued throughout the 1640s, for apocalyptic themes appeared in his other pronouncements, often in confident or combative tone. Preaching on Revelation 11:15 in 1643, he urged his people to note that "they being the Kingdom of Christ, they were bound to goe out against all people, to subdue all such unto themselves as are weaker then they." Praying for the coming of Christ's kingdom, he told Roger Williams in 1647, involved praying "for the comming downe of all opposite Kingdomes." To Cromwell in 1651 he wrote, "I am fully satisfyed, that you have all this while fought the Lords battells," adding a recommendation that he ponder Revelation 17:14 on the Lamb's victory over the Beast.[16] . . .

Although Cotton's may have been a primary influence in encouraging a sense of historical urgency in Massachusetts, his voice was certainly not alone. Ephraim Huit's *Whole Prophecie of Daniel explained* (1644) taught a visible Fifth Monarchy of the saints and speculated that its coming would follow the end of Turkish dominion over the Jews about 1650. A year later Thomas Parker of Newbury published his *Visions and Prophecies of Daniel Expounded*, going over the same ground and fixing on 1649 as a likely beginning to apocalyptic events.[17] Eschatological doctrine often colored other parts of divinity than commentary. Hooker's preface to *A Survey of the Summe of Church-Discipline*, for instance, stressed increasing perfection of the church's constitution as a sign of history's approaching consummation, and almost everything that Richard Mather wrote is "shot through with an eschatological expectation."[18] Even Roger Williams, although a skeptic about exact times of prophetic fulfillment, broke with Massachusetts partly because his faith in the Apocalypse left little room for allegiance to the king. Charles I, he implied, was "a friend of the Beast and an enemye of Jes[us] Ch[ris]t" who had "comitted Fornication with the whore, and shall bewayle her destruction."[19] Nor was this anxious inspection of history a concern only of the clergy. The earthquakes of 1638 and 1639 created general anxiety, and on the authority of Joel 2:30 and Revelation 6:12 were viewed as signs of a new stage in history's closing scenes.[20] In 1640 Lechford noted that the people cried out "of nothing but Antichrist and the Man of Sin," and his own career in the colony was damaged because he circulated his manuscript book expressing the eccentric belief that Antichrist was not the pope but was still to come.[21]

Yet in reputation Cotton stood foremost among transatlantic Puritans as prophet of the coming glory, and as the 1640s advanced, news from England must have vindicated his teaching and deepened an assured and militant adventist mood. Officially Massachusetts mobilized prayers for the brethren in England through fasts decreed by the General Court, but the temper of the colony may have been more faithfully expressed in the work of two lay figures, both influenced by Cotton. During the 1640s the poet Anne Bradstreet labored at her most ambitious work, "The Foure Monarchies of the World," an epic history following conventional divisions inspired by the seventh chapter of Daniel. This gigantic undertaking was never finished, but Bradstreet's religious imagination was concisely worded in "A Dialogue between Old England and New," completed in 1642. In this work the colony cheered the mother country in language both patriotic and martial, and confidently set forth the coming triumph when English armies would sack popish Rome and thus precipitate the final sequences to the millennium:

> This done, with brandished swords to Turkey go,
> For then what is't but English blades dare do,
> And lay her waste for so's the sacred doom,
> And do to Gog as thou hast done to Rome.[22] . . .

Eight years later this militant optimism reached its zenith in both Old and New England, and produced in Johnson's *Wonder-Working Providence of Sions Saviour* a fit parallel in faith, fervor, and even language to the army's contemporary Declaration on entering Scotland. Johnson's entire work was an exultant celebration of the coming divine government, New England Puritans serving as "the forerunners of Christs Army." All God's people, he counseled, must equip themselves with "Swords, Rapiers, and all other piercing weapons," for "the time is at hand wherein Antichrist will muster up all his Forces, and make war with the People of God: but it shall be to his utter overthrow." So strong was his certainty of the imminence of Christ's kingdom that Johnson rejoiced as if Armageddon were already won: "The Winter is past, the Raine is changed and gone, come out of the holes of the secret places, feare not because your number is but small, gather into Churches, and let Christ be your King."[23]

These vivid expectations of the latter-day glory must have suggested to some colonists the prospect of doing more than awaiting God's providence—indeed, of anticipating the divine kingdom by establishing God's law alone or by proclaiming Christ an immediate earthly king. Did such attempts in fact occur in New England as they did later in England? Only limited evidence exists on which to rest an affirmative case. Ordinarily, radical theocracy at the Bay was checked by conservative tendencies—the magistrates' moderation and pragmatism, a continuing regard for English law, and even the resistance of ordinary men to the difficult demands of Christ's monarchy. Inclinations toward a millennial social order may also have been aborted because governments commonly acnowledged theocratic responsibilities and thus reassured enthusiasts for the New Age. Samuel Symonds's complacent query to Winthrop suggests as much: "Is not government in church and Common weale (according to gods owne rules) that new heaven and earth promised, in the fullnes accomplished when the Jewes come in; and the first fruites begun in this poore New Eng:?"²⁴ Nonetheless, three familiar experiments during these early decades should be reexamined from the perspective of eschatological politics. Two of these—Cotton's proposed scriptural code for Massachusetts and the Antinomian exiles' earliest constitution for Portsmouth—may be treated briefly because they were early abandoned and were somewhat ambiguous in meaning. But about the third there can be no doubt. John Eliot's grand theocratic design for his Indian converts was to begin the transformation of earthly governments into the universal empire of the Lord and his saints, the glorious climax to human history.

A role for Cotton in Fifth Monarchy stirrings is an intriguing but uncertain possibility. That he expected a marvelous new age of saintly power is clear. It is also certain that he advocated a more expressly theocratic polity in Massachusetts than colonial leaders could be induced to install. In all his political works he taught that theocracy was the best polity, perhaps most clearly in the *Discourse about Civil Government in a New Plantation Whose Design is Religion* in which he envisioned magistrates, covenanted with the church and endowed with the Holy Spirit, ruling by God's laws in a new Israel. This same ideal explained his deep distrust of all merely human legislation: "The more any Law smells of man the more unprofitable."²⁵ While sharing Cotton's general outlook, Massachusetts magistrates were not so tied to biblical warrant or so scrupulous in framing positive law. Winthrop particularly, reflecting his English legal education, related civil law to natural law, honored it as a reflection of the Law of God, and was confident that God gave adequate "power and gifts to men to interprett his Lawes."²⁶

Cotton's more rigorous biblicism was apparent when the General Court appointed him to the committee to frame fundamental law for the colony in 1636. As is well known, Cotton fulfilled this assignment by drafting the scriptural code which Winthrop designated "a model of Moses his judicials, compiled in an exact method." While many provisions appeared without biblical citation, Cotton did rely heavily on scripture for constitutional and criminal law. Moreover, in a later defense of his proposal, "How Far Moses Judicialls Bind Massachusetts," Cotton argued that the colony must submit not only to the moral law of Moses but to much and perhaps all of the Mosaic judicial law as well. Although Cotton's code circulated in manuscript for five years, it was never adopted by the General Court.²⁷

Did Cotton press for systematic scriptural legislation in Massachusetts partly because he expected the transition to Christ's kingly rule soon to come? One must be cautious in answering because the Reformed tradition, stressing God's sovereignty and law, was able to inspire theocratic regimes without accompanying millennial excitement—as Calvin's Geneva amply demonstrates. But what makes Cotton's proposal intriguing is that four years after composing "Moses His Judicials" he was teaching that New England occupied a situation unprecedented in history, a society freed from the Beast, accepting the Lord as head, and looking for no laws but God's Word. Indeed, his language suggests that New England already dwelt on an eschatological rather than a historical plane. Afflictions might come, but they would be the death throes of the Beast which already "hath begun to fall before the Lamb." The millennium was about to begin, New England was in advance of all the earth, and its people must strike their covenant with God at once.[28]

Admittedly, there are ambiguities here that permit no settled conclusion. Cotton's millennial expectations may have been less pressing in 1636 than in 1640. His words, some of them hortatory in purpose, may have been exaggerated for effect. But it is significant that his 1641 lecture on the third vial of Revelation 16 pleaded for adoption of Mosaic laws and penalties in all kingdoms.[29] And at least one member of his Boston congregation repeatedly turned in later life to "Moses His Judicials" as an ideal instrument to accomplish Christ's perfect reign in Massachusetts. William Aspinwall, Boston magistrate and later Fifth Monarchy agitator, cherished the code, republished it in England in 1655, and in his last advice to the Bay once again recommended its acceptance:

> Remember you had an old Prophet of the Lord amongst you who is now at rest, and he . . . collected a whole Sisteme, or body of Laws . . . out of the word of God: with a divine stamp upon them. . . . I know you wil acknowledg your own Laws are not perfect (some capitals only excepted, wherein you followed the advice of that antient Prophet) and you wil also acknowledg that there is no imperfection in the Laws given by Jesus Christ our King.
>
> Therefore I beseech you again to revise what was commended to you by that faithful servant of Christ (Mr. Cotton I mean) and . . . be persuaded in the Lord to take his Laws for yours, and make them your Magna charta.[30]

About the second political experiment, the primitive order planned for the Antinomians' settlement on Aquidneck Island in Narragansett Bay, judgment must again be highly conjectural, although the circumstances justify the raising of brief query. The first government produced by the exiles on the island was avowedly theocratic in inspiration. Was it also millennial? While no certain answer can be given, the intense eschatological excitement among the Portsmouth founders deserves consideration. Not only were most of them from Cotton's church, but they were also caught up in the apocalyptic mood of the Antinomian crisis. Anne Hutchinson had emigrated to America preoccupied with the prospect of huge historical changes: shocked at her first sight of Boston, "she uttered these words, if she had not a sure word that England should be destroyed her heart would shake." Later in her long confessional narrative at her trial she hinted at a spiritualized eschatology, decrying the blindness of ministers in her own day in not recognizing that Christ had come in the flesh.[31] The conviction that spiritual apocalyptic combat was now at hand was also urged by John Wheelwright in his fast-day sermon when he stressed the destruction of Antichrist not through an "externall burning of Rome," but through "a Spirituall burning, . . . by the fire of the Gospell." "Why shold we not further this fire," he asked; "who knoweth not how soone those Jewes may be converted? Rev: 18 and 19 chap: after the burning of the whore followes, Alleluia, a praysing of the Lord in Hebrew."[32] Winthrop himself complained that many of Hutchinson's people looked upon her "as a Prophetesse, raised up of God for some great worke now at hand, as the calling of the Jewes, etc."[33]

Such anticipation may then have been responsible for the extremely simple and naive subordination to King Jesus and his laws contained in the solemn covenant endorsed by the Antinomian outcasts on the eve of their departure from Boston: "We whose names are underwritten do here solemnly in the presence of Jehovah incorporat our selves into a Bodie Politick and as he shall helpe will submit our persons lives and estates unto our Lord Jesus Christ, the King of Kings and Lord of Lords and to all those perfect and most absolute lawes of his given us in his holy word of truth, to be guided and judged thereby."[34] There may be some significance too in the adoption of the title of "Judge" for the chief magistrate, not only after the fashion of the Judges of the Israelites in their occupation of a new land, but perhaps also in preparation for the New Age when, according to I Corinthians 6:₂, the saints should judge the world.

If this "constitution" was an anticipation of Christ's rule through his saints, it failed in practice and was overthrown by a coup on April 30, 1639. Distrust of William Coddington and desire for the practical advantages of English law may have figured in this alteration, but erosion of the theocratic experiment may also have been the work of the deepening spiritual emphasis itself. In her final conflict at the Bay Hutchinson had at last become specific, shocking the ministers with speculation that the saints' resurrection was past and Christ had already come. "I desire to know," exclaimed an exasperated Peter Bulkeley, "whether you hould any other Resurection than that of . . . Union to Christ Jesus." Normally, a "realized eschatology" prompted renunciation of carnal instruments, and hence special significance may lie in Winthrop's 1639 report that William Hutchinson resigned his magistracy because his wife convinced him that the use of the sword was unlawful to Christians.[35] But although the Portsmouth theocracy failed, the rise of conventional magistracy did not end speculation "concerning the rising of Christs Kingdome after the Desolations by Rome" among many Narragansett settlers, especially those gathered in the primitive church at Newport. Twelve years later when three members of this Baptist meeting made their famous missionary journey to Massachusetts, they improved their Boston imprisonment by testifying to the coming of the Fifth Monarchy. And the most prominent of their number, John Clarke, was soon to contribute to Fifth Monarchy agitation in England.[36]

As examples of millennial politics, these experiments remain somewhat conjectural, since the theocratic urge in the principal actors may not have been primarily owing to millennial anticipations. But in the final enterprise, Eliot's attempt to plant Christ's monarchy among his Christianized Indians, we discover in high relief a New England endeavor to prepare for God's rule among the nations.

Massachusetts's ambivalent attitude toward missions to its native tribes has long been noted by historians, but the story has usually been regarded as a curiosity of missionary history or early American anthropology and never adequately linked to Puritan conceptions of providential design and eschatological expectancy.[37] Yet from the first planting New England leaders sought to accommodate Indians in the total scheme of human history, the church's triumph, and the final judgment. As early as 1630 Cotton preached that God may have "reared this whole Plantation" to accomplish the conversion of Indian peoples, and Winthrop before leaving England listed the same opportunity among the compelling reasons for migration.[38] Behind such reasoning lay the New Testament prediction that all the earth would hear the gospel before the End. Hence Eliot's toilsome study of the Algonquin tongue to enable him to begin an effective Indian ministry after 1646 was undertaken in faith that such labor advanced the great historical sequences toward their prophesied denouement. Toward the end of the 1640s these anticipations became more pronounced as news from Europe strengthened optimism that the last days were nigh. As Thomas Shepard (citing Brightman) hoped in 1647-1648, within the next few years Turkish power would collapse, the Jews return to Zion, and "these Westerne Indians . . . soon come in." These views were given elaborate publicity by the many missionary appeals of the English Society for the Propagation of the Gospel, founded in 1649, to support the work of Eliot, Jonathan Mayhew of Martha's Vineyard, and other evangelists among the Indians. By 1652 Eliot in one of these tracts, *Tears of Repentance*, had ceased to relegate these triumphs to the future: even now Christ's kingdom was "rising up in these Western Parts of the World," an encouragement for Cromwell to make Christ reign everywhere.[39]

Throughout this apocalyptic literature, divines in both England and America attempted to locate the conversion of the Indians in biblical prophecy by relating the time of their "coming in" to the calling of the Jews. This convention had not always yielded happy results. Lechford, resident in Boston in the late 1630s, had judged the Puritans to be indifferent to the Indians' salvation, ascribing their neglect to the doctrine that no new people could submit to Christ before the Jews were converted. Cotton himself promoted this interpretation and preached it in his lectures on Revelation 15 in 1641.[40] By 1652, however, a more favorable exegesis, supported by an epistle of fourteen eminent English divines, urged strenuous labors among the Indians since scripture prophesied two gentile conversions, one before and the other after the Jews came in.[41] Also by the 1650s prophecy had been given still another cast by news of vast stirrings in world Jewry. Well-publicized rabbinic calculations were foretelling the imminent appearance of the Messiah.

The influential *The Hope of Israel* by the Hispano-Dutch Jew, Menasseh ben Israel, was predicting the gathering of the Twelve Tribes and their restoration to Jerusalem. By mid-decade Cromwell was negotiating the Jews' admission to England—an event that would both fulfill the prophecy of Deuteronomy 28:64 concerning Israel's worldwide dispersal and introduce Jews to an evangelical English gospel to which they must surely respond. In Massachusetts Johnson exulted: "Oh! yee the antient Beloved of Christ, . . . looke here, behold him whom you have peirced, preparing to peirce your hearts with his *Wonder-working Providence.*"[42]

Eliot, already dazzled by the promise of coming glory and personally dedicated to winning Indians' souls, followed this speculation with consuming interest. Like others, he concluded that the Indians were even now coming to Christ and that this submission was a sign of the great transfiguration of history. But Eliot was singular in two respects. First, he added a new dimension to speculation about the Indians' place in eschatology by his conviction that they were Hebrews, retrograde descendants of the biblical patriarchs and the Ten Lost Tribes of Israel. Second, he believed that his own humble Indian flock at Natick was destined to take the first step toward the millennium.

Speculations identifying the Indians with Jewish tradition had become common earlier in the seventeenth century. Hugh Broughton (whose writings Eliot knew) developed the theory that the American natives were offspring of Eber, son of Shem (Genesis 10).[43] In the mid-century excitement concerning the coming Christ such theory took on new significance. At The Hague in 1644 John Durie, the ecumenical Puritan, heard a story about one Antonio de Montezinos who had come upon an Ecuadorian community of Indians who recited the Shema (Deuteronomy 6:4-9) and acknowledged Abraham, Isaac, and Jacob as their forefathers.[44] During these same years Thomas Thorowgood was gathering evidence that finally appeared in his comprehensive argument, *Jewes in America* (1650). To this work Thorowgood appended a long "Epistolicall Discourse" by Durie which repeated the tale of Andean "Jews" and published correspondence on the subject with Menasseh ben Israel, himself recently converted to the theory. Soon, exulted Durie, the yoke of oppression would be broken for both Jew and gentile, knowledge of Christ would fill the earth, and the Indians could go home to Judea.[45]

Eliot knew about this research of Durie, Menasseh, and Thorowgood, even before the publication of their theories in 1650, through his correspondence with Thorowgood and Edward Winslow, the Massachusetts agent in London. In the summer of 1649 Eliot wrote fervent letters to Winslow, not only demanding fresh information but confessing that the Indians' Hebrew origin placed his own work in new perspective and confirmed his faith in an imminent millennial dawn. In these ecstatic passages Eliot returned repeatedly to "the glorious coming of the Lord Jesus" both in the English Commonwealth and "among these poore Indians."[46] All these hopes were communicated to the English public in *The Glorious progress of the Gospel amongst the Indians* (1649) and *The Light Appearing More and More towards the perfect Day* (1651). In the latter work Eliot was even able to report that the pirate, "Captaine

Cromwell, who lately dyed at Boston," had seen "many Indians to the Southward Circumcised."[47]

In his excitement Eliot's mind constantly dwelt on Ezekiel's vision of the Valley of Dry Bones (Ezekiel 37). Did not those bones which, though dead and scattered, were miraculously restored to life by the preaching of God's word mean that these New World "Jews" must again be placed under their ancient covenant with God? Would not such a restoration, in which these Christian Indians would serve only God's law revealed in scripture, be an appearance of the coming kingdom? Eliot surveyed the Indians' situation and reasoned that no barrier stood in the way. Despite the claims of the Boston government, English law was not really applied to Indian disputes. Moreover, the tribes possessed no law or "wisdome of their own (I meane as other Nations have) wherein to stick." Consequently, Eliot clearly saw his task: "My scope is, to write and imprint no nother but Scripture principles in the *abrasa tabula scraped board* of these naked people, that so they may be in all their principles a choice people unto the Lord, owning none other Lord or law-giver, but the Lord alone, who is the King of Saints."[48]

Eliot was awed by his undertaking because he believed that his work would serve as a model for an expanding theocratic kingdom. The plan would go forth among the Indians "as a patterne and Copie before them, to imitate in all the Countrey." Moreover, he saw that although "humane wisdome in learned Nations will be loth to yeeld to Christ so farre," the Lord was even then shaking European peoples, readying them for their submission to God's law.[49] Proceeding with elaborate care "to lay a sure foundation for such a building," he worked out the plan to bring his Indians first into a proper political order and then into a visible church state. Significantly, he first "advised with Mr. Cotton and others" about valid principles for their civil government. Finally, after all preparations, the great day came on August 6, 1651. To the assembled natives Eliot offered prayer and read, as he had in earlier instruction, the account in Exodus 18 of the Hebrews' choice of rulers in the Sinai wilderness. Then the Indians themselves solemnly named magistrates and placed themselves under them as in the biblical pattern. A few weeks later they entered into high covenant with God: "We doe give our selves and our Children unto God to be his people, he shall rule us in all our affaires, not onely in our Religion . . . but also in all our works and affaires in this World, God shall rule over us . . . the Lord is our Judge, the Lord is our Law-giver, the Lord is our King, He will save us; the Wisedome which God hath taught us in his Booke, that shall guide us and direct us in the way." Observing the earlier ceremony, Eliot saw "scattered bones goe, bone unto his bone . . . and the Lord was pleased to minister no small comfort unto my spirit, when I saw it."[50]

Eliot turned next to building an Indian church, but already his imagination was dwelling on the European scene. To his mind this Indian theocracy must be extended to England where, since the death of the king, ancient political traditions had dissolved and a new order was forming. "Oh the blessed day in England when the Word of God shall be their Magna Charta and chief Law Book; and when all Lawyers must be

Divines to study the Scriptures," he had written to Winslow. Convinced that when everything was done by God's scriptural command, "then doth Christ reigne, and the great Kingdome of Jesus Christ which we weight for," Eliot composed an ardent appeal to the brethren at home.[51] *The Christian Commonwealth*, finished about 1651, was sent over the Atlantic to preach the Fifth Monarchy to Cromwell's England.

Eliot's haste to turn from his American experience to plead the cause of Christ's kingly government in Britain was not in any way unusual. The first generation in New England could not regard America as central. The Old World was the critical theater for the performance of the Last Things, and colonists never doubted that the cosmic scenes prophesied in scripture were soon to be revealed in European history. After the Puritan Revolution began to unfold, many planters returned to England resolved to be "helpfull in advancing the Kingdome of Christ, and casting down every strong house of sinne and Satan."[52] From this American devotion to the "English Jerusalem" developed a radical and partisan epilogue to New England's quest for Christ's monarchy—the contribution of several American Puritans to millenarian agitation in Interregnum England.

England had created what New England never produced—an articulate and organized Fifth Monarchy connection. Contrary to caricature, English Fifth Monarchy Men were neither absurd eccentrics nor rigid sectarians. The pedigree of their doctrines was respectable: they stood with the English Independents and with Cotton in looking for the rule of the Lord in their time. Nor were they an authentic sect. Instead, they sought the unity of all the godly. The party was unusual, however, in continuing to assert and even intensify the millennial faith after the apocalyptic mood had lifted from much of the Puritan leadership and community. For most Puritans in both Englands this awakening occurred in the early 1650s, and in this profound shift the Little Parliament played a central role. As a parliament of saints it fired imaginations and hopes. Its failure and abrupt dissolution by a Cromwell newly converted to constitutional conservatism led many to relinquish expectations of Christ's impending reign. But some English radicals, more determined, naive, or desperate, clung to the vision, remonstrated with authority, and finally organized opposition, propagandistic or even conspiratorial, to Cromwell's Protectorate.[53] To this remnant of believers in a once common faith a few New England men were attached in varying degrees.

For most of these colonial Puritans involvement was limited, peaceable, and primarily sympathetic. Hugh Peter, for instance, the most prominent of the repatriated divines, spoke out for government by perfect men, contributed an introduction to a Fifth Monarachy tract, Mary Cary's *Little Horns Doom and Downfall* (1651), and advocated burning "all the old Records" to make way for "the Moral Law . . . to which Moses's judicials added, with Solomon's Rules and Experiments, will be complete." Yet Peter was loyal to the Protector and avoided conspiracy.[54] Hanserd Knollys, exiled from Massachusetts as an Antinomian in 1638 and subsequently a controversial pastor on the New Hampshire frontier until he returned to England in 1641, was more committed. He preached an ardent millenarianism, attracted government surveillance, and inspired many in his Baptist congregation to sedition, although he himself remained clear.[55] The apothecary Thomas Tillam launched a new career as Baptist preacher and Fifth Monarchy advocate, although he publicly opposed brethren who engaged against the government.[56] A John Clarke, almost certainly the Rhode Island physician, was one of twelve laymen from Henry Jessey's London Baptist church to sign a Fifth Monarchy manifesto in 1654. Four years later he was tried "for speaking reproachfull and malitious scandalous words against his Highness."[57] Others there must have been, obscure men like Raphael Swinfield, who joined the cause because on returning from America he found himself "*walking* alone, and very *desolate* for want of such a society as this."[58] But New England's contribution was most prominently displayed in the work of three men: Eliot's *Christian Commonwealth* emerged from Livewell Chapman's Fifth Monarchy press, although Eliot himself remained in Massachusetts; William Aspinwall, repatriated in 1653, plunged into Fifth Monarchy agitation and issued numerous appeals for the immediate enthronement of Christ; and Thomas Venner, although less self-consciously identified with New England, conferred damaging notoriety on Massachusetts through revolutionary terrorism.

Aspinwall made the most impressive contribution, and it is strange that his fascinating career has never been properly studied. Arriving in Boston with the earliest settlers, he became merchant, deputy, and deacon before the Hutchinson controversy sent him into Narragansett exile. In Rhode Island he played a puzzling role. Although he had drawn up the Antinomian petition in 1637 and signed the theocratic covenant in 1638, he retained his tie with the Boston church, refused to attend the Portsmouth court, and was at length accused of sedition, his property being attached. After his submission and return to Boston in 1642, he again became prominent, serving as recorder and leading an exploratory expedition up the Delaware.[59] In 1653 he went back to England. In quick succession over the next five years he published six works, five of them desperate appeals for government of the saints and all of them issued by Chapman, the Fifth Monarchy bookseller. After 1657 he dropped from sight, although he must have been the "William Aspinall" of New England who was appointed minister of Kilcullen in 1659 in connection with the army's last attempt to Puritanize Ireland.[60] Throughout his later career Aspinwall seems to have seen himself as the last faithful disciple of Cotton.

Aspinwall published his first tract in the summer of 1653, shortly after he arrived in England. *A Brief Description of the Fifth Monarchy* vividly reveals the ideal England that is about to become reality, not through Christ's personal presence but through the dictatorship of his saints. The army, he argues, must begin the regime. "The Lambs Military Officers," who have proved their worth by "warring against the whore," must exercise supreme power until "the Churches be settled in Peace." Eventually, two kinds of power, legislative and magisterial, will maintain Christ's rule in the established Fifth Monarchy regime. Legislative power belongs to Christ alone and is never delegated. Hence every law must be based on divine command in scripture. Magisterial power Christ delegates to his saints who exercise it through a supreme Council of State and through subordinate officers—judges, overseers, exactors, and visitors—who bring theocratic oversight to the common level. All officials, high and low, are drawn from the churches which certify their faithfulness. For English constitutional traditions or the historic liberties of the subject Aspinwall clearly has no regard. Parliaments and diets are appropriate only to the *Fourth* Monarchy. To the objection that parliaments may be exercising powers delegated to them by the people there is an angry answer: "I demand what power have the people so to do? or when did Christ betrust the people with power to make laws?"[61]

During the next four years Aspinwall elaborated these themes in four more tracts: *An Explication and Application of the Seventh Chapter of Daniel* (1653), *Thunder from Heaven* (1655), *The Work of the Age; or, the Sealed Prophecies of Daniel opened and applied* (1655), and *The Legislative Power is Christs Peculiar Prerogative* (1656).[62] Apart from naive adornments, such as the recommendation that saints learn Hebrew because it is to be the accepted language in the coming age, and timely alterations, such as the declining estimate of Cromwell, these works added little to the conception. But while the later tracts raged at the Protector's "betrayal" and showed disappointment at delay, the author never lost faith that the day of power was near. Even in 1655 he reasoned that the Jews' conversion could not be more than nineteen years distant, and that the transition to the Fifth Monarchy would begin before that event.[63]

Eliot's *Christian Commonwealth* was also identified by contemporaries as a New England version of the Fifth Monarchy, and Aspinwall may have seen to its publication before he disappeared into Ireland. Although it was Eliot's only contribution to the English debate, the tract was assured prominence by its extravagant language, its author's fame, and especially the disastrous timing of its appearance. The work was issued in October 1659, just eight months before the return of Charles II, yet the Roxbury pastor had written the work about 1651, ostensibly as a reply to a Lancashire Presbyterian manifesto, Edward Gee's *A Plea for Non-Scribers.*[64] The long delay in publication cannot now be explained. Eliot himself insisted in 1661 that he had sent the manuscript to England "about nine or tenn yeares since" and that the book had eventually been submitted to the press "by others."[65] However, the title page stated only that the work was issued by "a Server of the Season" after the author's "consent given." The circumstances are puzzling, but suspicion arises that Eliot may have entrusted his manuscript to Aspinwall when the latter departed for England and that for some reason Aspinwall delayed placing it in the hands of the publisher, Chapman. Since Eliot's aim had been to mobilize contending Puritan factions behind a common program, Aspinwall or Chapman may have thought the book particularly useful in the desperate divisions after Cromwell's death when the nation was sliding toward a royalist restoration.

Whatever the reason for delay, *The Christian Commonwealth* clearly emerged from Eliot's earlier experiment with Indian theocracy, even repeating entire phrases from his missionary correspondence with the Society for the Propagation of the Gospel. The text does not deal at all with the usual themes—wicked rulers, pregnant prophecies, apocalyptic dating problems, or Mosaic legislation. Instead, it presents the extremely simple plan of political organization, already pioneered in the American wilderness in which godly rulers are set over decimal units of the people in tens, fifties, hundreds, thousands, and ultimately "myriads" or ten thousands, all functioning under a Supreme Council of seventy-one who rigorously enforce the law of God. The basis for the entire scheme is Eliot's favorite text, the Israelite "constitution" of Exodus 18:21, and hence the plan represents God's frame of government. It is not merely human. It is established over the saints in heaven and also over the angelic hierarchy, "according as it is applyable to their condition." Furthermore, the constitution has practical advantages. Drawn from the Old Testament, it will appeal to the Jews and hasten their conversion. Finally, Eliot brings to his argument the persuasion that this plan has already been successfully adopted by the Massachusetts Indians.

Eliot's long and impassioned preface also belonged to the early 1650s when Cotton, Cromwell, and hosts of others hoped that the millennial day was breaking. Addressed to "the Chosen, and Holy, and Faithful, who manage the Wars of the Lord, against Antichrist, in great *Britain*," this martial summons disclosed a full measure of exquisite millennial excitement. The saints were victorious; the Fourth Monarchy was in collapse; recent history was marching toward the glorious kingdom—events that tended to drive Eliot's prose into a kind of ecstatic litany: "The faithful Brethren in Scotland gave the first blow at the dirty toes, and feet of this Image; with whom the faithful brethren in England, presently concurred. But the Iron of the Civil State, stuck so fast to the miry clay, that . . . they are . . . both fallen together; they are fallen, they are fallen, they are both fallen together: Oh that men would therefore praise the Lord." In this marvelous moment England must grasp the chance to forswear all "humane Polities and Platformes," adopt biblical laws, and acknowledge Jesus as king: "Let him be your JUDGE, Let him be your LAW-GIVER, Let him be your KING!"[66] Such language revealed an obsessed religious personality already detached from mundane politics and dwelling in the expected millennial era, yet the idiom was not too distant from the enthusiastic expression of other Puritans earlier in the Revolution. Goodwin had "glimpsed Sion's glory"; Owen had rejoiced at the "shaking of the nations." Replying to a letter from Cotton, Cromwell had marveled, "What is the Lord a-doing? What prophecies are now fulfilling?"[67] The irony lay in the tract's tardy publication. Appearing in late 1659 as the nation moved toward historic English constitutional forms, *The Christian Commonwealth* won for Eliot a fanatic's place among Fifth Monarchy zealots. It is not surprising that Massachusetts soon found its "Apostle to the Indians" a source of embarassment in its relations with the Restoration government.

Lastly, Thomas Venner—to contemporaries the symbol of fanatic insurrection—completed New England's "trinity" in the Fifth Monarchy movement. Because he wrote nothing that showed dependence on his colonial experience, Venner's Massachusetts background and Fifth Monarchy violence may have been an adventitious connection. Yet for seven years he must have sat under Cotton's ministry, and at his trial he remembered that he was a New England man. His revolt, increasing Massachusetts's difficulties at the Restoration, deepened the colonial repudiation of apocalyptic politics.

A colonist of little consequence, Venner seldom appears in Massachusetts records. He settled in Salem as a cooper and was made freeman and church member in 1638. In both Salem and Boston (to which he moved in 1644) his residence was uneventful, although his advocacy of Puritan migration to the Isle of Providence may suggest restlessness and his enrollment in the artillery company may indicate martial ambitions.[68] By 1651 he was back in England, the subject of espionage reports submitted to Cromwell's secretary, John Thurloe. "A fellow of desperate and bloudy spirit," was Thurloe's conclusion, and Venner lost his place as wine cooper at the Tower on suspicion of a design to blow it up. Venner's aim is not clear, but the Tower's place as symbol of secular sovereignty and storehouse of legal records may have been involved. By 1656 he had become the leader of the congregation of revolutionary saints that met at Swan Alley, Coleman Street. More than that of other Fifth Monarchists, their style was military: they gathered arms, divided their forces into three bands after the example of Gideon and David, and chose officers by lot. In April 1657 they attempted a coup and were arrested by government soldiery. "One Vennour, not long since dwelling in your Boston," wrote a London friend to John Winthrop, Jr., behaved with "great impudence, insolence, pride and railing" before the Council. On the Protector's order he was sent to the Tower for the next two years.[69]

Venner's greatest fame was won eight months after the king's restoration in a final tragic episode that completed New England's ties to the Fifth Monarchy. On January 6, 1661, fifty of his fanatic followers poured out of their meetinghouse raising the cry, "The King Jesus and the heads upon the gates!" Bloody clashes with terrorized citizens and the trained bands occurred intermittently until final defeat on January 9. Nearly all the insurgents were killed or taken, although at least one managed to escape to refuge in Massachusetts. Venner himself, half dead from multiple stab wounds, was preserved for trial and a traitor's execution on January 19. Two days earlier he gave his last witness at the Old Bailey. Called upon to answer whether guilty or no, he "began an extravagant and bottomless discourse about the fifth monarchy, and his having had a testimony above twenty years in New-England."[70]

Although faith in a proximate millennium had subsided since the early 1650s, the Stuarts' return and the end of the Puritan age in England completed the destruction of the earlier hope. A full year before the Restoration John Davenport prophesied from New Haven that England might become "the popes asse againe," and the correspondence between Massachusetts and its London agent in the same era bore a similarly anxious cast. After 1661 the political necessity of quickly repudiating Venner hastened decisive rejection of millennial dreams. In London, Clarke, the Rhode Island representative, published a prompt condemnation of the rising, and not long after Massachusetts prepared an address to the king. "Venner (not to say whence he came to us) went out from us because he was not of us," the General Court assured Charles. "God preserve your Majestie from all emissaries agitated by an infernal spirit."[71] The plainest mark of the reaction was the Court's treatment of Eliot and his book. On May 22, 1661, the magistrates, formally considering *The Christian Commonwealth*, decided that "sundry passages and expressions thereof is justly offencive, and in speciall relating to kingly government in England." The book was suppressed and persons possessing copies were ordered to deliver them to the magistrates. Two days later the Roxbury minister himself submitted. "Freely and fully" acknowledging his fault to the Court, Eliot confessed that he had libeled government by king, lords, and commons as antichristian and had wrongfully justified "the late innovators." Then in a brief statement of principle, the Court approving, Eliot and Massachusetts together bade farewell to the alluring dream of Christ's kingdom on earth: "All formes of civil government deduced from Scripture, either expressely or by just consequence, I acknowledg to be of God, and to be subjected unto for conscience sake; and whatsoever is in the whole epistle or booke inconsisting herewith, I doe at once for all cordially disoune."[72]

At last the prophetic vision, that sense of the fullness of time for the fall of Antichrist, the conversion of the Jews, and the victory of the Lord and his saints which had so intoxicated Cotton, Eliot, and Aspinwall, passed away. Dying in 1652, Cotton alone among these three had probably not lived to see the collapse of hope. Eliot survived longest, until 1690, but his communities of "praying Indians," who were visibly to proclaim Christ's monarchy to all the world, were devastated in King Philip's War. Quickly the millennialism of the first generation became a pious memory, faithfully recorded by Cotton Mather but exotic to the religious life of the province. At the beginning of the eighteenth century a last quiet echo of the once militant faith was sounded in Samuel Sewall's Diary: "William Parsons of 88 years, is buried. Was in the fifth- monarchy fray in London: but slipt away in the Crowd."[73]

Indeed, as its second generation grew to maturity, New England in the mid-seventeenth century had entered on a changed mentality. The earlier sense of standing at the crisis-gates of history had weakened, while a new awareness of their geographical place and "wilderness mission" had settled over New England people. The Mathers themselves epitomized the change: Richard, preoccupied with the approaching apocalyptic ordeal for all God's people, had been geographically vague in justifying removal to "New [England], or to *some such like place*"; his grandson Cotton, by contrast, provided the classic account of a unique American mission entrusted to the Puritan fathers and their heirs.[74] In keeping with the change, the earlier expectation of sweeping revival and godly revolution throughout the world—John Cotton's longed-for "resurrection of the churches"—was replaced by a conservative determination to perpetuate the symbols and institutions of the colonial founders. And since the latter-day guardians of the tradition found their task doomed to failure, they gradually lost confidence in a corporate New England and developed the jeremiad as an appropriate literature for apostate generations.

As pursuit of the Fifth Monarchy faded from memory, New England "chiliasm" gradually assumed definition as an eschatological scheme fit for an age of "declension." "They, who of late were called fifth Monarchy-men," wrote Davenport in 1667, "did err . . . especially two ways. First by anticipating the time, which will not be till the pouring out of the sixth and seventh Vials [and] Secondly, By putting themselves upon a work which shall not be done by men, but by Christ himself."[75] No longer was history expected to bring forth Christ's perfect rule through holy magistrates and Spirit-filled assemblies; rather, it was to reveal deepening corruption until it terminated in cataclysm, judgment, and the miraculous resurrection of martyred saints. To a world abandoned in wickedness Christ would personally return, rescue his suffering people, and establish his divine imperium for a thousand years. Beginning with Increase's *Mystery of Israel's Salvation* (1669), the Mathers led New England in literary cultivation of the new apocalypticism, although it was left to Sewall's *Phenœmena quœdam Apocalyptica* (1697) to provide the perfect blending of millenarianism and provincial pride. Yet even before these works, New England's passage to this theological fashion was quietly marked in an exchange of letters after 1659 between Samuel Hutchinson of Boston and an English millenarian, probably the former colonist Thomas Tillam. To his friend's defense of Fifth Monarchists Hutchinson gave a cautious response: "I do not approve of such Fifth-Monarchy-Men as taking up Arms against Commonwealths and Governments" but only of "such Fifth-Monarchy-men that Daniel prophesied of . . . which will not be till Christ appear in the Clouds, for the Restitution of all things." If Tillam was the correspondent, he may never have read the reply. Unlike most Old and New England Puritans, he had declined to abandon hope in impending godly rule and, gathering a few steadfast recruits, had led a new Puritan migration to the Palatinate, intending to erect a new New England on the banks of the Rhine.[76]

The enthusiasm of an Edward Johnson or a John Eliot occasionally produced plans for a new Jerusalem. But they and other Puritan spokesmen devoted equal if not greater effort to the task of perfecting existing religious institutions. The Bible Commonwealths of New England achieved their distinctive character from their ecclesiastical organization as well as from the theology and zeal of their founders.

NOTES

1. J. Franklin Jameson, ed., *Johnson's Wonder-Working Providence 1628-1651*, Original Narratives of Early American History (New York, 1910), 34.

2. For medieval and Reformation backgrounds to eschatology see Norman Cohn, *Pursuit of the Millennium: Revolutionary Millenarians and Mystical Anarchists of the Middle Ages* (London, 1957). In Britain the chief influences establishing an apocalyptic historical perspective seem to have been early commentaries on Revelation, particularly those of John

Bale and John Napier, the various editions of the Geneva Bible, and John Foxe's *Book of Martyrs.* See Lewis Lupton, *A History of the Geneva Bible,* 4 vols. to date (London, 1966-   ), and William Haller, *The Elect Nation: The Meaning and Relevance of Foxe's Book of Martyrs* (New York, 1963).

3. For the vision of history in Cromwell's army see *A Declaration of the English Army now in Scotland, to the People in Scotland especially those among them that know and fear the Lord* (London, 1650). For Puritan obsession with the struggle against Antichrist see Hill, *Antichrist,* 41-145. . . .

4. Brightman's relevant works were *A Revelation of the Apocalyps* (Amsterdam, 1611), an English translation of an earlier Latin text published at Frankfurt in 1609 and Heidelberg in 1612; *A Most Comfortable Exposition of the Prophecie of Daniel;* and *A Commentary on the Canticles.* . . .

5. Alsted's great work was *Diatribe de mille annis Apocalypticis* (Frankfurt, 1627), translated and published by William Burton as *The Beloved City, or the Saints reign on earth a thousand yeares* . . . (London, 1643). His millennial views also appeared in *The Worlds Proceeding Woes and Succeeding Joyes* (London, 1642). Alsted was a celebrated Ramist logician; his *Encyclopaedia, septem tomis distincta* (Herborn, 1630) was read at Harvard and treasured by Cotton Mather. . . .

For Independent millennialism see Geoffrey F. Nuttall, *Visible Saints: The Congregational Way 1640-1660* (Oxford, 1957), 143-155, and John F. Wilson, *Pulpit in Parliament: Puritanism during the English Civil Wars 1640-1648* (Princeton, N. J., 1969), 223-230. Goodwin's expository discourses on Revelation were preached in Holland in 1639 but not published until after his death. His most influential sermon was the anonymous *A Glimpse of Sions Glory* . . . , preached in Holland in 1641. . . .

6. The 1559 edition of the Geneva Bible greatly expanded the note on Rom. II, emphasizing future Jewish conversion. Perkins's views were developed in his commentary on Galatians. The Jacobean Puritan divine, William Gouge, edited Sir Henry Finch's exposition on the subject, *The Worlds Great Restoration. Or, the Calling of the Jews* . . . (London, 1621). For Puritan interest in the Jews see Toon, ed., *Puritans,* 23-34, 115-125, and Nuttall, *Visible Saints,* 143ff. The general background of English Hebrew scholarship is treated in David Daiches, *The King James Version of the English Bible: An Account of the Development and Source of the English Bible of 1611 with Special Reference to the Hebrew Tradition* (Chicago, 1941), 88-166.

7. Nuttall, *Visible Saints,* 148. See also John C. Miller, ed., *The Works of Thomas Goodwin, D.D.* (Edinburgh, 1861-1866), III, 81-82, 122-133; XII, 74-75; and Thomas Hooker, *A Survey of the Summe of Church-Discipline* (London, 1648), "Preface." Goodwin served as co-pastor to the Arnhem church with John Archer, author of *The Personall Raigne of Christ upon Earth* (London, 1641). Independents' commitment to the millennium was made a charge against them by Robert Baillie, *A Dissuasive from the Errours of the Time* (London, 1645), 224. . . .

8. Thomas Tillam, "Uppon the first sight of New-England June 29 1638," in Harold S. Jantz, "The First Century of New England Verse," American Antiquarian Society, *Proceedings,* LIII (1943), 331. The text in Harrison T. Meserole, ed., *Seventeenth-Century American Poetry* (New York, 1968), 397-398, includes what Jantz omits—Tillam's important marginal reference to "Math 25:34"—but apparently neither editor appreciates the apocalyptic emotion of the poem. The sense of constructing a new historical order in Massachusetts is conveyed especially well in Jameson, ed., *Johnson's Wonder-Working Providence,* notably 49ff.

9. [Increase Mather], *The Life and Death of That Reverend Man of God, Mr. Richard Mather, Teacher of the Church in Dorchester in New-England* (Cambridge, Mass., 1670), esp. Argument VI of "Arguments tending to prove the Removing from *Old England* to *New.*" The narrative is set in context in Middlekauff, *The Mathers,* 20-34. For the "desolation" theme in Hooker and Hutchinson see Thomas Hooker, *The Danger of Desertion: or, A Farewell Sermon of Mr. Thomas Hooker* . . . (London, 1641), and David D. Hall, ed., *The Antinomian Controversy, 1636-1638* (Middletown, Conn., 1968), 336-338. The theme is also prominently displayed in "Arguments for the Plantation of New England," *Winthrop Papers,* II, 111-121.

10. For Cotton's eschatology see Emerson, *John Cotton,* 95-101, and Ziff, *Career of John*

Cotton, 170-202. Canticles, treated as an allegory of church history, was commonly looked to for apocalyptic meaning. Cotton's *A Brief Exposition of the Whole Book of Canticles, or, Song of Solomon* . . . (London, 1642) was influenced by Brightman's commentary. It is not possible to fix the precise dates of Cotton's Thursday lectures on Revelation. . . .

11. Cotton Mather, *Magnalia Christi Americana; or, The Ecclesiastical History of New-England* . . . (Hartford, Conn., 1853-1855 [orig. publ. London 1702]), I, 25-26; *Memoirs of Capt. Roger Clap* . . . (Boston, 1731), 24-25.

12. Although preached in 1639-1640, Cotton's *Exposition upon the Thirteenth Chapter* was not printed until 1655 when the Fifth Monarchy bookseller, Livewell Chapman, brought out an edition "taken from his mouth in Short-writing." Another edition, omitting pp. 109-112 but otherwise identical, was issued 17 months later by Timothy Smart. On internal evidence, *The Powring Out of the Seven Vials: or an Exposition of the 16. Chapter of the Revelation, with an Application of it to our Times* . . . (London, 1642) seems to have been delivered in 1641.

13. Cotton, *Exposition upon the Thirteenth Chapter*, passim; Cotton, *Churches Resurrection*, 3-21.

14. Cotton, *Exposition upon the Thirteenth Chapter*, 93; Cotton, *Powring Out*, 77-86, 138-140, 154-156.

15. Cotton, *Churches Resurrection*, 5-6, 15-21.

16. The report of the 1643 sermon is by Samuel Gorton, *Simplicities Defence against Seven-Headed Policy* . . . , in Peter Force, ed., *Tracts and Other Papers, Relating Principally to the Origin, Settlement, and Progress of the Colonies in North America, From the Discovery of the Country to the Year 1776* (Washington, D. C., 1836-1848), IV, 64; John Cotton, *The Bloudy Tenent, washed and made white in the bloud of the Lambe* . . . (London, 1647), 52-53. . . .

17. Ephraim Huit, *The whole Prophecie of Daniel explained by a paraphrase, analysis and briefe comment* (London, 1644), 181-202; Thomas Parker, *The Visions and Prophecies of Daniel Expounded* . . . (London, 1646).

18. Hooker, *Survey of the Summe of Church-Discipline*, "Preface." The statement about Richard Mather is Middlekauff's judgment, *The Mathers*, 372, n. 25. Mather's eschatology is most developed in the unpublished "Summe of Seventie Lectures," but it is also strongly expressed in John Eliot and Thomas Mayhew, *Tears of Repentance: Or, A further Narrative of the Progress of the Gospel Amongst the Indians in New-England* (London, 1653), "To the Christian Reader." Cotton Mather said of John Eliot that his discourses ran on "the coming of the Lord Jesus Christ" whatever his subject. *Magnalia*, I, 548. Typological use of eschatology is exemplified in Peter Bulkeley, *The Gospel-Covenant: or, the Covenant of Grace Opened* . . . (London, 1646), which opens with discussion of the calling of the Jews and then proceeds to apply "three other things as types to them" (the natural estate of all men in spiritual bondage, the captivity of the church under Antichrist, the servile condition of the Jews).

19. The language is Winthrop's and may exaggerate. Winthrop makes the charge in considerable detail, but it appears to have been overlooked as a factor in Williams's departure from Massachusetts. *Winthrop Papers*, III, 147-148.

20. References to the earthquakes are found generally. See, for example, James Kendall Hosmer, ed., *Winthrop's Journal, "History of New England, 1630-1649,"* Original Narratives of Early American History (New York, 1908), I, 270-271, 292; *Winthrop Papers*, IV, 37, 115; and Jameson, ed., *Johnson's Wonder-Working Providence*, 160, 185.

21. *Note-Book Kept by Thomas Lechford, Esq., Lawyer, in Boston, Massachusetts Bay, from June 27, 1638, to July 29, 1641*, Am. Antiq. Soc., *Transactions and Collections*, VII (Cambridge, Mass., 1885), 50.

22. "A Dialogue Between Old England and New; Concerning Their Present Troubles, Anno, 1642," in Jeannine Hensley, ed., *The Works of Anne Bradstreet* (Cambridge, Mass., 1967), 187-188. . . .

23. Jameson, ed., *Johnson's Wonder-Working Providence*, 33.

24. *Winthrop Papers*, V, 126. The date was Jan. 6, 1647.

25. The *Discourse*, not published until 1663, was written in 1637 to instruct John Daven-

port in sound political principles for New Haven. See Isabel M. Calder, "John Cotton and the New Haven Colony," *New England Quarterly*, III (1930), 82-94. For a brief summary of Cotton's political writings see Emerson, *John Cotton*, 141-151.

26. George Lee Haskins, *Law and Authority in Early Massachusetts: A Study in Tradition and Design* (New York, 1960), 120-162.

27. Ibid., 124-126; W. C. Ford, "Cotton's 'Moses His Judicials,' " Mass. Hist. Soc., *Proceedings*, 2d Ser., XVI (1903), 274-284, which includes the text of "How Far Moses Judicials Bind Massachusetts." The code was eventually published as *An Abstract of the Lawes of New-England* (London, 1641).

28. Cotton, *Exposition upon the Thirteenth Chapter*, 96-97, 111-112, and esp. 241-242; Cotton, *Churches Resurrection*, 14-16. Note also Cotton Mather's report that Cotton wrote to John Davenport that "the order of the churches and the commonwealth was now so settled in New-England, by common consent, that it brought into his mind the new heaven and the new earth, wherein dwells righteousness." *Magnalia*, I, 325.

29. Cotton, *Powring Out*, 48-49.

30. W[illiam] A[spinwall], *Thunder from Heaven against the Backsliders and Apostates of the Times. In some Meditations on the 24 Chapter of Isaiah* (London, 1655), 38.

31. Hall, ed., *Antinomian Controversy*, 336-338. See Geoffrey F. Nuttall, *The Holy Spirit in Puritan Faith and Experience* (Oxford, 1946), 102-133, concerning the manner in which preoccupation with the abiding presence of the Spirit often suggested the dawning of a new era with God's Spirit more bountifully shed in men's hearts.

32. Charles H. Bell, ed., *John Wheelwright. His Writings, Including His Fast-Day Sermon, 1637, and His Mercurius Americanus, 1645; with a Paper upon the Genuineness of the Indian Deed of 1629, and a Memoir* (Prince Soc., Pubs. [Boston, 1876]), 170.

33. Hall, ed., *Antinomian Controversy*, 308. Hutchinson herself claimed prophetic competence on the basis of eschatological description in Joel 2:28: "It is said, I will poure my Spirit upon your Daughters, and they shall prophesie, etc. If God give mee a gift of Prophecy, I may use it." *Ibid.*, 268. The apocalyptic atmosphere surrounding the Antinomian controversy has received inadequate comment, possibly because adventist excitement was present on both sides and the millennial promises were not a central issue. (But see Ziff, *Career of John Cotton*, 155-157, and Jesper Rosenmeier, "New England's Perfection: The Image of Adam and the Image of Christ in the Antinomian Crisis, 1634 to 1638," *WMQ*, 3d Ser., XXVII [1970], 456-457.) . . .

34. Howard M. Chapin, *Documentary History of Rhode Island*, II (Providence, R. I., 1919), 19. The date was Mar. 7, 1638. The first scriptural citation attached to the covenant was Exod. 24:3-4 concerning Israel's promise of obedience to the word of the Lord after Moses's descent from the Mount. Authorship of the covenant is not known, but William Aspinwall was secretary.

35. Hall, ed., *Antinomian Controversy*, 350-373, esp. 361-362. Note also the apparent mixture of legal and experiential imperatives in the resolve of Jan. 2, 1639, pledging the colony to biblical law but providing also that if any brother received "Light to the Contrary of whatt by the Judge and Elders hath been determined formerly: that then and there it shall be repealed as the Act of the Body." Chapin, *Documentary History*, II, 48-49. The report on William Hutchinson is found in both *Winthrop's Journal*, II, 39-41, and Baillie, *Dissuasive*, 150. Baillie had the story from Williams.

36. *Winthrop Papers*, V, 376-377. The quotation is from Williams's account of Clarke's preaching at Seekonk in 1649. John Clarke, *Ill Newes from New-England: or a Narrative of New-England's Persecution* . . . (London, 1652), 47-48. . . .

37. A recent example of this tradition, Ola Elizabeth Winslow's *John Eliot, "Apostle to the Indians"* (Boston, 1968), is an inadequate study that fails as an interpretation because it misses Eliot's passionate longing for the accomplishment of the millennial prophecies. The author does not know how to appraise *The Christian Commonwealth* (pp. 195-197), and dismisses Eliot's nearly hysterical appeal as a "by no means exciting book" (p. 197). For other treatments of Eliot that also fail to consider his millennialism see Alden T. Vaughan, *New England Frontier: Puritans and Indians, 1620-1675* (Boston, 1965); Francis Jennings, "Goals and Functions of Puritan Missions to the Indians," *Ethnohistory*, XVIII (1971),

197-212; and Neal Salisbury, "Red Puritans: The 'Praying Indians' of Massachusetts Bay and John Eliot," *WMQ*, 3d Ser., XXXI (1974), 27-54.

38. John Cotton, *Gods promise to His plantation* . . . (London, 1630), 19-20; *Winthrop Papers*, V, 114, 115-116.

39. Thomas Shepard, *The Clear Sun-shine of the Gospel breaking forth upon the Indians in New-England* (London, 1648), 30; Eliot and Mayhew, *Tears of Repentance*, "To His Excellency, the Lord General Cromwel." See also the preface by Richard Mather in the same volume, "To the Christian Reader."

40. Lechford, *Plain Dealing*, 21; *Winthrop's Journal*, II, 30. See also John Cotton, *The Way of the Congregational Churches Cleared* (London, 1648), Pt. I, 78. Williams reached the same conclusion, again on the basis of Rev. 15:8. See *The Hireling Ministry None of Christs* . . . (London, 1652) in Perry Miller *et al.*, eds., *The Complete Writings of Roger Williams* (New York, 1963), VII, 168.

41. *Strength Out of Weaknesse, Or a Glorious Manifestation of the Further Progresse of the Gospel among the Indians in New-England* (London, 1652), "To the Reader."

42. Jameson, ed., *Johnson's Wonder-Working Providence*, 59, 255.

43. Broughton's most influential work was *A Revelation of the Holy Apocalyps* ([Amsterdam?], 1610). See *Dictionary of National Biography*, s.v. "Broughton, Hugh."

44. Toon, ed., *Puritans*, 117-118.

45. Thomas Thorowgood, *Jews in America, or probabilities that the Americans are of that Race* . . . (London, 1650), "Epistolicall Discourse of Mr. Iohn Drury, to Mr. Thorowgood"; Hamon L'Estrange wrote a skeptical reply, *Americans no Jews, or Improbabilities that the Americans are of that race* (London, [1651]).

46. John Eliot, *The Light Appearing More and More towards the perfect Day, or a farther discovery of the present state of the Indians in New-England* . . . (London, 1651), 14-18, 24-25. See also John Eliot, *The Glorious progress of the Gospel amongst the Indians of New England.* . . . (London, 1649), "Epistle Dedicatory," 22-28. Winslow, like Durie, stressed the work of Menasseh and the theory of the Indians' Semitic origins in the preface.

47. Eliot, *Light Appearing*, 24.

48. *Ibid.*, 28; Thomas Thorowgood, *Jews in America, or Probabilities that those Indians are Judaical, made more probable by some additionals to the former conjectures* . . . (London, 1660), [27], misnumbered 23.

49. *Strength Out of Weakness*, 8-13; Eliot, *Light Appearing*, 23, 28.

50. *Strength Out of Weakness*, 12-15; Eliot, *Light Appearing*, 23.

51. Eliot, *Light Appearing*, 28-29.

52. Jameson, ed., *Johnson's Wonder-Working Providence*, 160-161.

53. The established study in the field has long been Louise Fargo Brown, *The Political Activities of the Baptists and Fifth Monarchy Men in England During the Interregnum* (Washington, D. C., 1912), a careful account but rather too accented on Baptist contributions and written in the belief that the 1650s—rather than the 1640s—were the zenith of English millennialism. Of two recent studies, P. G. Rogers, *The Fifth Monarchy Men* (London, 1966), and Capp, *Fifth Monarchy Men*, the latter is more thoroughly researched and more reliable. On the Little Parliament see H. A. Glass, *The Barbone Parliament* . . . (London, 1899), and Austin Woolrych, "The Calling of Barebone's Parliament," *English Historical Review*, LXXX (1965), 492-513. On the importance of the Little Parliament see Nuttall, *Visible Saints*, 148-153. . . .

54. Hugh Peter, *Good Work for a Good Magistrate, or a short cut to great quiet* (London, 1651), 32-33; Raymond Phineas Stearns, *The Strenuous Puritan: Hugh Peter 1598-1660* (Urbana, Ill., 1954), 368-369. Henry Jessey and Christopher Feake also wrote introductions to Mary Cary's tract. On Peter and law reform see Stuart E. Prall, *The Agitation for Law Reform during the Puritan Revolution 1640-1660* (The Hague, 1966), 66.

55. Capp, *Fifth Monarchy Men*, 92-93. For Knollys's own account see William Kiffin, ed., *The Life and Death of that old Disciple of Jesus Christ, and Eminent Minister of the Gospel, Mr. Hanserd Knollys* (London, 1692).

56. E. A. Payne, "Thomas Tillam," *Baptist Quarterly*, XVII (1957-1958), 61-66.

57. W. T. Whitley, "The English Career of John Clarke, Rhode Island," *ibid.*, I (1922-1923), 368-372. William H. Allison in *The Dictionary of American Biography*, s.v. "Clarke, John," doubts the identification, arguing that a Fifth Monarchy partisan could not have obtained the Rhode Island charter. However, it is probable that the author of *Ill Newes from New-England* would have worshipped with Henry Jessey's London church and supported Fifth Monarchy campaigns that remained free of sedition. Capp accepts the identification. *Fifth Monarchy Men*, 246. For Clarke's trial see *A Narrative, wherein is faithfully set forth the Sufferings of John Canne* . . . (London, 1658), and Abbott, ed., *Writings and Speeches of Cromwell*, IV, 786.

58. Quoted in Capp, *Fifth Monarchy Men*, 97. Even Roger Williams had sympathy for such millenarians as Canne and Archer. See Miller *et al.*, eds., *Writings of Williams*, I, 386, IV, 221. Of Thomas Harrison, the Fifth Monarchy leader, Williams wrote to John Winthrop, Jr., in 1654: "Surely, Sir, he is a very gallant, most deserving, heavenly man, but most high flown for the kingdom of the saints, and the fifth monarchy now risen, and their sun never to set again, etc." *Ibid.*, VI, 260.

59. The entry in the *DNB* is very brief and confused; the *DAB* has no entry. There are scattered references in the *New England Historical and Genealogical Register* and a century-old account in James Savage, ed., *A Genealogical Dictionary of the First Settlers of New England* . . . , I (Boston, 1860), 70-71. For Aspinwall's Rhode Island career there are frequent references in Chapin, *Documentary History*, II, 22, 33-51, 56, 87-90, 116, and *passim*. Aspinwall's alienation from the Narragansett colonists culminated in the order of the Portsmouth court, Feb. 7, 1639, enjoining him from building a shallop. The record implies some treasonable design. The Massachusetts court granted him a safe-conduct Oct. 7, 1641, to appear in Boston, and he submitted to Boston church and magistrates on Mar. 27, 1642. Nathaniel B. Shurtleff, ed., *Records of the Governor and Company of the Massachusetts Bay in New England* (Boston, 1853-1854), I, 338; *Winthrop's Journal*, II, 56.

60. The presentment coincided with the last revival of Fifth Monarchy expectations after Cromwell's death. St. John D. Seymour, *The Puritans in Ireland, 1647-1661* (Oxford, 1921), 175, 206.

61. William Aspinwall, *A Brief Description of the Fifth Monarchy or Kingdome that shortly is to come into the world* . . . (London, 1653), esp. 4-10. After the author's name on the title page are the letters "N. E.," presumably for "New England." Aspinwall's name is mentioned in Massachusetts records on May 18, 1653, with no indication that he had left the colony. Shurtleff, ed., *Mass. Bay Recs.*, III, 307. George Thomason, the London tract collector, had his copy of *A Brief Description* on Aug. 1, 1653. *Thomason Tracts Catalogue*, II, 30. The "N. E." and the brief residence in England before publication suggest the possibility that the tract was composed in New England.

62. All were published in London. Another title, *A Premonition of Sundry Sad Calamities Yet to Come* (London, 1655), has the text of *Work of the Age*. The *Abrogation of the Jewish Sabbath, or Sabbath of the 7th Day of the Week* (London, 1657) carries Aspinwall's name but displays no obsession with the millennium and shows no familiarity with New England.

63. Aspinwall's commentary on Daniel, written during the sessions of the Little Parliament, was admiringly dedicated to Cromwell. It identified the late king with the Little Horn of Dan. 7:8 and urged Cromwell to destroy the remaining royal authority and law that had developed over the centuries. By 1655 *Thunder from Heaven* warned darkly that "Christ takes a speedy course with that HIGH ONE and his host, which have been instrumental in all these sad changes, and have obstructed the work of Christ" (p. 29). The prediction of the Jews' conversion within 19 years occurs *ibid.*, "The Author to the Reader."

64. John Eliot *The Christian Commonwealth: or, The Civil Policy of the Rising Kingdom of Jesus Christ* (London, [1659]), "The Preface." On the title page of the copy in the Boston Public Library a 17th-century hand has written "5th Mon: form of Govrmt." Gee's work was published in London in 1650.

65. Shurtleff, ed., *Mass. Bay Recs.*, IV, Pt. II, 5-6.

66. Eliot, *Christian Commonwealth*, 3-9, 16, "The Preface."

67. Abbott, ed., *Writings and Speeches of Cromwell*, II, 482-483. The date was Oct. 2, 1651.

68. The fullest account of Venner is Charles Edward Banks, "Thomas Venner. The Boston

Wine-Cooper and Fifth Monarchy Man," *NEHGR*, XLVII (1893), 437-444. Venner's name is oddly juxtaposed with Aspinwall's in a controversy of both men with Thomas Gayner in Boston, Oct. 1651. Shurtleff, ed., *Mass. Bay Recs.*, III, 252-253.

69. Rev. William Hooke to John Winthrop, Jr., Apr. 13, 1657, in Banks, "Thomas Venner," *NEHGR*, XLVII (1893), 440; Thomas Birch, ed., *A Collection of the State Papers of John Thurloe . . .* , VI (London, 1742), 184-188; Brown, *Political Activities*, 106-111; Champlin Burrage, "The Fifth Monarchy Insurrections," *Eng. Hist. Rev.*, XXV (1910), 722-747.

70. *A Collection of Scarce and Valuable Tracts, on the Most Interesting and Entertaining Subjects* [*Somers Tracts*], VII (London, 1812), 470.

71. John Clarke, *The Plotters Unmasked* (London, 1661); Isabel MacBeath Calder, ed., *Letters of John Davenport, Puritan Divine* (New Haven, Conn., 1937), 139-140; *Hutchinson Papers*, II, 34-35, 40ff, 62.

72. Shurtleff, ed., *Mass. Bay Recs.*, IV, Pt. II, 5-6. However, Eliot's millennialism again appears in *Communion of Churches: Or, The Divine Management of Gospel-Churches by the Ordinance of Councils, Constituted in Order according to the Scriptures . . .* (Cambridge, Mass., 1665). In this tract, written to "Prepare for the hoped-for Resurrection of the Churches," Eliot refers to his plan for a theocratic political order (pp. 9-10), urges the civil power to put transgressors to death by the law of God (p. 33), and expects the setting up of Christ's glorious kingdom (esp. pp. 16-17). Although issued in 1665, the work may have been written several years earlier; it takes no account of the Restoration and looks like an ecclesiastical counterpart to the political scheme in *The Christian Commonwealth*. A likely date might be 1657, when Richard Baxter was pressing Eliot to develop a proposal that might unite Presbyterians and Independents. See F. J. Powicke, *Some Unpublished Correspondence of the Reverend Richard Baxter and the Reverend John Eliot, the Apostle of the American Indians 1656-1682* (Manchester, 1931), 21-22, 24. . . .

73. *Diary of Samuel Sewall*, Jan. 31, 1702 (Mass. Hist. Soc., *Collections*; 5th Ser., V [Boston, 1879]), 52. Aspinwall's life after the Restoration is unknown. A William Aspinwall, mercer of Halifax, died in 1660. Another William Aspinwall died in Chester in 1662. See Capp, *Fifth Monarchy Men*, 240-241.

74. [Increase Mather], *Life and Death of Richard Mather*, "Arguments Tending to Prove the Removing from *Old England* to *New*," Argument VI. Italics mine.

75. John Davenport, "An Epistle to the Reader," in Increase Mather, *The Mystery of Israel's Salvation, Explained and Applyed . . .* ([London], 1669).

76. S[amuel] H[utchinson], *A Declaration of a Future Glorious Estate of a Church to be Here upon Earth, at Christs Personal Appearance for the Restitution of All Things, a Thousand Years before the Ultimate Day of the General Judgement Set Forth by a Letter to a Friend* (London, 1667), 3.

5 | THE HISTORY OF A PURITAN CHURCH 1637-1736

KENNETH A. LOCKRIDGE

In Orthodoxy in Masssachusetts, Perry Miller maintained that the early settlers of Massachusetts were "non-separating Congregationalists" who brought their ecclesiastical principles with them from England; they had no need to emulate the Separatists of neighboring Plymouth. According to Miller, the Puritan church structure established by John Cotton and his colleagues ensured the congregational autonomy of the various churches. Edmund S. Morgan's Visible Saints: The History of a Puritan Idea (New York, 1963) brings an added dimension to the topic. Morgan convincingly demonstrates that congregational principles—particularly the requirement that prospective members demonstrate proof of saving grace—developed gradually within the Puritan communities in England, the Netherlands, and America. He also stresses the independency of individual churches, although the colonists' ambition to be a "City on a Hill" that would edify the world required that the independent congregations join together to offer a unified front.

The organization and structure of one Puritan church, the church in Dedham, Massachusetts, is the topic of the following essay.

I

For no other church as for that of Dedham does there exist so full a narration of the long, peculiar process of founding a Puritan congregation.[1] The Reverend John Allin's "brief history of the Church of Christ [gathered] in his name at Dedham in New England"[2] offered "for future ages to make use of" is a monument to the honesty and seriousness with which he and his fellows approached the task of beginning a church. This description of the events which began in 1637 and ended with the establishment of the church in late 1638 is a careful one. Every line speaks of a slow, agonizingly self-critical approach to God in which a firm hope of success was mixed with a terrible fear of failure.

It would be a mistake to assume that Allin and his friends knew step-by-step where they were going when they began their efforts. In later years, the classic form of the foundation process became that of (1) a decision to found a congregation of God's elect, those whom He had predestined for salvation, in order to offer to God the purest possible visible church devoted to His worship, (2) a series of mutual cross-examinations by the founders, out of which were to emerge seven "pillars," seven men truly and hopefully considered to have received the saving grace and (3) the admission of other members by these "pillars," in the form of a public examination of the candidates in which certain signs of the reception of grace were to be sought. But in 1637, in Dedham, no one, perfect form was known to be usual or acceptable.[3] The seekers after God groped their way through these same stages partly by the dim light of their intuitions, partly with help from other early congregations who had undergone the same experience. It was by no means undertaken mechanically or with an unthinking assurance of good results. Nor was the way taken considered the only way to reach the desired end. Allin noted that his account of Dedham's efforts was "no way intending hereby to bind the conscience of any to walk by this pattern or to approve of the practice of this church further than it may appear to be according to the rule of gospel."

Things began informally, with a series of meetings of "all the inhabitants who affected church communion . . . lovingly to discourse and consult together such questions as might further tend to establish a peaceable and comfortable civil society and prepare for spiritual communion." The chief object of these weekly discourses was that the townsmen, being "from several parts of England," might "be [come] further acquainted with the [spiritual] tempers and gifts of one another." After this they sought to "gain further light in the ways of Christ's Kingdom and government of his Church." In these get-acquainted meetings there was a regular procedure and a distinct tone. They met "the fifth day of every week at several houses in order." At each meeting the man of the house began and ended the proceedings with a prayer and initiated the discussion. Each person asked questions or talked as he saw fit, all "humbly and with a teachable heart not with any mind of cavilling or contradicting." "Which order," Allin notes, "was so well observed as generally all such reasonings were very peaceable, loving and tender, much to edification." These "tender" weeks of exploration probably spared them many later contentions.

"After which questions," Allin continues, "we proceeded to such as more properly concerned the chief scope of our meetings." Now facing directly the business of "the gathering of a church" those in attendance agreed upon thirteen questions and propositions in which the doctrinal base of their labors was set down. Starting from a position of nominal innocence, they asked whether Christian strangers such as themselves might thus assemble, speak, pray and fast together while not in a usual church order and community. This essential first question they answered affirmatively: "the right to pray, fast, consult and institute a church" flowed from the relation of each individual with Christ. Having affirmed their own legality, they next considered what kind of church they sought to institute and how this should be done. These problems were resolved through the dialectical process of twelve more questions and answers, each building upon the others.

Their "duties of Christian love" were pledged in the second proposition: "to exhort, admonish, privately comfort, to communicate and improve any gift . . . , to relieve the wants of each other etc." It is characteristic of these men that the spirit with which they were to regard one another was considered before doctrinal details. But the third question forced them to go beyond a mere promise of mutual love. It asked "whether having these privileges of christian communion [question one] and being bound to such duties [of love, question two], we may not rest in such a condition and look no further?" to which the reply was:

> Negatively, we may not, but [must] seek for a further union and communion even such as may . . . convey unto us all the ordinances of Christ's instituted worship both because it is the command of God that [the] whole Christ should be received and submitted unto . . . and also because the spiritual condition of every christian is such as stands in need of all instituted ordinances for the repair of the spirit and edification of the body of Christ Eph. 4.

With a skepticism about the nature of man and faith in institutions which distinguished Puritan from Quaker, the men of Dedham rejected an informal, loving communion as insufficient. They could not rest content with mere meetings, but must seek the "instituted ordinances" of God as required by the Bible.

The answer to the fourth proposition finally spelled out the nature of the formal church they were seeking. It was to be a "Church communion of the fellowship of a certain number of visible saints or believers agreeing to live together in spiritual communion . . . in the use of all the holy instituted ordinances and worship of the gospel." "This," they went on, "is an institution of Christ in the gospel that the saints of Christ [i.e. the elect] should be distributed into particular visible congregations enjoying their distinct officers etc." How then to locate the visible saints who would constitute the true church? Such was the subject of the fifth proposition, which itself gave the solution—"a profession of faith and holiness, [and] the fruit of it as makes it visible, makes a man fit matter for a visible church." True grace and true faith were matters between a man and Christ, hence invisible. But they gave certain signs which could make one acceptable as a church member. A profession of faith and the active fruits of that faith were not only visible, but evidence of the reception of grace. The sixth proposition proceeded to assert that a "covenant" would be the contract between the visible saints and God. The Lord "never took any people unto himself to worship . . . but by covenant, as appears in the stories of Abraham and his family constituted a church by covenant Gen. 15 and 17."

The last six propositions went back over the matter of the elect and of their church in greater detail, filling in the broad spaces of the first principles. To ensure that "the ordinances may be kept in purity" and "the persons knit firmly in the bond of love," it was found "requisite that the professors, being strangers to one another, . . . should be well acquainted with the hearts and states of one another." The first members were to "join by way of confession and profession of their faith" to each other in order to assure themselves that they were suitable founders of a congregation. "But," it was affirmed, "the number and what persons should first join it is not much material, so they be such as are living stones . . . and also be of that innocency of life as may invite other saints more willingly to join to them." Finally, there was reaffirmed the belief in "reverent respect" and "brotherly love" with which the meetings and questionings had begun. Not only before and during, but now after the exposition of doctrine these duties were emphasized. Best "for the better

settling of a body newly gathered . . . to be free and frequent in com-
municating to one another the inward workings and dealings of the Lord
with their souls." This faith in the healing virtue of love and honesty was
the alpha and the omega of their efforts. They evolved doctrine in detail,
with biblical citations and even legalistic turns of speech, but before and
after all doctrine came the rules of the spirit which they hoped would
guide them to a true and an enduring church.

So it came about that there "agreed to gather [to themselves] . . .
about eight persons more [in addition to Allin and Ralph Wheelock]
whom we had best hopes of for soundness and grace and meet gifts for
such a work." Then, "after solemn invocations and humiliation of
ourselves before the lord . . . everyone [of the ten proceeded] to open
their conditions and declare the workings of God in their souls . . . the
whole company [to] approve or leave out as the Lord should give us to
judge of every one's conditions or fitness for the work." The search for
the "stones" mentioned in the doctrinal passages had begun. It was to be
a tedious search with several turnings and reverses. The goal was a
mutual testing of each of the ten men who seemed likely candidates for
"soundness of grace," each speaking all he knew of himself or of the
others with neither ambition nor bashfulness.

After "many meetings," six of the ten were found suitable to be
founders of a church, though the four others still had not shown sufficient proof of grace. Though they now felt themselves ready to find a
minister, establish a church and admit members, the chosen six were
delayed by the refusal of John Phillips to join them as minister. In the
meantime they approved a newcomer, John Hunting, as a founder. In an
interesting move, they also submitted themselves to "a meeting or conference of the whole town." Of the town they asked that "if they had any
offences or grievances in their spirits from any of us and knew any just
cause which might move us to leave out any, that now they would
faithfully and plainly deal with such a one." On the day appointed to
hear the town's objections there were none, but several men from out of
town came to complain of offences at the hands of Edward Alleyn. These
were heard, along with Alleyn's replies—which satisfied all concerned.

When it became evident that Phillips would not join them, those approved as founders had to undertake things themselves. These were the
six first approved (Allin, Wheelock, John Luson, John Frary, Eleazer
Lusher, and Robert Hinsdell) plus Edward Alleyn (now cleared of all accusations) and John Hunting (the newcomer). The record only hints at
the questionings, pleas, and changes of heart that lay behind these selections, but they were there and in plenty. It was now November 1638, the
better part of a year since the first public discussions had begun, months
after the ten men set out to test one another's credentials as visible saints
and pillars of the church.

> The Lord thus far clearing up our way before us we agreed upon the 8th day
> of the 9th month 1638 to make our public profession and enter into solemn
> covenant with the Lord and one another, giving notice to the magistrates and
> by letters unto the several churches of this our purpose that we might enjoy

not only the countenance and encouragement of the magistrates therein, but also the advice and counsel of the churches in so weighty a work, that nothing might be done therein against the rule of the gospel. . . .

The private scrutiny over, the public review of the doctrines and men put forward by Dedham was to begin.

On the chosen day Allin began with a profession of faith, a profession of the confidence of the founders in the working of the Lord's grace within themselves. The ministers and elders present were invited to criticize this profession "faithfully and plainly." None offering to do so, the proposed covenant was read to the assembly. Obedience to Christ's precepts, faith in his saving grace, and mutual love were pledged. The eight "pillars" signed the document; the church was instituted at that moment. Yet not even this ended the process. Though other members could now be heard and admitted, there were as yet no officers. Without a minister, a teacher or an elder there could be no preaching and no communion. So there began another year-long search and mutual examination followed by still another public ceremony and scrutiny before Allin was ordained as minister, John Hunting as elder, and the church was a mature body.

Two things about the whole process, both already much underlined in the previous pages, are striking. One is the preoccupation with mutual love which transcended the usual platitudes. The other is the insistence upon the most perfect honesty at every turn. Each man and each point of doctrine went before the town, the founders, the state, and other ministers before being finally accepted. Time was taken when time seemed the only fair test. The criticism of others was voluntarily, almost eagerly sought out so that the greater certainty might be achieved. If the drive for perfection before the Lord led to narrowness, it also led to a fair, painful search for the right way. The cliches of religion were few and were overwhelmed by the desire to live and worship according to God's word as feeble man could understand it. It is possible to find fault with their understanding, but difficult to accuse them of insincerity or injustice.

II

If there had been great disturbances after this harmonious beginning, it is by no means sure that the records would have reflected them. But since neither church nor town or colonial records suggest any troubles within the Dedham church, it would be fair to suppose that the local congregation was not unusually contentious. Perhaps the founders' stress on mutual obligations gave rise to a lasting policy of amicable adjustment; Johnson's *Wonder Working Providence* contains the observation that the Dedham religious community "continued in much love and unity from their first foundation."[4] This was written in the early 1650's, about fifteen years after that "first foundation." How long this continued is anyone's guess.

The characteristic which at first dominated the church in this town was not strife, doctrinal schism or heresy. It was exclusiveness which distinguished the Dedham Puritans from their co-religionists and marked their congregation as different perhaps as late as 1691.

Exclusiveness was a common trait in the Massachusetts churches from the earliest years until 1662. It was inherent in the doctrine of a church of visible saints. To become a member one had to truly feel and truly relate before the congregation the workings of divine grace within the soul. For men and women who had felt intensely enough about their beliefs to pack up and move into a distant wilderness, this experience might not have been difficult to achieve. The great number of emigrants were seekers after God with their whole hearts. But what of their children, brought to America or born there without having experienced the heresies and persecutions of Anglican England? Would they be so fervent and so ready to feel the work of God's grace on their sinful souls? And if they did not, what would become of their children in turn, for the children of nonmembers could not even be baptized! What would become of the Puritan church in the colonies as fewer became members and fewer still were baptized into it? As the first generation died off, the covenant with God would lack adherents and the church would dwindle to a small handful of saints.[5]

Dedham experienced precisely this decline, as did many other congregations. At the beginning, the difficult test of membership did not stop the majority of adult townspeople from joining the church.[6] By the end of 1639, 48 people had been admitted—among them 23 men and 25 women. Since hardly more than 35 families had come to town by this time,[7] most families had at least one church member and several had two. Four of the 48 were servants, two men and two women. Baptisms proceeded apace, exceeding births over the years 1639-1643, as new members were able to have their children baptized into the church for the first time. By 1648, 61 of 87 male taxpayers were members, or about 70 per cent. Counting other families in which wives had joined but not husbands, about 77 per cent of all families had members. Between 1644 and 1653, baptisms averaged 80 per cent of total births—very close to what one would expect if 77 per cent of all families were eligible to have their children baptized.[8]

It was in 1648 that John Allin's *Defence of the Answer made unto the Nine Questions or Positions sent from New England . . .*[9] was published. In defending the practices of the New England churches against criticism by English Puritans, Allin singled out the church of visible saints as the major innovation of New England theology. He went to some length to defend the strict policy on membership. At that time he found it according to the gospel law and foresaw no unfortunate consequences. His own experience in Dedham offered no cause for doubt.

Warning signs, however, soon appeared. After 1653, the average number of infants baptized in Dedham began to decline. From 1654 until 1661, only 40 per cent of the children born in Dedham were baptized. Over half of the new souls in the town were being excluded from this introduction to the church. Behind this lay a decrease in membership which also began after 1653. In the eight years before 1662, only eight persons were admitted to membership, none after 1657. The result of these lean years is that by 1661, only 56 per cent of the male taxpayers were members of the church, and if this continued, nonmembers would soon outnumber members. The church was well on the way to exclusiveness. Why fewer people took membership after 1653 is not explained, but one can guess. The great majority of the members of 1648 were mature men and women recently fled from England. Those who failed to join after 1648 were the young men and women then coming of age. Numbers of these should be found enrolling as members, but they are not. Not even all of the eight admitted after 1653 were sons and daughters of the founding families—two or three were recent arrivals in the town. Thus it happened that the children of these same young men and women were not being baptized and the church was dwindling to an ageing minority of townspeople.

The divines of the colony had a remedy for the decline which was affecting many congregations. The deliberations of the synod called in 1662 to consider whether the strict position on membership should not be modified resulted in what became known as the "Half-Way Covenant."[10] Retreating from the espousal of the most perfect possible visible church, they provided for "half-way" membership in the church. Under this dispensation a person might become a member entitled to all the ordinances except communion by merely showing that he understood, believed in, and would obey the word of God as revealed in the Bible. Such a profession avoided the requirement of a profound inner experience of grace. It made baptism available to the children of those who would make this minimal affirmation of belief.

Sensible as it seems, in the face of a dwindling body of saints and a church embracing the lives of fewer and fewer people, the solution of the synod was opposed by many.[11] Those who were firmly attached to the idea of a church of the elect considered the synod's decision a retreat from a sound doctrine well based in the Bible. Their protests reached the point where Allin was asked to write a defence of the new position, even as he had defended the old in 1648. Like most of his fellow ministers, Allin had become convinced by the events of 1648-1661 that the old position was no longer tenable. In his *Animadversions on the Antisynodalia Americana* he vigorously defended the half-way covenant, not only against the writer of the original *Antisynodalia*, but also against all of its critics.[12]

Alas for Allin, his own congregation refused to accept the synod's decision. The first signs of this refusal are contained in the lists of new memberships. From 1662 to 1671, the congregation approved of only twenty-seven new members. This was still far below the number of admissions during the 1640's and early 1650's. No members of any kind were admitted from 1668 until 1671, when the record ends. Moreover, none of those admitted was listed as coming under the new covenant. The percentage of men paying taxes who were also church members remained just above 50 per cent.[13] Judging from the petition of the men of Dedham "being yet nonfreemen" in 1664, over half of the adult males in town were not yet admitted to "the holy institutions of Jesus Christ."[14] The continued narrowing of the Dedham church after 1662 is best summarized in the statistics of baptisms. The increase in unbaptized children which had prompted the synod to act went unchecked in Dedham. In 1662-1668, when admissions revived a little, the number of baptisms rose from 40 per cent to almost 60 per cent of infants born, though it never reached its previous high of 80 per cent of the 1640's. After 1668, baptisms plunged as admissions ceased altogether and of forty-one children born by 1672, only ten had been baptized into the church.

Documents from sources in Boston confirm Allin's dilemma and the continued exclusiveness of the Dedham church. In 1671, shortly before his death, Allin joined other prominent ministers in an address to the General Court.[15] The men of God chastized the Court for giving countenance and even aid to the prevailing antiministerial sentiment. Between the lines one may read of past opposition to the new covenant of 1662 on the part of many representatives to the General Court. Allin and the others now asked that the Court apologize for its wavering and vote full support of the clergy and of their authority. This was voted, but fifteen of the deputies dissented and among them were the representatives of Dedham, Daniel and Joshua Fisher. Evidently, this town remained in the hard core of resistance ten years after the Synod of 1662.

The most remarkable single document in the history of the local church is in the possession of the Massachusetts Historical Society.[16] By what path it came there is beyond knowing, but the paper, the script, and the words used are authentic. This sheet of closely covered paper is a formal recantation of opposition to the 1662 covenant by the members of the Dedham congregation of 1672. It begins somewhat ambiguously:

> The brethren of the church of Dedham in full communion . . . do judge and condemn ourselves for those sins both personal, family and church whereby we have grieved and provoked our most gracious and merciful God in a way of just judgement once and again to remove the ministry from us which we had enjoyed . . . not only to suspend but now at last almost quite cut off our hopes of a return and resettlement thereof and to leave us to so much disorder, confusion, distraction and frustration in all our transactions thereabout.

Since Allin's death, the congregation had been unable to find and keep a new minister. Now having been without one for months, they were beginning to despair of obtaining a man to lead them. Some sin on their part, they concluded, must be the cause of their afflictions. But what sin? The following paragraphs reveal the essence of their confusion:

> We acknowledge the fault to be ours, *not that of our pastor, who brought us up properly and showed the way and the word clearly and long* . . . [and especially the] *church duty to the children of the covenant* born of us and growing up with us as members of the church by divine instruction and so the proper subjects of church discipline and of all the other church privileges accordingly they did approve themselves and grow up to maturity and a due capacity unto a regular and orderly participation in them . . .

> *We are now under conviction of our total neglect of the practice of this doctrine* in the discharge of the great church duty . . . [which was] a great grief to those our faithful ministers as it was an obstruction to them in so great a part

of the work of the ministry . . . [and] also that it may have been one of the provoking and procuring causes of our woeful bereavement and long unsettlement which by sad expressions and consequences we are convinced of.

In a word, they had been unable to find a minister because no minister wanted a congregation which still refused to practice the doctrine of 1662, which refused to admit half-way members and to include their children in the church. They were renegades, as the doctrine had since been accepted throughout the colony and just recently had been given the sanction of the General Court. If they wanted a minister they would have to retreat, which they did:

> We do therefore hereby solemnly and in the fear of God declare that we do own and acknowledge all such children of the covenant with us both infant and adult to be joint members of this particular visible church together with ourselves, and that by a divine right of membership from God's holy covenant which [he] hath graciously provided . . .

> Such of you as shall not find your hearts so disposed to join unto us [as members in full communion], we yet exhort practically to own effort and improve your church membership by joining and acting together with us as church members in a church way and so far as according to the rules of church order you may and ought, in the great business of obtaining and upholding a settled ministry with us . . .

> We apply and cry earnestly unto God for his spirit and grace whereby we may be all enabled to stand fast in one spirit with one mind striving together not only in faith but the order of the gospel that both may abide with us from generation to generation forever.

The intensity of religious feeling in Dedham had not slackened perceptibly in the thirty-five years since the church was founded. It took a decade and the threat of deprivation of a minister before the townsmen would compromise with their first doctrine of a church of saints. When they did abandon it, they recanted with fierce self-condemnation and adopted the new way in equally strong language.

Shortly afterward they obtained a minister and the issue was buried. But when the Reverend William Adams died in 1685, it arose again. From 1685 to 1692, the town was once more without a minister. The manuscript records reveal repeated offers to likely young men, and repeated refusals. At least one of three candidates referred to some troubles and "uncomfortableness" within the congregation.[17] For over five years the search went on while the town had to rely on visiting preachers. Then, late in 1691, the church was moved to state:

> The church of Christ in full communion being assembled in the name and fear of God to consult and consider of such things as must be of concernment for them to practice and remembering and considering the declaration of the elders and messengers of churches convened in a synod [of 1662] and the doctrine of our late reverend Pastor . . . concerning children's interest in the covenant of God with their parents, do now by their vote declare their judgement is that the declaration of the synod and the doctrine of their late reverend Pastor is according to the mind of Christ and do resolve through his help and grace to practice accordingly.[18]

This suggests a virtual repetition of the situation of 1672, and of the declaration which followed from it. If it means what it seems to say, Dedham was reluctant to give full force to the half-way covenant for thirty years after it was promulgated! This again explains their difficulties in obtaining a minister, and the reference to "uncomfortableness" by one of the candidates. As on the earlier occasion, a declaration of obedience cleared the air and a minister was found not long after.

Such enduring exclusiveness is formidable evidence of the intensity with which the men of Dedham treated religion. Fathers would have had to pass the adherence to the old principle of membership on to their sons, and the sons who did not become members to have foregone opposition to the narrowness of the church. Yet that is what must have happened, if this statement is genuine. Perhaps the passion for a pure church was not as easily weakened by time and circumstance as might be thought.

III

About the members of the congregation from 1636 to 1671, little more remains to be said. In the beginning virtually every family contained a member; most adult males were admitted to the church; women joined in equal numbers with men; several of the town's few servants were admitted. On the other hand, the selectmen of the town as of July 1640 included John Haward, who is nowhere in the records of the church listed as a member. Likewise, Samuel Morse was a selectman in February of 1640, and he is not listed among the men admitted to the congregation.[19] In short, no restriction of any type or magnitude is evident.

As the years passed and as the membership narrowed, changes in the nature of the church were inevitable. Some of the settlers who trickled in after 1650 never became members—including most of a group of five or six poor Scots who arrived after 1659.[20] Relatively few of the children born or baptized into the church in the 1630's and 1640's became members upon reaching maturity. From 1655 until 1671 only thirty-five persons joined the church (about two persons a year), while double this number of children must have reached maturity in that span of time if the records of births and baptisms are any indication. Because of this, it is doubtful whether a majority of the men in town were members in 1671.

Yet these quantitative changes need not have brought conflict or implied restriction. Probably the slow rate of admission reflected the general sentiment of the town on the issue of membership. No protests were ever recorded, whether in Dedham or in Boston, against the changing character of the local congregation. Children of rich as well as of poor families grew up outside the church. Selectmen might or might not have been church members depending solely upon the decision of the town meeting, not upon any policy of exclusion. Moreover, in 1663, no fewer than sixty-nine townsmen petitioned the General Court in complete support of the established government though they, as nonfreemen (and as nonmembers almost to a man), were denied full participation in it. These men, some of them prominent within the town, were neither ashamed of nor embittered by their status. They stated their hopes of a future experience of grace and their regret that this had not yet come to them—but they placed no blame and asked no redress.[21]

There is one way in which a "minority church" could be said to have "dominated the town" (to state a cynical view in its extreme form). The old settlers of the town unquestionably *did* constitute a majority of the members of the church through the 1630's, 1640's, 1650's and 1660's. It is probable that both numbers and age enabled them to direct the affairs of the congregation. It is equally clear that, as late as the 1670's, the great majority of the selectmen elected by the town were older men and were church members. The truth is that the spiritual and political leadership of the town came to rest largely in the hands of a small group of ageing men. But it must be remembered that this was an elected political leadership and a leadership whose church aroused no popular protest. To say that the potential for an "oligarchy of saints" existed is very far from saying that there is the least evidence that it did exist, or that, if it did exist, it was not favored and respected by the town at large. After 1680 there is no longer any question of political oligarchy. The old leaders had died and selectmen were recruited from a wider group of somewhat younger men.[22]

IV

It is disappointing not to have any battles or spicy "morals cases" to report of the Dedham congregation. Disappointing, too, is the absence of any evidence of a radical change in the content of the local religion. All of these may have existed, but for all the record shows, they did not. But there did exist and were recorded features of the regular business of running a church which give a better sense of the relation of the church to the town.

When the town covenant was written, church and state were as close together as they could be short of having identical leadership. In a very real sense it was the church that lay behind the foundation of the town. The covenant made "the knowledge and faith of the Lord Jesus" the town's purpose. When Allin arrived in 1637, he became the first citizen of the village. His name was at the head of the list of those present at meetings. Later, elder John Hunting's name followed immediately after Allin's and both headed these lists and tax lists for some time.[23] Two of the pillars of the church, Edward Alleyn and Eleazer Lusher, were also leaders of secular society. Allin himself was consulted on matters of town business and was placed on a committee charged with managing a land purchase.[24] The interpenetration extended to the point that it was ordered that "our reverend Pastor and our reverend Elder . . . should advise with the seven men in the division of lands."[25]

The town was always generous with its minister. Land was heaped upon Allin. In every division before 1656, he received the largest share. In July 1639, he was given a farm of 150 acres which was to be forever free of taxes.[26] His salary in the 1660's was 60-80 Pounds per annum[27] and probably the same from the beginning. This was a huge sum in a town where an estate of 300 Pounds meant comfort and 500 Pounds wealth. Allin was wealthy enough to buy twenty-four acres of land in 1639 and he eventually obtained 200 acres from the General Court in return for twenty-five Pounds he had loaned the colony in its infancy.[28] At his death he had a nine-room house, well over 300 acres of land, twenty-one common rights in Dedham and others in Wrentham and Deerfield, eight cattle, seven swine and no less than twenty- eight sheep—a very large flock. His total worth was over 1,000 Pounds, far above anything achieved by his fellow first settlers and a sum equaled by no more than five or six men of the town before 1700. No other local minister was relatively as wealthy as John Allin.[29] He commanded respect for his education and for his calling, but his wealth alone would have inspired awe. And the town wanted it that way. They gave him land and money in handsome amounts because they wanted their minister to be wealthy.

But the intimate association of church and state deteriorated quickly. After 1642 Allin was almost never mentioned in the course of town meetings. After 1646 elder Hunting was less often given the place of honor beneath his minister on the various lists. In 1656 for the first time another man surpassed Allin in rated estate, 309 Pounds to 261 Pounds. As early as 1651 his was only the second largest house. After 1662 Eleazer Lusher was an Assistant of the colony and outranked Allin on the tax lists. Secular prominence continued to be placed above religious leadership thereafter.[30]

The separation of the church and of the minister from town affairs was nearly complete after 1650. In rare instances the minister would be consulted in a poverty case and he was usually among the school trustees, but other than this he might as well not have existed as far as the town record is concerned.[31] After 1671 he was no longer taxed, so he did not even appear on the annual lists. He was to all intents and purposes a respected employee of the town, a well-regarded consultant on religious affairs who did just that and nothing more. The town together with the elder and deacons proportioned out the amount of his salary due from each man and arranged the seating in the meetinghouse.[32] The town participated equally with the congregation in hiring new ministers, saw to it that the church and ministry were properly endowed and raised or lowered the minister's salary as they saw fit.[33] What the minister advised in private and on Sundays may have influenced the town, but he was in no way a regular part of secular affairs. Nor was his general religious influence evident in the records. Except for mention of "the afflicting hand of God upon us" in 1669, and a 1647 reference to "things with which God blessed his people [i.e. metals],"[34] the language used is quite without religious overtones. Business was business and church was church—in the record the twain seldom met.

The 60-80 Pounds given Allin each year represented a sacrifice on the part of every citizen. From 1638 until after his death in 1671, the average per capita "tax" for Allin's support almost equaled the taxes collected for all other purposes! For most of the same quarter-century this sum was raised by voluntary contributions. Barely a word about money for the pastor crept into the town records.[35] But like the close association of church and state and like the position of Allin as the most honored citizen, this was too perfect to endure. In 1670 "divers of the inhabitants coming this day to the selectmen and moved that some care might be taken that our reverend Pastor might have his salary yearly paid."[36] From this day forward the collection of the minister's salary was a running problem of the town, one which exemplifies the weakness of the flesh in the face of the pecuniary demands of the spirit.

They tried to preserve the old way at first,

> In reference to the present way of contribution in each Lord's day, these two questions were put. One: whether a proportion shall be made wherein each man shall be assessed what he is to pay and a committee chosen to make that proportion accordingly; voted in the negative. Two: whether, in consideration of what have been spoken from scripture and argument referring to the duty and rule of contribution as to conscience as in the sight and fear of God, the case may not at present be left in the same way of contribution that at present and for some time past we have practiced, hoping that every man will endeavor to keep a good conscience therein, at least for trial. The vote passed in the affirmative to this second question by general consent.[37]

But, by the next year, 1672, a compromise had become necessary. Under it each man had to be assigned a definite proportion of the minister's salary, but could pay this from Sunday to Sunday as he saw fit and could add to his share voluntary contributions. Somewhere between a tax levied by the town and a free personal offering, this arrangement represented a major breach in the unity of the spiritual community. And in fact it was far closer to a tax than to the old voluntary way, for it made public each man's debt to the ministry, assigned him that debt on the basis of his estate, and made the town reponsible for seeing that the minister received all that was due him. It left precious little room for the operation of "good conscience" in "the sight and fear of God."[38]

Despite the measures taken in and after 1672, difficulties multiplied. Reverend Mr. Adams' salary was most often late and the arrears owed by some of the townsmen sometimes dated back over two years. In 1686 a committee was appointed to investigate these arrears, hear the excuses offered in place of money, and try to collect what was due.[39] Adams was little aided by such attempts and had to take his salary when and as it was given him.

Joseph Belcher made an attempt to restore free contribution. He suggested to the town that three-quarters of his pay for 1696 be left off of the proportion-list and up to the consciences of his parishioners.[40] Despite several persons being behind even in the one-quarter proportion assigned to them in that year, Belcher renewed the proposal for the year 1697 "from the confidence he had in the town's love to him."[41] Some in the town responded to his appeal. Regularly until 1712 (when his salary was raised to 100 Pounds officially), most of the heads of families added 40 Pounds a year from among themselves to the 60 Pounds proportioned to him by the town.[42] Full free contribution, however, was never restored. The normal 60-Pound salary was proportioned as it had been under Adams, and as under Adams arrears accumulated.[43] People fell behind in supporting the ministry even though the burden of the minister's salary on the individual taxpayer was falling as the total population increased faster than that salary was raised.

By 1704 the fiction of any form of voluntarism was over.[44] After this date it became the practice of the town to assign all arrears on the proportions to the constables for collection. In demanding payment, these officers had the same authority they had in collecting other taxes. If a man did not pay in his assigned share on such Sundays as he might choose throughout the year, he would soon find a constable at his door with a warrant. The euphemistic "proportion" became "assessment" and finally was frankly called what it had become, a "rate,"[45] an ordinary tax. With few exceptions thereafter, "the minister's rate [was] . . . delivered into the hands of the constables"[46] for collection on the spot along with the other taxes. The town abandoned its idealistic free contributions reluctantly over a period of forty years, but abandon them it did. Another aspect of the original spirit of Dedham had been transmuted into routine.

V

Even with synods and councils of ministers, a church based on congregational autonomy might develop odd variations on the accepted theology. "Reverend Smith" off in "Upper Pocumtuck, Mass." was subject to little review by these infrequently assembled bodies. Unless one of his flock saw fit to complain, he might gently and over a period of years lead them all into heresy. No doubt this happened here and there in the backwoods, but there was a strong informal check on this where Dedham was concerned. Allin or Adams or whoever it might be at the time was far from the only voice heard from the pulpit of the First Church. The exchange of visits and sermons among ministers in the Boston area was a much-observed custom. As often as once a month a strange minister might preach at Dedham and Dedham's minister might give a sermon in some other town. If a man's theology developed a bulge in the wrong direction, it would be noticed sooner or later as he preached about the country. Likewise a congregation was not limited to the teachings of one minister. Where towns were close together, exchanges like these served to keep doctrine on the center track and ensure that any shifts would be slow and general.[47]

VI

There had been a day when Quakers were whipped in Dedham,[48] but there came a day when Quakers lived undisturbed within the limits of the old town grant. Among the founders of Bellingham in 1719 were several Quakers and possibly a Baptist or two. They kept up the pretense of supporting the established church and were not bothered.[49] Five years later an Anglican church was begun in Dedham.[50] Without the slightest objection the congregation allowed those professing the Church of

England to pay their minister's rates to that body.[51] The following year a Baptist was allowed a comparable privilege.[52] Quakers, Anglicans, and Baptists—it had taken them a century, but there they were.

From the foundation and the stubborn adherence to the half-way covenant to tolerance of three varieties of heresy is a long way. How the congregation moved from one to another is obscure. Part of the story is surely told in the transformation of "free contribution" into "rate." Another part may be the disruption of the church by sectional disputes which racked the town after 1725. Much of it was the work of intellectual and political changes before which the village was a straw in the wind. For all these reasons, and for others we cannot trace, the church in Dedham slowly became less a way of life and more one institution among several. To say this is not to question the piety of the later generations or the quality of the ministry. It is merely to assert that the high faith of the first generation was unique, too intense to last forever and not immune to the shift in man's attitude toward God which had been progressing since before the Reformation.

> *The Dedham church led a relatively trouble-free existence during the seventeenth century. Other congregations were not as fortunate; many were wracked by disputes over faith or discipline. And Dedham's pattern of church formation and practice was not matched point for point by all New England churches. There were few formal mechanisms for regulating such uniformity in the early decades of settlement. Yet gradually a system of informal clerical conferences and formal synods and assemblies of church representatives was developed to control the centrifugal force of congregational autonomy. Robert Scholz has described the importance of such gatherings in his study of "Clerical Consociation in Massachusetts Bay: Reassessing The New England Way and its Origins" (William and Mary Quarterly, ser. 3, XXIX [1972]). In Connecticut the concern for uniformity eventually produced a system of official clerical associations as recommended by the Saybrook Assembly of 1708. But in Massachusetts the laity's fear of presbyterianism kept the Bay Colony committed to congregational autonomy only slightly curtailed by clerical organizations.*

NOTES

1. The theological writers of the Congregational Church have long been aware of this account, which was probably written immediately after the events it describes. The genesis of the process on which it focuses is the subject of Professor Edmund S. Morgan's book, *Visible Saints: The History of a Puritan Idea* (New York, 1963). In addition, Professor Clarence Ver Steeg, in *The Formative Years* (New York, 1964), has made use of it, but he partially misunderstands both the general nature of the process and some of its details in attempting to use Dedham as an example of an otherwise valid point.

2. This and all quotations in the following paragraphs of section I are from the *Early Records of the Town of Dedham* (I-IV, Dedham, Mass., 1886-1936) II [records of the church and cemetery, hereafter cited *C.R.*], 1-21.

3. In *Visible Saints*, Morgan shows that the process of foundation and selection took several years to reach its mature and unique New World form.

4. Johnson's *Wonder Working Providence*, edited by J. F. Jameson (New York, 1910), 180.

5. See Perry Miller, "The Half-Way Covenant," in the NEW ENGLAND QUARTERLY, VI (1933), for a thorough discussion of the problem. Morgan's *Visible Saints* places the new Covenant in a broad perspective.

6. These data and those following are from *C.R.*, 20-30.

7. *C.R.*, 1 (Allin's narrative), "about 30 families" in late 1638. *T.R.*, [*Early Records of Dedham*, III-IV], III lists admissions to the town in the same period.

8. *C.R.*, 20-39, and *T.R.*, III, 152-153, tax list for 1648.

9. Reverend John Allin, *Defence of the Answer made unto the Nine Questions or Positions sent from New England . . .* (London, 1648); Houghton Library of Harvard University has a copy. Congregational autonomy and a church of the elect were the chief points of innovation which Allin was defending.

10. See Perry Miller's article cited in note 5.

11. The background and some details of this opposition will be found in Miller's article, above, and in his *Orthodoxy in Massachusetts, 1630-1650* (Cambridge, 1933) and *The New England Mind: The Seventeenth Century* (New York, 1939).

12. Rev. John Allin, *Animadversions on the Antisynodalia Americana* (Cambridge, Mass., 1664); also in the Houghton Library.

13. *C.R.*, and *T.R.*, III, tax lists for 1670.

14. *T.R.*, IV, 276-278 (appendix).

15. Massachusetts Historical Society manuscript in *Photostats* file, June 1671; and *The Records of the Governor and Company of Massachusetts Bay* (I-V, Boston, 1853-   ), IV (part 2), 492.

16. Massachusetts Historical Society manuscripts, in the catalogue under "Dedham 1672." Emphasis has been added in the passages below.

17. This was the Reverend Jonathan Pierpont in a letter in the Dedham Historical Society manuscripts.

18. Same location as in note 17.

19. *T.R.*, III July 6 and Feb. 22, 1640; *C.R.*, index and 1-26.

20. *T.R.*, IV, tax lists for 1658-1662 and index; *C.R.*, index. Dates are given as in the records, the new year beginning on March 25, and are listed instead of pages where precision and a sense of chronology demand.

21. *T.R.*, IV, 276-278 (appendix). The word "nonage" is not used as "majority," since many of these men were over 21. It seems to mean "maturity," most probably "spiritual maturity" in the context of the petition.

22. Kenneth A. Lockridge, "Dedham 1636-1736: The Anatomy of a Puritan Utopia" (PhD dissertation, Princeton University, 1965) is the basis for this and similar generalizations on Dedham that will be made here and there in this article.

23. *T.R.*, III, pages covering the dates 1635-1640 will verify this. The covenant is in *T.R.*, III, 1.

24. *T.R.*, III, 67 (1638) and 41 (1640).

25. *T.R.*, III, 92 (1642).

26. *T.R.*, III, 56 (1639).

27. *T.R.*, IV, 98 (1664).

28. *T.R.*, III, 56, 58 (1639); *T.R.*, IV, 237-238 (appendix).

29. The inventories of Allin, and the Reverends Belcher and Dexter are on file in the Probate Office of the Suffolk County Courthouse.

30. *T.R.*, III, 142 (1656); *T.R.*, III, 183 (1651).

31. *T.R.*, III, March 5, 1665; *T.R.*, V, Feb. 24, 1695, for example.

32. *T.R.*, IV, Jan. 9, 1670, for one example, and *T.R.*, V, Jan. 5, 1690, for another. The chapter on "Policy" in Lockridge, "Dedham" takes up the matter of seating as part of a discussion of social policy.

33. *T.R.*, III, Aug. 28, 1638; V, Jan. 4, 1685; VI, Aug. 26, 1723 and Oct. 14, 1723; *T.R.*, IV, June 11, 1660, Jan. 4, 1668; V, Jan. 17, 1686; *T.R.*, V, Dec. 31, 1694; VI, March 2, 1729.

34. *T.R.*, III, Feb. 8, 1647; IV, Aug. 6, 1669.

35. Exceptions being *T.R.*, IV, Jan. 1, 1662 and Jan. 2, 1664.

36. *T.R.*, IV, March 11, 1670.

37. *T.R.*, IV, Jan. 1, 1670.

38. *T.R.*, IV, July 12, 1672. Any of the many "ministers proportions" in *T.R.*, IV and after will verify this. The latter point is demonstrated by *T.R.*, V, Dec. 31, 1674.

39. *T.R.*, V, Jan. 3, Jan. 17, 1686.

40. *T.R.*, V, March 2, 1695.

41. *T.R.*, V, March 1, 1696.

42. *T.R.*, V, Aug. 17, 1705.

43. *T.R.*, V, March 7, 1697; *T. R.*, V, Nov. 29, 1703; VI, Feb. 16, 1710 are only examples.

44. *T.R.*, V, Nov. 20, 1704.

45. *T.R.*, VI, Nov. 2, 1708; *T.R.*, VI, March 7, 1714.

46. *T.R.*, VI, May 18, 1727.

47. This is based upon manuscript records containing information on the First Church in the possession of the Dedham Historical Society.

48. *Dedham Historical Register*, IV, 32 ff., "Quaker Persecutions in Dedham" by F. L. Gay, which mentions occasions from 1658 to 1663.

49. Bellingham had been an unincorporated and distant part of the original Dedham grant, lying on the Rhode Island border; G. Partridge, *History of Bellingham* (Boston, 1919).

50. *New England Historic-Genealogical Register* (Boston 1880–   ), XIV, 204 (1894).

51. As above, note 50, and manuscripts in the Dedham Historical Society.

52. *T.R.*, VI, April 8, 1735.

PART THREE |

IN SEARCH OF
SOCIAL ORDER

Since the beginnings of the American nation some New Englanders have claimed that their region was the cradle of American democracy. The credence given such claims by scholars has fluctuated widely. Early historians emphasized Puritan society's democratic institutions, particularly the town meeting. But historians in the late nineteenth century, some of whom were descendants of New England's founders, challenged the filio-pietistic interpretations on which they had been raised. Charles Francis Adams, in *Three Episodes of Massachusetts History* (Boston, 1892), and Brooks Adams, in *The Emancipation of Massachusetts* (Boston, 1919), advanced a new model of colonial Puritan society, which depicted the early Puritan leaders as a dictatorial band of theocrats who suppressed a citizenry striving to expand its rights.

Vernon Parrington's *Main Currents in American Thought* (New York, 1927) made the clash of theocrats versus democrats in early New England an essential part of the Progressives' interpretation of American history. But Parrington's assessment was soon undermined by the labors of three Harvard scholars. Samuel Eliot Morison's *Builders of the Bay Colony* (Boston, 1930), Kenneth Murdock's *Increase Mather* (Cambridge, Mass., 1925), and the works of Perry Miller rehabilitated the reputation of the "theocrats," humanized their image, and discredited the charge that they were unrepresentative of their society.

Later scholarship has not substantially challenged the broad outlines of the Harvard school's interpretation. But heated debates have developed over the significance of dissent, the extent and purpose of the franchise, and the roots of colonial institutions. Borrowing the methodology of the social sciences, historians have sharpened the focus of their investigations and brought us a better understanding of New England society.

6 | THE PURITANS' GREATEST ACHIEVEMENT: A STUDY OF SOCIAL COHESION IN SEVENTEENTH-CENTURY MASSACHUSETTS

TIMOTHY H. BREEN and STEPHEN FOSTER

In recent years historians have taken a fresh look at the Puritans' aspirations and achievements. Among others, Darrett Rutman has offered important revisions of long-held assumptions. In Winthrop's Boston *(Chapel Hill, 1965),* American Puritanism: Faith and Practice *(Philadelphia, 1970), and in a variety of articles, he has argued that agreement between colonial leaders and their followers on goals was at best tenuous and short lived. In Winthrop's* Boston *Rutman uses the ideals expressed by John Winthrop in his lay sermon "A Model of Christian Charity" as the standard against which he measures the rapid decline of Boston society. The Hutchinsonian controversy and growing economic diversification are offered as evidence of the breakdown in social harmony.*

Other social historians have challenged Rutman's reintroduction of the theme of conflict. The studies of community life by Philip Greven (Four Generations: Population, Land, and Family in Colonial Andover, Massachusetts *[Ithaca, N.Y., 1970]), Sumner Chilton Powell* (Puritan Village *[Middletown, Conn., 1963]), John Demos* (A Little Commonwealth *[New York, 1970]), and others raise the issue of how representative Boston's pluralism was. Other historians look for comparative measurements and see the Puritan colonies as relatively stable and peaceful. The following article examines the roots of that stability.*

Harmony is a condition societies always seem to lose in the transition from a peaceful past to a chaotic present. When peace is considered normal and natural, social history becomes the search for the causes of conflict rather than the causes of cohesion; and the achievement of a genuinely cohesive society is ignored in an exclusive concentration on whatever flaws in the surface calm have subsequently widened into contemporary chasms. Thus, historians of seventeenth-century Massachusetts have ignored the Bay Colony's most startling accomplishment, fifty years of relative social peace.[1]

No one alive in Europe or America between 1600 and 1700 could ever have made this particular mistake. Peace and order, stability and love, for the seventeenth century these were the attributes of another and happier time. On the continent nations experienced paroxysms of revolt and internal strife so severe and so widespread that contemporaries thought the world itself was coming apart. In 1656 James Harrington described the contagion of violence: "What is become of the Princes of Germany? Blown up. Where are the Estates or the power of the people in France? Blown up. Where is that of the people of Aragon and the rest of the Spanish kingdoms? Blown up. Where is that of the Austrian princes in Switz? Blown up. . . ."[2] England in the same period endured a major civil war, several smaller rebellions, and a "glorious revolution" along with a regular incidence of more localized upheavals growing out of food shortages and the complications of enclosure.[3]

Nor did the New World tame the Old Man. Virginians sent their royal governor packing in 1636, fought their own civil war in 1676, and disrupted the normal flow of trade with monotonous but violent regularity at every downward fluctuation in the price of tobacco.[4] Just to the north in Maryland, Protestant and Catholic factions contended with each other in a series of rebellions. Political chaos seems the rule in the seventeenth century until one comes to the Puritan colonies, especially to Massachusetts Bay under the old charter. Between 1630 and 1684 the Bay Colony avoided significant social and political disorder: no riots, no mobs, no disruptions of the judicial process by gangs of aggrieved plaintiffs. From the Ukraine to the Chesapeake few other polities in the Western world could claim as much, and it is no surprise that in 1643 *New Englands First Fruits* thanked the Lord specifically for bringing peace to Massachusetts "when almost all the world is on a fire."[5]

Not that Massachusetts was quite the happy, bishopless Eden the Puritan clergy represented to their English admirers. The records of the colony's General Court, as well as those of the various county courts, are filled with grisly accounts of murders, rapes, and assaults. There is no reliable way to compare rates of crime in seventeenth-century Massachusetts, Virginia, and England, but a rough scanning of available sources indicates that the New Englanders ran afoul of the law as frequently as did any of their contemporaries.[6] Moreover, they found it impossible to live in peace with the Indians, and on at least two occasions they declared all-out war on their Indian neighbors.[7]

What was exceptional about the Bay Colony was the absence of internal, organized violence. The scholarship dealing with this period has stressed the colony's divisiveness, contention, and faction—all things which seemingly would have sparked the kinds of extreme disorder found in the rest of the Western world.[8] The Antinomian crisis, for example, involved a substantial group of Bostonians, including several of the colony's more experienced military leaders. Yet despite the fierceness of the controversy surrounding Anne Hutchinson's religious convictions and the expulsion of her followers, there was never a real threat of organized violence against the state.[9] Throughout the century, other equally troublesome problems divided the Puritans. Sometimes townsmen disagreed so passionately about the proper way to distribute common land that they formed new villages rather than accept the majority will. Congregations split over everything from governance to building the meeting house, while colonists of all sorts argued about the character of magisterial authority.[10] Amazingly none of these disagreements generated serious disorder.

The peaceful resolution of these crises is harder to explain than the events themselves. Schism, for example, was hardly a novelty in English Protestantism, but the outcome of the Antinomian crisis and later disputes stands in marked contrast to the usual method of settling political and religious differences at the time. The harmonious working out of internal problems can hardly be explained on the basis of any innate irenic temper in the New Englanders themselves. The subsequent English careers of a whole variety of former Bay Colonists from Hugh Peter to Thomas Venner provide ample proof, if any is needed, that American Puritans were perfectly capable of picking up more than just the sword of faith in defense of any particular opinion passionately held.[11] With swarms of such opinionists and militia laws that required them and everyone else to own a gun, prudent English contemporaries had every reason to expect that Boston would become another Muenster.[12]

Yet it did not. Even at its worst moments Massachusetts Bay never lost its extraordinary stability. Under exceptional pressure, to be sure, the society could falter; anxiety might occasionally widen into hysteria and hysteria narrow into atrocity. Christian Indians, for example, were massacred in 1676 during King Philip's War, and their leading lay and clerical protectors were roundly abused by a war-weary populace.[13] It is not remarkable that such incidents should occur now and again. Rationality dissolves easily under the strain of heavy military casualties. Rather, historians should wonder at Massachusetts' resilience in overcoming such calamities. It would take no more than a glance at other contemporary crises, such as Bacon's Rebellion, to see that English society elsewhere did not recover so well or so quickly from such unfortunate episodes as did the Bay Colony.[14]

It is not the purpose of this essay to praise Massachusetts but only to point to a central problem in its early history. Why was conflict so restrained in the Bay Colony when serious political, economic, and religious issues were at stake and when all of Europe's wisdom combined with all of Europe's experience would have indicated that such issues must eventually lead to some sort of explosion?

Explosions or the threat of explosions hold an obvious fascination for contemporary social science. Over the last two decades political scientists and sociologists in particular have attempted to explain the incidence of internal violence, especially revolution, but rarely have they dealt directly with the causes of social cohesion.[15] In large part, therefore, the authors of this study have been forced to proceed negatively, to assume that the achievement of social cohesion lies in the absence of divisive agents. This is not quite the tautology it seems, for calm in itself is not sufficient proof of social unity. Any state willing and able to suppress dissent systematically can attain a peace of sorts and with it the appearance of social cohesion. Seventeenth-century Massachusetts was not such a state; for although Puritan rulers did not flinch at employing coercion when necessary, they could never have maintained social harmony without popular cooperation. The Massachusetts wilderness lacked the resources to establish a police state; its remarkable internal stability must be explained in terms other than simple oppression.

Only one possible source of stability has received the attention it merits: the famous nucleated towns which served as effective instruments of social control and military power. The most recent research into New England local history adds that the structure of the village families provided a second source of strength. Stable and patriarchal, at least in the earliest decades, the New England family guaranteed peace and good order.[16] In Europe the village or the family, singly or together, were the last refuges in periods of civil and religious strife, the permanent institution when all other things, even churches and monarchies might pass away. But it was precisely the failure of the larger society that made village and family so important; when the society did not fail the significance of the two institutions diminished.[17] Therefore, this essay will concentrate instead on the larger context. The existence of a widely accepted ideology strong enough to resist outside challenge, responsive political institutions, and general prosperity go a long way toward explaining the Bay Colony's peculiar social cohesion.

In the case of Massachusetts the ideology was Puritanism. To cite Puritanism as a possible cause or source of social tranquility would have shocked Charles I. The king and his allies viewed the "precisionists" as dangerous troublemakers determined to alter the traditional forms of church and state whatever the costs. But Charles and his bishops were thousands of miles away from Massachusetts, and with the Stuarts effectively removed from daily consideration, American Puritans lost the militancy that their coreligionists continued to show in England.[18] If the crown had been able to assert its authority over the Congregational preachers in New England, the history of the Bay Colony might well have been more violent.

Left to themselves, however, the Massachusetts colonists found Congregationalism a source of stability. Flexible enough to accommodate moderate differences of opinion, the orthodox faith still served as a useful test for detecting and expelling extremists, thereby precluding any prolonged clash over religious fundamentals. Irreconcilables quickly discovered the charms of Rhode Island and left the Bay Colony in relative peace. Nathaniel Ward, the colony's most exuberant propagandist, explained this phenomenon in his *Simple Cobler of Aggawam*: "True Religion is *Ignis probationis* [a testing fire] which doth *congregare homogenea & segregare heterogenia* [congregate homogeneity and segregate heterogeneity]."[19]

Ward was correct to emphasize the homogenizing effect of "true religion," any true religion, providing it could be widely and exclusively inculcated as in Massachusetts. The Bay Colony fortunately possessed an offical priestly caste supported at public expense and periodically replenished by the graduates of Harvard College. Unhampered by anything but the most futile and sporadic opposition, the authorized interpreters of the exclusive faith provided the citizens of the Bay Colony with meaning for their present, a mission for their future, and, what was more, and perhaps most of all, a synthetic but compelling past. The Apostles, the Lollards, Martin Luther, John Calvin, the Huguenots, and the Marian martyrs, these were all putative ancestors whose deeds collectively constituted a unifying tradition heavy with rights and responsibilities for those who partook of it.[20]

Later generations of colonists would add the founding generation to the roll of folk heroes. This New England ancestor worship really amounted to a potent variant on the corporate constitutionalism prevalent in most workable social units in Western Europe, a sense of a community which was founded on "history, law and achievement, on the sharing of certain common experiences and certain common patterns of life and behaviour," and "whose rights and liberties were embodied in written constitutions and charters, and kept alive in corporate memory."[21] Small wonder then Samuel Sewall's lament when the charter of 1629, the Bay Colony's most visible symbol of its communal existence, was suddenly struck down in 1684: "the foundations being destroyed what can the Righteous do."[22]

Puritanism gave to Massachusetts the same kind of provincial identity that was supplied by local tradition in the counties of seventeenth-century England. Indeed, in its physical situation no less than in its mental set the Bay Colony would have made a typical county community. The colony was small in extent, its population was about the right size and relatively compact in distribution, it possessed a coherent intellectual and gentry class, and it was ready to offer fierce resistance to central power emanating from London. If Massachusetts invoked the memory of the Marian martyrs and their own grandfathers alternately, so Kentish antiquarians attempted to rally their countrymen in the name of the kingdom of the Jutes and of their Jutish forebears who had preserved the ancient liberty of the Weald from the onslaught of the Conqueror in 1066. There were divisions in Kentish society even as there were in Massachusetts, and in both divisiveness would temporarily facilitate the intervention of the hated central power. But this power, be it a major general or royal governor, had to be maintained by the repeated use of force until the outraged community reunited behind its common tradition and its suspended traditional liberties. Seventeenth-century military and fiscal efficiency being what it was, force in the end would give way, and there would be a local restoration, in 1660 in Kent, in 1689 in Massachusetts.[23]

By contributing a common ideology to the Bay Colony, Puritanism did much to create in America the kind of community capable of maintaining order within its borders. If anything, the artificiality of Massachusetts "countyness" assisted its function. Conflicting loyalties to patrons, family, or guilds, which could tear apart even the most traditional European community,[24] were all comparatively weak or absent in New England. In this sense the social utility of Puritanism lay in its position as the monopoly faith rather than in its particular tenets. Hinduism might have served equally well if Harvard could have turned out genuine Brahmins trained in the learned exposition of the *Bhagavad-gita* and the printing press, pulpit, and schools been adapted to the inculcation of the Word in Sanskirt. But the specific preachings of the Puritan Word also had a contribution to make.

From the very first the leaders of New England spoke of love as the foundation of their society. While still aboard the *Arbella*, John Winthrop set the tone for life in the Bay Colony, urging the settlers to be "knitt together in this worke as one man" and warning that their failure to do so would make them "a story and a by-word through the world."[25] Winthrop and the other Puritans who moved to Massachusetts assumed that the Lord had made a covenant with them as He had once done for the people of England. This initial "national Covenant" was followed by a proliferation of other covenants on every level of life in New England. The Massachusetts Puritans organized churches, towns, indeed, the entire commonwealth upon the contractual model.[26] The essential ingredient in this contract was free will: the individual voluntarily promised to obey civil and scriptural law, for the seventeenth-century Puritans believed that meaningful obedience could only grow out of voluntary consent, never out of coercion. With this principle in mind, Thomas Hooker insisted that the man who desired to enter a social covenant had to "*willingly* binde and ingage himself to each member of that society . . . or else a member actually he is not."[27] The strong sense of communal responsibility that developed out of this voluntary commitment influenced the character of conflict within the Bay Colony. It was incumbent upon all men to work out their disputes as peacefully as possible, thinking always of their greater obligation to the commonwealth as a whole and ultimately to God himself. Thus, when the future townsmen of Dedham drew up their covenant, they pledged to practice "everlasting love," and should that bond ever be strained by local differences "then, such party or parties shall presently refer all such differences unto some one, two or three others of our said society to be fully accorded and determined without any further delay."[28]

The logic of the covenant determined that the towns and churches of New England would be homogeneous units. Puritan villagers excluded anyone from their midst whom they believed endangered their way of life, and unwanted strangers were frequently "warned out" when they failed to meet the community's standards.[29] In Winthrop's time the concern for social purity was so great that colonial authorities sometimes asked newcomers to present evidence of good character before allowing them to settle.[30] Such conscious self-selection strengthened social cohesion within Massachusetts by forcing potential troublemakers to find homes in other parts of America. Historians have often criticized the leaders of the Bay Colony for their intolerance of other men's opinions, but when one considers Catholics fighting Protestants in colonial Maryland or the Dutch quarreling with the English in New York, one begins to understand why the Puritan fathers acted as they did.

Within their exclusive, covenanted communities the Puritans allowed relatively broad participation in civil and ecclesiastical affairs, a practice which meant that government seldom remained long at odds with its constituents. the colony's numerous freemen elected all the civil leaders from governor to town selectmen.The many church members within the various villages chose ministers, and the men who served in the militia elected, at least until 1668, their own officers.[31] Sometimes, of course, groups were not happy about the selections that their neighbors made, but the losers rarely claimed that they had been denied a voice. Moreover, civil elections were held frequently, providing dissatisfied factions with ample opportunity to alter the character of government. The freemen of Massachusetts studied the behavior of their political representatives with care, especially in times of crisis, and the voters often wrote instructions telling their deputies in Boston how to handle specific legislation before the General Court.[32] Certainly no ruler could take continuance in office for granted. Even the powerful Winthrop was dropped from the governorship when he resisted the formation of the House of Deputies and thereby irritated a substantial part of the colony's freemen. And when Deputy Governor Roger Ludlow angered the citizens in 1635, they left him out of the magistracy altogether.[33]

The case of Sir Henry Vane dramatically revealed the importance of popular participation in thwarting political violence. The colonists gave the young Vane an enthusiastic welcome when he arrived in the New World in 1635. Everyone was well aware that he possessed impressive contacts in England which hopefully could be used to protect Massachusetts from possible Stuart interference. But to the Puritans, Vane's "right religion" was probably as important a consideration as his political connections. The freemen demonstrated their approval of Vane by electing him governor in 1636.[34]

It was not long, however, before Puritans began to reconsider the wisdom of their choice. The new governor allied himself with Hutchinson and her Antinomian followers, and according to Winthrop, Vane "went so far beyond the rest, as to maintain a personal union with the Holy Ghost."[35] After this shocking declaration, Vane's days as governor were numbered. Indeed, as the election of 1637 approached, it became clear that the voters, especially those living outside the Antinomian center of Boston, wanted a new chief magistrate. Some of the men from Newbury reportedly walked as far as forty miles "on purpose to be made free [freemen], and help to strengthen Govr. Winthrop's Party."[36] Although Vane worked to retain office, the orthodox Congregationalists swept the election; and within a year the defeated Vane quietly returned to England where he would achieve far greater notoriety as a leader of the Independents in the civil war.

The colonists were fortunate to have effected such a major transition in political leadership so peacefully. Perhaps if Vane had been an appointed royal governor not subject to the freemen's control or if only a very small number of persons had been permitted to vote, the proceedings of 1637 might have taken a more violent turn. To appreciate the unique conditions in Massachusetts, one only has to look at Virginia in this period. When the royal governor, John Harvey, became obnoxious to a number of local grandees, they arrested the man "on suspicion of treason to his majesty." The armed rebels forced Harvey to listen to their grievances, and as he was leaving for England one Virginia councillor warned that if he ever returned he would be "pistoled or shot." The leading Chesapeake planters regarded Harvey as an outsider, someone working counter to their interests and, therefore, someone to be resisted.[37] Whatever the faults of Winthrop, Thomas Dudley, and the other old charter governors of Massachusetts, no one could accuse them of being "outsiders."

The judicial system of the Bay Colony also contributed to the maintenance of social tranquility. As soon as the Puritans arrived in America, their leaders established clear procedure for handling legal disputes. In the early years of the colony's history, the Court of Assistants, composed of elected magistrates, heard all civil and criminal cases; but as the colony expanded both numerically and geographically new courts were created to meet the growing case load. Distant places such as Springfield and Maine never had to complain that they had been denied justice or that they had to travel great distances to receive redress for some wrong.[38] When the leaders of South Carolina, more than a century later, failed to provide the people on the western frontier with the basic institutions of justice, the Regulators forcefully reminded the Charleston gentry of the oversight and, thus, precipitated the type of political violence from which seventeenth-century New England had been spared.[39]

During the old charter period in Massachusetts an individual could appeal a decision of the county courts before the Court of Assistants, and if the need arose before the General Court. A few disgruntled persons argued from time to time that Massachusetts authorities should allow appeals from the General Court to the English Privy Council, but by stressing such exceptional cases historians have tended to overlook the fact that most settlers were pleased with the quality of the colony's justice.[40] The Puritans' confidence in the equity of their own courts is best revealed by their willingness to bring delicate cases, especially those involving rival land claims, before local justices. In Dedham the townsmen relied on a system of voluntary mediation, which in many disputes served as a complement to the colony's regular courts. The local mediators or arbitrators simply applied the golden rule and urged the contending parties to "live together in a way of neighborly love and do each other as they would have the other do themselves."[41] At no time before 1684 did groups of people try to settle their differences through violence or attempt to coerce judges through the force of arms. As long as the commonwealth provided an equitable means for hearing grievances, the citizens had little reason for disrupting the colony's internal harmony. By contrast the corruption and complexity of the law courts in England and Virginia gave the citizens of their polities little reason to place their faith in the established institutions of justice.[42]

A third factor that served to discourage social and political disorder was the region's general prosperity. The growth of commerce brought a steady source of income to the colony's inland agricultural communities, and the population of Massachusetts expanded rapidly during the seventeenth century, far more rapidly, in fact, than did the populations of most contemporary Western European nations.[43] The chief reason for this growth was not a greater fertility rate or an earlier average marriage age than that of Europe, but the absence of major disasters—lengthy international wars, severe epidemics, or continued famines. Men and women in the Bay Colony had less reason to fear hunger or epidemic than their European contemporaries.[44] In addition to the general healthiness of early New England there was an abundance of land, and although Puritan fathers sometimes slowed their sons' achievement of full economic independence the boys knew that someday they would possess a farm and home of their own. Younger sons usually enjoyed the same economic opportunities as their oldest brother did, and in any case, they never formed a floating, dispossessed group within society.[45] Examination of the Boston tax list of 1687 reveals that class divisions were not very distinct, certainly not as distinct as they were to become a century later, and a man on the lowest level of society could reasonably expect with perseverance to improve his lot in the community. It was no rarity for an indentured servant or person of obscure parentage to attain commercial or economic leadership.[46] The widespread prosperity and pervasive sense of well-being found in old charter Massachusetts removed many of the social grievances that might have generated mass discontent and in all probability open violence.[47]

During the mid-1680s the peaceful era in Massachusetts history ended, and the colony began to experience forms of social disruption common to Europe and the southern provinces. To understand this development, one must review the major events of the period, especially changes in the colony's constitution. The English government had long been annoyed by the unwillingness of the American Puritans to enforce the Navigation Acts, and in 1684 the Lords of Trade, goaded by the crown's officious agent Edward Randolph, convinced the Court of Chancery to annul the original Massachusetts charter. The Lords of Trade reorganized the government of all the New England colonies under a new administrative system called the Dominion of New England. A single royal governor, acting with the members of an appointed council, held complete executive and legislative authority over the people who lived within this jurisdiction, a vast territory stretching from New Hampshire to New Jersey. The imperial reformers made no provision for the continuance of elective or representative assemblies, and although some men warned the Dominion leaders that such an arbitrary government was not "safe for you or us" there seemed little chance of restoring the broad political participation that had characterized the old charter government. What was more, the new appointed rulers were instructed to gurarantee freedom of worship, to enforce the Navigation Acts, and to issue land grants only in the king's name. It was not long before James' governor, Edmund Andros, restricted the number of traditional town meetings to only one a year, and that only for the routine election of local officials.[48] When New Englanders turned to the courts for relief, they discovered that justice was now frequently sacrificed either to personal greed or to political expediency: in the words of Cotton Mather, "*Foxes* were made the Administrators of Justice to the *Poultrey*."[49]

The Dominion of New England disrupted Massachusetts society more deeply than historians have realized. Certainly, the tone of political and social action contrasted markedly to what it had been before the arrival of Andros. The government of appointed outsiders ultimately could be changed only through the use of organized force. When local militia units marched on Boston on the morning of April 18, 1689, there was no doubt about the nature of their business. Within a matter of hours groups of armed colonists had arrested Andros and most of his chief advisers. While the change of government occurred without any bloodshed, the New Englanders were clearly prepared to use force had there been resistance from the troops that Andros brought with him.[50] After the Dominion officials had been jailed, various colonial pamphleteers attempted to justify the overthrow of the Andros regime, claiming that the governor had "Invaded *Liberty* and *Property*" and therefore forfeited his office. Another writer, uneasy about the use of force, declared "that we have not so much *resisted the Ordinance of God*, as we have resisted an intollerable violation of His *Ordinance*."[51] These justifications may have reassured the colonists of the virtue of their cause, but the fact remained that they had employed arms to settle their political grievances, an unprecedented action in Massachusetts.

After the overthrow of the Dominion, the colonists recalled the old charter government headed by Simon Bradstreet, one of the original founders of New England. Everyone, especially Bradstreet, expected life to return to normal. But they soon discovered that the colony's former harmony had been seriously compromised. Political observers began writing of mobs—a new word in the New England vocabulary. One man, recounting the events of the Glorious Revolution, reported, "What moved my countrymen so rashly and violently I cannot yet learn, but think it very fortunate that so many prudent and able men interposed to prevent worse results from a giddy and enraged *mob*."[52] New Englanders were less willing to submit to mediation, less willing to take their grievances through proper channels. Increasingly, writers noted that disruption, disobedience, and violence had spread throughout Massachusetts. One of the more articulate examples of this new literature was an anonymous pamphlet entitled *Reflections upon the Affairs of New England*. The author explained that "as soon as the hurry of revolution was over," the colonists decided that they needed some form of civil authority and for that purpose "chose the men that had thrown themselves at the head of the action." But when the leaders "could not in all things run with the mad head strong multitude they began to be kicked at and when they endeavored a regulation of affairs that the law might have its course it was accounted intollerable."[53]

These writers may well have been guilty of hyperbole, but whatever their purpose they had witnessed sights new to Massachusetts. When Bradstreet's government made an unpopular decision, a mob of 150 men gathered menacingly in front of his house calling him an "Old Rogue." Some uneasy councillors reported "the tumult in the town is so great and sudden that no reason will be heard or regarded." This political mob was soon replaced by disgruntled soldiers demanding immediate enfranchisement and later by bitter veterans from the Canadian campaign threatening mutiny unless they received long overdue wages.[54] The character of New England political life appeared to have been somehow transformed. The respected Congregational minister, Samuel Willard, reflected the views of many men when he referred to the period of Bradstreet's rule as "the short *Anarchy.*"[55] Even popular broadsides reminded the colony's rulers that "the *Sword* now rules" and that the army which sent Andros packing could also remove his successors, since "in violent Changes the people can as well authorize *Civil* as Military Government."[56]

Conditions within Massachusetts did not improve with the arrival of a new charter in 1692. The colony's appointed governor, Sir William Phips, reflected in his own personality the disruptive changes that had occurred within the commonwealth since 1684. Phips was a violent man who apparently believed that the best way to settle arguments was with his fists or cane. On one occasion a large crowd on the Boston dock was treated to the spectacle of their chief magistrate wrestling an English naval officer who had dared to question the governor's authority. "I find great offence taken at your governor Phips, for beating the captain of the man of war there," a prominent Englishman explained to Increase Mather. The writer then added with unintended irony that it "seems to reflect on the whole plantation, for chusing a governor of no better principles or practices than to forget himself so far as to cane or strike a commission officer."[57] Phips' violent streak embarrassed the colonists, and anyone who reviews the character of the old charter magistrates will immediately discover that Puritan voters would never have selected Phips as governor.

The colonists were even more embarrassed in 1692 when a court at Salem executed twenty persons as witches. Historians have analyzed every scrap of evidence, borrowing tools from psychology, sociology, and anthropology,[58] and, while this research has yielded some provocative insights, it has failed to relate the witch trials to the previous fifty years of Massachusetts history. New Englanders had punished witches throughout the seventeenth century, and the intellectual and judicial issues involved in such cases were well established by 1692. During the old charter period executions had been infrequent, some towns choosing to live in peaceful coexistence with "known" witches.[59] The central issue at Salem was not witchcraft, but violence, fanaticism, and fear. Never before in the colony had the concern about evil spirits reached epidemic proportions. Contemporaries were intensely aware that the events at Salem were without precedent, and for the next fifteen years various major participants in the trial came forward to apologize for their actions.[60]

In little more than a decade Massachusetts had changed from a peaceful to a relatively turbulent society. During these years the conditions which had formerly minimized grievances and thus reduced the possibility of social disruption were systematically undermined. The overthrow of Andros, the mob at Bradstreet's home, the executions at Salem, all of these events revealed the loss of the elements that had once unified the commonwealth: a common ideology, a widespread trust in the colony's rulers, and a high level of prosperity.

The Puritan vision of an exclusive, covenanted society was the most obvious casualty of the revolutionary period. The revocation of the old charter in 1684 and the enforced religious toleration after that date all but destroyed any lingering sense among the colonists that they formed a special, divinely chosen community. As several historians have noted, commitment to the creation of "a city on a hill" never, not even in Winthrop's time, eliminated the petty bickering found in every society. The belief in a "national covenant" did, however, help to establish limits of acceptable behavior. The early Puritans may not have loved their neighbors, but they felt obliged to try to settle their differences as amicably as possible. There was clearly no place in old charter Massachusetts for political violence, mob action, and judicial terror. After the Glorious Revolution self-restraint became more a matter of individual concern than of communal responsibility. Indeed, as time passed men increasingly defined the common good in narrow, personal terms. Boston merchants, for example, won special commercial privileges that sometimes sacrificed the welfare of the many to the profits of the few, and Joseph Dudley, one of the early royal governors in Massachusetts, sold supplies to French and Indian forces who were killing New Englanders along the frontier.[61] During the 1690s one writer became so concerned about the apparent disintegration of social responsibility that he warned the colonists, in words that no Congregational Jeremiah would have used, that Massachusetts might soon be "Reduced to *Hobs* his state of *Nature,* which (says he) is a *state of War,* and then the *strongest* must *take* all."[62]

The very structure of civil government after 1684 contributed to the breakdown of social cohesion. As we have seen, the Dominion of New England allowed the freemen almost no voice in the selection of their rulers and, thus, destroyed the voluntarism that had been the foundation of political trust and obedience within the commonwealth. The new charter government established in 1692 provided for a popularly elected lower house, but the voters no longer had any direct control over the choice of the governor, the members of the upper house, the judges, or the military officers. These alterations in the constitution greatly affected the colonists' attitude toward all civil authority. The new charter governors were regarded as "outsiders," men possessing potentially dangerous prerogatives that the elected house had to restrict. The members of the lower house acquired an adversarial responsibility as the special guardians of the people's rights. The new charter government, unlike the old, contained inherent tensions, for it pitted the interests of the *elected* representatatives against those of the *appointed* rulers.[63] Of course, the political horizons of many colonists never extended beyond the boundaries of their own town; but even there it became increasingly difficult to ignore the influence of royal officials in Boston. Military officers, for example, once chosen by their own train bands, had become placemen, rewarded for considerations that had little to do with their military competence. Cotton Mather understandably complained of this practice: "The Influence which Preferments and Commissions have upon little Men, is inexpressible. It must needs be a Mortal Sin, to Disoblige a Governour, that has Inabled a Man to Command a *Whole Country*

Town, and to Strut among his Neighbours, with the Illustrious Titles of, *Our Major,* and, *The Captain,* or, *His Worship.*"[64] Such changes in themselves did not create political violence, but they did transform the trust of old charter days into suspicion and irritation.

Economic problems in Massachusetts further undermined the colony's social cohesion. As prosperity waned during the 1680s and 1690s, money matters increasingly became a cause of dissension. The merchants, for example, complained that the lack of specie in New England made it extremely difficult to carry on profitable business.[65] It is not certain how much the decay in trade affected the general populace, but the expense of the disastrous Quebec campaign quickly exhausted the colony's treasury. Thomas Hutchinson claimed that returning soldiers were on "the point of mutiny for want of their wages."[66] To meet this crisis the Bay Colony government printed thousands of pounds in paper currency, promising to redeem the notes at full value in specie when taxes next came due. Unfortunately, since the troops needed funds immediately, many of them sold the currency to speculators at reduced rates and, therefore, were never adequately compensated for their sacrifice.[67] At the same time that the merchants and soldiers were grumbling about depressed economic conditions, the state raised taxes far above any previous level. Doubtless the cause of the increase was the war against France, but the people were not happy about paying so much for military adventures that seemed so ill-conceived and poorly managed. Little wonder that a visitor in Massachusetts at this time reported "that many who had been for, were now inveterate enemies to the present Government."[68]

Eighteenth-century Massachusetts looked much like the rest of English society. No longer a peaceful anomaly, the Bay Colony began to experience sporadic internal disorders.[69] The rise of organized violence should be taken not so much as evidence of the Puritans' failure to create the ideal commonwealth, but as testimony that the Bay Colony had rejoined the Western world.

Breen and Foster's study of social cohesion in seventeenth-century Massachusetts is representative of a new thrust in Puritan studies. Scholars are increasingly asking questions about colonial society that were previously considered to be the province of the social anthropologist. Breen's recent work, such as his "Persistent Localism: English Social Change and the Shaping of New England Institutions" (William and Mary Quarterly, series 3, XXXII [1975]) and his "English Origins and New World Development: The Case of The Covenanted Militia in Seventeenth Century Massachusetts" (Past and Present, LVII [1972]), perhaps best represents this trend. Like other students of Puritan society, Breen not only employs new investigative approaches but is also heavily influenced by such English studies as Peter Laslett's "The Gentry of Kent in 1640" (Cambridge Historical Journal, 9 [1948]), Alan Everitt's Change in the Provinces: The Seventeenth Century (Leicester, 1972), and the essays in Joan Thirsk's The Agrarian History of England and Wales: 1500–1640 (Cambridge, Eng., 1967). In devoting their attentions to the lives and concerns of English villagers, these British historians have developed a new type of social history which recognizes both regional variations and the interaction of environment, tradition, ideology, political circumstances, and social institutions.

NOTES

1. For the problem of violence in early American history, especially in the eighteenth century, see Pauline Maier, "Popular Uprisings and Civil Authority in Eighteenth-Century America," *William and Mary Quarterly*, XXVII (Jan. 1970), 3-35; Gordon S. Wood, "A Note on Mobs in the American Revolution," *ibid.*, XXIII (Oct. 1966), 635-42; Richard Maxwell Brown, "Historical Patterns of Violence in America," and "The American Vigilante Tradition," Hugh Davis Graham and Ted Robert Gurr, eds., *The History of Violence in America: Historical and Comparative Perspectives* (New York, 1969), 45-84, 154-226; and Pauline Maier, "The Charleston Mob and the Evolution of Popular Politics in Revolutionary South Carolina 1765-1784," *Perspectives in American History*, IV (1970), 173-96.

2. Quoted in H. R. Trevor-Roper, "The General Crisis of the Seventeenth Century," Trevor Aston, ed., *Crisis in Europe 1560-1660* (Garden City, 1967), 68. See also E. J. Hobsbawm, "The Crisis of the Seventeenth Century," *ibid.*, 5-62. It is not necessary to accept the thesis of E. J. Hobsbawm and H. R. Trevor-Roper to recognize that the seventeenth century was a peculiarly violent era in European history. See also Perez Zagorin, *The Court and the Country: The Beginning of the English Revolution* (London, 1969), 1-9; J. H. Elliott, "Revolution and Continuity in Early Modern Europe," *Past & Present: A Journal of Historical Studies*, 42 (Feb. 1969), 35-56.

3. Max Beloff, *Public Order and Popular Disturbances 1660-1714* (Oxford, 1938), 9-91; C. S. L. Davies, "Revoltes populaires en Angleterre (1500-1700)," *Annales, XXIV* (Jan.-Feb. 1969).

4. Wesley Frank Craven, *The Southern Colonies in the Seventeenth Century, 1607-1689* (Baton Rouge, 1949), 154-55, 374-91, 398-99; Richard L. Morton, *Colonial Virginia: The Tidewater Period, 1607-1710* (Chapel Hill, 1960), 136-39, 260-77, 304-05, 307-08; Wilcomb E. Washburn, *The Governor and the Rebel: A History of Bacon's Rebellion in Virginia* (Chapel Hill, 1957).

5. Craven, *Southern Colonies in the Seventeenth Century*, 230-36, 257-61, 296-302, 411-15; Bernard C. Steiner, *Maryland During the English Civil Wars* (2 vols., Baltimore, 1906-1907); *Maryland Under the Commonwealth: A Chronicle of the Years 1649-1658* (Baltimore, 1911). For *New Englands First Fruits*, see Samuel E. Morison, *The Founding of Harvard College* (Cambridge, Mass., 1935), 441.

6. For a sophisticated study of the pattern of crime in the Bay Colony, see Kai T. Erikson, *Wayward Puritans: A Study in the Sociology of Deviance* (New York, 1966).

7. For Puritan-Indian relations see Alden T. Vaughan, *New England Frontier: Puritans and Indians 1620-1675* (Boston, 1965); Douglas Edward Leach, *Flintlock and Tomahawk: New England in King Philip's War* (New York, 1958); Charles H. Lincoln, ed., *Narratives of the Indian Wars, 1675-1699* (New York, 1913).

8. Darrett B. Rutman, "The Mirror of Puritan Authority," George Athan Billias, ed., *Selected Essays: Law and Authority in Colonial America* (Barre, Mass., 1965), 156-62; Bernard Bailyn, *The New England Merchants in the Seventeenth Century* (New York, 1964), 39-44, 123-24, 134-42, 160, 176-77; Michael G. Hall, *Edward Randolph and the American Colonies, 1676-1703* (Chapel Hill, 1960), 21-97.

9. For the Hutchinsonians, see Emery Battis, *Saints and Sectaries: Anne Hutchinson and the Antinomian Controversy in the Massachusetts Bay Colony* (Chapel Hill, 1962), 249-85, 299-328. For a full account of the issues at stake, see David D. Hall, ed., *The Antinomian Controversy, 1636-1638: A Documentary History* (Middletown, Conn., 1968), 4-20.

10. Darrett B. Rutman, "God's Bridge Falling Down: 'Another Approach' to New England Puritanism Assayed," *William and Mary Quarterly*, XIX (July 1962), 408-21; Sumner C. Powell, *Puritan Village: The Formation of a New England Town* (Middletown, Conn., 1963), 150-70; Timothy H. Breen, *The Character of the Good Ruler: A Study of*

Puritan Political Ideas in New England, 1630-1730 (New Haven, 1970), 35-133; Joshua Coffin, *A Sketch of the History of Newbury, Newburyport and West Newbury* (Boston, 1845), 74-76, 87, 101, 109. David D. Hall, *The Faithful Shepherd: A History of the New England Ministry in the Seventeenth Century* (Chapel Hill, 1972), 93-156, 227-48. See also references cited in note 8.

11. William L. Sachse, "The Migration of New Englanders to England, 1640-1660," *American Historical Review*, LIII (Jan. 1948), 251-78; Raymond P. Stearns, *The Strenuous Puritan: Hugh Peter 1598-1660* (Urbana, 1954); Charles E. Banks, "Thomas Venner, The Boston Wine-Cooper and Fifth-Monarchy Man," *New England Historical and Genealogical Register*, XLVII (Oct. 1893), 437-44.

12. For English strictures on the New England Way, see *A Letter of Many Ministers in Old England . . .* (London 1643); William Rathband, *A Briefe Narration of some Church Courses Held in Opinion and Practise in the Churches Lately Erected in New England* (London, 1644); Robert Baillie, *A Dissuasive from the Errours of the Time . . .* (London, 1645). For the background of this literature, see Stearns, *The Strenuous Puritan*, 204-14.

13. Vaughan, *New England Frontier*, 315-19.

14. For the aftermath of Bacon's Rebellion in Virginia and Leisler's Rebellion in New York, see Wesley F. Craven, *The Colonies in Transition 1660-1713* (New York, 1968), 149-53, 281-82; John D. Runcie, "The Problem of Anglo-American Politics in Bellomont's New York," *William and Mary Quarterly*, XXVI (April 1969), 191-217. By contrast Daniel Gookin, dropped from the magistracy for his advocacy of Indian rights in 1676, was reelected again in 1677 and annually thereafter, and was the leading vote getter in 1685. *Collections of the Massachusetts Historical Society, Fifth Series* (10 vols., Boston, 1871-1888), V, 77.

15. For current theories of revolution, see Lawrence Stone, *The Causes of the English Revolution, 1529-1642* (London, 1972), 3-25. See also Charles Tilly, "Collective Violence in European Perspective," Hugh Davis Graham and Ted Robert Gurr, *The History of Violence in America: Historical and Comparative Perspectives* (New York, 1969), 4-45; Harry Eckstein, *Division and Cohesion in Democracy: A Study of Norway* (Princeton, 1966), 225-88; Ted R. Gurr, "Sources of Rebellion in Western Societies: Some Quantitative Evidence," *Annals of The American Academy of Political and Social Science*, 391 (Sept. 1970), 128-44; Ted Robert Gurr, *Why Men Rebel* (Princeton, 1970); James C. Davies, "Toward a Theory of Revolution," *American Sociological Review*, XXVII (Feb. 1962), 5-19; Ivo K. Feierabend and Rosalind L. Feierabend, "Aggressive Behaviors Within Politics, 1948-1962: A Cross-National Study," *Journal of Conflict Resolution*, X (Sept. 1966), 249-71; H. L. Nieburg, "The Threat of Violence and Social Change," *American Political Science Review*, LVI (Dec. 1962), 865-73; Lewis A. Coser, *The Functions of Social Conflict* (New York, 1956); Lewis A. Coser, "Some Social Functions of Violence," *Annals of The American Academy of Political and Social Science*, 364 (March 1966), 10-12; Sheldon Hackney, "Southern Violence," *American Historical Review*, LXXIV (Feb. 1969), 906-25.

16. Powell, *Puritan Village*, 102-86; Kenneth A. Lockridge, *A New England Town, The First Hundred Years: Dedham, Massachusetts, 1636-1736* (New York, 1970); Philip J. Greven, Jr., *Four Generations: Population, Land, and Family in Colonial Andover, Massachusetts* (Ithaca, 1970), 21-99; John Demos, *A Little Commonwealth: Family Life in Plymouth Colony* (New York, 1970), 60-130; John Shy, "A New Look at the Colonial Militia," *William and Mary Quarterly*, XX (April 1963), 175-85.

17. Joan Thirsk, "The Family," *Past & Present: A Journal of Historical Studies*, 27 (April 1964), 116-22. See also Robert Mandrou, *Introduction a là France Moderne: (1500-1640) Essai de Psychologie historique* (Paris, 1961), 112-37, 165-82.

18. For a comparison of the revolutionary potentials of English and American Puritanism, see Stephen Foster, *Their Solitary Way: The Puritan Social Ethic in the First Century of Settlement in New England* (New Haven, 1971), 155-72.

19. Quoted in Perry Miller and Thomas H. Johnson, eds., *The Puritans* (2 vols., New York, 1963), I, 228.

20. For English Protestant hagiography in general, see William Haller, *Foxe's Book of Martyrs and the Elect Nation* (London, 1963); Richard Dunn, "Seventeenth-Century English Historians of America," James Morton Smith, ed., *Seventeenth-Century America:*

Essays in Colonial History (Chapel Hill, 1959), 195-225; Perry Miller, *The New England Mind: From Colony to Province* (Cambridge, Mass., 1963), 134-35.

21. Elliott, "Revolution and Continuity in Early Modern Europe," 49.

22. *Collections of the Massachusetts Historical Society, Fifth Series*, V, 139.

23. Alan Everitt, *The Community of Kent and the Great Rebellion 1640-60* (Bristol, 1966), 33-55; Peter Laslett, *The World We Have Lost* (London, 1965), 162-67.

24. Elliott, "Revolution and Continuity in Early Modern Europe," 51. For rival loyalties in early modern France, see Mandrou, *Introduction à la France Moderne*, 191-93; and for the decline of the French *commune* in the same period, see Ch. Petit-Dutaillis, *Les Communes Françaises: Caractères et Évolution, des Origines au XVIII Siècle* (Paris, 1947), 245-314.

25. John Winthrop, *Winthrop Papers* (5 vols., Boston, 1929-1947), II, 294, 295; Foster, *Their Solitary Way*, 41-64.

26. Perry Miller, *The New England Mind: The Seventeenth Century* (New York, 1939), 365-491; Edmund S. Morgan, *The Puritan Dilemma: The Story of John Winthrop* (Boston, 1958), 69-83, 93-95.

27. Thomas Hooker, *A Survey of the Summe of Church-Discipline* . . . (3 pts., London, 1648), pt. I, 50 (italics added). Peter Bulkeley explained, "When the Lord is in Covenant with a people, they follow him not forcedly, but as farre as they are sanctified by grace, they submit willingly to his regiment." Peter Bulkeley, *The Gospel-Covenant* (London, 1651), 220.

28. *Early Records of the Town of Dedham* (6 vols., Dedham, Mass., 1886-1936), III, 2.

29. *Early Records of . . . Dedham*, III, 2. See also Nathaniel Ward on Ipswich's policy of exclusion. Winthrop, *Winthrop Papers*, III, 216; Josiah H. Benton, *Warning Out in New England* (Boston, 1911).

30. John Winthrop, *The History of New England From 1630 to 1649*, James Savage, ed. (2 vols., Boston, 1853), I, 45.

31. Williston Walker, *The Creeds and Platforms of Congregationalism* (Boston, 1960), 214-15. On the militia, see Nathaniel B. Shurtleff, ed., *The Records of the Governor and Company of the Massachusetts Bay in New England.* Vol. II: *1642-1649* (Boston, 1853), 49-50, 117, 191; Morrison Sharp, "Leadership and Democracy in the Early New England System of Defense," *American Historical Review*, L (Jan. 1945), 244-60.

32. Kenneth W. Colegrove, "New England Town Mandates," *Publications of the Colonial Society of Massachusetts*, XXI (1919), 411-49.

33. Winthrop, *History of New England*, I, 152-53, 157, 188.

34. Breen, *Character of the Good Ruler*, 53-58.

35. Winthrop, *History of New England*, I, 246.

36. Samuel Sewall to Edward Calamy, Jan. 24, 1704, *Collections of the Massachusetts Historical Society, Sixth Series* (10 vols., Boston, 1886-1899), I, 295.

37. Craven, *Southern Colonies in the Seventeenth Century*, 154-55; Thomas J. Wertenbaker, *Virginia Under the Stuarts: 1607-1688* (Princeton, 1914), 60-84; Wilcomb E. Washburn, *Virginia Under Charles I and Cromwell, 1625-1660* (Williamsburg, 1957), 20-29; Bernard Bailyn, "Politics and Social Structure in Virginia," James Morton Smith, ed., *Seventeenth-Century America: Essays in Colonial History* (Chapel Hill, 1959), 96-98.

38. Breen, *Character of the Good Ruler*, 84-85; Joseph H. Smith, ed., *Colonial Justice in Western Massachusetts (1639-1702): The Pynchon Court Record* (Cambridge, Mass., 1961), 65-88.

39. See Richard Maxwell Brown, *The South Carolina Regulators* (Cambridge, Mass., 1963).

40. Smith, ed., *Colonial Justice in Western Massachusetts*, 89-200; George L. Haskins, *Law and Authority in Early Massachusetts: A Study in Tradition and Design* (New York, 1960), 113-231.

41. *Early Records of . . . Dedham*, IV, 118-19; Lockridge, *A New England Town*, 13.

42. For the complexity of English legal procedure in this period, see Stuart Prall, *The Agitation for Law Reform During the Puritan Revolution, 1640-1660* (The Hague, 1966);

Donald Veall, *The Popular Movement for Law Reform 1640-1660* (Oxford, 1970); Lawrence Stone, *The Crisis of the Aristocracy, 1558-1641* (Oxford, 1965), 240-42. For Virginia, see Warren M. Billings, "The Causes of Bacon's Rebellion, Some Suggestions," *Virginia Magazine of History and Biography*, 78 (Oct. 1970), 409-17, 434-35.

43. Darrett B. Rutman, "Governor Winthrop's Garden Crop: The Significance of Agriculture in the Early Commerce of Massachusetts Bay," *William and Mary Quarterly*, XX (July 1963), 396-415; Bailyn, *New England Merchants in the Seventeenth Century*; Kenneth Lockridge, "The Population of Dedham, Massachusetts, 1636-1736," *Economic History Review*, XIX (Aug. 1966), 318-44.

44. Lockridge, "The Population of Dedham," 334-39. See also Georges Duby and Robert Mandrou, *A History of French Civilization* (New York, 1964), 207-19.

45. Greven, *Four Generations*, 21-99.

46. James A. Henretta, "Economic Development and Social Structure in Colonial Boston," *William and Mary Quarterly*, XXII (Jan. 1965), 75-92; Miller, *New England Mind: From Colony to Province*, 41-52.

47. On this point Ted Gurr explained, "My basic premise is that the necessary precondition for violent civil conflict is relative deprivation, defined as actors' perception of discrepancy between their *value expectations* and their environment's apparent *value capabilities*. Value expectations are the goods and conditions of life to which people believe they are justifiably entitled. The referents of value capabilities are to be found largely in the social and physical environment: they are the conditions that determine people's perceived chances of getting or keeping the values they legitimately expect to attain." Ted Gurr, "Psychological Factors in Civil Violence," *World Politics: A Quarterly Journal of International Relations*, XX (Oct. 1967-July 1968), 252-53. For a seventeenth-century example of this phenomenon, see Hugh R. Trevor-Roper, *The Gentry, 1540-1640* (London, 1953).

48. Craven, *Colonies in Transition*, 213-23; Viola F. Barnes, *The Dominion of New England: A Study in British Colonial Policy* (New Haven, 1923), 5-70; Hall, *Edward Randolph and the American Colonies*, 79-117; Breen, *Character of the Good Ruler*, 134-50.

49. Cotton Mather, "The Life of His Excellency Sir William Phips," *Magnalia Christi Americana . . .* (7 bks., London, 1702), bk. 2, p. 43; Hall, *Edward Randolph and the American Colonies*, 110; Bailyn, *New England Merchants in the Seventeenth Century*, 180-81.

50. G. B. Warden, *Boston, 1689-1776* (Boston, 1970), 3-14.

51. Mather, "Life of Phips," 55; A. B., *An Account of the Late Revolution* (Boston, 1689), 1.

52. J. W. Fortescue, ed., *Calendar of State Papers, Colonial Series, America and West Indies 1689-1692* (London, 1901), 61.

53. *Collections of the Connecticut Historical Society* (Hartford, 1924), XXI, 324-25.

54. Theodore B. Lewis, Jr., "Massachusetts and the Glorious Revolution, 1660-1692" (doctoral dissertation, University of Wisconsin, 1967), 336; Thomas Hutchinson, *The History of the Colony and Province of Massachusetts-Bay*, Lawrence S. Mayo, ed. (3 vols., Cambridge, Mass., 1936), I, 340.

55. Samuel Willard, *The Character of a Good Ruler . . .* (Boston, 1694), 3.

56. "*The Case* of Massachusetts Colony *Considered, in a LETTER to a Friend at* Boston" and "The *COUNTREY-MAN's* ANSWER to a Gentleman in *BOSTON* Mr. N. N.'s LETTER to a Friend in the *Countrey*," Richard C. Simmons, ed., "The Massachusetts Revolution of 1689: Three Early American Political Broadsides," *Journal of American Studies*, II (April 1968), 8, 10.

57. Quoted in Breen, *Character of the Good Ruler*, 183-95; Hutchinson, *History of Massachusetts-Bay*, II, 60.

58. Chadwick Hansen, *Witchcraft at Salem* (New York, 1969); John Demos, "Underlying Themes in the Witchcraft of Seventeenth-Century New England," *American Historical Review*, LXXV (June 1970), 1311-26. See also Marion Starkey, *The Devil in Massachusetts: A Modern Enquiry into the Salem Witch Trials* (New York, 1949).

59. For New England witchcraft prior to 1692, see Demos, "Underlying Themes in Witchcraft of Seventeenth-Century New England," 1314-18; Starkey, *Devil in Massachusetts*, 207.

60. *Collections of the Massachusetts Historical Society, Fourth Series* (9 vols., Boston, 1852-1871), VIII, 646; *Collections of the Massachusetts Historical Society, Fifth Series*, V, 445; Starkey, *Devil in Massachusetts*, 258-70.

61. Warden, *Boston*, 66-68; G. M. Waller, *Samuel Vetch: Colonial Enterpriser* (Chapel Hill, 1960), 80-93.

62. "Some Considerations on the Bills of Credit Now passing in New England" (Boston, 1691), Andrew McFarland Davis, ed., *Colonial Currency Reprints 1687-1751* (4 vols., Boston, 1910-1911), I, 191-92.

63. Breen, *Character of the Good Ruler*, 195-99; Michael Zuckerman, *Peaceable Kingdoms: New England Towns in the Eighteenth Century* (New York, 1970), 17-24.

64. [Cotton Mather,] "The Deplorable State of New-England," *Collections of the Massachusetts Historical Society, Fifth Series*, VI, 118. On the intervention of the colonial government into local affairs, see Lockridge, *A New England Town*, 136-38; Edward M. Cook, Jr., "Social Behavior and Changing Values in Dedham, Massachusetts, 1700 to 1775," *William and Mary Quarterly*, XXVII (Oct. 1970), 577-78.

65. Bailyn, *New England Merchants in the Seventeenth Century*, 189; William B. Weeden, *Economic and Social History of New England, 1620-1789* (2 vols., Boston, 1890), I, 356, 379; Hutchinson, *History of New England*, II, 9.

66. Hutchinson, *History of New England*, I, 340.

67. *Ibid.*, 340-41.

68. Newton D. Mereness, ed., *Travels in the American Colonies* (New York, 1916), 8.

69. See Maier, "Popular Uprisings and Civil Authority in Eighteenth-Century America"; Lockridge, *A New England Town*, 112-14; *Collections of the Massachusetts Historical Society, Fifth Series*, VI, 280-81, 384; *Reports of the Boston Record Commissioners* (29 vols., Boston, 1880-1902), IX, 194, 196; Hutchinson, *History of New England*, II, 330-33; Edmund S. Morgan and Helen M. Morgan, *The Stamp Act Crisis: Prologue to Revolution* (Chapel Hill, 1953), 119-43; Wood, "A Note on Mobs in the American Revolution," 635-42.

7 | THE CONTROVERSY OVER THE FRANCHISE IN PURITAN MASSACHUSETTS, 1954 TO 1974

B. KATHERINE BROWN

One of the most important bonds of social unity—broad participation in government—has been subjected to extensive historical debate, especially during the past two decades. Starting with the early work of B. Katherine Brown, historians began to discard nineteenth- and early twentieth-century stereotypes of Puritan society as a narrow and repressive oligarchy. Students of colonial political structure agreed with the earlier interpretations of social and intellectual history forwarded by the Harvard school. But when scholars examined the extent of the franchise in New England towns and colonies, the amount of rotation of officeholding, and the function that participation in government played in Puritan society, they frequently disagreed over both facts and interpretations. Brown reviews below the literature that has developed on the subject and offers some new views.

Since the mid-1950s historians have engaged in a spirited debate over the extent of political democracy in Massachusetts before 1691. This debate has been concerned with the differences between local and provincial suffrage qualifications, and with changes in both over time; with differences of size between the potential electorate (the free adult males), the formally qualified electorate (the freemen), and the number of men who actually voted; with the significance of the religious qualification; with the problem of illegal voting; with difficulties in interpreting the language of records and laws; and with questions arising from the bias, incompleteness, and ambiguity of sources. The reason for exploring these issues is to determine by intelligent interpretation of the evidence whether the polity of the Bay Colony can be appropriately characterized as democratic or oligarchic.

One outcome of the discussion has been a great increase of our detailed knowledge of political policies and practices in early Massachusetts; another has been a shift of emphasis in the definition of the term political democracy. Earlier historians generally focused on the number who could vote or hold office, and pointed to the existence of large unenfranchised classes of people as a sign of oligarchy or lack of democracy. More recently, some scholars have doubted that the right to vote or hold office, even if widespread, signified a democratic polity. For them, such elements of the political culture as elitism, a spirit of deference, or the continuity or discontinuity of leadership provide the real keys to the question. Although these subjects should not be neglected, the fact remains that the definition of a polity as democratic depends fundamentally on the extent of the franchise. It is with the franchise, therefore, that we should be centrally concerned.

Contributions to the debate have been so numerous and scattered that the course of the controversy can be traced only with difficulty. This article attempts to rectify that situation by giving a short chronological survey of the recent historiography of the seventeenth-century Massachusetts franchise and by presenting new evidence that may help to clarify several important points relating to the extent of the suffrage, the meaning of the franchise laws, and how those laws actually worked. The original charter of the Massachusetts Bay Colony, granted in England in 1629 and used as a constitution by the first settlers, allowed a general court of stockholders and officials to make laws governing company affairs and provided rules for admitting new members (freemen). Over the years these rules were altered by legislation enacted by the General Court. A law of 1631 limited voting on provincial matters to church members who had taken the oath of freemanship, and four years later this ruling was applied to local or town voting as well. A 1647 law revised the qualifications for town voting by opening the local franchise to selected nonfreemen. In 1658 the parts of all former acts relating to nonfreemen were repealed and replaced by a new law giving the local franchise to all nonfreemen who possessed £20 of taxable property, a figure which was raised in 1670 to £80. The province voting rules were altered in 1664 to grant the franchise not only to all freemen but to some men who, though not members of a church, owned a stated amount of property and were sanctioned by their minister as "orthodox" in religion. In 1686 all franchise regulations were temporarily voided; reinstated or modified slightly in 1690, the rules were finally superseded by the new charter of 1691. These laws will be discussed more fully below.[1]

Until the current controversy began in 1954, most historians believed that Puritan Massachusetts was oligarchic and undemocratic, although their ideas varied as to the extent of the franchise during certain periods. John G. Palfrey (1864), George G. Haynes (1894), Albert E. McKinley (1905), James Truslow Adams (1921), and Perry Miller (1933) maintained that only about one-fourth or one-fifth of the adult males could vote. Vernon L. Parrington (1930) described early Massachusetts as a religious "oligarchy" where "the Saints were few and the sinners many." Samuel Eliot Morison (1930) agreed that Massachusetts was governed by an "oligarchy" based on religious qualifications and that the franchise was "narrow," but, unlike Adams, Morison insisted that a high percentage of the adult men were qualified voters during the early years—58 of 69 householders in Roxbury (1638-1640), for example, and 54 of 57 male church members in the same town in 1652. Morison agreed with Palfrey, however, that by 1670 perhaps only 20 or 25 percent of the adult men could vote. Writing in 1934, Charles M. Andrews found the Bay Colony undemocratic, especially in the early days, but believed that after 1647 all men had some share in local or general government. Thomas Jefferson

Wertenbaker (1947) reversed Andrews's conclusion by contending that Massachusetts was a Puritan oligarchy where most men had the vote in the early years but only a minority were enfranchised by the end of the century.[2] Except for Morison's few figures, these older estimates of the number of qualified voters were more inferential than factual and were grounded in an incomplete comprehension of the relation of church membership to voting.

Discussion of these matters began in earnest in 1954 with the publication of two articles by this writer. One short essay analyzed John Cotton's definition of "aristocracy" and concluded that, in practice, what Puritans called aristocracy closely resembled our representative democracy. Massachusetts officials—the "aristocrats"—were elected annually, were given authority by the people to "rule," and did not need hereditary privilege or great wealth to achieve their positions. The second article noted the differences among earlier interpretations and presented evidence suggesting that a majority of men had the vote and that freemanship had no social bounds.[3]

No major article or book squarely addressed these issues during the next few years, but in 1958 a trickle of publications began, some of which restated or supported the traditional view of a narrow franchise. Edmund S. Morgan, in *The Puritan Dilemma* (1958), described Massachusetts in 1630 as a "despotism" in which the freemen were allowed "to elect their despots every year," although he noted that at this date the freemen included "most, if not all, of the adult males, excluding servants." Morgan made no attempt to estimate the growth or decline of the suffrage. Without offering new evidence, George Lee Haskins maintained in 1960 that the 1631 law, which required every voter or "freeman" to be a member of a Puritan church, "imposed a drastic limitation on the franchise," putting the government on a "narrow religious basis." But Massachusetts was not a theocracy, Haskins claimed, for church and state were separate and the clergy did not have a formal or final voice in civil affairs. The towns were "oligarchies" similar to those in England, he believed, and eventually an "ecclesiastical oligarchy" developed comparable to the English "oligarchy of magistrates." Haskins pointed out, however, that these oligarchic magistrates had the confidence of the freemen who elected them to office year after year. In a study of Hingham (1961), John S. Coolidge stressed the domination of a ruling clique and asserted that Hingham's society was "patriarchal" but noted that the town had a high degree of economic equality. Contrary to Haskins and Coolidge, Darrett B. Rutman suggested in 1962 that the idea of an "absolute oligarchy" in Puritan Massachusetts was being relegated to the historical ash can. He predicted that more would be written on this issue in the future and urged that Morgan's plea for close examination of sources be heeded.[4]

The first direct challenge to my interpretation came in 1962 in an article by Richard C. Simmons who questioned the traditional ratio of freemanship but also disagreed with my general position. While stating that the percentage of freemen among the adult males before 1645 was "certainly higher than the traditional one-to-four or one-to-five," he ventured no ratio to replace the old estimate and he noted that the franchise laws were not always enforced. Simmons criticized my interpretation of the provincial franchise law of 1664, a subject to be discussed below, and suggested that in restricting the franchise to church members the colonial leaders were endeavoring to create "an orthodox and Godly state." In contrast to my view, he claimed that there was a marked though not absolute correlation of landed wealth with freemanship and officeholding. Simmons concluded that accurate generalizations about the Massachusetts franchise and its relationship to the social structure must rest on studies of individual communities.[5]

Two books, published in 1962, accepted without argument the idea of a tightly limited franchise. Writing on John Cotton, Larzer Ziff characterized the Bay Colony in the mid-1640s as an "oligarchy" where only 1,708 of the nearly 20,000 residents had citizenship.[6] Richard S. Dunn's study of the Winthrop "dynasty" offered no new evidence on the franchise, yet he stated that the 1631 law succeeded in barring a "majority of the colonists from any share in government."[7] Reviewer Lawrence Towner wrote that Dunn's book provided "food for thought on the old, and probably worn out, question of how democratic Puritan New England was."[8] The next decade would prove that though the question was old, it was far from worn out.

In 1963 Sumner Chilton Powell published his study of Sudbury which revealed wide participation in that town's government. He discovered that only 40 percent of the founders of the town were freemen, but that once a man was accepted as a "townsman" he could dissent and be heard. Powell concluded that Sudbury could not be called a theocracy: no exclusive borough council ruled; all townsmen had rights and responsibilities; and all inhabitants were granted land "free and clear." Powell also emphasized the participatory connotations of the language of the overwhelming majority of Sudbury's early laws, which stated boldly that what was done was "ordered and agreed by the inhabitants."[9]

My article on Cambridge, which also came out in 1963, showed a substantial measure of democracy in that town, too. I found that 75 percent of the adult men in the period 1652-1670 were church members who could have voted had they so desired, but that only 50 to 65 percent of them bothered to become freemen, a requirement for voting on the province level. The bulk of the townsmen appeared to be in the middle of the economic scale, although they generally elected those of better-than-average wealth to represent them. There was remarkable uniformity in religion in the town and overwhelming support on the part of both freemen and nonfreemen for the colony's government in 1664 when the government was challenged by Britain. Cambridge was extremely selective in admitting new settlers, but once inside, the inhabitants enjoyed much democracy.[10]

In the mid-1960s the trickle of writings became a flood. Two studies of particular communities agreed that the early years in Massachusetts were marked by considerable political democracy in town affairs. In his doctoral thesis (1964) on the family structure, inheritance patterns, and social mobility of Andover, Philip J. Greven, Jr., found that critical issues in the town seem to have been decided by freemen and nonfreemen alike.[11] A few months later, in 1965, Rutman published his study of Boston in the time of John Winthrop in which he pointed out that, regardless of the law and despite the fact that by 1649 fewer than half of the adult males were full church members, the town meeting gave "every indication of being an open body." Although he attempted to distinguish the "gentry" from the "generality," class divisions, he believed, were not strong and economic mobility was marked.[12]

Somewhat in contrast to Greven and Rutman, two other writers in 1965 appeared to uphold more traditional views. Morgan, in an introduction to a book of readings on Puritan political ideas, hesitantly accepted the view of limited suffrage in the Bay Colony. After the first few years, he wrote, "probably the majority of the population" was excluded from participation in the colony's government.[13] Late in 1965 Robert Wall challenged my idea that political power was widely distributed and concluded that the colony was governed by a political "elite" that drew its members from one class.[14]

Nineteen sixty-five also brought the completion of Simmons's doctoral thesis on the Massachusetts franchise, an enlargement of his 1962 article. Simmons maintained his revisionist view of the franchise but found a general decline over the years both in church membership and in eligibility to vote in province elections. Although he acknowledged that his calculations did not take into account the mortality rates or the uncertainty of estimates of the total number of adult males, and although he did not recognize the possibility that the official freemen's lists might be incomplete, Simmons concluded that the freemen may have numbered about 67 percent of the adult males in 1640 but declined to 40 percent by 1686. Since political rights were based on religious affiliation, Simmons held that Massachusetts was not a democratic society, and he suggested that the important consideration was not the quantity but the quality and power of the freemen. He expressed the hope that his study had "exhaustively and, hopefully, fully assessed" the issue of the extent of the provincial franchise and that "it should not be necessary to debate it further." On town voting, which had different qualifications after 1647 from province voting, Simmons very briefly noted that the religious restriction had never been widely observed and that by the last decade of the century all adult males with certain property holdings could vote in local affairs.[15]

Although Simmons's statistical findings on the franchise came closer to my estimates than to the traditional view, he disagreed forcefully with my general conception of the subject. He maintained that my analysis of previous interpretations was "unfair and demonstrably false"; that the extent of freemanship is not an adequate measure of democracy; that I did not present much evidence on the franchise during the last two decades of the Puritan period; that my analysis of the franchise law of 1664 was in error; that I did not understand the subtle political ramifications of the church membership qualification; that my sources on the widespread disobedience of the franchise laws were too few to be conclusive; that my remarks on the lack of distinction in contemporary records between freemen and nonfreemen were open to criticism; that my view of Puritan representative government as resembling our current political system was "whig history with a vengeance"; and that my idea that democracy could be seen in the rotation of offices without respect to wealth or heredity could not stand inspection. Finally, although Simmons thought my calculation of the extent of the franchise deserved "more respect," he rebuked me for my use of certain seventeenth-century statements on this subject by Nathaniel Ward and Thomas Lechford, and declared that my "simplistic" arguments represented an "anachronistic and mistaken view" of American historical development. In short, Simmons disagreed with the bulk of my interpretation.[16]

In 1966 Stephen Foster completed his doctoral dissertation on the Puritan social ethic which stressed the view that Massachusetts was not a democracy in spite of annual elections of officials and considerable economic equality. Foster held that the political structure of the Puritan period was dominated by John Winthrop's philosophy that the people should elect their officials, but that once elected those officials should take their orders from God. Foster maintained that it was this tradition of "aristocratic" rule and not some form of representative democracy which John Cotton meant by the word aristocracy. On the extent of the suffrage Foster's views varied. In his thesis abstract he indicated that Massachusetts had "mass white adult male suffrage" and a "much larger" freemanship than previously supposed; and in the thesis itself he claimed that "many, probably most, men could vote and hold office." Elsewhere, however, he stated that after the first generation the franchise "fell sharply," but then revised this generalization by suggesting that the period near the end of the century when only a minority could vote must have been a short one. Foster, like Simmons, disagreed with my interpretation of the 1664 law.[17]

Kenneth A Lockridge completed his doctoral dissertation on Dedham in 1965, and one of his first publications indicated wide political participation in that town. In 1966 Lockridge collaborated with Alan Kreider on an article about the evolution of Massachusetts town governments from 1640 to 1740, drawing their evidence primarily from Watertown and Dedham. They maintained that from 1648 to 1670 well over 90 percent of the adult males held the local suffrage in Dedham; that the supposedly higher qualifications for town voting from 1670 to 1690 were probably "fiction"; and that the town records gave no evidence that any voting qualification was rigidly enforced. "A wide town suffrage was very probably the normal and continuing state of affairs," they declared, "broken only in the years 1670-91 and possibly not even then."[18]

In 1967, unaware that Lockridge had written a dissertation on Dedham, I published a case study of the political structure of that town. Analysis of church and town records, tax lists, and other documents showed that in the early years most men in Dedham were church members and freemen but that the law restricting the vote to church members does not seem to have been rigidly enforced. As late as 1666, at least 75 percent of the adult males were freemen and thus could vote in provincial elections, and almost every adult male could vote for local officials. There seems to have been no great gap between rich and poor; there was easy economic mobility; and the choice of officials showed a pattern common today: a few men were elected year after year, but the majority served only a few terms. Although Dedham selectmen were generally in the upper half of the economic scale, there was no important correlation between being chosen selectman and great wealth. Like Cambridge, Dedham had a high degree of political and economic democracy and much religious unity.[19]

Nineteen sixty-seven brought other publications on the Bay Colony, some of which tended to support the traditional view. In an article on the church of Dedham, Lockridge began to retreat from the position taken in his dissertation. He did not deal with freemanship directly but did stress the "exclusiveness" of the church and noted that with the passing of the first generation the membership dwindled "to a small handful of saints,"[20] implying a decline of the franchise. Shortly thereafter Foster again questioned my interpretation of the law of 1664 but helpfully pointed out that recent as well as earlier studies of the franchise had relied exclusively on the official freemanship lists and that these lists were in fact incomplete—a matter, he noted, that I had considered in 1954 but had failed to develop. Foster neglected, however, to point out that this fact, if true, would in effect raise the estimates of the percentages of freemen. He concluded that "no one 'case study' proves much of anything," for research on a large number of towns must yield similar results before one could speak with confidence about the general extent of the franchise.[21]

Prompted by my 1967 article, Simmons, Lockridge, and Foster collaborated in 1968 on a lengthy knuckle-rapping letter-to-the-editor challenging my findings. After "correcting" my "repeated errors" and restoring my "omissions," they concluded that Dedham "had a shrinking eligibility for the provincial franchise, a narrow, wealthy base of leadership," and a diminishing town franchise, particularly after the local electoral law was changed in 1670. By 1686, near the end of the Puritan period, they wrote, "in all probability no more than 60 percent of the adult males" had the suffrage in either town or province, and they suggested that my concern for "irrelevant typology" had blinded me to the essence of the Massachusetts franchise—its "restrictiveness." They concluded that my "simplistic labels and mechanistic approach yield a classic case of *Hamlet* without the Prince," and they preferred to "approach history as historians" rather than as "intellectual antiquarians" seeking "particular examples of general categories that bear little relation to the reality" of other times. In reply, I noted among other things the need for calculating and deducting the number of young men (the nonvoters) from tax or militia rolls in estimating the percentage of freemen among the total adult males, and I reminded my critics that their figure of 60 percent freemen in 1686 was considerably higher than the traditional estimate of 20 or 25 percent.[22]

In 1967 Simmons published two articles amplifying the idea that it was not the quantity but the quality and power of freemanship that mattered. He stressed again that the purpose of the franchise legislation was to keep political control in the hands of the godly, not to enlarge the franchise. Although he now recognized that efforts to determine "even an approximate percentage of freemen" among the adult males were "fraught with danger," he nevertheless maintained that the records showed that freemanship declined in the later decades of the Puritan period to about one-third of the adult males and that "a flood of admissions" of freemen occurred when the law was changed in 1690. It should be noted that Simmons's figure of one-third is in decided contrast to the 60 percent estimate for the same period which he had offered in his letter published a few months earlier.[23]

Simmons's second article expressed the view that by 1689 the majority of men did not qualify for the vote, and he presented three broadsides published at that time that suggested ideas on the formation of a new government. The broadsides urged that voters in this proposed government should be "Free men," or HouseKeepers" with some taxable estate, or "trusty Freeholders." These qualifications were not new to the colony, but Simmons maintained that such proposals reflected the desire of the towns to expand the franchise. The evidence cited by Simmons indicates, however, that of the forty towns responding to an official query about the type of government the towns desired, only five mentioned the franchise—a response suggesting that increasing the number of voters was not a prominent issue.[24]

In 1969 Robert G. Pope published his study of church membership in seventeenth-century Massachusetts in which he challenged the generally accepted idea of a decline in piety. He pointed out that, contrary to the usual interpretation, few churches used the innovations in church membership proposed in the Half-Way Covenant, and that instead of a decline during the last three decades of the century, there was a major revival in church membership from 1675 to 1690. The primary causes of this revival, according to Pope, were the Indian problems of the 1670s and the loss of the charter in 1684 which deprived the Congregational churches of their favored status.[25] Since church membership was an important means of freemanship, Pope's findings have value for students of Puritan politics.

In 1970, in a perceptive survey of the controversy over the colonial suffrage in Massachusetts, James A. Thorpe found that issues other than the suffrage had come to dominate the debate. That a majority of adult males had the vote, or were capable of qualifying to vote, in provincial and town elections during the entire colonial period "now seems to be fairly well established," Thorpe maintained, but "the presence or absence of democratic *characteristics*" such as elitism and ease of reelection, as well as the definition of democracy itself, was still debatable. Thorpe predicted that the controversy would continue and possibly intensify, a prediction that soon proved accurate.[26]

Lockridge's monograph on Dedham, published in 1970, revealed that his views on the franchise varied considerably both within this book and from his previous writings. Without presenting new evidence, he stated that up to 70 percent of the male taxpayers of Dedham could vote in town affairs before 1647; he also noted that regardless of the law, probably most men, whether taxpayers or not, voted in these early informal meetings. After 1647, he claimed, the suffrage rose to "over ninety percent of adult males," and future laws changed that little. Two paragraphs later, however, Lockridge reversed himself. He concluded that the laws of the colony "imposed an increasing degree of narrowness on the right to political participation," so that by the end of the Puritan period "nearly half of the taxpayers" were not eligible to vote in town affairs. In province elections "full church members alone" could vote, Lockridge believed, and by 1662 only half of Dedham's male taxpayers were church members, and the number "continued to fall thereafter," implying a continuous decline in the suffrage. In his bibliographical essay Lockridge estimated without documentation that the early laws allowed 60 to 80 percent of the adult males of Massachusetts to vote in provincial elections and 60 to 90 percent in town affairs, but that by the 1680s these figures had fallen respectively to 30 to 60 percent and 40 to 70 percent. "It may be," he concluded, "that by this time in most towns a majority of men held no suffrage whatsoever." This statement was in decided contrast to his conclusion for Dedham alone that the town suffrage there was over 90 percent for most of the years after 1647, as well as to his statement four years earlier that a "wide town suffrage was very probably the normal and continuing state of affairs, broken only in the years 1670-91 and possibly not even then."[27]

On other aspects of politics and religion in Dedham, Lockridge also exhibited considerable inconsistencies. Although he characterized the church as "exclusive," he showed that 70 percent of the adult men were church members in 1648, that 80 percent of the children born in the town between 1644 and 1653 were baptized, and that even when these percentages declined, those outside the church voluntarily accepted the Puritan way. Although he maintained that the "selectmen enjoyed almost complete control over every aspect of local administration," that the town meeting was "passive" and "lacked initiative," and that its powers were largely "symbolic," he also contended that the very existence of the selectmen depended on the will of the town and that the "Wholl Towne" debated how much power to allow the selectmen, specified what power they were to have, repeated the process several times, and upon occasion voted out every incumbent selectman. Although Lockridge believed it "an injustice to the past" to suggest that the form of government in early Massachusetts was democratic, and "anachronistic" to look for anything resembling modern democracy in early Dedham, his own figures show that 83 of 91 male taxpayers were on the Dedham voting list of 1666 and that even the disfranchised usually supported the government. For Lockridge the political life of Puritan Massachusetts was "full of contradictions which the modern mind is hard put to resolve," and as he described it, this was true.[28]

In the same year Timothy H. Breen also presented inconsistent views on Puritan political ideas and practices. Relying mainly on a rereading of the laws, he focused on local political rights and, contrary to my view that nearly all men voted in the towns, attempted to prove that the General Court never sanctioned "anything like manhood suffrage" and that the failure of historians to distinguish between simple participation and actual voting may have been responsible for "inflated estimates" of the number who disobeyed the franchise laws. Breen questioned my inference that the wording in town records suggests wide participation, but he ignored the implications in his own quotation of a complaint by a subcommittee of the General Court that "'in all Elections wherin Freemen and non Freemen voat . . . scotch servants Irish negers and persons under one and Twenty years have liberty to vote.'" Breen concluded that the Bay Colony experienced no significant growth in democracy in the seventeenth century but rather a transition from a godly oligarchy to a propertied one. Yet in another work published the same year, he maintained that at no time "could the rulers of New England forget that they were only players before a large electoral audience."[29] And three years later, when Breen and Foster collaborated on an article, they pictured the polity as far more democratic than Breen had maintained in his first article. One of the main reasons for the peculiar social cohesion of the Bay Colony, they explained, was its "responsive political institutions." Although they noted that Massachusetts had a "gentry" class, they held that the colony had "relatively broad participation" in political and religious affairs: the "numerous freemen" elected all civil officials; the "many church members" chose their ministers; "civil elections were held frequently"; "no ruler could take continuance in office for granted"; the judicial system was fair and responsible; and there was widespread economic opportunity and prosperity.[30] This does not sound like the same community which Breen previously described as an "oligarchy" or the one Foster viewed as having a traditional "aristocratic" leadership.

Robert Wall, who had maintained in 1965 that the Bay Colony was governed by a political elite, now tried to answer the question of how many could vote by determining the percentage of freemen among all men in Massachusetts in 1647. He chose that year because it was the last one in which freemen alone could legally vote in town elections. Wall concluded that the freemen composed a majority of men in the towns close to Boston, but that the more remote communities contained fewer freemen and "in all probability" observed the franchise laws "in the loosest possible manner." Wall must be commended for trying a new approach to the problem of the franchise, although his statistics contained so many exceptions that one must question his generalization that the farther from Boston, the fewer the freemen.[31]

Wall's later writings reiterated the theme of elite domination, contending that the main conflict during the 1640s was between two groups of the elite, not between the elite and the common men. In a book on the "crucial decade," 1640-1650, published in 1972, he depicted a "struggle" for political control between two "distinct orders": the "great gentlemen" or magistrates and the "lesser gentry," whom Wall identified as a "group of economically and socially prominent men" who were far inferior to the great gentlemen but of a "higher social status than the freemen and nonfreemen," despite some common interests. He estimated that in 1647, 12 out of 27 Massachusetts towns had over 50 percent freemen among their adult male population. Apparently, however, there was no serious discord between the elite and the lower orders: even the "nonvoting minority" and the illegal voters were sympathetic to government policies. Despite this consensus, Wall suggested that the 1647 law was a measure instigated by the elite to curb illegal voting and thus to tighten their control, for the law permitted freemen alone to choose who should vote.[32] Since the majority of freemen who would be selecting the new political participants were not among the "elite," it is rather difficult to understand why Wall believed that elite control was enhanced by allowing them this power.

In the same year Wall published an article maintaining that the franchise in Massachusetts declined from 1647 to 1666. Since the conclusions in this short essay have been accepted by some later writers, it is worthwhile analyzing its thesis in detail. Wall presented statistics on the adult male population and on freemanship for most of Massachusetts in the years 1647 and 1666 and concluded that "all sections were moving toward a uniform decline in the number of voters and a uniform ratio of voters to adult male population of about 28 to 29 percent." But on close examination his statistics do not substantiate that conclusion. In the two counties where he claimed that complete records were available, the decline in the number of freemen, and thus of voters, varied considerably. In Essex County the change ranged from plus 5 percent in Gloucester to minus 24 percent in Wenham and minus 35 percent in Rowley. In Norfolk County the drop varied from 2 percent to 18 percent, and Springfield in the west actually gained 24 percent. These figures do not seem to indicate a "uniform" decline in the number of voters.[33]

Part of the answer to this problem may lie in Wall's statistics on the adult male population. Let us look carefully at his figures for two towns about which I have some knowledge. Wall concluded that Dedham in 1647 had 107 adult men, of whom 64, or 60 percent, were freemen. But in 1645 the town divided some land "according to the number of persons and mens estates," and only 83 persons, including one woman, were named. In 1648 a tax "valuation" of the houses in Dedham showed only 81 entries, including the names of 77 male householders, two of whom owned more than one structure; and the tax list for that year contained the names of 88 men, some of whom were undoubtedly too young to vote. Wall's figure of 107 adult men means either that a sizeable number of men were avoiding the tax assessor or that Wall overestimated the adult male population of Dedham for 1647.[34]

A similar discrepancy appears in Wall's figures for Dedham in 1666. He shows 107 adult men and 32 freemen in that year, but the tax list in 1666 included only 89 male taxpayers plus two more men who paid no tax. More complete records for the previous year, 1665, reveal that a sizeable number of the taxpayers were underage. Of the 90 men in town that year (86 male taxpayers and 4 non-taxpayers), 36 declared that they were "not yet past our Noneage" in a petition they signed supporting the government. In other words, only about 54 of the 90 men were adult males, of whom, according to my figures, 41 were freemen, a figure much closer to 75 percent than the 28 or 29 percent suggested by Wall.[35]

Wall's population statistics for Cambridge in 1666 also seem high. He claims that the town had 198 adult men and 75 freemen, but a land division list for 1665 contained only 134 names; and when we sort out the women, the estates, the college, and those with extra lots, only 119 men remain. Furthermore, a 1664 petition supporting the government, signed by 141 men, included 35 young men who chararacterized themselves as single but of the same "mynd with our parents, masters, and the aged men and householders," which means that about 106 adult males signed the petition. It seems unlikely that a land division list would omit almost half of the town's adult men. Discrepancies of this type in the figures on the adult male population in these two towns cast a long shadow over the accuracy of all of Wall's statistics. If his figures on adult male population are too high, his percentages of freemanship are too low, and his entire thesis would then be in serious doubt.[36]

Accepting Wall's data and using similar quantitative methods, Theodore B. Lewis and Linda M. Webb not only projected the view of a declining Massachusetts franchise into the later period but also maintained that power, not votes, was the key element in the polity. They estimated the percentage of freemen in the adult male population from 1674 to 1686 by calculating the number of adult males from militia rolls and tax lists and by comparing that total with the number *who voted*, not with those *who could vote*. They determined that approximately 30 percent of the adult male population were freemen, a figure similar to that of Wall. What their estimated minimum figures actually showed, however, was that 43 percent of the adult males were "freemen" in 1674, just over 38 percent in 1676, nearly 32 percent in 1682, and slightly less than 30 percent in 1686. Lewis and Webb concluded that although accurate statistics on the electorate would be "satisfying," they are not "vital" to understanding Massachusetts politics. "We have a reasonably satisfactory profile" of the voters from the 1630s to 1686, they maintained, which shows a declining percentage of voters among the adult males from "a small majority to a small minority." It was time, they believed, to stop counting heads under the impression that "the number of voters in a population measures the degree of 'democracy' in colonial society." The important question, they felt, concerned "the functions of power within the system," whether in colonial Massachusetts or in Miami in 1972.[37] One wonders how many politicians in 1672 or in 1972 would agree that the number of voters has no relation to "democracy" or to power.

From this brief survey it is clear that there are great disagreements and inconsistencies of interpretation among historians. Why? Somehow we all should be able to settle on an accurate description of the political structure of the Bay Colony with the sources we have available. When we reach conflicting conclusions, is it possibly a clue that our data are not complete or that we have gone astray in our estimates? Is the trouble that we have not let our sources speak for themselves? Let us take a deeper look at some of the points on which we disagree.

Central to the controversy are the issues of the extent of the franchise and the meaning of the franchise laws. For the period between 1631 and

1647, when local and provincial voting was limited to church members who had taken the required oath of freemanship, the main questions are how many men became church members and how many church members became freemen.

Historians now generally hold that most men were church members and freemen in the first years of the Bay Colony, and some have pointed out that even nonfreemen in that period participated in political affairs.[38] There is much evidence to support this latter view. In Watertown, for example, two of the eleven men chosen in 1636 as selectmen were not made legal freemen until eight months after they were elected.[39] Five of the twelve selectmen chosen in Dorchester in 1636, three of the ten elected in 1637, and five of the ten chosen in 1638 were not on the official list of freemen, indicating either that the town was lax in enforcing the law or that the freemen's list is not complete.[40] In Woburn two of the three surveyors of highways were nonfreemen in 1644,[41] and Dedham records show clearly that nonfreemen participated in town meetings before 1647.[42]

The language of the town records and laws also supports the view that nonfreemen were active in local politics before 1647. Dorchester records contain such phrases as "a Generall vote of all the Plantation" and "upon a generall and lawfull warning of all the inhabitants"; Woburn selectmen were elected in 1644 "with the general consent of all the freemen and other inhabitants then present." In 1646 Salem agreed "that all the towne's men and freemen" should join in town meetings, while Boston called its "Generall Meeting" by giving notice "from house to house" in 1639. Powell indicated that, with few exceptions, laws in Sudbury were ordered and agreed to by the "inhabitants." Finally, in 1639 Dedham records say, "Whereas the wholl towne wear warned to meete together this Daye to make Choyce of newe men for the Ordering of the Towne affayers according unto Courte Order in that behalfe. The greatest parte of the Inhabiting townsmen being assembled," the town proceeded with its business.[43] There is no hint in these records that the local franchise was restricted in practice to church members before 1647.

Other records also show that most men could participate in town affairs before 1647 if they so desired. According to Morison, 58 of the 69 householders in Roxbury in 1638-1640 were both church members and voters.[44] A Dedham land division list of February 1645, which apparently included all inhabitants, contained the names of 82 men, and a list of men who attended the "generall Meeting of the Whole Town" in January 1647 named 70. Seventeen of the men named on the land division list did not appear among the 70 who attended the meeting, but other records indicate that most of them could have done so.[45]

Breen argued that the terms "townsmen" and "inhabitants" were vaguely defined and may actually have denoted a restricted class during this period,[46] but the facts reveal his supposition to be only partially accurate. Generally, the towns defined the meaning of the term inhabitant in some way. In 1640 Boston stated that "John Palmer, Carpenter, now dwelling here, is to be allowed an Inhabitant, if he can gett an house, or land to sett an house upon (it being not proper to allowe a man an Inhabitant Withou[t] habitation)." Dedham and Sudbury had similar definitions of townsmen as men who owned property in the town.[47] But Breen was correct in saying that this group was a restricted class if by that he meant that no person could long dwell in a town without sanction. In fact, no newcomer could stay in Massachusetts more than three weeks without official "license," according to a General Court ruling.[48] And anyone who reads through the early Massachusetts town records cannot but be impressed by the care the towns took in selecting their new inhabitants and keeping out those whom they thought undesirable. In 1636 the Boston selectmen ordered that "noe Townsmen shall entertain any strangers into their houses for above 14 dayes, without leave" of the selectmen. And in March 1647 they declared that persons who intended to take up residence in the town must give the town officials notification within eight days of their arrival or be fined.[49] In Dedham, newcomers in these early years were required "according to the order of Courte" to produce certificates from the magistrates before the town would let them settle, and only with the consent of the town could a man acquire or sell land there.[50] This "restrictiveness" continued through the years. As late as 1671 Boston refused six men admittance as inhabitants.[51] In 1667 Dedham refused to let a man reside in his father-in-law's house even though his father-in-law put up the necessary bond to protect the town from damages, and the officials kept after the young man until he left the area.[52]

Some of the historians who accept the "oligarchic" interpretation erroneously assume that all adult men in the colony during the period 1631-1647 and after desired to become freemen and voters, but the fact is that many avoided freemanship. The reasons are quite obvious. Towns fined freemen who failed to attend town meetings or refused to serve in town offices when elected.[53] As a result, and even though it cost them the right to vote in provincial elections, some men apparently preferred to remain nonfreemen in order to avoid town responsibilities. This situation sometimes permitted able men to escape public work, while others were fined for refusal to accept election, a fact that provoked the General Court in 1643 to order the churches to deal with "members that refuse to take their freedom."[54] Neither forced attendance at town meetings nor refusal on the part of church members to become freemen speaks very loudly for an "oligarchic" interpretation.

The failure of church members to become freemen continued to be a problem until the General Court finally found a solution in 1647. A movement to enlarge the civil rights of nonchurch members, which began as early as 1644, culminated in 1646 when the Court drew up a law giving nonfreemen "equal power" with freemen in town affairs and also extending the vote in provincial elections to nonfreemen of specified estate.[55] Before this act became law, however, Robert Child and other opponents of the New England way presented the court with a controversial petition demanding more civil and religious rights for members of the Church of England, "godly" men who did not dissent from the late reformation in England and Scotland. The petitioners threatened to carry the issue to Parliament if their demands were rejected.[56]

Acting under the need to get more men to share local political responsibilities, to legalize the political activities of some nonfreemen, and to meet the threat from Child and his faction, the Court enlarged the suffrage for the towns in 1647. The new law allowed the freemen of the towns to grant the town franchise to "such Inhabitants (though non-Freemen)" who were twenty-one years of age or over and who had taken the oath of fidelity to the government. A few months later the Court ruled that whereas there were *many members of Churches who to exempt themselves from all publick service in the Common-wealth will not come in, to be made Freemen,*" such church members must henceforth, like freemen, accept election to offices or be fined for refusal.[57] It should be noted that while these laws forced church members to participate more actively in town government and allowed some nonchurch members more participation, they did not include a property requirement for nonfreemen, as did the proposed 1646 bill.

Opinions on the 1647 law vary widely. Rutman and Greven suggest that the law simply recognized and made legal what was already taking place in many towns: as Rutman puts it, "the law trailed the fact." Powell appears to agree that this was true for Sudbury. Foster, at one point, writes that after 1647 all men could serve on juries and in town offices; Lockridge considers the law "generous"; and Simmons finds the law liberalizing. Two other historians do not agree. Breen contends that in giving the freemen the power to enfranchise nonfreemen the Court desired only "a slight expansion" of the franchise; "colonial rulers" gave no indication in the language of the bill that they accepted equal status for nonfreemen. He reasons that if as many nonfreemen had been participating in community affairs before 1647 "as we have been led to believe," the 1647 law would not have been needed. Similarly Wall declares that the law was "riddled with restrictive clauses," and he, too, stresses the fact that it gave the freemen the power to admit nonfreemen. If nonfreemen were casting votes in large numbers, Wall supposes that the law "may" have been designed to eliminate these illegal voters.[58]

As we have seen, the evidence prior to 1647 supports the view of Rutman and Greven that the law trailed the fact, and there is also much evidence that, contrary to Wall's implication, the 1647 law did not restrict town voting after that date. An unsuccessful proposal of a General Court committee in the 1650s clearly suggests that, although the freemen still did the work, almost all adult men voted—freemen and nonfreemen, servants, and even those under twenty-one.[59] Voting records and tax lists also confirm that town suffrage after 1647 was very wide indeed. A January 1652 list of the "names of those Townesmen that are to be called at the generall Towne meeteing" in Dedham included twelve names that did not appear on the town rate made up the following month. Eleven of those twelve were younger sons or servants, three of whom were not officially admitted townsmen until 1655. A similar situation is found in 1652 in Cambridge.[60] Finally, a 1658 petition from some Ipswich nonfreemen acknowledged that it was the "alowed practice Throughout this Jurisdiction" for all men who had taken the oath of fidelity to vote and participate in town affairs, not just those selected by the freemen.[61] In the face of this evidence, one cannot accurately conclude that the 1647 law was restrictive, as Wall implied, or that the clause in the law allowing freemen to choose which nonfreemen could participate resulted in only a slight expansion of the suffrage, as Breen suggested.

The law of 1647 conflicted with other laws and after only eleven years was replaced by a new law that kept few if any adult men from the ballot box. In 1658, responding to an Ipswich petition that requested clarification of the 1647 law and recognizing that conflict existed among the laws then on the books, as the petition pointed out, the General Court repealed all acts as far as they related to the voting of nonfreemen and adopted a new one giving the town franchise and the right to hold town office to all nonfreemen who were settled inhabitants and householders of at least twenty-four years of age, who were rated at £20 estate, and who had taken the oath of fidelity.[62] As my findings for Dedham confirm and as Breen acknowledges, this property qualification was not restrictive.[63] Under the new law, almost every adult man could vote in town affairs.

Although the 1658 law on the local franchise remained unchanged until 1670, a major and controversial alteration in provincial voting occurred in 1664. At the insistence of the English government, the General Court repealed the 1631 law restricting the franchise to church members who became freemen and passed a new statute giving the vote in provincial elections not only to church members who took the freeman's oath but to all other "English men," at least twenty-four years of age, who presented a certificate from the minister of the town that they were orthodox, and who were settled inhabitants, householders, and certified freeholders "rateable [in addition to the poll tax] to the country in a single country rate, after the vsual manner of valuation in the place where they liue, to the full value of tenne shillings."[64] At the time of its passage, royal commissioners, who had been sent to the colony to investigate problems there and who were unhappy with what they found, condemned the law as merely complying on paper with the king's request. They warned that the king would not be pleased to find that the vote was allowed to "him only who pajeth ten shillings to a single rate to be of competent estate" because not three in a town of one hundred actually paid that amount. The General Court replied that the law was not "exclusive," and arguments on the subject persisted.[65]

Historians are still debating the meaning and effect of the 1664 law. On the basis of its wording and of its description by contemporaries— "rateable to the value of tenn shillings in a single country rate" or "Tenn Shillings ratable Estate," as many phrased it—I assumed in 1954 that the statute's property requirement for nonchurch members meant *assessed* valuation, not the amount *paid*, as the royal commissioners maintained, and that therefore the amount of property required was very small indeed.[66] This interpretation was challenged by Simmons in his 1962 article. He noted that, according to the certificates of orthodoxy and financial status of the prospective freemen now in the Massachusetts archives, few nonchurch members were admitted by rate up to 1684. Later Simmons claimed that the ten shillings was not a "rate" but a tax paid and that according to the General Court this meant a ratable estate of £120, which, he said, "was a large estate." He maintained, however, that it was not this requirement but the continued policy of allowing church members to become freemen regardless of property and the requirement of certificates of orthodoxy for nonchurch members that really circumvented the royal intention.[67]

Two other historians also questioned my interpretation. Believing the property requirement to be a "substantial sum," Foster cited the certification of Nathaniel Jacobs which used the word "paid" rather than "rated." Foster did not mention that this was the only certificate using the word "paid" among the many using "rated," nor did he say that the same selectman in the same town some years earlier had signed another certificate using the term "rated."[68] Another critic, Robert Wall, took an ambiguous position. He seemed to agree with me that the 1664 property qualification was not a high one and that not all of those who could meet it became freemen. But having said this, he called the law itself "restrictive" in that it put admission to freemanship "back in the hands of the deputies and magistrates" who composed the General Court, and he asserted his belief that historians who project the high percentage of voters found in earlier years into the middle or later Puritan periods "were quite wrong."[69]

Evidence now available on the meaning of the term "rate" indicates that while it was often used in general speech to refer to the payment of a tax—a country rate, a town rate, or a minister's rate—in the tax laws it almost always meant assessed value. In Watertown, for example, single persons were "rated" at £15 and cows were "rated" at £3.[70] However, "rate" and "pay" were sometimes used interchangeably. In 1642 the Watertown clerk, in recording assessed valuations, noted that "Land . . . shall pay ye Acre, 2 lb 10s," while in the same list cattle were "rated at 5 lbs,"[71] causing one to wonder whether the lone certificate of freemanship found by Foster which said "paid" may have been a similar aberration. Evidence from the final years of the old charter suggests, however, that it was not. In 1690 when the General Court revised the 1664 law, it ordered that the ten-shilling requirement be reduced to four shillings, and Samuel Sewall stated that under this ruling men who "pay 4s to a single rate," not counting their "head" or poll tax, could present themselves to the General Court to be admitted electors. Furthermore, the language of most of the town selectmen in presenting lists of men desiring freemanship under this new ruling used the term "pay," not "rated."[72]

But knowing whether the ten-shilling qualification was the amount paid or the assessed valuation does not answer the important question of how exclusive the 1664 law was in practice. How many people were affected by this qualification? It did not touch church members, and my previous research showed that in Cambridge in this period at least three-fourths of the adult men were full church members and could have been freemen had they so desired; that at least 75 percent of the adult men in Dedham were freemen; and that Boston in 1679 had about 61 percent freemen among the adult males.[73] If these percentages were generally true throughout the colony—and so far there is no detailed evidence on other towns to refute this[74]—only a minority would need to use the property qualification to become freemen. Moreover, the law was effective for only about twenty years, for with the coming of Andros in 1686 it became inactive.[75] As Simmons noted, few men apparently became freemen under the law's property qualification, if the number of certificates now existing in the state archives is any measure. Furthermore, when Edward Randolph, a Church of England sympathizer and leading critic of the Bay Colony, testified in England that the province franchise was limited to church members in spite of the 1664 law, Massachusetts' agents denied the charge. British officials accepted the agents' interpretation, which they would hardly have done had the law been exclusive. And why would Randolph ask the British government to institute a law limiting the vote in Massachusetts to those who paid ten shillings in a single rate if, by the guess of the royal commissioners, only three in a hundred could so qualify?[76] Surely not all of the Church of England people in the colony were wealthy. Finally, what exactly did the Massachusetts agents mean when they explained that a £120 ratable estate was an "estate competent" for the vote?[77] And how does this tally with Randolph's description of a freeman as a man "worth about £200"?[78]

A clue to these puzzles may be found in the tax assessment ratio. It appears doubtful that by counting only those who paid ten shillings on any country rate we can determine how many could vote, for the assessment ratios varied considerably.[79] The partial Boston country rate for 1674, which gives only total tax and no valuations or head count, contains about 52 men who paid more than the tax required to vote, or about 11 out of each 100 men, a number decidedly larger than the royal commissioners claimed but still far from a majority.[80] However, a partial Boston valuation list for 1676, which shows assessed property only, includes 201 men, 37 of whom had £120 or more of assessed valuation. Further investigation reveals that houses were assessed on this list at 20 percent of their true value.[81] When we adjust the houses to full value, 117 out of the 201 men, or 58 percent, had £120 of taxable estate. The 1687 Boston tax list—a complete list giving polls, valuations, and taxes—contained 1,140 male taxpayers of whom only 7 paid ten shillings on their property alone, and the valuation of property on this list had fallen dramatically to 6 percent of its true worth.[82] Thus in 1687 if a man paid a ten-shilling tax, which would be £120 assessed value, he needed £2,000 of taxable property, a very large estate. Lt. Thomas Clark, a prominent merchant and one of the richest men in Boston, had an estate worth at least £2,151 in 1678, and Dep. Gov. Samuel Symonds, who died the same year, was worth £2,103.[83]

What does this wide variation in assessment ratios mean for the 1664 franchise? When the assessed value was 6 percent of true value in 1687 but 20 percent in 1676, is it unreasonable to assume that it may have been 50 percent or even full value in 1664 when the law was passed? If this were so, the £120 ratable estate said by the Massachusetts officials to be competent for freemanship and Randolph's description of a freeman as a man "worth about £200" would be about the same.

Until we learn more about how property in the Bay Colony in this period was assessed and how officials interpreted the law, we cannot know for sure how exclusive the 1664 statute was. We do know that no one but a few Church of England men objected to it during its twenty-odd years of existence, and their objections were based mainly on religious rather than economic grounds. We also know that, almost to a man, freemen and nonfreemen in many towns backed their government during the trouble with England in 1664.[84] Finally the fact that a sizeable majority of the adult men were still freemen during this period,[85] and that almost all the rest of them could participate in town affairs, undoubtedly lowered any pressure for enlarging the provincial franchise, if such pressure did exist among the regular inhabitants.

The next change in the franchise concerned town voting and has caused less debate among historians than the 1664 ruling. Without explanation, the new law of 1670 raised the £20 ratable estate required of nonfreemen by the 1658 law to £80, but this provision was not to exclude any who already had the vote.[86] There is considerable evidence that the law kept few if any from the town ballot, and later actions by the General Court actually softened the impact of the law. In answer to a 1674 Marblehead petition, the Court ordered that persons approved by the selectmen and the county court could act in all town affairs "as if freemen" until further Court order. And in 1681 the Court declared that "any" inhabitant could be chosen constable, selectman, or juror, even though not rated according to law, and that any person so chosen was thereafter to have the same political privileges as any freeman in town.[87]

The most convincing evidence that the number of town voters did not decrease as a result of the 1670 law is to be found in the town records which show how the law was put into practice. In 1680 the general town meeting in Watertown ordered that "all house houlders" were to have the vote in town affairs.[88] In Ipswich a 1679 list of those allowed to vote in town affairs, when compared with a commoners list of 1678, reveals that at least 77.6 percent of the adult males of Ipswich had the franchise.[89] The records of Springfield show in detail how that town reacted to the law. In 1664 Springfield drew up a list of townsmen who were "allowed and admitted Inhabitants." This list contained the names of 72 men and 2 women, and 4 more men were admitted townsmen by 1667, making a total of 76 male inhabitants. In February 1672 the 1670 law was discussed at a general town meeting and the clerk was ordered to check the country rates and make a list of the legal town voters. Seventy-six men were on that list.[90] Although the names on these two lists are not entirely identical—some men may have left town or died; others may have arrived or come of age—the fact that there were 76 admitted inhabitants in 1667 and 76 voters in 1672 shows clearly that the 1670 law disfranchised almost no one in town affairs and refutes the idea of a decline in voting in Springfield.

If there was a sharp decrease in town voting or any resentment over restrictions on the franchise in these last years of the Puritan period, Samuel Sewall, one of Boston's leading politicians, seemed unaware of it.

Although Sewall meticulously recorded exact votes in many elections and frequently named unsuccessful candidates, he never mentioned any concern about limitation of the franchise, which suggests that this was not a problem. Furthermore, his figures on Boston elections reveal no significant drop in voting and little difference in the number of freemen voting for deputies and the number of townsmen voting for town officials (see Table I). It should be noted that the number who voted in Boston remained about the same before the old charter was finally condemned in 1686 and for several years after the new charter went into effect in 1691. For some unexplained reason, however, there was a major increase in 1698, six years after the lower qualifications of the new charter were put into practice. From this evidence one can only conclude that the town franchise did not decline radically even in the last years of the Puritan period, as suggested by Simmons, Foster, Lockridge, and Breen. Finally, the very small number of eligible voters who participated in the 1684/5 Boston election for deputy casts doubt on the work of Lewis and Webb who equate those who voted with those who could vote, for there were certainly more than one hundred voters in Boston during this period. It also refutes their suggestion that there was intense political activity in 1683 and a significant decline in voting between 1684 and 1686. Even their own figures on the elections do not indicate great activity or a decline. According to their chart, votes given the top candidates in 1683 totalled 17,539; in 1684, 17,763; in 1685, 17,813; and in 1686, 17,657.[91]

Table I   Samuel Sewall's Account of Voting in Boston Elections, 1685-1699

Election Date	Highest No. Votes for Any One Candidate	Office	Voters Present
Mar. 1684/5	90+[a]	deputy	--
Mar. 1685/6	86	selectman	--
May 1688	85	selectman	--
Mar. 1691/2	78	selectman	--
Mar. 1692/3	92	selectman	--
May 1693	77	assemblyman	--
May 1696	88	assemblyman	134
May 1698	218	assemblyman	340
May 1699	239	assemblyman	323

[a] Sewall records 90 "and odd." Samuel Sewall, *Diary*, Massachusetts Historical Society, *Collections*, 5th Ser., I (1878), 67, 124-125, 213, 358, 374-375, 378, 424-425, 478-479, 496. Sewall gives no figure for the number of voters present at the first six elections.

The revocation of the Massachusetts charter and the assumption of power by the new governor, Edmund Andros, in late December 1686 altered the franchise dramatically. The 1670 law on town voting was superseded by a rule permitting the "inhabitants" to vote in town meetings—a rule which those historians who maintain that the franchise was limited may view as an enlargement—but this was offset by limiting town meetings to only one a year. The province franchise was even more drastically curtailed by eliminating the General Court with consequent loss of political power on the province level for all freemen.[92] When Andros was overthrown in 1689, the 1670 law on town voting was reinstated without change, a province election by the "Freemen that are or shall be in the Colony" was ordered, and within two years the new charter was in effect, a charter which most historians now agree was liberal in its franchise requirements.[93]

Over the past two decades, then, there has been much controversy over the franchise in Puritan Massachusetts. Some historians found broad political participation; others accepted the traditional view of a restricted franchise, especially after 1647; still others changed their minds about the percentage who could vote. A few even maintained that the number who could vote made no real difference in the political power arrangement of the colony, a generalization which few if any American political candidates then or now would accept.

Examining the major points of disagreement, we find that the bulk of the primary evidence confirms the existence of an extensive franchise throughout the period. When we study not only the laws but how they actually worked, we find that almost all adult men had a vote in town affairs even in the later years of the old charter, and that a majority did or could vote in province elections except during the brief Andros regime in the 1680s. Objections to the franchise rules over the years were very few; instead, political apathy became at times a problem serious enough to require corrective legislation. The controversial 1664 law remains something of an enigma, but it affected only a very small percentage of voters on the provincial level and for a period of only about twenty years.

Such evidence does not permit us to describe early Massachusetts as an oligarchy or an aristocracy. Not only was the franchise extensive, but all political officials were subject to annual elections and no man had a hereditary right to office. How could any society with these characteristics, especially a society of small agricultural towns, be accurately called an oligarchy? When we feel the urge to attach an oligarchic label to the Bay Colony, we should remind ourselves of Samuel Sewall's description of his visit with a leader of that "oligarchy" in 1697 at Dorchester: "When I first saw the Lieut. Governour," wrote Sewall, "He was Carting Ears of Corn from the upper Barn."[94]

Brown and the scholars whose views she discusses are aware of the need to define the meanings which words such as "aristocracy" and "democracy" had for seventeenth-century Englishmen and Americans. Yet the works analyzed above are primarily concerned with evaluating Puritan political structure in terms of the numerical parameters of voter and officeholder participation. A different type of insight is provided by intellectual historians. Edmund S. Morgan's Puritan Political Ideas, 1558–1794 *(Indianapolis, 1965) is a collection of primary sources with an extensive analytical introduction that traces the evolution of key political concepts from the Elizabethan age through the era of the American Revolution. Timothy H. Breen's* The Character of a Good Ruler: Puritan Political Ideas in New England, 1630–1730 *(New Haven, 1970) focuses on shifting views of the proper relationship between the people and their elected leaders. Both of these works not only clarify the ideals behind the structures examined by Brown but also demonstrate the evolutionary nature of Puritan political thought.*

NOTES

1. Nathaniel B. Shurtleff, ed., *Records of the Governor and Company of the Massachusetts Bay in New England, 1628-1686* (Boston, 1853-1854), I, 87, 161, IV, pt. 2, 117-118, hereafter cited as *Mass. Records; The Laws and Liberties of Massachusetts* (Cambridge, Mass., 1929 [orig. publ. 1648]), 23, hereafter cited as *Laws of Mass.*; William H. Whitmore. ed., *The Colonial Laws of Massachusetts* (Boston 1889 [orig. publ., 1660]), 76; *The General Laws and Liberties of the Massachusetts Colony . . . May 15, 1672* (Cambridge, Mass., 1672), 148; Albert S. Batchellor, ed., *Laws of New Hampshire* (Manchester, 1904-1922), I, 218-221, 353, 355; Francis Newton Thorpe, *The Federal and State Constitutions, Colonial Characters and Other Organic Laws . . .* (Washington, D. C., 1909), III, 1878-1879.

2. John Gorham Palfrey, *History of New England* (Boston, 1858-1890), III, 41n; George H. Haynes, *Representation and Suffrage in Massachusetts, 1620-1691*, Johns Hopkins University Studies in Historical and Political Science, VII-IX (Baltimore, 1894), 14, 15, 23, 28-29, 49n, 57, 58-59, 83; Albert Edward McKinley, *The Suffrage Franchise in the Thirteen English Colonies in America* (Philadelphia, 1905), 302, 313, 334-335; James Truslow Adams, *The Founding of New England* (Boston, 1921), 143-144, 146, 154-156, 323, 394, 395; Perry Miller, *Orthodoxy in Massachusetts, 1630-1650: A Genetic Study* (Cambridge, Mass., 1933), 176-177, 227, 242-245; Perry Miller, *Errand into the Wilderness* (Cambridge, Mass., 1956), 143-144; Perry Miller, *The New England Mind: The Seventeenth Century* (New York, 1939), 439-440, 452-454; Vernon Louis Parrington, *Main Currents in American Thought: An Interpretation of American Literature from the Beginnings to 1920*, I (New York, 1927), 21; Samuel Eliot Morison, *Builders of the Bay Colony* (Cambridge, Mass., 1930), 86-87, 339-341; Charles M. Andrews, *The Colonial Period of American History*, I (New Haven, Conn., 1934), 459-460; Thomas Jefferson Wertenbaker, *The Puritan Oligarchy: The Founding of American Civilization* (New York, 1947), vii-viii, 67-69.

3. B. Katherine Brown, "A Note on the Puritan Concept of Aristocracy," *Mississippi Valley Historical Review*, XLI (1954), 105-112; B. Katherine Brown, "Freemanship in Puritan Massachusetts," *American Historical Review*, LIX (1954), 865-883.

4. Edmund S. Morgan, *The Puritan Dilemma: The Story of John Winthrop* (Boston, 1958), 91, 101-113. A similar view was expressed in Edmund S. Morgan, *Visible Saints: The History of a Puritan Idea* (Ithaca, N. Y., 1963). George Lee Haskins, *Law and Authority in Early Massachusetts: A Study in Tradition and Design* (New York 1960), 29, 52-53, 62-63, 74, 75, 87, 90, 99-103; John S. Coolidge, "Hingham Builds a Meetinghouse," *New England Quarterly*, XXXIV (1961), 439, 442, 448; Darrett B. Rutman, "God's Bridge Falling Down: 'Another Approach' to New England Puritanism Assayed," *William and Mary Quarterly*, 3d Ser., XIX (1962), 420-421.

5. Richard C. Simmons, "Freemanship in Early Massachusetts: Some suggestions and a Case Study," *WMQ*, 3d Ser., XIX (1962), 422-428.

6. Larzer Ziff, *The Career of John Cotton: Puritanism and the American Experience* (Princeton, N. J., 1962), 209, 210.

7. Richard S. Dunn, *Puritans and Yankees: The Winthrop Dynasty of New England, 1630-1717* (Princeton, N. J., 1962), 14 and Book I, *passim.*

8. Lawrence W. Towner's review of Dunn, *Puritans and Yankees, MVHR*, XLIX (1963), 689.

9. Sumner Chilton Powell, *Puritan Village: The Formation of a New England Town* (Middletown, Conn., 1963), 107, 111-112, 116, 124-129, 154, 158-161, 180.

10. B. Katherine Brown, "Puritan Democracy: A Case Study," *MVHR*, L (1963), 377-396.

11. Philip J. Greven, Jr., "Four Generations: A Study of Family Structure, Inheritance, and Mobility in Andover, Massachusetts, 1630-1750" (Ph.D. diss., Harvard University, 1964), I, 57-58. Greven published his revised dissertation as *Four Generations: Population, Land, and Family in Colonial Andover, Massachusetts* (Ithaca, N. Y., 1970).

12. Darrett B. Rutman, *Winthrop's Boston: Portrait of a Puritan Town, 1630-1649* (Chapel Hill, N. C., 1965), 72-75, 141-147, 156-163.

13. Edmund S. Morgan, ed., *Puritan Political Ideas, 1558-1794* (Indianapolis, 1965), xxix.

14. Robert Emmet Wall, Jr., "A New Look at Cambridge," *Journal of American History*, LII (1965), 599-605.

15. Richard C. Simmons, "Studies in the Massachusetts Franchise, 1631-1691" (Ph.D. diss., University of California at Berkeley, 1965), 36-39, 46, 75.

16. *Ibid.*, 139-147.

17. Stephen Foster, "The Puritan Social Ethic: Class and Calling in the First Hundred Years of Settlement in New England" (Ph.D. diss., Yale University, 1966), 65, 134-136, 141, 147-148, 173, 362-364, 368-371, 388. Foster published his revised dissertation as *Their Solitary Way: The Puritan Social Ethic in the First Century of Settlement in New England* (New Haven, Conn., 1971).

18. Kenneth A. Lockridge, "Dedham, 1636-1736: The Anatomy of a Puritan Utopia" (Ph.D. diss., Princeton University, 1965); Kenneth A. Lockridge and Alan Kreider, "The Evolution of Massachusetts Town Government, 1640-1740," *WMQ*, 3d Ser., XXIII (1966), 564-565.

19. B. Katherine Brown, "Puritan Democracy in Dedham, Massachusetts: Another Case Study," *WMQ*, 3d Ser., XXIV (1967), 378-395.

20. Kenneth A. Lockridge, "The History of a Puritan Church, 1637-1736," *NEQ*, XL (1967), 408-411. Lockridge also published an article on "The Population of Dedham, Massachusetts, 1636-1736," *Economic History Review*, XIX (1966), 318-344, in which he correctly warned of pitfalls in using vital statistics and indicated that tax lists provided a much more reliable measure of population.

21. Stephen Foster, "The Massachusetts Franchise in the Seventeenth Century," *WMQ*, 3d Ser., XXIV (1967), 613-623.

22. Letter to the Editor, *ibid.*, XXV (1968), 330-339. This same month and year Lockridge published an article, "Land, Population and Evolution of New England Society, 1630-1790," *Past and Present* (1968), 62-80, in which he noted that the suffrage "could not possibly have been above 90 per cent" (p. 68n).

23. Richard C. Simmons, "Godliness, Property, and the Franchise in Puritan Massachusetts: An Interpretation," *JAH*, LV (1968), 495-511.

24. Richard C. Simmons, "The Massachusetts Revolution of 1689: Three Early American Political Broadsides," *Journal of American Studies*, II (1968), 5-6, 8, 9, 12; Massachusetts Archives, State House, Boston, CVII, 21, 24b, 49, 49a, 50, *passim*.

25. Robert G. Pope, *The Half-Way Covenant: Church Membership in Puritan New England* (Princeton, N. J., 1969), 9, 274, 279-286, chap. 8, *passim*; see also Pope, "New England Versus the New England Mind: The Myth of Declension," *Journal of Social History*, III (1969-1970), 95-105.

26. James A. Thorpe, "Colonial Suffrage in Massachusetts: An Essay Review," *Essex Institute, Historical Collections*, CVI (1970), 169-181.

27. Kenneth A. Lockridge, *A New England Town, The First Hundred Years: Dedham, Massachusetts, 1636-1736* (New York, 1970), 47-49, 194; Lockridge and Kreider, "Evolution of Massachusetts Town Government," *WMQ*, 3d Ser., XXIII (1966), 564-565.

28. Lockridge, *A New England Town*, 30, 31, 33, 36, 37, 38, 40, 46, 47, 48, 54, 87; see also Don Gleason Hill, ed., *Early Records of the Town of Dedham* (Dedham, Mass., 1881-1894), III, 62, 126, IV, 13, 29-30, hereafter cited as *Dedham Town Records*.

29. Timothy H. Breen, "Who Governs: The Town Franchise in Seventeenth-Century Massachusetts," *WMQ*, 3d Ser., XXVII (1970), 460-474; T. H. Breen, *The Character of the Good Ruler: A Study of Puritan Political Ideas in New England, 1630-1730* (New Haven, Conn., 1970), 58, 170

30. Timothy H. Breen and Stephen Foster, "The Puritans' Greatest Achievement: A Study of Social Cohesion in Seventeenth-Century Massachusetts," *JAH*, LX (1973), 5-22; see also Breen, "Persistent Localism: English Social Change and the Shaping of New England Institutions," *WMQ*, 3d Ser., XXXII (1975), 19.

31. Robert Emmet Wall, Jr., "The Massachusetts Bay Colony Franchise in 1647," *WMQ*, 3d Ser., XXVII (1970), 136-144. Wall showed that Charlestown had 65% freemen, but so did remote Concord; Cambridge had 56%, but so did outlying Rowley and Hull; Watertown, very near Boston, had only 41% compared with a higher percentage for 14 towns much farther from Boston (Hull, Weymouth, Braintree, Dedham, Sudbury, Concord, Woburn, Salem, Wenham, Rowley, Andover, Newbury, Salisbury, and Haverhill). Furthermore, why would Rowley have 56% when Ipswich, just six miles south and nearer Boston, had only 29%, and Wenham, a few miles more to the south, had 53%? All of these were "remote" towns. Why did Wall pick Ipswich (29%) instead of Rowley (56%) for his comparison with Charlestown (65%)?

32. Robert Emmet Wall, Jr., *Massachusetts Bay: The Crucial Decade, 1640-1650* (New Haven, Conn., 1972), 21, 22, 25, 31, 32, 39-40, 162n, 170, 174, 230. Wall elaborated on the restrictive qualities of the 1647 and 1666 laws in "The Decline of the Massachusetts Franchise: 1647-1666," *JAH*, LIX (1972), 308-310.

33. Wall, "Decline of Massachusetts Franchise," *JAH*, LIX (1972), 304, 307.

34. *Ibid.*, 304; Brown, "Puritan Democracy in Dedham," *WMQ*, 3d Ser., XXIV (1967), 387-388; *Dedham Town Records*, III, 109-111, 153-154.

35. Wall, "Decline of Massachusetts Franchise," *JAH*, LIX (1972), 304; Brown, "Puritan Democracy in Dedham," *WMQ*, 3d Ser., XXIV (1967), 393-394; *Dedham Town Records*, III, 104-105, 119-120, 276-278. A total of 69 young men signed the 1665 Dedham petition of nonfreemen, but many of the signers not on the tax list appear to have been younger sons or servants. It is possible that Wall relied too heavily upon vital statistics, which can be misleading, rather than on the more accurate tax records. See Lockridge, "Population of Dedham," *Econ. Hist. Rev.*, 2d Ser., XIX (1966), 320; James K. Somerville, "Family Demography and the Published Records: An Analysis of the Vital Statistics of Salem, Massachusetts," Essex Inst., *Hist. Colls.*, CVI (1970), 251.

36. Wall, "Decline of Massachusetts Franchise," *JAH*, LIX (1972), 304; Brown, "Puritan Democracy: A Case Study," *MVHR*, L (1963), 385-389.

37. Theodore B. Lewis and Linda M. Webb, "Voting for the Massachusetts Council of Assistants, 1674-1686: A Statistical Note," *WMQ*, 3d Ser., XXX (1973), 625-634.

38. Although the 1631 law did not name any specific church, it was generally understood that membership in one of the Congregational churches was intended. Brown, "Puritan Democracy in Dedham," *WMQ*, 3d Ser., XXIV (1967), 385-387; Rutman, *Winthrop's Boston*, 160-161, 197; Powell, *Puritan Village*, 124-129, 180; Philip J. Greven, Jr., "Old Patterns in the New World: The Distribution of Land in 17th Century Andover," Essex Inst., *Hist. Colls.*, CI (1965), 135; Lewis and Webb, "Voting for the Council," *WMQ*, 3d Ser., XXX (1973), 628.

39. Watertown Historical Society, *Watertown Records . . . ,* (Watertown, Mass., 1894-1934), I, 2, hereafter cited as *Watertown Records*; *Boston Town Records*, in William Whitmore and William Appleton, eds., *The Report of the Record Commissioners of the City of Boston* (Boston, 1876-1909), XXIX, 133, 134, 136, 137, hereafter cited as *Boston Town Records*.

40. *Dorchester Town Records*, in Whitmore and Appleton, eds., *Report of the City of Boston*, IV, 9, 24, 35, hereafter cited as *Dorchester Town Records*; *Mass. Records*, I, 80, 366-379.

41. Samuel Sewall, *The History of Woburn, Middlesex County, Mass. From the Grant of Its Territory to Charlestown, in 1640, to the Year 1860* (Boston 1868), 25; *Mass. Records*, I, 366-379.

42. Brown, "Puritan Democracy in Dedham," *WMQ*, 3d Ser., XXIV (1967), 385-386.

43. *Dorchester Town Records*, 25, 54, 57, 83; Sewall, *History of Woburn*, 24; Joseph B. Felt, *The Annals of Salem from Its First Settlement* (Salem, Mass., 1827), I, 350; *Boston Town Records*, II, 41; Powell, *Puritan Village*, 116; *Dedham Town Records*, III, 62.

44. Morison, *Builders of the Bay Colony*, 340-341.

45. Brown, "Puritan Democracy in Dedham," *WMQ*, 3d Ser., XXIV (1967), 387-388.

46. Breen, "Who Governs," *ibid.*, XXVII (1970), 464-465.

47. *Boston Town Records*, II, 51; *Dedham Town Records*, III, 2, 135; Powell, *Puritan Village*, 128.

48. *Mass. Records*, II, 141.

49. *Boston Town Records*, II, 10, 90; see also *Watertown Records*, I, 1, 10.

50. *Dedham Town Records*, III, 24, 32-37, 55, 61, 162, IV, 208, 209, 224.

51. *Boston Town Records*, VII, 64.

52. *Dedham Town Records*, IV, 127, 130, 131, 156; for other material on townsmen and their admission see *ibid.*, III, 18, 20, 68, 162, IV, 4, 66, 123, 127, 169-170, 209.

53. See for example, *ibid.*, III, 4; *Dorchester Town Records*, 292-293; Wenham Historical Society, *Wenham Town Records* . . . (Wenham, Mass., 1927-1940), I, 23.

54. *Mass. Records*, II, 38; see also Edward Winslow, "New-Englands Salamander Discovered," Massachusetts Historical Society, *Collections*, 3d Ser., II (Cambridge, 1830), 137, 139.

55. James Kendall Hosmer, ed., *Winthrop's Journal, "History of New England," 1630-1649*, Original Narratives of Early American History (New York, 1908), II, 271-272.

56. John Childe, *New-Englands Jonas Cast up at London* . . . (London, 1647), in Peter Force, comp., *Tracts and Other Papers* . . . (Washington, D. C., 1846), IV, 11-13; Morison, *Builders of the Bay Colony*, chap. 8.

57. *Laws of Mass.*, 23, 50-51. The law in this widely used book gave the age as 21 years, but in the clerk's copy of the records it was 24 years. See *Mass. Records*, II, 197.

58. Rutman, *Winthrop's Boston*, 161, 197; Greven, "Old Patterns in the New World," Essex Inst., *Hist. Colls.*, CI (1965), 135; Greven, "Four Generations," I, 56-58; Foster, "Puritan Social Ethic," 65; Lockridge, *A New England Town*, 49; Simmons, "Studies in the Massachusetts Franchise," 94; Breen, "Who Governs," *WMQ*, 3d Ser., XXVII (1970), 466-469; Wall, "Decline of Massachusetts Franchise," *JAH*, LIX (1972), 308.

59. Cited in Rutman, *Winthrop's Boston*, 162, and in Breen, "Who Governs," *WMQ*, 3d Ser., XXVII (1970), 469.

60. *Dedham Town Records*, III, 190, 198; Brown, "Puritan Democracy: A Case Study," *MVHR*, L (1963), 383-384.

61. "A Petition from Some of the Inhabitants of Ipswich," Essex Inst., *Hist. Colls.*, XXXVI (1900), 245-246.

62. *Mass. Records*, IV, pt. 2, 335-336; Whitmore, ed., *Colonial Laws of Massachusetts*, 76.

63. Brown, "Puritan Democracy in Dedham," *WMQ*, 3d Ser., XXIV (1967), 387-388; Breen, "Who Governs," *ibid.*, XXVII (1970), 471.

64. *Mass. Records*, IV, pt. 2, 117-118, 134.

65. *Ibid.*, 205, 221.

66. Brown, "Freemanship in Massachusetts," *AHR*, LIX (1954), 880; letter of General Court to British, June 11, 1680, in *Mass. Records*, V, 287-288; Mass. answer to the king's letter, in R. N. Toppan and A. T. S. Goodrich, eds., *Edward Randolph including his Letters and Official Papers* . . . *1676-1703* (New York, 1967 [orig. publ. Boston, 1898-1909]), III, 192, hereafter cited as *Randolph Papers*.

67. Simmons, "Freemanship in Early Massachusetts," *WMQ*, 3d Ser., XIX (1962), 423-424n; Simmons, "Studies in the Massachusetts Franchise," 106-151.

68. Foster, "Massachusetts Franchise in the Seventeenth Century," *WMQ*, 3d Ser., XXIV (1967), 617-619; Mass. Archives, CVI, 500b and *passim*. Foster called the man Jacques and gave the certificate date as July 9, 1684, but in the document the name appears as Jacobs

and the date was Feb. 2, 1681. The second certificate was that of John Whiple dated 1668 (Mass. Archives, CVI, 485d). In this article Foster helpfully stressed the limitations of the official freemen lists.

69. Wall, "Decline of Massachusetts Franchise," *JAH*, LIX (1972), 309.

70. *Watertown Records*, I, 33; *Mass. Records*, IV, pt. 1, 388-389.

71. *Watertown Records*, I, 8.

72. Samuel Sewall, *Letter-Book*, Mass. Hist. Soc., *Colls.*, 6th Ser., I (Boston, 1895), 107; Batchellor, ed., *Laws of New Hampshire*, I, 385, 393, 455.

73. I say "at least" because these figures were based on the official freemen lists which have now been shown to be incomplete; therefore these percentages can only be minimum. Brown, "Puritan Democracy: A Case Study," *MVHR*, L (1963), 386-395; Brown, "Puritan Democracy in Dedham," *WMQ*, 3d Ser., XXIV (1967), 393-394; Brown, "Freemanship in Massachusetts," *AHR*, LIX (1954), 881-882.

74. Robert Wall has attempted to show that freemanship decreased from 1647 to 1666 in all towns by using estimated population figures and the official lists but has not made a detailed analysis of any one town. Wall, "Decline of Massachusetts Franchise," *JAH*, LIX (1972), 303-310.

75. Batchellor, ed., *Laws of New Hampshire*, I, 146-155.

76. *Randolph Papers*, II, 68, 281-283.

77. Mass. Archives, CVI, 94, quoted in Simmons, "Godliness, Property, and the Franchise," *JAH*, LV (1968), 510.

78. *Randolph Papers*, II, 201.

79. The problems of using tax lists to determine who could meet property requirements are many, as shown by Foster, "Massachusetts Franchise," *WMQ*, 3d Ser., XXIV (1967), 618, and by Breen, "Who Governs," *ibid.*, XXVII (1970), 471.

80. *Boston Town Records*, I, 20-53.

81. *Ibid.*, 60-67. In order to find the ratio of the assessment valuation to the true value of the property in 1676, it was necessary to find some taxpayer who purchased his property shortly before the valuation list was made up. Fortunately, two men on this list did just that. James Brading, an ironmonger of Boston, bought over eight acres and a house in Boston in Aug. 1672 for £250. Although Brading did buy a few small pieces of land in the Boston area and sold one parcel prior to 1676, he neither bought nor sold any house during this time, and on the 1676 valuation his house was listed as £50, or 20% of the sale value. (*Boston Town Records*, I, 60; *Suffolk Deeds*, VI, 329, VIII, 120, 159, 160, 163, 327, 334, IX, 306). The second man, John Wing, "shopkeeper" of Boston, bought a "big mansion" and brewery and wharves for £1,000 "in money" on Mar. 19, 1674/5. This property was rated at £200 on the 1676 valuation list, or 20% of its true sale value. (*Boston Town Records*, I, 61; *Suffolk Deeds*, IX, 151, 299). No other Brading (or Braden) appears in the deeds, and no other entries concerning property transfers are in the deeds for John Wing except a mortgage by which Wing borrowed £1,200 on the above property on Feb. 9, 1675/6.

82. *Boston Town Records*, I, 91-133, VII, 189. Not included in these figures are the outlying area of Muddy River which had 50 men, none of whom paid 10s or more without head tax, and Rumney Marsh which had 46 men of whom 12 paid 10s or more without head tax, but four of these were for "islands" and another was a tenant. The same method of determining assessed valuation to true worth of property was used for 1687 as for 1676. See materials on John Squire and Samuel Checkley, *ibid.*, I, 102, 126, VII, 183, 186, 191, 192, IX, 78; *Mass. Records*, V, 544; *Suffolk Deeds*, XIII, 145, 208, XIV, 31, and *passim*.

83. *Boston Town Records*, II, pt. 2, 127; *Mass. Records*, V, 257-258.

84. *Mass. Records*, IV, pt. 2, 132; Cambridge petition in Lucius R. Paige, *History of Cambridge, Massachusetts, 1630-1877, With a Genealogical Register* (Boston, 1877), 74-76; *Dedham Town Records*, IV, 119-120.

85. Brown, "Puritan Democracy: A Case Study," *MVHR*, L (1963), 389; Brown, "Puritan Democracy in Dedham," *WMQ*, 3d Ser., XXIV (1967), 393; Brown, "Freemanship in Massachusetts," *AHR*, LIX (1954), 881-882. Wall's figures on freemen, arrived at by a quantitative method, do not agree with mine. See Wall, "Decline of Massachusetts Fran-

chise," *JAH*, LIX (1972), 303-310. A 1673 ruling ordered a year's wait for freemen to be confirmed, but this law was repealed after 10 years and it is doubtful that it hindered many men from becoming freemen. See *Mass. Records*, IV, pt. 2, 562, V, 385.

86. *General Laws and Liberties*, 148.

87. *Mass. Records*, V, 306.

88. *Watertown Records*, II, 1.

89. Brown, "Freemanship in Massachusetts," *AHR*, LIX (1954), 882. Because the commoners list very likely included some men under 24 years of age and some estates, the 77.6% must be considered a minimum.

90. Henry M. Burt, *The First Century of the History of Springfield: The Official Records from 1636 to 1736* . . . (Springfield, Mass., 1898), I, 8, II, 72, 76, 114-115.

91. Lewis and Webb, "Voting for the Council," *WMQ*, 3d Ser., XXX (1973), 625-634.

92. Batchellor, ed., *Laws of New Hampshire*, I, 218-221, 353; Samuel Sewall, *Diary*, Mass. Hist. Soc., *Colls.*, 5th Ser., I (1878), 159-162.

93. Simmons stressed the importance of the number of men admitted to freemanship in 1690 when the province franchise requirement was lowered from ten to four shillings and the requirement for a minister's certificate was repealed. But of the 900 men admitted at that time, 296 were admitted on the basis of church membership, 387 by rate, and 217 unspecified. Furthermore, it was the town officials, not the individual men, who requested their admission to freemanship. And that the franchise was not a major issue is shown not only by the fact that just 5 of the 44 towns responded to the General Court's request in 1690 for their views on enlarging of the franchise, but also by the decrease in the number who actually did vote in the province elections after this enlargement. See Simmons, "Godliness, Property, and the Franchise," *JAH*, LV (1968), 502; Batchellor, ed., *Laws of New Hampshire*, I, 353, 355; Mass. Archives, CVII, 8a, 13a-27, 36a-41b, 43-51, 99, 109a, and *passim*, XXXV, 154, XXXVI, 54, 256; and Sewall, *Diary*, Mass. Hist. Soc., *Colls.*, 5th Ser., I (1878), 48, 77-78, 132, 136-137, 360. Evarts B. Greene and Virginia D. Harrington, *American Population before the Federal Census of 1790* (New York, 1932), 19-21, shows more towns than the 44 acknowledged by the officials at this time, but probably some towns were too small to send representatives.

94. Sewall, *Diary*, Mass. Hist. Soc., *Colls.*, 5th Ser., I (1878), 462.

8 | GOVERNOR WINTHROP'S GARDEN CROP: THE SIGNIFICANCE OF AGRICULTURE IN THE EARLY COMMERCE OF MASSACHUSETTS BAY

DARRETT B. RUTMAN

Timothy Breen and Stephen Foster demonstrate in their study of social cohesion in New England (see selection 6) that no matter how strong its religious fervor, the Puritan experiment required a viable economic base to succeed.

New England's coast had long been famous for cod and other fish, which the European and West Indian markets could absorb in almost limitless quantities. But as the colonial population grew, it inevitably moved inland, where farming had to be the principal livelihood not only to sustain the community but to produce a surplus to exchange for tools, weapons, nails, sugar, and other goods that could not be produced locally.

Much has been written about the Puritans' struggle with New England's recalcitrant soil, especially by Percy W. Bidwell and John I. Falconer, History of Agriculture in the Northern United States, 1620–1860 *(Washington, 1925); Robert R. Walcott,* "Husbandry in Colonial New England" *(New England Quarterly, IX [1936]); and Darrett B. Rutman,* Husbandmen of Plymouth: Farms and Villages in the Old Colony, 1620–1692 *(Boston, 1967). Much has also been written about early efforts at overseas trade and the emergence of a mercantile class. Bernard Bailyn's* The New England Merchants in the Seventeenth Century *(Cambridge, Mass., 1955) is the best and most recent account. The interconnection between farming and trade, a topic largely overlooked by earlier writers, is the focus of the following essay.*

There is a paradox in the history of early Massachusetts—indeed, one applicable to all of New England in the first decades. It is that of an agricultural land in which the trades of the sea are dominant; a land largely devoted to crops where—if the tenor of historical writing is to be accepted—profits are made in other endeavors.

On the one hand, there is the frequent description of New England's "cold climate and rocky soil" and the conclusion that agriculture was "not an encouraging business." The New Englanders simply made a good thing of a bad bargain during the first years of settlement, building a short-term prosperity by selling their agricultural surplus to new arrivals. But when the tide of newcomers ebbed and depression broke upon them in 1640, they turned to trade, shipbuilding, fish. In the words of a recent writer, they abandoned the plow "for the rising star of ocean commerce."[1]

On the other hand, there is the unavoidable fact that the land dominates town and commonwealth records both before and after 1640. The General Court of Massachusetts Bay regularly appointed land for new towns in the interior—away from the sea and ships. The towns themselves are always in the throes of a new distribution of land. Court records indicate farm after farm being leased, with the owner receiving agricultural products as rent; probate records show land passing from father to sons, while estate inventories list page on page of farm equipment.[2] Contemporary descriptions of the commonwealth reiterate the impression given by the records. Edward Johnson, writing in 1651, described the Bay settlement as a chain of agricultural communities. Dorchester, he wrote, boasted "Orchards and Gardens full of Fruit-trees, plenty of Corne-Lande"; Roxbury was "this fertill Towne" of "very goodly Fruit-trees, fruitfull Fields and Gardens, their Heard of Cowes, Oxen and other young Cattell of that kind about 350"; Ipswich was a "very good Land for Husbandry, where Rocks hinder not the course of the Plow." Even Boston, though its center on Shawmut Peninsula was by this time devoted exclusively to commercial pursuits, included purely agricultural areas at Muddy River, Winnisimmet, Rumney Marsh, and Pullen Point.[3]

Only occasionally have writers hinted at the resolution to this paradox. Charles M. Andrews, in surveying the extant cargo manifests of the period, concluded that ships from New England carried away cargoes consisting of one-third fish, one-third woodproducts, and one-third wheat and other grains. Bernard Bailyn, in examining the seventeenth-century New England merchant, noted the existence of a trade in provisions to the wine-producing islands of the eastern Atlantic (the Cape Verde Islands, Madeira, the Azores) and to the sugar-producing islands of the Caribbean.[4] Yet the extent of these agricultural exports and the interaction of commerce and agriculture—the fact that neither could have existed without the other, that New England itself could probably not have persisted without both—has been left unexplored.[5]

Such an exploration must begin with the peculiar and highly inflationary economy which had evolved in the 1630's—that economy based upon the production of an agricultural surplus and the consumption of the surplus by new arrivals.[6] Each year, prior to 1640, five, ten, twenty ships dropped anchor in Boston harbor. Every arrival was a signal: out from the town hurried the lighters carrying merchants and shopkeepers eager to take from the ships' inventories those English goods for which their customers on shore waited; back in the same lighters came the passengers from the ships. The newcomers brought little in the way of material goods, having transformed their possessions into cash in England. They were now eager to transform that cash into new possessions in Massachusetts. From the already established settlers, they bought the Indian corn and wheat, the timber and, particularly, the cattle needed to start life anew. For their part, the established settlers hastened to their local shops to transform the newcomers' cash into English pots and pans, plows and cloth, even lace and frills. From the towns and villages to the Boston merchants who served to supply the local communities, the coin made its way, and from the merchants to the ships which came in steady procession. Where cash was not sufficient, credit was obtained; the colony was prosperous and expanding; bills would eventually be paid.

In 1640, however, with surprising suddenness, the cycle collapsed. The three years prior had been tremendously prosperous. In 1637 and 1638 the tide of immigrants had run strong. But in 1639 there had been a slackening.[7] For a time the momentum of the earlier years kept the economy operating, though fatal cracks had opened. The settlers found their surplus harder to dispose of as the market created by the flood of newcomers contracted; the store of cash in the coffers of the Boston merchants diminished as the specie contributions of the newcomers failed to keep pace with the outgoing payments for imports.[8] In 1640 the ships entering the harbor from England, encouraged by "the store of money and quick markets" of prior years, carried enlarged inventories.[9] But the diminished supply of specie would not even cover old bills, let alone permit the contracting of new ones. Shippers found the market steadily worsening through the summer and fall and grumbled over poor profits. More important was the position of the settler. The market for his surplus, contracting since the previous year, all but disappeared. He offered his produce in payment of goods and debts, but the merchants "would sell no wares but for ready money."[10] In consequence, commodity prices plummeted, wheat from seven shillings a bushel in May to four shillings in October; Indian corn from five shillings to three, then, by June of 1641, to nothing.[11] Cattle prices fell from twenty and thirty pounds sterling a head to four and five pounds. But even at this price there was no market. The very land lost value.[12] In the disaster, the possibility arose of a wholesale desertion from the Puritan commonwealth of people who could not conceive of a way to live there."The times of the Unsettled Humyrs of many mens spirits to Returne for England," John Cotton called the early 1640's; "Why should a man stay untill the house fall on his head and why continue his being ther, where in reason he shall destroy his subsistence?" wrote Thomas Hooker; and John Winthrop: "They concluded there would be no subsisting here, and accordingly they began to hasten away."[13]

The crux of the economic problem facing the settlers was the existence of an unsaleable agricultural surplus. The newcomers had constituted one market for that surplus. Now that market had been lost. The solution in this situation—when, as a Puritan rhymester put it—"men no more the Sea passe o're, and Customers are wanting"[14]—was nothing other than finding new customers at home or abroad. The leaders of the commonwealth did not realize this. Their response to their plight was dictated by prevalent economic theory which accented the position of the merchant.[15] Reduce imports—hence the encouragement given to domestic cloth manufacturing, the ironworks, the passage of a series of sumptuary laws—and increase exports—thus the renewed attempts to spur a domestic fish industry, the support given to various trading ventures[16]—and the net result would be (in their minds) a favorable flow of trade, a consequent increase in the merchants' specie and credit, a quickening of imports from England, and prosperity. That the merchants could not import unless the general populace bought and that the general populace could not buy unless it could sell the products of the countryside did not occur to them.

The finding of new customers for excess agricultural products was, therefore, accidental. In 1640 and 1641, probably through their connections with English merchants, a few men in the Bay colony became cognizant of the existence of a market for woodproducts in Spain and the Atlantic islands—merchant George Story arranging for the shipment of 8,500 clapboards in 1640, presumably to the islands; Samuel Maverick, in 1641, dealing with William Lewis of Malaga, Spain, for the sale of clapboard.[17] Undoubtedly it was through such contacts that clever traders among the men of Massachusetts learned of a market across the Atlantic for the cheap wheat and other grains glutting the Bay area. Edward Gibbons, a leading Bay merchant, was early in seeing the possibility. In October of 1641, at his urging, the General Court gave official encouragement to the preparation of a grain ship. They commanded the colonists to forego bread and cakes made of wheat flour inasmuch "as it appeareth to this Court that wheate is like to bee a staple commodity, and that a ship is withall convenient speede to bee set fourth, and fraited with wheate, for the fetching in of such forraine commodities as wee stand in need of." Little is known of the actual shipment. Presumably the various towns of the colony "adventured" their local surplus under Gibbons's direction. Presumably, too, it sailed for Spain or the islands prior to May of 1642.[18] Certainly, however, the commonwealth had struck at the heart of its problem, though its approach in limiting consumption to create an exportable surplus when a surplus already existed displays the economic ignorance of the time. Grain values, minimal in 1641, steadied in 1642, the General Court in September reflecting the market price in ordering that wheat and barley be received for taxes at four shillings a bushel, rye and pease at three shillings four pence, and Indian corn at two shillings six.[19]

In the years immediately following, the trade in agricultural products grew quickly to major proportions: woodproducts, which had first found an overseas market and were in these years a product of the agricultural community as farmers cut timber in their off season and sold it to the coopers of Boston and elsewhere to be cut and shaped into pipe staves, treenails, clapboard, and the like;[20] grains, principally wheat but including also quantities of rye, barley, dried pease, and Indian corn; and packed and salted beef. The extent of the trade can be followed in the ship arrivals and departures from the Bay.[21] In the fall following the sailing of Gibbons's grain ship, John Winthrop recorded the departure of six ships "laden with pipe staves and other commodities of this country"; four others had sailed "a little before." At least one of these vessels had initiated its voyage in the new market itself, coming from Madeira with wine specifically to pick up and return with New England produce. During the winter following, as the governor reported, the "much corn spent in setting out the ships, ketches, etc." in addition to a bad crop in 1642, caused a reversal of the earlier market glut and created a temporary scarcity of grain.[22]

Indications of voyages in 1643 are confused, but it is evident that the trade continued and grew: at least five vessels returned to Boston harbor with wine and sugar and two ships sailed. Early in 1644, the sixty-ton *Hopewell* of Boston sailed for the Canaries with a cargo of wheat-in-bulk; at least six other identifiable vessels sailed in the trade that year. The year following, the *Edmund and John* of London carrying at least 3,000 bushels of pease, wheat, and Indian corn, the *Dolphin* of London with 7,000 bushels or more, and five other identifiable vessels, made the journey.[23] During this one year, 1645, a total of some 20,000 bushels of grain valued at approximately 4,000 pounds sterling in Boston prices were exported from the commonwealth; so much indeed that the provisions market in the Canary Islands was temporarily surfeited.[24] In terms of bulk this grain equaled the exports of fish and woodproducts, hence the average cargo would conform to Andrews's formula of equal thirds. But fish, while more substantial in terms of value—between 4,000 and 10,000 pounds sterling worth being exported this year[25]—was far less to the benefit of the area as a whole. Grains profited the farmers who produced them, the local merchants who sent them on to Boston, and the Boston merchants who sold them for shipment abroad; fish, on the other hand, profited a scattering of fishermen located primarily along the northern coast, the English houses which, as Bailyn and others have pointed out, controlled the trade in this early period, and those Boston merchants acting as agents for English firms.[26] Woodproducts were to the general profit of the Bay; but, subjected to heavy freight charges and bringing low prices in comparison to bulk, they were a poor third in terms of value. In one case, for example, pipe staves brought but eighteen pounds per 1,000 delivered at Madeira. At this price (which was probably high) it would have required roughly 225,000 pipe staves to equal the value of grain exports in 1645 and as much as one-half million to equal the value of fish. Yet the average shipment seldom exceeded 10,000.[27]

Thus far and through 1646 when six identifiable vessels made the journey to the Atlantic islands and the Iberian peninsula (including the locally built *Malaga Merchant*, a 250-300-ton ship whose name proclaimed her intended trade[28]) agricultural exports flowed principally eastward across the ocean. A second outlet, in the Caribbean, was opening up however.[29] From the early 1640's Massachusetts men had been sporadically exchanging provisions for raw cotton, tobacco, indigo, and sugar, John Winthrop reporting to his son relative to the 1646 trading season that "Our Pinnaces had very good receitts." But large-scale trading began in 1647. That year West Indian ships, particularly from Barbados, appeared in Boston harbor "to trade for provisions for the belly," a plague of six months' duration having struck the islands and the settlers there having become "so intent upon planting sugar [introduced in 1641] that they had rather buy foode at very deare rates than produce it by labour."[30] Boston merchants immediately responded, shipping out grain, beef, bread, fish, and eventually live cattle and horses.[31] The following year, for the second time in the decade, grain exports from the Bay, southward and across the Atlantic, were so great as to cause a local scarcity in the commonwealth. A temporary order of the General Court prohibited the export of Massachusetts-grown grain. Prices, which had been steadily rising—wheat from four shillings a bushel to four shillings six pence in 1647—turned sharply upward during the scarcity, then fell to five shillings as the 1649 crop relieved the situation, remaining at that level into the 1650's.[32]

The trade in agricultural produce, inaugurated by Massachusetts men, was very quickly incorporated into that evolving trade network emanating from the merchant houses of England. New Englanders moving out to barter for a profitable return in the peninsula and the island markets during the early 1640's found established English merchants already there. At times they were driven to make connections with these merchants by the reluctance of foreign traders and officials to deal with them as independents. The *Hopewell* of Boston, for example, on coming to Tenerife in the Canaries in 1643 found resident English agents there and an officialdom which refused to deal unless the ship gave bond through these agents that it would not trade on to Portuguese Madeira.[33]

More frequently, however, the Massachusetts merchants sought relations with English houses and their agents, selling their produce through them in order to build up credits in England against the purchase of goods for importation into the commonwealth. Samuel Maverick's first efforts in sending clapboard to William Lewis in Spain had been to build credits through Lewis with his London supplier. Subsequently, Massachusetts men were themselves sought out by English merchants to supply New England products to the Atlantic community in return for imports.[34] By the mid-1640's the local merchants were shipping abroad in their own and English ships in payment of goods advanced to them from England. Stephen Winthrop, for example, is found in partnership with Edward Gibbons and Thomas Fowle exporting 7,000 bushels of grain, 12,000 pipe staves, 40 hogsheads of packed beef and pork, and 1,000 kintals of fish to the Canary Islands for the account of a London firm, presumably in payment of earlier shipments of cotton goods, silk, window glass, iron, pewter, brass, shoes, and nails. In 1646, three Bostonians—Barnabas Fower, James Mattock, and John Spoore—agreed to deliver 60,000 pipe staves to the waterside at Boston as payment for linen and woolen cloth dispatched to them by Bristol merchants. The following year, Nicholas Davison of Charlestown shipped pipe staves and rye to Madeira to satisfy in part his account with the estate of a London merchant. Richard Ludlow, in 1648, received goods from an English merchant at Boston on condition that he load wheat and pease aboard a vessel to be dispatched to Boston by the merchant the following year. At about the same time, merchant Thomas Breedon entered the New England scene—where eventually he would rise to great heights—with a cargo loaded by an English house at Malaga on his promise to return "wheate fish or Tobacco" in payment.[35] The West Indian trade also became involved in this Atlantic complex, though it always remained more open to enterprising persons venturing small cargoes on their own than did the Atlantic trade. In 1649, for example, Ralph Woory of Charlestown, probably acting as agent for William Peakes of London, bought 5,000 quarter-pound loaves of bread from Bostonian James Oliver, paying with bills of exchange drawn on Peakes in London; the bread was to be carried on the ship *Planter* to Barbados and sold, presumably for sugar delivered to Peakes in England.[36]

All the while, too, as the trade developed, English ships were moving into Boston harbor to seek grain on an open market, paying in English goods or bills of exchange. This was apparently the case in 1645 when a "store of linen, woollen, shoes, stockings, and other useful commodities" was brought from England and "the ships took pay in wheat, rye, peas, etc." In 1651, Hezekiah Usher, the Boston bookseller who was to establish one of the leading merchant families in the Bay, was building credits with Londoner Thomas Bell by selling wheat to Bell's agent aboard the ship *Sarah*.[37]

Direct exports to the Caribbean or across the Atlantic constituted but one outlet for agricultural produce. Another outlet was the outfitting and provisioning of ships attracted to the Bay by the facilities and cheap foodstuffs there. Begun in 1641 and 1642 when privateers began outfitting in the port prior to operating in the Caribbean and when storm and accidents at sea forced more legitimate vessels to make port in a depressed Boston, outfitting and provisioning had become a major industry by the end of the decade.[38] Then, Edward Johnson could write of the "store of Victuall both for their owne and Forreiners-ships, who resort hither for that end."[39]

The activities of John Parris, the merchant-uncle of the future mintmaster John Hull, exemplify the extent of this branch of the agricultural trade of the commonwealth. Parris, having first visited the Bay in 1642 from Madeira, eventually based his operations in Barbados and, in the late 1640's, sent ship after ship to Boston to fit and provision for slave voyages to the African coast. On one occasion, 3,698 pounds of cured beef, 4,200 quarter-pound loaves of bread, 100 bushels of pease, and a variety of other commodities were loaded aboard a Parris vessel. Again, English ships voyaging to the fishing areas of the northern coast and Newfoundland, the Atlantic islands and the Caribbean, time after time are found making Boston a port of call—in part to load New England produce, but in part to outfit and provision. In 1649, for example, the owners of the ship *Mary* of London lodged a protest against Boston workmen "for delay of time (these eight dayes) to fitt and furnish her out uppon her voyage to fyall Maderas or else where and so to Virginia." Merchants such as bookseller Usher profited greatly in the trade: Usher and a partner on one occasion providing 850 pounds sterling in "wheate pease fish and other provissions" for the crew of the ship *Castle Frigate*.[40] But the whole port community of Boston and Charlestown profited—the shipwrights, cordwinders, smiths and carpenters and wharfers who fitted and loaded the ships; the butchers who transformed cattle into packed and salted beef; the coopers who built the casks to hold it; the millers and bakers who transformed wheat into bread and biscuits; even the doctor who on one occasion treated an injured sailor.

This thriving commercial community was intimately connected to the ·

surrounding countryside. For the trade in grain and provisions necessarily stretched not only outward from the harborside but inland into the very heart of the commonwealth and even beyond to the towns of Connecticut, Rhode Island, and New Haven. The records of the internal trade between port and country are scant, but clear: settlers in the outlying towns bought goods and paid their debts and taxes in grain and other produce; local merchants were supplied with their stock from Boston and forwarded the agricultural goods they had received from their own customers as payment. Prices at various places in Massachusetts reflect the flow, increasing as commodities passed from hand to hand. In 1647, wheat brought four shillings six pence at Boston, but far in the interior at Springfield it was three shillings ten, with prices for pease and Indian corn proportionately lower; in late 1648, wheat was five shillings in the port, but in the outlying areas around Boston it could be bought directly from the farmers for four shillings eight pence.[41] The monetary expressions were only a convenience, of course, for even in Boston, as Robert Keayne commented, "the way of trade" was "not so much for ready money as for exchange," cloth, tools, pewterware, and such items from England "for Corne, Cattle and other Comodities."[42]

In this constant exchange of goods transportation was a vital consideration, and the records show an intense interest on the part of the authorities to keep open vital lines of traffic. Roads were difficult to build and maintain, but the commonwealth even in this early period tried to insist on a minimum upkeep "so as a loaden horse carrying a sack of Corne may passe"—with a lessening effect as distance from the port increased. Produce moved easily into Boston from towns just back from the coast: Dedham's inhabitants found that the capital's "coyne and commodities" lured them into making "many a long walk" with their crops, and Ipswich, at the end of the decade, was sending "many hundred quarters" of beef to the Boston market yearly, as was Waymouth, whose constable in 1655 decided that woodproducts and grains were too difficult to transport. Collecting local taxes in cattle, he drove the herd to Boston to sell. (So great, indeed, was the influx of cattle that by 1648 Boston petitioned the General Court for two fairs a year, the second exclusively "for Cattle to make provision both for or selves and shipping.") On the other hand, Sudbury, nineteen miles west of Boston, was considered too far from the "Mart Towns" by Edward Johnson in 1651, though it made possible its continued existence by taking "in Cattell of other Townes to winter." Andover, twenty miles from Boston and fifteen from Salem, suffered from the same isolation.[43] The area of adequate land transportation steadily expanded, however, and in 1660 Samuel Maverick wrote of Rehoboth: "It is not above 40 Miles from Boston, betweene which there is a Comone trade, carrying and recarrying goods by land in Cart and on Horseback."[44]

Far easier were connections by water, and in this respect Long Island Sound was the great artery of the Bay's internal trade, imported goods moving along the Sound to as far down as Fairfield on the border of New Netherlands, and New England's agricultural produce moving eastward to the Bay for transshipment into the Atlantic community. In the late

1640's, the artery branched to the north at several points; at Narragansett Bay at the eastern entrance to the Sound, at Thames River to John Winthrop, Jr.'s, New London in Pequot Country, at the Connecticut to the River Towns and William Pynchon's Springfield in the far backcountry of Massachusetts, and at New Haven. It also branched to the south to Long Island; in 1649 wheat was moving along the artery from as far west on the island as Hempstead in Dutch territory.[45] The Connecticut River Towns were the most productive points along this route. Robert Child referred to them as "exceedingly abounding in corne. . . . the fruitfullest places in all new England," and as early as 1644 and 1645 the area was dispatching many thousands of bushels of grain to Boston.[46] Farther upriver, the account books of William Pynchon of Springfield show shipments of 1,500 bushels of grain in the single year 1652.[47]

Along the coast itself were located small merchants who bought in bulk from Boston, retailed among the coves and islands of the Sound, and collected produce to be returned to Boston—men like Richard Smith of Wickford, Rhode Island, who, in April 1649, is glimpsed leaving Providence "to Newport, bound for Block Iland and Long Iland and Nayantaquit for Corne," or the Quaker merchant Nathaniel Sylvester busy several years later retailing English goods for grain, pipe staves, and cattle at Shelter Island, Rhode Island, and New London.[48] Not all such shippers bringing grain into Boston were honest. In 1655 the Massachusetts General Court, "taking into . . . consideration the complaynts of severall in reference to the abuses committed by divers seamen, who, bringinge corne from Conectecott and other places, so measure the same as by experience is found will not yeeld so much, altho presently measured agayne, by fowre or five percent," empowered the selectmen to appoint official measurers of grain.[49] That same year, too, imports of wheat into the Bay were of such magnitude as to break the five shilling per bushel price which had been maintained since 1649.[50]

Typical of the operations of small resident merchants on the great artery were those of John Winthrop, Jr., at New London, a settlement intended from the beginning for agriculture and laid down on "fruit-bearing land without rocks, arable with a goodly number of planting fields."[51] In 1649, Robert Scott, a onetime servant, a member of the First Church of Boston, and in partnership with Robert Harding a large-scale exporter of grain, forwarded a bark laden with cloth and other imports to Winthrop for resale to the New London settlers: "if you send corne" in payment, Scott's agent wrote, "mr. scott will exspeckt wheate and Rye or pease as well as Indian an equall proportion of each." The relationship between Winthrop as the local merchant and Scott as his supplier was already an established one, for Winthrop is reminded that there are two pounds seventeen shillings "Resting upon the Booke of old." The year prior, Winthrop sent "soe many fatt Cattle" to Charlestown as to satisfy a debt there. The cattle were to be dispatched on the hoof to be butchered, salted, packed, and shipped in the Bay area. In 1649, Winthrop inquired about the price of beef in Boston and was advised by his father "not to sende any for it will not yeild above 3d the li. at most."

Somewhat later the younger Winthrop is making arrangements for the pickup of cattle at the mouth of Thames River. Still later he is meeting debts by the sale of beef packed and salted at New London.[52]

The internal trade of New England—the products of the land flowing one way to the harbor at the head of Massachusetts Bay, English imports the other way to the towns and villages of the hinterland—tied New England's agricultural and commercial communities together. The outward flow of grain, cattle, and other products provided a market for the agricultural community. In the Bay commonwealth alone there were, by 1650, some 15,000 people, perhaps 3,000 families.[53] If averages hold good, each family held between twenty and thirty acres, of which between ten and twenty were in cultivation, probably three or four planted in grain earmarked to be sold and ultimately exported.[54] These three or four acres would yield sixty to 100 bushels of wheat, or twelve to twenty pounds sterling in English goods per year when exchanged with the local merchant. This constituted probably the greater part of the annual income (discounting the home consumption of farm products) of the Bay family during these years, with additional income from the sale of stock, garden produce, and the like.[55] Yet this agricultural community was absolutely dependent on the merchants of the ports who sent its products away and returned to it the necessary imports from England and elsewhere, a dependence recognized by Captain Edward Johnson when he attributed the farmers' resistance to the sporadic attempts of the authorities to promote the home-manufacture of cloth to a fear that "if the Merchants trade be not kept on foot . . . their corne and cattel will lye in their hands." The magistrates of the commonwealth, too, recognized the dependence. In 1650 they drafted a letter to their agent in England: "Wee . . . have a Competencie of Cattle of all Sorts and allso of Corne for Subsistence and Some to spare, whereby with the help of some fish here taken wee formerly have procured Clothing and other necessaries for our families by means of some Traffique in bothe Barbadoes and some other places." But if this should fail—possibly by the Dutch underpricing New England commodities—we are undone, for then "the generallitie of people are exceedingly [distressed] and in small Capacitie to Carrie through their ocasions."[56]

This dependence of the agricultural community upon the commercial community centered in Boston and Charlestown extended beyond the Bay colony, however. For the fact that through the 1640's the Bay merchants, by virtue of their exports, constituted the largest market for the agricultural products of the settlements of Narragansett Bay, Long Island Sound, and Connecticut River gave to those merchants an economic domination over southern New England which would remain unbroken, a domination recognized in the common appellation of the time, "Boston in New England."[57] Only the Massachusetts men managed to develop the broad connections in the Atlantic trading complex necessary to expedite imports and exports; hence the other settlements had always to buy from the Bay and sell to her. Only the Bay was able to establish the complex internal trade necessary to the distribution of imported goods to the hinterland. John Eliot, for example, in 1650 advised those "who ever would send any thing to any Towne in New England" to send it to Boston or Charlestown "for they are haven Townes for all New England and speedy meanes of conveyance to all places is there to be had."[58] Ultimately a small direct trade from the southern settlements to the West Indies would develop, but largely as a branch of the Massachusetts commercial system.[59]

The commercial community was, conversely, just as dependent upon the countryside. A prosperous population in the hinterland constituted an indispensable market for the goods imported by the merchants from England. But more: the agricultural products of the hinterland afforded the merchants entree into the greater world of Atlantic commerce. Agricultural products largely filled the holds of the first Massachusetts-built ships; their export introduced the merchants to the profitable commerce of the Iberian peninsula, the Atlantic islands, the Caribbean; the availability of cheap provisions attracted Atlantic shippers to Boston for outfitting, contributing immeasurably to the port's development. In the Atlantic complex where the Bay merchants were establishing themselves, their greatest asset in these years was their control of the cattle and grains and woodproducts of New England's farms and villages—their staple products.[60] Without the produce which flowed into them from the countryside and out through them to the Atlantic, they would have been as unable to purchase the all-important English imports as they had been during the depression of 1640 and 1641.[61]

Already the merchants were expanding their activities beyond the trade in agricultural produce. They were developing and controlling a domestic fishing industry and tapping the timber and fish resources of the northern coast. But in expanding their operations they were proceeding generally from the strength of the agriculturally based economy and specifically from the strength of their own trade in agricultural goods. Merchants who first entered the fish trade as agents for English houses during the 1640's—men like Valentine Hill—were equally at home in the provisions trade and—like Thomas Fowle—they regularly resorted to grain to meet their obligations when fish failed them.[62] Again, as Massachusetts men began going abroad as resident agents for New England, they went first as agents of the provisions trade. Robert Harding, for example, a onetime resident of the Bay, operated from London after 1646 but retained his connections with Bay merchants and in 1648 in partnership with Boston and Ipswich men was collecting wheat for export. Stephen and Samuel Winthrop traveled to Tenerife early in 1646 with a cargo of wheat and fish. Stephen traded along the Spanish coast (at least in part on behalf of those at home) then went on to London. Samuel remained at Tenerife briefly, then moved on to the Caribbean on the advice of his father, setting up shop for a time at Barbados, fully expecting "imployment [from] my Freinds . . . especially our New england Marchants" in receiving their produce shipments. So many New Englanders were attracted south by the provisions trade that within a few years a Barbadan street would be referred to as "the New-England street."[63]

The expanding interests of the merchants should not cloud either the agricultural basis from which their expansion developed or the continued interaction between the world of commerce and the acres of corn and meadow. For though agriculture undoubtedly declined in the villages and towns along the immediate coast as the inhabitants turned to winter fisheries after 1650, the growing population of the inland areas had no other source of income but agriculture.[64] The internal commerce in farm produce and the export of that produce continued. Even the appearance of the wheat blight which destroyed the primary agricultural export—first along the Massachusetts coast in the summer of 1663, then gradually farther west until it struck the wheat of the River Towns and New Haven in 1665[65]—did not halt it. In that very year "pork, beef, horses, and corn" were indicated among the leading exports of New England by commissioners dispatched by the Crown; in 1675 a similar report cited "horses, beef, pork, butter, cheese, flour, peas, biscuit" as major exports of the section; in 1689 an anonymous writer commented that "the other *American plantations* cannot well subsist without *New England*" inasmuch as the section was supplying them "with provisions, beef, pork, meal, fish, etc."[66]

Commerce and agriculture—interacting, interdependent: it was on this basis that the economy recovered from the depression of the early 1640's. And it was from this basis that the economy proceeded. In the countryside, prices for grains, cattle, and woodproducts rose steadily through the second decade, though never to the inflated levels of 1639. In contrast to the dark days of ten years before, the General Court could comment in 1652 on "mens outward estates . . . increasing in their hands," and one New Englander could write of his land "being grown more worth: to such value as we though it was at the hiest."[67] In the port towns the foundations of widespread operations and family fortunes were being laid down by busy merchants and artisans.

"Let me tell thee who are like to reap benefite by transporting themselves to those colonies," a pamphleteer for New England wrote in 1648: merchants "skild in commerce with forraigne nations lying near the Indies," seamen "skild in Navigation, and "Husband-men" who "are like to benefit themselves much, all sorts of cattell increasing exceedingly, and tillage prospering, that thousands of Acres are broken up yearly."[68] Here was a new formula for prosperity to replace that which had failed in 1640: farmers to produce, merchants to deal in their products, and ships to carry the products to faraway markets. In this formula the paradox of an agricultural land where the pursuits of the sea predominated—a paradox posed by historians looking at commerce and agriculture separately—disappears.

Darrett Rutman's investigation of the interrelationship between agriculture and commerce focuses on the two most important props of the New England economy. Other economic endeavors have also received historical attention. Among the more valuable studies are E. N. Hartley's Ironworks on the Saugus *(Norman, Okla., 1957) and Charles F. Carroll's* The Timber Economy of Puritan New England

(Providence, 1974). A recent study that traces the interrelationship among land, commerce, farming, and the timber industry is David Vandeventer, The Emergence of Provincial New Hampshire, 1623–1741 (Baltimore, 1976).

NOTES

1. Max Savelle, *The Foundations of American Civilization* (New York, 1942), 145; George Lee Haskins, *Law and Authority in Early Massachusetts . . .* (New York, 1960), 109.

2. The conclusions here presented are drawn in part from the research for a study of Massachusetts Bay and particularly the town of Boston, 1630-50, undertaken with the assistance of research grants from the American Council of Learned Societies and the University of Minnesota.

3. J. Franklin Jameson, ed., *Johnson's Wonder-Working Providence, 1628-1651* (New York, 1910), 69-70, 72, 96. For Boston see the various town divisions, grants, and property transfers in "Boston Town Records, 1634-1661," and "The Book of Possessions," both in City of Boston, *A Report of the Record Commissioners*, II (Boston, 1877).

4. Charles M. Andrews, *The Colonial Period of American History*, I (New Haven, 1934), 516; Bernard Bailyn, *The New England Merchants in the Seventeenth Century* (Cambridge, Mass., 1955), 83 ff.

5. The best general work on agriculture in this period is still Percy W. Bidwell and John I. Falconer, *History of Agriculture in the Northern United States 1620-1860* (Washington, 1925), 5-66, though it fails to recognize any large export of agricultural products from New England and notes (p. 42) a regular import of wheat, rye, barley, and the like into the section "not entirely due to inability to raise a sufficient supply of these grains at home, but in part at least to the realization of the advantages of specialization in fishing, trading, and shipbuilding."

6. For descriptions of the economy as it developed in the 1630's and of the depression of the early 1640's see Massachusetts Historical Society, *The Winthrop Papers* (Boston, 1929-47), III, 166-168; James Kendall Hosmer, ed., *Winthrop's Journal "History of New England," 1630-1649* (New York, 1908), I, 112; II, 6 et passim; Jameson, ed., *Johnson's Wonder-Working Providence*, 209; Marion H. Gottfried, "The First Depression in Massachusetts," *New England Quarterly*, IX (1936), 655-659; Bailyn, *New England Merchants*, 32 ff., 45-49.

7. Charles E. Banks, *The Planters of the Commonwealth . . .* (Boston, 1930), 190, 201-202. 1638 was the peak year with 3,000 arrivals, but for 1639 Banks cites only three ship arrivals. In 1640 there was a recovery in the number of immigrants, 1,575 passengers aboard ten ships. (See William B. Weeden, *Economic and Social History of New England* [Boston and New York, 1890], I, 165.) But this was too late to contribute to a recovery from the recession which had already set in. And probably the arrivals of 1640 carried less specie than they had previously. (*Winthrop Papers*, IV, 212; *New Englands First Fruits . . .* [London, 1643] as reprinted in Samuel Eliot Morison, *The Founding of Harvard College* [Cambridge, Mass., 1935], 444.) The almost complete stoppage of immigrants came in 1641.

8. Repeated warnings of the shaky condition of the economy mark the correspondence of 1639-40. See *Winthrop Papers*, IV, 112-113, 249-252; "Report of Edmund Browne" to Sir Simonds D'Ewes, Sept. 1639, in Colonial Society of Massachusetts, *Publications*, VII (Boston, 1905), 78.

9. Hosmer, ed., *Winthrop's Journal*, II, 6.

10. *Ibid.*, 17. That at least some cash transactions took place this year is illustrated by the presence of 300 pounds sterling aboard the *Mary Rose* of Bristol when she exploded and sank in the harbor, July 27, 1640.

11. Nathaniel B. Shurtleff, ed., *Records of the Governor and Company of the Massachusetts Bay in New England* (Boston, 1853-54), I, 214, 304; hereafter cited as Shurtleff, ed., *Mass. Records*. Hosmer, ed., *Winthrop's Journal*, II, 31, 92; *Winthrop Papers*, IV, 279-280, 296.

12. The highest cattle price during the inflation of the late 1630's noted by the present writer was the sale of six cows for 301 pounds sterling payable over seven years. Thomas Mayhew's mortgage to Simon Bradstreet, Sept. 29, 1638, Chamberlain Manuscripts, Boston Public Library, A.1, 1-63. The decline can be traced in Edward E. Hale and others, eds., *Note-book Kept by Thomas Lechford, Esq., Lawyer in Boston, from June 27, 1638, to July 29, 1641* (Cambridge, Mass., 1885); *Winthrop Papers*, IV; Shurtleff, ed., *Mass. Records*, I; Hosmer, ed., *Winthrop's Journal*, II. On land values see Hosmer, ed., *Winthrop's Journal*, II, 17, 19.

13. Hooker to Thomas Shepard, Nov. 2, 1640, Hutchinson Papers, State House, Boston; [Cotton] to Richard Saltonstall, ca. 1649, Cotton Papers, Boston Public Library, Boston; Hosmer, ed., *Winthrop's Journal*, II, 82. Note, too, the specific incidents of ships carrying passengers out of New England, e.g., Hosmer, ed., *Winthrop's Journal*, I, 333-335; II, 11, 33-34, 207; Thomas Lechford, *Plain Dealing; or, News from New England*, ed. J. Hammond Trumbull (Boston, 1867), 113-114; Edward Winslow, *New-Englands Salamander . . .* (London, 1647) as reprinted in Massachusetts Historical Society, *Collections*, 3d Ser., II (Cambridge, 1830), 120. Note also Winslow's comment (p. 141) on "the many thousands . . . that came from New England" and were in old England at the time of his writing.

14. *Good News from New-England . . .* (London, 1648) as reprinted in Mass. Hist. Soc., *Colls.*, 4th Ser., I (Boston, 1852), 204.

15. Joseph Dorfman, *The Economic Mind in American Civilization 1606-1865*, I (New York, 1946), 6; E. A. J. Johnson, *American Economic Thought in the Seventeenth Century* (London, 1932), 150-153.

16. On cloth, see Gottfried, "The First Depression in Massachusetts," 664-666; on the ironworks, E. N. Hartley, *Ironworks on the Saugus . . .* (Norman, Okla., 1957), 47 ff.; on the fisheries, Harold A. Innis, *The Cod Fisheries* ([Toronto], 1954), 75 ff., and Raymond McFarland, *A History of the New England Fisheries* (New York, 1911), 53-69; on fur trade, Arthur H. Buffinton, "New England and the Western Fur Trade, 1629-1675," in Col. Soc. of Mass., *Publs.*, XVIII (Boston, 1917), 160-192, and Francis X. Moloney, *The Fur Trade in New England, 1620-1676* (Cambridge, Mass., 1931).

17. Hale and others, eds., *Note-book Kept by Thomas Lechford*, 327; *A Volume Relating to the Early History of Boston Containing the Aspinwall Notarial Records From 1644 to 1651*, in Registry Department of the City of Boston, *Records Relating to the Early History of Boston*, XXXII (Boston, 1903), 71-72; hereafter cited as *Aspinwall Notarial Records*.

18. Shurtleff, ed., *Mass. Records*, I, 337; William H. Whitmore, *A Bibliographical Sketch of the Laws of the Massachusetts Colony from 1630 to 1686 . . .* (Boston, 1890), xxiii. At the same time, the making of malt out of wheat was prohibited. The order was repealed May 20, 1642.

19. Shurtleff, ed., *Mass. Records*, II, 27; *New Englands First Fruits*, 444.

20. N. Sylvester to John Winthrop, Jr., Apr. 7, 1655, in Mass. Hist. Soc., *Proceedings*, 2d Ser., IV (Boston, 1889), 274; William B. Trask and others, eds., *Suffolk Deeds* (Boston, 1880-1906), I, 122-123; *Winthrop Papers*, IV, 304-305, 311-312; for the various efforts to regulate local cutting, see "Boston Town Records," in City of Boston, *A Report of the Record Commissioners*, II, passim.

21. Figures reflecting ship arrivals and departures in Boston harbor are drawn from a shipping list for the years 1640-50 being compiled by the present writer from ship-mentions in a variety of sources, most notably *Aspinwall Notarial Records*; *Winthrop Papers*, IV, V; Hosmer, ed., *Winthrop's Journal*, II; Hale and others, eds., *Note-book Kept by Thomas Lechford*; Trask and others, eds., *Suffolk Deeds*, I, II; and Massachusetts Archives, State House, Boston.

22. Hosmer, ed., *Winthrop's Journal*, II, 85, 89, 92.

23. For the *Hopewell* see *ibid.*, 154; for the *Edmund and John* and *Dolphin*, *Aspinwall Notarial Records*, 395, 397.

24. Hosmer, ed., *Winthrop's Journal*, II, 245; *Winthrop Papers*, V, 62.

25. Robert Child to Samuel Hartlib, Dec. 24, 1645, in Col. Soc. of Mass., *Publs.*, XXXVIII (Boston, 1959), 52, estimates a catch of 10,000 pounds sterling. But see Hosmer, ed., *Winthrop's Journal*, II, 42, 321—300,000 fish sent to market in 1642 (approximately 7,500 kintals worth about 6,750 pounds) and 4,000 pounds sterling worth taken in local fisheries during the winter season 1646-47.

26. Despite the occasional claims of writers on the subject—e.g., Innis's quoting with approval (in *Cod Fisheries*, 76) C. L. Woodbury's 1880 statement that "it was the winter fishery that placed on our coasts a class of permanent consumers, and gave to agriculture the possibility of flourishing. . . . It . . . gave to the industrious the great boon of independence, the foundation of character in the individual, and in the State. Agriculture followed with halting steps where it led the way"—the factual evidence presented by Innis, McFarland, Bailyn, and others fails to show the existence of any large fishing operations in southern New England or extensive profit to the settlers of the Bay during the first two decades. On the contrary, there is a great deal of evidence indicating that the fisheries brought very little profit to the colony.

27. *Aspinwall Notarial Records*, 244-245. This was in 1649. In 1646 a shipment brought 14 pounds per 1,000 delivered to the ship at Boston; in 1648, pipe staves were used to satisfy a debt on the basis of 3 pounds per 1,000. *Ibid.*, 47, 125. With regard to freight charges, note the shipment of 270 pounds sterling worth of pipe staves in 1646 at a charge of 91 pounds 16 shillings. *Ibid.*, 47. The same was true of other woodproducts—bolts, shaken casks, treenails.

28. *Ibid.*, 46, 47, 180-181, 403-404.

29. Contacts southward had existed during the 1630's, but were not of great importance. Hosmer, ed., *Winthrop's Journal*, I, 126, 222, 260, et passim; *Winthrop Papers*, III, 253, 450; Hale and others, eds., *Note-book Kept by Thomas Lechford*, 46-47.

30. *Winthrop Papers*, V, 161, 172.

31. See, e.g., *Aspinwall Notarial Records*, 80, 83-84, 140-141, 177-178; Trask and others, eds., *Suffolk Deeds*, I, 106; Hosmer, ed., *Winthrop's Journal*, II, 346. Similarly, a Virginia trade was developing through the 1630's and 1640's, though it too became a major factor only around 1647. See Hosmer, ed., *Winthrop's Journal*, I, 64 et passim; *Records of the Court of Assistants of the Massachusetts Bay: 1630-1692* (Boston, 1901-28), II, 25; *Winthrop Papers*, II, 337-338; III, 31, 156, 255, 276, 345; Virginia Colonial Records Survey Project, *Report No. 707*, 1; *Aspinwall Notarial Records*, 115-116, 236-238. By 1647, of 31 ships in Virginia at one time, 7 were New England vessels. *A New Description of Virginia* (London, 1649) in Mass. Hist. Soc., *Colls.*, 2d Ser., IX (Boston, 1832), 118.

32. Hosmer, ed., *Winthrop's Journal*, II, 341; Shurtleff, ed., *Mass. Records*, II, 215, 286; III, 212, 245, 359; *Winthrop Papers*, V, 346.

33. Hosmer, ed., *Winthrop's Journal*, II, 154.

34. The nature of the developing relationships between New England and English merchants is amply explored in the early chapters of Bailyn's *New England Merchants*.

35. *Aspinwall Notarial Records*, 75, 137, 202, 379-380, 394, 397.

36. *Ibid.*, 225.

37. *Ibid.*, 381; Hosmer, ed., *Winthrop's Journal*, II, 245.

38. Hosmer, ed., *Winthrop's Journal*, II, 55-56, 57, 153. Note, too, that in restricting the use of grain in 1642 prior to Gibbons's grain ship, the General Court exempted the making and selling of "bisket of wheate meale for the use of ships." (Shurtleff, ed., *Mass. Records*, I, 337.)

39. Jameson, ed., *Johnson's Wonder-Working Providence*, 71.

40. *Aspinwall Notarial Records*, 210, 285-287; Trask and others, eds., *Suffolk Deeds*, I, 45. Usher seems to have supplied the "payroll" for the ship's crew, receiving payment in bills of exchange drawn on London.

41. Mason A. Green, *Springfield, 1636-1886* . . . (Springfield, Mass., 1888), 95; Shurtleff, ed., *Mass. Records*, II, 215; *Aspinwall Notarial Records*, 188-189. The cost of transportation necessitated a part, but not all, of the differential.

42. "The last will and testament of me, Robert Keayne . . . ," in City of Boston, *A Report of the Record Commissioners*, X (Boston, 1886), 12.

43. County of Suffolk, *Records of the Court of Assistants*, II, 84 et passim. The subject of roads and bridges is continually stressed here and in Shurtleff, ed., *Mass. Records*, I, II, and III, passim; Jameson, ed., *Johnson's Wonder-Working Providence*, 96, 179, 196, 249; Petition of Nicholas Morton, late constable of Waymouth, Nov. 2, 1655, Photostats, Box 7, Mass. Hist. Soc.; Petition of the town of Boston to the General Court, ca. Oct. 1648, Massachusetts Archives, CXIX.

44. Samuel Maverick, "A Briefe Discription of New England and the Severall Townes therein . . . ," ca. 1660, in Mass. Hist. Soc., *Proc.*, 2d Ser., I (Boston, 1885), 243-244.

45. *Winthrop Papers*, V, 353; *Aspinwall Notarial Records*, 170, 202, 240, 386-388.

46. Robert Child to Samuel Hartlib, Dec. 24, 1645, in Col. Soc. of Mass., *Publs.*, XXXVIII, 51. The River Towns "the last yeare . . . spared 20000 bushell [of corn], and have already this yeare sent to the bay 4000 bushell at least."

47. Bidwell and Falconer, *Agriculture*, I, 12; Sylvester Judd, *History of Hadley . . .* (Springfield, Mass., 1905), 368.

48. *Winthrop Papers*, V, 326,; letters of Sylvester to Winthrop, Jr., 1654-55, in Mass. Hist. Soc., *Proc.*, 2d Ser., IV, 271-274.

49. Shurtleff, ed., *Mass. Records*, III, 375.

50. *Ibid.*, 394. At the time, the General Court temporarily barred imports of malt, meal flour, wheat, barley, biscuit, beer, and salted beef to protect local farmers from the competition of other areas of southern New England.

51. William R. Carlton, "Overland to Connecticut in 1645: A Travel Diary of John Winthrop, Jr.," *New Eng. Qtly.*, XIII (1940), 505.

52. *Winthrop Papers*, V, 240, 311, 314, 330-331, 373. On Scott see Manuscript Records of the First Church of Boston, Mass. Hist. Soc. copy, under date of Dec. 15, 1633; *Aspinwall Notarial Records*, 145-146, 188-189, 405.

53. Population figures for the colony vary, that in the text being calculated on the basis of ship arrivals to 1643—approximately 200; the average number of passengers carried computed from the passenger lists in Charles E. Banks, *Planters of the Commonwealth*—84; less estimated numbers of those returning to England or moving on to the settlements in Connecticut and Rhode Island—approximately 3,000 by 1638 according to a "Petition of Planters in Conecticut," Bancroft Transcripts, New England, I, 337-[342], New York Public Library, New York; plus a calculated natural increase to 1650. See Evarts B. Greene and Virginia D. Harrington, *The American Population Before the Federal Census of 1790* (New York, 1932), 12-13.

54. For average landholdings and land utilization see Bidwell and Falconer, *Agriculture*, 38; Jameson, ed., *Johnson's Wonder-Working Providence*, 154. These averages agree with actual property descriptions available in various town and probate records, though some extremely large holdings—e.g. Thomas Dexter of Lynn with 600 acres, 80 of which were "plowed up" (Trask and others, eds., *Suffolk Deeds*, I, 69)—and some extremely small holdings—e.g. "Bostian Ken Commonly called Bus Bus Negro of Dorchester" who, in 1656, was raising $4^1{}_2$ acres of wheat (*ibid.*, II, 297)—are in evidence.

55. For agricultural yield see Thomas Jefferson Wertenbaker, *The Puritan Oligarchy . . .* (New York and London, 1947), 4, which gives the English yield at 10 bushels of wheat per acre; John Winthrop's exaggerated estimate to the Earl of Warwick, ca. Sept. 1644, *Winthrop Papers*, IV, 492, of 30 to 40 bushels per acre; the General Court's underestimate of 6 to 8 bushels per acre in its draft of a letter to Edward Winslow, ca. 1650, Massachusetts Archives, CVI; and the 18th-century figure of 20 bushels in Lyman Carrier, *The Beginnings of Agriculture in America* (New York, 1923), 150. Reversing the figures in the text and multiplying the average yield by the number of families gives 18,000 to 30,000 bushels of wheat exported per year at the end of the decade, not an overly high estimate in view of the 20,000 bushels exported in 1645. That the great bulk of wheat grown was exported is indicated by Martha Johanna Lyon's comment to John Winthrop, Jr., Mar. 23, 1649 (*Winthrop Papers*, V, 323) that the use of wheat flour was above ordinary people. The best descriptions of the New England family farm unit are those of Wertenbaker in *Oligarchy* and *The First Americans 1607-1690* (New York, 1927), 56 ff.; of New England farm practices, Robert R. Walcott, "Husbandry in Colonial New England," *New Eng. Qtly.*, IX (1936), 218-252.

56. Jameson, ed., *Johnson's Wonder-Working Providence*, 211; Draft of a letter from the General Court to Edward Winslow in England, ca. 1650, Massachusetts Archives, CVI.

57. John Clark, *Ill Newes from New-England . . .* (London, 1652), reprinted in Mass. Hist. Soc., *Colls.*, 4th Ser., II (Boston, 1854), 23; Albert Matthews, "The Name 'New England' as Applied to Massachusetts," in Col. Soc. of Mass., *Publs.*, XXV (Boston, 1924), 382-390.

58. Letter to [?], ca. Spring, 1650, in Mass. Hist. Soc., *Proc.*, 2d Ser., II (Boston, 1886), 50. See also the "Answers of the General Court of Connecticut to Certain Queries of the Lords of the Committee of Colonies," July 15, 1680, in Mass. Hist. Soc., *Colls.*, 1st Ser., IV (Boston, 1795), 220-223. The smaller towns attempted to effect direct connections with the Atlantic community during the 1640's but failed.

59. For example, the position of Peleg Sanford of Rhode Island in the Hutchinson family complex, sketched by Bailyn, *New England Merchants*, 88-90.

60. Jameson, ed., *Johnson's Wonder-Working Providence*, 246-247; Samuel Danforth, *Almanac for 1648* (Cambridge, Mass., 1648), under November.

61. At which time the General Court had spurred on shipbuilding out of fear that the lack of returns would dissuade English shippers from making the colony a port of call.

62. *Aspinwall Notarial Records*, 8, 9.

63. William L. R. Marvin, "Robert Harding," *Bostonian Society Publications*, VI (Boston, 1910), 127-128; *Aspinwall Notarial Records*, 188-189; *Winthrop Papers*, V, 62-64, 97-98, 163, 320-321; "The Diaries of John Hull . . . ," in American Antiquarian Society, *Archaelogia Americana*, III (Worcester, Mass., 1857), 235.

64. Note the petition to the General Court of the inhabitants of the town of Lynn, ca. Oct. 27, 1648: "Wee wold not envy our neighbour townes which are of the risinge hand by tradinge or other wayes[.] we rather wish theyr prosperity[.] but for our selves we are neither fitted for or inured to any such course of trade but must awayt Gods blessing alone upon our Lands and Cattell." Massachusetts Archives, C.

65. "The Diaries of John Hull," 208, 210, 213, 218.

66. Noel Sainsbury, ed., *Calendar of State Papers, Colonial Series, America and West Indies, 1661-1668* (London, 1880), 346; *1675-1767* (London, 1893), 221; "A brief Relation of the Plantation of New England . . . 1689," in "Hutchinson Papers," Mass. Hist. Soc., *Colls.*, 3d Ser., I (Boston, 1825), 98.

67. Draft "Declaration concerning the advancement of learning in New Engl: By the genrall Court," Oct. 1652, and "A Replye to the resenes of Mr Philop Nelson" by Richard Dommer, May 1656, Massachusetts Archives, LVIII, and XV (B).

68. *Good News from New-England*, 218.

PART FOUR

CHALLENGES TO ZION

Every society at one time or another confronts internal criticism and disruption. How such challenges are handled tells much about the character and values of the society and helps to determine how posterity will judge it. The Puritans' determination to exclude those who were clearly unsympathetic to their basic tenets and to expel those who challenged the orderliness of the Bible Commonwealths has done much to tarnish their reputation among scholars and the general public.

No sooner had the Puritans established a foothold in New England than they exercised what they considered a moral and legal right—the former decreed by God, the latter by their charter—to eject overt dissenters. The Puritans' sense of community and mission would tolerate no threat to the success of their experiment. (Minor differences over doctrine and the governance of the church were another matter; there the permissible variety was wide.) The laws of Massachusetts restricted immigration to persons acceptable to the magistrates, and freemanship in the colony was limited to church members. When undesirables did somehow find their way into the Bay Colony, they were, if incorrigible, banished.

As early as 1629 Governor John Endecott sent several contrary-minded settlers home to England. In the next several decades Massachusetts and the Plymouth, Connecticut, and New Haven colonies expelled scores of real or potential troublemakers. The first prominent outcast was Roger Williams, a Puritan preacher whose religious and secular views often shifted during his long and productive life. Until the mid-nineteenth century most scholarly treatments of Williams portrayed him as a proponent of religious liberty who was unjustifiably persecuted by the narrow-minded Massachusetts authorities. More recently, studies of Williams's mind and rhetoric—especially by Perry Miller (*Roger Williams: His Contribution to the American Tradition* [Indianapolis, 1953]), Alan Simpson ("How Democratic Was Roger Williams?" *William and Mary Quarterly*, series 3, XIII [1956]), and Edmund S. Morgan (*The Puritan Dilemma: The Story of John Winthrop* [Boston, 1958]) and *Roger Williams: The Church and the State* [New York, 1967])—have placed Williams's disputes with his contemporaries in the context of seventeenth-century thought and the realities of the Puritan experiment. Williams emerges from these studies as no less admirable, perhaps, than in the earlier estimates, but his expulsion is no longer seen as a case of simple intolerance. His attack on the validity of the Massachusetts charter and his advocacy of Separatism threatened the colony's survival.

9 | CHURCH AND STATE IN SEVENTEENTH-CENTURY MASSACHUSETTS: ANOTHER LOOK AT THE ANTINOMIAN CONTROVERSY

RONALD D. COHEN

Perhaps the most complex instance of Puritan efforts to maintain civil and religious order is the case of Anne Hutchinson. She too has traditionally been pictured as a blameless victim of Puritan bigotry, exacerbated by the magistrates' contempt for an outspoken woman. In the late 1930s Edmund S. Morgan's "The Case Against Anne Hutchinson" (New England Quarterly, X [1937]) *and subsequently his* The Puritan Dilemma *(cited above), viewed the Hutchinsonians as a serious threat to the colony, especially to its theological integrity. Later, James F. Maclear's, " 'The Heart of New England Rent': The Mystical Element in Early Puritan History"* (Mississippi Valley Historical Review, XLII [1956] *stressed a point too often overlooked: that Anne Hutchinson's theological views were well within the spectrum of Puritan pietistic thought. In the early 1960s Emory Battis* (Saints and Sectaries: Anne Hutchinson and the Antinomian Controversy . . . [Chapel Hill, 1962]) *saw the threat much differently. According to Battis, Mrs. Hutchinson, somewhat cranky from menopausal complications, became a rallying point for a business-oriented faction that sympathized with her attacks on clergymen whose doctrines were antithetical to mercantile aspirations. More recently Ronald D. Cohen, in the following selection, has assessed Hutchinson and her followers in terms of their potential threat to civil order.*

The Erastian quality of church-state relations in seventeenth-century Massachusetts has been both damned and defended by historians. Recently, there has been a basic consensus in supporting the colony government's involvement in ecclesiastical affairs, viewing it as necessary in order to protect and insure congregational purity. Civil interference in religious affairs was not a violation of the ideals of the colony's founders, but in fact the only way they knew to accomplish their goal of establishing a city upon a hill composed of individual groupings of the elect. It is possible, however, to approach the government's ecclesiastical interests from a different angle. Such involvement was necessary to protect civil stability. The state, not the religious structure, was of paramount importance, and most civil actions were channeled primarily towards insuring the viability of the former, not the sanctity of the latter.

The Antinomian controversy provides us with a convenient laboratory in which to understand the driving impulse of the Massachusetts government to control ecclesiastical affairs for the sake of its own welfare. The common view is that the official response to the activities of Anne Hutchinson and her followers was essentially abstract in nature—concerned with conflicting notions of theology—and designed to enforce congregational purity.[1] This is in part true, for differences of religious opinion were a vital factor throughout the controversy, but by concentrating upon such matters historians have glossed over the dispute's central ingredient: the colony's search, not for religious uniformity, but for civil stability. And with the suppression of the Antinomians temporary success, of sorts, was achieved.

By 1637 a combination of past and present experience, Puritan ideals of the "good society," internal and external threats to colony stability, rendered Bay colony authorities incapable of tolerating excessive deviant behavior. It was not theoretical Puritan narrowmindedness that motivated John Winthrop and his colleagues to suppress the Antinomian heresy. Rather, they acted upon the sincere (and perhaps realistic) belief that their great experiment, the establishment of a godly, viable society in the New World wilderness, would crumble about them if the activities of the Hutchinsonians were not stemmed. Indeed, what is significant is not that the authorities responded as they did, but that the penalties inflicted were so mild. Such leniency is explicable, but only after the central controversy is put into proper context.[2]

. . .

If a wilderness environment seemed ideal as the setting for an experiment in social harmony and the successful practice of covenant theology, it also made harmonious communities imperative. According to Roderick Nash, the new surroundings not only held terrors and hardships for the colonies, but even provided them the opportunity "to behave in a savage or bestial manner." Such wilderness perils could only be combated by group action. Winthrop early recognized this added necessity when he warned his fellow adventurers that in order to insure prosperity, "wee must be knitt together in this worke as one man, wee must entertaine each other in brotherly Affeccion, wee must be willing to abridge our selves of our superfluities, for the supply of others necessities, wee must uphold a familiar Commerce together in all meekenes, gentlenes, patience and liberallity." Thus in the end their English experiences, their belief in the efficacy and binding nature of the social covenant, and the environmental dangers of the New World all combined to produce in the founders of Massachusetts an overwhelming desire to erect closely knit, socially harmonious, relatively homogeneous communities, dedicated to achieving earthly felicity and abiding by the Word of God. Discord (and dispersal) would destroy all.[3]

While dedication to the community was expected of all who settled within the Massachusetts Bay Company's jurisdiction, Winthrop and his colleagues were not so naive as to believe that deviant behavior would not be enountered. "Sathan," they knew, would bend "his forces against us," entrapping the weak in spirit. In their religious ethos, they would have to contend with the centrifugal force of an inherent individualism which one historian has called "the revolutionary dynamic contained in

English Protestantism." Moreover, the Massachusetts experiment was destined to include the regenerate and the reprobate alike, as Winthrop was well aware. This was to be no pure society, no exclusive haven for God's anointed. It was idle to think that any screening process, even if rigidly enforced, could winnow absolutely the wheat from the chaff, and so the attempt was never really made.[4]

. . .

Once past the initial problems of settlement and organization, the Bay colony did not experience grave internal problems until the middle years of the first decade. As prosperity waxed the Bay colonists "began to forget their Poverty, and verily could Purity, Peace and Plenty run all in one channell, Gods people here should have met with none other," wrote Edward Johnson, "but the still waters of Peace and Plenty for back and belly soone contract much mudde."[5] The Captain was referring to the plethora of difficulties that beset the colony beginning in 1634. Ostensible colony harmony began to crack when the freemen demanded an institutionalized voice in guiding colony affairs. Winthrop and the assistants gave in and permitted them to elect deputies from the separate towns, thereby resolving the first in a long series of controversies between the freemen and the more privileged assistants. In this same year an increasing influx of Englishmen necessitated stricter control of the population in order to insure that the newcomers would be dedicated to the ideal of community solidarity. An oath was required of all nonenfranchised males "of or above the age of twenty yeares" (later lowered to sixteen), obliging them to promise to obey all laws and "indeavor . . . to advance the peace & wellfaire of this body pollitique, and . . . seeke to devert & prevent whatsoever may tende to the ruine or damage thereof." Those who refused were subject to banishment. Freemen, who could be chosen only by the General Court from among church members, were required to take a similar oath. Originally the General Court had attempted to control immigration, but the growing magnitude of this duty soon made it evident that it could only be performed satisfactorily by the towns. They were eager to try. As Ipswich's Nathaniel Ward wrote in late 1635, "our Towne of late but somewhat too late have bene carefull on whome they bestowe lotts, being awakned therto by the confluence of many ill and doubtfull persons, and by their behaviour since they came in drinking and pilferinge." But the towns could not help but be remiss in their duty, for the previous trickle of newcomers had now reached flood proportions, and by early 1636 the colony was threatened seriously by heterogeneity.[6]

In Puritan Massachusetts church affairs were all but indistinguishable from civil affairs, and what affected one affected the other. Fearing religious anarchy, particularly after the Roger Williams affair (he was banished in October 1635), the Bay colony's congregations attempted to close ranks in order to prevent their own shattering. Evidence of saving grace, a most stringent requirement, soon became a necessary qualification for church membership; in February 1636 the members of the Boston congregation renewed their convenant, reaffirming their commitment "to the discipline and government of Christ in his Church"; and the following month the General Court decreed that it would not "approve of any such companyes of men as shall henceforthe joyne in any pretended way of church fellowshipp, without they shall first acquainte the magistrates, & the elders of the greater parte of the churches in this jurisdiction, with their intentions, & have their approbation herein.[7] Discipline and order were becoming increasingly necessary and desirable, but increasingly harder to accomplish.

While the colony was attempting to prevent disharmony and even chaos from entering by the front door, difficulties of a different sort were entering (or rather exiting) by the rear, further exacerbating colony frustration. For a variety of reasons, among them religious, economic, and personal, individuals and even entire towns began to seek relocation, first within the colony's confines, then soon beyond its vague boundaries. Colony authorities panicked, viewing population dispersal as destructive of community solidarity and strength. As they explained to Newtown's inhabitants, who were on the verge of removal to Connecticut, "in point of conscience, they ought not to depart from us, being knit to us in one body, and bound by oath to seek the welfare of this commonwealth." The crisis was temporarily averted, but in 1635 the colony could not prevent the opening of the floodgates of dispersal as groups from Watertown, Dorchester, and Newtown relocated along the Connecticut River far to the west. Helpless to prevent the exodus, Massachusetts yet attempted to retain nominal jurisdiction over the Connecticut River settlements. Anxious to keep their distance, however, the new towns were virtually independent within a year.[8]

Threatened from within, the Bay colony also encountered dangers from without, which further necessitated cohesion and solidarity. Since its founding the colony had been under scrutiny from those in England anxious "to pick a hole in your coats," and in 1634 a Commission for Regulating Plantations was organized within the king's Privy Council to reduce the colony's independence. Fearful that England might now "compel us, by force, to receive a new governor, and the discipline of the church of England, and the laws of the commissioners," Massachusetts resolved to strengthen further its fortifications, a move given divine sanction by the ministers in January 1635. Two months later a committee of eleven was deputed "to dispose of all millitary affaires whatsoever," as well as "to imprison or confine any that they shall judge to be enemyes to the commonwealth, & such as will not come under commaund or restrainte . . . it shalbe lawfull for the said commissioners to putt such persons to death."[9] In England, meanwhile, the attack upon the charter temporarily ground to a halt, then sprang to life in the spring of 1637. The issue came to a head with the successful nullification of the charter in the Court of King's Bench and the appointment of Sir Ferdinando Gorges, the colony's long-time foe, as royal governor of New England. Gorges never reached the New World and the charter remained safe in Boston, but as late as 1639 there lingered the threat of English intervention. During the period of gravest danger, 1634-1637, the Bay colony remained constantly alert and expectant, one colonist writing in late 1636 or early 1637 that they were "like to have warrs the next yeere with old

England."[10] In the face of such a threat, and considering their domestic broils, colony authorities naturally began to rely more upon coercion—as evinced by the power given the military affairs committee—rather than persuasion in order to maintain internal solidarity.

Disquieted by the news from England, Bay colonists were preoccupied further by an external danger from still another, and closer, quarter. The Pequot Indians of Connecticut had killed their first white victims in 1634. A peace was soon established with Massachusetts, but it was fraught with difficulties. By the spring of 1637 a full-scale war was in progress. . . . [11]

If we accept the contention that Massachusetts was in a precarious position by the summer of 1637, it might be argued that colony authorities were yet not justified in using what are currently regarded to be repressive measures—excommunication, disfranchisement, and banishment—to still the Hutchinsonians. A lenient response might have been more ameliorative. However, to place the Hutchinsonians' activities and convictions into their contemporary context will reveal their apparent threat to colony unity, a unity sanctioned by theory and practice and one that had to be maintained vigorously. In 1636 Bay colony authorities had come upon a forked road, the right branch of which led to a society in which deviancy would be leniently rebuked, the left veering towards the harsher suppression of nonconformity. John Winthrop initially advocated mildness, arguing "that in the infancy of plantation, justice should be administered with more lenity than in a settled state, because people were then more apt to transgress, partly of ignorance of new laws and orders, partly through oppression of business and other straits." But his colleagues, and subsequently Winthrop himself, chose the left fork, contending "that strict discipline, both in criminal offences and in martial affairs, was more needful in plantations than in a settled state, as tending to the honor and safety of the gospel.[12] Hereafter deviants would scarcely be trifled with.

The unique quality of the Hutchinsonian cause was that it pervaded many different aspects of Massachusetts society, everywhere undermining communal solidarity, everywhere disrupting ostensible colony harmony. "Yea, they employed their distinctions about a 'covenant of works,' and a 'covenant of grace,' at so extravagant a rate, as threatned a subversion to all the peaceable order in the colonies," Cotton Mather later commented. "The contention spread itself even into families, and all private and smaller societies, who were to be accounted under a 'covenant of works,' and so enemies unto the Lord Jesus Christ; and who were *not!* . . . The disturbance proceeded from thence into all the general affairs of the publick . . . and the magistrates began to be condemned as being of a *legal spirit*, and having therewithal a tang of Antichrist in them; nor could the ordering of town-lots, or town-rates, or any meetings whatsoever, escape the confusions of this controversie." Mather's account agreed substantially with contemporary opinion, which lamented "their boldnesse, pride, insolency, alienations from their old and dearest friends, the disturbances, divisions, contentions they raised amongst us, both in Church and State, and in families, setting division betwixt husband and wife." And only recently Darrett Rutman has written that they were "threatening the very foundations of society. Challenging magistrates and ministers alike, they had opened the door to a thrusting aside of all distinctions of birth, wealth, education.[13]

While the Hutchinsonians were a pervasive corrupting influence, there were a few specific areas in which their particularism appeared especially corrosive and dangerous to colony stability. For example, when the General Court attempted in May 1637 to regain control over immigration, a power it had relinquished to the towns a few years earlier, by stipulating "that no towne or person shall receive any stranger, resorting hither with intent to reside in this jurisdiction," without the approbation "of some one of the counsell, or of two other of the magistrates," its action was challenged immediately by Hutchinsonians William Coddington and former governor Henry Vane. Their criticism stemmed from their pique that the law was designed to screen out their sympathizers and, according to Vane, from a divergent concept of the relationship between the individual and colony authority—indeed, this was the heart of the whole Antinomian controversy. For Winthrop (and his colleagues) "the nature of such an incorporation [into a commonwealth] tyes every member thereof to seeke out and entertaine all means that may conduce to the wellfare of the bodye, and to keepe off whatsoever doth appeare to tend to theire damage." The commonweal came first, the individual second. Winthrop decried those who championed individualism under the guise of defending the sanctity of higher laws and who would disclaim the authority of their elected officials. Vane, on the other hand, believed that "members of a common wealth may not seeke out all meanes, that may conduce to the wellfare of the body, but all lawful and due meanes, according to the charter they hold by, either from God or the King, or from both." In using such rhetoric, Vane was stripping Massachusetts of its precious sovereignty and ostensible cohesiveness and fomenting anarchy by absolving the citizens of their allegiance to the colony government if it transgressed the laws of God or the English crown, both of which had prior claim to their loyalty. And he was propounding these views at a time when colony authorities still felt the hot breath of English intervention on their necks. In response, Winthrop could only add that "better it is some member should suffer the evill they bring upon themselves, than that, by indulgence towards them, the whole familye of God in this countrey should be scattered, if not destroyed.[14]

If the Antinomians seemed to weaken colony unity and its position in regard to England, they also disrupted directly its attempts to subdue the Pequot uprising. "Now the Lord be pleased to raise up the publick spirits of his servants (and where they are not to create them) that every heart and head and hand may be stirring and working in this case," John Higginson wrote from Saybrook at the height of the Pequot disturbance; "for the strength and sinnewes of these warres I take to lye in the combined abilities and united hearts and hands of all the servants of the Lord etc. (To omit that it cannot be expected that ever warres should prosper abroad, if civill [nay worse and religious] dissentions abound at home) yet all pertaking in the good and benifit of peace and in the danger and damage of a common warre should also be every way enlarged to their utmost for the procuring and preserving the one, removing and preventing of the other."[15] Higginson was only stating the obvious, that internal broils were dangerously debilitating during wartime. But he was also a prophet, for after the Massachussetts General Court voted in May 1637 to raise 160 soldiers for an expedition against the Pequots, appointing the Reverend John Wilson of the Boston congregation—the Hutchinsonians' archenemy—expedition chaplain, Boston "sent not a member, but one or two whom they cared not to be rid of, and but a few others, and those of the most refuse sort, and that in such a carelesse manner, as gave great discouragement to the service." Fortunately, they were not needed, for Connecticut troops dealt the Pequots a crushing blow in mid-May. But, as Emery Battis has noted, "had the Indian peril been greater, Boston's scruples might have endangered the existence of the entire colony."[16] Thus did the Hutchinsonians drive another nail into their coffin.

Winthrop and his colleagues' English and Puritan penchant for communal solidarity, reinforced by current needs of maintaining a united colony front against internal and external disintegrative forces, in the end convinced them "that those brethren [the Antinomians], etc., were so divided from the rest of the country in their judgment and practice, as it could not stand with the public peace, that they should continue amongst us." During the fall session of the Court, therefore, punishments were meted out, for "two so opposite parties could not contain in the same body, without apparent hazard of ruin to the whole."[17]

Bay colony authorities, especially John Winthrop, felt that their response to the Antinomians was eminently rational and realistic, necessarily preserving colony cohesiveness and strength. Recent sociological findings seem to vindicate such views. Kai Erikson, for one, has used his knowledge of the sociology of deviance to propound a unique interpretation of the Antinomian controversy. It was, he concludes, essentially functional, a necessary step towards delineating the Bay colony's dedication to a structured society free from individualism.[18]

More pertinent are Lewis Coser's studies of the functions of social conflict. Not concerned with the Antinomian controversy per se, Coser's conclusions yet are important because they make conflict a vital ingredient in promoting the growth and well-being of society. For example, he asserts that "groups engaged in continued struggle with the outside tend to be intolerant within. . . . Their social cohesion depends upon total sharing of all aspects of group life and is reinforced by the assertion of group unity against the dissenter." Moreover, he goes on to state that "the evocation of an outer enemy or the invention of such an enemy strengthens social cohesion that is threatened from within." Thus, external conflict tightens group solidarity, and conversely, group unity is vitally necessary in order to combat external threats. Significantly, John Higginson had foreshadowed both conclusions. He had not only warned Winthrop of the dangerous effects of internal disharmony during wartime, but earlier in the same letter opined that perhaps "the Lord" sent "the Indians upon his servants, to make them cleave more close togither, and prize each other, to prevent contentions of Brethren which may prove as hard to break as Castle barres, and stop their now beginning breaches before they be as the letting out of many waters that cannot be gathered in againe, etc."[19] During the Antinomian controversy both factors came into play, each reinforcing the other. Without such a resolution of is problems, Massachusetts might have fragmented, destroying root and branch Winthrop's "Citty upon a Hill."

It was necessary for Bay colony authorities to clamp down upon the Hutchinsonians, that much is certain. But if they were attempting in the only way they knew how, to prevent chaos and uphold the dictates of covenant theology, it was also true that their social and church covenants prevented them from inflicting undue punishments upon their neighbors. Although historians have been quick to castigate the Puritans for their severity, in the case of the Hutchinsonians the sentences were mild indeed. Three *were* banished, but only three, a mere eight disfranchised, and numerous others only disarmed; excommunication was also used sparingly, only four of Anne's hard-core followers suffering this ignominy. And of those who were punished many, including the banished William Aspinwall and John Wheelwright, later recanted and were pardoned.[20]

Generally speaking, Massachusetts used both civil and ecclesiastical punishments lightly and was quick to forgive. Recently, Jules Zanger has discovered that while the General Court might have handed out "relatively heavy penalties, heavy fines in particular," it frequently remitted them for one reason or another, thereby creating "a deceptive appearance of severity." Confession and repentance were usually enough to obtain remission. The same held true for ecclesiastical censure or excommunication. "Because an excommunicate person was always potentially penitent and might again become a church member in good standing, he was not to be treated as an enemy but as a brother in need of admonition, never as a 'common Sinner' who had always been outside the Church," Emil Oberholzer has written. "If he repented and offered an acceptable confession, the excommunicate was restored to church fellowship . . . for he had never ceased to be a member, although he had temporarily forfeited the privileges of membership."[21] Contrition, not punishment, was the congregation's goal, and all effort was made to bring the sinner back into the fold. Neither in secular nor sacral affairs were the Puritans a vindictive lot.

The Hutchinsonian controversy is a good example of the desire of both church and state to forgive and forget. Aside from the fact that the colony's troubles were diminishing by early 1638—internal cooperation had been ostensibly achieved in creating a phalanx against the Hutchinsonians and the Indian problem was solved—the basic reason why the Puritans were lenient was that they still felt themselves bound tightly by their covenants, church and social. A covenant was a two-way street, preventing the authorities from tolerating dissent in their zeal to maintain unity, but also predisposing them to labor to keep the individual within the bounds of the covenant. Mass banishment, disfranchisement, or excommunication would be as debilitating as uncontrolled deviancy, for neither would maintain the colony's organic unity. Massachusetts knew the dangers of fostering a class of pariahs, just as it knew that emigration sapped its strength. Moreover, the Puritans could not turn rigorously upon their long-standing friends and neighbors, for in so doing they would only be exposing the downfall of their attempt to establish a "Citty upon a Hill," a godly society in which harmony was generated from within, not imposed from without.

When, for instance, in November 1637 many of Anne's following were disarmed for having signed a petition defending the Reverend John Wheelwright, the General Court was also quick to stipulate "that if any that are to bee disarmed acknowledg their sinn in subscribing the seditious libell, or do not justify it, but acknowledg it evill to two magistrates, they shalbee thereby freed from delivering in their armes according to the former order." Forgiveness "was easily granted," commented one contemporary, "and their offence with a loving admonition remitted." Two years later the Court went so far as to order "that all that were disarmed, remaining amongst us, carrying themselves peaceably, shall have their armes restored to them."²² With the lapse of time deeds were as sufficient as words to mark a penitent spirit.

Those Antinomians who remained in Massachusetts were eventually reabsorbed into the life of the colony. The more zealous left, voluntarily. "I wos not willing to live in the fyer of contention with your selfe (and others whome I honored in the Lord)," William Coddington later wrote to John Winthrop, "haveing lived 7 years in place of Government with yow. But chose rayther to live in exsile."²³ "Chose" was the correct word, for neither Coddington (who was not disarmed) nor any of his cohorts, except Aspinwall and Anne herself, who journeyed to Rhode Island, were banished. Indeed, after voluntarily making the decision to leave, they used the proper official channels to obtain the colony's permission. Governor Winthrop thought it wise for most "to depart for a time, till they could give the Court satisfaction," but as for Coddington, a former magistrate, "he persuaded [him] earnestly to stay, and did undertake to make his peace with the court." Deputy Governor Dudley advised that five of the leading Hutchinsonians "shall have lycence to departe out of this Patent . . . and after to retourne at their pleasures to remoove their famyles, soe it be with in halfe a yeare from this day, onely Mr. Coddington and Mr. Wildboare [Samuel Wilbore] are to come and goe and trade and comerce and take their owne tyme for remoovall of their famylyes." The governor concurred with his deputy, but the General Court was not so lenient, granting Coddington and the others "licence to remove yourselves & your families out of this jurisdiction . . . before the next Generall Court" two months off. If not gone by then, they would be summoned "to answear such things as shalbee objected." The Court had made no direct move to oust these Hutchinsonians, but once they had requested the severing of their social covenant, it desired to be rid of them as soon as possible in order to prevent further broils. It did not confiscate any property, however, and both Coddington and Wilbore later returned, unmolested, to sell their holdings.²⁴

Experiencing some difficulty in breaking their social covenant, the Hutchinsonians faced stiff (but delayed) opposition when they attempted to smash their church covenant as well. Formal dismissal from one's congregation was an absolute necessity in Puritan New England. In the case of Coddington and his colleagues, while there was apparently no formal dismissal, they had the distinct impression that the Boston congregation had acquiesced in their removal. Since a majority of the congregation's members were at least sympathetic to the Hutchinsonians, they were apparently glad to see them depart in peace. By 1640, however, through force or cajolery, the congregation had been swung over to the side of orthodoxy and now took affront that the Rhode Islanders were flaunting their independency.[25] In February it attempted to refasten the binding nature of the church covenant upon them by delegating three messengers "to goe to the Iseland of Aquethnicke [Rhode Island] to inquyre of the state of matters amongst our brethren there, and to require some satisfactory Aunswer about such things as wee heare to be Offensive amongst them." Although the messengers were completely rebuffed, the Boston congregation hesitated to excommunicate the apostates even though "the elders and most of the church would have cast them out, as [for] refusing to hear the church," for it could not bring itself to accept the fact that they had unilaterally freed themselves from the covenant's iron grip. In August Coddington could inform Winthrop "that it doth remayne to be proved by the rules of the gosple, that any Church ever clamed power over their brethren removed, more then over those that wos never in fellowshipe with them," but three months later there was still hope in Boston that the strayed lambs would return to the fold. They never did. There is no record, however, that the congregation could ever bring itself to excommunicate or even censure its erstwhile members. The congregation was so anxious to maintain the covenant's efficacy that it could not admit defeat even in the face of adversity. It was not interested in chastisement, only unity and conformity.[26]

The Antinomian controversy ended as it had begun, with an attempt to maintain the social bond of covenant theology, not for abstract reasons but in order to maintain the colony's viability. By suppressing the Hutchinsonians and their inherent individualism, Massachusetts had achieved a modicum of stability, allowing it to enter its second decade of existence without undue turmoil. It had reasonably gauged the seriousness of the crisis, set against a background of internal disintegration and external threats, and resolved it forcefully, yet humanely.[27]

Throughout the seventeenth century and into the eighteenth, crisis after crisis emerged to threaten the New Englanders' dedication to (and partial establishment of) stable communities, free from the dangers of heterogeneity and rampant individualism. Some were dealt with successfully, others were not. But all were approached from the common viewpoint that civil intervention in both secular and religious affairs was vitally necessary if the state was to be preserved.[28]

The burgeoning interest in women's history in the 1970s has produced two studies that emphasize the sexist bias of the Massachusetts magistracy—Ben Barker-Benfield, "Anne Hutchinson and the Puritan

Attitude Toward Women," Feminist Studies, *I (1972); and Lyle Koehler, "The Case of the American Jezebels: Anne Hutchinson and Female Agitation During the Years of Antinomian Turmoil, 1636—1640,"* William and Mary Quarterly, *series 3, XXXI (1974). These articles convincingly demonstrate that the colonial leaders were angered by Mrs. Hutchinson's bold violation of traditional sex roles. The question remains, however, whether that was a causal influence or merely a minor irritant.*

Cohen's basic point—that the Hutchinsonians threatened civil order—could be applied as well to other episodes in the seventeenth century, especially to the persecution of the Baptists in the 1640s and the Quakers in the 1650s. (The plight of the former is covered in William G. McLoughlin, New England Dissent, 1630–1833: The Baptists and the Separation of Church and State *[Cambridge, Mass.; 1971]); the latter in Rufus M. Jones,* The Quakers in the American Colonies *[London, 1911].) In each case, it can be argued, the state acted to preserve itself and the church. But sociologist Kai Erikson, in* Wayward Puritans: A Study in the Sociology of Deviance *(New York, 1966), contends that the explanation for these and other forms of dissent lies less in the nature of the protests themselves than in society's need to define its own behavioral boundaries. This thesis has found favor with some historians, but not with all.*

NOTES

1. See, for example, Emery Battis, *Saints and Sectaries: Anne Hutchinson and the Antinomian Controversy in the Massachusetts Bay Colony* (Chapel Hill: University of North Carolina Press, 1962); Edmund Morgan, *The Puritan Dilemma: The Story of John Winthrop* (Boston: Little, Brown and Co., 1958), chap. 10; Morgan, "The Case Against Anne Hutchinson," *New England Quarterly* 10 (December 1937): 635-649; Norman Pettit, *The Heart Prepared: Grace and Conversion in Puritan Spiritual Life* (New Haven: Yale University Press, 1966), chap. 5; David Hall, ed., *The Antinomian Controversy, 1636-1638: A Documentary History* (Middletown, Conn.: Wesleyan University Press, 1968), pp. 3-20.

2. A multicausational approach has been attempted by previous historians, but their findings have been virtually ignored by recent scholars; see, for instance, Jane Pease, "On Interpreting Puritan History: Williston Walker and the Limitations of the Nineteenth-Century View," *New England Quarterly* 42 (June 1969): 242-244; John Gorham Palfrey, *History of New England,* 5 vols. (Boston: Little, Brown and Co., 1876-1890), 1:489-497; Charles M. Andrews, *The Colonial Period of American History,* 4 vols. (New Haven: Yale University Press, 1934-1938), 1:475-476; Perry Miller, *Orthodoxy in Massachusetts, 1630-1650* (Boston: Beacon Press, 1959), pp. 161-165. Emery Battis, while training his sociological insights upon Anne and her followers, is most one-dimensional in his treatment of her opposition, essentially resurrecting the theocracy bugbear.

3. Nash, *Wilderness and the American Mind* (New Haven: Yale University Press, 1967), p. 29, and see chaps. 1 and 2 in general; Winthrop, "A Modell of Christian Charity," *Winthrop Papers,* 2:294; Peter N. Carroll, *Puritanism and the Wilderness: The Intellectual Significance of the New England Frontier, 1629-1700* (New York: Columbia University Press, 1969), chap. 7 and passim. Cf. Kenneth A. Lockridge, *A New England Town: The First Hundred Years* (New York: W. W. Norton & Co., 1970), chap. 1.

4. John Winthrop to His Wife, 23 July 1630, Massachusetts Historical Society, *Winthrop Papers,* 5 vols. (Boston: The Massachusetts Historical Society, 1929-1947), 2:303; Gary B. Nash, *Quakers and Politics: Pennsylvania, 1681-1726* (Princeton: Princeton University Press, 1968), p. 170, and see in general pp. 168-170 for the problems Protestant individualism caused in early Pennsylvania; Darett B. Rutman, *Winthrop's Boston: Portrait*

of a Puritan Town, 1630-1649 (Chapel Hill: University of North Carolina Press, 1965), pp. 13-14.

5. J. Franklin Jameson, ed., *Johnson's Wonder-Working Providence, 1628-1651* (New York: Charles Scribner's Sons, 1910), pp. 101-102.

6. Nathaniel B. Shurtleff, ed., *Records of the Governor and Company of the Massachusetts Bay in New England*, 5 vols. (Boston: William White, 1853-1854), 1:115-117, 137 (hereafter cited as *Mass. Col. Records*); "Boston Town Records [1634-1660/1]," in City of Boston, *Report of the Record Commissioners*, 2 (Boston: Rockwell and Churchill, 1877), 5, 10; Nathaniel Ward to John Winthrop, Jr., 24 December 1635, *Winthrop Papers*, 3:216; Rutman, *Winthrop's Boston*, pp. 138-143, 156-157, 178-180; George L. Haskins, *Law and Authority in Early Massachusetts* (New York: The Macmillan Co., 1960), pp. 68-71, 78-79. For a contrary understanding of the state of the colony at this time see Battis, *Saints and Sectaries*, pp. 255-256.

7. "Church Covenant," ca. February 1635/36, *Winthrop Papers*, 3:223-225; James K. Hosmer, ed., *Winthrop's Journal: "History of New England"* 2 vols., (New York: Barnes and Noble, Inc., 1953), 1:175; *Mass. Col. Records*, 1:168; Edmund S. Morgan, *Visible Saints: The History of a Puritan Idea* (New York: New York University Press, 1963), pp. 98-106.

8. Hosmer, ed., *Winthrop's Journal*, 1:132-133; *Mass. Col. Records*, 1:148, 160, 170-171; Perry Miller, "Thomas Hooker and the Democracy of Connecticut," *Errand into the Wilderness* (Cambridge, Mass.: Harvard University Press, 1956), pp. 16-47; Mary Jeanne Anderson Jones, *Congregational Commonwealth: Connecticut, 1636-1662* (Middletown, Conn.: Wesleyan University Press, 1968), chap. 1; Carroll, *Puritanism and the Wilderness*, pp. 140-147.

9. Edward Howes to John Winthrop, Jr., 3 April 1632, 18 March 1632/33, *Winthrop Papers*, 3:76, 111-112; Hosmer, ed., *Winthrop's Journal*, 1:135, 145; *Mass. Col. Records*, 1:138, 146-147, 161, 168, 183.

10. ? to John Winthrop, ca. May 1637, *Winthrop Papers*, 3:398; Hosmer, ed., *Winthrop's Journal*, 1:221; Richard Dunn, *Puritans and Yankees: The Winthrop Dynasty of New England, 1603-1717* (Princeton: Princeton University Press, 1962), pp. 30-36.

11. Alden T. Vaughan, *New England Frontier: Puritans and Indians, 1620-1675* (Boston: Little, Brown and Co., 1965), chap. 5.

12. Hosmer, ed., *Winthrop's Journal*, 1:171-172. The following year John White, in England, cautioned Winthrop "to remember that as Liberty is sweet soe it is apte (as it is with sweet meats) to allure men to Excess. . . . You are wise to understand my meaning which is noe more but this that if the providence and wisdome of some prevent it not you may be as much endangered by your liberty as we are by our bondage." *Winthrop Papers*, 3:335-336. See also Morgan, *Puritan Dilemma*, pp. 101-116.

13. Cotton Mather, *Magnalia Christi Americana*, 2 vols. (New York: Russell and Russell, 1967). 2:509; [John Winthrop], *A Short Story of the Rise, Reign, and Ruine of the Antinomians, Familists & Libertines, that Infected the Churches of New England* (London: Ralph Smith, 1644), in Charles F. Adams, ed., *Antinomianism in the Colony of Massachusetts Bay, 1636-1638* (Boston: The Prince Society, 1894), p. 81; Rutman, *Winthrop's Boston*, pp. 125-126.

14. *Mass. Col. Records*, 1:196, 228; Hosmer, ed., *Winthrop's Journal*, 1:219, 226; [John Winthrop], "A Declaration in Defence of an Order of Court Made in May, 1637," and "A Reply in Further Defense of an Order of Court Made in May, 1637," ca. August 1637, *Winthrop Papers*, 3:423, 475; Henry Vane, "A Brief Answer to a certain Declaration, made to the intent and equitye of the Order of Court, that none should be received to inhabite within this jurisdiction, but such as should be allowed by some of the magistrates," William H. Whitmore, ed., *The [Thomas] Hutchinson Papers*, 2 vols. (Albany: The Prince Society, 1865), 1:85.

15. John Higginson to John Winthrop, ca. May 1637, *Winthrop Papers*, 3:406.

16. Hosmer, ed., *Winthrop's Journal*, 1:218; [Winthrop], *A Short Story*, p. 142; Battis, *Saints and Sectaries*, p. 156; Vaughan, *New England Frontier*, pp. 140-145.

17. Hosmer, ed., *Winthrop's Journal*, 1:239, 257; *Mass. Col. Records*, 1:211. For a narrative of these events see Battis, *Saints and Sectaries*, chaps. 13-15.

18. *Wayward Puritans: A Study in the Sociology of Deviance* (New York: John Wiley and Sons, 1966), pp. 68-107. See also Lewis Coser, *Continuities in the Study of Social Conflict* (New York: The Free Press, 1967), pp. 113-118. Professor Erikson's conclusions conflict with my own understanding of the problem, for where he sees the social covenant as a late Puritan innovation, I feel that it was an integral part of the initial Puritan thrust into Massachusetts.

19. *The Functions of Social Conflict* (Glencoe, Ill.: The Free Press, 1956), pp. 103, 110; John Higginson to John Winthrop, ca. May 1637, *Winthrop Papers*, 3:404.

20. See Battis, *Saints and Sectaries*, appendix 2. Battis is not always correct, occasionally attributing banishment to those who voluntarily left the colony. John Underhill was first disfranchised and only later (September 1638) banished, but was reinstated in 1640 after he "openly and humbly acknowledged & bewayled his offences against God & this common wealth." *Mass. Col. Records*, 1:301-302.

21. "Crime and Punishment in Early Massachusetts," *William and Mary Quarterly*, 3rd Ser., 22 (July 1965): 475-476; *Delinquent Saints: Disciplinary Action in the Early Congregational Churches of Massachusetts* (New York: Columbia University Press, 1956), p. 38.

22. *Mass. Col. Records*, 1:212, 278; [Winthrop], *A Short Story*, p. 183. See also "Acknowledgement of Samuel Wilbur [Wilbore]." 16 May 1639, *Winthrop Papers*, 4:121-122.

23. 22 May 1640, *Winthrop Papers*, 4:246.

24. Howard M. Chapin, ed., *Documentary History of Rhode Island*, 2 vols. (Providence: Preston and Rounds Co., 1916-1919), 2:22-23; Thomas Dudley to John Winthrop, 19 February 1637/38, *Winthrop Papers*, 4:14-15; *Mass. Col. Records*, 1:223. Compare the viewpoint in Battis, *Saints and Sectaries*, pp. 230-231. For the sale of Wilbore's land see "Boston Town Records [1634-1660/61]," p. 34; for Coddington's, [Thomas Lechford] *Notebook kept by Thomas Lechford, Esq., Lawyer, In Boston, Massachusetts Bay, From June 27, 1638 to July 29, 1641* (Cambridge: John Wilson and Son, 1885), pp. 63-67.

25. William Coddington to John Winthrop, 22 May 1640, *Winthrop Papers*, 4:245-246; Hosmer, ed., *Winthrop's Journal*, 1:324-325; Rutman, *Winthrop's Boston*, pp. 123-126.

26. Richard D. Pierce, ed., "The Records of the First Church in Boston, 1630-1868," in Colonial Society of Massachusetts, *Publications*, 39 (1961): 27; Hosmer, ed., *Winthrop's Journal*, 1:330-331; 2:14; Coddington to Winthrop, 25 August 1640, *Winthrop Papers*, 4:278; "Robert Keayne of Boston in New England his Book 1639," Adams, ed., *Antinomianism in the Colony of Massachusetts Bay*, pp. 393-402; Ziff, "Social Bond of the Church Covenant," pp. 457-460.

27. I have tried to explain why the Bay colony government reacted as it did to the Hutchinsonians. Given the above argument, what seems most peculiar is that Anne and her friends were able to reject the dominant values system in Massachusetts. Emery Battis (*Saints and Sectaries*, chap. 17) has put forth one explanation, which has its serious weaknesses; others are certainly called for. Indeed, there is need for more studies of deviant behavior in all of the New England colonies.

28. For a recent discussion of the continuation into the eighteenth century of a concern for social harmony and homogeneity in New England see Michael Zuckerman, "The Social Context of Democracy in Massachusetts," *William and Mary Quarterly*, 3rd Ser., 25 (October 1968): 523-544, and his *Peaceable Kingdoms: New England Towns in the Eighteenth Century* (New York: A. Knopf, Inc., 1970). For the disintegration of social harmony in early Boston, however, see Rutman, *Winthrop's Boston*; for the same in eighteenth-century Connecticut, Richard L. Bushman, *From Puritan to Yankee: Character and the Social Order in Connecticut, 1690-1765* (Cambridge, Mass.: Harvard University Press, 1967); and for the same in early Pennsylvania, Nash, *Quakers and Politics*.

10 | BLACK PURITAN: THE NEGRO IN SEVENTEENTH-CENTURY MASSACHUSETTS

ROBERT C. TWOMBLEY and ROBERT H. MOORE

A different sort of resistance to the authority of Puritan society came from its own lower economic classes—indentured servants, apprentices, slaves, and others bound by law to serve and obey a master. Servitude was not, of course, confined to the Puritan colonies. But as Lawrence W. Towner has shown in "'A Fondness for Freedom': Servant Protest in Puritan Society" (William and Mary Quarterly, series 3, XLX [1962]), the specific configurations of servitude and servant protest in seventeenth-century New England often reflected Puritanism's influence.

Towner's principal concern is with indentured servants rather than with slaves, if only because in New England the former vastly outnumbered the latter. Recently, however, resurgent interest in the origins and growth of racial slavery has brought new attention to the fate of blacks in Puritan society. A generation ago Lorenzo J. Greene, in The Negro in Colonial New England, 1620–1776 *(New York, 1942), argued that, on the whole, blacks fared better in New England than in most other British colonies because they were few and hence of little threat to the white majority, and because Puritanism ameliorated somewhat the conditions of bondage. Still, as "strangers" outside the Puritan fold (except for the very few who became church members), blacks presented a potential challenge to the founders' notion of a homogeneous holy commonwealth. Two scholars—a historian and a literary critic—have recently taken a fresh look at the attitudes and actions of white New Englanders toward the blacks in their midst. Their conclusions are summarized in the following selection.*

I

Historians have assumed that seventeenth-century Massachusetts was no different from other American colonies in its treatment of Negroes.[1] It has been easy to overlook a colony where, as late as 1715, there were only 2,000 Negroes in a population of 96,000, and where whites seemed to hold racial views similar to those of other settlers. But an analysis of Negro life in the Puritan Commonwealth reveals the inaccuracy of this view.

Most authorities agree that Negroes first came to Massachusetts in 1638, but it seems clear to us that at least one Negro had arrived as early as 1633. Contemporaries estimated that there were between 100 and 200 in 1680 and 550 by 1708.[2] Although Negroes were numerous enough to be familiar in the everyday affairs of many communities by the 1660's, most Puritans regarded blacks as strange and exotic creatures. Despite the inconsistent terminology used to refer to Negroes,[3] Massachusetts whites held certain derogatory attitudes.

John Josselyn noted that some New Englanders thought Negro blackness resulted from the African climate, while others believed it came from Ham's curse. Blackness was commonly associated with evil. During the witchcraft hysteria many people claimed to have seen the Devil in the form of a "Blackman"; white women accused of having evil spirits were sometimes called "black witches." Blackness connoted ugliness as well as evil. "Sea-Devils," a fish found off the Maine coast, were popularly called "Negroes" because they were a very "ugly," "hideous" species, "having a black scale."[4]

If some derogatory attitudes found expression in metaphor, others appeared in social relations. Whites were insulted when compared closely with a Negro. "A Lieutenant of a Man of War," the perturbed Cotton Mather wrote, "whom I am a Stranger to, designing to putt an Indignity upon me, has called his *Negro-Slave* by the Name of COTTON-MATHER." Samuel Sewall recorded in his diary that "Mr Cotton Mather came to Mr. Wilkins's shop, and there talked very sharply against me as if I used his father worse than a Neger; spake so loud that the people in the street might hear him." Such opinions sometimes led to bizarre actions. Josselyn wrote that fish did not respond to herring as quickly as they did for a "waggish lad at Cape-porpus [Maine], who baited his hooks with the drown'd Negro's buttocks." Puritan racial attitudes do not seem appreciably different from those held by other contemporary white men.[5]

One might expect the Puritans to have treated Negroes with an indignity matching their attitudes. But the real test of the colony's race relations must be based not on what whites thought and said but on what they did. How the Negro fared in day to day activity is the best indication of the nature of Negro life in the Puritan Commonwealth.

II

Central to the maintenance of order and stability in any society is the administration of justice. This was particularly true in Massachusetts where respect for the law was primary in the colonists' conception of a vigorous, stable, and godly society. A profound commitment to the law and the judicial process overpowered antipathetical racial views and assured fair and equal treatment, guaranteeing the basic legal rights of Englishmen to free, servant, and slave Negroes. These rights—including police protection, legal counsel, trial by jury, fair and considered hearings, and impartial justice—are very much expected in the twentieth century. In the seventeenth they were incipient concepts in much of the western world. But Massachusetts guarded these liberties jealously, applying them without regard for skin color. The Puritans did not hold advanced racial views but they did place a high priority on the universality of justice. Throughout the century Negroes and whites received essentially equal treatment before the law.

Important principles were observed even in minor offenses. In 1680, for example, Goodman Wolland accursed Daniel King's Negro boy of insulting him on a Boston street. When the boy denied the allegation, Wolland brought him to court where the case was thrown out for lack of witnesses. That the case went to court at all indicates a predilection to seek legal redress rather than to initiate private action. When, in 1653, "a contravercy" developed between John Smith of Plymouth and John Barnes's "neager maide servant," the Plymouth court listened to "whatsoever could bee saide on either side." Both were cleared of any misdemeanor, but they were admonished for public quarreling.[6]

Like whites, Negroes received police protection and were shielded from extralegal punitive action. When three Indians broke into the home of Angola, a free Negro, in 1672, he prosecuted. All three were given twenty stripes and ordered to remain in prison until they paid court costs. In another case Pelatiah Glover brought suit against Betty Negro for insulting his son and mother. Richard White and Tom, a Negro, testified against her. She was found guilty of slander and given ten stripes but by being taken to court Betty at least found a measure of protection. The principle of using judicial means rather than resorting to personal retribution extended to the colony's Maine jurisdiction where in 1686 George Norton prosecuted his own Negro for stealing his wool. Due process and a willingness to use the courts minimized expeditious extralegal punishment. Even masters recognized this principle.[7]

Other incidents establish that Negro testimony was admissible as evidence against whites. In 1673 a defendant challenged a witness's legal right to testify, but the plaintiff replied "that the negro was of such carriage and knowledge that her testimony had been accepted several times before this." Later, in 1679, Wonn Negro testified against Bridget Oliver, who was suspected of witchcraft. In 1680 Mingo the Negro was a witness in a suit involving warehouse arson. Instances of Negro testimony for and against both races are numerous.[8]

It is also evident from the records that Negroes had access to legal counsel. In 1679 Hannah, Negro servant, was convicted for stealing a box of "Chyrurgions Jnstrumts." From prison she persuaded three white men to post forty pounds bond for her release and petitioned the Suffolk County court for dismissal of her fines. Her appeal, a sophisticated legal argument, cited page and section numbers of the laws governing burglary. Although the jury dismissed it, Zachariah Chaffee, Jr., commenting on Hannah's appeal, noted the "refined distinctions" that could only have been "written by men accustomed to legal problems."[9]

An additional example of the many elements of justice accorded Negroes stemmed from the Salem witch controversy. In 1692 a warrant was issued for the arrest of Mary Black, a Negro owned by Lieutenant Nathaniel Putnam of Salem Village. Although maintaining her innocence, Mary was tried, convicted, and imprisoned for witchcraft. The next year, however, cooler heads had apparently prevailed, and Mary was not forgotten. Upon petition she was released from prison by proclamation of the Governor.[10]

These cases introduce important principles illustrating Negro legal rights. A Negro's word was admissible as evidence and his testimony could be as acceptable as that of whites. Charges against Negroes had to be documented and they received the thoughtful consideration of juries and magistrates. Negroes had police protection and were shielded from extralegal practices that would have denied them due process of law. They could appeal, use legal counsel, and receive gubernatorial pardons.

The principles operative in the cases described above were applicable when more abhorrent crimes were committed. Negroes were given the same judicial treatment as whites in all aspects of the case from indictment to punishment. Some crimes, like burglary, are impossible to analyze, for penalties were distributed on the basis of the kinds and amounts of items stolen; we were unable to find cases in which Negroes and whites appropriated exactly the same things. For this reason we have not attempted comparisons of thefts, but have analyzed arson, murder, manslaughter, and sexual offenses—the four main areas in which comparison between the races is possible.

Of the sexual crimes committed in Massachusetts, fornication, bastardy, and rape were most prevalent. According to the 1675 Laws and Ordinances of War—a compilation of previous statutes—rape, ravishment, and unnatural abuses were punishable by death. Fornication and other "dissolute lasciviousness" were penalized at the judge's discretion, taking into account the severity and circumstances of the case. Fornication, by both Negro and white, was a considerable problem in early Massachusetts, and the many recorded cases provide ample opportunity for comparative analysis.[11]

Essex County punished its Negro fornicators by whipping or fine, the choice sometimes being left to the offender. In 1660, Captain White's Negro Jugg was whipped; Grace and Juniper, convicted in 1674, were "to be fined or whipped." In 1678, two "neager" servants, David and Judith, chose to pay a fine rather than feel the last ten and five times respectively. The whites in Essex county received similar treatment. Mary Dane, an indentured servant, was whipped. The same year, 1654, Elizabeth Osgood was given thirty stripes and her mate twenty-five. Most infringers, regardless of race, received from ten to twenty stripes or were ordered to pay from forty to fifty shillings.[12]

Representative of Suffolk County's treatment of fornicators was the case of Mary Plumb, a white, who was punished with fifteen stripes and court and prison fees for "Lascivious carriage by being seene in bed with a man." For the same offense, Phoebe Lovell received ten stripes or a forty shilling fine plus court costs. Negroes in Suffolk County got the same penalties. Joan and her partner, Jasper Indian, were given their choice of fifteen stripes or a forty shilling fine plus court costs. In a significant case, Robert Corbet, a white, and George, a Negro, both servants of Stephen French, received identical sentences in 1679 for committing fornication with the Negro Maria: twenty stripes and court costs. Fornication between the races was not punished any more stringently than that between members of the same race. In Suffolk, as in Essex County, the most common penalty ranged from ten to twenty lashes or a forty to fifty shilling fine plus fees of court.[13]

Although there is no evidence that it was practiced, racial intermarriage was not illegal until 1705. Before then most miscegenation was illicit. It if led to bastardy, penalties for both races were generally the same as for simple fornication. In most cases the court sought to determine paternity in order to provide the child's support, and this led to additional costs for the father. Usually the woman was whipped from ten to twenty stripes or ordered to pay a forty to fifty shilling fine. The man was given a similar number of stripes and then bound to pay weekly support or a lump sum to be administered over the years. In 1682, for example, Richard Prior gave thirty pounds surety to save Ipswich from maintaining his illegitimate child. The same year John Tucker was fined six pounds and ordered to pay an undiscolosed amount for birth and support. In 1679 the court ordered John Hunkins to give his partner's father one shilling per week. When the races mixed the penalties were about the same: William Rane, father of a child by the Indian servant Ann, paid three shillings a week. For "haveing a bastard," the white Hannah Bonny was "well whipt"; her mate, Nimrod Negro, was also whipped and made to turn over eighteen pence weekly for his offspring. Illegitimate Negro children were generally awarded financial support in amounts similar to those paid to white and mixed offspring. In 1673 the Negro Silvanus provided two shillings six pence per week for his son's upbringing.

. . .

Rape, a more serious offense, could be punished by death. The two Negro cases in the published records reveal the severity dealt offenders. Basto Negro was convicted in 1676 of raping the three year old daughter of Robert Cox, his master. When Cox appealed Basto's death sentence, the jury substituted thirty-nine lashes and ordered him "allwayes to weare a roape about his neck, to hang doune two foot." If ever he was found without his rope Basto would feel an additional twenty lashes. Shortly thereafter John Negro confessed to "pulling Sarah Phillips of Salem off her horse and attempting to ravish her." John's penalty for attempted rape was a five pound payment to Miss Phillips, prosecution and court costs, and banishment from the colony.[14]

Whites also received stiff penalties. John Man, perhaps the Marquis de Sade of his time, for "wanton and lascivious carriages . . . and cruell beating" of his indentured servant, gave two hundred pounds sureties until the next court, paid prosecution costs and court fees, and terminated his girl's contract. John Kempe attempted rape on "3 yong girles [and] was censured to bee whiped both heare [Boston], at Roxberry and at Salem very severely and was Comitted for a slave to Lieft Davenport." Two other white rapists, William Cheny and Samuel Guile, were hanged until dead.[15]

. . .

Equitable treatment for Negroes extended to other capital offenses. According to the law, murder was to be "expiated with the death of the murderer." A measure of Massachusetts's concern for justice was the care with which she appraised murder cases, often meting out punishment for manslaughter instead. Thoughtful scrutiny reflected a recognition of extenuating circumstances. And this attitude did not exclude Negro assailants of whites.

The average penalty for manslaughter was a twenty pound fine and the costs of prosecution, court, and detention. Depending on the circumstances, part of the fine went to the colony and part to the deceased's relatives.[16] Both instances of Negro manslaughter, originally indictments for murder against whites, were handled equitably. A 1684 defendant, "Robert Trayes, negro," wounded the "legg of Daniell Standlake . . . , of which wound, and cutting the legg occationed therby, died. . . ." Since he had meant to fire at Standlake's door, the jury decided that Trayes was "an instrument of the death of Daniell Standlake by misadventure," and sentenced the defendant to pay the deceased's father five pounds or be whipped. The second case, in which the servant Robin was accused, is of particular note, not only for its dealing with manslaughter but also for its clear statement of Negro legal rights.[17]

Robin was guilty of giving John Cheeny of Cambridge "a mortall wound on the head with a stick" in 1689. His punishment was light: charges of prosecution, fees of court, and costs of prison where he was to remain until he paid. Robin had pled not guilty, but what extenuating circumstances had brought about the easy sentence are not recorded. More important, however, is that after the jury had been selected Robin was allowed to "make . . . challange against any of them." In addition, one juror, feeling as Hawthorne had in 1660, that Negroes did not deserve "the same distribution of Justice with our selves," refused to appear. In reply the court fined him five shillings. Through this concrete act the court clearly stated that shirking jury duty was inexcusable and that due process extended to blacks as well as whites.

The only recorded case in which a white killed a Negro took place in Maine in 1694 when a master's continual mistreatment of his servant led to her death. In the South well before this time, as Carl Degler points out, masters were without "any fear of prosecution" if they killed slaves; the law "allowed punishment for refractory slaves up to and including accidental death. . . ." But the Puritans showed more restraint. Indicted by a grand jury on suspicion of murder, Nathaniel Cane was convicted of manslaughter for "Cruelty to his Negro woman by Cruell Beating and hard usage." His fine—ten pounds ten shillings—was light. Nonetheless, a master could not mistreat, abuse, or murder his Negro without threat of legal action.[18]

Arson, an infrequent but serious offense, brought harsh penalties. Severity was demonstrated early in the colony's history when in 1640 Henry Stevens fired his master's barn and had his indenture extended by twenty-one years. Throughout the century the penalties were stiff; Jack, a Negro arsonist, was hanged in 1681. Two Negroes implicated in the Maria arson case the same year were banished and Maria was burned alive, the only punishment of its kind in Massachusetts history.[19] Maria's fire had caused the death of a baby girl. She had deliberately destroyed her master's house and had not intended murder. But since she had caused a death by burning she in turn was burned. Her severe sentence may have been prompted by uneasiness over a rash of fires in the Boston vicinity. Social pressure may have induced the court to be unduly harsh in this affair but it was not stampeded. The strict sentence was a response to a specific situation and did not become a precedent for future dealings with either arsonists, murderers, or Negroes. But the case stands as an ugly blot on Puritan history.[20]

This review of legal cases indicates that throughout the seventeenth century the Negro received due process and only in isolated incidents, like the Maria case, was he given unusual treatment. But even on that occasion it is questionable to what extent skin color dictated severity. In general, the Negro held the rights of Englishmen before the courts. The legal apparatus did not undergo subtle shifts when Negroes came before it.

III

If the Negro's legal status was not circumscribed by pigmentation neither were his economic opportunities. Several black men, servant and free, accumulated real and other property; the color of their skin did not by definition render them ineligible for economic gain. Although most Negroes were members of the servant class and therefore at the bottom of the economic ladder, some were able to carve out an enviable niche in the white business world.

The story of Angola illustrates the possibilities. In 1653 he was owned by Captain Robert Keayne, who in his will in 1656 left Angola a two pound legacy. Then the free Negro Bostian Ken purchased Angola and set him free by bonding his property to Mrs. Keayne. In 1670 Governor Richard Bellingham sold a piece of land bordered "Upon the North East with the land of Angola, the Negro." Bellingham had given him this fifty-foot square piece in the late 1660's when Angola, paddling in a river, had rescued the Governor from his sinking boat. When he died in 1675 Angola's will confirmed his house, land, and other possessions upon his widow Elizabeth, her children, and her heirs forever. In the twenty years before his death Angola had paid his eighteen pound obligation to Ken and had moved from a servant with a two pound legacy to a free Negro of means.[21]

Bostian Ken, Angola's benefactor, was another prosperous Negro. In order to purchase his friend's freedom in 1656 Ken bonded his house and land in Dorchester plus four and one half acres of wheat. In 1662 he sold his one-third share of the fourteen-ton ship *Hopewell* to his "loving Friend Francis Vernon" along with "one barrell of liquor one barr of Sugar one Barr mackerell and one Barr Codfish." From 1656 to 1662 Ken dealt in considerable amounts of property.[22]

Most of the other seventeenth-century Negro landowners received their holdings from their masters. In 1677 Increase Mather bought land bordered on the "Northwest by the land of Jethro the Negro." If Governor Bellingham and the Reverend Mr. Mather owned choice land, the bordering Negro holdings may have also been desirable.[23] Other Negroes held land, houses, and small businesses. When Thomas, owner of a chairmaking establishment, married Katherine in 1678, he drew up a lengthy document granting her his estate in case of his death and bound himself for one hundred pounds surety. Zippora Potter, daughter of one of Robert Keayne's Negroes, bought a twenty-eight by sixty-foot "parcell of land with a dwelling house thereupon" in 1670 for "forty Six pounds currant Mony of New England in hand paid." Although the number of successful Negroes was small, they came from a total Negro population in the colony that was at most only two hundred at this time.[24]

A few Negroes were property owners, but the majority were house servants living with white families. Many resided in Boston but those in the outlying areas and the Boston blacks who traveled about broadened interracial contact. Most Negroes lived in their masters' homes, were often left alone, and could come and go as they pleased when not working. They were not restricted to the towns in which they lived and in many cases moved freely about the countryside.[25]

Freedom of movement opened up certain options. One option, running away may have been a product of working class discontent; but running away was also encouraged by alternatives that lack of repression offered.[26] Freedom of movement permitted a certain amount of fraternization between races in the lower classes; the derogatory views of most whites did not preclude informal relations. Occasionally mutual activities were forms of antisocial behavior. In 1673, for example, "John Burrington, Edward Fish, Richard Hollingworths Negro Tom, Thomas [,] Clark Cliffords Servt," and a fifth man, stole saddles and bridles and "complotted to run away." About the same time "Gregory, Nath. Emerson, Arthur Abbot and a Negro" broke into a house, took wine, and improvised a drinking party. But not all interracial mingling was mischievous. For five years in the 1690's one of Boston's four chimney sweepers was "Jeremiah the Negro"; for one year, 1693, he was joined by "Negro Will," who along with Jeremiah brought token integration to Boston's public employ. During the smallpox epidemic in the 1680's Mary Heall, a seventy-four year old widow living alone, took the Negro Zanckey into her home to watch over his recovery. On another occasion, Jack, a runaway Negro, came to Anthony Dorchester's home. Jack was a stranger but Dorchester invited him in and made him welcome:

. . . after asking for a Pipe of Tobacco which I told him there was some on the Table he tooke my knife and Cut some and then put it in his Pocket, and after that tooke downe a Cutlass and offered to draw it but it Coming out stiff I closed in upon him. . . .

Jack was overpowered and taken to prison, but Dorchester's initial hospitality is noteworthy.[27]

The colony's mechanisms of social control which permitted easy interracial contact did not make Negroes full fledged citizens or the social equals of whites, but neither were the blacks shunted to another realm of existence. . . . The Negro hovered on the fringes of full participation in social and economic life.

IV

. . .

Except for militia policy, no laws were passed applying only to Negroes until the 1680's.[28] Old and New England had fitted the black man into the social system without legally recognizing slavery or a slave caste. Within the broad guidelines of the Common Law and Puritan religious views Massachusetts had extended century-old rights of Englishmen to Negroes. But in the 1680's the colony began to place restrictions upon them. The new Negro policies were responses to three social concerns: a widespread anathema for the slave trade, a pervasive uneasiness about the colony's economic future, and a growing anxiety about the Negro's behavior.

In spite of the unpopularity of slaving, several Massachusetts merchants were active traders in the 1680's, selling Negroes in Virginia for three to five thousand pounds of tobacco per head. Public pressure could not prohibit businessmen from dealing with Southerners but it could discourage the practice at home. Fear of public reprisal forced John Saffin, John Usher, James Wetcomb, and Andrew Belcher to import Negroes secretly in 1681. Fearing seizure, these merchants rerouted their Guinea trader from Swansea, Rhode Island, to Nantasket, Massachusetts, where, they wrote, "before you come in there take in such negroes . . . of ours and come up in the night with them, giveing us notice thereof wth what privacy you can. . . ." "Keepe your men Ignorant of your designe," the traders told their agent, and do nothing "prejudiciall to our mayne designe."[29]

Analyses of the economy seemed to demonstrate little benefit in the Negro's presence. In 1702 the General Court decided to promote "the bringing of White Servants and to put a period to Negroes being slaves." Beneath this admirable statement were more complex and mundane considerations. In 1708 Governor Joseph Dudley remarked that Negroes were costly to maintain during the winter months because they did little and demanded great amounts of clothing. Negroes "are usually the worst servants," he noted. . . .

The first regulations on Negroes were clauses inserted into general laws prohibiting Negroes, mulattos, Indians, servants, and apprentices from buying or being served alcoholic beverages. Later in the 1680's the same groups were warned about stealing or giving away stolen goods and whites who induced thefts or received stolen merchandise were similarly promised punishment.[30]

No further legislation appeared until after the turn of the century. In 1703 Indian, Negro, and mulatto servants and slaves could be on the streets after nine in the evening only with masters' consent. After 1703 no Negro or mulatto could be manumitted unless his master gave fifty pounds surety for the servant's welfare. The first law was directed toward night-time unrest, and the second prevented masters from throwing elderly, unemployable servants on the town charge. . . .

The most stringent new measure, "An Act for the Better Preventing of a Spurious and Mixt Issue" of 1705, drove a deep wedge between the races. Sexual intercourse and racial intermarriage were now specifically prohibited. Fixed penalties were imposed on both races. Fornication was no longer left to judicial decision: Negro offenders were banished and the white consort, male or female, assumed responsibility for the offspring. The law reemphasized the desirability of Negro marriages, presumably as part of an effort to minimize mulatto births.

The 1705 law also placed a four pound duty on Negroes imported into the colony, and set heavy penalties on violators. The new duty aimed to discourage the slave trade. Some Puritans wished to rid the colony of Negroes or prevent any more from coming but restrictions on importation did not rest on this basis alone. Seven years later, in 1712, the General Court prohibited the trade in Indians. Revulsion for the slave trade and suspicion of outsiders worked to prevent nonwhites from coming to the Puritan Commonwealth.

A five-part law in 1707 prevented free Negroes from harboring or entertaining nonwhite servants in their homes without masters' approval and ordered them to repair highways, clean streets, or perform other tasks equal in time and amount to military duty. Since free Negroes had "a share in the benefit" of common defense, they would also go to the parade ground "in case of alarm" and "perform such tasks as the first commission of the company shall direct. . . ." The several laws were supplemented by town ordinances which, throughout the eighteenth century, further limited Negro freedom of movement.[31]

V

The new Massachusetts statutes dealing with Negroes were responses to specific and observable colonial problems. The measures arose from what the Puritans thought were manifestations of social disorder. The legislation was not a premeditated program to debase the Negro, for the Puritans believed that their regulations were in the Negro's best interest. Some colonial leaders like Samuel Sewall and Cotton Mather wanted to incorporate Negroes more intimately into the colony's social and religious institutions; but men of narrower vision passed laws which overruled better intentions. The Bay Colony reluctantly accepted the black man's presence but believed by the 1700's that it precipitated social disorder. Legal restrictions on Massachusetts's Negroes neither followed from nor led to slavery. In the Bay Colony these restrictions were part of a hasty problem-solving endeavor that prevalent attitudes and predispositions made possible. The Negro felt the brunt of discriminatory laws but he was not without due process and never totally removed from participation in the white social and economic orbit. These advantages reflected an attitude that later enabled the Bay Colony to lead the way in constitutional prohibitions of slavery.

The extent of Puritanism's impact on attitudes toward blacks and on the conditions of servitude can be judged conclusively only through the comparative study of several British colonies. A major step in that direction was taken by Winthrop D. Jordan in White over Black: American Attitudes toward the Negro, 1550–1812 *(Chapel Hill, N. C., 1968). Also suggestive are David Brion Davis,* The Problem of Slavery in Western Culture *(Ithaca, N. Y., 1964), Edward J. McManus,* Black Bondage in the North *(Syracuse, 1973), and Lester B. Sherer,* Slavery and the Churches in Early America, 1619–1819 *(Grand Rapids, Mich., 1975). But none of these studies quite addresses the crucial question: how did the settlers' Puritanism—as distinct from their more broadly English heritage—influence their racial perceptions and policies. That remains a fruitful area of investigation.*

NOTES

1. Recent scholarship on early American slavery has ignored Massachusetts or assumed similarity with the South: Oscar and Mary Handlin, "Origins of the Southern Labor System," *The William and Mary Quarterly*, 3d Ser., VII (1950), 199-222, and Oscar Handlin, "The Origins of Negro Slavery," *Race and Nationality in American Life* (New York, 1957), 3-29, argue that discrimination developed because of the institutionalization of slavery. Carl N. Degler, "Slavery and the Genesis of American Race Prejudice," *Comparative Studies in Society and History*, II (1959), 49-66, reverses the Handlin thesis, attributing slavery to innate white discriminatory attitudes. Winthrop D. Jordan, "Modern Tensions and the Origin of American Slavery," *Journal of Southern History*, XXVIII (1962), 18-30, sees both slavery and discrimination as part of a worldwide debasement of the Negro. Other relevant works are: Jordan, "The Influence of the West Indies on the Origins of New England Slavery," *Wm. and Mary Qtly.* 3d Ser., XVIII (1961), 243-250; Lawrence W. Towner, " 'A Fondness for Freedom': Servant Protest in Puritan Society," *ibid.*, XIX (1962), 201-219; Towner, "The Sewall-Saffin Dialogue on Slavery," *ibid.* XXI (1964), 40-52; Jules Zanger, "Crime and Punishment in Early Massachusetts," *ibid.*, XXII (1965), 471-477; Emory Washburn, "Slavery as it Once Prevailed in Massachusetts," in *Early History of Massachusetts: Lectures Delivered . . . Before the Lowell Institute, in Boston* (Boston, 1869), 199-225; and Lorenzo J. Greene, *The Negro in Colonial New England, 1620-1776* (New York, 1942).

2. William Wood's 1634 *New-England's Prospect . . .* (1764 ed.), in *Publications of the Prince Society*, III (Boston, 1865), 86; and Deloraine P. Corey, *The History of Malden, Mass., 1633-1785* (Malden, Mass., 1899), 415, refer to a Negro living in Plymouth at least as early as 1633. Population estimates are taken from Simon Bradstreet to the Committee of Trade and Plantations, May 18, 1680, in Elizabeth Donnan, ed., *Documents Illustrative of the History of the Slave Trade to America* (Washington, D. C., 1930-35), III, 14-15; Edward Randolph's Report to the Lords of the Committee of the Colonies, Aug., 1681, in Samuel G. Drake, *The History and Antiquities of Boston . . .* (Boston, 1856), 441; Joseph Dudley to the Council of Trade and Plantations, Oct. 1, 1708, in Cecil Headlam, ed., *Calendar of State Papers, Colonial Series, America and West Indies, June, 1708-1709* (London, 1922), 110; and Evarts B. Greene and Virginia D. Harrington, *American Population Before the Federal Census of 1790* (New York, 1932), 14.

3. "Slave" was not precisely defined in seventeenth-century Massachusetts; its flexible usage permitted several meanings. The conventional definition was "one who is the property of, and entirely subject to, another person, whether by capture, purchase, or birth; a servant completely divested of freedom and personal rights." See W. A. Cragie, ed., *A New English Dictionary on Historical Principles* (Oxford, 1919), X, 182-184. The burden of this article is to demonstrate that Massachusetts never forced Negroes into this status. Puritans also used "slavery" to describe prisoners of war and criminals, and the term functioned as a rhetorical device to indicate dissatisfaction with government or authority. "Slave" and "servant" were used interchangeably in reference to Negroes: John Noble and John F. Cronin, eds., *Records of the Court of Assistants of . . . Massachusetts . . .* (Boston, 1901-28), I, 74; and John Josselyn, *An Account of Two Voyages to New-England, Made during the Years 1638, 1663* (Boston, 1865), 139-140.

4. The long history of black men in the European experience and the development of white racial opinion has been admirably treated in Winthrop D. Jordan, "White Over Black: the attitudes of the American colonists toward the Negro, to 1784" (unpubl. Ph.D. diss., Brown University, 1960), Ch. I. Puritan racial attitudes are illustrated in Josselyn, *Two Voyages*, 143; George L. Burr, ed., *Narratives of the Witchcraft Cases, 1648-1706* (New York, 1914), 309-310, 312, 425; and William S. Southgate, "History of Scarborough, from 1633 to 1783," Maine Historical Society, *Collections*, III (1853), 92.

5. Dec. 10, 1721, in Worthington C. Ford, ed., *Diary of Cotton Mather* (New York, 1957), II, 663; Barrett Wendell, *Cotton Mather: The Puritan Priest* (New York, [1891]), 153, quoting Samuel Sewall, Oct. 20, 1701; Josselyn, *Two Voyages*, 159; Jordan, "White Over Black," Ch. I.

6. George F. Dow, ed., *Records and Files of the Quarterly Courts of Essex County* (Salem, 1911-21), VII, 425; Nathaniel B. Shurtleff, ed., *Records of the Colony of New Plymouth in New England* (Boston, 1855-61), III, 39. To demonstrate racial equality before the law we shall compare the several kinds of criminal and civil offenses committed by Negroes to similar cases involving whites. We have appraised all the published records (falling between 1650 and 1690) in which Negroes appear; those presented here are not atypical. We believe these cases accurately reflect the temper of the Negro's participation in the legal process.

7. The Angola case is in Samuel Eliot Morison, ed., *Records of the Suffolk County Court, 1671-1680*, 2 vols., in *Publications of the Colonial Society of Massachusetts, Collections*, XXIX-XXX (Boston, 1933), I, 119. The Glover incident is listed in Joseph H. Smith, ed., *Colonial Justice in Western Massachusetts (1639-1702): The Pynchon Court Record* . . . (Cambridge, Mass., 1961), 375. A comparable case involving a white woman brought a penalty of twenty stripes and the order to wear a paper "pinned upon her forehead with this inscription in capital letters: 'A SLANDERER OF MR. ZEROBABELL ENDICOTT,' " in Dow, ed., *Essex Court Recs.*, I, 380. Norton and Peter appear in Robert E. Moody, ed., *Province and Court Records of Maine* (Portland, 1928-64), III, 226. Carl Degler, on the Southern administration of justice to Negroes, says: "As early as 1669 the Virginia law virtually washed its hands of protecting the Negro held as a slave. It allowed punishment of refractory slaves up to and including accidental death, relieving the master, explicitly, of any fear of prosecution. . . . ," in "Slavery and the Genesis of American Race Prejudice," 61. Compare this situation also with the 1694-95 Nathaniel Cane murder case cited in Moody, ed., *Maine Recs.*, IV, 34-35.

8. See Dow, ed., *Essex Court Recs.*, V, 179; VI, 225; VII, 329-330, 373, 410. For white testimony on behalf of Negroes see Noble and Cronin, eds., *Assistants Recs.*, III, 194.

9. Morison, ed., *Suffolk Court Recs.*, II, 1153-1157. Chaffee's remarks are in the Intro., I, xxv.

10. Charles W. Upham, *Salem Witchcraft* . . . (Boston, 1867), II, 128, 136-137.

11. The 1675 statutes are in Nathaniel B. Shurtleff, ed., *Records of the Governor and Company of the Massachusetts Bay in New England* (Boston, 1854), V, 49-50, Sections 13 and 14. Also see Jordan, "White Over Black," 119. Fornication and adultery were usually treated as one crime in the seventeenth century. Married men, engaging in sexual activity with women other than their wives, were often tried for fornication.

12. For Essex County Negro fornication cases see Dow, ed., *Essex Court Recs.*, II, 247; V, 411; VI, 73, 135; VII, 141, 411; for whites see I, 71, 80, 82, 337, 347, 404, 414, 420; III, 17, 61, 198-199; VII, 377-378, 398, 406, 410; VIII, 375, 377, 424. This list is by no means exhaustive.

13. Because the published records are incomplete, the only Suffolk County cases are from the 1670's. For Negro offenders see Morison, ed., *Suffolk Court Recs.*, I, 233; II, 991; for whites see, for example, I, 22, 80, 90-91, 114, 119, 185, 233-234; II, 885, 1012-1014, 1097-1099, 1102, 1153. The Courts sometimes required a couple fornicating before marriage to make public confession before the church. See I, 80, 90-91. In Maine fornicators usually received seven or more stripes or a fine ranging from fifteen to fifty shillings. See Moody, ed., *Maine Recs.*, IV, 268-269, 293, 340, 344-345, 358, 360, and 371 for examples.

14. Basto's case is in Noble and Cronin, eds., *Assistants Recs.*, I, 74, and Shurtleff, ed., *Mass. Recs.*, V, 117-118. John Negro is in Morison, ed., *Suffolk Court Recs.*, II, 1067.

15. *Ibid.*, II, 807; Noble and Cronin, eds., *Assistants Recs.*, I, 50, 199; II, 86; innocent whites are *ibid.*, I, 73, 158.

16. Shurtleff, ed., *Mass. Recs.*, V, 50, lists penalties for manslaughter and murder. White manslaughter cases are cited in Noble and Cronin, eds., *Assistants Recs.*, I, 54, 114, 188, 358-359.

17. The Trayes case is in Shurtleff, eds., *Plymouth Recs.*, VI, 141-142; Robin's in Noble and Cronin, eds., *Assistants Recs.*, I, 304-305, 321.

18. Moody, ed., *Maine Recs.*, IV, 34-35. We saw no published court records convicting Negroes of murder. But note the equality of sentence in this extract from Samuel Sewall's diary, June 8, 1693: "Elisabeth Emerson of Havarill and a Negro Woman were executed after Lecture, for murdering their Infant Children." Massachusetts Historical Society, *Collections*, 5th Ser., V (1878), 379.

19. The Stevens case is in Noble and Cronin, eds., *Assistants Recs.*, II, 100. The documents relating to Maria, her accomplices, and Jack have been brought together by John Noble. See *Publications of the Colonial Society at Massachusetts, Transactions, 1899, 1900*, VIII (Boston, 1904), 323-336.

20. Noble, *ibid.*, argues that Maria was hanged before burning, dismissing both Cotton and Increase Mather's assertions that she was burned alive. But Noble overlooked evidence that subtantiates the Mathers' contentions: a Milton minister who had witnessed Jack's and Maria's execution noted in his diary on Sept. 22, 1681: " . . . two negroes burnt, one of them was first hanged." "Rev. Peter Thacher's Journal" in Albert K. Teele, ed., *The History of Milton, Mass. 1640 to 1887* (Boston, 1887), 646. Increase Mather wrote: Maria was "burned to death,—the first that has suffered such a death in New England." Mass. Hist. Soc., *Proceedings*, III (1859), 320. Edgar Buckingham's allegation that in 1675 Phillis, a Negro slave, was burned alive in Cambridge, in "Morality, Learning, and Religion, in Massachusetts in Olden Times," *History and Proceedings of the Pocumtuck Valley Memorial Association, 1880-1889* (Deerfield, Mass., 1898), II, 20, seems unsupported.

21. *Suffolk Deeds* (Boston, 1880-1906), II, 297; III, 78; VII, 22, 144; VIII, 298-299; Morison, ed., *Suffolk Court Recs.*, II, 598; *Report of the Record Commissioners of the City of Boston Containing Miscellaneous Papers* (Boston, 1876-1909), X, 25.

22. Bostian Ken (Kine, Kajne), also known as Sebastian and Bus Bus, probably took his surname from the Keayne family. It was common for a Negro, if he had a last name, to use his master's or former master's. *Suffolk Deeds*, II, 297; IV, 111, 113.

23. Angola's land fronted on the main road between Boston and Roxbury and at least one man, James Pennyman, envied it. *Ibid.*, VIII, 298.

24. Property owning Negroes and master's gifts are *ibid.*, VII, 43; X, 278, 295; Dow, ed., *Essex Court Recs.*, II, 183; VIII, 434; *York Deeds*, IV, fol. 52; Ford, ed., *Diary of Cotton Mather*, I, 278; Henry A. Hazen, *History of Billerica, Mass.* (Boston, 1883), 170-171. Charles Taussig noted a Rhode Island Negro couple that had accumulated a 300 pound fortune and in 1735 sailed back to Guinea where they were independently wealthy; see *Rum, Romance and Rebellion* (New York, 1928), 33.

25. Horizontal mobility and freedom of movement are illustrated by the Maria case, discussed above; Dow, ed., *Essex Court Recs.*, VI, 255; VIII, 297-298; *Suffolk Deeds*, IV, x-xi; Ford, ed., *Diary of Cotton Mather*, II, 139; *Diary of Samuel Sewall*, Mass. Hist. Soc., *Coll.*, 5th Ser., VI (1879), 5; the travel account of an unknown Frenchman, *ca.* 1687, in Nathaniel B. Shurtleff, *A Topographical and Historical Description of Boston* (Boston, 1871), 48; James R. Trumbull, *History of Northampton* (Northampton, 1898), I, 376-377. Exemplifying freedom from masters' supervision is the case of a servant who persisted in wooing a young lady although repeatedly warned by *her* master to keep away. Both were later convicted for fornication. Dow, ed., *Essex Court Recs.*, VII, 141.

26. Revolts were never a problem in Massachusetts but runaways were frequent. Closest to a slave revolt was an unsuccessful 1690 attempt by a New Jerseyite with abolitionist tendencies to induce Negroes, Indians, and Frenchmen to attack several Bay Colony towns. See Joshua Coffin, *A Sketch of the History of Newbury . . .* (Boston, 1845), 153-154; and Sidney Perley, "Essex County in the Abolition of Slavery," *Essex-County Historical and Genealogical Register*, I (1894), 2.

27. On informal relations see Dow, ed., *Essex Court Recs.*, I, 287; V, 141; VII, 394-395;

VIII, 297; Morison, ed., *Suffolk Court Recs.*, I, 249; II, 648-649; Robert F. Seybolt, *The Town Officials of Colonial Boston, 1634-1775* (Cambridge, Mass., 1939), 77, 79, 83, 85, 87; Joseph Dudley to Gabriel Bernon, May 20, 1707, in George F. Daniels, *History of the Town of Oxford Massachusetts* (Oxford, 1892), 26-27. The quotation is from Smith, ed., *Colonial Justice in Western Massachusetts*, 298-299.

28. Massachusetts never formally denied Negroes the right to bear personal arms and specifically included them in the militia in 1652. But in 1656, without explanation, she reversed her policy, excluding Indians and Negroes from training. Shurtleff, ed., *Mass. Records*, IV, Pt. i, 86, 257.

29. William Fitzhugh, King George County Virginia, to Mr. Jackson of Piscataway, in New England, Feb. 11, 1683, in R. A. Brock, "New England and the Slave Trade," *Wm. and Mary Qtly.*, II (1894), 176-177; Saffin, Usher, Wetcomb, and Belcher to Welstead, June 12, 1681, in *New-England Historical and Genealogical Register*, XXXI (1877), 75-76.

30. Acts regulating alcoholic consumption are in the Records of the Council of Massachusetts under the Administration of President Joseph Dudley, "Dudley Records," Mass. Hist. Soc., *Proceedings*, 2d Ser., XIII (Boston, 1899, 1900), 252; Ellis Ames and Abner C. Goodell, eds., *Acts and Resolves of the Province of Massachusetts Bay, 1692-1714* (Boston, 1869-1922), I, 154; Moody, ed., *Maine Recs.*, IV, 51; Edward W. Baker, "The 'Old Worcester Turnpike,' " *Proceedings of the Brookline Historical Society* (Jan. 23, 1907), 29. Laws governing stolen goods are in Ames and Goodell, eds., *Acts and Resolves*, I, 156, 325; see also Greene, *The Negro in Colonial New England*, 130. The only other seventeenth-century statute aimed at Negroes was passed in 1680: that no ship of more than 12 tons should entertain any passenger, servant or Negro, without permit from the governor. *The Colonial Laws of Massachusetts. Reprinted from the Edition of 1672, With the Supplements through 1686* (Boston, 1887), 281.

31. The laws discussed in these paragraphs are in Ames and Goodell, eds., *Acts and Resolves*, I, 535, 578-579, 606-607; John B. Dillon, ed., *Oddities of Colonial Legislation in America . . .* (Indianapolis, 1879), 206-207, 211-212; *Report of the Record Commissioners of the City of Boston*, VIII, 173-177.

11 | PEQUOTS AND PURITANS: THE CAUSES OF THE WAR OF 1637

ALDEN T. VAUGHAN

The paucity of blacks in New England allowed the Puritan colonies from the outset to establish unilateral policies for their treatment and, when desired, for their enslavement. The Indians posed a far different challenge. Although an epidemic devastated the New England tribes a few years before the beginning of English colonization, the possibility—and often the reality—of armed conflict persisted throughout the seventeenth and eighteenth centuries. Warfare not only jeopardized life and property but it made more difficult the Puritans' efforts to convert the Indians to reformed Christianity. The prospect of widespread conversion, we know by hindsight, was slim; but the Puritan was not content to change only the Indians' beliefs; he insisted too on changing their entire way of life—a situation few Indians would accept. Meanwhile, the swelling colonial population acquired more and more of the Indians' land, thus alienating most Indian leaders and lessening the prospect of peaceful coexistence.

Two general interpretations of the Puritans' Indian policy have vied for acceptance during the past half-century. One sees the Puritans as essentially hostile to Indian survival: the settlers' insatiable land hunger and their determination to crush God's enemies ensured mounting hostility and belied the occasional professions by Puritan spokesmen of constructive or humane intentions. The other interpretation stresses the Puritans' efforts at conversion and education of the Indians and argues that until 1675 the colonies made sincere and partly successful efforts to deal fairly with their Indian neighbors. The schools of interpretation differ too over the causes of New England's wars. The following essay reviews earlier versions of the first major clash between the region's settlers and the Indians and concludes with an explanation that assigns responsibility to both sides.

The war of 1637 between the Puritans and the Pequot Indians was one of the most dramatic episodes in early New England history, possessing an intensity and a significance deserving of far more attention than it has usually been accorded. While more limited in scope than King Philip's War, and less tied to controversial issues than the Antinomian crisis or the banishment of Roger Williams, the Pequot War had unique elements which made it memorable in its own right. It resulted in the extermination of the most powerful tribe in New England, it witnessed one of the most sanguinary battles of all Indian wars—when some five hundred Pequot men, women, and children were burned to death in the Puritans' attack on Mystic Fort—and it opened southern New England to rapid English colonization. The war was not soon forgotten by the other tribes in the north-east, nor by the English who memorialized the victory in prose and poetry.[1] It even found its way into *Moby Dick* when Herman Melville chose the name of the vanquished tribe for Captain Ahab's ill-fated whaling vessel.[2]

As in the case of most wars, the conflict between the Pequot Indians and the Puritans of New England raises for its historian the twin problems of cause and responsibility. Involved is the whole question of Indian-white relations during the first century of English settlement in New England, the basic nature of the Puritan experiment, and the justice and humanity of the participants. Writers in eighteenth-century New England tended to side with their ancestors and view the conflict as a defensive maneuver on the part of the righteous forces of Puritanism prodded into action by the Pequot hordes, or, as Puritan rhetoric would have it, by Satan himself. Later historians sharing a popular antipathy toward Puritanism and all its works concluded that the war was a simple case of Puritan aggression and Pequot retaliation. Others would have us believe that it was fundamentally a manifestation of English land-hunger with the Pequots fighting for their lands as well as their lives.[3] The well-established facts seem to indicate that the proper explanation lies in none of these interpretations alone, but in a blend of the first two, modified by a radical restatement of the third.

Although the early history of the Pequot tribe is shrouded in obscurity, it is generally accepted that prior to the tribe's arrival in southern New England, it had inhabited lands in northern New Netherland close to the Mohawk Indians. For reasons that will probably always remain uncertain, the Pequot tribe, then called Mohegan, migrated into west central New England in the early seventeenth century and then turned southward until it reached the shores of the Atlantic Ocean. Unlike the Pilgrims who were exploring and settling Plymouth harbor at about the same time, the Mohegans gained their territory by force of arms. Along the route of their journey they made innumerable enemies and incurred such a reputation for brutality that they became known as "Pequots," the Algonquin word for "destroyers of men."[4] Animosity toward the Pequots was particularly strong among the small tribes of the Connecticut Valley who were forced to acknowledge the suzerainty of the intruders and to pay them annual tribute. Equally unfriendly were the Narrangansetts, the Pequots' nearest neighbors to the east, who resented the presence of a militarily superior tribe and refused to be cowed by it. The result was almost constant warfare between the Narragansetts and the Pequots, the final campaign of which was one phase of the Pequot War of 1637.

Not only were the Pequots unable to live peacefully with their Indian neighbors, they alienated the adjacent European settlers as well.[5] In 1634 the Pequots were at war with both Dutch New Netherland and the Narrangansetts. In the same year they made their first hostile move against the English with the assassination of Captain John Stone of Virginia and eight other Englishmen. Friendly Indians informed the Massachusetts authorities that the Pequots had assassinated the ship captain while he was sleeping in his bunk, had murdered the rest of his crew, and plundered his vessel. The Puritans could hardly let the murder of nine colonists go un-challenged if they intended to maintain their precarious foothold in a land where the natives vastly outnumbered them.

With the English demanding revenge for the murder of John Stone, the Pequots decided that this was one enemy too many, and late in October 1634 they sent ambassadors to Massachusetts to treat for peace and com-merce, reinforcing their appeal with gifts of wampum.[6] The Puritan authorities, after consulting with some of the clergy, demanded Stone's assassins as a prelude to negotiations. The Pequots replied with an account of Stone's death that differed markedly from the colonists' version. Stone, the Indians contended, had seized and bound two braves who had board-ed his ship to trade. It was after this, they said, that several of the braves' friends ambushed the captain when he came ashore. They also insisted that the sachem responsible for the ambush had since been killed by the Dutch and all but two of his henchmen had fallen victim to the pox.

The Pequots told their story "with such confidence and gravity" that the English were inclined to accept it, and after several days of negotiations the Pequots and the Bay Colony signed a treaty on November 1, 1634. By its terms the Indians agreed to hand over the two remaining assassins when sent for and "to yield up Connecticut," by which they probably meant as much of the valley as the English desired for settlement. In addi-tion, the Pequots promised to pay an indemnity of four hundred fathoms of wampum, forty beaver and thirty otter skins. Commercial relations were projected by an agreement that Massachusetts would send a trading vessel to the Pequots in the near future. Peace was thus maintained in New England. Commerce between the Bay Colony and the Pequots did not materialize, however. When John Oldham took his trading ship into Pe-quot territory the next spring, he found them "a very false people" and disinclined to amicable trade.[7]

Peace between the Bay Colony and the Pequots lasted until the fall of 1636, but those two years witnessed a rapid deterioration of the relations between the two. The Pequots failed to surrender the remaining assassins of Stone, the indemnity was paid only in part, and reports of further Pe-quot disingenuousness began to drift into Boston. By mid-summer of 1636, Massachusetts had lost patience and commissioned John Winthrop, Jr., then in Connecticut, to demand that Chief Sassacus of the Pequots sur-render at once the assassins of Captain Stone and reply to several other charges of bad faith. Should the Pequots fail to meet these demands, the Bay Colony threatened to terminate the league of amity and to "revenge the blood of our Countrimen as occasion shall serve."[8] But before Win-throp could fulfill his mission, an event occurred that put an end to all peaceful dealings with the Pequot tribe.

Late in July, John Gallop, en route by sea to Long Island, spied near Block Island John Oldham's pinnace, its deck crowded with Indians and no sign of a white man. When no one answered his hail, Gallop tried to board to investigate; a frenzied battle followed in which Gallop routed the Indians. On board he found the naked and mutilated body of Oldham.[9]

At first it appeared that the Narragansetts were responsible for Old-ham's murder. The Block Island tribe was subservient to them, and according to one report, all the Narragansett sachems except Canonicus and Miantonomo (the two leading chiefs) had conspired with the Block Islanders against Oldham because of his attempts to trade with the Pequots the previous year. The Massachusetts leaders contemplated war with the Narragansetts and warned Roger Williams "to look to himself." But Canonicus and Miantonomo speedily regained the confidence of the English by returning Oldham's two boys and his remaining goods from Block Island, and by assuring the Bay Colony, through Roger Williams, that most of the culprits had been killed by Gallop. Meanwhile the few surviving assassins sought refuge with the Pequots.[10]

The upshot of all this was a punitive expedition of ninety Massachusetts volunteers under magistrate John Endicott against Block Island. The troops were also ordered to visit Pequot territory to secure the remaining murderers of Stone and Oldham and assurances of future good behavior on the part of the Pequots. But when in early September the expedition made contact with the tribe, the Pequot spokesmen obstinately refused to comply with Puritan demands, first offering a new version of the killing of Stone that absolved them of any blame, then claiming that their leading chiefs were on Long Island, and finally insisting that they were still trying to discover who the culprits were. After a few hours of futile negotiations, the English became convinced that the delay was a camouflage for ambush, particularly when they observed the Pequots "convey away their wives and children, and bury their chiefest goods." A brief clash ensued in which a few Pequots were slain, several wounded, and much Pequot property seized or destroyed by the Massachusetts troops.[11]

The Pequots retaliated by torturing and slaying every Englishman they could find. Fort Saybrook at the mouth of the Connecticut River was put under virtual seige, and several of its garrison were ambushed during the next few months. English traders entering the Connecticut River fell victim to Pequot raiding parties. When reinforcements arrived from Massachusetts in the spring of 1637, the Pequots shifted their attacks to the unprotected plantations farther up the river.[12] Early on the morning of April 23, 1637, two hundred howling Pequot braves descended on a small group of colonists at work in a meadow near Wethersfield, Connecticut. Nine of the English were slain, including a woman and child; and the Pequots carried to their stronghold two young women whom the sachems hoped could make gunpowder for the tribe's few firearms. With some thirty Englishmen dead at Pequot hands, the New England colonies had no alternative but to wage war. Massachusetts Bay had in fact already declared war two weeks before the Wethersfield raid but had done nothing to stop the pattern of massacres. Connecticut could wait no longer, and on May 1, 1637, its General Court declared "that there shalbe an offensive warr against the Pequoitt."[13] Settlers as well as Pequots had engaged in the series of attacks, retaliations, and counter-retaliations preceding the formal declaration, but the wantonness, scope, and cruelty of the Indian raids cast upon them a very heavy burden of responsibility for the war that followed.

The reaction of the other Indian tribes to the outbreak of war reveals much about the nature of the conflict. The Narragansetts, thanks to some last-minute diplomacy by Roger Williams, had already made an offensive alliance with Massachusetts.[14] The Mohegans, a secessionist faction of the Pequot tribe that had revived the old tribal name and separated from Chief Sassacus the year before, also fought on the English side, against their blood brothers. The small valley tribes along the Connecticut River enthusiastically backed the Puritans, whom they had encouraged to settle in the valley as early as 1631 in hope of gaining protection against the Pequots.[15] Connecticut's declaration of war was, in fact, partly due to the urging of these tribes. "The Indians here our frends," wrote Thomas Hooker from Hartford, "were so importunate with us to make warr presently that unless we had attempted some thing we had delivered our persons unto contempt of base feare and cowardise, and caused them to turne enemyes agaynst us."[16] Of the hundreds of casualties the Pequots suffered, scores were inflicted by the Indians of southern New England and Long Island. As Captain John Mason, leader of the Connecticut forces observed, "Happy were they that could bring in their Heads to the English: Of which there came almost daily to Winsor, or Hartford."[17] And the greatest prize of all, the head of Chief Sassacus, was delivered by the Mohawks. Sassacus had sought asylum with his former neighbors, but afraid of the Englishmen's "hot-mouthed weapons," the Mohawks seized him and forty of his warriors, cut off their heads and hands, and confiscated their wampum.[18] The Pequots, for their part, were unable to find any important allies among the Indians. Clearly, this was no racial conflict between white man and red. Rather, the Pequot War saw the English colonies, eagerly assisted by several Indian tribes, take punitive action against the one New England tribe that was hated and feared by Indian and white alike.

The short career of the Pequots in history, then, was of a people apparently incapable of maintaining the trust and forbearance of any of their neighbors, red or white, English or Dutch. A prima facie case exists for the claims of Puritan apologists, and its partial validity is undeniable. Unfortunately, it is not the whole story.

The weightiest criticism of Puritan policy, and the one stressed most often by scholars hostile to the New Englanders, is that the conduct of the settlers was incessantly heavy-handed and provocative. It can even be argued that long before the Endicott expedition the English had treated the Pequots with something less than equity. For example, the character of Captain John Stone was such as to lend an air of plausibility to the Pequot version of his death.

Captain Stone, it seems, had piloted a shipload of cattle from Virginia to Boston in 1634. At each stop along the way he managed so to embroil himself with the local authorities that he was soon *persona non grata* in every community north of the Hudson. His first escapade was in New Amsterdam, where he attempted to steal a Plymouth bark and was thwarted only at the last minute by some Dutch seamen. Later, in Plymouth, he almost stabbed Governor Thomas Prence. He acted little better in Massachusetts Bay where he "spake contemptuously of [the] magistrates, and carried it lewdly in his conversation," in particular calling Judge Roger Ludlow "a just as." On top of this he was charged with excessive drinking and adultery. He was tried and acquitted for lack of evidence on the major charge, but his lesser indiscretions earned him a suspended fine of one hundred pounds and banishment from the colony under penalty of death.[19] Stone was on his way back to Virginia, accompanied by Captain Walter Norton and crew, when he stopped off to explore the trading prospects of the Connecticut River and there met his death. As might be expected, news of his fate did not elicit universal mourning: some of the English, secure in their piety, concluded with Roger Clap that "thus did God destroy him that so proudly threatened to ruin us."[20]

These circumstances perhaps explain why no military action was taken against the Pequots in 1634. It should be noted, however, that the treaty the Puritans extracted from the Pequots later that year was hardly a lenient one. Still, hostilities did not break out until the Bay Colony dispatched the Endicott expedition in 1636 to avenge the death of John Oldham. And here again, the Puritans' conception of just retribution was stern indeed. Endicott's instructions were to kill all Indian men on Block Island, seize the women and children, and take possession of the island. He was then to proceed to the Pequot territory and demand the murderers of Stone and Oldham, one thousand fathoms of wampum, and some Pequot children as hostages. Should the Pequots refuse to comply with the terms of this ultimatum, the expedition was to impose them by force.[21] And Endicott vigorously complied with these instructions. He secured a beachhead on Block Island in the face of brief resistance, routed the defenders, and devastated the island, While the Indians of Block Island sought refuge in the swamps, the Massachusetts troops burned wigwams, destroyed cornfields, and smashed canoes. Dissatisfied by the small number of Indian casualties, the English soldiers heartlessly "destroyed some of their dogs instead of men." After two busy days of destruction, the expedition set sail for Pequot territory.[22]

Four days later Endicott's fleet entered Pequot Harbor. The Indians greeted the fleet's appearance with "doleful and woful cries," for it was obvious to the Pequots that this was no friendly mission. And whatever chance there may have been for peaceful negotiations rapidly vanished. When the Pequots refused to meet his demands and began their annoying delays, Endicott landed his troops and took station on a commanding hilltop.[23] Some of the Indians' excuses for delay may have been legitimate, but the English rejected them, and Endicott interpreted a final Pequot suggestion that both sides lay down their arms as a dastardly ruse. "We rather chose to beat up the drum and bid them battle," recorded Captain John Underhill. A volley from the musketeers sent the Pequot warriors scurrying for shelter, and the pattern established on Block Island was repeated. The colonists spent the next two days in rampant destruction and looting. In deference to English firepower, the Indians kept a respectful distance.[24]

By the fourteenth of September, less than three weeks after their departure from Boston, the Massachusetts troops were back in the Bay Colony with but two casualties, neither fatal. The Pequots were mourning far greater losses: several killed and a score or more wounded in addition to the destruction of their property. Ironically, the first Pequot life may well have been taken by Chief Cutshamekin of the Massachusetts Indians, who had joined Endicott as an interpreter and guide.[25] In any event, harsh Puritan "justice" had been imposed; harsh Pequot retaliation soon followed.

The Endicott attack spurred the Pequots to seek retribution. Although the Pequots had suffered few casualties, it was inconceivable that this proud tribe would not insist on revenge. Its land had been invaded, its chief subjected to arrogant demands, and its tribesmen assaulted. The other Puritan colonies were quick to blame the Bay Colony for the massacres that ensued. Spokesmen for Plymouth, Connecticut, and Fort Saybrook (then under separate government) all condemned the Endicott expedition, and even Governor Winthrop later tacitly admitted that Massachusetts had provoked hostilities. Lion Gardiner, commander of the Saybrook garrison, expressed the prevalent opinion even before the Endicott expedition reached Pequot soil. "You come hither," he protested, "to raise these wasps about my ears, and then you will take wing and flee away."[26] His prophecy was accurate; Endicott upset the nest, but the stings were first felt by the few hundred settlers of Connecticut and Fort Saybrook.

There remains the question of why the Bay Colony had resorted to coercive action after having tolerated the crimes attributed to the Pequots prior to their harboring of Oldham's assassins. The explanation may be threefold. In the first place, the Bay Colony, now considering herself the dominant authority in New England, was determined strictly to enforce the peace, a policy more easily undertaken since she was the least likely to feel the brunt of any retaliation. Secondly, shortly before the Endicott expedition was formed Roger Williams had reported a heady boast of the Pequots that they could by witchcraft defeat any English expedition, a challenge hardly designed to soothe Puritan tempers.[27] Finally, Massachusetts was then in the throes of civil and religious controversy. Roger Williams had been ousted but a few months earlier for "divers dangerous opinions," the Crown had recently instituted quo warranto proceedings against the colony's charter, and the first rumblings of the Antinomian movement were faintly audible. If frustration is a prime cause of aggression, the Bay Colony had been overripe for Endicott's blow at Satan's horde.

Added to Pequot perfidy, then, was the harshness of Massachusetts's remedial action. Both contributed to the outbreak of the war.

That the war was a product of English land hunger and Pequot defense of its tribal territory, finds little documentation. It seems doubtful that in 1636 English settlers wanted land with which the Indians were unwilling to part. The Connecticut Valley tribes were welcoming the English and encouraging their settlement there. Neither the Narragansetts nor the Mohegans seem to have been disturbed by colonial expansion; the former had made sizable grants to Roger Williams, and the latter were to make the most vigorous Indian contribution to the downfall of the Pequots. Nor is there any evidence that the Pequots themselves feared immediate English encroachment on their tribal lands. It is true that the Pequots did try to gain Narragansett aid against Massachusetts Bay by raising the specter of future Indian extermination at the hands of the English, but they did not argue that the present danger of dispossession was great.[28] By the treaty of November 1634, the Pequots themselves had granted the Bay Colony the right to settle in Connecticut, though of course the local valley tribes would have denied the right of the Pequots to make such a grant. The English settlement nearest to Pequot territory was at Saybrook, which had a garrison of only twenty men. It was situated, in fact, in the Mohegans' territory after their secession in 1636.

A few historians have attempted to find evidence of a ravenous Puritan land hunger in the rhetoric of Puritan theology,[29] but the evidence presented in support of such a view appears to consist for the most part of theological generalizations—in many cases uttered by Puritan leaders before embarking for the New World—concerning the holiness of their venture and the certainty that God had laid aside for them the lands necessary for its fulfillment. It is far more germane to establish how the Puritans, once settled in New England and confronted with it realities, went about the mundane business of evolving and administering a practicable land policy. The records clearly demonstrate that the bulk of the settlers proceeded upon the assumption that the Indian—heathen or not—had legal title to the lands upon which he lived, a title that could be changed only through the civilized conventions of sale and formal transfer.[30] Only two instances exist in which the New Englanders acquired any substantial amounts of land from the Indians by means other than treaties. One was the Pequot War of 1637, the other King Philip's War of 1675-76; neither can reasonably be explained as campaigns for territorial expansion.

In seeking to identify the causes of the war and apportion responsibility for its outbreak, one must begin with the fact established by the testimony of all the whites and most Indians that the Pequots were blatantly and persistently provocative and aggressive. Perhaps brilliant diplomacy could have prevented the intransigence of the Pequots from leading to open warfare; but even Roger Williams, the most likely man for the role of arbiter, had no influence upon the Pequots. On the other hand, it is undeniable that Puritan severity in the Endicott campaign provided the spark that set off the ultimate conflagration. Although the harshness of the Bay Colony's policy in the summer of 1636 is understandable, it cannot be excused.

While land as such was plainly not at issue, the Endicott expedition may well have represented something even more fundamental at stake here—the struggle between Puritans and Pequots for ultimate jurisdiction over the region both inhabited. The Puritans, determined to prevent Indian actions that might in any way threaten the New World Zion, had assumed through their governments responsibility for maintaining law and order among all inhabitants, Indian and white. The Plymouth magistrates had accepted this responsibility to the full limit of their resources, and had labored to curb both Indian and English when either threatened the peace. Massachusetts Bay, at first too weak to exert its authority beyond its immediate area of settlement, was by 1636 ready to enforce its fiat on all Indians in southern New England. Prior to the formation of the Confederation of New England in 1643, each colony endeavored to exercise full authority over natives as well as its own people within its own borders; yet Massachusetts, in its dealings with the Narragansetts and Pequots, was obviously assuming jurisdiction over areas outside its charter limits. It did so for the simple reason that otherwise Indians could molest white men, and vice versa, with impunity.

At bottom it was the English assumption of the right to discipline neighboring Indians that led to war in 1637. The Endicott expedition of 1636 was sent primarily to act as a police force, with orders to inflict punishment upon Block Island and obtain sureties of good behavior from the Pequots. The Pequots naturally resented the interference of Massachusetts in an area over which they had but recently acquired hegemony, and rejected the Bay Colony's assumption of the right to impose authority. The result was war. It may be the Puritans of Massachusetts were begging for trouble by extending their authority beyond their chartered territory; but the other tribes of New England not only submitted to the exertion of authority by Massachusetts Bay to keep the peace but even appeared at times to invite it. As the alternative was anarchy outside the settled areas, it is difficult to condemn the policy of Massachusetts, except in its application by Endicott. In short, the Pequot War, like most wars, cannot be attributed to the unmitigated bellicosity of one side and the righteous response of the other. Persistent aggression by the Pequot tribe, the desire for autonomy from or revenge against the Pequots by various other tribes, the harshness of the Endicott campaign, and divergent concepts as to the Englishman's jurisdiction all contributed to the outbreak of New England's first Indian war.

The war itself was brief, brutal, and its outcome thoroughly satisfying to the English and their Indian allies. The toll in human life was extremely high and makes the Pequot War one of the most regrettable episodes in early New England history. Still, it is small, though real, consolation that the blame perhaps lies as heavily upon the Pequots as on the Puritans. It may also be hoped that the troubled conscience with which the modern American historian often views our past relations with the Indians can find some balm in contemplating an episode in which the white man groped for workable formulas of friendship and justice, and in which he was not solely responsible for their ultimate failure.

Vaughan's interpretation has been sharply contested by Francis Jennings in The Invasion of America: Indians, Colonialism and the Cant of Conquest *(Chapel Hill, 1975). Jennings blames the war on Puritan expansion into the Connecticut Valley and on what he sees as duplicity by the "Puritan oligarchy" in its dealings with the Pequots. He also denies the sincerity of most Puritan missionaries, especially John Eliot, whom Jennings characterizes as "the apostle who was not of peace."*

Such a view of Eliot and the Puritan missionary impulse is largely shared by Neal Salisbury in "Red Puritans: The 'Praying Indians' of Massachusetts Bay and John Eliot," (William and Mary Quarterly, series 3, XXXI [1974]), an assessment that differs at several points from the accounts by Samuel Eliot Morison in Builders of the Bay Colony (Boston, 1930) and Alden T. Vaughan in New England Frontier: Puritans and Indians, 1620–1675 (Boston, 1965). All historians agree, however, that in 1675 King Philip's War brought an effective end to peaceful relations between Puritans and Indians throughout New England. That holocaust, well covered in Douglas E. Leach's Flintlock and Tomahawk: New England in King Philip's War (New York, 1958), revealed the Puritans' tragic inability to transcend the assumptions and biases of their time or to create a society that accepted cultural diversity.

NOTES

1. See, for examples, Timothy Dwight, Greenfield Hill: A Poem in Seven Parts (New York, 1794), Bk. IV, and Samuel G. Drake, The Book of the Indians, 9th ed. (Boston, 1845), Bk. ii, 106-107.

2. For an explanation of Melville's familiarity with the history of the Pequot War and his reasons for employing the name of the tribe see the edition by Luther S. Mansfield and Howard P. Vincent (New York, 1952), 68, 631-633.

3. For a representative of the first view, see Benjamin Trumbull, A Complete History of Connecticut . . . (New Haven, 1818), I, chap. 5. The second viewpoint, prevalent among non-New England authors in the 19th century and among 20th-century historians regardless of locale, can be found in John R. Brodhead, History of the State of New York, I (New York, 1853), 237-273; William C. MacLeod, The American Indian Frontier (New York, 1928), 209-219; and William T. Hagan, American Indians (Chicago, 1961), 12-14. The latter two also see the Puritans coveting Indian lands; they thus have much in common with the third school of interpretation, which finds its most articulate presentation in Roy Harvey Pearce, The Savages of America (Baltimore, 1953), 19-35.

4. Roger Williams, "A Key into the Language of America . . . ," in Narragansett Club, Publications, I (Providence, 1866), 22n, 203.

5. See Brodhead, History of New York, I, 242; James Kendall Hosmer, ed., Winthrop's Journal, "History of New England," 1630-1649 (New York, 1908), I, 79, 139.

6. The details of these negotiations can be found in Winthrop's Journal, I, 138-140; Winthrop to John Winthrop, Jr., Dec. 12, 1634, in Allyn Bailey Forbes, ed., Winthrop Papers, III (Boston, 1943), 177; and Winthrop to William Bradford, n.d., in William Bradford, Of Plymouth Plantation, 1620-1647, ed. Samuel E. Morison (New York, 1952), 291.

7. Winthrop's Journal, I, 139-140; Winthrop to Bradford, Mar. 12, 1635, in Bradford, Of Plymouth Plantation, 291-292.

8. Jonathan Brewster to John Winthrop, Jr., June 18, 1636, in Winthrop Papers, III, 270-271; Colony of Massachusetts Bay to John Winthrop, Jr., July 4, 1636, ibid., 284-285.

9. Winthrop's Journal, I, 183-184; Thomas Cobbet, "A Narrative of New England's Deliverances," New England Historical and Genealogical Register, VII (1853), 211-212.

10. Winthrop's Journal, I, 184-185; Bradford, Of Plymouth Plantation, 292; William Hubbard, The History of the Indian Wars in New England . . . , ed. Samuel G. Drake (Roxbury, Mass., 1865), II, 11.

11. John Underhill, "News from America . . . ," in Massachusetts Historical Society, Collections, 3d Ser., VI (Boston, 1837), 4-10, is the only eyewitness account of the Endicott expedition. See also Winthrop's Journal, I, 187-189; and Lion Gardiner, A History of the Pequot War . . . (Cincinnati, 1860), 12-13.

12. Gardiner, *History of the Pequot War*, 14-21; *Winthrop's Journal*, I, 191-192, 194, 208, 212; Lion Gardiner to John Winthrop, Jr., Mar. 23, 1637, in *Winthrop Papers*, III, 381-382.

13. Underhill, "News from America," 12; J. Franklin Jameson, ed., *Johnson's Wonder-Working Providence, 1628-1651* (New York, 1910), 149; Nathaniel B. Shurtleff, ed., *Records of the Governor and Company of the Massachusetts Bay in New England*, I (Boston, 1853), 192; J. Hammond Trumbull, ed., *The Public Records of the Colony of Connecticut*, I (Hartford, 1850), 9.

14. Williams to John Mason, June 22, 1670, in Narragansett Club, *Publs.*, VI (Providence, 1874), 338; *Winthrop's Journal*, I, 192-194.

15. *Winthrop's Journal*, I, 62; Bradford, *Of Plymouth Plantation*, 258.

16. Hooker to John Winthrop, spring 1637, in *Winthrop Papers*, III, 407.

17. John Mason, "A Brief History of the Pequot War . . . ," in Mass. Hist. Soc., *Colls.*, 2d Ser., VIII (Boston, 1819), 148.

18. Philip Vincent, "*A True* Relation of the Late Battell Fought in *New-England*, between the English and the Pequet Salvages . . . " in Mass. Hist. Soc., *Colls.*, 3d Ser., VI (Boston, 1837), 40. *Winthrop's Journal*, I, 229.

19. *Winthrop's Journal*, I, 102-108; Bradford, *Of Plymouth Plantation*, 268-269; Roger Clap, "Memoirs of Capt. Roger Clap," in Alexander Young, *Chronicles of the First Planters of the Colony of Massachusetts Bay, from 1623 to 1636* (Boston, 1846), 363; *Records of Massachusetts Bay*, I, 108.

20. Bradford, *Of Plymouth Plantation*, 269-271; *Winthrop's Journal*, I, 118; Clap, "Memoirs," in Young, *Chronicles of the First Planters*, 363.

21. *Winthrop's Journal*, I, 186.

22. Underhill, "News from America," 7. Underhill reported that 14 Indians were killed and 40 wounded on Block Island. The Narragansetts later informed the English that there had been only one Indian fatality. (*Winthrop's Journal*, I, 189-190.) In any event, since the island was under the jurisdiction of the Narragansetts, this phase of the Endicott expedition was not considered as an attack on the Pequots; rather, it was as vengeful retaliation for the murder of Oldham.

23. Underhill, "News from America," 7.

24. *Ibid.*, 7-10; *Winthrop's Journal*, I, 188-189.

25. *Winthrop's Journal*, I, 189-190; Gardiner, *History of the Pequot War*, 13; Underhill, "News from America," 11. Gardiner claimed that only one Pequot had been killed, and that Cutshamekin was the slayer. Winthrop reports two killed, while Underhill referred to "certain numbers of theirs slain, and many wounded." The Narragansetts later told Winthrop that 13 Pequots had been killed and 40 wounded. While there is no way of knowing which of these figures is most accurate, it is interesting to note that the two earliest historians of the war accept the lowest figure, but do not place the blame on Cutshamekin. Hubbard, *History of the Indian Wars in New England*, II, 15; Increase Mather, *A Relation of the Troubles which have hapned in New-England, By reason of the Indians there . . . ,* ed. Samuel G. Drake under the title, *Early History of New England . . .* (Boston, 1864), 162.

26. *Winthrop's Journal*, II, 115-116; Gardiner, *History of the Pequot War*, 23-24; Jameson, ed., *Johnson's Wonder-Working Providence*, 164. Although there is no record of Roger Williams's opinion, he undoubtedly was appalled by the severity of the attacks on the Block Islanders and Pequots.

27. Williams to John Winthrop, ca. Sept. 1636, *Winthrop Papers*, III, 298. The text of the letter strongly suggests that it is misdated in the published collection; it was probably written in early Aug.

28. Bradford, *Of Plymouth Plantation*, 294.

29. For example, see Pearce, *Savages of America*, 20.

30. As the Commissioners of the United Colonies put it in 1653, "The English . . . did generally purchase to themselves from the Indians the true propriators a Just Right and title to the lands they ment to Improve if they found not the place a Vacuum Domicilium." Nathaniel B. Shurtleff and David Pulsifer, eds., *Records of the Colony of New Plymouth, in New England* (Boston, 1855-61), X, 13. While there existed, of course, much room for dispute over what land was occupied and what was *vacuum domicilium*, the Indians rarely seem to

have felt aggrieved. See also *ibid.*, IV, 19; IX, 11, 112; *Records of Connecticut*, I, 19; *Records of Massachusetts Bay*, III, 281-282; Charles J. Hoadley, ed., *Records of the Colony of Jurisdiction of New Haven* . . . (Hartford, 1858), 518, 593-594; *Winthrop's Journal*, I, 294. Unpublished evidence can be found in such depositories as Massachusetts Archives (vol. XXX), State House, Boston; Connecticut Archives (Indians, vols. I and II), State Library, Hartford; Mass. Hist. Soc. (Miscellaneous Bound Manuscripts, vols. I and II), Boston. For a different interpretation see Chester E. Eisinger, "The Puritans' Justification for Taking the Land," *Essex Institute Historical Collections*, LXXXIV (Salem, Mass., 1948), 131-143, and Wilcomb E. Washburn, "The Moral and Legal Justifications for Dispossessing the Indians," in James Morton Smith, ed., *Seventeenth-Century America: Essays in Colonial History* (Chapel Hill, 1959), 15-32.

PART FIVE |

PATTERNS OF
NEW ENGLAND LIFE
AND THOUGHT

Regardless of Puritanism's influence on everyday life—undoubtedly strong in some aspects, slight or perhaps nonexistent in others—New England gradually took on its own patterns of daily existence. The region's soil, climate, and commercial opportunities shaped the economy; a growing population, the availability of land, and concepts of community cohesion determined the structure of towns and families; and theological premises and the practical needs of a frontier environment molded attitudes toward birth, marriage, death, and human relationships.

In the seventeenth and eighteenth centuries, economic endeavor, especially agriculture, was predominantly a family enterprise. For a while some of the New England towns carried on communal farming traditions brought from old England, as Sumner Chilton Powell's *Puritan Village: The Formation of a New England Town* (Middletown, Conn., 1963) and Kenneth A. Lockridge's *A New England Town: The First Hundred Years* (New York, 1970) have shown, respectively, of Sudbury and Dedham, Massachusetts. But the abundance of inexpensive land encouraged individual ownership and the fencing of individual allotments—very rapidly in Dedham, somewhat more slowly in Sudbury. As a result, families rather than towns soon became the principal economic units. And from the outset, families were central to most other aspects of early New England society.

Studies of the Puritan family have proliferated in the past ten years. Edmund S. Morgan, in *The Puritan Family: Religion and Domestic Relations in Seventeenth-Century New England* (rev. ed., New York, 1966), made the initial major contribution by demonstrating the impact of Puritan theology on family functions and on the roles of each member. In *A Little Commonwealth: Family Life in Plymouth Colony* (New York, 1970), John Demos used demographic techniques and psychological concepts to investigate family structure and relationships in the several towns of Plymouth Colony. In contrast, Philip Greven (*Four Generations: Land, Population, and Family in Colonial Andover, Massachusetts* [Ithaca, N.Y., 1970]) studied the evolution of family and community in a single New England town.

One of the principal findings of these works has been that, contrary to long-held assumptions, the New England family from the outset was nuclear (i.e., consisting of husband, wife, and their children) rather than extended (i.e., containing in addition grandparents or married siblings of the husband or wife), But Greven found that Andover developed a pattern, neither exclusively nuclear nor extended, in which married sons lived in their own homes but on their father's property; in most instances the father retained until death the title to the land his sons occupied and tilled and thereby maintained a strong patriarchal influence. It appears that in family structure, as in so many aspects of life, Puritan New England encompassed considerable variety within its ostensible conformity.

Similarly, the inhabitants of colonial New England did not necessarily think alike about the roles of women, or death, or Satan's ability to enlist witches and wizards to do his evil work. Yet in these and other areas of human concern—family structure and town organization, for example—prevailing attitudes and practices distinguished the Puritan colonists from their non-Puritan contemporaries.

12 | VERTUOUS WOMEN FOUND: NEW ENGLAND MINISTERIAL LITERATURE, 1668-1735

LAUREL THATCHER ULRICH

There were distinctive patterns, as well as apparent inconsistencies, in Puritan society's attitudes toward women and in the lives women led. Accounts of Anne Hutchinson's trial suggest a pervasive sexism; however, works on colonial legal practices by Richard B. Morris (Studies in the History of American Law, with Special Reference to the Seventeenth and Eighteenth Centuries *[New York, 1930]) and on the status of colonial women by Roger Thompson* (Women in Stuart England and America: A Comparative Study *[London, 1974]) indicate that the Puritans were less culpable than their cousins in England or Virginia. The following essay examines selected Puritan writings to see how a segment of Puritan leadership reflected society's attitudes toward women.*

Cotton Mather called them "The Hidden Ones." They never preached or sat in a deacon's bench. Nor did they vote or attend Harvard. Neither, because they were virtuous women, did they question God or the magistrates. They prayed secretly, read the Bible through at least once a year, and went to hear the minister preach even when it snowed. Hoping for an eternal crown, they never asked to be remembered on earth. And they haven't been. Well-behaved women seldom make history; against Antinomians and witches, these pious matrons have had little chance at all. Most historians, considering the domestic by definition irrelevant, have simply assumed the pervasiveness of similar attitudes in the seventeenth century. Others, noting the apologetic tone of Anne Bradstreet and the banishment of Anne Hutchinson, have been satisfied that New England society, while it valued marriage and allowed women limited participation in economic affairs, discouraged their interest in either poetry or theology. For thirty years no one has bothered to question Edmund Morgan's assumption that a Puritan wife was considered "the weaker vessel in both body and mind" and that "her husband ought not to expect too much from her."[1] John Winthrop's famous letter on the insanity of bookish Mistress Hopkins has been the quintessential source. ". . . if she had attended her household affairs, and such things as belong to women, and not gone out of her way and calling to meddle in such things as are proper for men, whose minds are stronger, etc., she had kept her wits."[2]

Yet there is ample evidence in traditional documents to undermine these conclusions, at least for the late seventeenth and early eighteenth centuries. For the years between 1668 and 1735, Evans' *American*

Bibliography lists 55 elegies, memorials, and funeral sermons for females plus 15 other works of practical piety addressed wholly or in part to women.[3] Although historians have looked at such popular works as Cotton Mather's *Ornaments for the Daughters of Zion,* they have ignored the rest.[4] Thus, New England's daughters remain hidden despite the efforts of her publishing ministry. True, a collection of ministerial literature cannot tell us what New England women, even of the more pious variety, were really like, Nor can it describe what "most Puritans" thought of women. It can tell us only what qualities were publicly praised in a specific time by a specific group of men. Yet, in a field which suffers from so little data, there is value in that. A handful of quotations has for too long defined the status of New England's virtuous women. This interesting collection deserves a closer look.

Although 27 of the 70 titles are by Cotton Mather (who wrote more of everything in the period), the remaining 43 are the work of 21 authors. They range from a single sermon by Leonard Hoar, his only published work, to the six poems for women written over a 25-year period by ubiquitous elegist John Danforth. They include four English works republished in America. Only 12 of the titles were printed before 1700, but two others, Samuel Willard's short discourse on marriage from his *Complete Body of Divinity,* posthumously published in 1726, and Hugh Peter's *A Dying Father's Last Legacy*, first reprinted in Boston in 1717, originated earlier. Peter's treatise, written just before his execution, is especially interesting as a link to the first generation of New Englanders.

In spite of personal idiosyncracies and the acknowledged predominance of Mather, this literature is remarkable consistent. Thus, a crude woodcut decorating a broadside published for Madam Susanna Thacher in 1724 is identical to that ornamenting an elegy for Lydia Minot published in 1668. Nor are doctrinal distinctions of any consequence. Benjamin Colman could differ with his brethren over the precise meaning of New England, for example, yet share with them a common attitude toward women.[5] Because these works are so much of a piece, however, subtle shifts in emphasis between authors and across time become significant. A patient examination of this seemingly static and formulaic material reveals nuances in ministerial thought of considerable interest, demonstrating that for women's history, as for so many aspects of social history, the real drama is often in the humdrum.

. . .

In ministerial literature, as in public records, women became legitimately visible in only three ways: they married, they gave birth, they died. In the written materials, dying is by far the best documented activity. Although a minister might have had a specific woman in mind as he prepared an idealized portrait of the good wife for a wedding or espousal sermon or as he composed a comforting tract for parishioners approaching childbed, it is only in the funeral literature that he is free to name names and praise individual accomplishments. Not that a funeral sermon is ever very specific. Circumlocution, even a certain coyness in referring to "that excellent person now departed from us," is the rule. Still, it is a rare sermon that does not contain a eulogy, however brief. Some append fuller biographical sketches often containing selections from the writings of the deceased.[6] From these materials a composite portrait emerges.

A virtuous woman sought God early. Hannah Meigs, who died in New London at the age of 22, was typical. She began while still a child to pay attention in church, acquiring the habit of reading and praying at night when the rest of her family was asleep. Becoming preoccupied with her own salvation, she bewailed her sinfulness, at last receiving an assurance of God's mercy. In the sickness which eventually claimed her, she submitted her will to God, from her death bed meekly teaching her brothers and sisters and other "Relatives, Acquaintances, & Companions."[7] Praise of early piety was not confined to sermons for young women. In his eulogy for Mary Rock, who died at the age of 80, Cotton Mather devoted considerable space to her early religiosity and the wise education of her parents.[8] The women eulogized typically found God before marriage, having been, in Danforth's phrase, first "Polish'd and Prepar'd" by pious parents.[9]

A virtuous woman prayed and fasted. Jane Colman was said to have lain awake whole nights mourning for sin, calling on God, praying.[10] Mrs. Increase Mather regularly prayed six times a day. After her death her husband wrote a tribute to her from his study, a spot which had become endeared to him when he discovered in some of her private papers that during his four years absence in England she had "spent many whole Days (some Scores of them) alone with God there" in prayer and fasting for his welfare and that of her children.[11] Thomas Foxcroft characterized a praying mother as "One that *stood in the Breach* to turn away wrath" and concluded that the death of such women was a bad omen for the community.[12] Cotton Mather was fond of saying that good mothers travailed twice for their children, once for their physical birth, again for the spiritual.[13]

A virtuous woman loved to go to church. On the day of her death ailing Sarah Leveret went to hear the sermon even though the weather was bitter. When her friends tried to dissuade her, she answered: "If the Ministers can go abroad to Preach, certainly, it becomes the People to go abroad; and hear them."[14] Sarah was not alone among New England's pious matrons. The ministers who preached the funeral sermons for Anne Mason and Jane Steel both commented on the fact that they came to church even when they were ill.[15] Jabez Fitch said of Mrs. Mary Martin: "The feet of those that brought the glad Tidings of the Gospel, were always beautiful in her Eyes, and it was her great Delight to attend on the Ministry of the Word."[16]

A virtuous woman read. Throughout the eulogies reading is mentioned as often as prayer, and the two activities are occasionally linked as in John Danforth's praise of Hannah Sewall:

> *Observing Ladys* must keep down their Vail,
> 'Till They're as *Full* of Grace, & *Free* from Gall,
> As *Void* of Pride, as *High* in Vertue Rare
> As *much* in Reading, and as *much* in Prayer. [17]

After her children were grown, Maria Mather took renewed interest in reading the scriptures, more than doubling the prescribed pace by reading the Bible through twice in less than a year.[18] Her daughter Jerusha was a great reader of history and theology as well as scripture, having been given eyesight so excellent she could read in dim light.[19] Katharin Mather, Cotton's daughter, went beyond her grandmother and her aunt. She mastered music, penmanship, needlework, the usual accomplishments of a gentlewoman, "To which she added this, that she became in her childhood a Mistress of the Hebrew Tongue."[20]

A virtuous woman conversed. Mourning for Elizabeth Hatch, Joseph Metcalf lamented nothing so much as the loss of her pious discourse.[21] For John Danforth, Elizabeth Hutchinson's conversation was "sweeter than Hybla's Drops," while for Cotton Mather, the "fruitfulness" of Mary Rock's "Religious Conferences" made her sick room "A little *Anti-Chamber* of Heaven."[22] James Hillhouse said his mother could converse "on many subjects with the Grandees of the World, and the Masters of Eloquence" yet she was not haughty. "Her incessant and constant Reading, with her good Memory, and clear Judgment, made her expert (even to a degree) in the Bible. Insomuch, that she was capable on many occasions, very seasonably and suitably to apply it, and that with great facility and aptness, to the various Subjects of Discourse, that offered themselves."[23] James Fitch said that if he were to "rehearse the many Spiritual, Weighty, and Narrow Questions & Discourses" he had heard from Anne Mason, "it would fill up a large book."[24] Benjamin Wadsworth praised Bridget Usher for promoting "pious and savoury Discourse."[26] Godly matrons were meant to be heard.

A virtuous woman wrote. A quill as well as a distaff was proper to a lady's hand. Despite eight pregnancies in ten years, Katharin Willard was such a good manager and so industrious that she was "hindred not from the Use of her Pen, as well as of her Needle."[26] One form of writing was simply taking notes in church. Mary Terry wrote down the main points of the preacher's sermon, recalling the whole thing later from her notes, a habit which had apparently become less common by Foxcroft's time, for he commented that aged Bridget Usher and her associates had "practiced (even to the last) the good old way of *writing* after the Minister. They were *swift to hear*; and by this laudable (but not too unfashionable) Method, took care to hear *for the time to come*, as the Prophet Speaks."[27]

In preaching a funeral sermon Cotton Mather often included excerpts from the woman's writings. In Elizabeth Cotton's, for example, he drew from writings at several stages of her life, telling his audience that one of these selections was "so expressive and so Instructive, that it may well pass for the Best part of my Sermon, if I now give to you all, and particularly the Daughters of our *Zion*, the Benefit of hearing it Read unto you."[28] In 1711 he edited a selection of the writings of his sister Jerusha and published them with an introduction as *Memorials of Early Piety*. Such a practice was not uncommon. In 1681, Sarah Goodhue's husband published *The Copy of A Valedictory and Monitory Writing*, a letter of "sage counsel" and "pious instructions" which she had written for her family and hidden, having had a premonition of her death in childbirth.[29] Grace Smith's legacy to her children was supposedly "taken from her lips by the Minister of that Town where she died," a strange statement since it included in addition to predictable paragraphs of advice and motherly proverbs, two long passages in verse written in iambic tetrameter with a rather complex internal rhyme scheme.[30] Like the others, she had obviously been sharpening her pen after the spinning was done.

A virtuous woman managed well. Increase Mather said his father's greatest affliction was the death of his wife, "Which Afflication was the more grievous, in that she being a Woman of singular Prudence for the Management of Affairs, had taken off from her Husband all Secular Cares, so that he wholly devoted himself to his Study, and to Sacred Imployments."[31] Women were praised in the funeral sermons not only for being godly but for being practical. Even the saintly Jerusha Oliver was not above dabbling in investments. "When she sent (as now and then she did) her Little *Ventures to Sea*, at the return she would be sure to lay aside the *Tenth* of her gain, for Pious Uses."[32]

Anne Eliot's talents, which included nursing, were so valued that Danforth almost credited her with holding up the world:

> Haile! Thou *Sagacious & Advant'rous* Soul!
> Haile, Amazon Created to Controll
> Weak Nature's Foes, & T'take her part,
> The King of Terrours, Thou, (till the command
> Irrevocable came to Stay thy Hand,)
> Didst oft Repel, by thy Choice Art:
>   By High Decree
>   Long didst thou stand
> An Atlas, in Heav'n's Hand
> To th' World to be.[33]

Mrs. Eliot, like many of her sisters, was no less pious as an "Atlas."

A virtuous woman submitted to the will of God. Increase Mather told the story of a "Person of Quality" whose only son contracted smallpox. She called in the ministers to pray for him. When they prayed that if by God's will the child should die the mother would have the strength to submit, she interrupted, crying: "If He will Take him away; Nay, He shall the *Tear* him away." The child died. Sometime later the mother became pregnant, but when the time for delivery arrived the child would not come and was consequently "Violently *Torn* from her; so she Died."[34] For the godly woman rebellion was not worth the risks. She learned to submit to God, meekly acquiescing to the deaths of husband and children and ultimately to her own as well. Only one minister suggested that a departed sister was less than patient in her final sickness and Samuel Myles cautioned his reader lest he "Uncharitably, and Unchristianly impute that to the *Person*, which was justly chargeable on the *Disease*."[35] Cotton Mather's women were typically terrified of death until it approached, then they triumphed over the "King of Terrours." Jerusha Oliver sang for joy and sent a message to her sister in Roxbury telling her not to be afraid to die.[36] Rebeckah Burnet, age 17, expired crying, "Holy, Holy, Holy—Lord Jesus, Come unto Me!"[37] In her illness, Abiel Goodwin heard voices and music and was transported by the tolling of funeral bells. In her quieter moments she exhibited a wry sense of humor, agreeing with a visitor that, given her hydropical condition, she was "A going to Heaven by Water"and might soon sing that song with Jesus.[38]

Read directly, the qualities attributed to these women have little meaning. It is easy to conclude from the lavish praise bestowed upon them that they enjoyed an exalted position in the Puritan ethos. It is even more tempting to conclude the opposite, that the limited nature of their intellectual achievement and their continually lauded meekness and submission document a secondary role. It is helpful, then, to compare this portrait of a virtuous woman with a contemporary portrait of a godly man. Richard Mather, according to the eulogy written by his son Increase, found God early, prayed often, read the scriptures, and though he was learned "was exceeding low and little in his own eyes." Though well-educated, he was careful not to display his learning, and he always preached plainly. He loved to listen to sermons and in his last months continued to attend lectures in neighboring congregations until he was too sick to ride. "Yea and usually even to his old Age (as did Mr. Hildersham) he took notes from those whom he heard, professing that he found profit in it." He was patient in affliction, submitting to the will of God in death.[39] The inference is clear. While a godly woman was expected to act appropriately in all the relations in which she found herself, to be a dutiful daughter, an obedient and faithful wife, a wise parent and mistress, a kind friend, and a charitable neighbor, in her relationship with God she was autonomous. The portrait of Richard Mather, the first spiritual autobiography published in America, is duplicated in miniature in dozens of funeral sermons printed in Boston. But it didn't originate there. It is a pattern of godliness basic to the English reformed tradition.[40] This much should be obvious to anyone familiar with Puritan literature, yet it bears repeating in a time when qualities such as "meekness" and "submissiveness" are presumed to have a sexual reference. In a very real sense there is no such thing as *female* piety in early New England: in preaching sermons for women, the ministers universally used the generic male pronouns in enlarging their themes, even when the text had reference to a scriptural Bathsheba or Mary; the same Christ-like bearing was required of both male and female.

Because dying is an individual rather than a social act, it is in the funeral literature that we see most clearly the equality of men and women before God. It is important, then, to try to determine whether this acknowledged spiritual equality impinged on the prescribed social roles described in the general works of practical piety.

. . .

In 1709 there appeared in Boston a reprint of a wedding sermon preached at Sherbourn in Dorsetshire by a nonconformist minister named John Sprint. Called *The Bride-Woman's Counsellor*, it virtually ignored the groom. Marital troubles, the author concluded, were mainly the fault of women anyway. "You women will acknowledge that Men can learn to command, and rule fast enough, which as Husbands they ought to do, but tis very rare to find that Women learn so fast to Submit and obey, which as Wives they ought to do."[41] Like Sarah, women should call their husbands "Lord," never presuming to the familiarity of a Christian name lest they in time usurp his authority and place him under the discipline of an Apron-String. Although women might make light of this instruction to obey, he continued, "I know not of any duty belonging to any Men or Women, in the Whole Book of God, that is urged with more vehemency." Authority had been given to the husband as "absolutely and as peremptorily as unto Christ himself."[42]

This is a remarkable document, all the more remarkable because in the whole corpus of materials printed in Boston there is nothing remotely like it in content or in tone. It makes a useful reference point for looking at three other works printed about the same time: Benjamin Wadsworth's *The Well-Ordered Family*, 1712; William Secker's *A Wedding Ring*, an English pamphlet reprinted in Boston in 1690, 1705, 1750, and 1773; and Samuel Willard's exposition of the fifth commandment in *A Complete Body of Divinity*, 1726.

Wadsworth's treatise must be looked at structurally. Like Sprint he reminded wives to "love, honour and obey," but his entire essay was organized around the notion of mutual responsibility, mutual caring. He listed seven duties of husbands and wives. The first six are reciprocal: to cohabit, to love one another, to be faithful to one another, to help one another, to be patient with one another, to honor one another. It is only with the seventh duty that there is any differentiation at all: the husband is to govern gently, the wife to obey cheerfully. It was thus within an ethic of mutual concern and sharing that Wadsworth developed the obedience theme, and he maintained the parallel structure of the essay even in these paragraphs. Both mates were scolded if they should lift up their hands against the other. A woman who struck her husband usurped not just his authority but that of God. A man who twitted his wife affronted not just a Woman but God.[43] Wadsworth thus undercut the subjection of women to their husbands even as he upheld it.

The same tendency is apparent in Secker. *A Wedding Ring* is a frothy bit of writing, a tiny little book which would have fitted a pocket or pouch. Its intention was not so much instruction as celebration, and it appropriated attractive quotations and metaphors at random, regardless of inconsistency. Although there are traditional proverbs enjoining submission, the great weight of the imagery falls on the side of equality. Eve is a "parallel line drawn equal" with Adam. A husband and wife are like two instruments making music, like two streams in one current, like a pair of oars rowing a boat to heaven (with children and servants as passengers), like two milch kine coupled to carry the Ark of God, two cherubims, two tables of stone on which the law is written.[44]

Willard accepted this two-sided view of the marriage relation and in his short disquisition on the family attempted to harmonize it. "Of all the Orders which are unequals," he wrote, "these do come nearest to an Equality, and in several respects they stand upon even ground. These do make a Pair, which infers so far a Parity. They are in the Word of God called *Yoke-Fellows*, and so are to draw together in the Yoke. Nevertheless, God hath also made an imparity between them, in the Order prescribed in His Word, and for that reason there is a Subordination, and they are ranked among unequals." Yet, referring to the duties of the wife "as inferiour," he cautioned that "the word used there is a general word, and signified to be ordered under another, or to keep Order, being a Metaphor from a Band of Souldiers, or an Army." Further he explained that "the Submission here required, is not to be measured by the Notation or import of the Word itself, but by the Quality of the Relation to which it is applied." The husband-wife relation must never be confused with the master-servant or child-parent relation. A husband ought to be able to back his counsels with the word of God "and lay before her a sufficient Conviction of her Duty, to comply with him therein; for he hath no Authority or Compulsion." While in any relation it is the duty of inferiors to obey superiors unless a command is contrary to God, "a wife certainly hath greater liberty of debating the Prudence of the thing." Thus, the emphasis throughout is on discussion, on reasoning, on mediation. Wives as well as husbands have the responsibility to counsel and direct. Each should "chuse the fittest Seasons to Reprove each other, for things which their Love and Duty calls for."[45] The command to obedience, for Willard, was primarily a principle of order.

Sprint's sermon, bristling with assertive females and outraged husbands, is an oddity among the ministerial literature. Harmony, not authority, was the common theme. Thus, the marriage discourses support the implication of the funeral literature that women were expected to be rational as well as righteous, capable of independent judgment as well as deference, and as responsible as their spouses for knowing the word of God and for promoting the salvation of the family. A virtuous woman was espoused to Christ before she was espoused to any man.

. . .

That few tracts and sermons on childbirth survive is probably evidence in itself of the reluctance of the ministers to stress "feminine" or "masculine" themes over a common Christianity. The limited writing on parturition is worth examining, however, for here if anywhere authors had an opportunity to expound upon the peculiar failings or virtues of the weaker sex.

A pregnant woman in New England's godly community had two preparations to make for the day of her delivery. On the one hand she had to arrange for a midwife, ready a warm and convenient chamber, prepare childbed linen for herself and clothing for her infant, and plan refreshment for the friends invited to attend her. But she knew, even without a ministerial reminder, that these things could prove "miserable comforters." She might "perchance need no other linen shortly but a winding sheet, and have no other chamber but a grave, no neighbors but worms."[46] Her primary duty, then, was preparing to die. Female mortality is the most pervasive theme of the childbirth literature. The elegists loved to exploit the pathos of death in birth—the ship and cargo sunk together, the fruit and tree both felled, the womb became a grave. In his poem for Mary Brown, for example, Nicholas Noyes dwelt at length on the fruitless pangs of her labor "A BIRTH of *One*, to Both a Death becomes;/A Breathless Mother the *Dead Child* Entombs."[47] Thus, it was often in a very particular sense that the ministers spoke of the "fearful sex." In stressing the need for a husband's tenderness, for example, Willard had singled out those bodily infirmities associated with the "breeding, bearing, and nursing" of children.[48]

Yet these grim realities had their joyous side. Cotton Mather was fond of saying that though an equal number of both sexes were born, a larger proportion of females were reborn.[49] He wondered why. Perhaps they had more time to spend in godly activities, "although I must confess, tis often otherwise." No, he concluded, it was probably because in childbirth the curse of Eve had turned into a blessing.[50] Given the spiritual equality of men and women, the only possible explanation for a disparity in religious performance had to be physical. Benjamin Colman resolved the same problem in a similar way in a preface to one of his sermons. Writing later in the period than Mather, he could toy with the idea of a "natural Tenderness of Spirit" given to women through the election of God, yet he too focused upon their bodily experience. Pregnancy and childbirth, but turning female thoughts frequently "towards the Gates of Death, by which We all receive our Life," increased women's susceptibility to the comforts of Christ. Pregnancy was superior to regular human ills in this regard, thought Colman, because it continued for months rather than surprising the victim with an acute attack forgotten as soon as it was over.[51]

Even here the ministers were ready to stress similarities between men and women. Though John Oliver urged husbands to be kind to their pregnant wives because of their increased vulnerability to "hysterical vapours," his argument really rested on an analogy, not a contrast, between the sexes. Husbands should be tolerant of their wives, he insisted, because they "desire or expect the like favour to themselves in their own sickness, wherein all men are lyable to many absurdities, and troublesome humours."[52] Eve in her troubles was no more unstable than Adam.

Thus, the ministers were able to acknowledge the reproductive role of women without giving a sexual content to the psyche and soul. They stressed the *experience* of childbirth, rather than the *nature* of the childbearer. It is significant that the one place where they openly referred to the "curse of Eve" (rather than the more generalized "sin of Adam") was in dealing with the issue of birth. In such a context, Eve's curse had a particular and finite meaning, and it could be overcome. Stressing the redemptive power of childbirth, they transformed a traditional badge of weakness into a symbol of strength. Locating the religious responsiveness of women in their bodily experience rather than in their eternal nature, they upheld the spiritual oneness of the sexes. The childbirth literature, though fragmentary, is consistent with the marriage and funeral sermons.

. . .

When New England's ministers sat down to write about women, they were all interested in promoting the same asexual qualities: prayerfulness, industry, charity, modesty, serious reading, and godly writing. From 1660 to 1730 the portrait of the virtuous woman did not change. Her piety was the standard Protestant piety; her virtues were those of her brothers. Although childbearing gave her an added incentive to godliness, she possessed no inherently female spiritual qualities, and her deepest reality was unrelated to her sex. Yet an examination of the ministerial literature is not complete without consideration of an important but subtle shift, not in content but in attitude. This begins around the turn of the century in the work of Cotton Mather and continues, though less strikingly, in the sermons of Foxcroft and Colman. Mather's elegy for Mary Brown of Salem, "Eureka the Vertuous Woman Found, " marks the tone:

> Monopolizing HEE's, pretend no more
> Of wit and worth, to hoard up all the store.
> The Females too grow wise & Good & Great.[53]

Everything Mather said about Mary Brown had been said before by other ministers about other women. But his open championship of her sex was new. All of the ministers believed in the inherent equality of men and women, but for some reason first Mather, then others, seemed *compelled* to say so.

If we turn to the earliest of the advice literature, Hugh Peter's *A Dying Father's Last Legacy*, written for his daughter in 1660, this subtle shift becomes immediately apparent. The researcher who combs its tightly-packed pages looking for specific comments on women will come away disappointed. Yet the entire work is a profound comment on his attitude toward the subject. That he would write a long and detailed treatise to Elizabeth without reference to her sex is evidence in itself that he considered her basic responsibilities the same as his. Know Christ, he told her. Read the best books. Study the scriptures, using the annotations of divines. Pray constantly. Keep a journal; write of God's dealings with you and of yours with him. Discuss the workings of salvation with able friends. Seek wisdom. Speak truth. Avoid frothy words. Do your own business; work with your own hands. The one explicit reference to feminine meekness is inextricable from the general Christian context: "Oh that you might be God-like, Christ-like, *Moses*-like. *Michael* contesting with the Dragon, maintained his Meekness; and Paul says, it is the Woman's Ornament." For Peter, virtue had no gender. In putting on the woman's ornament, Elizabeth was clothed in the armor of a dragon-fighter as well. In a short paragraph on marriage, he reminded his daughter that while it was the husband's duty to lead, hers to submit, these duties "need mutual supports." Husbands and wives "need to observe each others Spirits; they need to Pray out, not Quarrel out their first Grablings; They need at first to dwell much in their own duties, before they step into each others." When he told her to stay much at home, he was applying a judgment to his own stormy career and troubled marriage. "For my Spirit it wanted weight, through many tossings, my head that composure others have, credulous, and too careless, but never mischievous nor malicious: I thought my work was to serve others, and so mine own Garden not so well cultivated."[54] Thus, Peter's treatise epitomized the central sermon tradition.

Thirty years later Cotton Mather was promoting the same qualities— but with a difference. Clearly, a contrast between inherent worth and public position was at the heart of his attitude toward women. "There are People, who make no Noise at all in the World, People hardly known to be in the World; Persons of the *Female Sex*, and under all the Covers imaginable. But the world has not many People in it, that are fuller of the Truest Glory."[55] That women made no noise bothered Mather, and he was continually devising metaphorical detours around the Pauline proscriptions. "Yes, those who may not *Speak in the Church*, does our Glorious Lord Employ to *Speak:* to *Speak* to us, and *Speak* by what we *see* in them, such Things as we ought certainly to take much Notice of."[56] He made much of the fact that Abiel Goodwin, a little damsel half his age, had taught him much of salvation, and in her funeral sermon he expressed pleasure that she could finally "without any Disorder" speak in the Church.[57]

But there was a route to worldly honor open to women, one which no epistle denied. "They that might not without *Sin*, lead the Life which old stories ascribe to *Amazons*, have with much Praise done the part of *Scholars* in the World."[58] A long section in *Ornaments for the Daughters of Zion* was devoted to the promotion of female writing. Mather combed the scriptures and the classics for precedents and applauded the efforts of near contemporaries such as Anna Maria Schurman, a Dutch feminist whose tract *The Learned Maid* probably influenced his decision to teach Katharin Hebrew. Schurman's argument, deeply imbedded in traditional piety, would have been congenial to Mather. She excluded from discussion "*Scriptural Theology*, properly so named, as that which without Controversie belongs to all Christians," directing her attention to that wider scholarship commonly denied women. If you say we are weak witted, she wrote, studies will help us. If you say we are not inclined to studies, let us taste their sweetness and you will see. If you say we have no colleges, we can use private teachers. If you say our vocations are narrow, we answer they are merely private; we are not exempt from the universal sentence of Plutarch: "It becomes a perfect Man, to know what is to be Known, and to do what is to be done."[59] She concluded by suggesting that young women be exposed from their infancy to the "encouragement of wise men" and the "examples of illustrious women." In his tracts and in his sermons, Mather enthusiastically provided both.

. . .

Cotton Mather's writings on women point to a . . . fundamental problem, a paradox inherent in the ministerial position from the first. This paper began by noting the obvious—that New England's women could not preach, attend Harvard, or participate in the government of the congregation or commonwealth. It went on to argue that this circumscribed social position was not reflected in the spiritual sphere, that New England's ministers continued to uphold the oneness of men and women before God, that in their understanding of the marriage relationship they moved far toward equality, that in all their writings they stressed the dignity, intelligence, strength, and rationality of women even as they acknowledged the physical limitations imposed by their reproductive role. Cotton Mather may not have been fully conscious of this double view, yet all his writings on women are in one way or another a response to it. Such a position requires a balance (if not an otherworldliness) that is very difficult to maintain. In the work of his younger contemporaries, Benjamin Colman and Thomas Foxcroft, this is even more clearly seen.

Colman's daughter Jane was apparently fond of the sermons of Cotton Mather for she composed a tribute to him on his death. Certainly in her own life she exemplified his teaching, spurning balls, black patches, and vain romances for godly scholarship. She had the run of her father's library, which included, in addition to edifying tomes, the poetry of Sir Richard Blackmore and of Waller. At eleven she began composing rhymes of her own and as a young bride she wrote letters to her father in verse which he sometimes answered in kind. Although intensely religious, she began to measure her own writing against a worldly as well as a heavenly scale, a tendency that must have contributed to her own self-doubts and frequent headaches. In a letter to her father, she expressed the hope that she had inherited his gifts. His answer epitomized the possibilities and the limitations of the ministerial position:

> My poor Gift is in thinking and writing with a little Eloquence, and a Poetical turn of Thought. This, in proportion to the Advantages you have had, under the necessary and useful Restraints of your Sex, you enjoy to the full of what I have done before you. With the Advantages of my liberal Education at School & College, I have no reason to think but that your Genious in Writing would have excell'd mine. But there is no great Progress or Improvement ever made in any thing but by Use and Industry and Time. If you diligently improve your stated and some vacant hours every Day or Week to read your Bible, and other useful Books, you will insensibly grow in knowledge & Wisdom, fine tho'ts and good Judgment.[60]

Both the "useful Restraints" and the encouragement of study are familiar themes. If Colman saw no possibility for a university education, neither did he deny her ability to profit by it. Like the other ministers, he made no attempt to extrapolate a different spiritual nature from a contrasting social role. But he fully accepted that role and expected Jane to fulfill it.

In 1735, Jane Colman Turrel died in childbirth. In her father's sermons and in the biography written by her husband, there is little to distinguish her from Katharin Mather or even Jerusha Oliver. But in a poem appended to the sermons, there is a fascinating crack in the portrait. The Reverend John Adams wrote:

> Fair was her Face, but fairer was her Mind,
> Where all the Muses, all the Graces join'd.
> For tender Passions turn'd and soft to please,
> With all the graceful Negligence of Ease.
> Her Soul was form'd for nicer Arts of Life,
> To show the Friend, but most to grace the Wife.[61]

Negligence, softness, ease! These are concepts alien to the virtuous woman. Jane Colman had been invited into her father's library as an intellectual equal, but to at least one of her male friends she had become only that much more attractive as a drawing-room ornament. It is tempting to conclude that by 1735, even ministers were seducing the Virtuous Woman with worldly standards. But the new prosperity was not entirely to blame. As an instrument of piety, scholarship had its limits. With no other earthly outlet available, dinner-party conversation had to do.

Thomas Foxcroft was either less comfortable with the intellectual role than Mather or Colman or more concerned about its limits. In *Anna the Prophetess* he went to great lengths to deny the implications of his own text, arguing on the one hand that women were worthy of the title of prophet and on the other that they certainly shouldn't be allowed to speak in church. His choice of a text and title were very much in the tradition of Mather, but his handling of it betrayed a discomfort his mentor never acknowledged. When he came to write of motherhood, however, his defense of women blossomed. In his sermon for his own mother, preached in 1721, he described women as the bastions of religion in the home and the community. "At the Gap, which the Death of a wise and good Mother makes, does many times enter a Torrent of Impieties and Vices." Some mothers were simply too good for this world: God might gather them home to prevent them seeing the "Penal Evils" about to befall their children. Foxcroft's praise overlay a more conservative base. He cautioned that the death of a mother might be a punishment for loving her too much as well as for loving her too little. But his own sermon is evidence of where he felt the greater danger lay. "Indeed Children's Love and Regard to their Parents living or dead, commonly needs a Spur, Tho' the Parents too often need a Curb."[62] As a good Puritan, he could not embrace mother love or any other form of human love as an unqualified good, but like Mather he was concerned that Boston's mothers receive the proper respect.

This is a crucial point. In the funeral literature there had been little mention of "motherhood" as opposed to the more generalized concept of "parenthood." Even Colman, who published a baptismal sermon entitled *"Some of the Honours that Religion Does Unto the Fruitful Mothers in Israel,"* was unable to maintain the sex differentiation much beyond the title. If a distinction between mothers and fathers is ever made in the literature, however, it is over the issue of respect. Wadsworth felt that "persons are often more apt to *despise a Mother*, (the weaker vessel, and frequently most indulgent) than a Father.[63] Despite its text, John Flavell's *A Discourse: Shewing that Christ's Tender Care of His Mother is an Excellent Pattern for all Gracious Children* is about parents rather than about mothers specifically. But the one direct comment on women echoes Wadsworth: "[S]he by reason of her blandishments, and fond indulgence is most subject to the irreverence and contempt of children."[64] Thus Boston's ministers showed a concern for neglect of women well before they identified or elaborated any sex-related virtues. Foxcroft built upon this concern, but with a subtle difference. Although his mother's piety was the traditional piety, it was as a *mother* rather than as a Christian that she was singled out. With a new set of values, a focus upon tenderness and love rather than on godliness and strength, Foxcroft's effusiveness would be indistinguishable from nineteenth-century sentimentality.

Thus, in New England sermons firmly rooted in the reformed tradition of the seventeenth century, we can see developing, as if in embryo, both the "genteel lady" of the eighteenth century and the "tender mother" of the nineteenth. Adams' poem for Jane Turrel shows the short step from Puritan intellectuality to feminine sensibility. Foxcroft's eulogy for his mother demonstrates how praise for a single virtue might obliterate all others. If Puritan piety upheld the oneness of men and women, Puritan polity in large part did not. Nor, we assume, did the increasingly mercantile world of early eighteenth-century Boston. Unwilling or unable to transfer spiritual equality to the earthly sphere, ministers might understandably begin to shift earthly differences to the spiritual sphere, gradually developing sexual definitions of the psyche and soul.

It is important to remember here that the sermon literature deals with a relatively small group of people, that it reveals attitudes not practices. Presumably, few women experienced the conflicts of Jane Turrel. Most housewives in provincial Boston were probably too occupied with the daily round to consider the nature of their position in society. Yet when a minister of the stature of Cotton Mather assumes a defensive tone, telling us that "those *Handmaids of the Lord,* who tho' they ly very much Conceal'd from the World, and may be called *The Hidden Ones,* yet have no little share in the *Beauty* and the *Defence* of the Land," as historians we ought to listen to him.[65] Attitudes are important. Subtle shifts in perception both reflect and affect social practice. Mather's advocacy of women suggests a real tension in early eighteenth century New England between presumed private worth and public position. It demonstrates the need for closer study of the actual functioning of women within congregation and community. But it has ramifications beyond its own time and place. Mather's work shows how discrete and ultimately confining notions of "femininity" might grow out of a genuine concern with equality. Finally, the ministerial literature to which it belongs illustrates the importance of the narrow study, the need to move from static concepts like "patriarchal New England society" to more intricate questions about the interplay of values and practice over time. Zion's daughters have for too long been hidden.

Ulrich's findings are interesting in their own right and an important insight into Puritan attitudes. However, in the search for a better understanding of women in Puritan society there remain other periods of New England history to explore (especially the 1630s through 1650s, when Puritanism was at its height) and other segments of the population to analyze (particularly the common people, including the women themselves). Much also remains to be learned about the lives of women in the Puritan colonies—their work, their leisure, and their relations with parents, husbands, and children. Recent studies of colonial families such as Demos s Little Commonwealth *and Morgan's* Puritan Family *(both cited above) have made important contributions to the understanding of women's roles, as have articles on more limited topics such as James T. Johnson's "The Covenant Idea and the Puritan View of Marriage" (*Journal of the History of Ideas, *XXXII* [1971]), and Alexander Keyssar's "Widowhood in Eighteenth- Century*

Massachusetts: A Problem in the History of the Family" (Perspectives in American History, VII]1974[). *But in general, the study of women in Puritan society has scarcely begun.*

NOTES

1. Edmund S. Morgan, *The Puritan Family: Religion and Domestic Relations in Seventeenth-Century New England* (New York: Harper and Row, 1966), p. 44. Recent works continue to rely on Morgan's study, which was first published in 1944. See, for example, John Demos, *A Little Commonwealth: Family Life in Plymouth* (New York: Oxford Univ. Press, 1970) p. 98. Morgan's description of male dominance within a loving marriage is consistent with descriptions taken from English prescriptive literature in Louis B. Wright, *Middle-Class Culture in Elizabethan England* (Chapel Hill, N. C.: Univ. of North Carolina Press, 1935), chapter VII, and in Charles H. and Katherine George, *The Protestant Mind of the English Reformation, 1570-1640* (Princeton, N. J.: Princeton Univ. Press, 1961), chapter 7.

2. The Winthrop quote appears in Morgan (p. 44) as in many lesser summaries of Puritan attitudes toward women from Thomas Woody, *A History of Women's Education in the United States*, Vol. I (New York: Science Press, 1929), pp. 106-07, to Lyle Koehler, "The Case of the American Jezebels: Anne Hutchinson and Female Agitation During the Years of Antinomian Turmoil, 1636-1640," *William and Mary Quarterly*, 3rd Ser., 31 (Jan. 1974), p. 58. Koehler's article exemplifies the common imbalance in favor of deviant women.

3. Charles Evans, *American Bibliography: A Chronological Dictionary of all Books, Pamphlets and Periodical Publications Printed in the USA, 1639-1820* (New York: P. Smith, 1941); Roger Bristol, *Supplement to Charles Evans' American Bibliography* (Charlottesville, Va.: Univ. Press of Virginia, 1970).

4. Mary Sumner Benson, in *Women in Eighteenth-Century America* (New York: Columbia Univ. Press, 1935), quotes extensively from Mather's *Ornaments*, using it as evidence that he believed in the "proper submission of women." Page Smith draws the opposite conclusion from the same document in *Daughters of the Promised Land* (Boston: Little, Brown, 1970), pp. 47ff. Two of the three main sources for Edmund Morgan's description of marital ethics belong to this group of materials: Willard's *Complete Body of Divinity* and Wadsworth's *The Well-Ordered Family*, although he quotes rather selectively from them. William Andrews, "The Printed Funeral Sermons of Cotton Mather," *Early American Literature*, 5 (Fall 1970), pp. 24-44, notes the high percentage of sermons on females and attempts some analysis of the materials but without relating it to the wider corpus of ministerial literature.

5. In his study of prescriptive literature in late seventeenth-century England, Levin L. Schucking noted a similar phenomenon. See *The Puritan Family: A Social Study from the Literary Sources* (London: Routledge and Kegan Paul, 1969), p. xiii. I have made no attempt to define the "Puritanism" of the authors. Although most of them belonged to the congregational majority, Samuel Myles was an Anglican. His eulogy for Elizabeth Riscarrick, though less detailed than many, follows the typical pattern.

6. The funeral sermon with its accompanying biographical "lean-to" was a venerable form by this time. See William Haller, *The Rise of Puritanism* (New York: Harper, 1938), p. 101.

7. John Hart, *The Nature and Blessedness of Trusting in God* (New London, 1728), p. 45.

8. Cotton Mather, *Nepenthes Evangelicum . . . A Sermon Occasion'd by the Death of a Religious Matron, Mrs. Mary Rock* (Boston, 1713), p. 41.

9. John Danforth, "An Elegy upon the much Lamented Decease of Mrs. Elizabeth Foxcroft," appended to Thomas Foxcroft's *Sermon Preach'd at Cambridge after the Funeral of Mrs. Elizabeth Foxcroft* (Boston, 1721), p. 53.

10. Benjamin Colman, *Reliquia Turellae, et Lachrymae Paternae. Father's Tears over his Daughter's Remains . . . to which are added, some Large Memoirs of her Life and Death by her Consort, the Reverend Mr. Ebenezer Turell* (Boston, 1735), p. 116.

11. Increase Mather, *A Sermon Concerning Obedience & Resignation To The Will of God in Everything* (Boston, 1714), p. ii, p. 39.

12. Foxcroft, *Sermon Preach'd*, pp. 14-15.

13. This is a common theme throughout Mather's funeral sermons. A typical example is in *Virtue in its Verdure. A Christian Exhibited as a Green Olive Tree . . . with a character of the Virtuous Mrs. Abigail Brown* (Boston, 1725), p. 23.

14. Cotton Mather, *Monica Americana, A Funeral-Sermon Occasioned by Death of Mrs. Sarah Leveret* (Boston, 1705), p. 27.

15. James Fitch, *Peace the End of the Perfect and Upright* (Cambridge, 1672), p. 12; Benjamin Colman, *The Death of God's Saints Precious in his Sight* (Boston, 1723), p. 23.

16. Jabez Fitch, *Discourse on Serious Piety. A Funeral Sermon . . . upon the Death of Mrs. Mary Martyn* (Boston, 1725), p. 18.

17. John Danforth, "Greatness & Goodness Elegized, In a Poem upon the Much Lamented Decease of the Honourable & Vertuous Madam Hannah Sewall" (Boston, 1717), Broadside, p. 1. 33ff.

18. Increase Mather, *A Sermon Concerning Obedience*, p. ii.

19. Cotton Mather, *Memorials of Early Piety* (Boston, 1711), pp. 3-4, 13.

20. "An Account of Mrs. Katharin Mather by Another Hand," in Cotton Mather, *Victorina: A Sermon Preach'd on the Decease and at the Desire of Mrs. Katharin Mather* (Boston, 1717), p. 50.

21. [Joseph Metcalf,] "Tears Dropt at the Funeral of . . . Mrs. Elizabeth Hatch" (Boston, 1710), Broadside.

22. John Danforth, "Honour and Vertue Elegized in a Poem Upon an Honourable, Aged, and Gracious Mother in Israel" (Boston, 1713), Broadside; Cotton Mather, *Nepenthes*, pp. 45-46.

23. James Hillhouse, *A Sermon Concerning the Life, Death, and Future State of Saints* (Boston, 1721), pp. 112, 117. Although Hillhouse's sermon was published in Boston after he had settled there, it was originally preached in Ireland.

24. James Fitch, *Peace*, p. 11.

25. Thomas Foxcroft, *The Character of Anna, The Prophetess Consider'd and Apply'd* (Boston, 1723), from the Preface by Benjamin Wadsworth, p. ii.

26. Cotton Mather, *El-Shaddai . . . A brief Essay . . . Produced by the Death of That Virtuous Gentlewoman, Mrs. Katharin Willard* (Boston, 1725), p. 22.

27. Thomas Reynolds, *Practical Religion Exemplify'd In The Lives of Mrs. Mary Terry . . . and Mrs. Clissould* (Boston, 1713, p. 4; and Foxcroft, *Anna*, p. 14.

28. Cotton Mather, *Ecclesiae Monilia. The Peculiar Treasure of the Almighty King Opened . . . Whereof one is more particularly Exhibited in the Character of Mrs. Elizabeth Cotton* (Boston, 1726), p. 25.

29. Sarah Goodhue, *The Copy of a Valedictory and Monitory Writing . . . Directed to her Husband and Children, with other Near Relations and Friends*, reprinted in Thomas Franklin Water, *Ipswich in the Massachusetts Bay Colony* (Ipswich, Mass.: Ipswich Historical Society, 1905), pp. 519-24.

30. Grace Smith, *The Dying Mother's Legacy, or the Good and Heavenly Counsel of that Eminent and Pious Matron* (Boston, 1712).

31. Increase Mather, *The Life and Death of Richard Mather* (Cambridge, 1670), p. 25.

32. Cotton Mather, *Memorials of Early Piety*, p. 45.

33. John Danforth, "A Poem Upon the Triumphant Translation of a Mother in Our Israel," appended to *Kneeling to God* (Boston, 1697), p. 64.

34. Increase Mather, *Sermon Concerning Obedience*, p. 34.

35. Samuel Myles, *Sermon Preach't At the Funeral of Mrs. Elizabeth Riscarrick* (Boston, 1698).

36. Cotton Mather, *Memorials of Early Piety*, p. 49.

37. Cotton Mather, *Light in Darkness, An Essay on the Piety Which by Rememb'ring the Many Days of Darkness, Will Change Them Into a Marvelous Light* (Boston, 1724), p. 20.

38. Cotton Mather, *Juga*, pp. 31-32.

39. Increase Mather, *Richard Mather*, pp. 33, 34.

40. See for example, Cotton Mather, *A Good Man Making A Good End* (Boston, 1698), on the death of a minister; and Thomas Foxcroft, *A Brief Display of Mordecai's Excellent Character* (Boston, 1727), on the death of a public official. For the English tradition (which placed less emphasis on early piety), see Haller, *Rise of Puritanism*, p. 93ff. Robert Middlekauff and David Hall both stress the prototypal quality of Richard Mather's biography. See *The Mathers: Three Generations of Puritan Intellectuals, 1596-1728* (New York: Oxford Univ. Press, 1971), p. 101-02, and *The Faithful Shepherd: A History of the New England Ministry in the Seventeenth Century* (Chapel Hill, N. C.: Univ. of North Carolina Press, 1972), p. 179.

41. John Sprint, *The Bride-Woman's Counsellor, Being A Sermon Preached at a Wedding at Sherbourn, in Dorsetshire* (Boston, 1709), p. 2.

42. Ibid., pp. 16, 11.

43. Benjamin Wadsworth, *The Well-Ordered Family: or, Relative Duties, Being The Substance of Several Sermons About Family Prayer, Duties of Husband & Wives, Duties of Parents & Children, Duties of Masters & Servants* (Boston, 1712), p. 28.

44. William Secker, *A Wedding Ring* (Boston, 1690), unpaged.

45. Samuel Willard, *A Complete Body of Divinity in Two Hundred and Fifty Expository Lectures* (Boston, 1726), pp. 609-12.

46. John Oliver, *A Present for Teeming American Women* (Boston, 1694), p. 3. This was an American edition of a pamphlet first printed in London in 1663. The Evans film is very short and probably includes just the preface.

47. Nicholas Noyes, poem for Mrs. Mary Brown in Cotton Mather, *Eureka the Vertuous Woman Found*, I, 15; see also "Upon the Death of the Virtuous and Religious Mrs. Lydia Minot" (Cambridge, 1668), an anonymous broadside.

48. Willard, *Complete Body of Divinity*, p. 611.

49. See for example, *Tabitha Rediviva, An Essay to Describe and Commend The Good Works of a Virtuous Woman* (Boston, 1713), p. 21.

50. Cotton Mather, *Ornaments for the Daughters of Zion* (Cambridge, 1692), p. 45.

51. Benjamin Colman, *The Duty and Honour of Aged Women* (Boston, 1711), pp. ii-iii.

52. John Oliver, *Teeming Women*, p. 4.

53. Cotton Mather, *Eureka*, p. 1.

54. Hugh Peter, *A Dying Father's Last Legacy* (Boston, 1717), pp. 22, 34, 83. Lyle Koehler quotes merely the phrase "Woman's Ornament" in attempting to show that Hugh Peter shared a general Puritan belief in the subjection of women. See "The Case of the American Jezebels," p. 59.

55. Cotton Mather, *Bethiah. The Glory Which Adorns the Daughters of God and the Piety, Wherewith Zion Wishes to see her Daughters Glorious* (Boston, 1722), p. 34.

56. Cotton Mather, *Undoubted Certainties, or, Piety Enlivened* (Boston, 1720), p. 26.

57. Cotton Mather, *Juga*, p. 24.

58. Cotton Mather, *Ornaments*, pp. 5-6.

59. Anna Maria Schurman, *The Learned Maid: or, Whether a Maid may be a Scholar? A Logick Exercise* (London, 1659), pp. 1, 37.

60. Colman, *Reliquiae Turellae*, p. 69.

61. Ibid., p. v.

62. Foxcroft, *Sermon*, pp. 14, 20.

63. Wadsworth, *Well-Ordered Family*, p. 92.

64. John Flavell, *A Discourse* (Boston, 1728), p. 5.

65. Cotton Mather, *El-Shaddai*, p. 31.

13 | DEATH AND THE PURITAN CHILD

DAVID E. STANNARD

*Two very recent areas of scholarly concern are childhood and death,
which David E. Stannard fuses in the next essay, "Death and the
Puritan Child." The topic of childhood achieved sudden prominence
with the publication of Philippe Ariès's* Centuries of Childhood: A
Social History of Family Life *(New York, 1962), a study of European
attitudes toward childhood. Ariès's book has stimulated a similar interest among American historians, some of it directed at investigations
of Puritan New England. John Demos's* A Little Commonwealth *(cited
above) offers a provocative model for understanding the develop-
mental stages of growth. In addition, several historians have examined
demographic aspects such as mortality rates, numbers of children per
family, and the frequency of orphanage.*

*Death, as a field of scholarly research, has barely begun. David
Stannard's "Death and Dying in Puritan New England" (*American
Historical Review, *LXXVIII [1973]) was the first modern study of the
subject. Stannard's article included here is the first to explore Puritan
society's approach to the prospect of early death. Although recent
studies of demographic patterns in colonial America show that the life
span of a child born in New England was likely to be appreciably
longer than that of a child born in most other colonies, especially in
Maryland or Virginia, pre-adult mortality everywhere was high by
modern standards. The possibility of childhood death, especially from
smallpox or other epidemics, remained an ominous reality.*

From time to time in the history of man a new idea or way of looking at
things bursts into view with such force that it virtually sets the terms for
all relevant subsequent discussion. The Copernican, Darwinian and
Freudian revolutions—perhaps, as Freud on occasion noted, the three
most destructive blows which human narcissism has had to endure—are
among the extreme examples of such intellectual explosions. Others have
been of considerably more limited influence: the concept of culture in anthropology is one example, the frontier thesis as an explanatory device
for American history is another. At still another level is the seminal
study of a particular problem. An instance of this is the fact that
throughout the past decade historians of family life have conducted their
research in the shadow of Philippe Ariès' monumental study, *Centuries
of Childhood*, a work that established much of the currently conventional wisdom on the subject of the family in history.

One of Ariès' most original and influential findings was that childhood
as we know it today did not exist until the early modern period. "In
medieval society," he observed, ". . . as soon as the child could live
without the constant solicitude of his mother, his nanny or his cradle-

rocker, he belonged to adult society."[1] It was not until the 16th and 17th centuries, and then only among the upper classes, that the modern idea of childhood as a distinct phase of life began to emerge.

The picture Ariès sketched, drawing on such diverse sources as portraiture, literature, games and dress, was predominantly one of French culture and society; but it was clear that he felt his generalizations held true for most of the Western world. Recent studies in colonial New England have supported Ariès' assumption of the representativeness of his French findings in extending his observations on medieval life to 17th and 18th century Massachusetts; but the support for this contention is unsteady, balanced as it is on much less substantive data than that on which Ariès argument rests. The clothing of children as adults—only one strand of evidence in Ariès' historical tapestry—has been seized by some colonial historians and used as the principal basis for claiming that in 17th and 18th century Massachusetts there was little or no distinction between children and adults. "If clothes do not made the man," writes Michael Zuckerman, "they do mark social differentiations"; and, adds John Demos, "the fact that children were dressed like adults does seem to imply a whole attitude of mind."[2] The phenomenon that both writers accurately describe, the similarity of dress for children and adults, may well suggest social differentiations and/or imply a whole attitude of mind—but not necessarily the one claimed.

In the first place, to argue in isolation of other data that the *absence* of a distinctive mode of dress for children is a mark of their being viewed as miniature adults is historical presentism at its very best; one might argue with equal force—in isolation of other facts—that the absence of beards on men in a particular culture, or the presence of short hair as a fashion shared by men and women, is a mark of that culture's failure to fully distinguish between men and women. In all these cases there are alternative explanations, explanations that do not presuppose that special clothing for children, or beards for men, or different hair lengths for adults of different sexes, are universally natural and proper cultural traditions. As to the specific matter of dress, children in New England were treated much the same as children in England. Until age six or seven they generally wore long gowns that opened down the front; after that, they were clothed in a manner similar to that of their parents. Rather than this stage marking an abrupt transition from infancy to adulthood, as Alan Macfarlane has pointed out it more likely was merely a sign that children had then reached an age where sexual differentiation was in order.[3]

Second, and most important, the supporting evidence that Ariès brings to bear in making his case for the situation in medieval France generally does not exist for colonial New England; when it does, it makes clear the fact that there was no confusion or ambiguity in the mind of the adult Puritan as to the differences between his children and himself. Puritan journals, autobiographies and histories are filled with specific references to the differences between children and adults, a wealth of parental advice literature exists for the 17th century that gives evidence of clear distinctions between adults and children well into their teens, and a large body of law was in effect from the earliest years of settlement that made definitive discriminations between acceptable behavior and appropriate punishment for children, post-adolescent youths and adults.[4]

The matter of children's literature is one case in point. Ariès has argued, both in *Centuries of Childhood* and elsewhere, that in France "books addressed to and reserved for children" did not appear until "the end of the 17th century, at the same time as the awareness of childhood." Recently Marc Soriano has supported Ariès' contention by showing that prior to the stories of Perrault in the 1690s, French literature and folk tales were directed "almost entirely" at an adult audience, though of course children were exposed to them as well.[5] The situation was quite different in both old and New England in the 17th century, as William Sloane showed almost twenty years ago. Limiting himself to a definition of a child's book as "a book written *only* for children"—a limitation which excludes books which subsequently became children's fare and "works which are the tools of formal instruction"—Sloane compiled an annotated bibliography of 261 children's books published in England and America between 1557 and 1710.[6] It is true that most of the books listed would not meet Zuckerman's definition of a child's book as one which provides "a sequestered simplicity commensurate with a child's capacities, " but that is not because children were viewed as synonymous with adults; rather, it is because 17th century New Englanders had a different view from that held by Zuckerman or other 20th century parents of the nature and capacities of children.[7]

The differentness of that view is crucial to this essay, and it will be developed at some length. But first it must be recognized that there were indeed children at home and in the streets of Puritan New England, and that this was a fact recognized—and never questioned—by their parents, ministers and other adults in the community. In many ways those children were seen and treated as different from children of today. In many ways they *were* different: to analyze, as this essay will, the Puritan child's actual and anticipated confrontation with death is but one of many ways in which the extent of that difference can be seen. But it is too much of a leap, and there is no real evidence to support the contention that in 17th century New England, as in 15th and 16th century France, there was little or no distinction between children and adults.

Probably at no time in modern history have parents in the West agreed on the matter of the correct and proper approach to child-rearing. Certainly this is true of our own time, but it was equally so in the age of the Puritan.

"A child is a man in a small letter," wrote John Earle in 1628,

> yet the best copy of *Adam* before hee tasted of *Eve* or the Apple. . . . Hee is natures fresh picture newly drawne in Oyle, which time and much handling dimmes and defaces. His soule is yet a white paper unscribled with observations of the world, wherewith at length it becomes a blurr'd Notebooke. He is purely happy, because he knowes no evill, nor hath made meanes by sinne, to be acquainted with misery. . . . Nature and his Parents alike dandle him, and tice him on with a bait of Sugar, to a draught of Worme-wood. . . . His

father hath writ him as his owne little story, wherein hee reads those dayes of his life that hee cannot remember; and sighes to see what innocence he ha's outliv'd.[8]

In view of this attitude among certain Englishmen of the 17th century—an attitude that, it appears, became prevalent in colonial Maryland and Virginia—it should come as no surprise to read in the report of a visiting Frenchman at the end of the century that "In England they show an extraordinary complacency toward young children, always flattering, always caressing, always applauding whatever they do. At least that is how it seems to us French, who correct our children as soon as they are capable of reason." This judgment was echoed a few years later by an Englishman reflecting on the customs of his people: "In the *Education* of *Children*," wrote Guy Miege in 1707, "the indulgence of Mothers is excessive among the *English*; which proves often fatal to their children, and contributes much to the Corruption of the Age. If these be Heirs to great Honours and Estates, they swell with the Thoughts of it, and at last grow unmanageable." Had Miege been writing a bit later in the century he might have sought evidence for his assertion in the life of Charles James Fox who, at age five, had been accidentally deprived of the privilege of watching the blowing up of a garden wall; at his insistence his father had the wall rebuilt and blown up again so that the boy might witness it. On another occasion, when the young Charles announced his intention of destroying a watch, his father's reply was: "Well, if you must, I suppose you must."[9]

But neither John Earle in 1628, nor Charles Fox in 1754 were Puritans; and neither Henri Misson in 1698, nor Guy Miege in 1707 were commenting on Puritan attitudes toward children. Had they been, their reports would have read very differently.

In 1628, the same year that John Earle was rhapsodizing on the innocence and purity of children, and on parental accomodation to them, Puritan John Robinson wrote:

> And surely there is in all children, though not alike, a stubborness, and stoutness of mind arising from natural pride, which must, in the first place, be broken and beaten down. . . . This fruit of natural corruption and root of actual rebellion both against God and man must be destroyed, and no manner of way nourished, except we will plant a nursery of contempt of all good persons and things, and of obstinacy therein. . . . For the beating, and keeping down of this stubbornness parents must provide carefully for two things: first that children s wills and willfulness be restrained and repressed. . . . The second help is an inuring of them from the first, to such a meanness in all things, as may rather pluck them down, than lift them up.[10]

In place of Earle's child, seen as "yet the best copy of Adam before hee tasted of Eve or the Apple," the Puritan child was riddled with sin and corruption, a depraved being polluted with the stain of Adam's sin. If there was any chance of an individual child's salvation, it was not a very good chance—and in any case, the knowledge of who was to be chosen for salvation and who was not to be chosen was not a matter for earthly minds. "Because a small and contemptible number are hidden in a huge multitude," Calvin had written," and a few grains of wheat are covered by a pile of chaff, we must leave to God alone the knowledge of his church, whose foundation is his secret election."[11] The quest for salvation was at the core of everything the devout Puritan thought and did; it was the primary source of the intense drive that carried him across thousands of miles of treacherous ocean in order to found a Holy Commonwealth in the midst of a wilderness; it was his reason for being. And yet, despite his conviction of God's purposeful presence in everything he did or encountered, from Indian wars to ailing livestock, full confidence in his own or anyone else's salvation was rendered impossible by the inscrutability of his God. He was driven to strive for salvation at the same time that he was told his fate was both predetermined and undetectable.

To be sure, Puritans believed there were signs or "marks," indications of God's will, that laymen and ministers alike could struggle to detect in their persons and in those of members of the congregation. But these signs were subject to interpretation and even feigning, and could never be regarded as more than *suggestions* of sainthood. Further, only very rarely was an apparent childhood conversion accepted as real by a congregation. Thus, Jonathan Edwards devoted a great deal of attention to youthful conversions during the stormy emotionalism of the Great Awakening, but only after first noting: "It has heretofore been looked on as a strange thing, when any have seemed to be savingly wrought upon, and remarkably changed in their childhood." And even James Janeway, whose *A Token For Children: Being an Exact Assessment of the Conversion, Holy and Exemplary Lives, and Joyful Deaths of Several Young Children*, was one of the best-read books of 17th and 18th century Puritans, admitted in a later edition that one of his examples of early spiritual development—that of a child who supposedly began showing signs of salvation between the ages of two and three—seemed to many "scarce credible, and they did fear [it] might somewhat prejudice the authority of the rest."[12]

But if conversion was unlikely at an early age, it was at least possible. Given the alternative, then, of apathetic acceptance of their children as depraved and damnable creatures, it is hardly surprising that Puritan parents urged on their offspring a religious precocity that some historians have interpreted as tantamount to premature adulthood. "You can't begin with them *Too soon*," Cotton Mather wrote in 1689,

> They are no sooner *wean'd* but they are to be *taught*. . . . Are they *Young?* Yet the *Devil* has been with them already. . . . They go astray as soon as they are born. They no sooner *step* than they *stray*, they no sooner *lisp* than they *ly*. Satan gets them to be proud, profane, reviling and revengeful, as *young* as they are. And I pray, why should you not be afore-hand with *him?*[13]

Puritan children, even "the very best" of whom had a "Corrupt Nature in them, and . . . an Evil Figment in their Heart," were thus driven at the earliest age possible both to recognize their depravity and to pray for their salvation. In the event that children proved intractable in this regard the first parental response was to be "what saies the Wise man, *A Rod for the fools back*"; but generally more effective—and more insidious—was the advice "to watch when some *Affliction* or some *Amazement* is come upon them: then God opens their ear to Discipline."[14] If Puritan parents carried out these designs with fervor it was of course out of love and concern for their children. But at least some of the motivation may well have had guilt at its source; as Mather and others were frequently careful to point out: "Your Children are Born Children of Wrath. Tis *through you,* that there is derived unto them the sin which Exposes them to infinite Wrath."[15]

We should not, however, pass too quickly over the matter of the Puritan parent's genuine love for his children. Even a casual reading of the most noted Puritan journals and autobiographies—those of Thomas Shepard, Samuel Sewall, Cotton Mather—reveals a deep-seated parental affection for children as the most common, normal and expected attitude. The relationship between parents and children was often compared with that between God and the Children of God. "That God is often angry with [his children]," Samuel Willard wrote in 1684, "afflicts them, and withdraws the light of his countenance from them, and puts them to grief, is not because he loves them not, but because it is that which their present condition requires; they are but Children, and childish, and foolish, and if they were not sometimes chastened, they would grow wanton, and careless of duty."[16] Indeed, in the same work in which Cotton Mather referred to children as "proud, profane, reviling and revengeful," he warned parents that "*They must give an account of the souls that belong unto their Families. . . .* Behold, thou has *Lambs* in the *Fold,* Little ones in thy House; God will strain for it,—if wild beasts, and Lusts carry any of them away from the *Service* of God through any neglect of thine thou shalt smart for it in the fiery prison of God's terrible Indignation."[17]

Children, then, were on the one hand deeply loved, "Lambs in the Fold"; as Willard noted: "If others in a Family suffer want, and be pincht with difficulties, yet the Children shall certainly be taken care for, as long as there is anything to be had: they are hard times indeed when Children are denied that which is needful for them."[18] On the other hand they were depraved and polluted; as Benjamin Wadsworth wrote: "Their Hearts naturally, are a meer nest, root, fountain of Sin, and wickedness."[19] Even most innocent infants, dying before they had barely a chance to breathe, could at best be expected to be given, in Michael Wigglesworth's phrase, "the easiest room in Hell."[20]

If the state of a child's spiritual health was an extremely worrisome and uncomfortable matter for the Puritan parent, the state of his physical health was not less so. In recent years historians of colonial New England have convincingly shown that the colonists of certain New England towns in the 17th and early 18th centuries lived longer and healthier lives than did many of their countrymen in England. This finding and the many others by these new demographic historians are important to our understanding of life in early New England; but in acknowledging the relative advantages of life in some New England communities compared with parts of England and Europe in the 17th century, we should be careful to avoid blinding ourselves to the fact that death was to the colonist, as it was to the Englishman and Frenchman, an ever-present menace—and a menace that struck with a particular vengeance at the children of the community.

. . .

. . . A young couple embarking on a marriage did so with the knowledge and expectation that in all probability *two or three* of the children they might have would die before the age of ten. In certain cases, of course, the number was more than two; Philip J. Greven discusses instances when parents lost six of eleven children in rapid succession, including four in a single month, and four of eight children in less than a year— and this in a town remarkable for the relative health and longevity of its residents.[21] In Boston the rate was much higher and even the most prominent and well cared for residents of that city were constantly reminded of the fragility of life in childhood. Thomas Shepard, for instance, had seven sons, three of whom died in infancy; the other four outlived their father, but he died at 43—having in that short time outlived two wives. As Joseph E. Illick has recently pointed out, Samuel Sewall and Cotton Mather each fathered fourteen children: "One of Sewall's was stillborn, several died as infants, several more as young adults. Seven Mather babies died shortly after delivery, one died at two years and six survived to adulthood, five of whom died in their twenties. Only two Sewall children outlived their father, while Samuel Mather was the only child to survive Cotton."[22]

It is important for us to recognize that conditions for living in colonial New England were sometimes superior to those in 17th century England and Europe. But it is equally important for us not to lose sight of the fact that the Puritan settlements were places where "winter was to be feared," as Kenneth Lockridge has written, where "harvests were a gamble that kept men's minds aware of Providence, plague arose and subsided out of all human control and infants died in numbers that would shock us today."[23]

It has often been noted by writers on the Puritan family that the prescribed and common personal relationship between parents and children was one of restraint and even aloofness, mixed with, as we have seen, an intense parental effort to impose discipline and encourage spiritual precocity. Parents were reminded to avoid becoming "too fond of your children and too familiar with them" and to be on their guard against "not keeping constantly your due distance."[24] Edmund S. Morgan has shown how this "due distance" worked in both directions, as when Benjamin Colman's daughter Jane wrote to her father requesting forgiveness for the "flow of affections" evident in some of her recent letters. Colman responded by urging her to be "careful against this Error, even when you say your Thoughts of Reverence and Esteem to your Father, or to a Spouse, if ever you should live to have one," and commended her for having "done well to correct yourself for some of your Excursions of this kind toward me."[25] Morgan has also seen the common practice of "putting children out," both to early apprenticeship and simply extended stays with other families, often against the child's will, as linked to the maintenance of the necessary distance between parent and child; "these economically unnecessary removals of children from home," he writes, probably resulted from the fact that "Puritan parents did not trust themselves with their own children, that they were afraid of spoiling them by too great affection."[26]

Morgan's suggested explanation for this practice seems logical and convincing, but there may have been an additional, deeper source for both this practice and the entire Puritan attitude toward severely restrained displays of fondness between parents and children. For children, despite the natural hold they had on their parents' affection, were a source of great emotional discomfort for them as well. In the first place, there was a very real possibility, if not a probability, that parental affection would be rewarded by the death of a child before it even reached puberty; the "due distance" kept by Puritan parents from their children might, at least in part, have been an instinctive response to this possibility, a means of insulating themselves to some extent against the shock that the death of a child might bring. This, of course, would be potentially true of any society with a relatively high rate of childhood mortality. But to the Puritan the child was more than a loved one extremely vulnerable to the ravages of the environment; he was also a loved one polluted with sin and natural depravity. In this, of course, he was no different from any other members of the family or community, including those Visible Saints viewed as the most likely candidates for salvation: Original Sin touched everyone, and all were considered polluted and not worthy of excessive affection. What is important her, however, is not that this dictum touched everyone, but that in the process it touched those most emotionally susceptible to its pernicious effects—the children of the zealous and devoted Puritan.

The Puritans of New England held as doctrine the belief that they were involved in a binding contract or "covenant" with God. This belief was complex and multifaceted, but one aspect of it viewed the entire community as having contracted a "social covenant" with God by which they promised strict obedience to his laws. Failure to obey on the part of any individual within the community could result in God's wrath being vented on the entire community. . . .

The depraved and ungodly child was, it is true, naturally repellent in his sinfulness; but more than that, the activity that might easily grow out of that sinfulness posed a very real danger to the well-being of the community. In response, understandably enough, the Puritan parent strove mightily to effect conversion or at the least to maintain a strict behavior code, but at the same time—when these effects were combined with the love he felt for his child, the tenuous hold the child had on life, the natural repulsiveness of sin—he may well have been driven to find ways of creating emotional distance between his offspring and himself.[27]

But if separation was emotionally beneficial to the Puritan parent, it may have had precisely the opposite effect on the Puritan child. John Demos has recently speculated on the "profound loss" experienced by many Puritan children in the second and third years of life because of the fact that they were probably weaned at the start of the second year and very often witnessed the arrival of a younger brother or sister at the start of the third year.[28] This in itself, it might be argued, does not make Puritan children unique: the spacing of children at two-year intervals is common among many of the world's cultures, and weaning at twelve months is hardly an exceptional custom. But added to these practices was the conscious effort of Puritan parents to separate themselves from an excessively intimate relationship with their children. If this normal practice of separation was not enough, Cotton Mather was probably echoing a fairly common sentiment in viewing as "the sorest Punishment in the Family" the banishment of the child from the parents' presence.[29] Separation, however, can be both real and imagined, can be both present and anticipated. And, of course, the ultimate separation is death. This was a fact of which the Puritan parent was well aware and which the Puritan child, from the earliest age possible, was never allowed to forget.

May of 1678 was a month of great apprehension in Boston. The smallpox plague referred to earlier had entered the city some months before and had begun its relentless slaying of the population. By May hundreds had died and the governments of the colony and the town were hurriedly passing legislation aimed at holding down the spread of the deadly infection—people were directed not to hang out bedding or clothes in their yards or near roadways, and those who had been touched by the disease and survived were forbidden contact with others for specified periods of time.[30] The worst was yet to come: by the time it was over it was as though, proportionate to the population, an epidemic were to kill over a million and a half people in New York City during the next eighteen months. The city girded for it.

Only two years earlier New England had endured the devastation of King Philip's War, in which—not counting the enormous numbers of Indian dead—greater casualties were inflicted in proportion to the population than in any other war in subsequent American history.[31] Death was everywhere in 1678 when, on May 5, Increase Mather addressed his Boston congregation and prayed "for a Spirit of Converting Grace to be poured out upon the Children and *Rising Generation* in *New England.*"[32] A decade later Increase's son Cotton would write, as I have noted earlier, that a particularly effective means of disciplining children was "to watch when some *Affliction* or *Amazement* is come upon them: then God opens their ear to Discipline." On May 5, 1678, the then teen-aged young man probably witnessed a particularly effective demonstration of this principle as it was directed toward an entire congregation.

Some years earlier—at first against Increase Mather's will, then later with his support—the churches of New England had succumbed to the need for what its detractors later called the "Half-Way Covenant," in which as yet unconverted adult children of church members were acknowledged as church members (with the right to have their own children baptized) but not as full communicants. Bound up with this change in the notion of Puritan exclusivity was the growing belief that, in his covenant with his holy children, God had promised to "be thy God, and the God of thy seed after thee."[33] In his sermon of May 1678,

Mather alluded to this belief very early: "Now God hath seen good to cast the line of Election so, as that it doth (though not wholly, and only, yet) for the most part, run through the loins of godly Parents." It is well to remember here that before any comforts could be gained from this doctrine the Puritan parent had also to face the impossibility of ever being truly assured of his own election. But that is not the reason Mather cluttered his sentence with such awkward qualifications—"though not wholly, and only, yet . . . for the most part." God remained inscrutable, and it was heresy to think otherwise; but also: "Men should not think with themselves (as some do) if their children do belong to God, then he will convert them, whether they pray for him or no, but should therefore be stirred up to the more fervency in cries to Heaven, for the blessing promised. *I* (saith the Lord) *will give a new heart to you, and to your Children* yet you must pray for it."[34]

When he turned to address the youth of the congregation Mather mentioned explicitly the "affliction and amazement" that was at hand:

> Young men and young Women, O be in earnest for Converting Grace, before it be too late. It is high time for you to look about you, deceive not yourselves with false Conversions (as many young men do to their eternal ruine) or with gifts instead of Grace. . . . Death waits for you. There is now a Mortal and Contagious Disease in many Houses; the Sword of the Lord is drawn, and young men fall down apace slain under it; do you not see the Arrows of Death come flying over your heads? Why then, Awake, Awake, and turn to God in Jesus Christ whilst it is called today, and know for certain that if you dy in your sins, you will be the most miserable of any poor Creatures in the bottom of Hell.[35]

But Mather's most determined and terrifying words were reserved for the youngest and most vulnerable members of the congregation, those of less "discretion and understanding" than the other youths addressed. It was with them that the specter of parental and ministerial separation and betrayal was merged with the promise of death and damnation. "Beg as for your lives that the God of your Fathers would pour his Spirit upon you," he exhorted these littlest of children.

> Go into secret corners and plead it with God. . . . If you dy and be not first new Creatures, better you had never been born: you will be left without excuse before the Lord, terrible witnesses shall rise up against you at the last day. Your godly Parents will testifie against you before the Son of God at that day: And the Ministers of Christ will also be called in as witnesses against you for your condemnation, if you dy in your sins. As for many of you, I have treated with you privately and personally, I have told you, and I do tell you, and make solemn Protestation before the Lord, that if you dy in a Christless, graceless estate, I will most certainly profess unto Jesus Christ at the day of Judgement, Lord, these are the Children, whom I spake often unto thy Name, publickly and privately, and I told them, that if they did not make themselves a new heart, and make sure of an interest in Christ, they should become damned creatures for evermore; and yet they would not repent and believe the Gospel.[36]

If there is one thing on which modern psychologists have agreed concerning the fear of death in young children it is that such fear is generally rooted in the anticipation of separation from their parents. Time and again experimental studies have shown that, as one writer puts it, "the most persistent of fears associated with death is that of separation—and the one which is most likely to be basic, independent of cultural, religious, or social background." "In children," this writer adds, "dread of separation seems to be basic."[37]

There are, certainly, ways that children seem to have of defending against separation anxiety resulting from anticipation of death. One of these—one that has inspired poets down through the ages—is the expectation of reunion in death, a defense that makes separation a temporary matter.[38] But this was a defense denied the Puritan child. As if addressing this question directly, Increase Mather in 1711 remarked on

> What a dismal thing it will be when a Child shall see his Father at the right Hand of Christ in the day of Judgment, but himself at His left Hand: And when his Father shall joyn with Christ in passing a Sentence of Eternal Death upon him, saying, Amen O Lord, thou art Righteous in thus *Judging:* And when after the Judgment, children shall see their Father going with Christ to Heaven, but themselves going away into Everlasting Punishment![39]

As Edmund S. Morgan has pointed out, this verbal "picture of parent and child at the Day of Judgment . . . was a favorite with many Puritan ministers, for it made the utmost of filial affection."[40] It was probably not of much comfort to the Puritan child to hear that, if he was to be separated from his parents, he would at least still have the companionship of certain playmates—given the circumstances. For, as Jonathan Edwards put it in one of his sermons specifically addressed to young children: "How dreadful it will be to be all together in misery. Then you won't play together any more but will be damned together, will cry out with weeping and wailing and gnashing of teeth together."[41]

Another common defense against childhood fear of separation and death that is mentioned in the psychological literature is supplied by parental interjection that only old people die, not children.[42] Puritan children met precisely the opposite advice. The young "may bear and behave themselves as if imagining their hot blood, lusty bodies, activity, beauty, would last alwayes, and their youthful pleasures never be at an end," acknowledged Samuel Wakeman at a young man's funeral in 1673; "but," he warned, *"Childhood and Youth are vanity:* Death may not wait till they be grayheaded; or however, the earliest Morning hastens apace to Noon, and then to Night." From the moment they were old enough to pay attention children were repeatedly instructed regarding the precariousness of their existence. The sermons they listened to, the parents who corrected them, the teachers who instructed them, and eventually the books they read, all focused with a particular intensity on the possibility and even the likelihood of their imminent death. Further, those who died young, it was often noted, died suddenly—"Death is oftentimes as near the young man's back as it is to the old man's face," wrote Wakeman—and matter-of-fact repetitions of this ever-present threat joined with burning pictures of Judgment Day to hammer the theme home. "I know you will die in a little time," the esteemed Jonathan

Edwards calmly told a group of children, "some sooner than others. 'Tis not likely you will all live to grow up."[43] The fact that Edwards was only speaking the very obvious truth did not help matters any.

Nor did the literalness with which Puritan children must have taken the descriptions of depravity, sin, imminent death, judgment and hell offer anything in the way of relief. At least since the early writing of Piaget psychologists have been familiar with the various stages of the child's sense of causal reality, one central and persistent component of which is termed "realism." Realism, as one writer puts it, "refers to the fact that initially all things are equally real and real in the same sense and on the same plane: pictures, words, people, things, energies, dreams, feelings— all are equally solid or insubstantial and all mingle in a common sphere of experience. . . . Realism does not imply fatalism or passive resignation, but simply a failure [on the part of the young child] to doubt the reality of whatever comes into awareness."[44] The children observed in the psychological experiments that gave rise to the identification of these stages of reality awareness were the children of 20th century parents, children living in, if not a secular universe, at least one in which a fundamentalist view of divine creation and judgment is largely absent. Puritan children, however, lived in a world in which their parents—indeed, the greatest scientific minds of the time: Bacon, Boyle, Newton— were certain of the reality of witches and subterranean demons. In 1674, surprised at Spinoza's skepticism regarding spiritual entities, a correspondent of the freethinking philosopher doubtless spoke for most men of his time, the famed "Age of Reason," when he replied: "No one of moderns denies specters."[45]

It has long been known that one component of death in the Middle Ages was concern over the fate of the body of the deceased, and worry that a fully disintegrated corpse or one that had been destroyed in war might be unable to be present at the Judgment.[46] It is less well known, or less often acknowledged, that a similar literalism retained a hold on the Puritan mind into the 18th century. Thus in 1692 a highly respected New England minister could effectively deal with questions concerning the Last Judgment in the following manner:

Where will there be room for such a Vast Multitude as Adam, with all his Children? The whole surface of the earth could not hold them all? Ridiculous exception! Allow that this World should Last no less than *Ten-Thousand Years*, which it *will not*; Allow that there are at once alive a *Thousand Millions* of men, which there *are not*; Allow all these to march off every *Fifty years*, with a New Generation rising up in their stead; and allow each of these Individuals a place *Five Foot* Square to stand upon. I think these are Fair Allowances. I would now pray the Objector, if he have any skill at *Arithmetick*, to Compute, Whether a Spot of Ground, much less than *England*, which contains perhaps about Thirty Millions of Acres, but about a *Thousandth Part* of the Terraqueous Glob, and about the *Three Hundred thirty third* part of the Habitable Earth, would not hold them all.[47]

In a world in which the presence of early death was everywhere, and in which the most sophisticated and well regarded adults expressed such a literal sense of spiritual reality, it is hardly surprising that children would respond with a deadly serious mien to reminders of "how filthy, guilty, odious, abominable they are both by nature and practice," to descriptions of parental desertion at the day of Judgment and subsequent condemnation to the terrors of hell where "the Worm dyeth not . . . [and] the Fire is not quenched," and to the exhortations of respected teachers to "Remember Death; think much of death; think how it will be on a death bed."[48] In such a world it is far from surprising that a girl of seven should react "with many tears"—and her father with tears of sympathy—to a reading of Isaiah 24, in which she would have encountered:

> Therefore hath the curse devoured the earth, and they that dwell therin are desolate: therefore the inhabitants of the earth are burned, and few men left. . . . Fear, and the pit, and the snare, are upon thee, O inhabitant of the earth. And it shall come to pass, that he who fleeth from the noise of the fear shall fall into the pit; and he that cometh up out of the midst of the pit shall be taken in the snare: for the windows from on high are open, and the foundations of the earth do shake.

Nor, in such a world, should we consider it unusual that later in her youth this same girl would again and again "burst out into an amazing cry . . . [because] she was afraid she should goe to Hell," would "read out of Mr. Cotton Mather—why hath Satan filled thy heart, which increas'd her Fear," and would eventually be unable to read the Bible without weeping, fearing as she did "that she was a Reprobat, Loved not God's people as she should."[49]

The case of young Elizabeth Sewall is by no means unique. Puritan diaries and sermons are filled with references to similar childhood responses to the terrors of separation, mortality and damnation. As with so many other things Puritan, these fears seem to have reached a crescendo with the emotional outpourings of the Great Awakening in the 1740s.[50] But the fears were always present, following children into adulthood and combining there with the diquieting complexities of Puritan theology and Christian tradition to produce a culture permeated by fear and confusion in the face of death.

The Christian tradition that the Puritans had inherited counseled peace and comfort in one's dying hour. Elaborate procedures for coping with the fear of death had been devised throughout long centuries of experience. Extreme unction, the viaticum, indulgences, requiem masses, the prayers of family and friends—all these served the Catholic as a cushion against an excessively fearful reaction in the face of death. The relative optimism that grew out of this tradition was passed on, in different form, to much of Protestantism during the Renaissance and Reformation. Thus, Renaissance poetry on the theme of death, Edelgard Dubruck observes,

> . . . stressed immortality and the afterlife. The word "death" was often avoided and replaced by euphemisms . . . [and] depiction of the realistic aspects of death was carefully suppressed. . . . In the early sixteenth century, poets dwelt upon fame and immortality rather than death, and in the Reformation

writings death had at least lost its sting, and both Lutherans and Calvinists insisted that death was at long last vanquished with the help of Christ.[51]

Although the Puritans inherited, and tried to live with, the *prescription* that a peaceful death was a good death, the deterministic pessimism of the faith was contradictory to Christian tradition and caused exceptional discomfort as the devout Puritan awaited the end of his life.[52] To the adult Puritan the contemplation of death frequently "would make the flesh tremble."[53] To the Puritan child it could do no less.

Puritan New England, in this respect at least, seems a far cry from England in the same period, at least if Peter Laslett is correct when he writes that people there were "inured to bereavement and the shortness of life."[54] But in recognizing this, we should also be wary of finding in Puritan attitudes and behavior too much grist for our psychological mills. The fear of death, to many Freudians, is "closely interwoven with castration fear," a fear which "is so closely united with death fear that it has often been described as its origin." It is, writes psychoanalyst J. D. Howard, "purely. . . a secondary substitutive phenomenon of the castration fear which grew out of an inadequately resolved Oedipal conflict."[55] Turning to Freud himself, a more sophisticated interpreter with some knowledge of Puritanism might seize on the similarity between the Puritan requirement for uncertainty and his preoccupations with death, and Freud's treatment of uncertainty and obsessional neurosis.[56] But interpretations of this type are hopelessly bogged down by the arrogance and myopia of the historical present.[57]

The world of the Puritan—child and adult—was a rational world, in many ways, perhaps, more rational than our own. It is true that it was a world of witches and demons, and of a just and terrible God who made his presence known in the slightest act of nature. But this was the given reality about which most of the decisions and actions of the age, throughout the entire Western world, revolved. When the Puritan parent urged on his children what we would consider a painfully early awareness of sin and death, it was because the well-being of the child and the community *required* such an early recognition of these matters. It merits little to note that the Puritans (and Bacon and Boyle and Newton) were mistaken in their beliefs in hobgoblins; the fact is they were real to men of the 17th century, as real as Ra and his heavenly vessels were to the ancient Egyptians, and at least as real as the unconscious is to devout followers of Freud; and the responses to that reality were as honest and as rational, in the context of the times, as are the responses to reality of any parent today.

If children were frightened, even terrified, by the prospects of life and death conjured up by their parents and ministers, that too was a natural and rational response. As more than one Puritan writer suggested, to fail to be frightened was a sure sign that one was either spiritually lost, or stupid, or both.[58] Death brought with it, to all but a very few, the prospect of the most hideous and excruciating fate imaginable. One necessary though by itself insufficient sign of membership in that select company of saints was the taking to heart of the warning to "beware of indulging yourselves in a stupid secure frame."[59] Thus, wrote Samuel Willard with remarkably cool detachment and insight,

> Here we see the reason why the People of God are so often doubtful, disquiet, discontent, and afraid to dy (I put things together). The ground of all this is because they do not as yet see clearly what they shall be: It would be a matter of just wonderment to see the Children of God so easily and often shaken, so disturbed and perplexed in hours of Temptation, were it not from the consideration that at present they know so little of themselves or their happiness: Sometimes their sonship itself doth not appear to them, but they are in the dark, at a loss about the evidencing of it to the satisfaction of their own minds, and from hence it is that many doubtings arise, and their souls are disquieted.[60]

Willard knew first hand of what he spoke. He was often the one chosen to try to calm the fears of those who found the prospect of death too much to bear; Judge Sewall in fact called him in to help with young Elizabeth's disconsolate weeping. It may be, despite their experience, that ministers and parents like Willard were unaware of all the components that went into the making of the Puritan child's fear of death. It was, as we have seen, a complex problem touching on a variety of matters which Puritan children and adults alike had to face every day of their lives. But they did at least know that when a young Betty or Sam Sewall broke down in tears over the prospects of death and damnation, the children— and they were children, not miniature adults—were most often acting normally, out of their own experience in the world, and in response to their parents' solemn, reasoned warnings.

As studies of death—its frequency, causes, and attitudes toward it—become more numerous, opportunities to compare New England patterns with those of other colonies and of European nations should make current findings more meaningful. So too will studies of the visual symbols of death, such as Allen Ludwig's Graven Images: New England Stonecarving and its Symbols, 1650–1815 *(Middletown, Conn., 1966). But for the present, students of American Puritanism must work with fragmentary evidence and tentative conclusions about a subject that weighed heavily on the Puritan mind.*

NOTES

1. Philippe Ariès, *Centuries of Childhood: A Social History of Family Life* (New York: Random House, 1962), p. 128.

2. Michael Zuckerman, *Peaceable Kingdoms: New England Towns in the Eighteenth Century* (New York: Random House, 1970), p. 73; John Demos, *A Little Commonwealth: Family Life in Plymouth Colony* (New York: Oxford Univ. Press, 1970), p. 139.

3. Alan Macfarlane, *The Family Life of Ralph Josselin, A Seventeenth Century Clergyman* (Cambridge: Cambridge Univ. Press, 1970), pp. 90-91.

4. For a convenient collection of some of this material see Robert H. Bremner, ed., *Children and Youth in America* (Cambridge, Mass.: Harvard Univ. Press, 1970), 1:27-122.

5. Philippe Ariès, "At the Point of Origin," in Peter Brooks, ed., *The Child's Part* (Boston: Beacon Press, 1972), p. 15; Marc Soriano, "From Tales of Warning to Formulettes: The Oral Tradition in French Children's Literature," ibid., pp. 24-25.

6. William Sloane, *Children's Books in England & America in the Seventeenth Century* (New York: Columbia Univ. Press, 1955).

7. Zuckerman, p. 77. It should be acknowledged that some of Ariès' contentions have been challenged within the French historical setting. On the matter of the presence or absence of an adolescent stage, for example, see the important essay by Natalie Z. Davis, "The Reasons of Misrule: Youth Groups and Charivaris in Sixteenth Century France," *Past and Present*, 50 (Feb. 1971); an extension of Davis' argument to 17th century London is Steven R. Smith, "The London Apprentice as Seventeenth-Century Adolescent," *Past and Present*, 61 (Nov. 1973).

8. *Micro-cosmographie or, A Piece of the World Discovered in Essays and Characters* (London, 1628), p. 5.

9. Henri Misson, *Mémoires et Observations Faites par un Voyageur en Angleterre* (Paris, 1698), p. 128; Guy Miege, *The Present State of Great Britain* (London, 1707), p. 222; John Drinkwater, *Charles James Fox* (London: Ernest Benn, 1928), pp. 14-15. On the leniency of parental discipline in some families in the American colonial South see Edmund S. Morgan, *Virginians at Home* (Charlottesville: Univ. Press of Virginia, 1952), pp. 7-8, where an English traveler is quoted as saying of Maryland and Virginia: "The Youth of these more indulgent Settlements, partake pretty much of the *Petit Maitre* Kind, and are pamper'd much more in Softness and Ease than their Neighbors more Northward."

10. *New Essays: Or, Observations Divine and Moral*, in Robert Ashton, ed., *The Works of John Robinson* (Boston: Doctrinal Tract and Book Soc., 1851), 1:246-48.

11. John Calvin, *Institutes of the Christian Religion*, ed. John T. McNeill (Philadelphia: Westminster Press, 1960), 2:1013.

12. Jonathan Edwards, *A Faithful Narrative of the Surprising Work of God*, in *The Works of Jonathan Edwards*, ed., C. C. Goen (New Haven: Yale Univ. Press, 1972), 4:158; James Janeway, *A Token for Children* [1679] (Boston: Caleb Bingham, 1802), p. 59.

13. *Small Offers Towards the Service of the Tabernacle in this Wilderness* (Boston, 1689), p. 59.

14. Cotton Mather, *The Young Mans Preservative* (Boston, 1701), p. 4; *Small Offers*, p. 62.

15. *Cares About the Nurseries* (Boston, 1702), p. 32.

16. *The Child's Portion* (Boston, 1684), p. 31.

17. *Small Offers*, pp. 18-19.

18. Willard, p. 16.

19. "The Nature of Early Piety as it Respects God," in *A Course of Sermons on Early Piety* (Boston, 1721), p. 10.

20. *The Day of Doom* (London, 1687), stanza 181.

21. *Four Generations: Population, Land, and Family in Colonial Andover, Massachusetts* (Ithaca: Cornell University Press, 1970).

22. "Parent-Child Relations in Seventeenth-Century England and America," in Lloyd de Mause, ed., *The History of Childhood* (New York: Psychohistory Press, 1974). I am grateful to Professor Illick for allowing me to examine his manuscript prior to publication.

23. Lockridge, "The Population of Dedham, Massachusetts, 1636-1736," *Economic History Review*, 19 (1966), 343.

24. Thomas Cobbett, *A Fruitfull and Usefull Discourse . . .* (London, 1656), p. 96.

25. *The Puritan Family* (New York: Harper & Row, 1966), p. 107.

26. Ibid., p. 77; cf. Demos, p. 74.

27. There is a large body of psychological and anthropological literature on related phenomena and it has been helpful in formulating some of the ideas in this section. On the effects of pollution fear see Mary Douglas, *Purity and Danger: An Analysis of Concepts of Pollution and Taboo* (London: Routledge & Kegan Paul, 1966); on the psychological problem of "approach-avoidance conflict," see, among many relevant monographs, W. N.

Schoenfeld, "An Experimental Approach to Anxiety, Escape, and Avoidance Behavior," in P. H. Hoch and J. Zuber, eds., *Anxiety* (New York: Grune & Stratton, 1950), pp. 70-99; and Murray Sidmas, "Avoidance Behavior," in W. K. Honig, ed., *Operant Behavior* (New York: Appleton-Century-Crofts, 1966), pp. 448-98.

28. Demos, p. 136.

29. "Diary," in Massachusetts Historical Society *Collections*, series 7, 7:535.

30. Boston Record Commissioners, *Report*, VII, 119. Cited in John B. Blake, *Public Health in the Town of Boston, 1630-1822* (Cambridge, Mass.: Harvard University Press, 1959), p. 19; see also Carl Bridenbaugh, *Cities in the Wilderness: Urban Life in America, 1625-1742* (New York: Capricorn Books, 1964 [orig. pub. 1936]), p. 87.

31. See Douglas Edward Leach, *Flintlock and Tomahawk: New England in King Philip's War* (New York: W. W. Norton, 1958), p. 243.

32. *Pray for the Rising Generation* (Boston, 1678).

33. John Cotton, *The Covenant of Gods Free Grace* (London, 1645), p. 19.

34. Increase Mather, *Pray for the Rising Generation*, p. 12.

35. Ibid., p. 22.

36. Ibid.

37. Marjorie Editha Mitchell, *The Child's Attitude To Death* (London: Barrie & Rockham, 1966), p. 100; cf. Sylvia Anthony, *The Discovery of Death in Childhood and After* (London: Allen Lane, 1971), esp. chap. 8; Roslyn P. Ross, "Separation Fear and the Fear of Death in Children," Diss. New York University 1966; Eugenia H. Waechter, "Death Anxiety in Children With Fatal Illness," Diss. Stanford University 1968; and the now almost classic studies of J. Bowlby, esp. "Separation Anxiety," *International Journal of Psychoanalysis and Psychiatry*, Vols. 41 and 42 (1961), and "Childhood Mourning and Its Implications for Psychiatry," *American Journal of Psychiatry*, Vol. 118 (1961).

38. Anthony (see note 37), p. 151.

39. *An Earnest Exhortation to the Children of New England to Exalt the God of their Fathers* (Boston, 1711), p. 35.

40. Morgan, pp. 178-79.

41. Jonathan Edwards, unpublished sermon in Edwards' manuscripts in Yale University Library. Quoted in Sanford Fleming, *Children and Puritanism* (New Haven: Yale Univ. Press, 1933), p. 100.

42. Anthony, p. 153.

43. Samuel Wakeman, *A Young Man's Legacy* (Boston, 1673), pp. 6, 41; Edwards quoted in Fleming, p. 100.

44. Joseph Church, *Language and the Discovery of Reality* (New York: Random House, 1961), pp. 15-16. For full discussion of this and other stages see Jean Piaget, *The Construction of Reality in the Child* (New York: Basic Books, 1954), and *The Child's Conception of Physical Causality* (Totawa, N.J.: Littlefield, Adams, 1966) esp. pp. 237-58.

45. On the belief of 17th century scientists in the reality of the invisible world, see Lynn Thorndike, *A History of Magic and Experimental Science* (New York: Columbia Univ. Press, 1951), Vols. 7 and 8. The reference quoted is from 8:570.

46. On this, with special reference to the catechistic treatment of such matters in the medieval text *La Lumiere as lais*, see C. V. Langlois, *La Vie en France au Moyen Age* (Paris: Librairie Hachette, 1928), 4:111-19.

47. Samuel Lee, *The Great Day of Judgment* (Boston, 1692), pp. 19-20.

48. Benjamin Wadsworth, "The Nature of Early Piety," p. 15; Solomon Stoddard, *The Efficacy of the Fear of Hell to Restrain Men From Sin* (Boston, 1713), p. 24; Joseph Green, *The Commonplace Book of Joseph Green* (1696), ed., Samuel Eliot Morison, Colonial Society of Massachusetts *Publications*, 34 (1943), 204.

49. Samuel Sewall, "Diary" in Massachusetts Historical Society *Collections*, series 5, V, 308, 419-20, 422-23, 437. See also the terrified reaction of Sewall's young son Sam to the death of a companion and his father's reminding him of the "need to prepare for Death," ibid., pp. 308-9.

50. See the numerous references to violent childhood reactions to death in *The Christian History*, I, and II (Boston, 1743-44); cited in Fleming.

51. Edelgard Dubruck, *The Theme of Death in French Poetry of the Middle Ages and the Renaissance* (The Hague: Mouton, 1964), pp. 152, 154.

52. For an extended treatment of this matter, see David E. Stannard, "Death and Dying in Puritan New England," *American Historical Review*, 78 (Dec. 1973), 1305-30.

53. James Fitch, *Peace the End of the Perfect and Upright* (Boston, 1673), p. 6.

54. Peter Laslett, *The World We Have Lost: England Before the Industrial Age* (New York: Scribner's, 1965), p. 96.

55. J. D. Howard, "Fear of Death," *Journal of the Indiana State Medical Association* (1962), quoted in Hattie R. Rosenthal, "The Fear of Death as an Indispensable Factor in Psychotherapy," in Hendrik M. Ruitenbeek, ed., *Death: Interpretations* (New York: Delta Books, 1969), p. 171; the previous quotation is from Mary Chadwick, "Notes Upon the Fear of Death," in Ruitenbeek, p. 75.

56. Sigmund Freud, "Notes Upon a Case of Obsessional Neurosis," Part II, *The Standard Edition of the Complete Psychological Works of Sigmund Freud.* James Strachey, ed. (London: Hogarth Press, 1957), 10:229-37.

57. A particularly egregious example of this, with specific bearing on the subject at hand, is the apparent raison d'être of a new journal, *History of Childhood Quarterly*, as the interminable psychoanalytic explication of the theme that: "The history of childhood is a nightmare from which we have only recently begun to awaken." It is the insistent and quite serious claim of the founder and editor of this journal that prior to the 18th century there did not exist in Western history a single "good mother."

58. See, for example, Leonard Hoar, *The Sting of Death* (Boston, 1680), pp. 11-12.

59. Ibid.

60. Willard, *The Child's Portion*, p. 67.

14 | UNDERLYING THEMES IN THE WITCHCRAFT OF SEVENTEENTH-CENTURY NEW ENGLAND

JOHN DEMOS

The one dramatic episode in early New England in which females appear in disproportionate numbers and in a variety of roles is the Salem witchcraft frenzy of 1692. That strange and brutal experience has always attracted popular and scholarly attention. It has probably been the subject of more stories and plays than any other aspect of early New England, and in the past decade it has received a fresh outpouring of historical analyses. For almost a quarter-century the standard interpretation was Marion Starkey's The Devil in Massachusetts *(Boston, 1950), which stressed Puritanism's repressive influence and the hysteria of the girls who initiated the witch hunt. Chadwick Hansen's* Witchcraft at Salem *(New York, 1969) has largely displaced Starkey's account, partly because it offered several important revisions and partly because Hansen claimed that in a society that holds such a belief, witchcraft* can *happen. By practicing certain rituals believed by both the "witch" and the victim to be harmful, Hansen concludes, real damage was done. Against this psychogenic approach, John Demos in the following essay offers an explanation based on a different set of psychological concepts, and at the same time he fuses recent scholarly interest in women, children, and generational tensions.*

It is faintly embarrassing for a historian to summon his colleagues to still another consideration of early New England witchcraft. Here, surely, is a topic that previous generations of writers have sufficiently worked, indeed overworked. Samuel Eliot Morison once commented that the Salem witch-hunt was, after all, "but a small incident in the history of a great superstition"; and Perry Miller noted that with only minor qualifications "the intellectual history of New England can be written as though no such thing ever happened. It had no effect on the ecclesiastical or political situation, it does not figure in the institutional or ideological development."[1] Popular interest in the subject is, then badly out of proportion to its actual historical significance, and perhaps the sane course for the future would be silence.

This assessment seems, on the face of it, eminently sound. Witchcraft was not an important matter from the standpoint of the larger historical process; it exerted only limited influence on the unfolding sequence of events in colonial New England, Moreover, the literature on the subject seems to have reached a point of diminishing returns. Details of fact have been endlessly canvassed, and the main outlines of the story, particularly the story of Salem, are well and widely known.

There is, to be sure, continuing debate over one set of issues: the roles played by the persons most directly involved. Indeed the historiography of Salem can be viewed, in large measure, as an unending effort to judge the participants—and, above all, to affix blame. A number of verdicts have been fashionable at one time or another. Thus the ministers were really at fault; or Cotton Mather in particular; or the whole culture of Puritanism; or the core group of "afflicted girls" (if their "fits" are construed as conscious fraud).[2] The most recent, and in some ways most sophisticated, study of the Salem trials plunges right into the middle of the same controversy; the result is yet another conclusion. Not the girls, not the clergy, not Puritanism, but the accused witches themselves are now the chief culprits. For "witchcraft actually did exist and was widely practiced in seventeenth-century New England"; and women like Goody Glover, Bridget Bishop, and Mammy Redd were "in all probability" guilty as charged.[3]

Clearly these questions of personal credit and blame can still generate lively interest, but are they the most fruitful, the most important questions to raise about witchcraft? Will such a debate ever be finally settled? Are its partisan terms and moral tone appropriate to historical scholarship?

The situation is not hopeless if only we are willing to look beyond the limits of our own discipline. There is, in particular, a substantial body of interesting and relevant work by anthropologists. Many recent studies of primitive societies contain chapters about witchcraft, and there are several entire monographs on the subject.[4] The approach they follow differs strikingly from anything in the historical literature. Broadly speaking, the anthropological work is far more analytic, striving always to use materials on witchcraft as a set of clues or "symptoms." The subject is important not in its own right but as a means of exploring certain larger questions about the society. For example, witchcraft throws light on social structure, on the organization of families, and on the inner dynamics of personality. The substance of such investigations, of course, varies greatly from one culture to another, but the framework, the informing purposes are roughly the same. To apply this framework and these purposes to historical materials is not inherently difficult. The data may be inadequate in a given case, but the analytic categories themselves are designed for any society, whether simple or complex, Western or non-Western, past or contemporary. Consider, by way of illustration, the strategy proposed for the main body of this essay.

Our discussion will focus on a set of complex relationships between the alleged witches and their victims. The former group will include all persons accused of practicing witchcraft, and they will be called, simply, witches.[5] The category of victims will comprise everyone who claimed to have suffered from witchcraft, and they will be divided into two categories to account for an important distinction between different kinds of victims. As every schoolchild knows, some victims experienced fits—bizarre seizures that, in the language of modern psychiatry, closely approximate the clinical picture of hysteria. These people may be called accusers, since their sufferings and their accusations seem to have carried the greatest weight in generating formal proceedings against witches. A second, much larger group of victims includes people who attributed to witchcraft some particular misfortune they had suffered, most typically an injury or illness, the sudden death of domestic animals, the loss of personal property, or repeated failure in important day-to-day activities like farming, fishing, and hunting. This type of evidence was of secondary importance in trials of witches and was usually brought forward after the accusers had pressed their own more damaging charges. For people testifying to such experiences, therefore, the shorthand term witnesses seems reasonably appropriate.

Who were these witches, accusers, and witnesses? How did their lives intersect? Most important, what traits were generally characteristic and what traits were alleged to have been characteristic of each group? These will be the organizing questions in the pages that follow. Answers to these questions will treat both external (or objective) circumstances and internal (or subjective) experiences. In the case of witches, for example, it is important to try to discover their age, marital status, socioeconomic position, and visible personality traits. But it is equally important to examine the characteristics attributed to witches by others—flying about at night, transforming themselves into animals, and the like. In short, one can construct a picture of witches in fact and in fantasy; and comparable efforts can be made with accusers and witnesses. Analysis directed to the level of external reality helps to locate certain points of tension or conflict in the social structure of a community. The fantasy picture, on the other hand, reveals more directly the psychological dimension of life, the inner preoccupations, anxieties, and conflicts of individual members of that community.

Such an outline looks deceptively simple, but in fact it demands an unusual degree of caution, from writer and reader alike. The approach is explicitly cross-disciplinary, reaching out to anthropology for strategy and to psychology for theory. There is, of course, nothing new about the idea of a working relationship between history and the behavioral sciences. It is more than ten years since William Langer's famous summons to his colleagues to consider this their "next assignment";[6] but the record of actual output is still very meager. All such efforts remain quite experimental; they are designed more to stimulate discussion than to prove a definitive case.

There is a final point—about context and the larger purposes of this form of inquiry. Historians have traditionally worked with purposeful, conscious events, "restricting themselves," in Langer's words, "to recorded fact and to strictly rational motivation."[7] They have not necessarily wished to exclude non-rational or irrational behavior, but for the most part they have done so. Surely in our own post-Freudian era there is both need and opportunity to develop a more balanced picture. It is to these long-range ends that further study of witchcraft should be dedicated. For witchcraft is, if nothing else, an open window on the irrational.

The first witchcraft trial of which any record survives occurred at Windsor, Connecticut, in 1647,[8] and during the remainder of the century the total of cases came to nearly one hundred. Thirty-eight people were executed as witches, and a few more, though convicted, managed somehow to escape the death penalty. There were, of course, other outcomes as well: full-dress trials resulting in acquittal, hung juries, convictions reversed on appeal, and "complaints" filed but not followed up. Finally, no doubt, many unrecorded episodes touching on witchcraft, episodes of private suspicion or public gossip, never eventuated in legal action at all.[9]

This long series of witchcraft cases needs emphasis lest the Salem outbreak completely dominate our field of vision. Salem differed radically from previous episodes in sheer scope; it developed a degree of self-reinforcing momentum present in no other instance. But it was very similar in many qualitative aspects: the types of people concerned, the nature of the charges, the fits, and so forth. Indeed, from an analytic standpoint, all these cases can be regarded as roughly equivalent and interchangeable. They are pieces of a single, larger phenomenon, a system of witchcraft belief that was generally prevalent in early New England. The evidence for such a system must, of course, be drawn from a variety of cases to produce representative conclusions. For most questions this is quite feasible; there is more evidence, from a greater range of cases, than can ever be presented in a single study.

Yet in one particular matter the advantages of concentrating on Salem are overwhelming. It affords a unique opportunity to portray the demography of witchcraft, to establish a kind of profile for each of the three basic categories of people involved in witchcraft, in terms of sex, age, and marital status. Thus the statistical tables that follow are drawn entirely from detailed work on the Salem materials.[10] The earlier cases do not yield the breadth of data necessary for this type of quantitative investigation. They do, however, provide many fragments of evidence that are generally consistent with the Salem picture.

There is at least minimal information about 162 people accused as witches during the entire period of the Salem outbreak.[11]

Sex	Total	Marital Status	Male	Female	Total	Age	Male	Female	Total
Male	42	Single	8	29	37	Under 20	6	18	24
Female	120	Married	15	61	76	21–30	3	7	10
		Widowed	1	20	21	31–40	3	8	11
Total	162					41–50	6	18	24
		Total	24	110	134	51–60	5	23	28
						61–70	4	8	12
						Over 70	3	6	9
						Total	30	88	118

These figures point to an important general conclusion: the witches were predominantly married or widowed women, between the ages of forty-one and sixty. While the exceptions add up to a considerable number, most of them belonged to the families of middle-aged, female witches. Virtually all the young persons in the group can be identified as children of witches and most of the men as husbands of witches. In fact this pattern conformed to an assumption then widely prevalent, that the transmission of witchcraft would naturally follow the lines of family or of close friendship. An official statement from the government of Connecticut included among the "grounds for Examination of a Witch" the following:

> if ye party suspected be ye son or daughter the servt or familiar friend; neer Neighbor or old Companion of a Knowne or Convicted witch this alsoe a presumton for witchcraft is an art yt may be learned & Convayd from man to man & oft it falleth out yt a witch dying leaveth som of ye aforesd. heirs of her witchcraft.[12]

In short, young witches and male witches belonged to a kind of derivative category. They were not the prime targets in these situations; they were, in a literal sense, rendered suspect by association. The deepest suspicions, the most intense anxieties, remained fixed on middle-aged women.

Thirty-four persons experienced fits of one sort or another during the Salem trials and qualify thereby as accusers.

Sex	Total	Marital Status	Male	Female	Total	Age	Male	Female	Total
Male	5	Single	5	23	28	Under 11	0	1	1
Female	29	Married	0	6	6	11–15	1	7	8
		Widowed	0	0	0	16–20	1	13	14
Total	34					21–25	0	1	1
		Total	5	29	34	26–30	0	1	1
						Over 30	0	4	4
						Total	2	27	29

Here again the sample shows a powerful cluster. The vast majority of the accusers were single girls between the ages of eleven and twenty. The exceptions in this case (two boys, three males of undetermined age, and four adult women) are rather difficult to explain, for there is little evidence about any of them. By and large, however, they played only a minor role in the trials. Perhaps the matter can be left this way: the core group of accusers was entirely composed of adolescent girls, but the inner conflicts so manifest in their fits found an echo in at least a few persons of other ages or of the opposite sex.

Eighty-four persons came forward as witnesses at one time or another during the Salem trials.

Sex	Total		Marital Status	Male	Female	Total		Age	Male	Female	Total
Male	63		Single	11	3	14		Under 20	3	2	5
Female	21		Married	39	16	55		21–30	13	4	17
			Widowed	3	1	4		31–40	14	6	20
Total	84							41–50	18	7	25
			Total	53	20	73		51–60	11	1	12
								61–70	2	1	3
								Over 70	2	0	2
								Total	63	21	84

Here the results seem relatively inconclusive. Three-fourths of the witnesses were men, but a close examination of the trial records suggests a simple reason for this: men were more likely, in seventeenth-century New England, to take an active part in legal proceedings of any type. When a husband and wife were victimized together by some sort of witchcraft, it was the former who would normally come forward to testify. As to the ages of the witnesses, there is a fairly broad distribution between twenty and sixty years. Probably, then, this category reflects the generalized belief in witchcraft among all elements of the community in a way that makes it qualitatively different from the groupings of witches and accusers.

There is much more to ask about external realities in the lives of such people, particularly with regard to their social and economic position. Unfortunately, however, the evidence is somewhat limited here and permits only a few impressionistic observations. It seems that many witches came from the lower levels of the social structure, but there were too many exceptions to see in this a really significant pattern. The first three accused at Salem were Tituba, a Negro slave, Sarah Good, the wife of a poor laborer, and Sarah Osbourne, who possessed a very considerable estate.[13] Elizabeth Godman, tried at New Haven in 1653, seems to have been poor and perhaps a beggar;[14] but Nathaniel and Rebecca Greensmith, who were convicted and executed at Hartford eight years later, were quite well-to-do;[15] and "Mistress" Ann Hibbens, executed at Boston in 1656 was the widow of a wealthy merchant and former magistrate of the Bay Colony.[16]

What appears to have been common to nearly all these people, irrespective of their economic position, was some kind of personal eccentricity, some deviant or even criminal behavior that had long since marked them out as suspect. Some of them had previously been tried for theft or battery or slander;[17] others were known for their interest in dubious activities like fortunetelling or certain kinds of folk-healing.[18] The "witch Glover" of Boston, on whom Cotton Mather reports at some length, was Irish and Catholic, and spoke Gaelic; and a Dutch family in Hartford came under suspicion at the time the Greensmiths were tried.[19]

More generally, many of the accused seem to have been unusually irascible and contentious in their personal relations. Years before her conviction for witchcraft Mrs. Hibbens had obtained a reputation for "natural crabbedness of . . . temper"; indeed she had been excommunicated by the Boston church in 1640, following a long and acrimonious ecclesiastical trial. William Hubbard, whose *General History of New England* was published in 1680, cited her case to make the general point that "persons of hard favor and turbulent passions are apt to be condemned by the common people as witches, upon very slight grounds." In the trial of Mercy Desborough, at Fairfield, Connecticut, in 1692, the court received numerous reports of her quarrelsome behavior. She had, for example, told one neighbor "yt shee would make him bare as a bird's tale," and to another she had repeatedly said "many hard words." Goodwife Clawson, tried at the same time, was confronted with testimony like the following:

> Abigal Wescot saith that as shee was going along the street goody Clasen came out to her and they had some words together and goody Clason took up stones and threw at her: and at another time as shee went along the street before sd Clasons dore goody Clason caled to mee and asked mee what was in my Chamber last Sabbath day night; and I doe afirme that I was not there that night: and at another time as I was in her sone Steephens house being neere her one hous shee folowed me in and contended with me becase I did not com into her hous caling of me proud slut what—are you proud of your fine cloths and you love to be mistres but you neuer shal be and several other provoking speeches.[20]

The case of Mary and Hugh Parsons, tried at Springfield in 1651, affords a further look at the external aspects of our subject. A tax rating taken at Springfield in 1646 records the landholdings of most of the principals in the witchcraft prosecutions of five years later. When the list is arranged according to wealth, Parsons falls near the middle (twenty-fourth out of forty-two), and those who testified against him come from the top, middle, and bottom. This outcome tends to confirm the general point that economic position is not, for present purposes, a significant datum. What seems, on the basis of the actual testimonies at the trial, to have been much more important was the whole dimension of eccentric and anti-social behavior. Mary Parsons, who succumbed repeatedly to periods of massive depression, was very nearly insane. During the witchcraft investigations she began by testifying against her husband and ended by convicting herself of the murder of their infant child. Hugh Parsons was a sawyer and brickmaker by trade, and there are indications that in performing these services he was sometimes suspected of charging extortionate rates.[21] But what may have weighed most heavily against him was his propensity for prolonged and bitter quarreling; many examples of his "threatening speeches" were reported in court.

One other aspect of this particular episode is worth noting, namely, the apparent influence of spatial proximity. When the names of Parsons and his "victims" are checked against a map of Springfield in this period, it becomes very clear that the latter were mostly his nearest neighbors. In fact nearly all of the people who took direct part in the trial came from the southern half of the town. No other witchcraft episode yields such a detailed picture in this respect, but many separate pieces of evidence suggest that neighborhood antagonism was usually an aggravating factor.[22]

We can summarize the major characteristics of the external side of New England witchcraft as follows: First, the witches themselves were chiefly women of middle age whose accusers were girls about one full generation younger. This may reflect the kind of situation that anthropologists would call a structural conflict—that is, some focus of tension created by the specific ways in which a community arranges the lives of its members. In a broad sense it is quite probable that adolescent girls in early New England were particularly subject to the control of older women, and this may well have given rise to a powerful underlying resentment. By contrast, the situation must have been less difficult for boys, since their work often took them out of the household and their behavior generally was less restricted.

There are, moreover, direct intimations of generational conflict in the witchcraft records themselves. Consider a little speech by one of the afflicted girls during a fit, a speech meticulously recorded by Cotton Mather. The words are addressed to the "specter" of a witch, with whom the girl has been having a heated argument:

> What's that? Must the younger Women, do yee say, hearken to the Elder?—
> They must be another Sort of Elder Women than You then! they must not
> bee Elder Witches, I am sure. Pray, do you for once Hearken to mee.—What
> a dreadful Sight are You! An Old Woman, an Old Servant of the Divel![23]

Second, it is notable that most witches were deviant persons— eccentric or conspicuously anti-social or both. This suggests very clearly the impact of belief in witchcraft as a form of control in the social ordering of New England communities. Here indeed is one of the most widely-found social functions of witchcraft; its importance has been documented for many societies all over the world.[24] Any individual who contemplates actions of which the community disapproves knows that if he performs such acts, he will become more vulnerable either to a direct attack by witches or to the charge that he is himself a witch. Such knowledge is a powerful inducement to self-constraint.

What can be said of the third basic conclusion, that witchcraft charges particularly involved neighbors? Very briefly, it must be fitted with other aspects of the social setting in these early New England communities. That there was a great deal of contentiousness among these people is suggested by innumerable court cases from the period dealing with disputes about land, lost cattle, trespass, debt, and so forth. Most men seem to have felt that the New World offered them a unique opportunity to increase their properties,[25] and this may have heightened competitive feelings and pressures. On the other hand, cooperation was still the norm in many areas of life, not only in local government but for a variety of agricultural tasks as well. In such ambivalent circumstances it is hardly surprising that relations between close neighbors were often tense or downright abrasive.

"In all the Witchcraft which now Grievously Vexes us, I know not whether any thing be more Unaccountable, than the Trick which the

Witches have, to render themselves and their Tools Invisible."[26] Thus wrote Cotton Mather in 1692; and three centuries later it is still the "invisible" part of witchcraft that holds a special fascination. Time has greatly altered the language for such phenomena—"shapes" and "specters" have become "hallucinations"; "enchantments" are a form of "suggestion"; the Devil himself seems a fantasy—and there is a corresponding change of meanings. Yet here was something truly remarkable, a kind of irreducible core of the entire range of witchcraft phenomena. How much of it remains "unaccountable"? To ask the question is to face directly the other side of our subject: witchcraft viewed as psychic process, as a function of internal reality.

The biggest obstacles to the study of psycho-history ordinarily are practical ones involving severe limitations of historical data. Yet for witchcraft the situation is uniquely promising on these very grounds. Even a casual look at writings like Cotton Mather's *Memorable Providences* or Samuel Willard's *A briefe account* etc.[27] discloses material so rich in psychological detail as to be nearly the equivalent of clinical case reports. The court records on witchcraft are also remarkably full in this respect. The clergy, the judges, all the leaders whose positions carried special responsibility for combatting witchcraft, regarded publicity as a most important weapon. Witchcraft would yield to careful study and the written exchange of information. Both Mather and Willard received "afflicted girls" into their own homes and recorded "possession" behavior over long periods of time.

A wealth of evidence does not, of course, by itself win the case for a psychological approach to witchcraft. Further problems remain, problems of language and of validation.[28] There is, moreover, the very basic problem of selecting from among a variety of different theoretical models. Psychology is not a monolith, and every psycho-historian must declare a preference. In opting for psycho-analytic theory, for example, he performs, in part, an act of faith, faith that this theory provides deeper, fuller insights into human behavior than any other. In the long run the merit of such choices will probably be measured on pragmatic grounds. Does the interpretation explain materials that would otherwise remain unused? Is it consistent with evidence in related subject areas?

If, then, the proof lies in the doing, let us turn back to the New England witches and especially to their "Trick . . . to render themselves and their tools Invisible." What characterized these spectral witches? What qualities were attributed to them by the culture at large?

The most striking observation about witches is that they gave free rein to a whole gamut of hostile and aggressive feelings. In fact most witchcraft episodes began after some sort of actual quarrel. The fits of Mercy Short followed an abusive encounter with the convicted witch Sarah Good. The witch Glover was thought to have attacked Martha Goodwin after an argument about some missing clothes.[29] Many such examples could be accumulated here, but the central message seems immediately obvious: never antagonize witches, for they will invariably strike back hard. Their compulsion to attack was, of course, most dramatically visible in the fits experienced by some of their victims. These fits were treated as tortures imposed directly and in every detail by witches or by the Devil himself. It is also significant that witches often assumed the shape of animals in order to carry out their attacks. Animals, presumably, are not subject to constraints of either an internal or external kind; their aggressive impulses are immediately translated into action.

Another important facet of the lives of witches was their activity in company with each other. In part this consisted of long and earnest conferences on plans to overthrow the kingdom of God and replace it with the reign of the Devil. Often, however, these meetings merged with feasts, the witches' main form of self-indulgence. Details are a bit thin here, but we know that the usual beverage was beer or wine (occasionally described as bearing a suspicious resemblance to blood), and the food was bread or meat. It is also worth noting what did not happen on these occasions. There were a few reports of dancing and "sport," but very little of the wild excitements associated with witch revels in continental Europe. Most striking of all is the absence of allusions to sex; there is no nakedness, no promiscuity, no obscene contact with the Devil. This seems to provide strong support for the general proposition that the psychological conflicts underlying the early New England belief in witchcraft had much more to do with aggressive impulses than with libidinal ones.

The persons who acted as accusers also merit the closest possible attention, for the descriptions of what they suffered in their fits are perhaps the most revealing of all source materials for present purposes. They experienced, in the first place, severe pressures to go over to the Devil's side themselves. Witches approached them again and again, mixing threats and bribes in an effort to break down their Christian loyalties. Elizabeth Knapp, bewitched at Groton, Massachusetts, in 1671, was alternately tortured and plied with offers of "money, silkes, fine cloaths, ease from labor"; in 1692 Ann Foster of Andover confessed to being won over by a general promise of "prosperity," and in the same year Andrew Carrier accepted the lure of "a house and land in Andover." The same pattern appears most vividly in Cotton Mather's record of another of Mercy Short's confrontations with a spectral witch:

> "Fine promises!" she says, "You'l bestow an Husband upon mee, if I'l bee your Servant. An Husband! What? A Divel! I shall then bee finely fitted with an Husband: . . . Fine Clothes! What? Such as Your Friend Sarah Good had, who hardly had Rags to cover her! . . . Never Dy! What? Is my Life in Your Hands? No, if it had, You had killed mee long before this Time!—What's that?—So you can!—Do it then, if You can. Come, I dare you: Here, I challenge You to do it. Kill mee if you can. . . ."[30]

Some of these promises attributed to the Devil touch the most basic human concerns (like death) and others reflect the special preoccupations (with future husbands, for example) of adolescent girls. All of them imply a kind of covetousness generally consistent with the pattern of neighborhood conflict and tension mentioned earlier.

But the fits express other themes more powerfully still, the vital problem of aggression being of central importance. The seizures themselves have the essential character of attacks: in one sense, physical attacks by the witches on the persons of the accusers and in another sense, verbal attacks by the accusers on the reputations and indeed the very lives of the witches. This points directly toward one of the most important inner processes involved in witchcraft, the process psychologists call "projection," defined roughly as "escape from repressed conflict by attributing . . . emotional drives to the external world."[31] In short, the dynamic core of belief in witchcraft in early New England was the difficulty experienced by many individuals in finding ways to handle their own aggressive impulses. Witchcraft accusations provided one of the few approved outlets for such impulses in Puritan culture. Aggression was thus denied in the self and attributed directly to others. The accuser says, in effect: "I am not attacking you; you are attacking me!" In reality, however, the accuser is attacking the witch, and in an extremely dangerous manner, too. Witchcraft enables him to have it both ways; the impulse is denied and gratified at the same time.

The seizures of the afflicted children also permitted them to engage in a considerable amount of direct aggression. They were not, of course, held personally responsible; it was always the fault of the Devil at work inside them. Sometimes these impulses were aimed against the most important—and obvious—figures of authority. A child in a fit might behave very disobediently toward his parents or revile the clergy who came to pray for his recovery.[32] The Reverend Samuel Willard of Groton, who ministered to Elizabeth Knapp during the time of her most severe fits, noted that the Devil "urged upon her constant temptations to murder her p'rents, her neighbors, our children . . . and even to make away with herselfe & once she was going to drowne herself in ye well." The attacking impulses were quite random here, so much so that the girl herself was not safe. Cotton Mather reports a slight variation on this type of behavior in connection with the fits of Martha Goodwin. She would, he writes, "fetch very terrible Blowes with her Fist, and Kicks with her Foot at the man that prayed; but still . . . her Fist and Foot would alwaies recoil, when they came within a few hairs breadths of him just as if Rebounding against a Wall."[33] This little paradigm of aggression attempted and then at the last moment inhibited expresses perfectly the severe inner conflict that many of these people were acting out.

One last, pervasive theme in witchcraft is more difficult to handle than the others without having direct recourse to clinical models; the summary word for it is orality. It is helpful to recall at this point the importance of feasts in the standard imaginary picture of witches, but the experience of the accusers speaks even more powerfully to the same point. The evidence is of several kinds. First, the character of the "tortures" inflicted by the witches was most often described in terms of biting, pinching, and pricking; in a psychiatric sense, these modes of attack all have an oral foundation. The pattern showed up with great vividness, for example, in the trial of George Burroughs:

It was Remarkable that whereas Biting was one of the ways which the Witches used for the vexing of the Sufferers, when they cry'd out of G.B.

biting them, the print of the Teeth would be seen on the Flesh of the Complainers, and just such a sett of Teeth as G.B.'s would then appear upon them, which could be distinguished from those of some other mens.[34]

Second, the accusers repeatedly charged that they could see the witches suckling certain animal "familiars." The following testimony by one of the Salem girls, in reference to an unidentified witch, was quite typical: "She had two little things like young cats and she put them to her brest and suckled them they had no hair on them and had ears like a man." It was assumed that witches were specially equipped for these purposes, and their bodies were searched for the evidence. In 1656 the constable of Salisbury, New Hampshire, deposed in the case of Eunice Cole,

> That being about to stripp [her] to bee whipt (by the judgment of the Court att Salisbury) lookeing uppon hir brests under one of hir brests (I thinke hir left brest) I saw a blew thing like unto a teate hanging downeward about three quarters of an inche longe not very thick, and haveing a great suspition in my mind about it (she being suspected for a witche) desiered the Court to sende some women to looke of it.

The court accepted this proposal and appointed a committee of three women to administer to Goodwife Cole the standard, very intimate, examination. Their report made no mention of a "teate" under her breast, but noted instead "a place in her leg which was proveable wher she Had bin sucktt by Imps or the like." The women also stated "thatt they Heard the whining of puppies or such like under Her Coats as though they Had a desire to sucke."[35]

Third, many of the accusers underwent serious eating disturbances during and after their fits. "Long fastings" were frequently imposed on them. Cotton Mather writes of one such episode in his account of the bewitching of Margaret Rule: "tho she had a very eager Hunger upon her Stomach, yet if any refreshment were brought unto her, her teeth would be set, and she would be thrown into many Miseries." But also she would "sometimes have her Jaws forcibly pulled open, wherupon something invisible would be poured down her throat . . . She cried out of it as of Scalding Brimstone poured into her."[36] These descriptions and others like them would repay a much more detailed analysis than can be offered here, but the general point should be obvious. Among the zones of the body, the mouth seems to have been charged with a special kind of importance for victims of witchcraft.

In closing, it may be appropriate to offer a few suggestions of a more theoretical nature to indicate both the way in which an interpretation of New England witchcraft might be attempted and what it is that one can hope to learn from witchcraft materials about the culture at large. But let it be said with some emphasis that this is meant only as the most tentative beginning of a new approach to such questions.

Consider an interesting set of findings included by two anthropologists in a broad survey of child-rearing practices in over fifty cultures around the world. They report that belief in witchcraft is powerfully correlated with the training a society imposes on young children in regard to the control of aggressive impulses.[37] That is, wherever this training is severe and restrictive, there is a strong likelihood that the culture will make much of witchcraft. The correlation seems to suggest that suppressed aggression will seek indirect outlets of the kind that belief in witchcraft provides. Unfortunately there is relatively little concrete evidence about child-rearing practices in early New England; but it seems at least consistent with what is known of Puritan culture generally to imagine that quite a harsh attitude would have been taken toward any substantial show of aggression in the young.[38]

Now, some further considerations. There were only a very few cases of witchcraft accusations among members of the same family. But, as we have seen, the typical pattern involved accusations by adolescent girls against middle-aged women. It seems plausible, at least from a clinical standpoint, to think that this pattern masked deep problems stemming ultimately from the relationship of mother and daughter. Perhaps, then, the afflicted girls were both projecting their aggression and diverting or "displacing" it from its real target. Considered from this perspective, displacement represents another form of avoidance or denial; and so the charges of the accusers may be seen as a kind of double defense against the actual conflicts.

How can we locate the source of these conflicts? This is a more difficult and frankly speculative question. Indeed the question leads farther and farther from the usual canons of historical explanation; such proof as there is must come by way of parallels to findings of recent psychological research and, above all, to a great mass of clinical data. More specifically, it is to psychoanalytic theory that one may turn for insights of an especially helpful sort.

The prominence of oral themes in the historical record suggests that the disturbances that culminated in charges of witchcraft must be traced to the earliest phase of personality development. It would be very convenient to have some shred of information to insert here about breast-feeding practices among early New Englanders. Possibly their methods of weaning were highly traumatic,[39] but as no hard evidence exists we simply cannot be sure. It seems plausible, however, that many New England children were faced with some unspecified but extremely difficult psychic tasks in the first year or so of life. The outcome was that their aggressive drives were tied especially closely to the oral mode and driven underground.[40] Years later, in accordance with changes normal for adolescence, instinctual energies of all types were greatly augmented; and this tended, as it so often does, to reactivate the earliest conflicts[41]—the process that Freud vividly described as "the return of the repressed." But these conflicts were no easier to deal with in adolescence than they had been earlier; hence the need for the twin defenses of projection and displacement.[42]

One final problem must be recognized. The conflicts on which this discussion has focused were, of course, most vividly expressed in the fits of the accusers. The vast majority of people in early New England— subjected, one assumes, to roughly similar influences as children— managed to reach adulthood without experiencing fits. Does this pose serious difficulties for the above interpretations? The question can be argued to a negative conclusion, in at least two different but complementary ways. First, the materials on witchcraft, and in particular on the fits of the accusers, span a considerable length of time in New England's early history. It seems clear, therefore, that aggression and orality were more or less constant themes in the pathology of the period. Second, even in the far less bizarre testimonies of the witnesses—those who have been taken to represent the community at large—the same sort of focus appears. It is, above all, significant that the specific complaints of the accusers were so completely credible to so many others around them. The accusers, then, can be viewed as those individuals who were somehow especially sensitive to the problems created by their environment; they were the ones who were pushed over the line, so to speak, into serious illness. But their behavior clearly struck an answering chord in a much larger group of people. In this sense, nearly everyone in seventeenth-century New England was at some level an accuser.

Since the publication of Demos's article, Paul Boyer and Stephen Nissenbaum have presented a still different interpretation. In Salem Possessed: The Social Origins of Witchcraft *(1974), they attempt to account for something earlier scholars failed to explain—why the outbreak came when and where it did. If belief in witchcraft was pervasive in New England and if generational hostility was normative, outbreaks of witchcraft should have been frequent and widespread. Boyer and Nissenbaum trace the tangled history of Salem Village and its social frictions with Salem Town, frictions reflected in two prominent families that took opposite sides before and during the witchcraft cases. Critics of this latest effort to explicate the events of 1692 contend that the enormity of the outbreak is still not satisfactorily explained. There is general agreement, however, that Salem witchcraft had something to do with profound changes in the Puritan experience, particularly with its social or psychological equilibrium.*

NOTES

1. S. E. Morison, *The Intellectual Life of Colonial New England* (Ithaca, 1956), 264; Perry Miller, *The New England Mind: From Colony to Province* (Boston, 1961), 191.

2. Examples of these varying interpretations may be found in Charles W. Upham, *Salem Witchcraft* (Boston, 1867); Winfield S. Nevins, *Witchcraft in Salem Village* (Salem, 1916); John Fiske, *New France and New England* (Boston and New York, 1902); W. F. Poole, "Witchcraft in Boston," in *The Memorial History of Boston*, ed. Justin Winsor (Boston, 1881); Marion L. Starkey, *The Devil in Massachusetts* (Boston, 1950); Morison, *Intellectual Life of Colonial New England*, 259 ff.

3. Chadwick Hansen, *Witchcraft at Salem* (New York, 1969). See especially x, 22 ff., 64 ff., 226-67.

4. Those I have found particularly helpful in developing my own approach toward New England witchcraft are the following: Clyde Kluckhohn, *Navajo Witchcraft* (Boston, 1967); E. E. Evans-Pritchard, *Witchcraft, Oracles, and Magic Among the Azande* (Oxford, 1937); M. G. Marwick, *Sorcery in its Social Setting* (Manchester, 1965); *Witchcraft and Sorcery in East Africa*, ed. John Middleton and E. H. Winter (London, 1963); Beatrice B. Whiting, *Paiute Sorcery* (New York, 1950).

5. This usage is purely a matter of convenience, and is not meant to convey any judgment as to whether such people actually tried to perform acts of witchcraft. Chadwick Hansen claims to show, from trial records, which of the accused women were indeed "guilty"; but in my opinion his argument is not convincing. The testimony that "proves" guilt in one instance seems quite similar to other testimony brought against women whom Hansen regards as innocent. There may indeed have been "practicing witches" in colonial New England, but the surviving evidence does not decide the issue one way or another.

6. William L. Langer, "The Next Assignment" (*AHR*, LXIII [Jan. 1958], 283-304), in *Psychoanalysis and History*, ed. Bruce Mazlish (Englewood Cliffs, N. J., 1963).

7. *Ibid.*, 90.

8. See John M. Taylor, *The Witchcraft Delusion in Colonial Connecticut* (New York, 1908), 145 ff.

9. Some of these episodes are mentioned, in passing, among the records of witchcraft cases that came before the court. See, for example, the references to Besse Sewall and the widow Marshfield, in the depositions of the Parsons case, published in Samuel G. Drake, *Annals of Witchcraft in New England* (Boston, 1869), 218-57. It is clear, too, that many convicted witches had been the objects of widespread suspicion and gossip for years before they were brought to trial.

10. These findings are based largely on materials in the vital records of Salem and the surrounding towns.

11. In some cases the information is not complete—hence the variation in the size of sample among the different tables. Still the total for each table is large enough to lend overall credence to the results.

12. An early copy of this statement (undated) is in the Ann Mary Brown Memorial Collection, Brown University.

13. The proceedings against these three defendants are included in the typescript volumes, *Salem Witchcraft, 1692*, compiled from the original records by the Works Progress Administration in 1938. These volumes—an absolutely invaluable source—are on file in the Essex County Courthouse, Salem.

14. See *Records of the Colony of New Haven*, ed. C. J. Hoadly (Hartford, 1858), II, 29-36, 151-52, and *New Haven Town Records 1649-1662*, ed. Franklin B. Dexter (New Haven, 1917), I, 249-52, 256-57.

15. Some original records from this trial are in the Willys Papers, Connecticut State Library, Hartford. For good short accounts see Increase Mather, *An Essay for the Recording of Illustrious Providences*, in *Narratives of the Witchcraft Cases*, ed. G. L. Burr (New York, 1914), 18-21, and a letter from John Whiting to Increase Mather, Dec. 10, 1682, entitled "An account of a Remarkable passage of Divine providence that happened in Hartford, in the yeare of our Lord 1662," in *Massachusetts Historical Society Collections*, 4th Ser., VIII (Boston, 1868), 466-69.

16. See *Records of Massachusetts Bay*, ed. Nathaniel B. Shirtleff, IV, Pt. I (Boston, 1854), 269; William Hubbard, *A General History of New England* (Boston, 1848), 574; Thomas Hutchinson, *The History of the Colony and Province of Massachusetts Bay*, ed. Lawrence S. Mayo (Cambridge, Mass., 1936), I, 160-61.

17. For example, Giles Corey, executed as one of the Salem witches, had been before the courts several times, charged with such offenses as theft and battery. Mary Parsons of Springfield was convicted of slander not long before her trial for witchcraft.

18. For example, Katherine Harrison, prosecuted for witchcraft at Weathersfield, Connecticut, in 1668, was reported to have been given to fortunetelling; and a group of ministers called to advise the court in her case contended that such activity did "argue familiarity with the Devil." See John M. Taylor, *The Witchcraft Delusion in Colonial Connecticut* (New York, 1908), 56-58. Evidence of the same kind was offered against Samuel Wardwell of Andover, Massachusetts, in 1692. See the proceedings in his case in the typescript volumes by the Works Progress Administration, *Salem Witchcraft, 1692*, in the Essex County Courthouse, Salem. Margaret Jones, convicted and executed at Boston in 1648, was involved in "practising physic." See Winthrop's *Journal*, ed. J. K. Hosmer (New York, 1908), II, 344-45. Elizabeth Morse, prosecuted at Newbury, Massachusetts, in 1679, was alleged to have possessed certain occult powers to heal the sick. See the depositions published in Drake, *Annals of Witchcraft*, 258-96.

19. Cotton Mather, *Memorable Providences, Relating to Witchcraft and Possessions*, in *Narratives*, ed. Burr, 103-06; Increase Mather, *An Essay* etc., 18.

20. Hutchinson, *History of the Colony and Province of Massachusetts Bay*, I, 160; Hubbard, 574. There is a verbatim account of the church proceedings against Mrs. Hibbens in the journal of Robert Keayne, in the Massachusetts Historical Society, Boston. I am grateful to Anita Rutman for lending me her transcription of this nearly illegible document. Manuscript deposition, trial of Mercy Desborough, Willys Papers; manuscript deposition, trial of Elizabeth Clawson, Willys Papers.

21. The tax list is published in Henry Burt, *The First Century of the History of Springfield* (Springfield, Mass., 1898), I, 190-91; a long set of depositions from the Parsons case is published in Drake, *Annals of Witchcraft*, 219-56; see also 224, 228, 242. Mary Parsons herself offered some testimony reflecting her husband's inordinate desire "for Luker and Gaine."

22. See Burt, *First Century of the History of Springfield*, I, for just such a map; see Increase Mather, *An Essay* etc., 18 ff., on the case of the Greensmiths. Also Richard Chamberlain, *Lithobolia*, in *Narratives*, ed. Burr, 61, on the case of Hannah Jones at Great Island, New Hampshire, in 1682.

23. See Cotton Mather, *A Brand Pluck'd Out of the Burning*, in *Narratives*, ed. Burr, 270.

24. See, for example, Whiting, *Paiute Sorcery*; Evans-Pritchard, *Witchcraft, Oracles, and Magic Among the Azande*, 117 ff.; and *Witchcraft and Sorcery in East Africa*, ed. Middleton and Winter.

25. For material bearing on the growth of these acquisitive tendencies, see Philip J. Greven, Jr., "Old Patterns in the New World: The Distribution of Land in 17th Century Andover," *Essex Institute Historical Collections*, CI (April, 1965), 133-48; and John Demos, "Notes on Life in Plymouth Colony," *William and Mary Quarterly*, 3d Ser., XXII (Apr. 1965), 264-86. It is possible that the voluntary mechanism of colonization had selected unusually aggressive and competitive persons at the outset.

26. Cotton Mather, *The Wonders of the Invisible World*, in *Narratives*, ed. Burr, 246.

27. Cotton Mather, *Memorable Providences* etc., 93-143; Samuel Willard, *A briefe account of a strange & unusuall Providence of God befallen to Elizabeth Knap of Groton*, in Samuel A. Green, *Groton in the Witchcraft Times* (Groton, Mass., 1883), 7-21.

28. The best group of essays dealing with such issues is *Psychoanalysis and History*, ed. Mazlish. See also the interesting statement in Alexander L. George and Juliette L. George, *Woodrow Wilson and Colonel House* (New York, 1964), v-xiv.

29. See Cotton Mather, *A Brand Pluck'd Out of the Burning*, 259-60, and *Memorable Providences* etc., 100.

30. Willard, *A briefe account* etc., in *Groton in the Witchcraft Times*, ed. Green, 8; deposition by Ann Foster, case of Ann Foster, deposition by Andrew Carrier, case of Mary Lacy, Jr., in Works Progress Administration, *Salem Witchcraft, 1692*; Cotton Mather, *A Brand Pluck'd Out of the Burning*, in *Narratives*, ed. Burr, 269.

31. This is the definition suggested by Clyde Kluckhohn in his own exemplary monograph, *Navajo Witchcraft*, 239, n. 37.

32. See, for example, the descriptions of the Goodwin children during the time of their affliction, in Cotton Mather, *Memorable Providences* etc., 109 ff., 119.

33. Willard, *A briefe account* etc., 9; Cotton Mather, *Memorable Providences* etc., 108, 120.

34. Cotton Mather, *Wonders of the Invisible World*, 216-17.

35. Deposition by Susannah Sheldon, case of Philip English, in Works Progress Administration, *Salem Witchcraft, 1692*; manuscript deposition by Richard Ormsbey, case of Eunice Cole, in Massachusetts Archives, Vol. 135, 3; manuscript record, case of Eunice Cole, in *ibid.*, 13.

36. Cotton Mather, *Memorable Providences* etc., 131.

37. John W. M. Whiting and Irvin L. Child, *Child Training and Personality* (New Haven, 1953), Chap. 12.

38. John Robinson, the pastor of the original "Pilgrim" congregation, wrote as follows in an essay on "Children and Their Education": "Surely there is in all children . . . a stubborn-

ness, and stoutness of mind arising from natural pride, which must be broken and beaten down. . . . Children should not know, if it could be kept from them, that they have a will in their own: neither should these words be heard from them, save by way of consent, 'I will' or 'I will not.' " Robinson, *Works* (Boston, 1851), I, 246-47. This point of view would not appear to leave much room for the free expression of aggressive impulses, but of course it tells us nothing certain about actual practice in Puritan families.

39. However, we can determine with some confidence the usual time of weaning. Since lactation normally creates an impediment to a new conception, and since the average interval between births in New England families was approximately two years, it seems likely that most infants were weaned between the ages of twelve and fifteen months. The nursing process would therefore overlap the arrival of baby teeth (and accompanying biting wishes); and this might well give rise to considerable tension between mother and child. I have found only one direct reference to weaning in all the documentary evidence from seventeenth-century New England, an entry in the journal of John Hull: "1659, 11th of 2d. My daughter Hannah was taken from her mother's breast, and, through the favor of God, weaned without any trouble; only about fifteen days after, she did not eat her meat well." American Antiquarian Society, *Transactions*, III (Boston, 1857), 149. Hannah Hull was born on February 14, 1658, making her thirteen months and four weeks on the day of the above entry. Hull's choice of words creates some temptation to speculate further. Was it perhaps unusual for Puritan infants to be "weaned without any trouble"? Also, does it not seem that in this case the process was quite abrupt—that is, accomplished entirely at one point in time? (Generally speaking, this is more traumatic for an infant than gradual weaning is.) For a longer discussion of infancy in Puritan New England see John Demos, *A Little Commonwealth: Family-Life in Plymouth Colony* (New York, 1970), Chap. 8.

40. I have found the work of Melanie Klein on the origins of psychic conflict in infancy to be particularly helpful. See her *The Psycho-Analysis of Children* (London, 1932) and the papers collected in her *Contributions to Psycho-Analysis* (London, 1950). See also Joan Riviere, "On the Genesis of Psychical Conflict in Earliest Infancy," in Melanie Klein *et al.*, *Developments in Psycho-Analysis* (London, 1952), 37-66.

41. See Peter Blos, *On Adolescence* (New York, 1962). This (basically psychoanalytic) study provides a wealth of case materials and some very shrewd interpretations, which seem to bear strongly on certain of the phenomena connected with early New England witchcraft.

42. It is no coincidence that projection was so important among the defenses employed by the afflicted girls in their efforts to combat their own aggressive drives. For projection is the earliest of all defenses, and indeed it takes shape under the influence of the oral phase. On this point see Sigmund Freud, "Negation," *The Standard Edition of the Complete Works of Sigmund Freud*, ed. J. Strachey (London, 1960), XIX, 237, and Paula Heimann, "Certain Functions of Introjection and Projection in Early Infancy," in Klein *et al.*, *Developments in Psycho-Analysis*, 122-68.

PART SIX |

PURITAN AESTHETICS

Spurred by the works of Perry Miller, the discovery of Edward Taylor's poetry, the rise of American studies as an academic field, and the increasing modern interest in societal myths, scholarship dealing with the aesthetic dimension of the New England mind has flourished in the past few decades. Studies of Edward Taylor, the seventeenth-century Connecticut Valley clergyman whose poems were first published in 1939, gave notice of this new direction. Among the more influential of such studies were Donald Stanford's *Edward Taylor* (Minneapolis, 1965), Douglas Grant's "Edward Taylor: Poet in a Wilderness" (in his *Purpose and Place: Essays on American Writers* [London, 1965]), Michael Colacurcio's "God's Determinations Touching Half-Way Membership: Occasion and Audience in Edward Taylor" (*American Literature*, XXXIX [1967]), and the essays in the special Edward Taylor issue of *Early American Literature* (IV, no. 3 [1969]). As Sacvan Bercovitch, one of the leaders in the revaluation of Puritan literature, has stated of this work on Taylor, "These studies taught us, first, to understand the poet as Puritan; then, to understand the Puritan as poet."

The new investigations of early New England authors and their works reflect the influence of the multidisciplinary approach to American studies, which blends aesthetic, intellectual, and historical concerns. Scholars such as Bercovitch, Everett Emerson, Jesper Rosenmeier, Cecelia Tichi, Norman Grabo, David Levin, Sargent Bush, Mason Lowance, and Richard Reinitz have almost created a new field of study. The best introduction to its variety is to be found in Sacvan Bercovitch, ed., *The American Puritan Imagination:Essays in Revaluation* (New York, 1974), which includes an excellent bibliography as well as a stimulating collection of articles.

The following essays focus on three important genres of Puritan literature: history, poetry, and autobiography. Whereas these are representative of the Puritans' aesthetic impulses, they only begin to indicate the diversity of New England art forms. Tombstone carving, cabinet making, architecture, quilting, and a host of other crafts offered opportunities for self expression. And while painting and music were fairly rare in early New England, examples also exist of those creative forms. Studies of these diverse modes of cultural expression—on which much work remains to be done—should reinforce the image of the Puritan New England that emerges from the new studies of its literature.

15 | THE HISTORIOGRAPHY OF JOHNSON'S WONDER-WORKING PROVIDENCE

SACVAN BERCOVITCH

Recent work in this field is distinct from earlier studies of Puritan literature in at least two ways. One distinguishing mark is that while older assessments examined colonial writings either to blame the Puritans for what was deplorable in the American literary tradition or to gain insights into Puritan theological or political thought, the new approach tries to understand the works in their own right. Scholars no longer feel compelled to apologize for the Puritan artist. We now appreciate that seventeenth-century New England may have produced more poets per capita than any other society in history, and we are becoming aware that the works of an Anne Bradstreet or an Edward Taylor contain much literary merit. The other significant dimension of the new literary studies is their sophisticated analysis of the Puritan use of allegory and symbolism.

The following selection by Sacvan Bercovitch analyzes Edward Johnson's Wonder-Working Providence. *His interpretation marks a sharp departure from the more traditional studies of Puritan historians such as Kenneth Murdock's* Literature and Theology in Colonial New England *(Cambridge, Mass., 1949) and Peter Gay's* A Loss of Mastery: Puritan Historians in Colonial America *(Berkeley, 1966). Murdock surveys the colonial historians to see how they reflect religious beliefs, and Gay seeks to place them in the evolution of the discipline of history. Bercovitch, in contrast, analyzes Johnson's work not simply as a piece of historical writing but also as an attempt to explain the place of the Puritan story in God's design. Bringing to his study an impressive command of the Bible and of Reformation modes of scriptural analysis, he illuminates the imagery of the* Wonder-Working Providence *and thus explains its significance in the evolution of the Puritans' concept of mission and their sense of identity.*

History has dealt harshly with Edward Johnson's *Wonder-Working Providence.* The first full-scale account of the Massachusetts theocracy could find no publisher for almost three years after its completion; its initial printing (London, 1654) was anonymous, mistitled, and marred throughout by typographical defects; then, having failed to sell, it was appended to a prosaic geographical report on America and attributed to Sir Fernando Gorges, a persecutor of the Puritans and life-long enemy of the New England colony. In the mid-seventeen hundreds it could not interest enough subscribers to warrant republication, and the Massachusetts Historical Society hardly improved the situation when some seventy-five years later it scattered the work through five volumes of its *Collections.* Perhaps the unkindest cut of all has come from twentieth-century scholars. J. Franklin Jameson, who arranged the standard edition, warns the reader in his introduction that "we have in him [Johnson] a striking example of the hot zealotry, the narrow partisanship, the confident dogmatism, which characterized so much of Puritanism. . . . [His] rhetorical flights . . . are turgid, bombastic, and tedious. . . . With whatever helps an editor may supply, the *Wonder-Working Providence* remains hard reading."[1] The recent renascence of Puritan studies has done little to alter this view. Historians have continued to speak of the "zealousness and superstition" pervading this "turgid . . . militant propaganda tract." Literary scholars have shown somewhat more sympathy, only to damn the book with faint praise: "it is . . . not without a certain charm," write Perry Miller and Thomas E. Johnson, but for them as for its earlier readers it remains an "ornate, windy, and verbose" work written by a "slighter figure than either Winthrop or Bradford."[2]

This sustained criticism has unfortunately obscured Johnson's achievement. That Winthrop and Bradford were greater men than the Woburn woodworker scarcely denigrates the merit of his writing. In a sense, indeed, that fact lends it a special interest. For all its stylistic imperfections and substantive deficiencies (in "statistics of immigration, of population, of the growth of settlements, of . . . products and prices") his History remains "representative of the rank and file" colonists' outlook, like a "rustic trumpet," in Charles L. Sanford's engaging simile, "sounding loud among the common folk" and echoing "the finer trumpets of . . . [the] respected leaders of the saints." As such, it offers a valuable insight into their concept of "the errand of Planting this Wilderness" and, by extension, into American Puritan culture.[3]

The distinctive qualities of Johnson's outlook become evident in his introductory description of the Great Migration:

> When England began to decline in Religion, like lukewarme Laodicea . . . in so much that the multitude of irreligious . . . persons spred the whole land like Grasshoppers, in this very time Christ . . . raises an Army out of our English Nation, for freeing his people from their long servitude . . . [before He would bring upon their adversaires a] sudden, and unexpected destruction. . . .
>
> Christ Jesus intending to manifest his Kingly Office toward his Churches more fully than ever yet the Sons of men saw, even to the uniting of Jew and Gentile Churches in one Faith . . . in the yeere 1628, he stirres up his servants as the Heralds of a King to make this proclamation . . . as followeth.
>
> *"Oh yes! oh yes! oh yes! all you the people that are here Oppressed! . . . gather yourselves together, your wives and little ones . . . [to] be shipped for his service, in the Westerne World. . . ."*
>
> [Thus, Christ calls His] . . . little remnant [to] . . . create a new Heaven, and a new Earth in, new Churches, and a new Common-wealth together. (pp. 23-25).

The passage in many ways characterizes the History as a whole: in its flamboyance, its awkwardness, its dramatic vitality, and perhaps most important in its constant recourse to the Bible. Clearly, whatever its stylistic defects, it sets forth an impassioned vision of New England's destiny; and clearly, the import of that vision lies in the deliberate inter-relationship of the immediate narrative with corresponding events in the Old and New Testaments.

In this light, the passage further reveals the essentials of Johnson's method and intent. In the first paragraph, the "Grasshoppers" and "luke-warm Laodicea" (familiar figures of degeneracy in Puritan literature[4]) identify "irreligious" Anglicanism with both Israelite and Christian apostasy;[5] and the emigrants, correspondingly, become associated with the faithful "little remnant" heralded by the Prophets and Apostles. They are another chosen Israel freed "from their long servitude" and, simultaneously, the redeemed Gentiles fleeing their "bondage" amidst the "great trespasses" of persecuting "kings and priests" in order to restore the Promised Land (Ezra 9: 7-9; Isa. 11: 10-16). In short, they are the in-heritors of the Hebrews' covenant: the "*Remnant* that . . . the Lord promised to *preserve*," as William Adams put it in 1685, reiterating Johnson's phrases, for "the *Removal* of . . . his Kingdom from them [the Hebrews] to *another* People," in America.[6]

The last part of the passage elaborates upon the significance of this promise. The "new Heaven and new Earth," we know (Rev. 21: 1-2), represent the New Jerusalem. St. John tells us that its arrival—entailing the sudden and final "fall of Babylon"—will be proclaimed by "a great voice out of heaven saying . . . they shall be his [God's] people" (Rev. 21: 3); Thomas Taylor, commenting on the prophecy, extends its mean-ing to the "Calling all Gods People out of Romish BABYLON," linking the "Saintly Commonwealth" with the "primitive Christians," the "elect warned . . . by a voice in Jerusalem . . . before the destruction of the City," and *Moses* [who] called not only the heads of the families from *Corah*, but their wives, sons, and little children." This is the "heavenly voice," Johnson imputes to the "Heralds" summoning "the *People of Christ* [to] . . .*the Westerne World*." It is a divine call to win the Second Paradise and bring about the Conversion of the Jews: their "uniting" with the "Gentile Churches in one Faith" so that, as John Cotton ex-plained in a work from which Johnson quotes (p. 88), they may "upon their conversion, marshall and ranke themselves into armies against Gog and Magog . . . for the establishment of the Kingdome . . . of Christ."[7] In sum, the migration marks the apex of a foreordained movement— pro-ceeding through the ancient Hebrews and the early Christian Church— toward the millenium.

Viewed thus in their own terms, the introductory paragraphs of *Wonder-Working Providence* form a cogent statement of purpose. If they fail to render the actual situation in 1628, they nonetheless effective-ly place that situation in what for its author was its total perspective. His reliance on the Scriptures to achieve his end presents difficulties only for his later readers. His contemporaries, for whom "the fundamental source book of history, as of all truth, was the Bible," would instantly have recognized his allusions. Moreover, they would have shared the ap-proach he sketches here and applies throughout the work. Kenneth Murdock has discussed "Johnson's efforts at allegory" as "a way of elevating New England history above the level of 'small things' so that its people could forget their 'low conditions, little number, and remoteness of place' and think instead of the glories of heroic deeds in Christ's army."[8] Certainly, Johnson elevates his material in a manner that tends toward the allegorical and the didactic. But these qualities do not adequately describe his method. His History expresses above all the historiography commonly adopted by the whole American Puritan colony: a historiography rooted in biblical exegesis, embracing all of history, and fundamentally derived from the principles of typological interpretation.

These principles, as Johnson understood them, may be briefly outlined. Originally used to spiritualize the Old Testament into a foreshadowing of Christ, typology established itself through the middle ages and into the Reformation as a prominent mode of historical analysis and prediction. Scriptural "types," early distinguished from allegory by their concern with "*littera-historia*," came to serve as signs prophetic of current happenings and of "the concrete future." As Jesus had fulfilled the past so too He foreshadowed things present and to come; and the story of the Hebrews, figuratively perceived, became a key to the "providential history of the world." Thus "the notion was current . . . that the Messiah would be a second Moses, that his redemption would be a second exodus from Egypt in which the miracles of the first would be repeated." Upon this basis, Eusebius and Orosius "constructed a Roman 'history of salvation' modeled on that of the Biblical Israel," which unfolded "the prospect of an ever triumphant and ever improving [Christian] society." Over a thousand years later Luther similarly portrayed the Germans as God's particular people marching toward a new Canaan, and English Puritans in turn repeated his words with respect to *their* nation—sometimes adding to the earlier notion of endless progress the imminency of the chiliasm, as revealed in the Johannine Apocalypse.[9]

In seventeenth-century America, as I have tried to show in an earlier essay,[10] this outlook consituted a crucial element in the definition of the theocracy. Shortly before he left for America, John Winthrop speculated that the country might be the "refuge" set apart for the righteous "whom he [God] meanes to save out of this generall callamitie." In the following decade, John Cotton amplified and extended the idea through the *figura* of Babylon:

> as there was in old *Babel*, sundry of God's *Israel* . . . so will there be in new Babel sundry of God's chosen people . . . Unto whom as the Lord hath sent his Angels to hasten *Lot* out of *Sodome* . . . so he hath sent . . . the voyce of his Messengers to hasten his people . . . out of new *Babel* (as he did out of old) before that sodaine destruction fall upon the City.
>
> . . .
>
> [Therefore,] such fellowship as the Church of the Jewes had with Christ coming out of Babylon, the same have we . . . coming out of Romish Babylon. . . . [in an enterprise] *pointing at the Gloriousnesse of the restored Estate of the Church of the Jewes, and the happy accesse of the Gentiles in the approaching dayes of Reformation.*

Unmistakably, Johnson's version of the migration reflects those of Win-

throp and Cotton; it finds comparable parallels throughout American
Puritan literature. Peter Bulkeley's *Gospel-Covenant*, for example—to
which Johnson alludes (pp. 110-11)—employs "the captivity of the Jews
. . . as a resemblance and type" of contemporary events; John Norton,
noting how "the New Testament giveth light unto the Old," argues his
belief in the church-state from the premise that the "Promises given unto
the *Saints* in the old Testament belong unto [us];" and Richard Mather
begins his "Apology" for the New England Way by announcing the
return of "the Gentiles" from "Jewish Bondage. . . . For . . . many things
that literally concerned the Jewes were types and figures, signifying the
like things concerning the people of God in these latter days . . . in their
returne . . . to the true Sion."[11]

These statements by the leading emigrant divines, all but one of which
were published before *Wonder-Working Providence*, indicate the tradition which Johnson inherited: the "linear typology"[12] which joined the
chosen Israelites, the "primitive Christians," and the New England
Puritans in a developmental-millenarian view of history. Johnson's
familiarity with typology is apparent on virtually every page of the
book. He quotes from typological tracts by Cotton, Parker, and Bulkeley
(pp. 88-89, 98, 110-11); he recurs constantly to such standard tropes and
figures as the Suffering Servant, the Altar, the Lion, the Cup of Salvation, the Vessel of New Wine, the Tables in the Wilderness, and the Bride
of Christ (*e.g.* pp. 56-57, 151-52, 157, 239, 246, 259); and he continually
uses numbers for their "typical significance,"[13] especially *three* and *seven*,
an emblem of the continuity between the biblical Jewish state, the
Church, and the "true Sion" of the elect.[14] Toward the close of the work,
we read that "the Wonderworking providence of Sions Savior . . . in
three seven years is comprised though very weakly, in this little book,
[for] there's in one seven year [so much to tell that it] would require
volumes" (p. 256). In fact the "little book" comprises twenty-three years
of history, but for Johnson such calculation is beside the point. Though
he tries to be reasonably accurate, primarily he employs numbers as
metaphors, as it were, to light up the larger providential plan. With this
intent, he divides the History into three parts: Book I discusses the seven
churches established in the first fourteen years; Book II enumerates
events covering the next three years; Book III, concerning "These Latter
Seven Years," moves forward through the "last Church that compleated
the number of 30" (chapter seven) to the proclamation issued in the
twelfth chapter that "*the time* [approaches] *of the fall of Antichrist, and
. . . the provoking of the twelve Tribes* [of Israel] *to submit to the
Kingdom of Christ*" (pp. 234, 251, 268).

The careful numerical pattern suggests the unity of the narrative itself.
Despite the "breathless confusion of [its] worst passages," in sum the
History has far more organization than its critics have acknowledged,[15]
an organization perhaps dictated by the coherence of its vision. The first
Book begins with the departure from England and ends with the formation of the civil government; Book II delineates the settlers' economic,
military, and spiritual progress; the last Book reviews the colony's accomplishments and their implications. Within this structured develop-

ment, Johnson methodically expands upon the various aspects of his theme, and, at the same time, always keeps before us the full import of New England's success by speaking of its inhabitants as at once an Army of Christ and a "wandering race of Jacobites" (e.g., pp. 74-75, 145-47, 227-34): by identifying them, that is, at every stage, as God's new "covenant-people," the ancient Israelites transformed in the image of the upright Gentile remnant.

The opening chapters deal with the divine impulse behind the first migration. As Johnson pictures them, the details of preparation for the voyage take on vast symbolic proportions. Every financial contribution, for example, becomes a "mite . . . cast into [Christ's] Treasury" in defiance of "Ananias and Saphirah" (p. 55)—an allusion to the faith of the Hebrews and of the Apostles which (as Cotton and Thomas Parker observe[16]) denotes the elect from Moses to Paul who "forsook Egypt" for the good land "prepared for them" in the wilderness—and similar parallels throughout the section, from the scenes of Anglican persecution to those of leave-taking, reinforce this configuration.[17] The voyage itself is for Johnson a final exodus from heathendom. He paints England, as we have seen, as Corah and Sodom, Egypt and Babylon; here he extends the comparison by equating the Atlantic with the Red Sea. Many other Puritans draw upon the comparison: Increase Mather, for one, when he recalls how "God hath . . . brought [us] by a mighty hand . . . over a greater than the Red sea."[18] But Johnson is the first to weave it into the texture of a comprehensive history. "Christs Providence," he writes,

> in delivering this his people in their Voyages by Sea . . . expresses the tender care Christ hath of his [chosen ones], to free them from all dangers, [so that] those that occupy their business in the deepe, and see the Wonders of God upon the waters, are taken with great astonishment to behold the extraordinary hand of the most High . . . [Who] misses not to be an exact Pilot in . . . [making for them a] path through the Waters. (pp. 61-62).

The Red Sea deliverance is of course the central precedent here, but it functions less as analogy or model (in our sense) than as an adumbration of the Atlantic crossing, which types out its broad historic context. In this characteristic fusion of direct narrative and scriptural allusion, the Puritans both participate in and surpass the miraculous biblical event: they reenact the Israelites' sea passage in a way which points forward to their larger purpose. Now, Johnson intimates, it is Christ who pilots the saints over the watery "path,"[19] and the Prophets of the New Zion who assure their success:

> For your sake have I sent to Babylon, and have brought down all their nobles . . . I am . . . the creator of Israel . . . which maketh a way in the sea, and a path in the mighty waters. . . . Behold, I will [now] do a new thing . . . I will even make a way in the wilderness, and rivers in the desert. (Isa. 43: 14-19).
>
> . . .
>
> They that go down to the sea in ships, that do business in great waters; these see the works of the Lord, and his wonders in the deep. For he commandeth, and . . . bringeth them out of their distresses. He maketh the storm a calm . . [and] turneth the wilderness into a standing water. . . . And there he

maketh the hungry to dwell, that they may prepare a city for habitation. (Psalms 107: 23-36).

The building of the city in the wilderness, which occupies much of the first Book, sustains this sense of historic progression. Johnson portrays the colony's foundation through two related figures of Christ: the Rock—a "token" of God's "special aid" to His saints in the Old and New Testaments—and the Israelites' Temple, "A Type . . . signifying the *visibility* of the *Church*" which also "applies . . . mystically to the *New Jerusalem*."[20] Johnson reports that their initial difficulties spurred "this Wildernesse-People" all the more resolutely to their "Temple-worke" (pp. 87, 92). Despite lack of food and shelter, they at once "began to hew stones . . . for building the Temple;" at night, "like true Jacobites they rest them one [on] the Rocks;" their magistrates and ministers "under-prop the building . . . as living stones, Elect and Pretious" (pp. 46, 62, 75, 113). And in token of His approval, the Lord helps them through their tribulations with "signs" and miracles:

> As the Lord surrounded his chosen Israel with dangers deepe to make his miraculous deliverance famous throughout, and to the end of the World, so here behold the Lord Christ, having egged a small handful of his people forth in a forlorne Wildernesse, stripping them naked from all humane helps. . . . But as his chosen Israel . . . in building the Temple and City . . . valiantly waded through [all difficulties], So these weake wormes . . . were most wonderfully holpen . . . [and thus remained] perswaded that Christ will . . . raine bread from Heaven. (pp. 151, 82, 75).

The varied references in this passage all apply directly to the "Temple-worke," and further open its meaning as metaphor. The gift of manna (the bread rained from heaven) pertains to the desert trials of Christ and the Hebrews; the "end of the World" and the "weak wormes" affirm the return of the Blessed Remnant to Zion, to erect "*the Kingdom of our Lord Jesus*," as Shepard said, in "*our present Wilderness state . . . in these Ends of the Earth*." John Norton had argued that "*David* lived not to build the Temple, but he left the patern thereof to his Son *Solomon:* And lo we have the patern."[21] Johnson's images form a lucid typological design joining the Puritans' *penuries of a Wildernesse*" (p. 75) with this high destiny. "These poore afflicted people desire . . . that the Mountains in the way of Zerubbabel may become a plane," he writes, alluding through that "typical" king to the way of the "worm Jacob, and men of Israel . . . [who will] thresh the mountain . . . [and] give to Jerusalem . . . good tidings" (Isa: 41: 14-27); and in the concluding chapter of Book I he invites us to contemplate the triumphant beginnings of their venture: "See heere the *Wonder-working Providence of Sions Savior* . . . in gathering together stones to build up the walls of Jerusalem (that his Sion may be surrounded with Bulworkes and Towres)" (p.141).[22]

The "penuries" do not end, however, with the conquest of the wilderness; indeed, they grow in scope and intensity through the Indian hostilities and the ferment caused by "heretics." In Book I and more forcefully in Books II and III, Johnson depicts these conflicts as a series of Wars of the Lord in which the builders prove themselves worthy of their

Temple. The "Erronious and Heticall persons," such as Samuel Gorton, Roger Williams and Anne Hutchinson, stand united as "Enemies of Christs Kingdome" (pp. 126, 94). Their "damnable Doctrines"—the "filthy vomit of Hels Dragon"—are "so many dreadfull Engines set by Satan . . . to hurt or destroy . . . Gods holy Mountaine;" "knowing right well that at the fall of Antichrist hee must be chained up for a thousand years [Rev. 20 :3]," the Devil strives to make each of them a "Captaine over [the Puritans], that they may returne againe into Egypt" (pp. 177, 147, 140, 122, 159).

The echoes of these phrases in Milton's work, as well as that of New England divines,[23] testify to the conventionality of Johnson's comparisons; suggest how readily his readers would have grasped the terms in which he heightens the theological dissensions into acts of cosmic significance. The orthodoxy's measures against the rebels are similarly translated. The reference to the Devil's "vomit" associates the colonists with the "woman in the Wilderness who may have the vomit of the Dragon cast in her face"—an image of "Sion the Outcast."[24] Johnson further pictures them as a series of types of an embattled Christ: Job overcoming Satan's temptations, Joshua destroying the heathen armies, Jeptha defending his towns, David dealing with Shimei, "Jehu . . . execut[ing] the judgements of the Lord upon Ahabs bloudy household" (pp. 122, 145-45, 155, 153). In expelling the heretics, they wield "the sharpe sword of the Word" and, "sounding forth their silver trumpets," they cast those "great Mountaines of proud erronious judgement . . . into the depth of the sea," clearing the "smoak which of a long time hath filled the Temple" (pp. 121, 136, 152, 174). Christ's sword, the mountains, the silver trumpets—none of Johnson's contemporaries could fail to see his meaning.[25] He makes it as explicit as necessary, at the end of a general discussion of "all sorts of Sectaries," in a single phrase: "the downfall of Antichrist is at hand" (pp. 144, 146).

While the heretics are thus effectually disposed of, the Indian wars persist well into the third book. The "cruell Cannibals" (p. 79) are represented as another, more dangerous flank of the powers of darkness. Like the heretics, they antitype the Israelites' enemies—the Assyrians, Babylonians, and Philistines (pp. 79, 160-61, 165-66, 256)—but in a more dire aspect: they are "not only men, but Devils," whose "quarrell" with the Puritans is "as antient as Adams time" (pp. 165, 148). As usual, the comparison is carefully placed. When God tells the snake in Eden that Adam's seed "shall bruise thy head" (Gen. 3: 15) He predicts, according to typology, the triumph of the Israelites over the heathen, of the Church over Babylon and of the Second Adam over "that old serpent" at the end of time (Rev. 20). For Johnson, the "tawny fiends or snakes" stand for the furthest (and hence most desperate) stage of the struggle. "[Our] feet shall soon be set on their proud necks," he declares (p. 166); and in the wars of 1645 he finds his anticipations justified. Invoking the figure of Jacob and Esau—frequently expounded as an allegory of the division of the elect and damned[26]—he records the Puritan successes in a paean that brings together the concept of Gog and Magog with those of the "remnant," the "golden candlestick," and the "ends of the earth:"

hearing prophane Esau [*i.e.*, the Indians] had mustered up all the Bands he could . . . this wandering race of Jacobites . . . acknowledg unto the Lord . . . the manner of his wonderful providence extended toward them . . . [so] as to lay them sure in thy Sion, a building, to be the wonder of the world. . . . [But] as Jacobs fear was, the seed of Christs Church in the posterity of Israel should be cut off . . . so these people at this very time pleaded not only the Lords promise to Israel, but to his only son Christ Jesus: Lord, hast thou not said . . . *I will give thee the Heathen for thine inheritance, and the uttermost ends of the earth for thy possession;* and now . . . the appointed time is at hand . . . [for Him] who walks in the midst of his golden Candlesticks. . . . [In defeating the Indians,] the poor remnant of Gods people . . . have heard the noyse of the great fall . . . [and] may reap with joy the glorious harvest . . . which is hard at hand. (pp. 237-39, 256; see also pp. 227, 232).

The strongest evidence that the harvest was at hand lay in the flourishing of the church-state. Under "the covet of Christ's wings" (p. 246), the American Zion blooms into a second Garden of God. John Cotton had informed the emigrants that when God "warms us with . . . [His ordinances] as with wings, there is a Land of Promise. . . . Acceptance of David's purpose to build God an House" will make Him their "Planter . . . Husbandman . . . [and] Gardener" and them His "Vineyard and Red Wine. . . . The Temple [is] Typified . . . when he plants us, when he gives us root."[27] Johnson testifies to the fulfilment of the promise. What a "miraculous work," he cries, for "this barren desart" to become "for fertilness in so short a space . . . the wonder of the world . . . ; [for] the most hideous, boundless, and unknown Wilderness in the world in an instant" to become a "Vineyard of the Lord"! What a "wonderful providence . . . such as was never heard of, since that Jacobs sons ceased to be a people, that . . . a Nation [should] . . . be born in a day" (pp. 209-11, 244, 248). All aspects of this development, civic and ecclesiastical, appear in the mythical illumination of the Garden image. In their consolidation the churches form "a defenced city, an iron pillar, a wall of brass" (see Deut. 8 and Isa. 26, 60) to protect "the fruit . . . of the goodly branches of Christs vines, . . . the flourishing trees planted in the house of the Lord, . . . [and the] Orchards of . . . Christs Garden . . . growing upon his root" (pp. 174, 126). The same Edenic colors brighten the *tableaux* of economic progress: in the border settlements as in the towns, the Puritans ("pitching their Tabernacles neare the Lords Tent") create another Canaan, "well watered with many pleasant streames, [and] abounding with Garden fruits" (p. 179). And the founding of Harvard College—that "Fountain" flowing with "the sweet waters of Shilo's streams" and "garden duly tended . . . with fruit full hung" (pp. 199, 205)—moves Johnson to a doggerel-verse tribute which summarizes his view of the new Paradise. "You that have seen these wondrous works," he exclaims,

> The noble Acts Jehova wrought, his Israel to redeem.
> Surely this second work of his shall far more glorious seem;
>
>   . . .
> The ratling bones together run with self-same breath that blows,

Of Israels sons long dead and dry, each joynt their sinews
grows,
Fair flesh doth cover them, and veins (lifes fountain) takes there
place. (p. 203)²⁸

As this passage suggests, Johnson draws New England's leaders as exemplary heroes. The brief elegaic portraits of the eminent theocrats
which punctuate the narrative attempt less to provide adequate
biographies than to integrate the individual and the community through
the use of figural parallels. These in part designate the Puritans as
"Israels sons" reborn in the blood of Christ ("lifes fountain"). Zachary
Simmes, for example, has "Moses zeale stampt" upon him, and Wareham
like another David slings his stones at the Goliath-heretics (pp. 101, 107).
In part, too, they serve to locate the minister or magistrate within the
larger typological scheme. John Allen "warre[s] for him [Christ] . . . in's
Vineyard;" Isaac Johnson is "a pillar to support this new erected
building;" Thomas Dudley cuts down with his figural two-edged "sword
. . . those Wolvish sheep, [that] amongst flocks do creep;" and John
Fiske, whom "Christ hath . . . in his vineyard plac't," labors so that
"Sions strong Mount [may] . . . now again be built" (pp. 180, 65, 81,
227).

Predominantly, the imagery is meant to fuse the colonist and the colony, so that the former becomes a microcosm of the latter. When
Johnson speaks of Hugh Peters as "Shiloes soft streames" or of Partridge
as the divinely nourished Tree of God (pp. 109, 119), his language
deliberately blurs the distinction between the man and the church-state.
What better grounds could there be for acclaiming New England's mission? The redeemed Christian, Cotton observes, resembles Jesus "as . . .
the Image of a Seal in the Wax," and both he and his fellow-congrega-
tionalists magnified the image to include His people as a whole. "What
Moses once said to the children of Israel," writes Hooker, and what "the
people of Israel [did] . . . in the land of Canaan . . . was a *type* of
Christ's redeeming thee that art a believer." The divine Seal, that is, is
impressed equally upon the covenanted community and upon the individual saint: both find their antitype, their "substance," in Christ. In
John Higginson's blunt expression of the matter, "We do *all* commit our
[collective] cause unto the Lord in the *same way* as we do *every one*
commit unto him the Salvation of our Soules."²⁹

Wonder-Working Providence from this standpoint eulogizes the
representative hero, who reenacts in his own life the *agon* of Christ, as a
symbol of the people of Israel in America. Thus Pelham "batter[s] downe
. . . All Heresies, and Errors" in order to win "Israels quite peace," and
the "troublous" lives of Saxton, Lenten, and Whitefield demonstrate that
the "Harvest is come . . . / A Harvest large of Gentil and of Jew" (pp.
189, 194). In each case, the saint and the community-in-Christ stand as
reflections of one another. This "People of Israel gather together as one
Man," writes Johnson, referring both to the "Seal" and its social-personal
"Image," and "grow together as one Tree" (p. 60; see also p. 152).

Against this background, Johnson in Book II turns his attention to the

English Reformation. By 1650 it seemed clear that the Puritan Revolution would succeed, that the reason for the flight from European "bondage" had disintegrated. Consequently, the whole *rationale* of his History is put to test and stands out in high relief. If at the start the emigrants "were not . . . refugees seeking a promised land," as Perry Miller contends, "but English[men] . . . taking the long way round in order that someday they . . . might rule in Lambeth," *Wonder-Working Providence* reveals that by the mid-seventeenth century their purpose had perceptibly changed. Since the colony had retraced and redeemed the progress of Israel, its attainments signalized the end of human history. They took on international ramifications now, as the focal point of what Nicholas Noyes called a world-wide "Revolution and Reformation."[30] "How came it to passe," Johnson demands of the English Puritans, "that the Lord put it into your hearts to set upon a Reformation . . . ?" (p. 155). His answer is unequivocal:

> No wonder . . . at the sudden and unexpected downfall of these domineering Lords [in the Church of England]. . . . No enemy of theirs [seemed] in sight, onely there appears a little cloud about the bignesse of a mans hand out of the Westerne Ocean, I [ay] but the Lord Christ is in it, out of Sion the perfection of beauty hath God shined. Our God shall come . . . and mighty tempests shall be moved about him. Now [that] . . . the Children of Sion rejoyce in their King, for the Lord hath pleasure in his people . . . the whole Earth may know [at last that] . . . he will ordaine Armies both by Sea and Land to make Babilon desolate. (pp. 157, 160).

The New World theocracy, then, was to Johnson not a "flank attack" on Europe,[31] but the vanguard of universal history. As early as 1638, he informs us, "the Ministers of Christ . . . could say . . . from [the Book of] Revalation . . . that if the Churches of New England were Gods house, then suddenly there would follow great alternations in the Kingdomes of Europe" (p.185). Correspondingly, in a rather daring (but not uncommon[32]) inversion, he treats the relationship of the American to the English movement as that of harbinger or leader to successors or followers: of John the Divine to later Christians, of Jacob to his descendants, of Queen Esther to Mordecai, and of Moses praying in Sinai to Joshua fighting in the vallies (pp. 155-56, 160). "The Lord hath . . . sent this people to . . . this Wilderness," he explains, "to proclaime to all Nations, the neere approach of the most wonderfull workes that ever the Sonnes of men saw" (p.61).

It is New England's destiny, in short, to lead the way for the Reformation, by radiating its glories back across the Atlantic. Is not the colony that "little cloud" (I Kings 18: 44) which represents Elijah on the top of Carmel, Moses on Sinai, the chosen people marching toward Canaan, and ultimately, through all these types of Christ, the rising of the Son of Man? (Exod. 24: 15-18, 13: 21 ff; Luke 21: 27.) Has it not been "set as lights upon a Hill more obvious than the highest Mountaine in the World," as the rebuilt "glorious Edifice of Mount Sion in a Wilderness" (pp. 29, 52)? Unmistakably, its covenant renews those made on Ararat, on Pisgah, and on the Mount of the Transfiguration (Gen. 8: 4, Deut. 3:

27, Mat. 17: 2), embodying as it does *"the pattern shewed . . . in the Mount"* to Moses and later by "our Saviour . . . unto his disciples." And by that token, as many divines had "proved," it signifies the "holy Mountain of his inheritance" and looks forward to the covenant confirmed with the "140000 [by] . . . *the lamb upon Mount Sion"* at the Second Coming.[33]

Johnson restates this progression time and again in addressing the English Puritans. In "gathering together his Saints" in America, he declares, "the Lord himselfe [has] roared from Sion; or again: "these weake wormes instrumentality had a share in the great desolation the Lord Christ hath wrought," as signified by a "terrible Earthquake . . . [which] taking rise from the West . . . made its progress to the Eastward" (pp. 159-60).[34] Upon this basis, he points to the theocracy as a paradigm for the particular institutions of the English Commonwealth (pp. 156, 159), and in general, as a sure sign of "his glorious comming."

The millenarian strain runs thoughout *Wonder-Working Providence*. As I have implied, it is integral to the descriptions of the Indians and heretics as well as of the Puritan heroes, and it is made part of the narrative through the phrases, reiterated with almost formulaic persistency, announcing the fall of Babylon and of Jericho, the cities "signifying the Kingdome of the Beast."[35] In the third book this strain becomes predominant. Each of the colony's successes is reviewed and epitomized in light of the approaching event: the civil ordinances herald "the speedy accomplishment of . . . the overthrow of Antichrist;" the synods' decrees "prepare for the . . . calling of the Jews, which in all likelyhood is very suddainly to be performed;" Rev. Moxon "takes up truths sword" to "be aveng'd on Satan . . . [whom] Christ will under thy feet . . . tread;" and the founding of "[our] *three last Churches"* bears witness that "The day's at hand, [wherein] both Jew and Gentile shall/ Come crowding in his Churches, Christ to preach,/ And last for aye, none can cause them to fall" (pp. 245, 255, 237, 249-50). As for "Antichrists Armies," their very fury here "hath declared some sudden blow to be given to this bloodthirsty monster . . . for who can expect a victory without a battel?" (pp.268-69).

Johnson occasionally interweaves these prophesies in Book III with complaints about backsliding. In so doing he strikes some of the major chords of the later jeremiads—Indian hostilities caused by "[our] sinful provacations of the Lord," the deaths of famous ministers expressing God's frowns *"upon his N. E. people,"* "unwonted disease" resulting from the spiritual neglect of children (pp. 238, 252, 254)—but he uses these factors to support his major theme. First, due repentence invariably brings "a multitude of marvellous mercies" (p. 238). Secondly, the afflictions serve to augment the settlers' determination: in all cases they are seen as a *"correcting hand. . . to awaken, rouze up, and quicken [us]* with the rod of his power . . . to prosecute [His] work . . . with the greater zeal and courage" (pp. 252-53, 255-56). Most important, God's chastisements reassert the meaning of the colony. As Increase Mather points out, "God hath Covenanted with his people, that Sanctified afflictions shall be their portion. . . . This is *Immanuels Land . . .* here the

Lord hath caused as it were *New Jerusalem* to come down from Heaven
. . . [and] *therefore* we may conclude that he will scourge us for our
backsliding. So doth he say . . . As many as I love I rebuke and chasten."
If the church-state sometimes provokes divine anger, that serves to
demonstrate its special calling.

> If our Nation forsake the God of their Fathers never so little God presently
> cometh up on us with one Judgement or other, that so he may *prevent* our
> destruction.
>
> . . .
>
> The Lord by the Prophet [Isaiah] declares the Judgement inflicted on his Peo-
> ple should be sanctified to their Reformation. He would Turn his Hand upon
> them . . . in Mercy, so as purely to *Purge away their Dross.*

For Johnson as for Mather and others,[36] New England's ultimate redemption, the consummation in its theocracy of the pledge made to Abraham,
becomes all the more evident through God's quick reprimands and high
expectations.

The concluding chapter of the History affirms this view in what is in
effect a prolonged invocation to the millennium. In the Massachusetts
election sermon for 1677, Increase Mather noted the "Opinion that when
New Jerusalem should come down from Heaven *America* would be the
seat for it," and exulted: "Where was there ever a place so like unto New
Jerusalem as New England hath been? . . . Truly that such a Type and
Embleme of New Jerusalem should be erected in so dark a corner of the
world, is a matter of deep Meditation and Admiration."[37] Such meditation was familiar fare both to the audience and the minister. His father-
in-law had set the date for the descent of the Holy City 1655, his colleague William Aspinwall for "not . . . later than 1673," and his son (using the same *"Prophetical* as well as . . . *Historical Calendar")* for
"about" 1697.[38] Johnson is not as specific as this, but he voices their
belief with equal fervency through the "Types and Emblems" which
characterize his work as a whole:

> As it was necessary that there should be a Moses and Aaron, before the Lord
> would deliver his people and destroy Pharaoh lest they should be wildred in-
> deed in the Wilderness; so now it was needfull that the Churches of Christ
> should first obtain their purity, and the civill government its power to defend
> them, before Antichrist come to his finall ruine: and because you shall be sure
> the day is come indeed, behold the Lord Christ marshalling of his invincible
> Army to the battell: some suppose this onely to be mysticall, and not literall
> at all. . . . [But] these N. E. people, who are the subject of this History . . .
> [have literally] ingaged with the main battell of Antichrist . . . [and] what the
> issue will be, is assuredly known in the generall already. Babylon is fallen.
> . . . And now you antient people of Israel look out of your prison grates, let
> these Armies of the Lord Christ Jesus provoke you to acknowledge he is cer-
> tainly come . . . that . . . you may enjoy that glorious resurrection-day, the
> glorious nuptials of the Lamb. (pp.270-71).

On this note Johnson ends the book, with a long poem (pp. 272-75)
pleading for the conversion of the Jews. No doubt he found some
aesthetic satisfaction in thus completing the circle: the Israel *redivivus*-in-

Christ calling the "antient Hebrews to the "nuptials of the Lamb." It stands as the last stage in the long mystical *and* literal development he charts, and recalls once more the momentous reference to Isaiah with which the History begins:

> I will bring forth a seed out of Jacob, and out of Judah an inheritor of my mountains; and mine elect shall inherit it, and my servants shall dwell there. . . . For, behold, I create new heavens and a new earth: and the former shall not be remembered, nor come into mind. But be glad and rejoice for ever in that which I create: for, behold, I create Jerusalem a rejoicing, and her people a joy. And they shall build houses, and inhabit them; and they shall plant vineyards, and eat the fruit of them. . . . They shall not labour in vain . . . for they are the seed of the blessed of the Lord. . . . [dwelling] in all my holy mountain. (65: 9-25).

This lofty vision of New England, and the historiography behind it, express an important element in colonial Puritanism and in its legacy to the national mind. Professor Peter Gay, who dismisses Johnson's work as a "naive military tract," charges that the study of divinity led to the "tragedy of Puritan historiography. . . . American Puritans did not write history as Americans. The two urgent questions that have obsessed Americans at least since the days of the Revolution—what does America mean? and, what does it mean to be an American?—hardly troubled them."[39] *The Wonder-Working Providence of Sions Saviour in New England* displays, on the contrary, a profound concern with both questions. Certainly it is rooted in biblical interpretation and in an eschatology expounded from the church fathers to the Reformation; and strictly speaking it pertains only to the isolated Bay theocracy. Yet in its presentation of the theocracy—of its holy wars and exemplary heroes, its destiny to usher in a new golden age for the world, its "vast undertaking" which, in John Higginson's words, might "dazzle the eyes of Angels, daunt the hearts of devils, ravish and chain fast the Affections of all the Saints"[40]—this first history of Massachusetts vividly formulates the Puritan concept of the colonial venture, and establishes a pattern which may be traced in secular form through many of the subsequent urgent and obsessive definitions of the meaning of America.

Important in most of Bercovitch's work, including the above essay, is his understanding of Puritan uses of typology. Typology was an important element of the colonists' symbolic vision and gave them a means of relating their history to that of God's first chosen people, the Israelites, and a way of determining their own place in the providential scheme. Perry Miller's studies of Roger Williams *(Indianapolis, 1953) and* Jonathan Edwards *(New York, 1949) were the first to demonstrate the importance of typology in Puritan biblical exegesis, but his analyses have been superseded largely by the work of Bercovitch ("Typology in Puritan New England,"* American Quarterly, *XIX [1967]), Jesper Rosenmeier ("The Teacher and the Witness: John Cotton and Roger Williams,"* William and Mary Quarterly, *series 3, XXV [1968]), and others.*

NOTES

1. Introduction to *Johnson's Wonder-Working Providence*, 1628-1651 (New York, 1910), pp. 16, 12, 11. All references to the History are from this edition. For a review of the early editions, see William F. Poole's Introduction to *Wonder-Working Providence of Sions Saviour* (Andover, 1867), p. v.

2. Michael Kraus, *A History of American History* (New York, 1937), p. 47; Richard S. Dunn, "Seventeenth-Century English Historians of America," in *Seventeenth-Century America: Essays in Colonial History*, ed. James M. Smith (Chapel Hill, 1959), pp. 204-05; Miller and Johnson, *The Puritans* (New York, 1963), I, 90.

3. Poole, Introduction to *Wonder-Working Providence*, p. i (a recent restatement of the complaint about "Johnson's frequently inaccurate . . . account" appears in Harvey Wish, *The American Historian* [Oxford, 1960], p. 16); Miller and Johnson, *Puritans*, I, 89; Sanford, *The Quest for Paradise* (Urbana, Ill., 1961), p. 83; John Oxenbridge, *New England Freemen Warmed and Warned* (Boston, 1673), p. 19.

4. See, for example, F. B. [Francis Bridges], *Gods treasure displayed . . . for the awakening of the Laodicean-like secure* (London, 1630); and in New England literature, Joshua Scottow, *A Narrative of the Planting of Massachusetts Colony* (1694), in *Massachusetts Historical Society Collections*, 4th series, IV (1858), 319; and Urian Oakes, *New England Pleaded With* (Cambridge, 1673), p. 27.

5. Amos 7, Rev. 3. All references to the Bible are to the King James Version, unless otherwise stated, though they have been checked with the Geneva translation.

6. *Gods Eye on the Contrite* (Boston, 1685), p. 1. See also William Stoughton, *New England's True Interest* (Cambridge, 1670), pp. 27, 33, and Samuel Hooker, *Righteousness Rained From Heaven* (Cambridge, 1677), p. 2.

7. Taylor, *The Parable of the Sower, and of the Seed* (London, 1659), pp. 276, 280; Cotton, *A Briefe Exposition Of . . . Canticles* (London, 1648), p. 196.

8. Edmund S. Morgan, *Roger Williams: The Church and the State* (New York, 1967), p. 7; Murdock, "Clio in the Wilderness: History and Biography in Puritan New England," *Church History*, XXIV (1955), 234, 231. I am indebted to Professor Murdock's comments in this essay (pp. 234-35) on typology in Puritan New England.

9. Erich Auerbach, "*Figura*," in *Scenes from the Drama of European Literature* (New York, 1959), pp. 47, 59, 70, 50; Robert W. Hanning, *The Vision of History in Early Britain* (New York, 1966), pp. 39, 29-30; Ernest L. Tuveson, *Millennium and Utopia* (Berkeley, 1949), p. 27; C. A. Patrides, *The Phoenix and the Ladder* (Berkeley, 1964), p. 47; William Haller, *The Rise of Puritanism* (New York, 1938), pp. 173-76; William G. Madsen, "Typological Symbolism in *Paradise Lost*," *PMLA*, LXXV (1960), 525; Alan Simpson, *Puritanism in Old and New England* (Chicago, 1955), pp. 75-79.

10. "Typology in Puritan New England: The Williams-Cotton Controversy Reassessed," *AQ* (1967), 166-92. Jesper Rosenmeier has studied the background and development of Cotton's typology in "The Image of Christ: The Typology of John Cotton" (unpublished Harvard dissertation, 1965), and Thomas M. Davis is now completing a dissertation entitled "Typology in New England Puritanism" (Southern Illinois University).

11. Winthrop, "Conclusions for the Plantation in New England," in *Old South Leaflets* (Boston, [n.d.]), II, no. 50, p. 4; Cotton, "A Reply to . . . Williams" (1646), in *The Complete Writings of Roger Williams* (New York, 1959), II, 229, 143-44; Cotton, *Briefe Exposition Of Canticles*, p. 182 and title page; Bulkeley, *The Gospel-Covenant* (London, 1646), pp. 2-3; Norton, *The Heart of New-England Rent* (Boston, 1659), p. 19; Richard Mather, *An Apology of the Churches in New-England* (London, 1643), pp. 1-2. A typical demonstration of the New Englanders' view of the development from the Hebrews to the early Church to the Reformation appears in John Cotton's *Discourse Concerning Civil Government* (Cambridge, 1663), where the rules of conduct are derived from the "*Jews* . . . and the *Christian Churches* persecuted by the *Roman Emporeurs*" (p. 4). Cf. Peter Folger, *A Looking Glass for the Times* (1675?), in *Rhode Island Historical Tracts*, XVI (1883), p. 17.

12. See Hanning's *Vision of History*, pp. 32-37, for a clear summary of the differences between Augustinian "vertical typology" and Eusebius' "linear typology;" and cf. Theodor E. Mommsen's "Saint Augustine and the Christian Idea of Progress," *JHI*, XII (1951), which contrasts Augustine and such "Christian progressivists" as Eusebius (pp. 373-74).

13. For example: *ten*, "a sign of perfection" (*e.g.*, pp. 88, 100, 213, 261); and *forty*, (*e.g.* pp. 18, 69, 99), "a figure of the Kingdom of Heaven," referring to Moses on Sinai, Elias in Horeb, Christ and the Israelites in the wilderness. John Bunyan, *Soloman's Temple Spiritualized* (Hartford, 1802), p. 74; John Speed, *A Cloud of Witnesses* (London, 1616), pp. 7, 15, 36, 89; John Norton, *The Evangelical Worshipper*, in *Three Choice . . . Sermons* (Cambridge, 1664),·p. 35.

14. See John Cotton, *The Powring Out of the Seven Vials* (London, 1642), p. 3—one of works to which Johnson expressly refers (pp. 88-89)—and Exod. 25; 31, Zech. 4: 2, and Rev. 1: 11 and 8: 2. For the chiliastic meaning of *twelve*, noted below, see John Eliot's Preface to his *Christian Commonwealth* (London, 1659), p. B4 verso. Jean Daniélou discusses the significance of "holy" numbers in typology in *From Shadows to Reality*, tr. Wulstan Hibberd (Westminster, Md., 1960), pp. 184-85.

15. Kenneth Murdock, *Literature and Theology in Colonial New England* (New York, 1963), p. 90. The usual view is that "Johnson enumerates a succession of 'wonder-working providences' which ripple along for the duration of the book." (Perry Miller, *New England Mind: From Colony to Province* [Cambridge, Mass., 1953], p. 31.)

16. Parker, *Visions and Prophecies of Daniel* (London, 1646), p. 15; Cotton, *A Briefe Exposition . . . Of Ecclesiastes* (London, 1657), pp. 35-36 (*cf. Cotton Mather, Psalterium Americanum* [Boston, 1718], pp. 371-72). The relevant biblical references are, respectively: Acts 5: 1-3, Heb. 11: 16-27, Isa. 33: 5-6. Johnson refers to Parker's work on p. 111. See also (regarding Ananias) Samuel Danforth, *Cry of Sodom* (Boston, 1674), p. 10, and (regarding the "Treasury") Jonathan Mitchel, *Nehemiah on the Wall* (Cambridge, 1671), p. 7. With respect to the reference to the colonists as "Jacobites," *cf.* Edmund S. Morgan, *Visible Saints* (New York, 1963), p. 78.

17. For example, Johnson describes how the Puritans, in "passing through the Floods of Persecution, . . . go [by way of] . . . the doore thou [Christ] has opened upon our earnest request, and we hope it shall never be shut" (pp. 29, 53). This is the "opened door" or the "door of hope" which typology tells us will "allure" the saints "into the wilderness . . . [to God's] vineyards . . . as in the day when she [Israel] came up out of the land of Egypt." (See John Cotton, *The Way of the Churches* [London, 1645], p. 111—another of Cotton's books from which Johnson quotes—and Hos. 2: 15-19). The "flood of persecution" refers to the race of Jacob whose enemies "shall fear the name of the Lord from the west . . . [when] the Redeemer shall come to Zion" (Isa. 59: 19-21), and also to "the woman [bearing] . . . the remnant of her seed" who fled into the wilderness (see Rev. 12: 15-17), a type of the Church often applied by New England writers to their colony: *e.g.*, by John Norton in *Sion the Outcast*, in *Three Sermons*, p. 15.

18. *The Day of Trouble is Near* (Cambridge, 1675), p. 27; Johnson might have known John Cotton's discussion of this parallel in his sermon, *God's Promise to His Plantations* (Boston, 1686); first delivered in 1634), p. 3.

19. The tradition behind the concept of Christ as Pilot is outlined in Ralph E. Hone, "The Pilot of the *Galilean* Lake," *SP*, LVI (1959), 60-61. For applications of this conception and that of the "path through the Waters" to the American Puritan experience, see Samuel Danforth's *A Brief Recognition of New Englands Errand into the Wilderness* (Cambridge, 1671), p. 21, and Thomas Shepard's *Eye Salve* (Cambridge, 1673), p. 49.

20. Cotton Mather, *The Bostonian Ebenezer* (1698), in *Old South Leaflets*, III, no. 67, pp. 3 ff.; Increase Mather, *A Discourse Concerning Baptism* (Boston, 1675), p. 7; Samuel Mather, *The Figures or Types of the Old Testament* (London, 1705), p. 346. Striking typological applications of the Temple and the Rock to the New England theocracy appear in John Davenport's *Gods Call to His People* (Cambridge, 1669), p. 2, and in Norton's *Evangelical Worshipper*, pp. 30-34.

21. Thomas Shepard, Preface to Danforth, *Brief Recognition*, p. A2 recto; Norton, *Evangelical Worshipper*, p. 37. The American Puritan habit of identifying the theocracy as the "ends of the earth" persists from Richard to Cotton Mather: see *A Farewell Exhortation* (Cambridge, 1657), p. 7, and *Magnalia Christi Americana*, ed. Thomas Robbins (Hartford, 1853), I, 25. The phrase "weake wormes" pertains not only to Jacob but to Isaiah's prophecy (41: 8-29) concerning the redeemed remnant. With regard to Zerubbabel as type, noted below, see Samuel Mather's *Figures or Types*, pp. 91, 115, 339; John Higginson's *The Cause of God* (Cambridge, 1663), p. 7, and James Allin's description of "that Wonder-working

providence" which has removed from New England "such Mountaines as cannot be removed by humane might" (*New Englands Choicest Blessing* [Boston, 1679], p. 13). It is relevant to Allin's and to Johnson's meaning that Zerubbabel has a vision of the golden seven-branched candlestick, symbolizing the New Zion (Zech. 4: 2).

22. The reference is to Isa. 26, and something of the continuity of figural thought in American Puritan culture may be seen in Cotton Mather's almost identical comments on this text in a sermon on Boston delivered nearly a half century after Johnson's History (*Bostonian Ebenezer*, p. 6). An important explication of the "Wilderness" image which pervades American Puritan literature is found in Shepard's *Eye-Salve* which "opens" five "metaphorical" uses of the term (pp. 3-5), and then explains:

> Though this place (as a Wilderness) hath been a place at times, of the same temptation as that Wilderness, Mat. 4. 1 to Christ . . . the Lord hath proved and tryed his People above forty years together [as He did the Israelites], yet (blessed be his Name!) they have had his gracious presence as a Pillar of Protection with them. (p. 14).

23. Regarding the false "Captain," see Northrup Frye, "The Typology of *Paradise Regained*, *MP*, LIII (1955-56), 233; and, in New England writing, Thomas Shepard's "Election Sermon" (1638), in *New England Historical and Genealogical Register*, XXIV (1870), 363. Merritt Y. Hughes, in his edition of *John Milton: Complete Poems and Major Prose* (New York, 1957), traces the concept of the "devilish Engines" in *Paradise Lost*, IV, 475 ff. to Spenser and other writers (p. 335 n.), but probably the source lies in a typological reading of Ezek. 26: 9, as Shepard's son intimates in describing the Anabaptist "Engines" (*Eye Salve*, p. 25).

24. John Norton, *Sion the Outcast*, p. 15. This image (from Rev. 12) was often attached to heretics in seventeenth-century New England: by Cotton Mather, for example, in condemning the Antinomians (*Magnalia*, II, 522).

25. See Samuel Mather, *Figures or Types*, pp. 436, 480; Roger Williams, *The Bloody Tenent Yet More Bloody*, in *Complete Writings*, IV, 277, 354; *Paradise Lost*, VI, 194-98, 646-53 (and cf. Mather's *Magnalia*, II, 566); Cotton Mather, *Midnight Cry* (Boston, 1692), p. 36; Increase Mather, *The Times of Men* (Cambridge, 1675), p. 19.

26. See Cotton, *Briefe Exposition of Ecclesiastes*, p. 34; and Samuel Torrey, *Exhortation Unto Reformation* (Cambridge, 1674), p. 14 (and cf. Auerbach, "Figura," p. 38). With respect to the continuity of this view of the Indians, see Increase Mather, *A Brief History of the Warr* (Boston, 1676), p. 47, and Cotton Mather, *Magnalia*, II, 553, 579. Johnson does turn briefly to the missionary efforts (pp. 261, 264), but primarily he sees the Indians within this typological framework.

27. *Gods Promise*, pp. 6, 17, 13. See also Danforth's description of the New Englanders "dwelling in the House of the Lord . . . under the shadow of the wings of the God of *Israel*" (*Brief Recognition*, p. 18), John Whiting, *The Way of Israels Welfare* (Boston, 1686), p. 32, and, for a full explication of the concept in these terms, Shepard's complaint against the "Laodicean frame of Spirit [that] prevails . . . in these ends of Earth," despite the fact that the inhabitants dwell "under the wings of the Covenant," since God has "given you Manna to the full, the Rock hath followed you, and you have had the Pillar . . . in all your Journeyings" (*Eye Salve*, pp. 24, 49). For a review of the various Garden types cited below (in a work Johnson knew) see Cotton's *Briefe Exposition of Canticles*, pp. 27, 72 (Vine), 55-56, 131-32 (Fruit, Wine, Plants, 129-36, 171-80 (Garden and Paradise). Gurton Saltonstall applies them to the theocracy in a way almost identical to Johnsons, and then adds: "These Figurative Terms . . . are obvious; and need not much to be said for their Explication." (*A Sermon Preached Before the General Assembly* [Boston, 1697], p. 11).

28. The "fountain" is of course an image of Christ (*e.g.*, John Cotton's *Christ the fountaine of life* [London, 1651], and Samuel Willard's *The Fountain Opened* [Boston, 1700]; and cf. *Paradise Lost*, IV, 225 ff. describing the "Fountain" and Earth's "veins" in the Garden of Paradise). The more complex meaning of the "ratling bones" is explained by John Winthrop: "love . . . workes like the Spirit upon the drie bones; (Ezek. 37) bone came to bone, it gathers together the scattered bones of perfect old man Adam and knitts them into one body again in Christ" ("Christian Charitie, A Modell Hereof," in *Puritan Political Ideas*, ed. Edmund S. Morgan [New York, 1965], p. 86). Regarding the familiar figure (from John 10: 12) of the "wolf" as heretic, quoted below, see John Cotton's *The Keyes of the Kingdom of Heaven* (London, 1644), p. 9.

29. Cotton, *A Treatise . . . of Faith* (London, 1713), p. 16; Thomas Hooker, *The Saints . . .*

Dutie (London, 1651), pp. 33, 38; Higginson, *Cause of God*, pp. 18-19 (my italics). See also, for example: Davenport's *God's Call*, p. 20; Samuel Torrey, *A Plea for the Life of Dying Religion* (Boston, 1684), p. 41; and Cotton's *Discourse about Civil Government*, p. 22. The union-in-Christ of the chosen people as a whole and the individual saint implies a meeting of the Puritans' social covenant and the very different covenant of grace, a question I discuss briefly in "Typology in Puritan New England," pp. 188-89.

30. Miller, *Colony to Province*, p. 5; Noyes, quoted in Mather's *Magnalia*, II, 653. See further Cotton Mather, *Things for a Distressed People to Think Upon* (Boston, 1696), pp. 32-35.

31. Miller, *Colony to Province*, p. 5. At one point, indeed, Johnson suggests that the English Reformation may itself be a "flank attack" on Satan's forces, instigated by Christ in order to help the colonists against "the Lording Bishops, and other Malignant adversaries . . . who exasperated against them" (p. 154; see also p. 155).

32. See for example William Hooke, *New England's Teares for Old England's Feares* (London, 1640), pp. 9, 21-22; and Increase Mather, *Day of Trouble*, p. 28. For an explication of Johnson's meaning in speaking of Esther and Mordecai, below, see Norton's *Sion the Outcast*, p. 11, and *cf.* Cotton's discussion of the Queen as type in *Briefe Exposition of Canticles*, pp. 185-86.

33. Cotton, *Gods Promise*, p. 60 Norton, *Evangelical Worshipper*, pp. 29, 37; Cotton Mather, *Midnight Cry*, p. 23; Higginson, *Cause of God*, pp. 13, 11. The implications of the "little cloud" are noted in Increase Mather's *David Serving His Generation* (Boston, 1698), pp. 22-23, and set forth in a general way in Speed's *Cloud of Witnesses*, *passim*. Regarding the "holy Mount" as type, see Samuel Mathers *Figures or Types*, p. 326, and John Cotton's *The Way of Congregational Churches Cleared* (London, 1648), Treatise I, p. 46 (from which Johnson quotes); quite frequently, too, the "holy Mount" appears as an emblem of the church-state, the "Mount of God" upon which "*Moses* and *Aaron* kissed each other," thus demonstrating once for all that "the Lord held the Magistracy and Ministry in Unity" (Scottow, *Narrative*, p. 290). Higginson shows the typological progression, in these terms, from the "Reformed Churches coming out of Popery" to the millennium on "*Mount Zion, Rev.* 14. 1 . . . *Rev.* 15. 2," in *Cause of God*, p. 11. The concept of the colony as lights "set . . . upon a Hill" (from Mat. 5: 14) is found, explicitly and implicitly, throughout seventeenth-century New England writings, from Winthrop's lay sermon through *New-England Rent*, p. 58 and Shepard's *Eye Salve*, pp. 45-46 to Cotton Mather's *Wonderful Works of God* (Boston, 1690), p. A3 verso. *Cf.* William Bradford, *Of Plymouth Plantation*, ed. Worthington C. Ford (Boston, 1912), II, 117.

34. *Cf.* Jonathan Edward's pronouncement that the Sun of Righteousness "*shall rise in the West*, contrary to the course of this world" (quoted in Sanford, *Quest for Paradise*, p. 98). Johnson was of course speaking of an actual earthquake, but in the context of his work it clearly has symbolic overtones. As Cotton Mather wrote, "I am verily perswaded, we are now Entred into those Earth-quakes which are to attend and assist, *The Resurrection of our Lords Witnesses, Ezr. 3: 3*" (*Midnight Cry*, pp. 60-61; or again: "I have the confidence to tell you, that the *Mystical Babylon*, is just entring into . . . *Vintage* . . . and that we are got . . . into these *Earth quakes* which will shake . . . the *Papal Empire* to pieces" [*The Serviceable Man* (Boston, 1690), pp. 52-53]).

35. Oxenbridge, *New-England Freemen*, p. 20; *cf.* William Hubbard, *The Happiness of a People* (Boston, 1676), p. 59. In addition to the instances already cited, see especially pp. 30, 50, 59-60, 151, 203-04; and the verses on Rogers (p. 184), Brown (p. 196), Hough (p. 226), Ward (p. 235), and Matthews (p. 251).

36. Mather, *Day of Trouble*, pp. 4, 26-27, and *The Great Blessing of Primitive Counsellors* (Boston, 1693), p. 9. See also Cotton, "Reply to Williams," p. 131; Adams, *Gods Eye*, p. 27; Norton, *Heart of New-England Rent*, pp. 5, 22-23; Higginson, *Cause of God*, p. 24; John Williams, *Warning to the Unclean* (Boston, 1699), pp. 21, 30. An interesting example of this view—which also demonstrates the common usage of the figures Johnson employs (the "Temple-Worke . . . Corner-stones . . . defenced Cities, Iron pillars and Brazen-Walls . . . Candlestick," etc.)—appears in Danforth's *Brief Recognition*, pp. 19-22. The contrast between the "curing" afflictions described in these works and the punishments meted out to the ungodly may be seen in Johnson's description (pp. 265-67) of an Indian attack upon a Virginia settlement which had just ejected several Puritan ministers; and the theory behind the contrast is presented in Increase Mather's *Day of Trouble*, p. 27, and *Times of Men*, p. 16. It should be noted, however, that the jeremiads could also express a less comforting

doctrine, as when Mather recalls that "the Troubles preceding the destruction of the Jewish Church and State may be applied to the Troubles of the last time [in New England], the former being a Type of the latter" (*Day of Trouble*, p. 20). For Johnson, backsliding denotes God's particular interest; in the jeremiad in general it becomes a more complex matter, one which I hope to examine in another essay.

37. *A Discourse Concerning . . . Apostacy* (Boston, 1685), p. 77. In his *Discourse Concerning Faith . . . and the Glorious Kingdom of the Lord . . . on Earth, Now Approaching* (Boston, 1710), Increase Mather claims that the reign of Antichrist is "almost finished" (pp. 96-98); and he expresses a similar conviction, in terms very close to those of Johnson, in *The Mystery of Israels Salvation* (London, 1669), *passim*.

38. John Cotton, *Exposition of Revelation* (London, 1656), p. 93 (quoted in Rosenmeier, *Image of Christ*, p. 16); Cotton Mather, *Midnight Cry*, pp. 30-32, 62; Aspinwall, *A Brief Description of the . . . Kingdom that Shortly Is to come into the World* (London, 1653), quoted in Ira V. Brown, "Watchers for the Second Coming: The Millenarian Tradition in America," *Mississippi Valley Historical Review*, XXXIX (1952-53), 445. Professor Brown notes further millenarian works by Cotton, Shepard, Parker (who in his *Visions of Daniel* fixed the year 1859 for the end of the world), and John Davenport who expected New Haven "to be the seat of the millennial kingdom" (p. 447).

39. *A Failure of Mastery: Puritan Historians in Colonial America* (Berkeley, 1966), pp. 53, 24-26.

40. *The Cause of God*, pp. 11-12.

16 | ANNE BRADSTREET: DOGMATIST AND REBEL

ANN STANFORD

Ann Stanford's essay on Anne Bradstreet is concerned less with the mythmaking aspects of Puritan literature and more with the relations between a Puritan poet and society. Anne Bradstreet, the daughter of Massachusetts governor Thomas Dudley and the wife of magistrate Simon Bradstreet, was nevertheless expected, as a woman, to refrain from public activities. Avoiding the pitfall of treating Bradstreet purely from a feminist perspective, Ann Stanford treats that issue as part of the larger question of the role of the writer in his or her culture.

Commentators on America from de Toqueville on have remarked the tensions, the simultaneous existence of opposing tendencies, within American life and literature. De Toqueville ascribed these tensions in part to the lack of mediating institutions between the individual and the state or the individual and his God. Other writers find the tensions rooted in spiritual conflicts rising out of economic developments;[1] in the pull between the will to believe and the need to be shown;[2] in theoretical principles, which, if consistently followed, lead to frustration in practice.[3] The conflict shows up in literature through the individual's struggle to remain himself, to maintain his own inner values in the face of social pressure—or, as D. H. Lawrence sees it, to maintain his spiritual energy in the face of dogma[4]—and in many works of American literature these conflicts are never brought into balance or resolved.[5]

It is into this pattern of unresolved antitheses that much of the work of Anne Bradstreet fits. Though she occasionally resolves the conflict, it breaks out again and again. And it is this pattern of tension, which has often been demonstrated to be characteristic of later American literature, that explains much of her work as well.

When in the summer of 1630 Anne Bradstreet looked from the deck of the *Arabella* at the crude settlement of Salem, Massachusetts, it was no doubt a dismal sight compared to her own homeland—the flat, fen country of Lincolnshire, with its towns and great estates. She later told how she "came into this Country, where I found a new world and new manners, at which my heart rose," that is, her heart rebelled. "But after I was convinced it was the way of God, I submitted to it and joined to the church at Boston."[6]

The elements of this first reaction were to be repeated again and again during Anne Bradstreet's pilgrimage through the new world. There was the rising of the heart either in dismay or rebellion and the assertion of the self against the dogma she encountered. Next, there was the need for conviction. It was only after persuasion that she could ever submit to the "way." Rebellion and a struggle for or against conviction form a pattern which runs through her writing. It is the statement of dogma and the concurrent feeling of resistance to dogma that give much of that writing the vitality we are still conscious of today.

The very fact that she wrote, that she considered herself a poet, that she continued to write in spite of criticism, indicates that she was willing to act independently in spite of the dogmatic assertions of many of her contemporaries, even those of the venerable John Winthrop. Winthrop recorded in his journal for April 13, 1645, the following comment on Anne Hopkins:

> Mr. Hopkins, the governour of Hartford upon Connecticut, came to Boston, and brought his wife with him, (a godly young woman, and of special parts,) who was fallen into a sad infirmity, the loss of her understanding and reason, which had been growing upon her divers years, by occasion of her giving herself wholly to reading and writing, and had written many books. Her husband, being very loving and tender of her, was loath to grieve her; but he saw his errour, when it was too late. For if she had attended her household affairs, and such things as belong to women, and not gone out of her way and calling to meddle in such things as are proper for men, whose minds are stronger &c. she had kept her wits, and might have improved them usefully and honourably in the place God had set her.[7]

And Thomas Parker wrote to his sister in a public letter, published in London, 1650, "your printing of a Book, beyond the custom of your Sex, doth rankly smell."[8]

Anne Bradstreet had already encountered such attitudes when, in 1642, she wrote in her "Prologue" to "The Four Elements":

> I am obnoxious to each carping tongue
> Who says my hand a needle better fits,
> A Poets pen all scorn I should thus wrong,
> For such despite they cast on Female wits:
> If what I do prove well, it won't advance,
> They'l say it's stoln, or else it was by chance.

She goes on to point out that to the Greeks the Nine Muses were women and Poesy itself was *"Calliope's* own Child." But, she says, to this argument her critics reply that "the Greeks did nought, but play the fools & lye." She then makes her customary concession to current dogma:

> Let Greeks be Greeks, and women what they are
> Men have precedency and still excell,
> It is but vain unjustly to wage warre;
> Men can do best, and women know it well
> Preheminence in all and each is yours.

The pre-eminence of man over woman was for both Anglican and Puritan a God-given condition. St. Paul had asserted it, and the authority of the man, especially in the state of marriage, was the subject of much discussion among Protestant ministers. This subject was of particular theological interest because of the development of the Protestant idea of a married clergy. Anne Bradstreet had doubtless heard sermons to this effect, and perhaps had read books on domestic relations such as those of Thomas Gataker: *A Good Wife, God's Gift* (1620), and *Marriage Duties Briefly Couched Together* (1620).[9] She was as well aware as Milton that men and women were

> Not equal, as thir sex not equal seemd;
> For contemplation hee and valour formd,
> For softness shee and sweet attractive Grace
> Hee for God only, shee for God in him.   (*P. L.*, iv, 296-299)

And she, like Eve, knew

> How beauty is excelled by manly grace
> And wisdom.   (*P. L.*, iv, 490-491)

Yet for Anne Bradstreet this dogma did not mean that women were not to use their wits at all. After admitting that men are superior, she asks them to "grant some small acknowledgement of ours." In other words, she would not have women confined to household affairs to the extent expected by John Winthrop.

In the following year, in her elegy on Queen Elizabeth, she stated her belief in the intellectual capacity of women much more strongly:

> Nay Masculines, you have thus taxt us long,
> But she, though dead, will vindicate our wrong.
> Let such as say our Sex is void of Reason,
> Know tis a Slander now, but once was Treason.

And despite the carping tongues, she kept on writing.

Two years earlier (1641) she had given evidence of a professional sense of dedication to her writing and a determination to continue with it. She said in her poem in honor of Du Bartas:

> But barren I my Dasey here do bring,
> A homely flour in this my latter Spring,
> If Summer, or my Autumn age do yield,
> Flours, fruits, in Garden, Orchard, or in Field,
> They shall be consecrated in my Verse,
> And prostrate offered at great *Bartas* Herse.

She showed her liberalism also in the wide range of books that she thought fit to read, among them, romances. The Puritan minister Richard Baxter expressed a common view of romances when he said of his youthful reading: "I was extremely bewitched with a Love of Romances, Fables and Old Tales, which corrupted my affections and lost my time." Though Anne Bradstreet admitted that Sidney's romance *The Arcadia* was in part rubbish, she at the same time defended it by saying

> But he's a Beetle-head that can't descry
> A world of wealth within that rubbish lye.

However, Anne Bradstreet was careful not to make the mistake of Anne Hopkins. She did not neglect her domestic affairs. The author of the preface to her book, *The Tenth Muse*, assures the "Kind Reader" that this is the "Work of a Woman, honoured, and esteemed where she lives, for her gracious demeanour, her eminent parts, her pious conversation, her courteous disposition, her exact diligence in her place, and discreet managing of her Family occasions." Furthermore, the author assures the reader that these poems were not written during hours which should have been devoted to work, but "are the fruit but of some few houres curtailed from her sleep and other refreshments."

Thus, because she did observe in her conduct an exact conformity to the mores of her community, Anne Bradstreet was able to continue to write though the practice of writing by women was disapproved of by many in the community and by the governor himself.

Her first book *The Tenth Muse* was published in London in 1650, the year that Thomas Parker criticized his sister for the "printing of a Book." Anne Bradstreet was protected from such criticism by the fact that the book was brought out without her knowledge, as her editor is careful to assert. Her reaction to the publication, however, was not so much annoyance at having her poems "expos'd to publick view" as it was that they were brought to public view "in raggs, halting to th' press." Her concern was with the blemishes in her work, and with the fact that the printer increased the errors. She set out to correct these flaws; the second edition, published six years after her death, states on the title page that it is "Corrected by the Author."

Thus in her determination to write and in her defense of the capability of women to reason, to contemplate, and to read widely, she showed herself capable of taking a stand against the more conservative and dogmatic of her contemporaries. It was a quiet rebellion, carried on as an undercurrent in an atmosphere of conformity.

Further examples of this tendency toward independence carried on under the guise and beneath repeated statements of dogma occur in the case of the three early elegies and the poems she wrote to her husband. The elegies are written in the form of funeral poems for Sir Philip Sidney, Queen Elizabeth and the French poet, Du Bartas. They are modeled on similar elegies found in Joshua Sylvester's work. But Sylvester concludes his elegies with a Christian apotheosis: the reader should not mourn, since the dead is with the saints in heaven. There is little of heaven in Anne Bradstreet's elegies. The apotheosis for the three characters she celebrates is not a higher Christian transformation, but fame. In such promise, she is closer to the classic poets and the Cavaliers than to the other Puritan writers. The Sidney epitaph concludes:

> His praise is much, this shall suffice my pen,
> That *Sidney* dy'd 'mong most renown'd of men.

The Du Bartas elegy elaborates the theme:

> Thy haughty Stile and rapted wit sublime
> All ages wondring at, shall never climb.
> Thy sacred works are not for imitation,
> But Monuments to future Admiration.
> Thus *Bartas* fame shall last while starrs do stand,
> And whilst there's Air or Fire, or Sea or Land.

The idea of fame also permeates the elegy on Elizabeth, which begins:

> Although great Queen thou now in silence lye
> Yet thy loud Herald Fame doth to the sky
> Thy wondrous worth proclaim in every Clime,
> And so hath vow'd while there is world or time.

It continues on the note of fame and glory to the final epitaph:

> Here lyes the pride of Queens, Pattern of Kings,
> So blaze it Fame, here's feathers for thy wings.
> Here lyes the envi'd, yet unparalled Prince,
> Whose living virtues speak, (though dead long since)
> If many worlds, as that Fantastick fram'd,
> In every one be her great glory fam'd.

These poems promise a continuation of the individual life on this earth through fame. The same attitude runs through the poems to her husband and children, though the earthly fame is to be continued in a different manner. One of the interesting poems with regard to this point is that titled "Before the Birth of one of her Children." The poem suggests she may die, and the reader assumes she is thinking of the possibility of death in childbirth. She asks her husband to forget her faults and remember what virtues she may have had. Here, as in so many of her poems, there is a conflict between her acceptance of Puritan dogma, and her own warm personality. She states her awareness that life is brief and joys are apt to be followed by adversity. But she also says

> love bids me
> These farewell lines to recommend to thee,
> That when that knot's unty'd that made us one,
> I may seem thine, who in effect am none.

It was the Puritan belief that a marriage was dissolved at death. Marriage was for the earthly life only, and in after life any union between spirits was no longer in effect. A person must not love any earthly thing too much, and even excessive grief for a departed spouse or child was contrary to God's command, since it showed that one had too much regard for the things of this world.[10] Anne Bradstreet voiced the Puritan view when she spoke of untying the knot "that made us one," just as she expressed it in the last line of another poem to her husband when she said, "Let's still remain but one till death divide." But she tries to get around the idea of the complete severance of death by writing lines so that "I may seem thine, who in effect am none." Despite the Puritan idea of the end of love in death, she wants to be remembered on this earth; she admits that her husband will probably marry again, as was customary, but she still hopes that

> if chance to thine eyes shall bring this verse,
> With some sad sighs honour my absent Herse;
> And kiss this paper for thy loves dear sake.

Further, she requests that

> when thou feel'st no grief, as I no harms,
> Yet love thy dead, who long lay in thine arms.

A comparable passage in another of the love poems attempts to circumvent the finality of love in death at the end of "To my Dear and Loving Husband":

> Then while we live, in love lets so persever,
> That when we live no more, we may live ever.

There are two possible interpretations of these lines: first, she may mean that they may have children, who will produce descendants, so that they may live on in their line. This is similar to the idea of some of Shakespeare's sonnets, for example. Second, it may mean that they will become famous as lovers, and live in fame. This would hardly seem to be a good Puritan idea, but the Cavalier idea of immortality through fame is not one Mistress Bradstreet would scorn.

Anne Bradstreet is also hopeful that her earthly memory will be kept green by her children. In a later poem, "In reference to her Children" (1658), which begins "I had eight birds hatcht in one nest," she reiterates her desire to be remembered:

> When each of you shall in your nest
> Among your young ones take your rest,
> In chirping language, oft them tell,
> You had a Dam that lov'd you well,
> That did what could be done for young,
> And nurst you up till you were strong.

She explains this desire for remembrance on the basis that she may continue to be a good influence upon her children and their grandchildren:

> And 'fore she once would let you fly,
> She shew'd you joy and misery;
> Taught what was good, and what was ill,
> What would save life, and what would kill?
> Thus gone, amongst you I may live,
> And dead, yet speak, and counsel give.[11]

But the over-all tone indicates that the remembrance itself is important to her. The desires for fame, honor, and worldly remembrance, indeed, seem to be special temptations for Anne Bradstreet. In her dialogue between "The Flesh and the Spirit" these are included among the temptations that Flesh sets forth:

> Dost honour like? acquire the same,
> As some to their immortal fame:
> And trophyes to thy name erect
> Which wearing time shall ne're deject.

The Spirit properly and dogmatically rejects such temptations:

> Thy sinfull pleasures I doe hate,
> Thy riches are to me no bait,
> Thine honours doe, nor will I love;
> For my ambition lyes above.

My greatest honour it shall be
When I am victor over thee.

The Spirit here has taken the proper Puritan attitude toward earthly things, but the Flesh clings to the visible. The struggle is recorded by Anne Bradstreet in prose as well as in poetry. God and his world to come are invisible, and Anne Bradstreet is reluctant to place her trust in either the actuality of God or the reality of life after death. She wrote in her notebook: "Many times hath Satan troubled me concerning the verity of the scriptures, many times by Atheisme how I could know whether there was a God; I never saw any miracles to confirm me, and those which I read of how did I know but they were feigned." These questions are not unique in Anne Bradstreet; other good Puritans such as Thomas Shepard and John Bunyan also asked them. But the elaborateness with which Anne Bradstreet formulates her answers indicates that for her too they were genuine problems. It is true that in the complete passage she does resolve her doubts through a determination to rely upon faith: "Return, O my Soul, to thy Rest, upon this Rock Christ Jesus will I build my faith." But she adds, "and, if I perish, I perish." So it takes one more assertion to close the argument: "But I know all the Powers of Hell shall never prevail against it. I know whom I have trusted . . . and that he is able to keep that I have committed to his charge."

Her distrust of death as the gateway to the supreme life is indicated more personally in an entry in the notebook for August 28, 1656:

Now I can wait, looking every day when my Saviour shall call for me. Lord graunt that while I live I may doe that service I am able in this frail Body, and bee in continuall expectation of my change, and let me never forgett thy great Love to my soul so lately expressed, when I could lye down and bequeath my Soul to thee, and Death seem'd no terrible Thing. O let me ever see Thee that Art invisible, and I shall not bee unwilling to come, tho: by so rough a Messenger.

Once more in this passage, the experience described seems to be one of conviction attempting to conquer feeling, but the final complaint of "so rough a Messenger" indicates that the delight in the future glorified state is not enough to offset earthly doubts and fear of death.

The struggle between dogma and feeling reaches its apex in the seven poems composed between 1665 and 1670, the last years of Anne Bradstreet's life. These include two personal poems and four memorial elegies upon members of her family.

These last poems present the arguments of the Flesh and the Spirit in relation to real occurrences. The Flesh argued for the visible against the invisible, and for honor, wealth, and pleasure. But what the real woman wants, rather than riches, is a home with its comforts and memories; rather than honor and pleasure, the lives of loved ones; and finally life itself. In these poems, Anne Bradstreet presents her own conflict in regard to these desires. Her feelings about her home represent the most material conflict. In 1666, when the Bradstreet home at Andover burned down, she wrote a poem about the conflagration and her own feelings. She describes her awakening to the "shreiks of dreadfull voice" and going

out to watch "the flame consume" her "dwelling place." But she comforts
herself with good Puritan dogma:

> And, when I could no longer look,
> I blest his Name that gave and took,
> That layd my goods now in the dust:
> Yea so it was, and so 'twas just.
> It was his own: it was not mine;
> Far be it that I should repine.
>
> He might of All justly bereft,
> But yet sufficient for us left.

This is an argument that Spirit might have used; the burning of the
house was God's doing, and his doings should not be questioned. But she
does question in the next three stanzas, where she lovingly goes over the
contents of the house—the questioning being through feeling tone rather
than statement. As she passes the ruins, she re-creates the pleasant things
that had been there:

> When þy the Ruines oft I past,
> My sorrowing eyes aside did cast,
> And here and there the places spye
> Where oft I sate, and long did lye.
>
> Here stood that Trunk, and there that chest;
> There lay that store I counted best:
> My pleasant things in ashes lye,
> And them behold no more shall I.
> Under thy roof no guest shall sitt,
> Nor at thy Table eat a bitt.
>
> No pleasant tale shall 'ere be told,
> Nor things recounted done of old.
> No candle 'ere shall shine in Thee,
> Nor bridegroom's voice ere heard shall bee.

In its progress the poem becomes almost another dialogue of dogma
and feeling, or of Flesh and Spirit, for she chides her own heart in the
manner of the Spirit:

> Then streight I 'gin my heart to chide,
> And did thy wealth on earth abide?
> Didst fix thy hope on mouldring dust,
> The arm of flesh didst make thy trust?
> Raise up thy thoughts above the skye
> That dunghill mists away may flie.
>
> Thou hast an house on high erect,
> Fram'd by that mighty Architect,
> With glory richly furnished,
> Stands permanent tho: this bee fled.

Despite the reasonable arguments that her goods belonged to God and
whatever God does is just, there is in the poem an undercurrent of regret
that the loss is not fully compensated for by the hope of treasure that lies
above.

The undercurrent is even stronger in the elegies on her grandchildren. Though dogma could reason that God could take away her possessions, and though she could accept this on a rational level, even though it ran counter to her feelings, what could Spirit say when God took away her dearest relatives? The questioning extends over the last four elegies. But we must first look back to the elegy on her father written some years before. There, in contrast to the early elegies which lacked the Christian apotheosis, her aged father is seen as being among the Saints:

> Ah happy Soul, 'mongst Saints and Angels blest,
> Who after all his toyle, is now at rest.

In this elegy, there is no question of the rightness of death; her father is "timely mown," for he is "fully ripe." It is otherwise in the poems on the deaths of her grandchildren. There is in these a strong note of personal bereavement, which goes beyond the impersonal tone of earlier poems, and that of the period generally: there is an inclination to use "self-expression," in itself a move in the direction of later writers, in interpreting these deaths in their relation to herself. The first elegy is on Elizabeth who died at the age of one and a half. It is incidentally one of the finest elegies in American literature. Her she admits in keeping with dogma that her heart was set too much on one who was after all only one of God's creatures:

> Farewel dear babe, my hearts too much content,
> Farewel sweet babe, the pleasure of mine eye,
> Farewel fair flower that for a space was lent,
> Then ta'en away unto Eternity.

She concludes the stanza with a conventional question:

> Blest babe why should I once bewail thy fate,
> Or sigh the dayes so soon were terminate;
> Sith thou art setled in an Everlasting state.

This should lead into a conventional Christian apotheosis, but the problem for Anne Bradstreet is that she cannot properly, i.e. dogmatically, answer the question. She answers it by stating how she really feels instead of how she *should* feel. The reply is closer to Herrick and the Cavaliers than to most Puritan poetry:

> By nature Trees do rot when they are grown.
> And Plumbs and Apples throughly ripe do fall,
> And Corn and grass are in their season mown,
> And time brings down what is both strong and tall.
> But plants new set to be eradicate,
> And buds new blown, to have so short a date . . .

How can she end the stanza? How can she retreat from this approach to criticism of God who orders all things? Only by saying it is God's will. So she concludes, not by joy in the Christian transformation, but by a backing down from her near-criticism of the deity, and says that the taking away of this fair flower "is by his hand alone that guides nature and fate."[12]

The elegy on the next dead grandchild is a fairly conventional one, concluding properly:

> Farewel dear child, thou ne're shall come to me,
> But yet a while, and I shall go to thee;
> Mean time my throbbing heart's chear'd up with this
> Thou with thy Saviour art in endless bliss.

But when the third grandchild, Simon, died that same year at the age of one month, she once more came closer to expressing her strong feelings:

> No sooner come, but gone, and fal'n asleep,
> Acquaintance short, yet parting caus'd us weep,
> Three flours, two scarcely blown, the last i'th 'bud,
> Cropt by th' Almighties hand . . .

Thus she lists in seemingly objective fashion what has happened. Continuing the burden of her earlier poem on Elizabeth, which implies regret that "buds new blown" should "have so short a date," these lines also imply that something is wrong. And the lines which follow convert this statement into irony, for they dwell on the goodness and power of God:

> Cropt by th' Almighties hand; yet is he good,
> With dreadful awe before him let's be mute,
> Such was his will, but why, let's not dispute,
> With humble hearts and mouths put in the dust,
> Let's say he's merciful as well as just.

Merely to state Puritan dogma about the power of God here after the ample description of what God has done is to question God's ways on the level of feeling. The words "Let's say" placed before "he's merciful as well as just" suggest doubt; the clause, "but why, let's not dispute" indicates there could be room for question. Anne Bradstreet is trying to stifle her doubt and grief by a statement of dogma. That she was aware of the irony at some level is perhaps shown by the fact that the rest of the poem is spent in a quiet settling down to a conventional and innocuous statement:

> He will return, and make up all our losses,
> And smile again, after our bitter crosses.
> Go, pretty babe, go rest with Sisters twain
> Among the blest in endless joyes remain.

Her last dated poem, the poem on the death of the mother of the children, is also conventional.

Of more interest in showing the final real outcome of the dialogue of Flesh and Spirit is the poem written in the summer of 1669, usually called "A Pilgrim." It was composed in the same summer as the conventional and world-weary poem on the death of her second grandchild. In it she considers the loss of the flesh itself, that is her own earthly life. Here the Flesh has already lost out; there is no internal conflict; only the inconveniences of the Flesh are considered:

> This body shall in silence sleep
> Mine eyes no more shall ever weep

> No fainting fits shall me assaile
> nor grinding paines my body fraile
> With cares and fears ne'r cumbred be
> Nor losses know, nor sorrowes see.

There is joyous acceptance of the promise of immortality:

> What tho my flesh shall there consume
> it is the bed Christ did perfume
> And when a few yeares shall be gone
> this mortall shall be cloth'd upon
> A Corrupt Carcasse downe it lyes
> a glorious body it shall rise.
> In weaknes and dishonour sowne
> in power 'tis rais'd by Christ alone
> The soule and body shall unite
> and of their maker have the sight
> Such lasting ioyes shall there behold
> as eare ne'r heard nor tongue e'er told
> Lord make me ready for that day
> then Come deare bridgrome Come away.

In the final analysis the spirit wins because it can outlast the flesh, and the individual submits to the loss of the flesh and the hope of the resurrection because he must. As when she first came into the country, Anne Bradstreet was always willing to submit to the inevitable during her long pilgrimage, but she did it only after using the full faculties of the soul— the imagination, the affections, and the will—and it is this clash of feeling and dogma that keeps her poetry alive. True, her tension is often resolved, and it is without the darkness, alienation, and disorder that grows out of the tension in later American writers. But Anne Bradstreet went as far as her place in a society which condemned Anne Hutchinson and Anne Hopkins would allow. And in this respect she sets the tone for a long line of American writers who would follow her, who could press farther against the limitations of society, who would express what D. H. Lawrence has called the "duplicity" of the American literary mind. These writers—men such as Cooper, Hawthorne, and Melville—according to Lawrence own "a tight mental allegiance to a morality which all their passion goes to destroy."[13] No better description could be found for the poetry of Anne Bradstreet.

As a Puritan, Anne Bradstreet came to accept her struggles as part of the condition of the saint. Her resolution of her doubts and the importance of the Puritan themes in her poetry are analyzed in Robert D. Richardson, "The Puritan Poetry of Anne Bradstreet," Texas Studies in Literature and Language, *IX (1967). More complete studies of her life and work are Elizabeth Wade White,* Anne Bradstreet, "The Tenth Muse" *(New York, 1971) and Ann Stanford,* Anne Bradstreet: The Worldly Puritan. An Introduction to Her Poetry *(New York, 1974).*

Notes

1. Marius Bewley, "Fenimore Cooper and the Economic Age," *American Literature*, XXVI, 166-195 (May, 1954).

2. Leon Howard, *Literature and the American Tradition* (Garden City, N. Y., 1960), ch. VI.

3. Henry Bamford Parkes, *The Pragmatic Test* (San Francisco, 1941, 3-38).

4. D. H. Lawrence, *Studies in Classic American Literature* (Garden City, N. Y., 1951).

5. Richard Chase, *The American Novel and Its Tradition* (Garden City, N. Y., 1957), ch. I.

6. *The Works of Anne Bradstreet in Prose and Verse*, edited by John Harvard Ellis (Charlestown, Mass., 1867), 5. All quotations from Anne Bradstreet's work cited in this essay are from this source.

7. John Winthrop, *The History of New England from 1630 to 1649*, edited by James Savage (Boston, 1826), II, 216.

8. Thomas Parker, *The Coppy of a Letter Written . . . to His Sister* (London, 1650), 13. Quoted from Edmund S. Morgan, "Puritan Love and Marriage," *More Books*, 44-45 (Feb., 1942).

9. The place of women in Puritan domestic relations is discussed in William and Malleville Haller, "The Puritan Art of Love," *Huntington Library Quarterly*, V, 235-272 (1941-1942), and in William Haller, " 'Hail Wedded Love,' " *English Literary History*, XIII, 79-97 (1946).

10. Morgan, 49.

11. Anne Bradstreet is here using a paraphrase of Hebrews xi:4 in which Abel by faith "being dead yet speaketh." This phrase, according to Harrison T. Meserole, was often used by Puritan writers to justify the publication of works not to gain worldly fame, but for the "fame in heaven" of Milton's *Lycidas*. Anne Bradstreet is using the phrase here, however, to refer to earthly remembrance.

12. Kenneth B. Murdock in Robert E. Spiller *et al.*, *Literary History of the United States* (New York, 1953), 64, notes of this poem that "Anne Bradstreet realizes that she is perilously close to writing rebelliously against God's decrees. She pulls herself up in the last line."

13. Quoted by Chase, 9.

17 THE ART AND INSTRUCTION OF JONATHAN EDWARDS'S PERSONAL NARRATIVE

DANIEL B. SHEA, JR.

One of the most important literary activities in Puritan society was the composition of diaries and autobiographies. Next to the sermon, these were the most didactic efforts of Puritan writers. Both the great and the humble kept diaries, which offer informative glimpses into the daily concerns of Puritan settlers. Diaries customarily charted their authors' spiritual progress and at the same time preserved a record of their perceptions of human frailty and God's graciousness. In addition to serving this autodidactic function, the diaries provided raw material for the composition of autobiographies designed to edify the writer's children and often a wider audience.

Jonathan Edwards, a leader of the eighteenth-century Great Awakening, was a careful student of man's progress toward grace. In treatises on Original Sin, Freedom of the Will, and the Religious Affections he addressed the general questions of the nature and destiny of man. His autobiography, analyzed below, was a carefully structured narrative of his personal experience designed to supplement his more theoretical works.

Although the first editor of Jonathan Edwards's *Personal Narrative* described this spiritual autobiography as written for "private Advantage," he also seems to have felt that Edwards had given him implicit permission to make the document serve a public purpose. The sometimes baffling resemblance between authentic and fraudulent spirituality was, said Samuel Hopkins, "a point about which, above many other[s], the protestant world is in the dark, and needs instruction, as Mr. Edwards was more and more convinced, the longer he lived; and which he was wont frequently to observe in conversation."[1] As Hopkins was aware, Edwards's essential act throughout a large body of his published work had been to set nature apart from supernature in the domain of religious experience. The act was no less central to the *Personal Narrative* than it was to other works in which its author promoted experimental religion and instructed readers on its glories and pitfalls.

In the controversy between himself and opposers of the Great Awakening, Edwards had put to good use his accounts of the gracious experience of Abigail Hutchinson, Phebe Bartlett, and his own wife Sarah. But a narrative told in the first person, as Sarah's had been originally,[2] was immensely more valuable to his cause than even the best job of evangelistic reporting. Let the reporter be a "true saint," said Edwards, he can only judge "outward manifestations and appearances," a method "at best uncertain, and liable to deceit."[3] No such objection could have been made against his *Account* of the life of David Brainerd, in which Edwards allowed the Indian missionary's diary to speak for itself. A reader's view of "what passed in [Brainerd's] *own heart*" would thus be cleared of such obstacles as an impercipient narrator; yet the reader would be in the hands of a perfectly reliable guide. As a student, Brainerd may have been rash in remarking that one of his Yale tutors had "no more grace than this chair," but Edwards could only praise the discretion he revealed when considering "the various exercises of *his own mind*":

> He most accurately distinguished between real, solid piety, and enthusiasm; between those affections that are rational and scriptural—having their foundation in light and judgment—and those that are founded in whimsical conceits, strong impressions on the imagination, and vehement emotions of the animal spirits.[4]

In the *Personal Narrative* Edwards had performed exactly those functions for which in 1749 he was praising Brainerd. Both men gave their readers, as Edwards said of Brainerd, an "opportunity to see a confirmation of the truth, efficacy, and amiableness of the religion taught, in the practice of the same persons who have most clearly and forcibly taught it."[5]

Because Edwards could not have introduced his own autobiography in such glowing terms, Samuel Hopkins admiringly supplied the deficit in 1765. But set next to the cautious distinction-making of the narrative itself, his words were superfluous. Since the manuscript of the *Personal Narrative* is lost, we shall never know just how much care Edwards took in composing it. In fact, the text printed by Hopkins gives the appearance of hurried writing.[6] But if Edwards spent only a day with his spiritual autobiography, he had spent twenty years or more arriving at the criteria by which he judged his experience. It is possible, of course, that we read precision back into the *Personal Narrative* after watching the author at work in, say, the *Treatise Concerning Religious Affections*, but the distinction between autobiography and formal argument, especially for an eighteenth-century New England divine, should not be exaggerated. Edwards's narrative is not identical with his spiritual experience but represents a mature articulation of that experience, its form and language determined in varying degrees by the author's reading of sacred and secular writers, interviews with awakened sinners, and his concerns at the time of composition. The Edwards of the *Personal Narrative* bears more resemblance to the author of the *Religious Affections* than to the young student at Yale who entered the perplexing data of daily spiritual upheavals in his diary.[7]

Once it is accepted, then, that Edwards set down his spiritual autobiography with more than "private Advantage" in mind, the *Personal Narrative* can be seen as governed by the purposes that informed most of his work during the period of the Great Awakening. By narrative example he will teach what is false and what is true in religious experience, giving another form to the argument he carried on elsewhere;

and he hopes actually to affect his readers by both the content and the presentation of his exemplary experience.

I

Something of what Edwards was trying to accomplish in the *Personal Narrative* emerges from a comparison with the *Diary*, which he kept regularly from the last year of his studies at Yale until his settlement in Northampton. The two are profitably read together, but not as if they formed a continuous and coherent piece of writing. A sense of their separate identities is necessary, not only to preserve the distinction that the *Diary* instructed Edwards alone, while the *Personal Narrative* extends and formalizes its instruction, but also because Edwards was bound to tell his story differently after twenty additional years of introspection and a good deal of pastoral experience. In 1723, for instance, he was greatly troubled by "not having experienced conversion in those particular steps, wherein the people of New England, and anciently the Dissenters of Old England, used to experience it."[8] Subsequent events, however, revealed a great variety in the Sprirt's operations, so that in 1741 Edwards allowed that a given work might be from the Spirit even though it represented a "deviation from what has hitherto been usual, let it be never so great."[9] He may even have reached by this time the more radical conclusion, announced in the *Religious Affections*, that although Satan can only counterfeit the Spirit's saving operations, he has power to imitate exactly the order in which they are supposed to appear (pp. 158-159). In any case, the *Personal Narrative* reveals no more brooding on Edwards's part over the absence of "particular steps."

The *Diary* exhibits, in general, considerably more doubt, sometimes approaching despair, than could be inferred from an isolated reading of the *Personal Narrative*. Periods of spiritual crisis were marked by such tortured complaints as: "This week I found myself so far gone, that it seemed to me I should never recover more"; and "Crosses of the nature of that, which I met with this week, thrust me quite below all comforts in religion."[10] There are, in addition, all the entries in which, as a kind of running theme, Edwards agonizes over dead, dull, and listless frames of mind. The *Personal Narrative* reflects little of the intensity or number of these entries. Edwards mentions only that at New Haven he "sunk in Religion" as a result of being diverted by affairs; and in a subsequent paragraph he rounds off a similar recollection with the comment that these "various Exercises . . . would be tedious to relate" (pp. 32-33).

The difference between the two versions is striking, yet understandable, if we assume that as Edwards grew in his assurance of grace, these drier seasons lost, in recollection, their original impact. But since he seems to have consulted his diary as he wrote ("And my Refuge and Support was in Contemplations on the heavenly State; as I find in my Diary of *May* 1,1723"), it is more likely that deletions and new emphases were intentional—the choice, for example, to minimize emotions arising from dulness and insensibility in a narrative intended to be affecting. The lingering memory of his uncle Hawley's suicide in 1735 would certainly have enforced Edwards's decision:

> He had been for a Considerable Time Greatly Concern'd about the Condition of his soul; till, by the ordering of a sovereign Providence he was suffered to fall into deep melancholly, a distemper that the Family are very Prone to; he was much overpowered by it; the devil took the advantage & drove him into despairing thoughts.[11]

Whatever the proximate reason, Edwards felt strongly enough about the dangers of melancholy to edit out any hint of it in the record of his conversion experience, just as in the preface to Brainerd's memoirs he forewarned readers that melancholy was the sole imperfection in an otherwise exemplary man, and just as in his *Thoughts* on the revival of 1740-1742 he excepted melancholy as the "one case, wherein the truth ought to be withheld from sinners in distress of conscience."[12] It was sufficient for readers to know that a Slough of Despond existed, the foul and miry by-product, as John Bunyan explained, of conviction of sin. Nothing was to be gained, and much would be risked, by bringing on stage the youth who once found himself "overwhelmed with melancholy."[13]

Seen from another point of view, the youth of the *Diary* might by the very miserableness of his seeking illustrate an important lesson. The characteristic of the *Diary* which the author of the *Personal Narrative* apparently found most repugnant was its tendency toward spiritual self-reliance. For even as he reminded himself that effort was ineffectual without grace, the young diarist had also been busy drawing up his "Resolutions," seventy of them eventually. In the *Personal Narrative*, Edwards reached back twenty years to untangle these cross purposes, simplifying his experience somewhat as he fitted it for instruction. Spiritual industry could not be despised; its products were real and of value: "I was brought wholly to break off all former wicked Ways, and all Ways of known outward Sin." What had to be emphasized was that the sum of resolutions and bonds and religious duties was not salvation. Edwards spoke beyond the limits of his own case when he concluded, "But yet it seems to me, I sought after a miserable manner: Which has made me some times since to question, whether ever it issued in that which was saving; being ready to doubt, whether such miserable seeking was ever succeeded."[14]

II

While the pattern that emerges from Edwards's reshaping of some of the materials of his diary helps suggest the more formal, public nature of the autobiography, the later document represents in most ways a fresh beginning on the analysis of his spiritual experience. The first sentence of the *Personal Narrative* reveals Edwards's anxiety to get at major issues, prefacing the entire narrative with a declaration that nearly sums it up:

> I Had a variety of Concerns and Exercises about my Soul from my Childhood; but had two more remarkable Seasons of Awakening, before I

met with that Change, by which I was brought to those new Dispositions, and that new Sense of Things, that I have since had.

A Northampton reader ought not to have missed the distinctions being made, or the ascending order of importance in the three clauses. Certainly he would have known that in the 1735 awakening more than 300 persons appeared to have been "savingly brought home to Christ," but that in the minister's *Faithful Narrative* of the work he had dismissed some as "wolves in sheep's clothing," while discovering in those for whom he was more hopeful "a new sense of things, new apprehensions and views of God, of the divine attributes." For the reader of shorter memory, who might have withdrawn from a battle he thought won at an early age, Edwards was ready at the end of the paragraph to deny that a boy who prayed five times a day in secret, who abounded in "religious Duties," and whose affections were "lively and easily moved" had anything of grace in him. He had already explained in "A Divine and Supernatural Light" (1734) that emotions raised by the story of Christ's sufferings or by a description of heaven might be no different in kind from those elicited by a tragedy or a romance.[15] And it was unnecessary to introduce psychology here, since the course of the narrative itself revealed the nature of these early affections. In time, Edwards says, they "wore off," and he "returned like a Dog to his Vomit." It was characteristic of him not to hesitate in applying a text (Proverbs 26:11) to himself, but he may already have conceived an extended application for this simile. In 1746, after his last awakening had ebbed, he used the same expression in charging that persons "who seemed to be mightily raised and swallowed with joy and zeal, for a while, seem to have returned like the dog to his vomit."[16]

When Edwards testifies that a sickness so grave it seemed God "shook me over the Pit of Hell" had only a passing effect on resolution, the implication is undoubtedly both personal and general. The emotion aroused by this image could have no other name but terror, but at almost the same time that he preached "Sinners in the Hands of an Angry God" (1741), he was disclosing that terror had been irrelevant in his own experience. Whatever moved him in his New Haven years, "it never seemed to be proper to express my Concern that I had, by the name of Terror" (p. 24). Thus an important distinction was laid down. The experience of terror gave no cause for self-congratulation, since there were persons, like the younger Edwards, "that have frightful apprehensions of hell . . . who at the same time seem to have very little proper enlightenings of conscience, really convincing them of their sinfulness of heart and life."[17]

Edwards's technique through the intitial paragraphs of the *Personal Narrative* is to separate the "I" of the narrative from his present self and to characterize the younger "I" as a less reliable judge of spiritual experience than the mature narrator. Thus, Edwards the boy takes much "self-righteous" pleasure in his performance of religious duties, or Edwards the young man seeks salvation as the "main Business" of his life, unaware that his manner of seeking is "miserable." Soon the reader must adjust his attitude even more carefully, for the mature Edwards will begin to describe genuinely gracious experience, while the "I" remains largely ignorant of what has happened. Edwards compiles sufficient evidence for a reader to draw his own conclusions from the passage, but subordinates himself to the mind of a youth who was not yet ready to draw conclusions when he says, "But it never came into my Thought, that there was any thing spiritual, or of a saving Nature in this" (p. 25).

One reason for so oblique an approach may be traced, not to the autobiographer's ignorance of his subject, but to the pastor's close acquaintance with the hypocrite, a brash, colloquial figure who appears often in the *Religious Affections*, drawn no doubt from models near at hand. That part of Edwards's purpose which was public and exemplary dictated that he give a wide margin to the "bold, familiar and appropriating language" of those who condemned themselves by announcing, " 'I know I shall go to heaven, as well as if I were there; I know that God is now manifesting himself to my soul, and is now smiling upon me' " (pp. 170-171). At the same time, Edwards remains faithful to personal experience, accurately reflecting the uncertainty and inconclusiveness he could see in his diary; and by preserving intact the uncertain young man he provided a character with whom readers similarly perplexed could identify.

The evidence that counters and overwhelms the disclaimers attached to these paragraphs emerges from the history Edwards gives of his assent to the doctrine of God's sovereignty. Even after childhood, his mind, which was "full of Objections," and his heart, which found the doctrine "horrible," had struggled against accepting the notion that God in his sovereign pleasure should choose to save some and leave the rest to be "everlastingly tormented in Hell." Suddenly and inexplicably the objections had evaporated, but at the time Edwards found it impossible to describe "how, or by what Means." Only the effects were clear: "I saw further, and my Reason apprehended the Justice and Reasonableness of it" (p. 25). Because the next and most significant stage of his conviction deserved separate treatment, Edwards is content for the moment to imply its essential difference: the doctrine that was now reasonable would later appear "exceeding pleasant, bright and sweet." In short, common grace had assisted natural principles by removing prejudices and illuminating the truth of the doctrine; saving grace had infused a new spiritual foundation that underlay a wholly different mode of perception through the "new sense" or "sense of the heart" that characterized genuinely spiritual experience.[18]

III

How far Edwards surpassed his Puritan predecessors in the art of uniting instruction with spiritual autobiography, the one reasoned and objective, the other felt and subjective, appears most impressively when he begins to document the experience of the "new man." As he relives the first instance of an "inward, sweet Delight in GOD and divine Things," his prose rises gradually to a high pitch of joyous emotion, sustained by characteristic repetitions and parallelisms and by an aspiring and exultant vocabulary. The paragraph takes its shape so naturally that one nearly overlooks the emergence of relationships that received their fullest elaboration in the *Religious Affections*. Edwards's first ejaculation, "how excellent a Being that was," is a response to the first objective ground of gracious affections, "the transcendently excellent and amiable nature of divine things." When he continues, "and how happy I should be, if I might enjoy that GOD and be wrapt up to GOD in Heaven, and be as it were swallowed up in Him," he proceeds according to the order of true saints, whose apprehension of the excellency of divine things "is the foundation of the joy that they have afterwards, in the consideration of their being theirs." The affections of hypocrites, on the other hand, are aroused in a contrary order; they find themselves "made so much of by God" that "he seems in a sort, lovely to them."[19]

To make clear the order of his own affections became crucial as he went on to report his visions, "or fix'd Ideas and imaginations." He ran the risk, after all, of becoming a chief exhibit in the case against enthusiasm should his narrative have fallen into the wrong hands. Nevertheless, when judging experiences similar to his own he was satisfied that lively imaginations could arise from truly gracious affections; and in adding, "through the infirmity of human nature,"[20] he claimed less for his "visions" than some who read him later. Class distinctions and hierarchies in spiritual experience held little interest for him, because all distinctions resolved finally into the ultimate one between the old and the new man. It was less difficult, however, to point out what was not spiritual experience, even in personal narrative, than it was to render the perceptions of the "new sense" with an instrument so imperfect as human language and so indiscriminate in itself as to be the common property of both spiritual and natural men. Moreover, narrative prose was only Edwards's second choice to convey what he felt. Insofar as the medium approached anything like satisfactory expression it was by compromise with another that seemed more natural: "to sing or chant forth my Meditations; to speak my Thoughts in Soliloquies, and speak with a singing Voice." In admitting that the "inward ardor" of his soul "could not freely flame out as it would," Edwards reconciled himself to one kind of defeat, but the attempt, if skilfully managed, might prove affecting to others.

The impossible aim Edwards set for himself in the *Personal Narrative* was to articulate his new delight in "things of religion" for readers who could have "no more Notion or idea" of it than he had as a boy, no more "than one born blind has of pleasant and beautiful Colours." He might have taken solace in the consideration that since all expression was in this case equally imperfect, any expression would do. The prose of the *Personal Narrative* deserves respect to the degree that he refused to avail himself of this consolation or to accept language that by this time flowed easily from his pen. Edwards's continual use of the word "sweet," for instance, points up some of the difficulty of judging his art and rhetorical effectiveness in the narrative. If the word seems at one moment to derive from a sensationalist vocabulary, we may regard it use as part of his unique project to make Lockean psychology serve the interests of experimental religion. Simply through repetition the word tends to gather to itself all the sensible difference Edwards was trying to express when he said that the easily moved affections of his youth "did not arise from any Sight of the divine Excellency of the Things of GOD; or any Taste of the Soul-satisfying and Life-giving Good, there is in them." But Edwards's reading of Locke only added new significance to scriptural passages long familiar to him. In the *Religious Affections* he refers the reader to Psalm 119 for a striking representation of "the beauty and sweetness of holiness as the grand object of a spiritual taste" (p. 260), and goes on to paraphrase verse 103 ("How sweet are thy words unto my taste! Yea, sweeter than honey to my mouth"). In this light he appears only to be indulging in the kind of reverent plagiarism common to many spiritual autobiographies of the period, among them that of Sarah Edwards.[21]

Occasionally, too, Edwards declines the full potential of personal narrative by taking over, with little change, passages from his 1737 account of Northampton conversions, making them his own by the mechanical act of altering the pronoun. He could not have avoided reporting that in his own experience, as in that of the converts, "the Appearance of every thing was altered"; but he expands the point by again simply listing natural phenomena over which the "new sense" played, without vitalizing and re-viewing them through personal expression: "God's Excellency, his Wisdom, his Purity and Love, seemed to appear in every Thing; in the Sun, Moon and Stars; in the Clouds, and blue Sky; in the Grass, Flowers, Trees; in the Water, and all Nature; which used greatly to fix my Mind."[22] However, when Edwards dramatizes a new kind of perception and so involves divine attributes with natural phenomena that abstraction is made vivid and concrete, he begins to communicate something of what it was to confront nature as, in the strictest sense, a new beholder:

> I used to be a Person uncommonly terrified with Thunder: and it used to strike me with Terror, when I saw a Thunder-storm rising. But now, on the contrary, it rejoyced me. I Felt GOD at the first Appearance of a Thunder-storm. And used to take the Opportunity, at such Times, to fix myself to view the Clouds, and see the Lightnings play, and hear the majestick & awful Voice of God's Thunder: which often times was exceeding entertaining, leading me to sweet Contemplations of my great and glorious GOD. (p. 27)

Taken together, these successive views of nature in its placid and then terrible beauty would adumbrate the symmetry of the divine attributes. Edwards noted as much in another manuscript not published in his lifetime,[23] but the narrative of his conversion imposed special conditions on viewing "shadows of divine things." When he scrutinized his own spiritual "estate," it was absolutely necessary that he be able to acknowledge a view of God's loveliness and majesty in conjunction, for even "wicked men and devils" were sensible of His "mighty power and awful majesty." Against the background of the recent awakening Edwards was moved to observe in the *Religious Affections* that "too much weight has been laid, by many persons of late, on discoveries of God's greatness, awful majesty, and natural perfection . . . without any real view of the holy, lovely majesty of God" (p. 265). To express the ideal vision in the *Personal Narrative*, Edwards chose the language of theological paradox over that of sensationalism, although we do hear symmetry and can observe the proportion Edwards maintains through a dexterous manipulation of his terms. The passage also reveals an infiltration into prose of the "singing voice," whose rhythms were still alive in the memory, inseparable from the experience that originally provoked them:

> And as I was walking there, and looked up on the Sky and Clouds; there came into my Mind, a sweet Sense of the glorious Majesty and Grace of GOD, that I know not how to express. I seemed to see them both in a sweet Conjunction: Majesty and Meekness join'd together: it was a sweet and gentle, and holy Majesty; and also a majestic Meekness; an awful Sweetness; a high, and great, and holy Gentleness. (p. 26)

Through heightened paradox the unawakened reader might be brought to see dimly and to seek the same sense of God's natural and moral pefections balanced and intermingled with each other. Edwards strove to make the path clearer and more inviting as well when he singled out for relatively extensive treatment that which constituted "in a peculiar manner the beauty of the divine nature." At its center the *Personal Narrative* focuses on the experiential realization that holiness is the divine attribute which primarily elicits the love of the true saint. God's underived holiness could not, of course, be encompassed by words; it could only be loved. But the holiness of creatures, deriving from the divine object of their love, yielded to definition in the *Religious Affections* as "the moral image of God in them, which is their beauty" (p. 258).

In the *Personal Narrative*, Edwards had already embodied the relationship between the holiness of God and the holiness of man in two successive and integrally related "moral images." The first describes the soul as "a Field or Garden of GOD," its multitude of flowers representative of individual moral excellencies. Since holiness comprehends all these excellencies, as its beauty sums up their individual loveliness, Edwards closes in immediately on a single consummate flower:

> . . . such a little white Flower, as we see in the Spring of the Year; low and humble on the Ground, opening its Bosom, to receive the pleasant Beams of the Sun's Glory; rejoycing as it were, in a calm Rapture; diffusing around a sweet Fragrancy; standing peacefully and lovingly, in the midst of other Flowers round about; all in like Manner opening their Bosoms, to drink in the Light of the Sun. (pp. 29-30)

Each felt quality that Edwards noted in his perception of holiness— "Purity, Brightness, Peacefulness & Ravishment to the Soul"—finds its correspondent physical detail in the image. The life of the flower, as it drinks in light and sustenance from the sun and returns its own fragrance, is the life of grace, continuous in God and the regenerate man; and the second image is finally enlarged to the scope of the first to include a fellowship of saints. Edwards's tendency toward pathetic fallacy, the flower's "rejoycing as it were, in a calm rapture," only reminds the reader that this is personal narrative and not an exercise in typology.

IV

Not every sight to which the "new sense" gave access evoked an ecstasy of joy. Acuteness of spiritual perception could also compel disgust and nausea when eyes seeing for the first time began to search the depths of one's depravity. So hideous a view as Edwards reported would have taxed any vocabulary, but his own had so far been richest and most novel when he expressed the affection of love. For this other task he might have been forced to depend entirely upon the communal vocabulary of Calvinists vis-à-vis man's corruption had his sensitivity to language not intervened. Edwards's awareness of the problems involved in verbal self-chastisement compares with that of his fictional fellow minister, Arthur Dimmesdale, who found that he could excoriate himself as the "vilest of sinners," not only with impunity but with the ironic dividend of being revered the more for his sanctity. Regardless of their denotative content, formulary expressions, given wide currency, were quickly emptied of meaning—as Edwards well knew from his experience with hypocrites, men fluent in "very bad expressions which they use about themselves . . . and we must believe that they are thus humble, and see themselves so vile, upon the credit of their say so."[24]

Even when Edwards is most likely to suggest to present-day readers an inverse pride in his corruption rather than the "evangelical humility" (the sixth sign of gracious affections) he hoped he had, we discover that a problem of language is at the root of the difficulty. It is not the rank of "chief of sinners" that he covets, nor is Edwards vying with his fellow townsmen for a place in the last ring of hell when he rejects their expression, "as bad as the Devil himself," because it seemed "exceeding faint and feeble, to represent my Wickedness." The full text of this passage, as printed by Hopkins, makes clear that Edwards is in fact rejecting language he thought inadequately proportioned to its object:

> I thought I should wonder, that they should content themselves with such Expressions as these, if I had any Reason to imagine, that their Sin bore any Proportion to mine. It seemed to me, I should wonder at my self, if I should express *my* Wickedness in such feeble Terms as they did. (p. 37)

The rationale that lies behind Edwards's greater dissatisfaction with attempts to convey a sense of his wickedness than with parallel attempts to express his delight in divine things is given fully in the *Religious Affections*. There Edwards explained that to the saint the deformity of the least sin must outweigh the greatest beauty in his holiness, because sin against an infinite God is infinitely corrupt, while holiness cannot be infinite in a creature (p. 326). No expression, then, could take the measure of infinite corruption, but before accepting a simile that only traded on the reputation of Satan, Edwards preferred to draw on the resources of his own rhetoric. He begins by bringing together two images that suggest physical immensity, and then associates them with the key word "infinite," which is extracted at last from its concrete associations and made to reproduce itself rhythmically:

My Wickedness, as I am in my self, has long appear'd to me perfectly inef-
fable, and infinitely swallowing up all Thought and Imagination; like an infinite Deluge, or infinite Mountains over my Head. I know not how to express better, what my Sins appear to me to be, than by heaping Infinite upon
Infinite, and multiplying Infinite by Infinite. I go about very often, for this
many Years, with these Expressions in my Mind, and in my Mouth, "Infinite
upon Infinite. Infinite upon Infinite!" (p. 37)

Even if he had improved on pallid representations of wickedness, Edwards only pushed the question one step further. Did the improvement
arise from a greater conviction of sin or from a natural ability in prose
expression? Just how rigorously Edwards dealt with himself in answering
such questions appears in a subsequent reflection that immediately
dissipated any complacency in mere verbal skill: "And yet, I ben't in the
least inclined to think, that I have a greater Conviction of Sin than ordinary. It seems to me, my Conviction of Sin is exceeding small, and
faint." Typically enough, his ruthlessness here is a double-edged sword
that also cuts away from himself. As a public document, the *Personal
Narrative* might only provide hypocrites with a new model for their
deceptions, a thesaurus of expressions (such as "infinite upon infinite")
that proclaimed conviction or other classic signs of grace. Edwards could
not prevent a prostitution of his narrative, but he knew that the
hypocrite found it difficult to claim anything in small amounts, and he
would explain in the *Religious Affections* how mimicry eventually con-
founded itself:

But no man that is truly under great convictions, thinks his conviction great
in proportion to his sin. For if he does, 'tis a certain sign that he inwardly
thinks his sins small. And if that be the case, that is a certain evidence that his
conviction is small. And this, by the way, is the main reason, that persons
when under a work of humiliation, are not sensible of it, in the time of it.[25]

Simultaneously, then, Edwards convinces the reader that his self-
scrutiny has been unremittingly honest, while he offers instruction that is
meticulous in its distinctions and affecting in its language. The *Personal
Narrative* is relatively brief, set against Cotton Mather's *Diary* or John
Bunyan's *Grace Abounding;* but it is not incomplete. Like all auto-
biographers, secular or spiritual, Edwards fashioned a coherent narrative
by using his total experience selectively; we judge it incomplete only by
our curiousity about the interior life of his last harrowing years. He
could scracely have added a word to the experiential summing-up of all
he ever thought on all that finally mattered.

*Edwards was a pastor and theologian, not a poet. Yet in his efforts to
communicate he drew extensively upon the recognized stylistic devices
of his time. Like Anne Bradstreet and Edward Johnson, Edwards was
influenced by the same currents of thought that produced Donne,
Shakespeare, Milton, and Bunyan. All employed similar literary and
analytical tools, though not always with the same skill. It is important
to remember that the same Puritans who struggled against the*

wilderness and the Indians, and against their own darker impulses, at the same time helped to shape the American literary imagination.

NOTES

1. *The Life and Character of the Late Reverend Mr. Jonathan Edwards* (Boston, 1765), p. iii.

2. *The Works of President Edwards: With a Memoir of His Life*, ed. Sereno E. Dwight (New York, 1829-1830), I, 171-186; hereafter cited as *Works*. Sarah's original relation was drawn up, according to Dwight, at the request of her husband. Edwards then retold her experiences as part of his attempt to vindicate experimental religion in *Some Thoughts Concerning the Present Revival of Religion* (*Works*, IV, 110-118).

3. *A Treatise Concerning Religious Affections*, ed. John E. Smith (New Haven, 1959), p. 181. All references to the *Religious Affections*, including those given parenthetically in the text, are to this edition.

4. From Edwards's "Preface" to the *Account* of Brainerd's life, "chiefly taken from his own diary and other Private Writings," *Works*, X, 29.

5. *Ibid.*, X, 27.

6. Although anthologies of American literature continue to reprint the *Personal Narrative* from the Austin (Worcester, 1808) or Dwight editions, the text printed by Hopkins in his 1765 *Life* of Edwards is clearly preferable. As was their habit, the nineteenth-century editors "improved" the style and also omitted several important passages. All my references are to the Hopkins text, but it is beyond the scope of this study to call attention to all the omissions and revisions of later editions. The indications in the Hopkins text of relatively hasty composition are: 1) the number of sentences lacking a pronominal subject ("On one Saturday Night, in particular, had a particular Discovery . . ."), more than appear in later editions; 2) redundancy of a sort that invites improvement and that Edwards might have revised himself had he taken a second look ("my Concern that I had," or the phrase just quoted). If Edwards intended to make the manuscript more fit for posthumous publication, he apparently never found time to do so.

7. It is very doubtful that the *Personal Narrative* was written after the *Religious Affections* appeared in 1746, but it might conceivably have been written as Edwards prepared the series of sermons given in 1742-1743 on which the *Religious Affections* is based. The only absolute certainty, of course, is that he did not conclude the narrative before January, 1739, the date he mentions in its final paragraph.

8. *Works*, I, 93.

9. *Ibid.*, III, 561.

10. Entries for April 7, 1723, and Sept. 12, 1724, *ibid.*, I, 84, 104.

11. *Jonathan Edwards: Representative Selections*, ed. Clarence Faust and Thomas Johnson, rev. ed. (New York, 1962), p. 83.

12. *Works*, IV, 163.

13. Entry for Jan. 17, 1723, *ibid.*, I, 81.

14. Hopkins, *Life of Edwards*, p. 24. By deleting "was" from the final phrase of this sentence, editors after Hopkins also silenced the passive voice that reminded readers, however awkwardly, whence grace originates.

15. *Works*, VI, 175-176.

16. *Religious Affections*, p. 119.

17. *Ibid.*, p. 156.

18. The full context for these distinctions may be found in the "Miscellanies" published in *The Philosophy of Jonathan Edwards From His Private Notebooks*, ed. Harvey G. Townsend (Eugene, Oregon, 1955), pp. 249-251. See especially numbers 397, 408, 628.

19. *Religious Affections*, pp. 240-250.

20. *Ibid.*, p. 291.

21. The word "sweet" is used frequently in Sarah's first person narrative.

22. The comparable passage in the *Faithful Narrative* reads: "The light and comfort which some of them enjoy . . . cause all things about them to appear as it were beautiful, sweet, and pleasant. All things abroad, the sun, moon, and stars; the clouds and sky, the heavens and earth, appear as it were with a cast of divine glory and sweetness upon them" (*Works*, IV, 50).

23. "As thunder and thunder clouds, as they are vulgarly called, have a shadow of the majesty of God, so the blue skie, the green fields, and trees, and pleasant flowers have a shadow of the mild attributes of God, viz., grace and love of God, as well as the beauteous rainbow" (*Images and Shadows of Divine Things*, ed. Perry Miller, New Haven, 1948, p. 49).

24. *Religious Affections*, pp. 316-317.

25. *Ibid.*, p. 334. The relationship between Edwards's personal experience and his public pronouncements on experience often presents interesting problems. In the passage quoted above, he almost seems to be settling for himself the question of why he could record no more conviction of sin than we find described in the *Personal Narrative*. But another cross reference, a sentence from the narrative, printed only by Hopkins, contains the essential logical distinction he employed to discuss conviction in the *Religious Affections* (pp. 323-336): "That my Sins appear to me so great, don't seem to me to be, because I have so much more Conviction of Sin than other Christians, but because I am so much worse, and have so much more Wickedness to be convinced of" (p. 37).

PART SEVEN |

DIFFUSION AND AWAKENING

The first generation of New England Puritans vigorously pursued its "errand into the wilderness." Although not everyone in the Bible Commonwealths shared the founders' religious and social fervor, a substantial majority did. And the second generation (i.e., the sons and daughters of the first wave of immigrants) apparently inherited their parents' enthusiasm, for they continued to advocate the same objectives in civil and religious life. True, the jeremiads preached by some of the clergy as early as the mid-seventeenth century insisted that there had been a tragic lapse in commitment which, if not quickly reversed, would invite God's vengeance. And in 1680 a gathering of leading lay and clerical spokesmen issued the ultimate jeremiad. "That God hath a controversy with His New England people," the Reforming Synod declared, "is undeniable, the Lord having written His displeasure in dismal characters against us." But Puritan rhetoric and New England reality did not necessarily coincide.

There is no doubt that by 1680 New England was in some ways a very different place than it had been a half century before. Most obvious was the phenomenal growth in population, partly a result of immigration, partly of high birth and low death rates. From a few thousand inhabitants in the early 1630s, New England's population swelled to about 150,000 by 1675. If nothing else, such growth meant geographic dispersal and greater economic and political complexity. It also meant a less homogeneous population, much of it impervious to Puritan social and theological prescriptions—as court records make abundantly clear. Moreover, the failure of the Puritan Revolution in England inevitably altered New England's role in the international Puritan movement and undermined many New Englanders' sense of mission. Such changes did not necessarily imply either a decline in religious zeal or a failure to observe the standards established by the first generation of Puritan settlers. But many of the clergy suspected the worst, and many historians have interpreted New England's history in the late seventeenth and early eighteenth centuries largely from the clergy's perspective.

18 | NEW ENGLAND VERSUS THE NEW ENGLAND MIND: THE MYTH OF DECLENSION

ROBERT G. POPE

Did the Puritans in the latter half of the seventeenth century stray from the religious fervor and communal ideals of the founders? Some historians argue that during the third quarter of the seventeenth century a "declension" in piety marked the effective end of Puritanism's influence, or at least the start of its decline. Other students of Puritanism, most notably Darrett B. Rutman (in Winthrop's Boston: Portrait of a Puritan Town *[Chapel Hill, N.C., 1965] and other works) contend that the decline began almost as soon as the founders arrived. Still others see Puritanism's hold on New England remaining strong, though uneven, through most of the eighteenth century. The following essay examines the controversy over "declension" and presents the results of the author's own research into trends in church membership.*

If any single concept pervades the historiography of seventeenth-century New England, it is clearly the idea of "declension." Regardless of their intellectual predispositions or their overall assessment of Puritan society, historians have agreed on one thing—New England Puritanism had fallen on bad days by the time Increase Mather brought home the new charter of 1691. Some historians have cheered the change; others have lamented it; but all have accepted it as fact.

The religious filiopietists like Leonard Bacon and Henry Martyn Dexter bemoaned the loss of purity and pointed accusing fingers at their forbears' willingness to sacrifice principle to expediency. Both men singled out the adoption of the half-way covenant in 1662 as a turning point for New England, the beginning of the innovations which had continued unto their own day.[1] More hostile secular historians, and one thinks here of the triumvirate of Adamses—Brooks, Charles Francis, and James Truslow—applauded the transformation. If their attitude toward the first generation oligarchy was ambivalent, they were openly contemptuous of the second and third generation elite and in its fall they saw the opening of a brighter new day.[2] In recent decades a far more sophisticated analysis of declension has supplanted the views of these men. In the monumental work of America's finest intellectual historian, the late Perry Miller, and that of his disciples, the dissection of the New England mind has revealed a far more subtle and complex alteration than any of their predecessors imagined.[3] Since the 1930s the history of seventeenth-century New England has been almost exclusively the province of the intellectual historian. When others intruded, they found their problems already defined and their vocabulary delimited. That in many instances the intellectual historians were remarkably gifted and perceptive men has, ironically, compounded the problem. Our wholesale devotion to the intricate process of the New England mind—something that earlier generations rarely acknowledged even existed—has given us a distorted view of New England's transformation from the world of John Winthrop into the world of Cotton Mather. We have, in effect, made New England over in the image of its literature. Swayed by the Puritans' rhetoric we have lost track of New England's realities.

Probably no other generation of Americans has had its writing scrutinized more carefully or taken more seriously. The enormous scholarly exegesis of Miller in particular has noted, explained, and amplified almost the entire corpus of Puritan literature. All other aspects of cultural and institutional change are made intelligible through this key. Unfortunately the attempt to extrapolate social history from intellectual sources has created some misconceptions about New England. For example, Solomon Stoddard is regularly enshrined in New England's pantheon for his supposed role in revitalizing Congregationalism with a daring innovation which discarded the regenerative experience and opened the church to all godly inhabitants.[4] But several Congregational ministers in Connecticut anticipated "Stoddardeanism" by at least a decade and they applied the practice far more successfully than Stoddard himself had in Northampton. A generation before Stoddard and Mather filled the Boston presses with tracts on church membership and sacraments, Connecticut churches faced and resolved the same issues.[5] But Connecticut's innovators have been relegated to historical limbo because they failed to leave behind the theological literature upon which historians have reconstructed New England.

Obviously history cannot be divorced from the realm of ideas without rendering it as sterile as an accountant's ledger. But when intellectual history attempts to interpret social change it must occasionally look to the external realities. When these are ignored the basis for the critical judgment of ideas is lost. The interpretation of New England Puritanism that has emerged in the last two decades reveals the dangers of extrapolation and suggests that historians need to reread the literature of Puritanism in a new light.

The traditional portrait of New England's declension depicts a period of increasing religious apathy—a spiritual deadness and loss of piety which was manifested in steadily declining church membership. That stream of new saints envisioned by the founding generation simply failed to materialize in the free air of the new world. The ministers, in order to cope with the threat this represented to the continued institutional life of the churches and their own influence in the community, supposedly devised a succession of innovations which made church membership more easily attainable. These innovations not only compromised the original toughness and intellectual integrity of the first generation, but also contributed to further attenuation of religious zeal.[6]

Foremost on the list of innovations is the half-way covenant, the change in polity which permitted baptized but unconverted children of the saints to retain partial membership and have their own children baptized.[7] Virtually everyone accepts the thesis that the churches immediately filled with half-way members who found their limited status completely satisfactory and would have been incapable of attaining full church membership had they desired it. Two decades later, in the face of continuing decline, the ministers compromised again with the mass covenant renewal, first for church members and then for the entire community, hoping vainly to achieve through a communal rite what apparently lay beyond the power of individuals.[8] To fill their churches ministers cheapened the covenant beyond recognition and it was left to Solomon Stoddard to tell the emperor he had no clothes. Once the historian has absorbed the contemporary Puritan literature, with Miller's aid, he finds all around him obvious examples which reinforce the impression of declension. The half-way covenant, the mass covenant renewals, the admission of strangers into the covenant, all become indices of a weakened religious life. That John Cotton would have scorned them and that later generations were uncomfortable in their apostasy are ample proofs that they are, de facto, declension.

Three basic objections can be raised to this portrait of declension: first, it assumes that at some point the Puritans achieved an ideal intellectual and social system; secondly, the term itself is value laden; and finally, it misrepresents the realities of Massachusetts history.

In *The New England Mind* Miller first recreates the Puritan's all-encompassing world view, and then he details the demise of that view and the creation of a New England provincial mentality. For Miller, the transformation began in the late 1640's, accelerated with the Half-Way Synod (in fact, he calls 1662 the end of the medieval mind in America),[9] and then hurtled toward its nadir in the first decades of the eighteenth century. More recently, in a detailed study of Boston, Darrett Rutman has suggested that the process of declension began very early and was almost fully accomplished by Winthrop's death in 1649.[10] As we gradually push the beginnings of declension back toward the founding of the colony, we reveal the inadequacy of the concept. If decline began when John Winthrop and his fellow travellers stepped ashore from the *Arbella* and transformed the idea into reality (and this seems the logical conclusion), then all we are saying is that from the very start Puritans adapted and changed to fit the environment. The only absolute from which they declined was a theoretical one and that may exist only in that twentieth-century imaginative construct called "the New England mind."

The term itself suggests the imposition of a set of values on the historical context. Declension implies a retrogression or fall from a higher state to a lower. But clearly the concept cannot apply to decline from what an individual historian perceives as "ideal" religion; if it is to have meaning it must apply to the nature of change itself. But who decides when change is progress or decline à la Spengler and Henry Adams? Declension has become a shorthand device that perpetuates misunderstanding; it categorizes the quality of change without analyzing the substance of it.

The most serious shortcoming, however, is that the concept conflicts with social and institutional realities. It totally misconstrues what was going on in Massachusetts churches in the seventeenth century. The half-way covenant, on which so much of the "proof" of declension has depended, simply did not produce the results that historians have attributed to it. Despite the stamp of approval from the ministers and from the General Court, neither churches nor individuals flocked to take advantage of more generous baptism. By 1675, only two-fifths of the churches in Massachusetts had adopted even the *principle* of the innovation. Only a few churches used the half-way covenant extensively or had fully integrated it into their polity as the synod had envisioned. A large number of those that had endorsed the principle had never had a member "own the covenant."[11] The remarkable element after 1662 is not the way in which members took advantage of the easier way into the church, but rather their intransigence. In a majority of Massachusetts churches the members simply refused to give their assent to the innovation, despite the pleas of the clergy. Even where the principle was accepted it often came out of deference to the minister, and the congregation refused to use it within their own families, thus effectively nullifying the innovation. Most Massachusetts Congregationalists apparently remained convinced that only one right way existed to qualify their children for baptism and that was through full communion and the required regenerative experience—even if that meant that their own children remained unbaptized. This is the quality of religious scrupulosity that most historians have lost sight of.[12]

A good example of this occurred in Dorchester where Richard Mather had fruitlessly devoted twenty years to convincing his congregation to accept the half-way covenant. In 1668 he told the members of the desire of one woman, baptized in the Dorchester church, to own the covenant and have her children baptized. After considerable debate the congregation asked Mather to speak with her to see if she would join in full communion instead (which would, of course, also have qualified her children for baptism). Mrs. Taylor refused: "She did not judge her self as yet fitt for ye Lords Supp & therefore durst not adventure ther uppon, but yet did desier baptizme for her Children." The church reluctantly refused.[13] Had she been less scrupulous, had she wanted baptism for her children above all, Mrs. Taylor could easily have joined in full communion.

Those who mark the half-way covenant as certain proof of declension might well consider this second dimension of scrupulosity. In Mrs. Taylor it appeared as reluctance to come to communion when asked, although she qualified by all external evidence. More frequently scrupulosity appeared as the unwillingness to use the half-way covenant even when it became available. Testified regenerate membership had become so ingrained that parents would rather stay out than take the proffered shortcut. Nor was this simply a matter of waiting a few years until lay resistance dissipated; at the rate Massachusetts churches were proceeding it would have taken two generations or more before the half-way covenant became an integral part of the New England Way. The general reaction was particularly dismaying to the clergy; as John Woodbridge described it, "the churches are such a heavy stone at the ministers' legs that they cannot fly their own course."[14] In other words, after almost three decades of agitation and thirteen years as part of the official "orthodoxy" the half-way covenant had had almost no measurable effect on church membership in Massachusetts.

Only after 1675 did the half-way covenant come into its own as part of the new orthodoxy. In 1675 the colony stood on the brink of a traumatic social upheaval. In the decade and half of crisis which began with King Philip's War, church after church adopted and utilized the half-way principle until by 1690 probably less than one church in five still followed the older practice. The half-way covenant no longer generated controversy; in fact, the propositions of the Half-Way Synod represented a moderate position. A large number of churches, as they confronted a radically altered religious context, introduced innovations which broadened the covenant beyond anything conceived in 1662 or for the thirteen years thereafter.

In 1675 God's judgment fell on New England and the jeremiads seemed fulfilled in ample measure. But no one could have prophesied the terror of King Philip's War. Half the towns in Massachusetts and Plymouth suffered Indian attacks and at least ten towns were abandoned. The war decimated the militia and left the colony reeling. No sooner had this scourge passed than new signs of God's wrath appeared: two great fires in Boston; a small pox epidemic; an outbreak of the fever; and threats to the charter and the economy in the person of Edward Randolph. The 1680s proved even more disastrous to the existing order. The political confusion which followed the revocation of the charter and culminated in the Andros regime threatened every element of stability in the colony; land tenure, self-government, Congregationalism, all appeared marked for major revision. The broad implementation of the half-way covenant can only be understood as response to crisis. Insecurity and anxiety convinced church members, as the ministers had never been able to do, that they must re-interpret their relation to the church.

In fact, what happened in Massachusetts in these fifteen years can only be described as a major revival in church membership—a turning to religion and the churches on a scale that had not been experienced since the first decade of settlement. The assumption that church membership steadily declined in the last three decades of the century is totally inaccurate. Data from research on all the churches in Massachusetts and Connecticut for which material is still available lead to one firm conclusion—the middle of the century, not the end, marks the lowest ebb in church membership. In three Boston area churches—Charlestown, Roxbury, and Dorchester—the average increments of new communicants in the fifteeen years of crisis almost doubled the levels of the 1660s, and they are higher than at any time since the churches were founded. All three of these churches almost certainly had a higher percentage of the inhabitants in full communion in 1690 than they had had twenty years earlier.[15]

A second aspect of church membership that supports this thesis of revival in response to crisis or social disruption is the religious involvement of the men. Traditionally in stable Western societies religious activity becomes the province of the woman; she handles that part of the socializing process. In every Massachusetts church examined, the women consistently became a numerical majority of the church within the first five years of its foundation. By 1640 women constituted a majority of church members and the ratio of women to men progressively increased until 1675. When the crisis began there is evidence of a shift. Two of the three churches mentioned above noted quite radical changes. In Roxbury the percentage of men joining in full communion increased from 19 percent between 1670 and 1676 to 46 percent between 1680 and 1689; in Dorchester it went from 38 percent to 49 percent and in this church 56 percent of the half-way members were men. Although some improvement also occurred in Charlestown, it was less dramatic (an increase from 25 percent to 30 percent).[16] Men were most likely to suffer from the social dysfunction of the period and they came into the churches in numbers unequalled since the 1630s.

Religion is in part the human response to contingency and powerlessness; as these factors increase in any given era, the overt religious response is almost certain to increase. From 1675 on, and particularly after 1684, the churches of Massachusetts offered to men a solace and stability that had disappeared in their normal context. The implementation of the half-way covenant after 1675 must be understood in the same light—as a religious response to crisis. Massachusetts was uniquely prepared psychologically for internal and external disaster. The jeremiads had conditioned the Puritan mind to the logic of the covenant: sin, affliction, confession, restoration.[17] When the calamities, even more fearful than the ministers had dared predict, befell Massachusetts, the people recognized them for what they were—judgments of God. The response of the churches and the people could not have come out of an apathetic society; it was not a sign of declension, as we are so frequently told, but of piety.

But we cannot simply jettison the misleading concept of declension, for that only renews the conceptual void that Miller was striving to fill and makes the processes of change as mysterious as ever. Two concepts from the sociology of religion, when they are used in conjunction, offer new possibilities for understanding what happened in seventeenth-century Massachusetts. One is the "church-sect" typology developed by Ernst Troeltsch and elaborated upon by Weber, Wach, Wilson, and Niebuhr,[18] and the other is functional analysis. The remainder of this essay will explore church membership in the role of the churches and their relationship with society at large. Here it seems the evolution of the "church-sect" typology is most apparent.

The original Puritan vision of their holy commonwealth contained a dual mission: first, they wanted to create in the new Israel a moral, covenanted society where men abided by God's laws; second, they wanted to erect truly reformed churches containing only visible saints. At the time of their migration the Puritans embodied the Calvinistic union of both church and sect, with some functions tending to be more sectarian and others more churchly. The churches themselves were both national *and* free—a holy community and an institution—and the society itself had a concrete mission which gave it a cultural unity that was enforced by the state. Thus from the outset there existed an inherent tension and conflict between the goal of a covenanted community and that of the covenanted churches, since they were not coextensive as they had been in Geneva or in medieval Christianity. In the first few years in Massachusetts the Congregational churches appear to have followed the Separatist example to determine church membership, for after all few of them had known the opportunity in England to determine who was and who was not a visible saint. The tests imposed in the Massachusetts churches—decent civil behavior, knowledge of the principles of the faith, and a desire to join the church—minimized the tension by leaving the doors of the churches open to most men of good-will thereby reducing the gap between the religious and the civil communities. But the Puritan zeal for a purer church brought an innovation that tightened the requirements. By 1640 almost every church required a candidate for admission to relate to the assembled congregation the process of his conversion. Good behavior, knowledge, and desire no longer sufficed.[19]

The morphology of conversion, initially developed by English Puritan divines as a guide for the individual soul, was transformed into a yardstick to measure the faithful. Testified regenerate membership put beyond the grasp of all but a few what had once been within the reach of most men. The strictness of the new test—and, of course, it quite rapidly became routinized and even more difficult to experience—made entry into the church so limited that few persons qualified. But Congregational policy, devised in a simpler era, limited baptism and church discipline to members and their children. Here was Congregationalism's quandary: it had predicated the continuing life of the church and the religious mission of the community upon a hereditary growth of faith, but the new test put a barrier between the children and the church. The primacy which Puritans placed on visible conversion as the basis for church membership destroyed the initial equilibrium between church and sect and turned New England toward sectarianism.

The emphasis on the doctrine of preparation[20] which underlies the entire antinomian controversy may represent an attempt to ameliorate the rigidity of the new test and preserve the essentially communal aspects of striving for sanctification. But preparation by itself was inadequate in the new environment. The religious history of seventeenth-century Massachusetts is the the story of the struggle to live with a concept of purity within the context of a covenanted community.

In part the clergy devised the half-way covenant to restore the equilibrium, although they were not completely conscious of this function. By creating a dual membership—the first for baptized believers who would be subject to church discipline and given a reason to strive for holiness, and the second for the core of regenerate believers—they preserved what they considered a real advance in reformation and they also closed the broadening gulf between the churches and the community. They achieved this revolution only by compromising the original concept of the covenant of grace and by attributing to the unregenerate capabilities they had previously denied existed. The chief opponents of the half-way covenant, John Davenport and Charles Chauncy, did not lack theological sophistication, nor were they short-sighted purists. They understood the issues clearly, but preferred marching the churches out of the world to compromising purity for the sake of the city on a hill.[21]

Perhaps the only reason New England was able to maintain its ideals as long as it did—compare it to England where the same idealism was shattered by the Civil Wars and the idea of free churches became a reality—was because of the state. For Massachusetts the state served as church and the churches served as sects within it. The state made it possible for the churches to behave as sectarians by keeping the entire community in line with God's laws and by serving many of the roles normally fulfilled by the church. The greatest catastrophe of the century for the colony's mission was the revocation of the charter in 1684.[22] For a half-century the state had bound the whole community in covenant with God. When Massachusetts lost the charter and with it the "due forme of government" that Winthrop and his friends had established, only the churches remained to fulfill the mission of the covenanted community.

Revocation of the charter destroyed the protective shield of a sympathetic state which had permitted the churches to retain their sectarian practices. The loss thrust new burdens on the churches and forced them to redefine their relationship to society. The old tribalism that had contented itself with familial Christianity could not preserve the covenanted community. The Congregational churches faced an unpleasant dilemma: they could either bring themselves more fully into the community, or they ran the risk of losing control completely. If Massachusetts was to meet the internal and external threats to the Puritan way, the churches had to speak to and effectively influence a segment of the population they had previously ignored. This meant developing a new evangelism, taking a different attitude toward the unchurched, and further revising the standards for church membership.

The churches met the challenge fairly successfully. The expansion of church membership which had begun after 1675 with "crisis" conversions and implementation of the half-way covenant continued and even expanded. Some New Englanders who had tenuous church connections but who had hitherto hung back from church membership because of religious scruples, doubts, or disinterest now came forward to strengthen by their membership the principal institution that remained for the expression of the Puritan way. It became an act of fealty.[23] Prior to revocation most new members were the descendants of the saints and the easing of requirements was directed primarily at those who had "holy roots." After 1684 the appeal was directed to the people with or without church connections. Mass covenant renewals and a broader half-way covenant meant that almost every adult in the community had a way into the church.[24] It is probably quite true that the "quality" or rigor of the conversion experience required for admission to communion declined with this new outreach, although that does not signify that people were less religious. In 1635 the Puritans feared the pollution of the sanctuary; in 1690 their survival depended on filling the sanctuary. A share in the covenant had become a political, social, and religious obligation by the end of the century and the evolution of Massachusetts from sect to church was complete. The man who most fully recognized the implications of the previous eighty years was not Cotton Mather but Solomon Stoddard.

The Puritans confronted in Massachusetts what every sect has faced in its children, and it should not surprise us that they, like others, failed to understand what was happening. H. Richard Niebuhr has suggested that it may be impossible for a sect to survive beyond the first generation[25] and the Massachusetts experience tends to support that thesis. Revision was inescapable, yet revision created the anxiety and guilt that permeated the rhetoric of the age.

The majority of the men and women who settled Massachusetts in the first decade represented an extraordinary religious experience. They were "twice-winnowed": first they had dared or had felt inwardly compelled to advocate Puritanism in the hostile English environment, and second they had risked lives and estates to create a new Israel in the wilderness. It appears from Michael Walzer's superb study[26] that Puritanism appealed most directly to those who sensed in early Stuart England a profound disorder verging on chaos and turned to Puritanism for meaning or an internal gyroscope. (Witness, for example, John Winthrop's increasing anxiety in the 1620s.) As a group or party the Puritans anticipated their rise to power as an opportunity to restore order and stability—in private lives and public lives—through what Walzer calls repression. Although in old England the attempt to bring order out of chaos failed dramatically, in New England it was a triumphant success.

For their success in establishing order however the Puritans paid an unexpected price. The second generation, the children of the saints, grew to maturity in the stable religious environment of New England. For them there were no counterparts to Laud's pursuivants, the Tower, or the exodus, and their parents may well have thanked God for that. But where elders and magistrates enforced God's laws with the general approbation of the people, it became less and less likely that the rising generation would experience the "soul-shattering" conversion. That wrenching out of the world's sin so common to their parents in religiously contentious England appeared all too rarely in the holy commonwealth. The challenge to the children of the saints lay in conquering the physical wilderness in accordance with God's laws.

The introduction of testified regenerate membership thus placed an added burden on the children; it demanded what they were least capable of realizing. Further the testimony of regeneration became an obstacle to conversion as the churches quickly routinized it: guidelines became hard lines. Not that churches denied membership to those that applied, for this happened very rarely, but the children had a model before them, a normative experience. When their own religious experiences failed to conform, they questioned their validity and waited. The conversion experience established by the first generation was a "patterning" based on an English environment which bore little resemblance to the "mature" faith that came from stability and habit.

A second aspect of the dilemma facing the second and third generation

Puritans came from their distorted historical perspective. They engaged in an oppressive filiopietism that transformed the founding generation into paragons of social virtue, wisdom, and saintliness. Although this is a common tradition, for Massachusetts it was nearly disastrous. It not only established difficult standards to live up to, but it also reflected a failure to understand what the founders had, in fact, done in Massachusetts. Later generations never seemed to realize that in the first two decades of the colony's history the founders had more or less continuously experimented, adapted, and changed their politics and their polity to fit the new environment. Only in 1648 had they set down their "final" thoughts in the Cambridge Platform, outlining and justifying the New England Way. Subsequent generations saw only this contruct, achieved at one point in time, and read it back into the colony's history. They saw themselves as stewards of that "truth" and judged themselves by how far they strayed from the straight and narrow orthodoxy. They never understood that change was normative; it had been for the founders, it was for them, and it would be for those that followed.

Thus the jeremiads are not only a rhetorical plea to the covenanted people, they are also the sounds of confusion. "All is flux," they seem to say. By invoking the past, they found some balm for living in the present but at a heavy psychological price. They are not unlike Marvin Meyers' Jacksonians sanctifying the Jeffersonian past while scrambling for the entrepreneurial gains of a new world.[27]

The process which historians have labelled declension is nothing more than the maturation of a sectarian movement. The churches of Massachusetts developed new functions which fulfilled the changing needs of a community they wished to preserve—a process as old as Christendom itself. The difference between the Massachusetts of 1630 and that of 1690 is the difference between Paul preaching conversion in Christ and II Peter pondering the problems of electing a bishop. It is important for us to recognize that the Massachusetts clergy who lived through this transformation understood it as declension, but it is even more important for us to stop letting the seventeenth-century mind define the processes of change which it only dimly perceived.

If Puritanism did not decline in the late seventeenth century, it at least diffused. Of course the New England Way had never been monolithic. A variety of beliefs and forms of worship existed among English Puritans and were carried to America, where they partly withstood efforts at standardization. Even after the promulgation of the Cambridge Platform in 1648 and the Half-Way Covenant in 1662, differences persisted (as Pope has shown). And as time passed, ecclesiastical distinctions between the several colonies increased, especially after Connecticut in 1708 adopted the Saybrook Platform. That document (reprinted with extensive historical introduction in Williston Walker, Creeds and Platforms of Congregationalism [New York, 1893; repr. Boston, 1960]) molded Connecticut's churches into a quasi-presbyterian structure.

The latter half of the seventeenth century also witnessed a breakdown in Puritanism's monopoly of New England theology. Rhode Island, from its inception in 1636, had been a haven for Baptists, Quakers, and other dissenters from orthodox Puritanism, but the other New England colonies labeled it an "island of errors" and excluded it from their definition of New England. But gradually even the staunchly Puritan colonies had to acknowledge the growing heterogeneity of their populations. Many immigrants after the 1640s cared little for Puritan precepts, and some descendants of the founders acquired theological convictions at odds with their ancestors.' Both trends were especially pronounced among the merchant community, as Bernard Bailyn has shown in The New England Merchants in the Seventeenth Century *(Cambridge, Mass., 1955). By the 1680s Boston's Puritan congregations had to vie for adherents with a Baptist meetinghouse and an Anglican church. A Quaker meetinghouse opened in 1710. New England was no longer an exclusively Puritan domain.*

NOTES

1. Bacon, *Thirteen Historical Discourses* (New Haven, 1839); Dexter, "Two Hundred Years Ago in New England," *Congregational Quarterly* 4 (1862).

2. Brooks Adams, *The Emancipation of Massachusetts*, Sentry Ed. (Cambridge, Mass., 1962); Charles Francis Adams, *Three Episodes of Massachusetts History*, 2 vols. (Boston, 1892); James Truslow Adams, *The Founding of New England* (Boston, 1921).

3. The best examples of Miller's exploration of Puritanism are *The New England Mind: The Seventeenth Century* (Cambridge, Mass., 1939) and *The New England Mind: From Colony to Province* (Cambridge, Mass., 1953).

4. Miller, "Solomon Stoddard, 1643-1729," *Harvard Theological Review* 34 (1941): 277-320; Thomas Schafer, "Solomon Stoddard and the Theology of the Revival," in *A Miscellany of American Christianity*, ed. Stuart Henry (Durham, 1963), pp. 328-361; and "Stoddardeanism," *The New Englander* 4 (1846): 350-355. Prof. Lucas of Indiana Univ. should now be adding a major reassessment of Stoddard to this limited literature.

5. See my *The Half-Way Covenant* (Princeton, 1969), chap. 4; also, "Correspondence of John Woodbridge, Jr., and Richard Baxter," ed. Raymond Stearns, *New England Quarterly* 10 (1937): 557-583; Northampton Church Records, microfilm (Forbes Library, Northampton).

6. The case is most thoroughly and carefully developed in Miller, *From Colony to Province*, pp. 3-118. Quite often readers of Miller's volumes are guilty of a simplification that he warily avoided with his knowledge of New England's complexity.

7. The full text of this revision in Congregational polity can be found in Williston Walker, *The Creeds and Platforms of Congregationalism*, Pilgrim Ed. (Boston, 1960), pp. 301-339. Prior to adoption of the half-way covenant only those children whose parents were full communicants could be baptized; thus the baptized child of a saint could reach maturity, marry, and, if he failed to experience conversion, find his children excluded from the church. The Half-Way Synod provided for the continuation of baptism for generations as long as the recipients descended from regenerate stock.

8. Mass covenant renewals usually brought together the entire community to reaffirm its covenant with God and pledge itself to moral reform. Originally only church members participated in the ceremony, but as time passed and dangers increased all the inhabitants were invited to participate. Frequently it became the occasion for children to own the half-way covenant. See Miller, *From Colony to Province*, pp. 105-118; Pope, *Half-Way Covenant*, chap. 9.

9. "Solomon Stoddard," p. 318.

10. *Winthrop's Boston* (Chapel Hill, 1965).

11. Pope, *Half-Way Covenant*, chaps. 5 and 8.

12. Edmund S. Morgan, "New England Puritanism: Another Approach," *William and Mary Quarterly* 18 (1961): 241, raises this issue and points out a number of new directions that need exploration.

13. *Records of the First Church at Dorchester; 1636-1734*, ed. Charles Pope (Boston, 1891), p. 55.

14. "Woodbridge-Baxter Correspondence," p. 574; Cotton Mather, *Magnalia Christi Americana* (Hartford, 1855), 2, bk. 5: 266; William Hubbard, *A General History of New England* (Boston, 1840), p. 570. Among the churches which had serious reservations about the half-way covenant were Dorchester, Charlestown, Roxbury, and First Church Boston; Pope, *Half-Way Covenant*, chaps. 5-7.

15. Pope, *Half-Way Covenant*, chap. 8, appendix.

16. Pope, *Half-Way Covenant*, chap. 8, appendix.

17. Miller, *From Colony to Province*, p. 192.

18. Troeltsch, *Social Teachings of the Christian Churches*, trans. Olive Wyon, 2 vols. (New York, 1931); Joachim Wach, *Sociology of Religion* (Chicago, 1944); *From Max Weber: Essays in Sociology*, trans. Hans Gerth and Don Martindale (Glencoe, 1952); H. Richard Niebuhr, *Social Sources of Denominationalism*, Meridian Ed. (New York, 1963); Bryan Wilson, *Sects and Society* (Berkeley, 1961).

19. Edmund S. Morgan, *Visible Saints* (New York, 1963), pp. 36-47, 77-93.

20. On preparation and its place in New England theology see Norman Pettit, *The Heart Prepared* (New Haven, 1966), which revises the views of Miller, "Preparation for Salvation," *Journal of the History of Ideas* 3 (1943): 253-286.

21. Pope, *Half-Way Covenant*, chap. 2; Walker, *Creeds and Platforms*, pp. 244-280.

22. The loss of the corporate charter of 1629 meant the transfer of political power from the hands of the saints to the rising merchants and imperial administrators who had far less interest in religion than in their own pocket-books. It meant Congregationalism faced new restraints both from Boston and London.

23. An example of this delayed religious affiliation is Wait Winthrop, grandson of John Winthrop: he joined Third Church Boston in 1689 after nearly a decade of involvement in politics (Richard Dunn, *Puritans and Yankees* [Princeton, 1962], p. 257.)

24. Miller, *From Colony to Province*, pp. 105-118, 209-225; Pope, *Half-Way Covenant*, chap. 9; Morgan, *Visible Saints*, pp. 142-150.

25. Pp. 17-19.

26. "Puritanism as a Revolutionary Ideology," *History and Theory* 3 (1961): 59-90.

27. *The Jacksonian Persuasion*, Vintage Ed. (New York, 1960); Meyer's restoration theme is strikingly similar to rhetoric of the jeremiads and suggests a profitable area for analysis.

19 | "AN APPEAL TO THE LEARNED": THE MIND OF SOLOMON STODDARD

PAUL R. LUCAS

Signs of Puritanism's diffusion in the late seventeenth century appeared not only in new church polities and rival denominations but also within Puritan strongholds. Harvard College, it seemed to many observers, was becoming a hotbed of liberalism. Equally disturbing was the opening in 1699 of Boston's Brattle Street Church, which maintained more lenient admissions requirements and allowed a wider participation by its members in church affairs—including, for example, participation by female members in the selection of church officers.

Still another sign of Puritanism's growing diversity appeared in the Connecticut Valley. There Solomon Stoddard, pastor of the congregation in Northampton, Massachusetts, emerged during the 1660s as the principal spokesman for innovations in the New England Way. The following essay reviews the traditional interpretations of Stoddard's role and places him more accurately in the context of evangelical Christianity.

Solomon Stoddard, minister of the First Congregational Church of Northampton, Massachusetts, from 1669 to 1729, is considered one of the most important ministers of early New England, and the reasons for his importance are fixed firmly in the minds of students of the period. It is generally believed that by 1700 his personality, ecclesiology, and theology dominated the laymen and clergy of western Massachusetts and much of Connecticut. Moreover, it is argued that among a clergy obsessed by church discipline, and especially Congregationalism, Stoddard's Presbyterian-like "Instituted Church" with its "converting" ordinances and open communion represented a radical alternative to the Puritan "New England Way" and did much to cause its destruction. Finally, it is believed that Stoddard, grandfather of Jonathan Edwards, formulated many of the evangelical notions which led to the Great Awakening.[1]

. . .

The key to understanding Solomon Stoddard is not to be found in New England Congregationalism, Old World Presbyterianism, frontier "experience," or frontier democracy. Nor is it fair, or sensible, to view him solely as an actor in the historian's saga of the rise, reign, and fall of the New England Way. Stoddard's complaint went far beyond New England Congregationalism to the whole of the Protestant Reformation, in which New England represented but one isolated outpost. As he often wrote, he was a soul-winner, an evangelical, and he rejected not only

New England's, but also the Reformed tradition's, seventeenth-century preoccupation with church discipline. That was Stoddard's significance for his time, a fact overlooked by most modern scholars.[2] He was a lonely but vocal colonial exponent of doctrine over discipline. His sympathies always lay with the early reformers, the propounders of doctrine, never with the later reformers, the architects of church discipline. He, alone among New England's clergy, disagreed with Thomas Hooker's admonition that the Protestant Reformation proceeded in two stages, one doctrinal and one disciplinary.[3] For Stoddard the latter was an aberration, an insult to divine and earthly intelligence.

Coming of age at a time when it was generally believed that religion in New England was dying, Stoddard blamed the prevailing polity, Congregationalism. But he went much farther, noting that religion waned in all Protestant areas, a fact he attributed to an obsession with discipline. No Presbyterian, he rejected all forms of church government that purported to represent the pattern of the primitive Christian church. In their stead, and as an antidote to spiritual decline, he offered his Instituted Church, a sacramental church neither Protestant nor Catholic, but rooted in his own peculiar and solitary conception of the meaning of scripture and the evolution of God's plan for mankind.

Consequently, for much of his life Stoddard was a maverick, revered personally but opposed by nearly everyone, including the members of his own church. The notion of the "pope" of the Connecticut Valley is a myth. Stoddard's influence, and it was considerable, stemmed from his personality, not from his theology or ecclesiology. His Instituted Church, while it generated much controversy, accomplished little more, and, contrary to legend, he never controlled either the clergy or the laity of the Valley.

In the last fifteen to twenty years of his life, however, Stoddard underwent an intellectual transformation of startling proportions, a fact which has also eluded modern scholarship. He did not alter his allegiance to soul-winning or his violent hostility to discipline and its particularly onerous New England form, Congregationalism, but he changed his tactics. He scrapped the Instituted Church with its institutionalized salvation, heaped abuse on the churches of New England for their preoccupation with church discipline, and chose the role of evangelical preacher. As a result, in his last years he developed a following among clergy he had not had before and played an important role in bringing about the Great Awakening.

Stoddard presented the Instituted Church to New England in 1700 with the London publication of his first and only comprehensive treatise on church polity, *The Doctrine of Instituted Churches.* Although brief, it contained the essentials of his position and showed quite clearly that he was at odds not only with the New England Way but with some of the main tenets of Reformed thought. While the Reformation sought the revival of primitive Christianity, Stoddard rejected all attempts to model polity on the supposed nature of the early Christian church. The Congregational tradition held that the authority of Christ passed to the early congregations of Rome, Antioch, and elsewhere as autonomous units. Hence, the true church was a congregation of true believers in which decisions were made by the members. Presbyterians contended that Christ's authority passed to the Apostles, who formed the first consistory of elders. The modern clergyman, they argued, was the descendant of those early "ministers" and possessed ultimate authority in Christ's visible church.

Stoddard also sought purity, but he denied that it was to be found only in the primitive church. God's church, he believed, formed a continuum from Old to New Testaments, and if one wished the restoration of the "pure" church, one looked first at the polity of God's church among the ancient Israelites. According to Stoddard, the church of Israel represented an Instituted Church created, or instituted, by God for the salvation of men. But what form did that salvation assume? According to Stoddard's exegesis, God made a covenant with the Israelites that if they lived according to His law they would be saved. Christ's death, however, changed the rules for salvation, for in death Christ atoned for the sins of men; to be saved, a man had only to accept Christ as his savior.

In Stoddard's view, man was, of course, powerless to effect his own salvation, for that was the province of the Almighty. Stoddard emphasized instead the process whereby grace was conveyed from God to man through the ordinances of the Instituted Church. They were Christ's legacy and, as a consequence, the real historical significance of primitive Christianity. Christ died to redeem mankind and provided the means of redemption in the ordinances of baptism, prayer, scripture, preaching, censure, and the Lord's Supper.

This, then, represented the heart of Stoddard's complaint against the churches of New England and much of the Reformed tradition as well. Too much time was wasted in speculation about the precise form of the primitive Christian church, for the significance of early Christianity was doctrinal not disciplinary. New England's failure was obvious. Prevailing theories concerning "pure" churches and the sacraments as only "Seals" of the Covenant of Grace caused God's anger and the country's decline, so that New Englanders starved for lack of spiritual nourishment.

Stoddard's conception of the Instituted Church represented an amalgamation of Old Testament form and New Testament function. The church of Israel was a national church comprising only the Jewish nation. In Christ, God extended his rule and benefits to all men. However, he retained the form of the church of Israel, changing only the rules for salvation. While adherence to the moral law had been sufficient justification for the Jews, a nation of believers, God now confronted a multitude of unbelievers who knew nothing of His power or His law. Obviously, new means were required for their salvation. The Jewish church had existed primarily as a vehicle for divine worship. The new church was that and much more. Its purpose was evangelistic, the saving of sinners, for whom God sacrificed His Son, then "instituted" his church—through the ordinances—to convey the message and the gift to the world.[4]

Unfortunately, Stoddard sounded occasionally as though he favored universal redemption, that his Instituted Church was, in truth, meant for all, and that no man could or would be barred from admission. In reality, although he often implied it, he did not mean it. His argument would have made much more sense had he stated that Christ died for all "visible saints," for that was his intent. In discussing the "fit matter" for church membership, he always made it clear that membership and the sacraments were intended only for visible saints.

By the standards of most New England Congregationalists, however, Stoddard's definition of a visible saint was so broad and loose that, by comparison, his communion did appear to be "open" to almost anyone. His definition proceeded directly from his analysis of the function of the Instituted Church. There were three churches, he argued. The invisible church encompassed the elect. The visible or "catholic" church included all who professed "the true faith in Christ." These made their sainthood visible through a blameless life and a sincere desire to close with Christ, not through church membership or proof of regeneration. Thus, it was possible for a man to be a visible saint and not a member of any particular congregation.

The third church was the Instituted Church, which provided the institutional means for the dissemination of grace. The basic purpose of that church was obvious: to bring all professing Christians to the ordinances so that they might be saved. Thus, for Stoddard, no obstacles should be placed in the path of professing Christians, or visible saints, desiring union with the institutional church.[5] He rejected New England's efforts to insure church purity through tests of regeneration. The ordinances lay open to all who wanted and could qualify for their benefits, and a man who thought himself a reprobate had as much right to them as the man who believed himself a saint. The reasons for this were twofold. First, Stoddard found no warrant in either Testament for any practice limiting membership to proven regenerates. Second, he believed that although a minister could aid in the search for "signs" of redemption, no external test could be devised to determine the condition of something so intangible as the human soul. Moreover, an over-zealous attempt to separate wheat from chaff violated the nature and function of the Instituted Church. Men desired membership because they sought the church's saving ordinances, and any attempt to keep them out for reasons other than immorality or ignorance of Christian doctrine represented a denial of the meaning of Christ's death.[6]

Thus, Stoddard could not accept the Congregational doctrine of the autonomous congregation as a community of saints drawn together out of society to worship God and celebrate the sacraments, bound together and to God by a covenant. The particular church, he argued, was a manifestation of the visible catholic church, and membership in one church constituted membership in all churches. For Stoddard, as for Presbyterians, a particular church was an institution whose "members were bound" by the appointment of God to assemble in one place in a constant way for the celebration of "Publick Worship." The church's importance lay in the dispensation of the sacraments. Particular churches were appointed by God as places where members of the universal catholic church came together to celebrate the sacraments.

In the absence of a binding covenant, the authority of the particular church came from its membership in the national church. Stoddard believed that the church of ancient Israel had been a national unit. God had made a covenant with the Jews and that relationship applied to the Christian church as well. Each Christian nation was in covenant with God, promising obedience to Him in return for His blessing. Consequently, as in the case of the Jewish church, spiritual authority and power flowed from God through the national covenant to the ruling body of the national church and from there to particular churches.

The Congregational doctrine of independent churches seemed to Stoddard "too lordly a principle." The experience of New England proved to him that the implementation of such a principle led to ecclesiastical anarchy with congregations working constantly at cross purposes. The Instituted Church, as he portrayed it, had but a single purpose—the salvation of sinners. To accomplish its mission, it needed effective coordination of the activities of local churches through a centralized governing body. The "light of nature" suggested to Stoddard that the Church of Scotland most resembled the Old Testament model and God's will.[7]

Here Stoddard showed his indebtedness to Samuel Rutherford, the Scottish Presbyterian whose books he had read and admired while a student and tutor at Harvard. Stoddard asserted that ultimate authority in the national church should be vested in a synod composed of all the elders of the churches, or, if the country were too large, of a few elders representing all the churches. The power of that national synod was both specific and pervasive. It would have full authority in the determination and dissemination of sound doctrine and in the fight against error and heresy. It would judge complaints and impose ecclesiastical censures when necessary. It would also oversee the training and placement of ministers, appointing groups of elders to examine each prospective minister to determine proper qualifications.

To facilitate the government of particular churches, Stoddard urged the division of the national church into provinces, each controlled by a body of elders immediately subordinate to the national synod. In turn, each province was to be divided into a number of classes, bodies composed of elders whose duties were to implement, on the local level, the decisions of the national synod.[8]

Turning to the polity of the local church, Stoddard wrote that the minister and ruling elders had complete authority in matters of doctrine and discipline. These officers formed a "presbytery" with total control over church affairs, total because the minister's power came from God through the national covenant and the hierarchical structure of church government. But Stoddard, like New England's Presbyterians, could not totally escape Congregational theory. The brethren, he concluded, were not without rights. They had the authority to choose their ruling elders and thus had considerable power in church affairs.

The pastor administered the sacraments of the church and decided who would be admitted to them and who would not. Baptism lay open to any person who was a visible saint. Membership in a particular church was not a prerequisite, nor was it necessary for the applicant to be the child or grandchild of a member. The prerequisites for communion were much the same. A prospective member need only be a visible saint, that is, to "walk blamelessly" and "profess faith in Christ." Yet Stoddard did have another condition: prospective communicants were to have knowledge of the principles of religion. This latter qualification barred infants from the Table.[9]

This was the core of Stoddard's "Presbyterianism." His attacks on restrictive membership requirements, church covenants, and congregational government, and his advocacy of open communion, converting ordinances, synodical government, and national churches were tied together neatly in a package labeled the Instituted Church. Was the Instituted Church also the church of New England's Presbyterians? Was Stoddard their spokesman, or was he a maverick whose views were peculiarly his own? Edward Taylor, who knew Stoddard well, favored the latter explanation. He and Stoddard maintained a friendly but serious argument over church discipline throughout the last three decades of the seventeenth century, and no one understood the significance and meaning of the Instituted Church better than the Westfield clergyman. In a 1687 letter Taylor commented on Stoddard's desire to open the Lord's Supper to "all above fourteen years of age, that live morally, and hav[e] Catechisticall knowledge of the Principalls of Religion," and on his views on polity in general. Taylor argued that Stoddard's position reflected the thoughts of no other New England clergymen and represented a dangerous apostasy likely to lead to the pollution of the churches. Yet, while he labeled Stoddard's scheme as new to New England, he recognized precedents in the history of Reformed thought, although, as he cautioned, "you [have] so few of the Non-Conformists for you, and therefore it is a thing well to be suspected.[10]

Boston's Increase Mather disagreed with Taylor, at least at first. As Miller points out, Mather believed that Stoddard led and spoke for a horde of Valley Presbyterians, especially after the protracted debate between the two at the synod of 1679 when Stoddard defended the "Broad Way" or Presbyterian approach to church membership and seemed to have so many clerical supporters.[11]

. . .

But when Mather read *The Doctrine of Instituted Churches*, his notion of the relationship of Stoddard to the Presbyterians quickly changed and he endorsed Taylor's view that, despite its Presbyterian-like quality, Stoddard's ecclesiology was unlike that of any other New England divine. To counter the *Instituted Churches*, Mather rushed into print a treatise written some years before by an English Presbyterian, John Quick, offering a different view of the nature of the sacraments.[12] In his introduction, which was longer than Quick's text, Mather warned the reader of the peril lurking in the hinterland of Massachusetts. Stoddard endangered the "Happy Union" of the New England churches, he announced, and represented a force more pernicious than all the Presbyterians combined. Compared to the Northampton cleric, the Brattle Street group was harmless. Obviously something Mather read in the *Instituted Churches* had taken him by surprise.[13]

. . .

Mather buttressed his attack with evidence that no major Protestant group accepted Stoddard's position. He cited the *Heads of Agreement* as proof that neither Congregationalists nor Presbyterians deviated from the doctrine of the "Seals."[14] He used Samuel Rutherford as further proof of Presbyterian rejection.[15] Even the Church of England, which in many respects conformed to Stoddard's notion of a national church, kept unregenerates from the Lord's Table. The opposition of New England's Congregationalists was well known, and he doubted that New England Presbyterians would be any more sympathetic. For Mather, Reformation polity represented an attempt to recreate primitive Christianity. Reformed theology sought the same end, rejecting the institutionalized salvation of Catholicism for the more personalized view of the confrontation of God and man without earthly mediators. Stoddard's polity and divinity came close to the institutionalized salvation of the "Papists." Thus, Mather rejected Stoddard because Stoddard questioned the Reformation.[16]

. . .

. . . To assess the true strength of Stoddard's ecclesiology one must scrutinize the clergy and brethren of the Connecticut Valley, for if Stoddard's views swept that region, extant records would reveal it. But they do not, at least not in Connecticut, where few ministers endorsed Stoddard.[17] Most of Connecticut's clergymen were Congregationalists of various hues, while a minority were Presbyterians, although not sympathetic to Stoddard. If any sizeable support existed for the Instituted Church in Connecticut, it would have emerged in connection with the synod of Connecticut churches at Saybrook in 1708, for that meeting took place during the Stoddard-Mather debate. But no such support was evident.[18]

In preparation for the synod the general court instructed each county to collect the desires of member churches and present a platform of discipline for consideration by the synod. Led by Timothy Woodbridge, Hartford and Fairfield counties, the centers of Presbyterianism in Connecticut, called for synodical rule and the adoption of a Presbyterian constitution. All other counties endorsed some form of Congregationalism. The representatives, meeting in the summer of 1708, worked in a remarkable spirit of compromise and with little disagreement endorsed the theological position of the *Heads of Agreement* of 1691, the joint declaration of London Congregationalists and Presbyterians. There was more argument on a confession of faith. The Presbyterians favored the Westminster Confession while the Congregationalists preferred the Savoy Confession of 1658. After some debate the Presbyterians gave in.[19]

The real struggle occurred over the issue of church government as the representatives perused the drafts presented by the counties. Presbyterians tended to favor Woodbridge's plan, while Congregationalists drifted toward the plan circulated by Nicholas Noyes of New Haven County. The majority preferred the New Haven plan, "but some Clauses were put into it, in Conformity to Mr. Woodbridge of Hartford and some others, who were inclined to the Presbyterian Side."[20] The resulting plan of church government became part of the Saybrook Platform. A general council or synod of all the churches was to meet yearly to discuss common problems and to make recommendations, although no substantive powers were assigned to the body. The plan envisioned the creation of county councils to determine cases of discipline and render decisions in church disputes, as well as "associations" of ministers to license and regulate the clergy and "consider and resolve questions and cases of Importance which shall be offered by any among themselves or others."[21]

Nothing in the records of Saybrook suggests the influence of Solomon Stoddard or his Instituted Church. None of the conclusions of the synod, except for the yearly synod and area associations, was even remotely similar to Stoddard's, and the associations received considerably less authority than Stoddard wanted. The Presbyterians at Saybrook, among whom Stoddard ought to have been influential, followed their own leaders, especially Woodbridge, and pursued a course conforming to the intent of the authors of the *Gospel Order Revived*, not the *Instituted Churches*.[22]

Similarly, there is no evidence that Stoddard had influence among the laymen of Connecticut's churches. No Connecticut church adopted a polity conforming to Stoddard's or endorsed his notion of converting ordinances. Presbyterianism in general was treated suspiciously by the laity. Some churches did follow practices similar to those proposed by Stoddard but to attribute them solely to his influence is unwarranted.[23]

One such practice was "open communion," which is often assumed to have been a Stoddardean innovation. Stoddard's view that any man or woman above the age of fourteen years could be admitted to the church and to the Lord's Supper if morally upright and possessing sound knowledge of Christian doctrine was adopted by the Northampton church in 1690.[24] The Windsor church of John Warham had dropped the same practice in 1647.[25] The First Church of Hartford adopted it probably in the 1660s and continued it at least until the death of Woodbridge in 1730. In the Hartford area it became known as "Mr. Woodbridge's Way," although it antedated the beginning of his ministry. Hartford's adoption of an open communion had nothing to do with Solomon Stoddard or his converting ordinances. The Hartford church continued to endorse the doctrine of the "Seals" and, despite Woodbridge's Presbyterianism and his opposition to such practices, maintained "Half-Way" and "Full Communion" designations for members as well as zealously guarding the governing rights of the membership.[26]

The ecclesiastical records of the churches and clergy of the Connecticut Valley of western Massachusetts, while scant, do not support the supposition of Stoddard's intellectual dominance over the area, although they do attest to the power of his personality. In the early years of his ministry he was surrounded by hostile Congregational ministers. Besides the opposition of Edward Taylor, Stoddard faced one of the oldest and ablest of the Valley clergy, John Russell of neighboring Hadley. Russell, who had led the migration of Connecticut families from Wethersfield, Windsor, and Hartford to Hadley in the 1650s, was once labeled a "Presbyterian" by those of Wethersfield who disliked both his views on ministerial authority and his advocacy of the "broad way" in admitting new members. In 1679 he and Stoddard attended the founding of Taylor's Westfield church and, after witnessing the public professions of religious experience of the seven "pillars" of that church, Russell called it the most ludicrous display he had ever seen, and Stoddard concurred. But Russell was no Presbyterian and no supporter of Stoddard's views, as he made clear in a 1681 letter to Increase Mather. He reported on Stoddard's activities and expressed his disgust not only for Stoddard but for all who deviated from the doctrine espoused by the synod of 1662. "Our good Brother Stoddard," he wrote, "hath bin strenuously promoting his position concerning that right which persons sound in the doctrine of faith, and of (as he calls it) a holy Conversation, have to full Communion." He thought it was time for the members of the synod of 1662 to defend their fourth proposition "for the securing of the churches: from pollutions by unprepared ones incroaching upon full Communion in the Lord's Supper and voting. . . . the doctrine of those propositions in the Synod 62 doth tend in the end of the worke . . . to shake and undermine the fundamentall doctrine and practise of the Congregationall way, viz. that visible Saints are only matter of a church of Christ."[27]

The clearest indication of the ecclesiastical views of the clergymen closest to Stoddard comes from the scattered remains of the Hampshire Association of churches, an organization formed largely at Stoddard's instigation in 1714. Six ministers drew up the proposal for its creation: Stoddard, John Williams of Deerfield, William Williams of Hatfield, Isaac Chauncey of Hadley, Daniel Brewer of Springfield's First Church, and Nathaniel Collins of Enfield. The wording of the document indicated that all of the men favored Presbyterianism, although not necessarily Stoddardeanism. The rationale for the existence of the Association was Presbyterian, particularly the concluding sentence: "we judge it our duty, to be subject to a Council of the County, until there be some Superiour Council set up in the Province unto which we may appeal.[28] Yet no evidence links any of these ministers to Stoddard's Instituted Church. This was true even of William Williams, who, next to Stoddard, was probably the most widely known minister in western Massachusetts in the early eighteenth century. His extant writings—a few sermons and letters—give no hint of sympathy for Stoddard's position, only that he was a Presbyterian. Moreover, he was the sole Valley minister to publish a treatise during the Stoddard-Mather debate. That treatise, while devoted largely to the nature of the Lord's Supper, was no defense of Stoddard, for Williams made it clear that he did not believe in converting ordinances.[29]

The extant records of the churches of the Valley do not manifest any sympathy for Stoddard's Instituted Church or, for that matter, Presbyterianism. Several churches refused to join the Hampshire Association even though it did not vest in a ministerial organization the kind of power Stoddard called for in the *Instituted Churches.*[30] The Hampshire Association imitated the associations created by the Saybrook Platform. Although its constitution upheld the Presbyterian conception of a covenanted national church and suggested that individual churches ought to bow to higher ecclesiastical authority, it contained no provisions to make such authority effective.[31] Yet lay opposition to the Association caused dissension and, even among churches whose ministers assented to the Association, one resisted participation. Nathaniel Collins of Enfield faced the loss of his pastorate because of his support. His flock refused to allow him to serve communion, complained bitterly of the quality of his preaching, and criticized him for involving them in the Association.

. . .

The failure of Stoddard's Hampshire Association to resolve amicably the Enfield dispute reflected the true extent of Stoddard's influence over the churches of the Connecticut Valley. Although Stoddard was personally revered, even feared, his idea of the Instituted Church fell on deaf ears. Nor was his own church a significant exception, for he had only slightly greater success with his own congregation than with neighboring ones. His attempts to remold his church into a model of the Instituted Church were quietly and consistently resisted throughout his pastorate, although, because of his personal influence, he achieved some success and retained the good will of his flock.

The First Church of Northampton had been formed in 1661. Stoddard arrived in 1669 as replacement for the first minister, Eleazer Mather, who had died the same year. The church had been organized under Mather's watchful eye, and its polity reflected his Congregationalism. But in 1667 Mather became bedridden with a serious illness and was unable to continue his pastoral duties. The church used his absence as an opportunity to change certain aspects of its polity that the brethren disliked. The church underwent what it called a "reformation," designed to bring its practices into conformity with the prevailing opinions of the country. The "reformation" ended shortly before Stoddard assumed the pulpit.[32]

Northampton's reformation centered on the adoption of the Half-Way Covenant, which Mather had opposed. In addition, the church adopted a new and enlarged church covenant which spelled out out in greater detail the obligations of members. The covenant stressed the congregation's duty toward the children of the church and established provisions for their care and edification. Also, the church sought to extend its watch to persons baptized in the Northampton church who remained nonmembers. These persons were allowed to enter a special "state of education" where they could be disciplined and catechized until such time as they could meet the requirements for full communion. The church approved a new profession of faith defining the nature of the Lord's Supper according to the doctrine of the "Seals," and reaffirmed its traditional position on admission to communion. All prospective members were required to make a "relation of experience" designed to reveal the "special worke of Gods Grace" to the assembled members.[33]

Stoddard began to agitate for changes in the church's constitution soon after his arrival. After his ordination in 1672 he achieved some success when the church agreed to a significant liberalization of membership requirements by allowing children of the church almost automatic membership upon reaching adulthood. "Such as grow up to adult age in the church shall present themselves to the Elders," the church affirmed, "and if they be found to understand and assent unto the doctrine of faith, not to be scandalous in life, and willing to subject themselves to the government of Christ in this Church, shall publickly own the Covenant and be acknowledged members of this church.[34] This was a momentous decision for a church which had shown so much concern four years earlier to bring its practices into conformity with the general practices of the country. In one day a significant group of potential members was released from the obligation of relating an experience of conversion before the congregation.

Stoddard probably hoped for more. If he did, he was disappointed, for the polity of his church remained unchanged for the next eighteen years. During that time he no doubt placed his entire church in a state of education," urging them to accept the reforms he so ardently proposed.[35] Finally, in the winter of 1690 he offered two motions to the church. First, he called for the abolition of a public confession of religious experience in order "to bring all to the Lords Supper that had a knowledge of [the] Principles of Religion, and not Scandalous by open Sinfull Living." Second, he asked the church to approve his contention that the Lord's supper was a converting ordinance. Stoddard won the first motion and the public profession—a church practice for thirty years—was abolished. The second motion lost by a small majority; the younger members supported Stoddard while the older ones, including the ruling elders, voted against him.[36]

Stoddard's dream of an Instituted Church was not to be realized. The church retained its covenant as well as a half-way status for baptized adults not reared in the town. Members continued to be designated as being in "full communion," and the brethren retained an equal voice with the minister in matters of doctrine and discipline, a situation inconsistent with Stoddard's beliefs. Moreover, the church never gave official sanction to his notion of the Lord's Supper as a converting ordinance although Stoddard had one final victory. In 1714, the forty-fifth year of his pastorate, the church endorsed the formation of the Hampshire Association and acknowledged the validity of a national church in covenant with God, one in which local congregations recognized that in some areas their powers gave way to those of "ecclesiastical councils." Also, the church agreed to bring all baptized persons in the town under the discipline of the church regardless of whether they had ever owned the covenant.[37] By that vote the Northampton church endorsed a form of Presbyterianism familiar to New England. It was not, however, "Stoddardeanism."

At seventy-two, some men might have been content with a small victory, but not Stoddard. Too devoted to his private struggle, he never considered either surrender or armistice. Always the strategist, he recognized that any objective could be approached from different directions just as he knew the value of masking intentions before the eyes of opponents. Therefore he was not above an occasional display of intellectual trickery, such as a public affirmation of something he did not believe or a public denial of something he did believe.

. . .

Stoddard's craftiness, his occasional attempts at subterfuge, and his skill as a polemicist not only confused contemporaries but have baffled modern scholars as well. Thus it is not surprising to find that students have missed his most important alteration in form, the decision to abandon the Instituted Church around 1708. Attacting little support from any quarter, lay or clerical, and attacked from press and pulpit, Stoddard published a treatise entitled *The Inexcusableness of Neglecting The Worship of God, Under A Pretence of being in an Unconverted Condition.* In it he returned to the position of *Safety of Appearing,* arguing that he had never meant that any ordinance, least of all Communion, existed primarily for conversion. Rather, he continued, the sacraments were intended mainly for preparation, although it was possible that in attending the Table a sinner could be converted. Concerning Communion, on which much of his debate with Mather had centered, he argued that it was no more than a "Memorial of Christs Death."[38]

As he had in 1685, he again urged that open communion was necessary because of the importance of the ordinances in preparatory work. But rather than admit a change of heart, he simply stated that he had been misconstrued by critics who punished anyone daring to "depart from the ways of our Fathers . . ."[39] He continued the same refrain the next year in another pamphlet, *An Appeal to the Learned . . . ,*[40] and then he stopped. He wrote no more on the Instituted Church.

Why he stopped is the object of considerable historical debate. Some students have argued that he defeated Increase Mather and, knowing it, retired. Others, believing the laments of *Inexcusableness* and *Appeal to the Learned,* have ventured the opinion that Stoddard grew tired of being misunderstood and misconstrued and simply gave up.[41] In a way he did, but not for these reasons. Stoddard had lost and knew it, and, although he continued to press his own church for reforms for a time, he was eager to extricate himself from further public debate. *Inexcusableness* and *Appeal to the Learned* were designed to allow him an honorable retreat.

Although he lost a battle, he retained his intense desire to reach New England's unconverted, as well as his hostility to church discipline, especially Congregationalism. He saw continued signs of religion's decay and, as always, he blamed New England Congregationalism and the Reformed mentality which had fostered it. Too long a frontier minister to be foiled by adversity, Stoddard developed a new plan for New England's redemption.[42] In 1718, he explained his decision to drop the Instituted Church in a blistering little pamphlet entitled *An Examination of the Power of the Fraternity.*[43] *An Examination,* a savage attack on Congregationalism and the Cambridge Platform, sounded typically Stoddardean, but it was not. He wrote it to confess publicly a serious error in judgment. For decades he had assumed that New England Congregationalism represented the collective thoughts and actions of the clergy, so, in seeking reform, he had attempted to alter the thinking of his colleagues. Few had accepted his program, but many had come to agree that change was necessary and had worked actively to bring it about. Their efforts, and his, had reached fruition in such devices as the Saybrook Platform and the Hampshire Association.

In retrospect, Stoddard lamented, they achieved nothing, for the real power in the churches lay with the brethren, and they resisted every attempt at reform, no matter how innocuous. The brethren, Stoddard argued, were the true paladins of Congregationalism, although it was not the Congregationalism of clergy, synods, or the Reformed tradition. Rather, it masked the very godlessness he and others had labored so long to destroy. The brethren were hypocrites, claiming to protect their rights and privileges in God's name while seeking only self-interest. They labeled all existing practices and beliefs traditional and therefore sacrosanct, and resisted reform even when shown how, in the name of the "power of the fraternity," their recalcitrance contributed to the collapse of true religion.[44] For the first time, Stoddard drew a sharp distinction between lay and clerical conceptions of a congregational polity. The former, not the latter, constituted the real enemy. The Instituted Church foundered not as a result of Increase Mather's logic but because of the ignorance and hostility of the laity. Smug and secure in their churches, fearful of change in any form, the brethren cloaked worldliness in the guise of Congregationalism while arguing that no alteration in either doctrine or discipline was possible without the approval of the fraternity—approval the fraternity never granted.

The brethren rationalized the "power of the fraternity" with constant appeals to the Cambridge Platform, and Stoddard turned his fury on that document and its creators. "The mistakes of one Generation," he announced, "many times become the calamity of succeeding Generations. The present Generation are not only unhappy by reason of the darkness of their own Minds, but the errors of those who have gone before them, have been a foundation to a great deal of Misery." The Platform was contrary to the "experience" of the churches in that it was written "before they had much time to weigh those things . . . and some of their Posterity are mightily devoted to it, as if the Platform were the Pattern in the Mount." And what was the "experience" of the churches? A century of life in New England demonstrated that the "community" was unfit to judge and rule in the church. The brethren lacked both understanding and wisdom, for few had "read or studied." "If the Multitude were to be judges in Civil causes," Stoddard warned, "things would quickly be turned up-side down."[45]

Stoddard offered "practical" objections to the Platform as well, evidently assuming that laymen would respond to that approach. He devoted his energies to refuting specific arguments against clerical rule, repeating a litany he had uttered for half a century. He chided those willing to let elders act only as "moderators" of meetings. To those who feared "corrupt" elders he replied that lay power was a poor defense against corruption since corrupt rulers always indicated a corrupt people. He spoke also of those who feared rule by elder because it tended to "exalt the Minister or debase the Brethren." In that, he added sarcastically, there was no more danger than in "the confining of Preaching to the Minister."[46]

More than ever Stoddard blamed New England's preoccupation with church discipline for the sad state of religion. By 1718 he believed he possessed a clearer understanding of the problem, and it was far worse than even he had imagined. Buttressed by the Cambridge Platform, clerical Congregationalism had wrought a social revolution. The brethren, blindly following the dictates of deluded minds, used the Platform to justify godless ways and protect them from all clerical attempts at reform. Trapped by ancient rhetoric, the clergy continued to seek a solution in discipline, little realizing that synodical decisions paled before the "power of the fraternity." Stoddard was just as critical of his own thinking. His Instituted Church, an alternative to Congregationalism and Presbyterianism, had been aimed at clerical ears. That it had generated no enthusiasm meant little, for he realized now that, even had he won hosts of ministerial supporters, the fraternity would have stopped him, just as it had in Northampton. Thus, perhaps sadly, Stoddard wrote the epitaph for his sacramental church.

To destroy the grip of the brethren on the structure of the churches, to resurrect clerical authority, and to reach New England's ever-growing multitudes of unconverted, Stoddard adopted a new tactic and gave it theological justification. By his own claim one of New England's most successful soul-winners, Stoddard measured his ministerial experience to find the secret of his success. His own personality, he decided, was the key. Not that he attributed any special power to his own efforts—for whatever he possessed was God's—but he had been the agent in the conversion of many souls and, he concluded, whatever he had done must have been right in the sight of God.

The position that Stoddard now adopted was not so much new as an elaboration of skeletal ideas presented in *Safety of Appearing*. The gospel was the sole means to conversion. Before conversion, however, every sinner underwent preparatory work, although that work had no saving power in itself. Preparatory work proceeded in two stages, humiliation and contrition, and its progress was aided by the ordinances of the church: baptism, preaching, the Word, Communion, and the like.[47]

His new evangelicalism was patterned on this outline, although in a considerably modified form. Searching his own experience in Northampton, he decided that God most often used the ordinance of preaching as the vehicle for the dispensation of grace.[48] Thus he concluded that if religion in New England languished it did so primarily because of the low quality of ministers and their lack of training in the workings of the Spirit, often due to their own unconverted state. Also, it languished because of the pathetic state of preaching and the shortage of "powerful preachers.[49]

Simply stated, Stoddard's plan involved little more than an attempt to upgrade the quality of ministers by conveying to them what he, in his success, had learned of the true nature of the ministerial function. What he passed on by book and pamphlet between 1713 and 1729 were his secrets. In *A Guide to Christ* he explained the workings of the Spirit and the "varieties of religious experience" and offered to young clergymen his wisdom and expertise in guiding sinners through preparatory work. In the same book he emphasized the absolute necessity of a converted ministry, arguing that no one could understand another's travail until he had followed the same path. Only six years earlier he had written that a converted ministry was not really necessary to do God's work.[50]

In the writings of his last years, Stoddard devloped his conception of "powerful preaching," including the proper use of emotionalism and the fear of damnation. Schafer and others have noted its distinctive characteristics.[51] Stoddard stressed constantly the correct manner of preaching—his manner. The gospel, while the only means of conversion, seemed most "efficacious" in the hands of the experienced and converted minister of the Lord who developed its truths in the manner used by Stoddard. Such a message was not novel in New England, for it invoked images of Shepard and Hooker, as well as an earlier Stoddard.[52] Yet for the aged warrior it represented a real breakthrough, for it suggested a tactic that would simultaneously reach the unconverted, raise the level of ministerial importance by making clergy vital in conversion, and provide a lever to unhinge the "power of the fraternity" and diminish the importance of church discipline in the minds of both clergy and laity.

Meanwhile other Valley clergymen began to share Stoddard's contempt for ecclesiastical discipline and synodical decisions. As their writings suggest, they flocked to his new plan. The Word was the only source of salvation, and it was most "efficacious" when applied by the "powerful preacher." The ministry must be upgraded, not by formal education, but through experience of the workings of the Spirit and practice in guiding souls through preparation. Suddenly, as never before, ministerial writings discovered Paul as the archetype of the powerful preacher and agent of conversion. He was described as an itinerant evangelist, dispensing the Word and bringing souls to Christ. Paul had argued, the evangelicals believed, that there were two principal ingredients in conversion, minister and Word. Properly handled, they were devastating.[53]

As Stoddard hoped, the Connecticut evangelicals' emphasis upon gospel preaching led them to open hostility toward Congreational discipline. Their intent was to create a "Great Awakening" and, to facilitate its coming, they advocated an itinerant, evangelical ministry. The realization of this ideal began haltingly in efforts like Stoddard's Hampshire Association's establishment of weekly public lectures around 1712 in which members exchanged pulpits and gave "reforming sermons" designed to stimulate religious revivals.[54] In the 1720s the practice became more informal and subject to abuse by laymen who travelled about posing as trained clergy. Ultimately, of course, the trend toward an itinerant ministry would find fruition in the career of George Whitefield.

Evangelicals continually looked for signs of an "Awakening." In the 1720s, revivals and mass conversions or, in the ministerial rhetoric, great "outpourings of the Spirit" appeared frequently. In 1721, for example,

Eliphalet Adams of New London traveled to Windham, Connecticut, to mark a revival in that community and praise the minister whose preaching brought it about. He told a throng that revivals, although still widely scattered, were no longer uncommon and that a "great Awakening" appeared imminent.[55]

Adams, of course, was correct, although it is doubtful whether the results were those intended or expected by the clergy. In Norwich, for example, evangelicalism only added fuel to the deep-seated personal and institutional antagonisms already present in church and community, especially those between church and minister, church and town, and brethren and brethren. Instead of reviving religion and restoring ministerial authority, revivalism in Norwich resulted in the destruction of the church.[56] In Northampton where Stoddard's grandson and successor, Jonathan Edwards, gave revivalism and intellectual justification far superior even to Stoddard's, Edwards's reward was missionary work among the Indians.

The pattern in Norwich and Northampton was the pattern of the Great Awakening in New England.[57] The institutional cement of many churches—Stoddard's lay Congregationalism—cracked, although the result was not so much heightened religiosity as social and ecclesiastical chaos. A plethora of new sects emerged and anticlericalism remained, as did the trend toward secularism or "worldliness." Moreover, the fragmenting effects of the Awakening appeared in secular institutions, disrupting traditional patterns of authority, weakening institutional relationships, and, some have argued, creating fertile ground for a revolutionary mentality.

Had he lived, Stoddard would have decried the results as loudly as any. Yet New England's traditional preoccupation with discipline suffered irrevocable harm, and revivalism and evangelicalism became permanent features of American religious history. Solomon Stoddard, New England's often lonely pioneer advocate of doctrine over discipline, deserved much of the credit although the irony of his final victory would not have escaped him. A persistent foe of Reformed ecclesiology, his most effective weapon proved to be Reformed theology. Long the champion of the institutional church, Solomon Stoddard nearly brought about its demise.

The argument advanced in the foregoing article is developed at greater length in Paul Lucas's recent book, Valley of Discord: Church and Society along the Connecticut River, 1636–1725 *(Hanover, N. H., 1976). There Lucas stresses the long course of dissent and conflict in western New England that began with the first settlements and intensified as the Puritan century progressed. If Lucas's conclusions about the Connecticut Valley can be applied to the rest of New England—a question that awaits further study—the extent of Puritanism's decline in the late seventeenth and early eighteenth centuries may have been less precipitous than many scholars have assumed.*

NOTES

1. Some of the more important treatments of Stoddard are Perry Miller, "Solomon Stoddard, 1643-1729," *Harvard Theological Review*, XXXIV (1941), 277-320, as well as his *The New England Mind From Colony to Province* (Cambridge, Mass., 1953), hereafter cited as *From Colony to Province* (I have used the 1961 paperback edition published by Beacon Press); Edmund S. Morgan, *Visible Saints: The History of a Puritan Idea* (New York, 1963); Norman Pettit, *The Heart Prepared: Grace and Conversion in Puritan Spiritual Life* (New Haven, Conn., 1966); Robert G. Pope, *The Half-Way Covenant: Church Membership in Puritan New England* (Princeton, N. J., 1969); Thomas A. Schafer, "Solomon Stoddard and the Theology of the Revival," in Stuart C. Henry, ed., *A Miscellany of American Christianity: Essays in Honor of H. Shelton Smith* (Durham, N. C., 1963), 328-361; and James P. Walsh, "Solomon Stoddard's Open Communion: A Reexamination," *New England Quarterly*, XLIII (1970), 97-114. Some of the ideas presented in this article were outlined in Paul Lucas, "The River Gods: Mr. Stoddard's Valley, 1650-1730" (a paper delivered at the meeting of the American Historical Association, Dec. 30, 1967, Toronto, Canada).

2. One who flirted with that notion was Joseph Haroutunian, *Piety versus Moralism: The Passing of the New England Theology* (New York, 1932), 197-198.

3. See Thomas Hooker, *A Survey of the Summe of Church Discipline* (London, 1648), Introduction, A2-A4.

4. Stoddard, *The Doctrine of Instituted Churches, Explained and Proved from the Word of God* (London, 1700), 1-5, 22, 25-28; see also Increase and Cotton Mather's analysis of Stoddard's position, "A Defence of Evangelical Churches," introduction to John Quick, *The Young Mans Claim unto the Sacrament of the Lords-Supper. Or, the Examination of a Person approaching to the Table of the Lord* (Boston, 1700) [orig. publ. London, 1691]).

5. In his chapter on Stoddard in *From Colony to Province*, Miller was correct in asserting that Stoddard differed from most New England divines in that his God was more Old Testament than New. However, Miller was wrong in arguing that Stoddard upheld a capricious, irrational God. Stoddard's God was perhaps more terrible than the God of most of his colleagues, yet he was still bound by the "law," and although above it, agreed to abide by it (the binding Covenant of Grace and Christ's atonement). Stoddard, *The Safety of Appearing at the Day of Judgement, In the Righteousness of Christ: Opened and Applied* (Boston, 1687), 205. If anything, Stoddard's notion of God made the Deity a very rational being. Stoddard believed that God's plan for man was perfectly clear and understandable and represented an unbroken chain from creation to the present. Although all-powerful, God acted rationally and man could easily interpret His plan as it was revealed in history. This was Stoddard's message in both *Safety of Appearing* and *Instituted Churches*.

6. Stoddard, *Instituted Churches*, 5-6, 18-19, 22. Stoddard did not leave the decision to seek membership to chance. Although most ordinances existed only for visible saints, the "Scandalous" were not ignored. They were to be impelled to reform and seek membership through another ordinance, enlightened preaching. Stoddard dwelt very little on preaching in his early treatises, although his Northampton revivals or "harvests" were common knowledge. However, from occasional remarks it is known that he envisioned preaching as primarily an educative function designed to instruct the sinner in Christian doctrine and morality, thus qualifying him for church membership. Later, however, Stoddard altered radically his conception of the preaching function, giving it a position of preeminence in the process of conversion. Simultaneously, he deemphasized the saving power of other ordinances, especially the Lord's Supper. See pp. 288ff. and n. 78. See also *ibid.*, 22-25, and Stoddard, *The Inexcusableness of Neglecting The Worship of God, Under a Pretence of being in an Unconverted Condition* (Boston, 1708), 27.

7. Stoddard, *Instituted Churches*, 7-8, 25-29.

8. *Ibid.*, 29-32.

9. *Ibid.*, 12, 18-22.

10. Edward Taylor to Solomon Stoddard, Feb. 13, 1687/8, Edward Taylor's Notebook, Massachusetts Historical Society, Boston.

11. Miller, "Solomon Stoddard," *Harvard Theo. Rev.*, XXIV (1941), 299-302, and Miller, *From Colony to Province*, 231-247.

12. Quick, *Young Mans Claim*.

13. Increase and Cotton Mather, "Defence of Evangelical Churches," introduction to Quick, *Young Mans Claim*, 9-11. Herein, the elder Mather argued that his *Order of the Gospel* (Boston, 1700) ought to be construed as an answer to Stoddard and that he meant it as such. Yet it seems apparent from his argument in the "Defence" that much of what Stoddard wrote took him by surprise. Why else would he have appended a 62-page treatise to Quick's pamphlet, if he had said all that was necessary in the *Order of the Gospel*?

14. According to the doctrine of the "Seals," the Lord's Supper was a commemoration or "Seal" of the Covenant of Grace between God and man. Therefore, it was argued that admission to the Supper ought to be restricted to known regenerates.

15. Mather hints that Samuel Rutherford once flirted with the notion of "converting" ordinances.

16. *Ibid.*, 43-46.

17. I have searched the libraries of both Connecticut and Massachusetts for any evidence linking Connecticut clergymen to Stoddard's views and found practically nothing. Only two may be connected to Stoddard with any certainty. Gurdon Saltonstall of New London— Governor Saltonstall after 1707—supported Stoddard in his Sermon Preached before the First Church of New London, Dec. 26, 1703, "Sermons of Gurdon Saltonstall," Mass. Hist. Soc. Stephen Mix of Wethersfield, Stoddard's son-in-law, made a request in his will that all his daughters receive copies of Stoddard's works (see Sherman W. Adams and Henry R. Stiles, *The History of Ancient Wethersfield, Connecticut* [New York, 1904], I, 330-332) and partially endorsed Stoddard in his *Extraordinary Displays of the Divine Majesty and Power* (New London, Conn., 1728), 29.

18. The best discussion of the Saybrook synod and Platform remains Williston Walker, *The Creeds and Platforms of Congregationalism* (Boston, 1960 [orig. publ. New York, 1873]), 495-516. . . .

19. Walker, *Creeds and Platforms*, 498-502, and J. Hammond Trumbull and Charles J. Hoadly, eds., *The Public Records of the Colony of Connecticut* . . . (Hartford, Conn., 1850-1890), V, 51.

20. The passage is from the Ezra Stiles MS, Yale University Library, New Haven. Conn., and is quoted in Walker, *Creeds and Platforms*, 501.

21. Walker, *Creeds and Platforms*, 505. The Platform's section on church government is to be found on 502-506.

22. The existence of an independent "Presbyterian" faction in Connecticut in 1708 is ably documented by Walker, *Creeds and Platforms*, 495-516. Its leader was Timothy Woodbridge, not Stoddard. Presbyterians formed a solid minority of the Connecticut clergy as early as 1660, antedating the arrival of Stoddard in the Valley by a decade. For a discussion of the emergence of Connecticut Presbyterianism, see Pope, *Half-Way Covenant*, 75-95, and Paul R. Lucas, "Presbyterianism Comes to Connecticut: The Toleration Act of 1669," *Journal of Presbyterian History*, L (1972), 129-147. For a recent analysis of the Saybrook synod and Platform, see Richard Bushman, *From Puritan to Yankee: Character and the Social Order in Connecticut, 1690-1765* (Cambridge, Mass., 1967), 150-155.

23. This conclusion is based on extensive research among extant church records available in manuscript or on microfilm at the Connecticut State Library, Hartford. The notion of Stoddard's influence is predicated largely on the number of clergymen and churches in Massachusetts and Connecticut in the late 17th century apparently sharing his view on an open communion. Scholars have assumed that the idea originated with Stoddard, but, as Pope suggests and my research bears out, it was common to Presbyterians and some Congregationalists long before Stoddard. Stoddard was not innovating but adopting a familiar belief. The innovative elements in Stoddard's ecclesiology were twofold: (1) his peculiar interpretation of the relationship of Old and New Testaments, and (2) his attempt to link open communion to "converting" ordinances. Thus, for documentation of Stoddard's influence, I have scanned church records not for evidence of open communion, for that would be meaningless, but for attempts to link open communion and converting ordinances. I have found no such evidence, except in Stoddard's own church. See Pope, *Half-Way Covenant*, 251-258, and Lucas, "Presbyterianism Comes to Conn.," *Jour. Pres. Hist.*, L (1972), 140-145.

24. Entry dated "1690," Edward Taylor's Notebook.

25. See the Windsor "Creed and Covenant," adopted Oct. 23, 1647, and Rev. Henry

Rowland's brief illuminating history of the Windsor church in Windsor Church Records, III, Conn. State Library. See also Henry R. Stiles, *The History of Ancient Windsor, Connecticut* (New York, 1859), 172-173, and George L. Walker, *History of the First Church in Hartford, 1633-1883* (Hartford, Conn., 1884), 429-431.

26. Woodbridge's method for admitting new members is described in the records of the First Church of Wethersfield, II, Jan. 2, 1703, Conn. State Library. The date of its adoption is not known, since the Hartford records do not go back earlier than the beginnings of Woodbridge's ministry in 1684. There is no record of a change of the practice under Woodbridge, thus suggesting that it antedated him. Most likely it stemmed from the 1650s or 1660s, for it is known that Samuel Stone, Hooker's colleague, endorsed a position identical to the later practice. See Stone, "Against a Relation of Experience" (n.d.), Notebook of Joseph Gerrish, 1697, Mass. Hist. Soc., which was partially responsible for a violent controversy in the church in the 1650s and 1660s. The controversy is outlined in G. Walker, *Hartford*, 150-180. See also Records of the First Church of Hartford, X, Accounts and Records, 1685-1772, Conn. State Library.

27. John Russell to Increase Mather, Mar. 28, 1681, "The Mather Papers," Mass. Hist. Soc., *Collections*, 4th Ser., VIII (1868), 83-84. The story of Russell's problems with the church in Wethersfield may be found in Adams and Stiles, *Wethersfield*, I, 159-163. Russell's reactions to the relations of experiences by the Westfield members is recounted in John H. Lockwood, *Westfield and its Historic Influences, 1669-1919* . . . (Westfield, Mass., 1922), 114-117.

28. Northampton Church Records, I, Dec. 9, 1714, Forbes Library, Northampton, Mass.

29. Williams's conception of the Lord's Supper is outlined in *The Danger of Not Reforming Known Evils Or, The Inexcusableness of a Knowing People Refusing to be Reformed* (Boston, 1707). See also Williams, *The Honour of Christ Advanced by the Fidelity of Ministers and their being received as sent by Him* (Boston, 1728).

30. Missing from the list of original churches were, for example, Westfield, West Springfield, and Northfield.

31. The charter of the Association made no mention of any machinery for the enforcement of decisions of the council and gave no evidence that local churches were being asked to surrender their sovereignty. Northampton Church Records, I, Dec. 9, 1714.

32. Trumbull, *Northampton*, I, 70-105, 214-215.

33. Northampton Church Records, I, Jan. 9, Feb. 16, and Feb. 22, 1668.

34. *Ibid.*, Nov. 5, 1672.

35. See, for example, Russell to Increase Mather, Mar. 28, 1681, "Mather Papers," Mass. Hist. Soc., *Colls.*, 4th Ser., VIII, 83-84; see also Edward Taylor to Solomon Stoddard, Feb. 13, 1687/8, Edward Taylor's Notebook, and Stoddard's reply of June 4, 1688, in Taylor's Notebook.

36. Entry dated "1690," Edward Taylor's Notebook.

37. Northampton Church Records, I, Dec. 9, 1714.

38. Stoddard, *Inexcusableness of Neglecting The Worship*, 11-12, 16-17, 25-27. Cf. Stoddard's argument in *Instituted Churches*, 22, where he states emphatically that all ordinances, and especially the Lord's Supper, exist primarily for conversion.

39. Stoddard, *Inexcusableness of Neglecting The Worship*, Preface.

40. Stoddard, *An Appeal to the Learned. Being A Vindication of the Right of Visible Saints to the Lords Supper, Though they be destitute of a Saving Work of God's Spirit on their Hearts: Against the Exceptions of Mr. Increase Mather* (Boston, 1709).

41. Miller suggested that Stoddard won the argument: *From Colony to Province*, Chap. 17. Walsh supports Stoddard's contention that no one understood his position. See "Stoddard's Open Communion," *NEQ*, XLIII (1970), 111-112.

42. Stoddard's continuing concern for the unconverted as well as his fear of impending doom for New England is ably demonstrated in *The Efficacy of the fear of Hell, to restrain Men from Sin* (Boston, 1713), 5-10. The elements of his new plan for reaching the unconverted were sketched in two sermons bound with *Efficacy*. These sermons, undated, were delivered during a revival in Northampton. One was entitled "Minister's had need have the Spirit of the Lord upon them, in order to the reviving of religion among the people." The other was "To Preach the Gospel to the Poor."

43. Appended to Stoddard, *The Presence of Christ with the Ministers of the Gospel* (Boston, 1718).

44. *Ibid.*, 1-3.

45. *Ibid.*, 1-2, 11.

46. *Ibid.*, 7, 14-15, 16.

47. Stoddard, *Safety of Appearing*, 119-125; his argument should be compared with his *Guide to Christ* (1714), Preface, 3-23, and *The Nature of Saving Conversion, and the Way wherein it is Wrught* (Boston, 1719), 81-83, for obvious similarities.

48. This is the essence of *Guide to Christ*. Throughout the sacramental phase of his career Stoddard emphasized that preaching was meant primarily to edify those not able to qualify as visible saints, while other ordinances were to prepare and convert professing Christians. Thus, in downgrading the converting power of some ordinances, he enlarged and enhanced the meaning and scope of gospel preaching. See, for example, *Inexcusableness*, 27, and n.18 above.

49. Stoddard's argument, repeated often between 1713 and 1729, may be gleaned from several of his writings. In addition to *Guide To Christ* and *Efficacy*, see *Presence of Christ, The Defects of Preachers Reproved* (New London, Conn., 1724), and *The Duty of Gospel-Ministers to preserve a People from Corruption* (Boston, 1718). The most concise statement I have found of his position is the sermon, "Minister's had need have the Spirit," given around 1712, printed with Stoddard's *Efficacy* and also appended to the 1816 edition of *Guide To Christ* (Northampton, Mass.), 157-175.

50. Stoddard, *Guide To Christ*, XXI. Cf. his argument in *The Falseness of the Hopes of Many Professors . . .* (Boston, 1708), 16.

51. Schafer, "Solomon Stoddard," in Henry, ed., *Miscellany of American Christianity*, esp. 333-335, 340-342, is outstanding in this regard and, while devoted largely to analyzing his theory of conversion, takes notice of Stoddard's belief in the efficacy of emotional preaching and the proper presentation of the Word. Schafer's article, while generally excellent, should be followed by Pettit's discussion of Stoddard as a preparationist in *Heart Prepared*, 200-207, which displays a keener understanding of the position of Stoddard in the evolution of the notion of preparation for grace in New England.

52. Stoddard paraphrased Hooker when he wrote, "The word of God is an hammer, and men must smite with strength to make the nail enter, or the rock to break. If the word of God be preached in a dull dead way, it is not like to have much efficacy." "Minister's had need have the Spirit," in *Guide to Christ* (1816), 159. See also the sermon following, "To whom is the gospel to be preached?," 163-169, 176-183. Other passages illustrating Stoddard's doctrine of minister and Word are quoted by Schafer, "Solomon Stoddard," in Henry, ed., *Miscellany of American Christianity, passim*.

53. Stoddard's evangelicalism was matched by that of his colleague at Hatfield, William Williams, in *The Great Salvation Revealed and Offered in the Gospel* (Boston, 1717). . . .

54. The reference to the Hampshire County Weekly Lecture is from Warham Williams, *Journal*, 1712, Mass. Hist. Soc. A Hartford County Weekly Lecture began soon after and is discussed in G. Walker, *Hartford*, 268-270.

55. Adams, *Sermon at Windham*, ii-iv.

56. See J. M. Bumsted, "Revivalism and Separatism in New England: The First Society of Norwich, Connecticut, as a Case Study," *WMQ*, 3d Ser., XXIV (1967), 588-612.

57. An exception to the pattern of disruption is noted and analyzed by James Walsh, "The Great Awakening in the First Congregational Church of Woodbury, Connecticut," *ibid.*, XXVIII (1971), 543-562.

20 | JONATHAN EDWARDS AND PURITAN CONSCIOUSNESS

RICHARD L. BUSHMAN

The controversy aroused by Solomon Stoddard, both during his lifetime and after, is mild compared to that generated by his grandson and successor to the Northampton pulpit—Jonathan Edwards. Besides being the foremost Puritan theologian of his day, Edwards was also the central figure in New England's Great Awakening of the 1730s and 1740s. His espousal of revivalism made it respectable in much of New England; his "Sinners in the Hands of an Angry God" is probably the most famous sermon in American history; and his dismissal from the Northampton congregation in 1750 marked the end of the Awakening in New England.

From what source and for what reasons the Awakening came to New England have long been disputed. In the 1720s many Dutch reformed congregations in the middle colonies experienced a harvest of converts and a general rise in piety. In the mid-1730s Edwards had comparable success in Northampton and neighboring towns. By the 1740s the revival was at a peak, encouraged by a triumphant visit from George Whitefield, the great English evangelist. But the then current explanations—that God had moved the hearts of sinners (according to the Awakening's supporters) or that a perfect madness had befallen New England (according to its critics)—have not satisfied historians. Some, such as John C. Miller in "Religion, Finance, and Democracy in Massachusetts" (New England Quarterly, VI [1933]) see the roots of the movement in social conflict; others, including Ernest Caulfield in A True History of the . . . Throat Distemper *(New Haven, 1939) find an epidemiological cause for the sudden upsurge in religiosity; still others, notably Richard Bushman in* From Puritan to Yankee: Character and Social Order in Connecticut, 1690–1765 *(Cambridge, Mass.; 1967), advocate a psychological explanation. Probably the most widely read survey of the movement is Edwin S. Gaustad's* The Great Awakening in New England *(Chicago, 1957), which stresses the breadth of its geographical and social appeal. It was not confined to the frontier or small towns or the lower classes, Gaustad argues, but was a universal phenomenon. Gaustad attributes its origin to a deeply felt reaction against Puritanism's drift toward excessive rationalism during the previous several decades. In the 1740s Puritan piety reasserted itself.*

All interpretations of the Awakening must attempt to explain Edwards's role—as an instigator, a catalyst, or a charismatic leader. Biographies of Edwards are abundant, including such outstanding though not unchallenged interpretations as Ola E. Winslow's Pulitzer Prize-winning Jonathan Edwards, 1703–1758: A Biography *(New*

York, 1940) and Perry Miller's Jonathan Edwards *(New York, 1949).*
Scholarly articles on the subject are legion. The following selection ex-
amines Edwards's Puritan roots.

The writings of Jonathan Edwards contain the most complete description
we have of the piety of eighteenth-century American Puritans. Events
made Edwards a specialist in Puritan consciousness. As he said, "It is
a subject on which my mind has been peculiarly intent, ever since I
first entered on the study of divinity."[1] Besides inquiring into his own
heart, he was chief defender and interpreter of the Great Awakening and
closely studied revival conversions to distinguish God's work from mere
emotions.

He recorded the fruits of his research in a variety of documents. His
"Diary" and *Personal Narrative* tell of his own quest for holiness; *A
Treatise Concerning Religious Affections, The Distinguishing Marks of a
Work of the Spirit of God,* and *Some Thoughts Concerning the Present
Revival of Religion in New England* were his answers to critics and
frauds. He also edited and commented on *An Account of the Life of the
Late Reverend Mr. David Brainerd,* for the edification of concerned
souls, and described the Northampton revivals of 1735 in *A Faithful Nar-
rative of the Surprising Work of God.* Taken together these works fully
describe the religious consciousness of his day.[2]

Edwards used himself as the chief source of information about conversion. His personal writings reveal how occupied he was with dark intruders from the cellars of his soul and the sweet and glorious visitations
of grace. He wrote at length of the contrasting moods they brought and
of his earnest efforts to keep his house in order. By reconstructing Edwards' dominant states of mind and by following his will's struggle to
regulate the powers of heaven and self circulating in his soul, we can
recover much of Puritan consciousness, making it available for translation into modern terms for our better understanding.[3]

The reconstruction and translation of Puritan experience is a task well
worth the effort. In an age so distant as our own, Calvinist theology may
be conceived as a stately but desolate mansion. We think of doctrinal
treatises as houses of intellect only and are baffled to know why men
shed blood in their defense. We also may glibly connect our modern
revival of Calvinism with the pristine variety, when actually the meaning
of the two are quite different. Perhaps most important to historians, the
significance of the passing of Puritanism is misunderstood if we do not
understand the structure of feeling lying behind it. Calvinist doctines lost
their vitality because old passions faded and new ones emerged. The
changing shape of personal experience motivated the intellectual
developments of the eighteenth and nineteenth centuries. Unless we have
a clear conception of the Puritan consciousness, we will not see what
died and what lived on, and why, in the mentality of the new era. Edwards' discourses on piety fix a base line for measuring ensuing changes.

Edwards' close attention to the condition of his soul began when he
was 16 and in his last year of college. In the two years after graduation
while studying divinity in New Haven his "sense of divine things"

gradually increased. In August of 1722 he finished his preparations and accepted a temporary pulpit in New York where he preached for a year and a half before returning to his father's house in East Windsor. Soon after he was appointed tutor at Yale. All this time his ecstatic experiences were growing more intense. Many years later he said that he enjoyed more "constant delight and pleasure" in God then than ever afterwards.[4]

This time of conversion from age 16 to 20 is described in both the "Diary" and the *Personal Narrative*. The *Narrative* was written after the revival had already swept through the Connecticut Valley once, beginning at Edwards' pulpit in Northhampton. It recounted his experiences of 20 years earlier, as a guide to parishioners who had newly discovered the excruciating pleasure of grace, and also presented his religious credentials, as it were, to critical observers in America and Europe. As such, the story stressed the moments of exaltation when Edwards felt close to God and drank deeply of the joys of grace.

The "Diary," or what remains of it, begins in December of 1722, near the midpoint of the conversion period. It was written for Edwards' own use, not for publication, and more frankly discloses how the peaks of rapture were regularly followed by valleys of despair. Essentially it is a record of the uphill struggle for piety. Those high thoughts of Christ's excellence which infused him with heavenly delight were exceedingly elusive, and he was determined to strengthen his hold at all costs. In one sense the "Diary" is a handbook of Edwards' "inventions," as he called them, and their success in producing spiritual enjoyments.[5] He was continually searching for ways of sustaining himself on the heights or of lifting himself from the depths. The "Resolutions" accompanying the "Diary" are the restraints and spiritual exercises he imposed on himself to achieve a lasting piety.

The highs and lows in Edwards' consciousness were two distinct frames of mind, characterized by clear contrasts in spiritual operations. The graceless consciousness he variously called dull, dead, lifeless, sunken, decayed. He never enlarged upon the meaning of these words as he did with those describing his delights, but they suggest a depressed state characterized by a flat emotional tone. In his "Diary" he equated deadness with listlessness and spiritual lethargy. At one point he said that during times of dullness he was not easily affected, his emotions were sluggard and bound.[6] He also said in his *Treatise Concerning Religious Affections* that hardness of heart was the opposite of piety, and hardness "meant an unaffected heart, or a heart not easy to be moved with virtuous affections, like a stone, insensible, stupid, unmoved, and hard to be impressed," in short "a heart void of affections."[7]

The misery of spiritual decay arose also from the paralysis of the righteous will. Edwards despised the listlessness which "unbends and relaxes" the mind "from being fully and fixedly set on religion." In times of spiritual depression he lamented that his "resolutions have lost their strength." Apparently when he began to sink, all his powers to act decayed. "I do not seem to be half so careful to improve time, to do every thing quick, and in as short a time as I possibly can." He was not "half so vigorous" and moved slowly, meanwhile placating his conscience by thinking of religion. He resolved the next time he was lifeless to force himself "to go rapidly from one thing to another, and to do those things with vigour." When all else failed, he worked arithmetic or practiced shorthand, anything to keep active.[8] Feeling his powers bogging down, he drove them on to keep his will from stalling.

To Edwards' mind a mired will and bound affections were two aspects of the same spiritual malfunction. The will was the faculty inclining the soul to like or dislike, to choose or reject, and all its movements were accompanied by some degree of pleasure or displeasure. Will and emotion were organically bound together. The will could not act without arousing emotion to some degree, and the affections were still only when the will stood at dead center, in a state of "perfect indifference."[9]

Thus conceived, the affections were symptomatic of the state of the soul. Joyous sensations of love for God meant the heart was strongly inclined toward heaven, while listless affections revealed an unconcern for religion. Edwards despised dullness because it signified "perfect indifference" to God.

He also knew that the will might pass beyond neutral indifference and incline lustfully toward worldly objects. The heart hard to holy affections was perfectly capable of indulging wicked passions.[10] The diary is a record of the evil inclinations that tugged persistently at Edwards' will. He readily admitted that "without the influences of the Spirit of God, the old serpent would begin to rouse up himself from his frozen state, and would come to life again."[11] The lethargy of will, even in merely dull frames, was not simple laziness as Edwards sometimes supposed, but the pull of inadmissable desires straining against his purer inclinations. When he did arithmetic or practiced shorthand he was struggling to deny forbidden demands from the emotional underworld.

His plans for invigorating the will are closely related to the central impulse of the Protestant Ethic. Cotton Mather probably had the same experience in mind when he urged a vocation on his parishioners as a means of avoiding the snares of sin. Devotion to a calling, even practicing shorthand, kept the Puritan a step ahead of the dullness and sin dogging his heels.

These artificial devices for controlling the will were forgotten when Providence lifted Edwards from his sunken condition to his other, happier frame of mind. Grace liberated the emotions and will from their prison. Filled with the Spirit, he joyously exercised the powers of his soul with perfect freedom. "Wherever true religion is," he said, "there are vigorous exercises of the inclination and will towards divine objects."[12] High thoughts of Christ made "unusual repentance of sin" easy, and he pressed forward in the struggle with alacrity and zeal. All of his work went better once the will was freed. "I can do seven times as much in the same time now, as I can at other times, not because my faculties are in better tune; but because of the fire of diligence that I feel burning within me."[13] The startling change confirmed the doctrine of rebirth, the creation of a new man in the old.

When downcast, Edwards complained most about his will, but when exalted he spoke more of affections. While lifeless, all he could manage was to drive on the stubborn will, knowing the affections would revive if the will inclined toward God. In gracious times, the affections rolled forth so powerfully that the will was carried effortlessly on their crest.[14] Obeying God, mortifying the self, and all the acts of will were the natural outcome of gracious love. Will and affections, of course, sprang from the same source, but overwhelmed as he was by love for God, it seemed fitting to stress one side more than the other. In the treatise on affections he underscored the proposition that "true religion, in great part, consists in holy affections."[15]

Above all Edwards experienced a consuming love of God. When he walked in the fields softly singing God's praises, his heart overflowed with adoration. Sometimes he imagined himself alone in the mountains with Christ, "and wrapt and swallowed up in God. The sense I had of divine things," he wrote, "would often of a sudden kindle up, as it were, a sweet burning in my heart; an ardor of soul, that I know not how to express." Even then his passions were not so free as he wished:

> The inward ardor of my soul, seemed to be hindered and pent up, and could not freely flame out as it would. I used often to think how in heaven this principle should freely and fully vent and express itself. Heaven appeared exceedingly delightful, as a world of love; and that all happiness consisted in living in pure, humble, heavenly, divine love.[16]

The love that began in God, overflowed into His creations, and encompassed all men. "God's excellency, his wisdom, his purity and love, seemed to appear in every thing," he wrote. He delighted to think of heaven where "reigns heavenly, calm, and delightful love, without alloy . . . where those persons who appear so lovely in this world, will really be inexpressibly more lovely, and full of love to us."[17] Brainerd's love was not only ardent for his friends but for his enemies, Edwards noted, and he could happily report that the Northampton converts put away their differences and treated one another lovingly.[18]

The whole world was bathed in affection while Edwards lived in the "sweet sense of the glorious *majesty* and *grace* of God."[19] The contrast with his sunken condition is perhaps best epitomized in the two words, sweet and vile. When despondent, insofar as he felt emotions, they were bitter and dark: anger, fretting, despair, melancholy, and scorn. They made him feel vile and odious, and he sought to extinguish or at least hold them back, covering them with an appearance of benignity.[20] In grace, his feelings were calm and sweet, the two words he used over and over. His emotions pleased and satisfied him, giving joy as they poured from his heart.

Eventually these sweet enjoyments always departed, and Edwards found himself decaying. His "Diary" entries most often occur at these times when he was sinking and remorsefully examining himself to discover why. His response then is important to understand, for it was characteristic of his psychic structure and basic to his theology. He always blamed himself, lamenting, "O how weak, how infirm," and set about to regain grace. In a letter to a young Christian he advised the practice he always followed himself: "If at any time you fall into doubts about the state of your soul, in dark and dull frames of mind . . . apply yourself with all your might, to an earnest pursuit after renewed experience, new light, and new lively acts of faith and love." At the same time, he knew he could not earn grace by himself. His full lament was, "O how weak, how infirm, how unable to do anything of myself!" The very cause of his downfall was a pretension to independence. "While I stand, I am ready to think that I stand by my own strength . . . when alas! I am but a poor infant, upheld by Jesus Christ."[21] Even the thought of becoming pious by his own efforts was prideful and offensive to the Spirit.

What then could he apply himself to in the pursuit of renewed experience? The answer was obvious to a Puritan. He must work to be more dependent on God: "O let it teach me," continues the lament, "to depend less on myself, to be more humble, and to give more of the praise of my ability to Jesus Christ."[22] The heart of Edwards' piety was humility before God carried to the point of self-abasement. His exertions all aimed to make less of himself and more of God.

Humility began with the extinction of the vile self, the lazy, lustful, proud, angry, and morose self which had to be wholly denied, utterly annihilated with all its corruptions to make room for the "contrary sweetness and beauties." He continually looked for more stringent forms of self-denial, convinced that "great instances of mortification, are deep wounds, given to the body of sin." With every blow he grows weaker and more cowardly, "until at length, we find it easy work with him, and can kill him at pleasure."[23]

To set a demanding standard, he once considered the supposition that there was to be but one person on earth at a time "who was properly a complete Christian, in all respects of a right stamp," and resolved "to act just as I would do, if I strove with all my might, to be that one, who should live in my time."[24] That sort of conscientiousness called for the complete elimination of every trace of sin. By the time Edwards began the "Diary" the grosser forms of sensuality were completely vanquished and never merited a comment. Instead he regularly rebuked himself for eating, drinking, and sleeping too much. He decided to skip meals entirely if called to the table when deeply engaged in study.[25] He could not permit himself any display of untoward emotions either. He worried especially over an inclination to find fault and resolved that he must "refrain from an air of dislike, fretfulness, and anger in conversation," and constantly exhibit an air of "love, cheerfulness, and benignity."[26] Of course, he assiduously attended to all his religious duties such as prayer and scriptural study, requiring of himself the most intense concentration and heartfelt devotion. When he wrote that he was lax in not "forcing" himself upon "religious thoughts," he was looking for total immersion in his meditations.[27]

Occasionally the constant exertion was too much and without willing it, his strength gave way. He even wondered if "this being so exceedingly careful, and so particularly anxious, to force myself to think of religion, at all times, has exceedingly distracted my mind, and made me altogether unfit for that, and every thing else." But then his strength returned and it

seemed he could not do enough. Sometimes he discovered himself looking forward to a suspension of effort, thinking he had earned a release as
his due. But he knew his lot was different, that he must "live in continual
mortification without ceasing, and even to weary myself thereby, as long
as I am in this world, and never to expect or desire any worldly ease or
pleasure."[28]

Talking about his wickedness seemed to strengthen him for the struggle and he avidly enlarged upon his corruption. His sin, he said, was
"like an infinite deluge, or a mountain over my head." Or, reversing the
metaphor, "when I look into my heart, and take a view of my
wickedness, it looks like an abyss infinitely deeper than hell."[29] These
were sincere expressions of his feelings, but he also knew that pointing to
his sinfulness empowered him to hate and destroy those qualities that
were, after all, still part of himself. When he said, "What a foolish, silly,
miserable, blind, deceived, poor worm am I, when pride works," he confirmed his determination to cut out a cancer in his own flesh, however
painful. One of his early resolves was "to act in all respects, both speaking and doing, as if nobody had been so vile as I."[30] Confessing his sins
passionately and in detail permitted him better to "abhor" himself and
brought him closer to the total abasement he sought.[31]

For all its difficulty, the destruction of evil impulses was the easiest
part of Christian humility. The more demanding task was to give up
every desire, every aspiration, every action that was not wholly for the
glory of God, even if ostensibly innocent. The Christian's duty was "freely, and from his very heart, as it were [to] renounce, and annihilate
himself."[32] Edwards wanted to destroy his sins and then give everything
else to God.

He once asked himself if he could permit any delight or satisfaction
that was not religious. His first answer was yes, for otherwise there
would be no rejoicing in friends or any pleasures in food. But on second
thought he concluded, "We never ought to allow any joy or sorrow, but
what helps religion." That degree of self-denial was characteristic. One of
his first resolutions was "never to do any manner of thing, whether in
soul or body, less or more, but what tends to the glory of God." Comprehensive as the statement was, it did not satisfy him. Every time he
received an honor or prospered in any way, he worried that he exalted
himself at God's expense. He regularly added resolutions blocking any
loopholes where pride could sneak through.[33] In one of his high moments
of dedication he entered into a covenant with God that was meant to be
absolutely binding and complete.

> I have been before God, and have given myself, all that I am, and have, to
> God; so that I am not, in any respect, my own. I can challenge no right in
> this understanding, this will, these affections, which are in me. Neither have I
> any right to this body, or any of its members—no right to this tongue, these
> hands, these feet; no right to these senses, these eyes, these ears, this smell, or
> this taste. I have given myself clear away, and have not retained any thing as
> my own.[34]

Abasement was not merely an unpleasant prerequisite for enjoying
God's love, a device for opening oneself to grace, ending when the walls

of the self were broken and the Holy Spirit flowed in. Humility was the desirable condition in itself, one of the sweetest fruits of grace, and came to culmination in times of spiritual joy. Edwards prayed for constancy in the pleasures of humility, for they were "the most refined inward and exquisite, delights in the world." He loved to be "a member of Christ, and not anything distinct, but only a part, so as to have no separate interest, or pleasure" of his own.[35] Some of his most fervent contemplations were of himself as a child being led by Christ. In a famous passage he pictured the soul of a Christian as "a little flower as we see in the spring of the year low and humble on the ground, opening its bosom to receive the pleasant beams of the sun's glory." "There was no part of creature holiness," he went on to say, "that I had so great a sense of its loveliness, as humility, brokenness of heart and poverty of spirit; and there was nothing that I so earnestly longed for. My heart panted after this, to lie low before God, as in the dust, that I might be nothing, and that God might be ALL, that I might become as a little child."[36]

The impulse for self-abasement brought Edwards to the verge of mysticism but it never carried him over. The passages that ring most mystically express a *longing* to lie low in the dust, a *yearning* to be "emptied and annihilated" and "full of Christ alone," without claiming consummation.[37] Edwards could never forget the corruptions of the flesh blocking the influx of the Spirit. The Northampton converts after experiencing God's glory had "a far greater sight of their vileness, and the evil of their hearts."[38] The more grace they enjoyed, the more they recognized how their sins separated them from God.

Edwards' conception of the regenerative process also stood in the way of self-annihilation. The Spirit of God did not absorb the person; it altered his nature and more particularly his perceptions. Through his senses he saw the beauty of God and his creations, and this vision was the source of holy love. The whole process was supernatural, originating in God, yet it was natural too, working through the faculties of the creature. Through all, the individual mind was held inviolate. Indeed regeneration depended on the independent functions of perceiving minds beholding and loving God's excellence.[39]

The preservation of individuality, however, was not Edwards' reason for advocating this conception of regeneration. Its beauty was that it diminished the role of the self in redemption. Humility not individualism was still the prevailing spirit. The schemes of Arminians and radical Separates, the targets of Edwards' arguments in *A Treatise Concerning Religious Affections*, began with selfishness. The Arminians thought men chose God to achieve their own happiness, and the Separates said converted men loved God because he first loved and saved them.[40] Edwards opposed both for justifying man's cardinal sins, pride and self-love. Men came to true faith only by obliterating the self and occasionally at least loving God purely for his own sake.

By affording a glimpse of God's beauty and excellency, grace gave men this selfless experience. Seeing His beauty, brightness, and glory, they adored Him without thinking of themselves. Saints "do not first see that God loves them, and then see that he is lovely; but they first see that God is lovely, and that Christ is excellent and glorious." "False affections begin with self." "The hypocrite lays himself at the bottom of all," while "the saints' affections begin with God." "In the love of the true saint, God is the lowest foundation."[41]

Edwards lived for those moments when the sight of God's glories so overwhelmed him that self fell away and he stood awestruck in love and admiration. "A true saint, when in the enjoyment of true discoveries of the sweet glory of God and Christ, has his mind too much captivated" to think of himself. "It would be a loss which he could not bear to have his eye taken from the ravishing object of his contemplation and turned back on his own person."[42]

The same power to humble also confirmed Edwards' belief in conventional Calvinistic doctrines. The value of belief in divine sovereignty, original sin, and free grace was that they allowed nothing to human powers and attributed all to God. They tore away the shields of human self-confidence and laid a man bare, exposing his sinfulness, helplessness, and utter dependence. An Arminian could hold on to some small portion of pride and self-righteousness. Calvinism compelled a man to abase and abhor himself totally.

Edwards' conviction that complete humility was man's only hope for enjoying divine love, a regulated will, and salvation was the theme of his life. He announced it in his maiden sermon before the Boston ministry, entitling his address, *God Glorified in Man's Dependence*. He elaborated a sophisticated and exalted statement of the same theme in *The Nature of True Virtue*, the work occupying him in his closing years. His personal devotions, his polemical works, and his sermons constantly returned to God's overpowering glory and dominion, and man's nothingness.

This picture of Edwards' consciousness raises many questions about his character. Perhaps the most obvious is what relationship existed between his deep yearning for self-abasement and his two most common spiritual conditions: the emotional lethargy of the dull states and the passionate love of the exalted? Why did self-annihilation seem the most natural way from lethargy to love? How can we explain his spiritual dynamics in terms meaningful for our generation?

To suggest a tentative answer, as well as to sketch briefly Edwards' place in the subsequent development of the New England mentality, we must set him in a wider context of Puritan consciousness. Edwards devoted most of his writing to the converted man, but he also described the condition of hardhearted sinners. Actually the misfortunes of this state were implicit in all of his writings, for only in contrast to the miseries of wickedness did the joys of grace achieve poignancy. Though not invidiously, the gracious person constantly contrasted present light to his previous deplorable darkness.

In the years before the Great Awakening, preachers addressed many a sermon to sleepy sinners. A drowsy insensibility seemed to have fallen over their parishioners and blinded them to the unfortunate condition of their souls. These everyday Puritans listened to the sermons about sin and damnation without taking them to heart. In one way or another they warded off the threats descending from the pulpit and maintained their equanimity. Some thought their righteousness was sensible proof of grace. Others may have taken enough comfort from the multiplication of flocks and herds not to worry over their estate in the hereafter. Edwards was well aware of "the stupifying influence of worldly objects."[43]

The apparent complacence, however, was not solid confidence. For years before the Awakening, ministers noted that an earthquake, a sudden death, or a shipwreck would set their congregations to inquiring into the state of their souls. Any sort of dramatic destruction seemed to resonate in the hearts of people and awaken fears of God's intentions for them. Two deaths in Northampton "contributed to the solemnizing of the spirits of the Young People" there. And when one person was seized with a concern for his soul, soon others were too. Observers from neighboring towns came to look and went away with "wounded spirits."[44] The sudden precipitation of concern up and down the Connecticut Valley in 1735 showed how the previous complacency covered a powerful dread.

The realization that burst upon these people was a horrifying conviction of their own sin. They saw clearly "their dreadful pollution, enmity, and perverseness: their obstinacy and hardness of heart." They could not forget their guilt in the sight of God and saw that with perfect justification "the great God who has them in his hands" was "exceedingly angry." He appeared "so much provoked and his great wrath so increased" that He must "forthwith cut them off" and send them down to "the horrible pit of eternal misery."[45]

The revival ministers pressed hard on these fears, teaching what was called "legal humiliation." They underscored the hopelessness of the state of the unconverted, tried by the law of God and found worthy of unending torment. The picture of God they drew was a Being of wrath and terror, unflinching in his determination to crush sinners. Small wonder that some listeners were buried in black despair. Weighed down by concern, Edwards' Uncle Hawley killed himself in the midst of his spiritual turmoil. Others clamored to "extinguish their fears of hell," and find some "confidence of the favour of God."[46] They grasped at every evidence of righteousness in themselves, every image of holy things crossing their minds, eager to see grace in it. The Separates made the assurance of the Saints a cardinal point of doctrine. Edwards thought their hopes were obstacles to true humility, but he himself brooded about his own state, at last resolving simply to trust in God's good intentions for him.[47]

Edwards wondered why he had never passed through the state of terror. Missing this step worried him a little, for it was standard in the conversion process.[48] But if he never felt terror consciously, there is reason to believe it worked its effects on some level. Like other Puritans he was seized with concern when destruction threatened, in his case a bout with pleurisy that brought him "nigh to the grave." Before his conversion nothing was more terrible to him than thunder and lightning flashing from the heavens, and he admitted that from childhood, no point of doctrine bothered him more than that of "God's sovereignty, in choosing whom he would to eternal life, and rejecting whom he pleased; leaving them eternally to perish, and be everlastingly tormented in hell." "It used

to appear like a horrible doctrine to me," he confessed.[49] Perhaps as
revealing as anything is the sermon, *Sinners in the Hands of an Angry
God.* It is difficult to conceive of anyone portraying the terrors so
forcefully who had not experienced them somewhere in his being.

> The God that holds you over the pit of hell much as one holds a spider, or
> some loathsome insect over the fire, abhors you, and is dreadfully provoked;
> his wrath towards you burns like fire; he looks upon you as worthy of
> nothing else, but to be cast into the fire; he is of purer eyes than to bear to
> have you in his sight; you are ten thousand times more abominable in his
> eyes, than the most hateful venomous serpent is in ours. . . . You hang by a
> slender thread, with the flames of divine wrath flashing about it, and ready
> every moment to singe it and burn it asunder.[50]

Those are the words of a man who had felt the wrath of God.

This component of terror was as characteristic of Puritan consciousness, Edwards not excepted, as love or lethargy, and must be included in an explanation of Puritan personality. Altogether the picture is
suggestive to anyone with a psychoanalytic orientation, though
understandably very complex. So compelling an experience as conversion necessarily operated on many levels of the personality, and brought
to the surface feelings shaped in all the earliest stages of life. Edwards' cycle of depression and exhilaration, for example, is reminiscent of an infant's experience of fright and estrangement when separated from the
mother and of the return of well-being when reunited. The wooden
restraint of feeling is a mode of handling emotion characteristic of those
taught to fear vile outbursts when first learning self-control. The com-
pulsive element in Edwards' preoccupation with will restraining the affections is unmistakable. Conversion permitted a safe and joyous release of
emotions somehow purified by submission to God.

But the central issue, judging from Edwards' own account, was reconciliation with the great and terrible God. The doctrine of God's
sovereignty in punishing whom he wished was the major intellectual
obstacle to conversion—and acceptance of God's right to judge prepared
the way. The scripture that precipitated the first outpouring of grace was
I Timothy 1:17: "Now unto the King eternal, immortal, invisible, the only wise God, be honor and glory forever and ever, Amen." Immediately
after the glory of the declaration struck him, Edwards saw God as an object to be loved rather than feared. His heart was caught up to Christ and
he rejoiced in the loveliness of the Divine Being.

In many ways this reconciliation of Father and son paralleled the
resolution of the Oedipal crisis, and perhaps Edwards' conversion may
be considered, on one level, primarily as an effort to repeat and master
that difficult ordeal. The similarities between Puritan theological images
and common childhood images of father and son suggest how easily the
tensions of the early conflict could be transferred to the adult conversion
experience. The qualities of the revival preachers' terrible God, for example, resemble those a boy often attributes in his imagination to his father-
rival. In the boy's fear-inspired fancy, even a kind and meek father is
credited with omnipotence and horrible wrath. The boy's own transgres-

sions also, though chiefly imaginary, may be painted in darkest hues, like those of the concerned sinner. Edwards' sense of sinfulness fits the childhood pattern particularly well. Partly he deplored specific faults like sensuality, anger, or faultfinding, departures from some ideal standard. But more wicked than disobedience was pride, the vaunting of the self over God. The young boy likewise worries about disobeying the father, especially about indulging sensuous desires that seem like forbidden approaches to the pleasures of the mother's love. But his most wicked ambition is to displace the father, to rise above him, perhaps to kill him. Pride is the boy's most offensive sin, too.

Some of Edwards' comments on hidden sinful desires reveal how deeply he probed for the roots of wickedness.

> You object against your having a mortal hatred against God; that you never felt any desire to kill him. But one reason has been, that it has always been conceived so impossible by you, and you have been so sensible how such desires would be in vain, that it has kept down such a desire. But if the life of God were within your reach, and you knew it, it would not be safe one hour.[51]

He could never consciously contemplate this act himself, of course, but pride in the world, or self-confidence, anything but abasement, pulled down God and exalted man in symbolic patricide.

This analogy between the spiritual vicissitudes of childhood and maturity helps explain the emotional lethargy of Edwards' dull frames of mind. The repression of emotion is connected with the assimilation of the wrathful father image. He becomes part of the boy and in a sense constantly rebukes him for his wicked desires. This judging part of the self demands the containment of evil thoughts, repressing them below the level of consciousness. Thus whenever Edwards' pride or sensuality raised their heads, his internal monitor suppressed them, closing subterraneously the valves of all feeling even remotely related to the forbidden actions. His experience of dullness was actually a struggle between unconscious desires and the countervailing powers of conscience.

Edwards made peace with this conscience as boys make peace with their fathers, by relinquishing the ambition to overcome and by striving to imitate instead. The significance of abasement was that he felt assured of God's love only when sin and pride were utterly denied, when he offered no threat to God's supremacy. Only when utterly humble was he confident of divine approval. Then his conscience released the emotions of the gracious times and he loved heartily and freely. Blessed with God's love, his soul glowed with affection. Humility was the surest way to circumvent the wrath of God and recover full use of will and emotions.

One reward of humility was a return to a harmony with all of Being, reminiscent of the infant's most blissful exchanges of love with its mother. Edwards longed to be a child again, or a little flower, opening itself "to drink in the light of the sun," eagerly consuming nourishment from the center of warmth and affection. One of the signs of true conversion was the awakening of sensory delight in divine things, which often seems like a hungry absorption of 'love through all the nerve endings, as if the usual consumption organs would not suffice. God's perfections in these joyous moments assumed at times a maternal cast. Edwards sang of the beauty, grace, and holiness of God, and longed to be "wrapt" up in Him. Indeed much of Edwards' model for the ideal harmony with God seemed to be drawn from the selfless union of mother and child.[52]

The meaning of conversion in psychoanalytic terms was that men accepted Edwards' solution to a basic problem. The preachment of legal humiliation brought the crisis to a head. The images of terror and the condemnation of sinners revived long-buried fears by starkly confronting the listener with a reflection of his inner self. The preachers coined words for feelings that before were mute, and gave archaic despair currency in the adult consciousness.

The wounds thus opened began to heal when the convert under the influence of grace ceased to fight God and started to love Him. By giving way entirely, as Edwards had, the sinner escaped divine terror and indeed found it beautiful.[53] Edwards sometimes saw a passive calm come over sinners as they gave up the struggle and surrendered to God. In his own case, the doctrine of divine sovereignty that once appeared horrible became "exceedingly pleasant, bright, and sweet." After that, thunder entertained rather than terrified and led to "sweet contemplations of my great and glorious God."[54]

The big difference in the converted man was that love swallowed fear. Natural men stood in awe of God and fearfully strove to obey Him, but they did not voluntarily "abase themselves and exalt God alone. This disposition," Edwards said, "was given only in evangelical humiliation, by overcoming the heart, and changing its inclination, by a discovery of God's holy beauty." Natural men may be "subdued and forced to the ground;" converted men "are brought sweetly to yield, and freely and with delight to prostrate themselves at the feet of God."[55] The crux of conversion was the willing renunciation of all ambition to rival God, and submission to Him out of selfless love.

The resolution of the old conflict brought peace and joy and a great tenderness of heart, but not perfect stability. The price of freer emotions and heightened self-awareness was the painful oscillation between dullness and grace. Edwards observed that among all converted men, love decayed and fear arose in persistent alternation. Conversion reconciled the soul to God without purging entirely the former fears of the terrible Divinity. The old terror remained at some level and properly so, Edwards thought, because it stirred men up to watchfulness, excited them to "care for the good of their souls," and restrained them from sin.[56] Conscience repeatedly drove them to the abasement and self-denial which preceded the return of gracious love, the dominant mode of Puritan consciousness.

Pointing to the parallel between boy-father and man-God relations does not fully explain the movements of the Puritan consciousness. At best the comparison suggests the sources of energy feeding the quest for piety. The theological and moral symbols—God, terror, pride, sin, abasement, love, beauty—tapped primary reservoirs of emotional power. The flow of childhood feelings into the adult struggle gave it urgency and endurance. But after saying that much the psychoanalyst can only congratulate Edwards for attempting to resolve an ancient and fundamental human dilemma.

The bald statement that the dramas of the Puritan consciousness were no more than a reenactment of the Oedipal trauma grossly distorts the truth. No simple link can be forged between childhood and adult life. Among other objections, there are logical flaws in such a contention. The most important is that all children pass through Oedipal crises, but not all adults are Puritans. The task of the historian is to explain why Oedipal problems were so prominent in the Puritan consciousness and why their resolution took the form it did.[57]

The inquiry obviously leads toward a study of Puritan family life and the conditions that magnified the boy's fear of his father.[58] It also leads toward a new look at Puritan culture to discover the elements that drew out this particular configuration of feelings from the varied experiences of childhood. It should be clear at this point how influential Calvinist doctrine was in the shaping of character. The conceptions of divine sovereignty, original sin, and free grace all stressed man's lowliness, God's power, and the necessity of submission. Those doctrines were bound to select from the legacy of childhood the patterns surrounding the Oedipal crisis and give them standing in the adult world. In the years when a young person was looking for the components of the private self that were negotiable in public, he could name and talk about these feelings. The doctrine helped him to choose them from his large store and award them a permanent place in his adult identity. Thus the Puritan encountered fewer obstacles to feeling sinfulness, despair, and holy wrath than, for example, a lad bred on optimism and rugged individualism in the late nineteenth century.

The Puritan consciousness began to decline in Edwards' own lifetime. By the end of the eighteenth century Puritans were in the minority even in New England. Either Edwards or the psychoanalyst could explain why. Calvinism required men to abase themselves totally in the hopes of reaching God, and few could meet the test. Edwards knew that pride and selfishness lay at the very bottom of the soul. Natural men had always constructed ingenious doctrinal defenses against God's demands for absolute humility. The psychoanalyst knows that boys who cease to compete overtly with their fathers continue the rivalry under various guises. No one surrenders entirely, and most will more or less openly protect their pride against the extreme demands of conscience.

Edwards lived to see eighteenth-century thinkers devising ways of stifling the voice of judgment and terror in themselves. The Enlightenment provided various notions of sufficient cultural strength to counterbalance the humbling doctrines of Calvinism. Reason was one of these. By virtue of its power Benjamin Franklin, a fugitive from Puritan Boston, held God to strict compliance with moral rules and could appease his conscience with good works. Benevolence was another. Charles Chauncy, Edwards' archfoe during the Awakening, said divine love and eternal punishment were contradictory. God desired the well-being of His children and punished to teach goodness. When the lesson was learned, the punishment ended. No one needed to fear permanent internment in the pit of misery. These two, reason and benevolence, helped many a Yankee to calm his fear of judgment and to avoid the humiliation of total surrender.[59]

The sons of the Puritans who resorted to these devices, however, did not enjoy perfect equanimity. Though its commands were muffled, conscience continued to drive men. They worried that their good works fell short, that pride had carried them too far, and that they must serve others more selflessly. They became zealous reformers, determined to exterminate from the world the evil they could not remove from their own hearts. However tightly they sealed the passage leading to the past, the voice of their fathers' God still resounded in their hearts. Even adherence to optimistic doctrines of progress only demonstrated how they feared their world would sometime collapse and God would have them in His awful power.

For many the cost of restraining God was the loss of internal freedom. Unable to face God in all his terror, they could never know Him in His glory. They held Him strictly to a reasonable morality and consequently were bound themselves. They enjoyed the small pleasures of decorous worship and worldly prosperity, and passed over the raptures of envelopment in heavenly love.

A few grandsons of the Puritans sensed they were cheated of their inheritance. A reasonable faith and moral propriety with quiet hopes for a good estate hereafter palled them. They hungered for sweeter, stronger nourishment. In this generation the transcendental prophets once again lost themselves in visions of divine excellence and felt the surge of holy love in their souls. They did not practice Edwards' humility; Emerson thought Puritanism a religion of "privation, self-denial and sorrow."[60] But they taught their own forms of discipline and surrender, and they avidly sought the moments of ecstasy and insight which as heirs of Edwards they knew were accessible to human consciousness.

Few others, however, tasted of the divine glory and so most forgot what Puritanism once meant. They saw only the terrors of a wrathful God and gladly buried the Puritan Divinity in the graves of their ancestors. Edwards was remembered chiefly for inhuman strictness and his debasement of human powers. Puritanism came to stand for dreary self-restraint and joyless piety. The latter-day generation lost touch entirely with the vital heart of Edwards' religion. They failed to see that unending spiritual exertions and absolute surrender were nought beside the sweetness of beholding and selflessly loving the great and glorious God.

Part of the fascination with Edwards comes from his diversity. Specialists in American literature have studied his prose; intellectual historians have examined his philosophical and scientific writings; and church historians have assessed his theological tracts and their impact on the evolution of New England Congregationalism. Edwards is also a likely subject for interdisciplinary investigation, as in Richard D.

Bushman's "Jonathan Edwards as Great Man: Identity, Conversion, and Leadership in the Great Awakening" (Soundings: An Interdisciplinary Journal, LII [1969]).

There is no indication that interest in Edwards is lagging. Books and articles on various aspects of his mind and career continue to appear with remarkable frequency, and Yale University Press is publishing a definitive edition of his complete works. Such efforts hold promise not only of a deeper understanding of the man but also of a better grasp of the causes and character of the Great Awakening.

NOTES

1. *The Works of President Edwards, in Four Volumes. A Reprint of the Worcester Edition.* 4 vols., New York: Leavitt, Trow & Co., 1843, vol. III, p. ix. Hereafter referred to as *Works.* John E. Smith explicates Edwards' definition of true religion in the introduction to Jonathan Edwards, *Religious Affections,* John E. Smith, Ed., New Haven: Yale University Press, 1959.

2. The guide to the literature on the English branch of the subject is William Haller, *The Rise of Puritanism,* New York: Columbia University Press, 1938.

3. For a comparable discussion of English Puritanism, see Richard Rogers and Samuel Ward, *Two Elizabethan Diaries,* M. M. Knappen, Ed., Chicago: American Society of Church History, 1933, pp. 1-16. Erik Erikson, *Young Man Luther: A Study in Psychoanalysis and History,* New York: W. W. Norton, 1958, is a much more sophisticated and complex discussion of Luther's piety. William James, *The Varieties of Religious Experience,* London: Longmans, Green, 1902, is still fundamental for anyone seeking psychological understanding of religion.

4. *Works,* I, pp. 16, 23.

5. The most complete versions of the "Diary" and the "Resolutions" appear in S. E. Dwight, *The Life of President Edwards,* New York: G. & C. & H. Carrill, 1830, hereafter referred to as *Life.* The reference is to p. 77.

6. Dwight, *Life,* p. 87.

7. *Works,* III, p. 16.

8. Dwight, *Life,* pp. 72, 81, 78, 91, 100.

9. *Works,* III, pp. 3-4.

10. *Ibid.,* III, p. 18.

11. Dwight, *Life,* p. 77.

12. *Works,* III, p. 6.

13. Dwight, *Life,* pp. 78, 83.

14. *Works,* I, pp. 17-18.

15. *Ibid.,* III, p. 2.

16. *Ibid.,* I, pp. 16, 18.

17. *Ibid.,* I, pp. 16-17, 19-20.

18. *Ibid.,* I, p. 659; III, p. 235; cf., I, p. 549.

19. *Ibid.,* I, p. 16.

20. Dwight, *Life,* p. 87.

21. *Ibid.,* pp. 81, 151.

22. *Ibid.,* p. 81.

23. *Ibid.,* pp. 85, 80.

24. *Ibid.,* p. 72.

25. *Ibid.,* pp. 78, 82, 83, 86, 87, 102, 103, 106.

26. *Ibid.,* p. 72.

27. *Ibid.,* pp. 77, 78.

28. *Ibid.*, pp. 81, 82, 77, 80.

29. *Works*, I, p. 22.

30. Dwight, *Life*, p. 68.

31. *Ibid.*, p. 90.

32. *Works*, III, pp. 139-140.

33. Dwight, *Life*, pp. 79-80, 68, 83, 69, 71, 72.

34. *Ibid.*, pp. 78-79.

35. *Ibid.*, pp. 83, 80.

36. *Works*, I, pp. 21, 18.

37. *Ibid.*, I, p. 22.

38. *Ibid.*, I, p. 550.

39. Miller, Perry. *Jonathan Edwards*. New York: William Sloane, 1949, pp. 67-68, 193-194.

40. *Works*, III, pp. 91-95.

41. *Ibid.*, III, pp. 93, 96.

42. *Ibid.*, III, p. 100.

43. *Ibid.*, III, p. 72.

44. *Ibid.*, III, p. 236.

45. *Ibid.*, I, p. 548; III, p. 549; cf. III, pp. 240-246.

46. *Ibid.*, I, p. 66.

47. Dwight, *Life*, pp. 76, 93, 99, 105.

48. *Ibid.*, p. 76; *Works*, I, pp. 15, 661-662.

49. *Works*, I, p. 15.

50. *Ibid.*, IV, p. 318.

51. *Ibid.*, IV, p. 48.

52. *Ibid.*, I, p. 18.

53. *Ibid.*, III, pp. 246-249; I, pp. 548-549.

54. *Ibid.*, I, pp. 15, 17.

55. *Ibid.*, III, p. 138.

56. *Ibid.*, III, p. 56.

57. I also hold with those who maintain a psychoanalytic interpretation of religion does not exclude a supernatural one.

58. Morgan, E. S. *The Puritan Family: Essays on Religion and Domestic Relations in Seventeenth Century New England*. Boston: The Trustees of the Public Library, 1944.

59. Haroutunian, J. *Piety versus Moralism: The Passing of the New England Theology*. New York: H. Holt, 1932, describes this development in theological terms.

60. Emerson, R. W. *The Complete Works of Ralph Waldo Emerson*. Concord Edition, Boston: Houghton, Mifflin, 1904, Vol. I, p. 220. My argument here follows that of Perry Miller in his essay, "From Edwards to Emerson," in *Errand into the Wilderness*, Cambridge: Harvard University Press, 1956, pp. 184-203.

PART EIGHT |

THE PURITAN LEGACY

No precise date marks the end of Puritan New England and the beginning of Yankee New England. The former faded slowly and unevenly; the latter emerged cautiously, at first as a subculture within Puritan society, until eventually—at some indefinable moment—it became dominant. But Puritanism as an intellectual force and as a religious persuasion lingered far beyond its theoretical demise.

The Puritan legacy, especially in the realm of literature, can be traced well into the nineteenth century and perhaps to the present. It is evident in various forms in the writings of Ralph Waldo Emerson, Nathaniel Hawthorne, and Herman Melville, to name only a few of the most prominent writers who often employed Puritan motifs and reflected Puritan attitudes. Moreover, as Sacvan Bercovitch has argued in *Puritan Origins of the American Self* (New Haven, 1975), Puritanism affected not only the way many nineteenth-century Americans wrote but also the way they saw the American past and future and how they saw themselves.

Historians have, on the whole, been only slightly less willing than literary critics to credit Puritanism with a significant impact on the nineteenth and twentieth centuries. Book titles—for example, William Allen White's *Puritan in Babylon: Calvin Coolidge* (New York, 1938), David L. Larson's *The Puritan Ethic in United States Foreign Policy* (Princeton, 1966), and Alan P. Grimes's *The Puritan Ethic and Woman Suffrage* (New York, 1967)—reflect that temptation. A few historians have even attributed democracy and the separation of church and state to seventeenth-century New Englanders. In 1947 Clifford Shipton ("Puritanism and Modern Democracy," *New England Historical and Genealogical Register*, CI [1947]) announced that "Puritanism has been probably the most important single factor in the shaping of the United States of today, and thus the most important factor in shaping the world of the immediate morrow." Few scholars would claim so much.

And yet there is a widespread conviction that Puritanism, in one form or another, had some influence not only on the subsequent development of New England but also on the mainstream of American history. The problem is to find causal connections rather than tangential or chronological affinities. It was once intellectually fashionable to blame late nineteenth-century Victorian attitudes on Puritan mores; the causal link, however, proved untenable. So have many other reputed ties between seventeenth-century Puritanism and later American history.

21 | THE PURITAN ETHIC
AND THE AMERICAN REVOLUTION

EDMUND S. MORGAN

*One connection that many, perhaps most, historians do acknowledge is between Puritanism and the American Revolution. The Puritans' legacy seems most demonstrable in the ideology of New England's patriots and especially (not surprisingly) among its Congregational clergymen. Charles W. Akers finds such a connection in the thought of Boston's Jonathan Mayhew (*Called unto Liberty: A Life of Jonathan Mayhew, 1720–1776 *[Cambridge, Mass.; 1964]). Alice M. Baldwin (*The New England Clergy and the American Revolution *[Durham, N.C.; 1928]) discerned a similar influence on New England clergymen in general and through them on the whole region. From a very different perspective, Alan Heimert has explored the interplay of religious and political ideologies in* Religion and the American Mind: From the Great Awakening to the Revolution *(Cambridge, Mass.; 1966), a work that has stimulated extensive debate. The following selection investigates one of the links between Puritanism and Revolutionary thought.*

The American Revolution, we have been told, was radical and conservative, a movement for home rule and a contest for rule at home, the product of a rising nationality and the cause of that nationality, the work of designing demagogues and a triumph of statesmanship. John Adams said it took place in the minds and hearts of the people before 1776; Benjamin Rush thought it had scarcely begun in 1787. There were evidently many revolutions, many contests, divisions, and developments that deserve to be considered as part of the American Revolution. This paper deals in a preliminary, exploratory way with an aspect of the subject that has hitherto received little attention.[1] Without pretending to explain the whole exciting variety of the Revolution, I should like to suggest that the movement in all its phases, from the resistance against Parliamentary taxation in the 1760's to the establishment of a national government and national policies in the 1790's was affected, not to say guided, by a set of values inherited from the age of Puritanism.

These values or ideas, which I will call collectively the Puritan Ethic,[2] were not unconscious or subconscious, but were deliberately and openly expressed by men of the time. The men who expressed them were not Puritans, and few of the ideas included in the Puritan Ethic were actually new. Many of them had existed in other intellectual contexts before Puritanism was heard of, and many of them continue to exist today, as they did in the Revolutionary period, without the support of Puritanism. But Puritanism wove them together in a single rational pattern, and

Puritans planted the pattern in America. It may be instructive, therefore, to identify the ideas as the Puritans defined and explained them before going on to the way in which they were applied in Revolutionary America after they had emerged from the Puritan mesh.

The values, ideas, and attitudes of the Puritan Ethic, as the term will be used here, clustered around the familiar idea of "calling." God, the Puritans believed, called every man to serve Him by serving society and himself in some useful, productive occupation. Before entering on a trade or profession, a man must determine whether he had a calling to undertake it. If he had talents for it, if it was useful to society, if it was appropriate to his station in life, he could feel confident that God called him to it. God called no one to a life of prayer or to a life of ease or to any life that added nothing to the common good. It was a "foul disorder in any Commonwealth that there should be suffered rogues, beggars, vagabonds." The life of a monk or nun was no calling because prayer must be the daily exercise of every man, not a way for particular men to make a living. And perhaps most important, the life of the carefree aristocrat was no calling: "miserable and damnable is the estate of those that being enriched with great livings and revenues, do spend their days in eating and drinking, in sports and pastimes, not employing themselves in service for Church or Commonwealth."[3]

Once called to an occupation, a man's duty to the Maker Who called him demanded that he labor assiduously at it. He must shun both idleness, or neglect of his calling, and sloth, or slackness in it. Recreation was legitimate, because body and mind sometimes needed a release in order to return to work with renewed vigor. But recreation must not become an end in itself. One of the Puritans' objections to the stage was that professional players made recreation an occupation and thereby robbed the commonwealth of productive labor. The emphasis throughout was on productivity for the benefit of society.

In addition to working diligently at productive tasks, a man was supposed to be thrifty and frugal. It was good to produce but bad to consume any more than necessity required. A man was but the steward of the possessions he accumulated. If he indulged himself in luxurious living, he would have that much less with which to support church and society. If he needlessly consumed his substance, either from carelessness or from sensuality, he failed to honor the God who furnished him with it.

In this atmosphere the tolerance accorded to merchants was grudging. The merchant was suspect because he tended to encourage unnecessary consumption and because he did not actually produce anything; he simply moved things about. It was formally recognized that making exchanges could be a useful service, but it was a less essential one than that performed by the farmer, the shoemaker, or the weaver. Moreover, the merchant sometimes demeaned his calling by practicing it to the detriment rather than the benefit of society: he took advantage of his position to collect more than the value of his services, to charge what the market would bear. In short, he sometimes engaged in what a later generation would call speculation.

As the Puritan Ethic induced a suspicion of merchants, it also induced, for different reasons, a suspicion of prosperity. Superficial readers of Max Weber have often leapt to the conclusion that Puritans viewed economic success as a sign of salvation. In fact, Puritans were always uncomfortable in the presence of prosperity. Although they constantly sought it, although hard work combined with frugality could scarcely fail in the New World to bring it, the Puritans always felt more at ease when adversity made them tighten their belts. They knew that they must be thankful for prosperity, that like everything good in the world it came from God. But they also knew that God could use it as a temptation, that it could lead to idleness, sloth, and extravagance. These were vices, not simply because they in turn led to poverty, but because God forbade them. Adversity, on the other hand, though a sign of God's temporary displeasure, and therefore a cause for worry, was also God's means of recalling a people to Him. When God showed anger man knew he must repent and do something about it. In times of drought, disease, and disaster a man could renew his faith by exercising frugality and industry, which were good not simply because they would lead to a restoration of prosperity, but because God demanded them.

The ambivalence of this attitude toward prosperity and adversity was characteristic of the Puritans: it was their lot to be forever improving the world, in full knowledge that every improvement would in the end prove illusory. While rejoicing at the superior purity of the churches they founded in New England, they had to tell themselves that they had often enjoyed more godliness while striving against heavy odds in England. The experience caused Nathaniel Ward, the "simple cobbler of Aggawam," to lament the declension that he was sure would overtake the Puritans in England after they gained the upper hand in the 1640's: "my heart hath mourned, and mine eyes wept in secret, to consider what will become of multitudes of my dear Country-men [in England], when they shall enjoy what they now covet."[4] Human flesh was too proud to stand success; it needed the discipline of adversity to keep it in line. And Puritans accordingly relished every difficulty and worried over every success.

This thirst for adversity found expression in a special kind of sermon, the Jeremiad, which was a lament for the loss of virtue and a warning of divine displeasure and desolation to come. The Jeremiad was a rhetorical substitute for adversity, designed to stiffen the virtue of the prosperous and successful by assuring them that they had failed. Nowhere was the Puritan Ethic more assiduously inculcated than in these laments, and it accordingly became a characteristic of the virtues which that ethic demanded that they were always seen to be expiring, if not already dead. Industry and frugality in their full vigor belonged always to an earlier generation, which the existing one must learn to emulate if it would avoid the wrath of God.

These ideas and attitudes were not peculiar to Puritans. The voluminous critiques of the Weber thesis have shown that similar attitudes prevailed widely among many groups and at many times. But the Puritans did have them, and so did their descendants in the time of the

Revolution and indeed for long after it. It matters little by what name we call them or where they came from. "The Puritan Ethic" is used here simply as an appropriate shorthand phrase to designate them, and should not be taken to imply that the American Revolutionists were Puritans.

The Puritan Ethic as it existed among the Revolutionary generation had in fact lost for most men the endorsement of an omnipresent angry God. The element of divinity had not entirely departed, but it was a good deal diluted. The values and precepts derived from it, however, remained intact and were reinforced by a reading of history that attributed the rise and fall of empires to the acquisition and loss of the same virtues that God had demanded of the founders of New England. Rome, it was learned, had risen while its citizens worked at their callings and led lives of simplicity and frugality. Success as usual had resulted in extravagance and luxury. "The ancient, regular, and laborious life was relaxed and sunk in Idleness," and the torrent of vices thus let loose had overwhelmed the empire. In modern times the frugal Dutch had overthrown the extravagant Spanish.[5] The lesson of history carried the same imperatives that were intoned from the pulpit.

Whether they derived their ideas from history thus interpreted or from the Puritan tradition or elsewhere, Americans of the Revolutionary period in every colony and state paid tribute to the Puritan Ethic and repeated its injunctions. Although it was probably strongest among Presbyterians and Congregationalists like Benjamin Rush and Samuel Adams, it is evident enough among Anglicans like Henry Laurens and Richard Henry Lee and even among deists like Franklin and Jefferson. Jefferson's letters to his daughters sometimes sound as though they had been written by Cotton Mather: "It is your future happiness which interests me, and nothing can contribute more to it (moral rectitude always excepted) than the contracting a habit of industry and activity. Of all the cankers of human happiness, none corrodes it with so silent, yet so baneful a tooth, as indolence." "Determine never to be idle. No person will have occasion to complain of the want of time, who never loses any. It is wonderful how much may be done, if we are always doing."[6] And Jefferson of course followed his own injunction: a more methodically industrious man never lived.

The Puritan Ethic whether enjoined by God, by history, or by philosophy, called for diligence in a productive calling, beneficial both to society and to the individual. It encouraged frugality and frowned on extravagance. It viewed the merchant with suspicion and speculation with horror. It distrusted prosperity and gathered strength from adversity. It prevailed widely among Americans of different times and places, but those who urged it most vigorously always believed it to be on the point of expiring and in need of renewal.

The role of these ideas in the American Revolution—during the period, say, roughly from 1764 to 1789—was not explicitly causative. That is, the important events of the time can seldom be seen as the result of these ideas and never as the result solely of these ideas. Yet the major developments, the resistance to Great Britain, independence, the divisions among the successful Revolutionists, and the formulation of policies for the new nation, were all discussed and understood by men of the time in terms derived from the Puritan Ethic. And the way men understood and defined the issues before them frequently influenced their decisions.

I. THE ORIGINS OF AMERICAN INDEPENDENCE

In the first phase of the American Revolution, the period of agitation between the passage of the Sugar Act in 1764 and the outbreak of hostilities at Lexington in 1775, Americans were primarily concerned with finding ways to prevent British authority from infringing what they considered to be their rights. The principal point of contention was Parliament's attempt to tax them; and their efforts to prevent taxation, short of outright resistance, took two forms: economic pressure through boycotts and political pressure through the assertion of political and constitutional principles. Neither form of protest required the application of the Puritan Ethic, but both in the end were affected by it.

The boycott movements were a means of getting British merchants to bring their weight to bear on Parliament for the specific purpose of repealing tax laws. In each case the boycotts began with extralegal voluntary agreements among citizens not to consume British goods. In 1764-65, for instance, artisans agreed to wear only leather working clothes. Students forbore imported beer. Fire companies pledged themselves to eat no mutton in order to increase the supply of local wool. Backed by the nonconsumers, merchants of New York, Philadelphia, and Boston agreed to import no British goods until the repeal of the Stamp Act. The pressure had the desired effect: the Stamp Act was repealed and the Sugar Act revised. When the Townshend Acts and later the Coercive Acts were passed, new nonconsumption and nonimportation agreements were launched.[7]

From the outset these colonial boycott movements were more than a means of bringing pressure on Parliament. That is to say, they were not simply negative in intent. They were also a positive end in themselves, a way of reaffirming and rehabilitating the virtues of the Puritan Ethic. Parliamentary taxation offered Americans the prospect of poverty and adversity, and, as of old, adversity provided a spur to virtue. In 1764, when Richard Henry Lee got news of the Sugar Act, he wrote to a friend in London: "Possibly this step of the mother country, though intended to oppress and keep us low, in order to secure our dependence, may be subversive of this end. Poverty and oppression, among those whose minds are filled with ideas of British liberty, may introduce a virtuous industry, with a train of generous and manly sentiments. . . ."[8] And so it proved in the years that followed: as their Puritan forefathers had met providential disasters with a renewal of the virtue that would restore God's favor, the Revolutionary generation met taxation with a self-denial and industry that would hopefully restore their accustomed freedom and simultaneously enable them to identify with their virtuous ancestors.

The advocates of nonconsumption and nonimportation, in urging austerity on their countrymen, made very little of the effect that self-denial would have on the British government. Nonimportation and non-consumption were preached as means of renewing ancestral virtues. Americans were reminded that they had been "of late years insensibly drawn into too great a degree of *luxury* and *dissipation*."⁹ Parliamentary taxation was a blessing in disguise, because it produced the nonimporta-tion and nonconsumption agreements. "Luxury," the people of the col-onies were told, "has taken deep root among us, and to cure a people of luxury were an Herculean task indeed; what perhaps no power on earth but a British Parliament, in the very method they are taking with us, could possibly execute."¹⁰ Parliamentary taxation, like an Indian attack in earlier years, was thus both a danger to be resisted and an act of prov-idence to recall Americans from declension: "The Americans have plen-tifully enjoyed the delights and comforts, as well as the necessaries of life, and it is well known that an increase of wealth and affluence paves the way to an increase of luxury, immorality and profaneness, and here kind providence interposes; and as it were, obliges them to forsake the use of one of their delights, to preserve their liberty."¹¹ The principal ob-ject of this last homily was tea, which, upon being subjected to a Parliamentary duty, became luxurious and enervating. Physicians even discovered that it was bad for the health.¹²

In these appeals for self-denial, the Puritan Ethic acquired a value that had been only loosely associated with it hitherto: it became an essential condition of political liberty. An author who signed himself "Frugality" advised the readers of the *Newport Mercury* that "We may talk and boast of liberty; but after all, the industrious and frugal only will be free,"¹³ free not merely because their self-denial would secure repeal of Parliamentary taxes, but because freedom was inseparable from virtue, and frugality and industry were the most conspicuous public virtues. The Americans were fortunate in having so direct and easy a way to preserve liberty, for importations, it now appeared, were mainly luxuries, "Baubles of Britain," "foreign trifles."¹⁴ By barring their entrance, "by consuming *less* of what we are not really in want of, and by industrious-ly cultivating and improving the natural advantages of our own country, we might save our *substance, even our lands*, from becoming the proper-ty of others, and we might effectually preserve our *virtue* and our *liberty*, to the latest posterity." Americans like Englishmen had long associated liberty with property. They now concluded that both rested on virtue: while liberty would expire without the support of property, property itself could not exist without industry and frugality. "Our enemies," they were assured, "very well know that dominion and proper-ty are closely connected; and that to impoverish us, is the surest way to enslave us. Therefore, if we mean still to be free, let us unanimously lay aside foreign superfluities, and encourage our own manufacture. SAVE YOUR MONEY AND YOU WILL SAVE YOUR COUNTRY!"¹⁵

There was one class of Americans who could take no comfort in this motto. The merchants, on whom nonimportation depended, stood to lose by the campaign for austerity, and it is not surprising that they showed less enthusiasm for it than the rest of the population. Their lukewarmness only served to heighten the suspicion with which their calling was still viewed. "Merchants have no country," Jefferson once remarked. "The mere spot they stand on does not constitute so strong an attachment as that from which they draw their gains."[16] And John Adams at the Continental Congress was warned by his wife's uncle that merchants "have no Object but their own particular Interest and they must be Contrould or they will ruin any State under Heaven."[17]

. . .

The merchants actually had more than a short-range interest at stake in their reluctance to undertake nonimportation. The movement, as we have seen, was not simply a means of securing repeal of the taxes to which merchants along with other colonists were opposed. The movement was in fact anticommercial, a repudiation of the merchant's calling. Merchants, it was said, encouraged men to go into debt. Merchants pandered to luxury. Since they made more on the sale of superfluous baubles than on necessities, they therefore pressed the sale of them to a weak and gullible public. What the advocates of nonimportation demanded was not merely an interruption of commerce but a permanent reduction, not to say elimination, of it. In its place they called for manufacturing, a palpably productive, useful calling.

The encouragement of manufacturing was an accompaniment to all the nonimportation, nonconsumption movements. New Yorkers organized a society specifically for that purpose, which offered bounties for the production of native textiles and other necessaries. The nonconsumption of mutton provided new supplies of wool, which housewives turned into thread in spinning matches (wheelwrights did a land-office business in spinning wheels). Stores began selling American cloth, and college students appeared at commencement in homespun. Tories ridiculed these efforts, and the total production was doubtless small, but it would be difficult to underestimate the importance of the attitude toward manufacturing that originated at this time. In a letter of Abigail Adams can be seen the way in which the Puritan Ethic was creating out of a Revolutionary protest movement the conception of a self-sufficient American economy. Abigail was writing to her husband, who was at the First Continental Congress, helping to frame the Continental Association for nonimportation, nonexportation, and nonconsumption:

> If we expect to inherit the blessings of our Fathers, we should return a little more to their primitive Simplicity of Manners, and not sink into inglorious ease. We have too many high sounding words, and too few actions that correspond with them. I have spent one Sabbeth in Town since you left me. I saw no difference in respect to ornaments, etc. etc. but in the Country you must look for that virtue, of which you find but small Glimerings in the Metropolis. Indeed they have not the advantages, nor the resolution to encourage their own Manufactories which people in the country have. To the Mercantile part, tis considerd as throwing away their own Bread; but they must retrench their expenses and be content with a small share of gain for they will find but few who will wear their Livery. As for me I will seek wool and flax and work willingly with my Hands, and indeed their is occasion for all our industry and economy.[18]

In 1774 manufacture retained its primitive meaning of something made by hand, and making things by hand seemed a fitting occupation for frugal country people who had always exhibited more of the Puritan Ethic than high-living city folk. Abigail's espousal of manufactures, with its defiant rejection of dependence on the merchants of the city, marks a step away from the traditional notion that America because of its empty lands and scarcity of people was unsuited to manufactures and must therefore obtain them from the Old World. Through the nonimportation movements the colonists discovered that manufacturing was a calling not beyond the capacities of a frugal, industrious people, however few in number, and that importation of British manufactures actually menaced frugality and industry.

. . .

While engaged in their campaign of patriotic frugality, Americans were also articulating the political principles that they thought should govern free countries and that should bar Parliament from taxing them. The front line of defense against Parliament was the ancient maxim that a man could not be taxed except by his own consent given in person or by his representative. The colonists believed this to be an acknowledged principle of free government, indelibly stamped on the British Constitution, and they wrote hundreds of pages affirming it. In those pages the Puritan Ethic was revealed at the very root of the constitutional principle when taxation without representation was condemned as an assault on every man's calling. To tax a man without his consent, Samuel Adams said, was "against the plain and obvious rule of equity, whereby the industrious man is intitled to the fruits of his industry."[19] And the New York Assembly referred to the Puritan Ethic when it told Parliament that the effect of the sugar and stamp taxes would be to "dispirit the People, abate their Industry, discourage Trade, introduce Discord, Poverty, and Slavery."[20] In slavery, of course, there could be no liberty and no property and so no motive for frugality and industry. Uncontrolled Parliamentary taxation, like luxury and extravagance, was an attack not merely on property but on industry and frugality, for which liberty and property must be the expected rewards. With every protest that British taxation was reducing them to slavery, Americans reaffirmed their devotion to industry and frugality and their readiness to defy the British threat to them. Students of the American Revolution have often found it difficult to believe that the colonists were willing to fight about an abstract principle and have sometimes dismissed the constitutional arguments of the time as mere rhetoric. But the constitutional principle on which the colonists rested their case was not the product either of abstract political philosophy or of the needs of the moment. In the colonists' view, it was a means, hallowed by history, of protecting property and of maintaining those virtues, associated with property, without which no people could be free. Through the rhetoric, if it may be called that, of the Puritan Ethic, the colonists reached behind the constitutional principle to the enduring human needs that had brought the principle into being.

We may perhaps understand better the urgency both of the constitutional argument and of the drive toward independence that it ultimately generated, if we observe the growing suspicion among the colonists that the British government had betrayed its own constitution and the values which that constitution protected. In an earlier generation the colonists had vied with one another in praising the government of England. Englishmen, they believed, had suffered again and again from invasion and tyranny, had each time recovered control of their government, and in the course of centuries had developed unparalleled constitutional safeguards to keep rulers true to their callings. The calling of a ruler, as the colonists and their Puritan forbears saw it, was like any other calling: it must serve the common good; it must be useful, productive; and it must be assiduously pursued. After the Glorious Revolution of 1688, Englishmen had fashioned what seemed a nearly perfect instrument of government, a constitution that blended monarchy, aristocracy, and democracy in a mixture designed to avoid the defects and secure the benefits of each. But something had gone wrong. The human capacity for corruption had transformed the balanced government of King, Lords, and Commons into a single-minded body of rulers bent on their own enrichment and heedless of the public good.

. . .

By the time the First Continental Congress came together in 1774, large numbers of leading Americans had come to identify Great Britain with vice and America with virtue, yet with the fearful recognition that virtue stands in perennial danger from the onslaughts of vice. Patrick Henry gave voice to the feeling when he denounced Galloway's plan for an intercolonial American legislature that would stand between the colonies and Parliament. "We shall liberate our Constituents," he warned, "from a corrupt House of Commons, but thro[w] them into the Arms of an American Legislature that may be bribed by that Nation which avows in the Face of the World, that Bribery is a Part of her System of Government."[21] A government that had succeeded in taxing seven million Englishmen (with the consent of their supposed representatives), to support an army of placeholders, would have no hesitation in using every means to corrupt the representatives of two and one half million Americans.

When the Second Congress met in 1775, Benjamin Franklin, fresh from London, could assure the members that their contrast of England and America was justified. Writing back to Joseph Priestley, he said it would "scarce be credited in Britain, that men can be as diligent with us from zeal for the public good, as with you for thousands per annum. Such is the difference between uncorrupted new states, and corrupted old ones."[22] Thomas Jefferson drew the contrast even more bluntly in an answer rejecting Lord North's Conciliatory Proposal of February 20, 1775, which had suggested that Parliament could make provisions for the government of the colonies. "The provisions we have made," said Jefferson, "are such as please our selves, and are agreeable to our own circumstances; they answer the substantial purposes of government and of justice, and other purposes than these should not be answered. We do not mean that our people shall be burthened with oppressive taxes to provide sinecures for the idle or the wicked. . . ."[23]

When Congress finally dissolved the political bands that had connected America with England, the act was rendered less painful by the colonial conviction that America and England were already separated as virtue is from vice. The British Constitution had foundered, and the British government had fallen into the hands of a luxurious and corrupt ruling class. There remained no way of preserving American virtue unless the connection with Britain was severed. The meaning of virtue in this context embraced somewhat more than the values of the Puritan Ethic, but those values were pre-eminent in it. In the eyes of many Americans the Revolution was a defense of industry and frugality, whether in rulers or people, from the assaults of British vice. The Puritan Ethic, in the colonists' political as in their economic thinking, prepared the way for independence.

II. WHO SHOULD RULE AT HOME

Virtue, as everyone knew, was a fragile and probably fleeting possession. Even while defending it from the British, Americans worried about their own uneasy hold on it and eyed one another for signs of its departure. The war, of course, furnished the conditions of adversity in which virtue could be expected to flourish. On the day after Congress voted independence, John Adams wrote exultantly to Abigail of the difficulties ahead: "It may be the Will of Heaven that America shall suffer Calamities still more wasting and Distresses yet more dreadfull. If this is to be the Case, it will have this good Effect, at least: it will inspire Us with many Virtues, which We have not, and correct many Errors, Follies, and Vices, which threaten to disturb, dishonour, and destroy Us.—The Furnace of Affliction produces Refinement, in States as well as Individuals."[24] Thereafter, as afflictions came, Adams welcomed them in good Puritan fashion. But the war did not prove a sufficient spur to virtue, and by the fall of 1776 Adams was already observing that "There is too much Corruption, even in this infant Age of our Republic. Virtue is not in Fashion. Vice is not infamous."[25] Sitting with the Congress in Philadelphia, he privately yearned for General Howe to capture the town, because the ensuing hardship "would cure Americans of their vicious and luxurious and effeminate Appetites, Passions and Habits, a more dangerous Army to American Liberty than Mr. Howes."[26]

Within a year or two Americans would begin to look back on 1775 and 1776 as a golden age, when vice had given way to heroic self-denial, and luxury and corruption had not yet raised their heads. In revolutionary America as in Puritan New England the virtues of the Puritan Ethic must be quickened by laments for their loss.

Many of these eighteenth-century lamentations seem perfunctory—mere nostalgic ritual in which men purged their sins by confessing their inferiority to their fathers. But in the years after 1776 the laments were prompted by a genuine uneasiness among the Revolutionists about their own worthiness for the role they had undertaken. In the agitation against Britain they had repeatedly told themselves that liberty could not live without virtue. Having cast off the threat posed to both liberty and virtue by a corrupt monarchy, they recognized that the republican governments they had created must depend for their success on the virtue, not of a king or of a few aristocrats, but of an entire people. Unless the virtue of Americans proved equal to its tasks, liberty would quickly give way once again to tyranny and perhaps a worse tyranny than that of George III.

As Americans faced the problems of independence, the possibility of failure did not seem remote. By recalling the values that had inspired the resistance to British taxation they hoped to lend success to their venture in republican government. The Puritan Ethic thus continued to occupy their consciousness (and their letters, diaries, newspapers, and pamphlets) and to provide the framework within which alternatives were debated and sides taken.

Next to the task of defeating the British armies, perhaps the most urgent problem that confronted the new nation was to prove its nationality, for no one was certain that independent Americans would be able to get on with one another. Before the Revolution there had been many predictions, both European and American, that if independence were achieved it would be followed by bloody civil wars among the states, which would eventually fall prostrate before some foreign invader. The anticipated civil war did not take place for eighty-five years. Americans during those years were not without divisions, but they did manage to stay together. Their success in doing so, exemplified in the adoption of the Constitution of 1787, demonstrated that the divisions among them were less serious than they themselves had realized. Without attempting to examine the nature of the debates over the Constitution itself, I should like to show how the Puritan Ethic, while contributing to divisions among Americans, also furnished both sides with a common set of values that limited the extent and bitterness of divisions and thus helped to make a United States Constitution possible.

In the period after 1776 perhaps the most immediate threat to the American union was the possibility that the secession of the United States from Great Britain would be followed by a secession of the lower Mississippi and Ohio valleys from the United States. The gravity of the threat, which ended with the fiasco of the Burr Conspiracy, is difficult to assess, but few historians would deny that real friction between East and West existed.

The role of the Puritan Ethic in the situation was characteristic: each side tended to see the other as deficient in the same virtues. To westerners the eastern-dominated governments seemed to be in the grip of speculators and merchants determined to satisfy their own avarice by sacrificing the interests of the industrious farmers of the West. To easterners, or at least to some easterners, the West seemed to be filling up with shiftless adventurers, as lazy and lawless and unconcerned with the values of the Puritan Ethic as were the native Indians. Such men were unworthy of a share in government and must be restrained in their restless hunt for land and furs; they must be made to settle down and build civilized communities where industry and frugality would thrive.

The effects of these attitudes cannot be demonstrated at length here, but may be suggested by the views of a key figure, John Jay. As early as

1779, the French Ambassador, Conrad Alexandre Gérard, had found Jay one of the most reasonable members of Congress, that is, one of the members most ready to fall in with the Ambassador's instructions to discourage American expansion. Jay belonged to a group which suggested that Spain ought to close the Mississippi to American navigation in order to keep the settlers of the West "from living in a half-savage condition." Presumably the group reasoned that the settlers were mostly fur traders; if they were prevented from trading their furs through New Orleans, they might settle down to farming and thus achieve "an attachment to property and industry."[27] Whatever the line of reasoning, the attitude toward the West is clear, and Jay obliged the French Ambassador by volunteering the opinion that the United States was already too large.[28]

In 1786 Jay offered similar opinions to Jefferson, suggesting that settlement of the West should be more gradual, that Americans should be prevented from pitching their tents "through the Wilderness in a great Variety of Places, far distant from each other, and from those Advantages of Education, Civilization, Law, and Government which compact Settlements and Neighbourhood afford."[29] It is difficult to believe that Jay was unaffected by this attitude in the negotiations he was carrying on with the Spanish envoy Gardoqui over the right of the United States to navigate the Mississippi. When Jay presented Congress with a treaty in which the United States agreed to forego navigation of the Mississippi in return for commercial concessions in Spain, it seemed, to westerners at least, that the United States Secretary for Foreign Affairs was willing to sacrifice their interests in favor of his merchant friends in the East.

Fortunately the conflict was not a lasting one. Jay was misinformed about the West, for the advance wave of fur traders and adventurers who pitched their tents far apart occupied only a brief moment in the history of any part of the West. The tens of thousands of men who entered Kentucky and Tennessee in the 1780's came to farm the rich lands, and they carried the values of the Puritan Ethic with them. As this fact became apparent, conflict subsided. Throughout American history, in fact, the West was perpetually turning into a new East, complete with industrious inhabitants, spurred by adversity, and pursuing their callings with an assiduity that the next generation would lament as lost.

Another sectional conflict was not so transitory. The South was not in the process of becoming northern or the North southern. And their differing interests were already discernible in the 1780's, at least to an astute observer like James Madison, as the primary source of friction among Americans. The difference arose, he believed, "principally from the effects of their having or not having slaves."[30]

The bearing of the Puritan Ethic on slavery, as on many other institutions, was complex and ambivalent. It heightened the conflict between those who did and those who did not have slaves. But it also, for a time at least, set limits to the conflict by offering a common ground on which both sides could agree in deploring the institution.

The Puritans themselves had not hesitated to enslave Indian captives or to sell and buy slaves. At the opening of the Revolution no state prohibited slavery. But the institution obviously violated the precepts of the Puritan Ethic: it deprived men of the fruits of their labor and thus removed a primary motive for industry and frugality. How it came into existence in the first place among a people devoted to the Puritan Ethic is a question not yet solved, but as soon as Americans began complaining of Parliament's assault on their liberty and property, it was difficult not to see the inconsistency of continuing to hold slaves. "I wish most sincerely," Abigail Adams wrote to her husband in 1774, "there was not a Slave in the province. It allways appeard a most iniquitous Scheme to me—fight ourselfs for what we are daily robbing and plundering from those who have as good a right to freedom as we have."[31] Newspaper articles everywhere made the same point. As a result, slavery was gradually abolished in the northern states (where it was not important in the economy), and the self-righteousness with which New Englanders already regarded their southern neighbors was thereby heightened.

Although the South failed to abolish slavery, southerners like northerners recognized the threat it posed to the values that all Americans held. Partly as a result of that recognition, more slaves were freed by voluntary manumission in the South than by legal and constitutional abolition in the North. There were other reasons for hostility to slavery in both North and South, including fear of insurrection, humanitarianism, and apprehension of the wrath of God; but a predominant reason, in the South at least, was the evil effect of slavery on the industry and frugality of both master and slave, but especially of the master.

A perhaps extreme example of this argument, divested of all considerations of justice and humanity, appeared in a Virginia newspaper in 1767. The author (who signed himself "Philanthropos"!) proposed to abolish slavery in Virginia by having the government lay a prohibitory duty on importation and then purchase one tenth of everyone's slaves every year. The purchase price would be recovered by selling the slaves in the West Indies. Philanthropos acknowledged that slaves were "used with more barbarity" in the West Indies than in Virginia but offered them the consolation "that this sacrifice of themselves will put a quicker period to a miserable life." To emancipate them and leave them in Virginia would be fatal, because they would probably "attempt to arrive at our possessions by force, rather than wait the tedious operation of labour, industry and time." But unless slavery was abolished in Virginia, the industry and frugality of the free population would expire. As it was, said Philanthropos, when a man got a slave or two, he sat back and stopped working. Promising young men failed to take up productive occupations because they could get jobs as overseers. By selling off their slaves in the West Indies, Virginians would get the money to import white indentured servants and would encourage "our own common people, who would no longer be diverted from industry by the prospect of overseers places, to [enter] agriculture and arts."[32]

Few opponents of slavery were so callous, but even the most humane stressed the effect of slavery on masters and the problems of instilling the values of industry in emancipated slaves. Thomas Jefferson hated slavery, but he hated idleness equally, and he would not have been willing to abolish slavery without making arrangements to preserve the useful activity it exacted from its victims. He had heard of one group of Virginia slaves who had been freed by their Quaker owners and kept as tenants on the land. The results had been unsatisfactory, because the ex-slaves had lacked the habits of industry and "chose to steal from their neighbors rather than work." Jefferson had plans to free his own slaves (after he freed himself from his creditors) by a gradual system which provided means for educating the Negroes into habits of industry.[33] But Jefferson never put his scheme into practice. He and most other Southerners continued to hold slaves, and the result was as predicted: slavery steadily eroded the honor accorded work among southerners.

During the Revolutionary epoch, however, the erosion had not yet proceeded far enough to alienate North from South. Until well into the nineteenth century Southerners continued to deplore the effects of slavery on the industry and frugality at least of the whites. Until the North began to demand immediate abolition and the South began to defend slavery as a permanent blessing, leaders of the two sections could find a good deal of room for agreement in the shared values of the Puritan Ethic.

. . .

The party divisions of 1778-79 seem to indicate that although most Americans made adherence to the Puritan Ethic an article of faith, some Americans were far more assiduous than others in exemplifying it. Since such men were confined to no particular section, and since men active in national politics could recognize their own kind from whatever section, political divisions in the early years of the republic actually brought Americans from all over the country into working harmony within a single group. And parties, instead of destroying the union, became a means of holding it together.

Recent studies have shown that there was no continuity in the political divisions of the 1770's, 1780's, and 1790's, by demonstrating that the split between Federalists and Republicans in the 1790's cannot be traced to the preceding splits between reluctant and ardent revolutionaries of 1776 or between Federalists and Antifederalists of 1789. The continuity that a previous generation of historians had seen in the political history of these years has thus proved specious. It is tempting, however, to suggest that there may have been a form of continuity in American political history hitherto unnoticed, a continuity based on the attitudes we have been exploring. Although the divisions of 1778-79 did not endure, Americans of succeeding years continued to show differing degrees of attachment to the values of the Puritan Ethic. By the time when national political parties were organized in the 1790's, a good many other factors were involved in attracting men to one side or the other, far too many to permit discussion here. But the Puritan Ethic remained a constant ingredient, molding the style of American politics not only in the 1790's but long afterwards. Men on both sides, and seemingly the whole population, continued to proclaim their devotion to it by mourning its decline, and each side regularly accused the other of being deficient in it. It served as a weapon for political conflict but also as a tether which kept parties from straying too far apart. It deserves perhaps to be considered as one of the major reasons why American party battles have generally remained rhetorical and American national government has endured as a workable government.

III. AN ECONOMIC INTERPRETATION OF THE CONSTITUTION

As the Puritan Ethic helped to give shape to national politics, so too it helped to shape national policy, especially in the economic sphere. Before 1776 the economic policy of the American colonies had been made for them in London: they had been discouraged from manufacturing, barred from certain channels of trade, and encouraged to exploit the natural resources of the continent, especially its land. After 1776 the independent states were free to adopt, singly or collectively, any policy that suited them. At first the exigencies of the war against England directed every measure; but as the fighting subsided, Americans began to consider the economic alternatives open to them.

There appeared to be three possible kinds of activity: agriculture, manufacturing, and commerce. Of these, agriculture and commerce had hitherto dominated the American scene. Americans, in accepting the place assigned them under the British Navigation Acts, had seen the force of their own environment operating in the same direction as British policy: as long as the continent had an abundance of unoccupied land and a scarcity of labor, it seemed unlikely that its inhabitants could profitably engage in manufacturing. The nonimportation agreements had done much to dispel this opinion in America; and the war that followed, by interdicting trade in some regions and hindering it in others, had given a further spur to manufactures. By the time peace came numerous observers were able to point out fallacies in the supposition that manufacturing was not economically feasible in the United States. From England, Richard Price reminded Americans that their country contained such a variety of soils and climates that it was capable of "producing not only every *necessary* but every *convenience* of life," and Americans were quick to agree.[34] They acknowledged that their population was small by comparison with Europe's and the numbers skilled in manufacturing even smaller. But they now discovered reasons why this deficiency was no insuperable handicap. People without regular employment, women and children for example, could be put to useful work in manufacturing. Moreover, if Americans turned to manufactures, many skilled artisans of the Old World, losing their New World customers, would move to America in order to regain them. Immigrants would come in large numbers anyhow, attracted by the blessings of republican liberty. And scarcity of labor could also be overcome by labor-saving machinery and by water and steam power.[35]

A few men like Thomas Jefferson continued to think manufacturing neither feasible nor desirable for Americans, but the economic vicissitudes of the postwar years subdued the voices of such men to a whisper. No one suggested that the country should abandon its major commitment to agriculture in favor of manufacturing, but it became a commonplace that too many Americans were engaged in commerce and that the moral, economic, and political welfare of the United States demanded a greater attention to manufacturing. The profiteering of merchants during the war had kept the old suspicions of that calling very much alive, so that long before the fighting stopped, people were worried about the effects of an unrestrained commerce on the independent United States. A Yale student reflected the mood in a declamation offered in July 1778. If the country indulged too freely in commerce, he warned, the result would be "Luxury with its train of the blackest vices, which will debase our manliness of sentiment, and spread a general dissolution of manners thro the Continent. This extensive Commerce is the most direct method to ruin our country, and we may affirm that we shall exist as an empire but a short space, unless it can be circumscribed within narrow limits."[36]

The prophecy seemed to be on the way to swift fulfillment within a year or two of the war's end. As soon as the peace treaty was signed, American merchants rushed to offer Americans the familiar British goods which they had done without for nearly a decade. The British gladly supplied the market, extending a liberal credit, and the result was a flood of British textiles and hardware in every state. As credit extended from merchant to tradesman to farmer and planter, Americans were caught up in an orgy of buying. But at the same time Britain barred American ships from her West Indies possessions, where American cattle, lumber, and foodstuffs had enjoyed a prime market. The British could now buy these articles in the United States at their own prices and carry them in their own ships, depriving the American merchant and farmer alike of accustomed profits. Hard cash was rapidly drained off; debts grew to alarming proportions; and the buying boom turned to a sharp depression.[37]

Casting about for a remedy, some states turned to the old expedient of paper money. But to many Americans this was a cure worse than the disease and no real cure anyhow. The root of the trouble, they told themselves, was their own frivolity. Newspapers and pamphlets from one end of the continent to the other lamented the lost virtues that had inspired resistance to tyranny a few short years before. While Rome had enjoyed a republican simplicity for centuries, the United States seemed to have sunk into luxury and decay almost as soon as born. And who indulged this weakness, who coaxed Americans into this wild extravagance? It was the merchants. Shelves bulging with oversupplies of ribbons, laces, and yard goods, the merchants outdid themselves in appealing to every gullible woman and every foolish fop to buy. There was an oversupply, it seemed, not merely of ribbons and laces but of merchants, a breed of men, according to Hugh Williamson of North Carolina, "too lazy to plow, or labour at any other calling."[38] "What can we promise ourselves," asked another writer, "if we still pursue the same extensive trade? What, but total destruction to our manners, and the entire loss of our virtue?"[39]

The basic remedy must be frugality. The laments over luxury were a summons to Americans to tighten their belts, as they had done before in the face of adversity. And as they had also done in the earlier campaigns, they again linked frugality with nonimportation and with manufacturing for themselves, but this time with somewhat more confidence in the result. Manufacturing was now freed of the restrictions formerly imposed by the British; if once firmly established in the United States, it would help protect the very virtues that fostered it. An industrious, frugal people would manufacture for themselves, and in turn "Manufactures will promote industry, and industry contributes to health, virtue, riches and population."[40] Although the riches thus gained might constitute a danger to the virtues that begot them, they would not be as great a danger as riches arising from trade or speculation: "the evils resulting from opulence in a nation whose inhabitants are habituated to industry from their childhood, will never be so predominant as in those nations, whose riches are spontaneously produced, without labour or care. . . ."[41]

As manufactures were linked to virtue, so both were linked to the independent republican government for which Americans had been fighting. "America must adopt [a] new policy," David Ramsay insisted in 1785, "or she never will be independent in reality. We must import less and attend more to agriculture and manufactures."[42] It was now possible to see a new significance in England's old restraints on colonial manufacturing. Why had she prevented Americans from "working up those materials that God and nature have given us?" The answer was clear to a Maryland writer: because England knew "it was the only way to our real independence, and to render the habitable parts of our country truly valuable. What countries are the most flourishing and most powerful in the world? Manufacturing countries. It is not hills, mountains, woods, and rivers that constitute the true riches of a country. It is the number of industrious mechanic and manufacturing as well as agriculturing inhabitants. That a country composed of agricultivators and shepherds is not so valuable as one wherein a just proportion of the people attend to arts and manufactures, is known to every politician in Europe: And America will never feel her importance and dignity, until she alters her present system of trade, so ruinous to the interests, to the morals, and to the reputation of her citizens."[43]

Britain's extension of credit to American merchants, it now seemed, was only part of a perfidious plan to undermine through trade the independence she had acknowledged by treaty. Samuel Adams had once detected a British plan to destroy American liberty by introducing luxury and levity among the people. Having been thwarted in 1776, the British were now on the verge of success. As a South Carolina writer charged, they had let loose, "as from Pandora's box, a ruinous luxury, speculation, and extravagance, vitiated our taste, corrupted our manners, plunged the whole state into a private debt, never before equalled, and thro' the means of their trade, luxury, influence, and good things, brought the Republic into a dilemma, an example of which has not before happened in the world."[44] From France, where he was serving as ambassador, Thomas Jefferson could see that Britain by her liberal credits had put the whole United States in the same economic thralldom in which her merchants had held (and still held) the Virginia tobacco planters. From economic thralldom back to political thralldom was only a step. Unless the United States could break the grip, her experiment in independence was over.

Jefferson, while joining in the hymns to frugality (he thought extravagance a "more baneful evil than toryism was during the war"),[45] had a peculiar prejudice against manufacturing and hoped to break the British grip and achieve economic independence by gaining new commercial treaties with other countries.[46] But few of his countrymen shared his prejudice. In every state they told themselves to manufacture. Even if it cost more to make a coat or a pair of shoes or a plow or a gun in America, the price of foreign imports was independence. "No man," warned Hugh Williamson, drawing upon another precept of the Puritan Ethic, "is to say that a thing may be good for individuals which is not good for the public, or that our citizens may thrive by cheap bargains, while the nation is ruined by them." Considered in the light of the national interest, "every domestic manufacture is cheaper than a foreign one, for this plain reason, by the first nothing is lost to the country, by the other the whole value is lost—it is carried away never to return."[47]

. . .

There were, of course, many forces working simultaneously toward the establishment of an effective national government in the 1780's, and perhaps economic forces were not the most important. It has been shown that Charles Beard's interpretation of the economic forces leading to the Constitution was without adequate foundation, and economic interpretations thus far advanced in place of Beard's have been only more complex versions of his. But another economic interpretation of the Constitution may be suggested: Americans from the time of their first nonimportation agreements against England had been groping toward a national economic policy that would bestow freedom from domination by outsiders. Long before the country had a national government capable of executing it, the outlines of that policy were visible, and the national government of 1789 was created, in part at least, in order to carry it out. Only an independent national economy could guarantee the political independence that Americans had declared in 1776, and only an independent national economy could preserve the virtue, the industry, frugality, and simplicity that Americans had sought to protect from the luxury and corruption of Great Britain. By 1787 it had become clear that none of these objectives could be attained without a national government empowered to control trade—and through trade all other parts of the national economy.

It is altogether fitting that the United States, which first acted as a government when the Continental Congress undertook the nonimportation, nonexportation, nonconsumption Association of 1774, gained a permanent effective government when Americans again felt an urgent need to control trade. There was in each case an immediate objective, to bring pressure on the British, and in each case a larger objective, to build American economic and moral strength. As the Philadelphia Convention was drafting its great document, Tench Coxe expressed a hope which many members of that body cherished equally with the members of the First Continental Congress, that the encouragement of manufacturing would "lead us once more into the paths of virtue by restoring frugality and industry, those potent antidotes to the vices of mankind and will give us real independence by rescuing us from the tyranny of foreign fashions, and the destructive torrent of luxury."[48] Patriotism and the Puritan Ethic marched hand in hand from 1764 to 1789.

The vicissitudes of the new national government in carrying out a national economic policy form another story, and one full of ironies. Alexander Hamilton, the brilliant executor of the policy, had scarcely a grain of the Puritan Ethic in him and did not hesitate to enroll the merchant class in his schemes. Hamilton, for purely economic and patriotic reasons, favored direct encouragement of manufactures by the national government; but the merchants whom he had gathered behind him helped to defeat him. Thomas Jefferson, devoted to the values of the Puritan Ethic but prejudiced against manufactures, fought against governmental support of them, yet in the end adopted the measures that turned the country decisively toward manufacturing.

The Puritan Ethic did not die with the eighteenth century. Throughout our history it has been there, though it has continued to be in the process of expiring. One student of the Jacksonian period has concluded that politics in the 1830's and 1840's was dominated by an appeal for restoration of the frugality and simplicity which men of that generation thought had prevailed in the preceding one. The most popular analysis of American society after the second World War was a lament for the loss of inner-directedness (read simplicity, industry, frugality) which had been replaced by other-directedness (read luxury, extravagance). The Puritan Ethic has always been known by its epitaphs. Perhaps it is not quite dead yet.

A problem that Morgan raises but does not entirely solve is the extent to which the ethic he discerns in the Revolutionary mind is Puritan or simply Protestant or Christian or even universal. There is also an increasing awareness that much of the Puritan legacy—where it can be identified as such—may have been more harmful than beneficial to American development. Richard Slotkin, in Regeneration Through Violence: The Mythology of the American Frontier, 1600–1800 (Middletown, Conn., 1973), has argued forcefully that much of what is deplorable in the American experience can be traced to Puritan modes of thought.

Disagreement over the Puritan legacy—both its extent and its desirability—is not likely to lessen. The debate will last as long as the American past is studied by scholars of diverse backgrounds, assumptions, and disciplines. From such debate, however, should come a still better understanding of the nature of Puritan New England and of the legacy it bequeathed to the American nation.

NOTES

1. The author is engaged in a full-scale study of this theme. The present essay is interpretative, and citations have for the most part been limited to identifying the sources of quotations.

2. I have chosen this term rather than the familiar "Protestant Ethic" of Max Weber, partly because I mean something slightly different and partly because Weber confined his phrase to attitudes prevailing while the religious impulse was paramount. The attitudes that survived the decline of religion he designated as the "spirit of capitalism." In this essay I have not attempted to distinguish earlier from later, though I am concerned with a period when the attitudes were no longer dictated primarily by religion.

3. William Perkins, *Workes* (London, 1626-31), I, 755-756.

4. Nathaniel Ward, *The Simple Cobbler of Aggawam in America* (London, 1647), 41.

5. Purdie and Dixon's *Virginia Gazette* (Williamsburg), Sept. 5, 1771. Cf. *Pennsylvania Chronicle* (Philadelphia), Feb. 9-16, May 4-11, 1767; *Newport Mercury*, Mar. 7, 1774; and *Boston Evening Post*, Nov. 30, 1767.

6. To Martha Jefferson, Mar. 28, May 5, 1787, in Julian Boyd *et al.*, eds., *The Papers of Thomas Jefferson* (Princeton, 1950-), XI, 250, 349.

7. Arthur M. Schlesinger, *The Colonial Merchants and the American Revolution, 1763-1776* (New York, 1918), remains the best account of these movements.

8. To [Unknown], May 31, 1764, in James C. Ballagh, ed., *The Letters of Richard Henry Lee* (New York, 1911), I, 7.

9. *Boston Evening Post*, Nov. 16, 1767.

10. *Va. Gazette* (Purdie and Dixon), June 1, 1769 (reprinted from *New York Chronicle*).

11. *Newport Mercury*, Dec. 13, 1773.

12. *Ibid.*, Nov. 9, 1767, Nov. 29, 1773, Feb. 14, 28, 1774.

13. *Ibid.*, Feb. 28, 1774.

14. *Boston Evening Post*, Nov. 9, 16, 1767; To Arthur Lee, Oct. 31, 1771, in H. A. Cushing, ed., *The Writings of Samuel Adams* (New York, 1904-08), II, 267.

15. *Boston Evening Post*, Nov. 16, 1767; *Pennsylvania Journal* (Philadelphia), Dec. 10, 1767.

16. To Horatio Spafford, Mar. 17, 1817, quoted in Boyd, ed., *Jefferson Papers*, XIV, 221.

17. Cotton Tufts to John Adams, Apr. 26, 1776, in L. H. Butterfield *et al.*, eds., *Adams Family Correspondence* (Cambridge, Mass., 1963-), I, 395.

18. Oct. 16, 1774, in Butterfield, ed., *Adams Family Correspondence*, I, 173.

19. [*Boston Gazette*, Dec. 19, 1768] in Cushing, ed., *Writings of Samuel Adams*, I, 271.

20. E. S. Morgan, ed., *Prologue to Revolution: Sources and Documents on the Stamp Act Crisis, 1764-1766* (Chapel Hill, 1959), 13.

21. Sept. 28, 1774, in L. H. Butterfield *et al.*, eds., *Diary and Autobiography of John Adams* (Cambridge, Mass., 1961), II, 143.

22. July 6, 1775, in E. C. Burnett, ed., *Letters of Members of The Continental Congress* (Washington, 1921-36), I, 156.

23. July 31, 1775, in Boyd, ed., *Jefferson Papers*, I, 232.

24. July 3, 1776, in Butterfield, ed., *Adams Family Correspondence*, II, 28.

25. John to Abigail Adams, Sept. 22, 1776, *ibid.*, II, 131.

26. Same to same, Sept. 8, 1777, *ibid.*, II, 338. Cf. pp. 169-170, 326.

27. John J. Meng, ed., *Despatches and Instructions of Conrad Alexandre Gérard . . .* (Baltimore, 1939), 531. Gérard reported of this group in February, 1779, "qu'ils desiroient fortement que Sa Majesté Catholique tint la clef du Mississippi de sorte que personne n'entrat du Mississippi dans l'Ocean ni de l'Ocean dans ce fleuve; mais qu'il falloit du Commerce aux peuplades dont il s'agit; que par là seulement on pourroit les empêcher de demeurer à demi Sauvages en les attachant à la propriété et à l'industrie."

28. *Ibid.*, 433-434, 494.

29. Dec. 14, 1786, in Boyd, ed., *Jefferson Papers*, X, 599.

30. In Convention, June 30, 1787, in C. C. Tansill, ed., *Documents Illustrative of the Formation of the Union of the American States* (Washington, 1927), 310.

31. Sept. 22, 1774, in Butterfield, ed., *Adams Family Correspondence*, I, 162.

32. Reprinted in *Pa. Chronicle*, Aug. 31-Sept. 7, 1767. The Virginia paper in which it originally appeared has not been found.

33. To Edward Bancroft, Jan. 26, 1788, in Boyd, ed., *Jefferson Papers*, XIV, 492.

34. Richard Price, *Observations on the Importance of the American Revolution . . .* (London, 1785), 75. Cf. *New Haven Gazette and Connecticut Magazine*, Nov. 16, 23, 1786; *American Mercury* (Hartford), Aug. 13, 1787.

35. Hugh Williamson, *Letters from Sylvius to the Freemen Inhabitants of the United States . . .* (New York, 1787); Tench Coxe: *An Address to an Assembly of the Friends of American Manufactures . . .* (Philadelphia, 1787); *An Enquiry into the Principles on which a commercial system for the United States of America should be founded . . .* (Philadelphia, 1787); and *Observations on the Agriculture, Manufactures and Commerce of the United States . . .* (New York, 1789).

36. Declamation, July 18, 1778, Yale University Archives, New Haven, Conn.

37. This picture of the economic history of the 1780's seems to have been universally accepted at the time. A typical statement is in Coxe, *Observations*, 59-64.

38. Williamson, *Letters from Sylvius*, 30.

39. *The American Museum*, I (Feb. 1787), 124.

40. *Am. Mercury*, Aug. 13, 1787.

41. *New Haven Gazette and Conn. Mag.*, Nov. 23, 1786.

42. R. L. Brunhouse, ed., *David Ramsay, 1749-1815, Selections from his writings*, American Philosophical Society, *Transactions*, LV, Pt. 4 (1965), 87.

43. *Am. Museum*, I (Feb. 1787), 124-125.

44. [Anonymous], *A Few Salutary Hints, pointing out the Policy and Consequences of Admitting British Subjects to Engross our Trade and Become our Citizens* (Charleston printed, New York reprinted, 1786), 4.

45. To John Page, May 4, 1786, in Boyd, ed., *Jefferson Papers*, IX, 445.

46. These views are scattered throughout Jefferson's letters during his stay in France. See Boyd, ed., *Jefferson Papers*, VIII-XV. For a typical statement see letter to Thomas Pleasants, May 8, 1786, *ibid.*, IX, 472-473.

47. Williamson, *Letters from Sylvius*, 13-14.

48. Coxe, *An Address to Friends of Manufactures*, 29-30. Coxe was not a member of the Convention. He was addressing, in Philadelphia, a group "convened for the purpose of establishing a Society for the Encouragement of Manufactures and the Useful Arts."

CHRONOLOGY

Events in the World of the Puritans, from the English Reformation through the Great Awakening

1534—Act of Supremacy recognizes the king of England as the supreme head of the church in England

1547—Death of Henry VIII; accession of Edward VI

1549—Publication of First Edwardean Prayer Book brings the Church of England closer to the continental Reformation

1552—Second Edwardean Prayer Book reflects further movement toward continental Protestantism

1553—Death of Edward VI; accession of Mary Tudor, who seeks to suppress Protestantism and return England to Roman Catholicism; the queen's policies lead to the arrest and later execution of Protestants such as John Hooper and Thomas Cranmer; other Protestants flee to the continent

1558—Death of Mary Tudor; accession of the Protestant queen Elizabeth

1559—Acts of Uniformity and Supremacy restore Anglican Church; Book of Common Prayer represents a more conservative settlement than that of 1552; Thomas Parker appointed archbishop of Canterbury

1563—Convocation approves the Thirty-Nine Articles, the doctrinal creed of the Anglican Church

1570—Thomas Cartwright preaches controversial lectures on the Acts of the Apostles and is removed as Professor of Divinity at Cambridge; he travels to the continent and is influenced by the presbyterian views of Theodore Beza

1571—Parliament approves the Thirty-Nine Articles

1572—John Field and Thomas Wilcox publish the *First Admonition to Parliament,* which seeks to enlist Parliamentary support for reform of the church

1576—Edmund Grindal succeeds Thomas Parker as archbishop of Canterbury; Grindal relaxes pressure on reformers and clashes with Elizabeth over the value of prophesyings

1577—Grindal suspended by the queen, pressure on reformers renewed

1583—Grindal dies and is succeeded by John Whitgift

1587—Walter Travers finishes his *Book of Discipline,* the model for the Presbyterian reforms sought by some in the Puritan faction

1588—Defeat of the Spanish Armada

　—John Field, a key organizer of Elizabethan Puritanism, dies

　—Publication of the "Martin Marprelate tracts," anonymous attacks on the Anglican hierarchy

1590—Thomas Cartwright and other presbyterian leaders arrested for their activities in trying to reform the church

1592—Cartwright and his fellow presbyterians released from prison on condition that they desist from further efforts to alter the church

1593—Execution of Separatist leaders Henry Barrow and John Greenwood

1597—Francis Johnson and a group of English Separatists fail to establish a colony at the mouth of the St. Lawrence

1601—William Perkin's *Treatise of the Vocations, or Callings of men* published

1603—Death of Elizabeth; James VI of Scotland becomes James I of England

—"Millenary Petition," seeking reforms in the church, presented to James I

1604—James I meets with the Puritan leaders at the Hampton Court Conference and agrees to only minor reforms; Richard Bancroft, strong opponent of the Puritans, succeeds Whitgift as archbishop of Canterbury

1606—Probable formation of the Scrooby Separatist congregation under John Smyth and Richard Clifton

1608—Scrooby congregation seeks to avoid persecution by migrating to Amsterdam

1609—Division in the community of English Separatists in Amsterdam leads Scrooby group to move to Leyden; Clifton remains and the congregation chooses John Robinson as its new pastor

1611—William Abbot succeeds Bancroft as archbishop of Canterbury; publication of King James' *Authorized Version* of the Bible

1612—Death of Prince Henry, thought to be sympathetic to the reform cause; Prince Charles becomes heir

1618—Execution of Sir Walter Raleigh

—Bohemian Revolt, the start of the Thirty Years War

1620—Severe slump in the cloth trade

—Thomas Weston and Associates receive patent from the Virginia Company under which the Scrooby Separatists will settle in the New World; group of Separatists (Pilgrims) depart for England in the *Speedwell* and with non-Separatists recruited by Weston they sail to America in the *Mayflower*; *Mayflower Compact* provides a voluntary bond of government when they establish the Plymouth colony outside of Virginia's boundaries

1621—Plymouth's governor John Carver dies and is succeeded by William Bradford, who holds the office all but five years until his death in 1657

1623—Dorchester Company formed to establish fishing bases in New England

—Strawberry Bank (later Portsmouth, New Hampshire) founded by colonists sent by John Mason

1625—Formation in England of the Feofees for Impropriation, a group of clergy, merchants, and lawyers (including Richard Sibbes and John Davenport) who intend to purchase livings for Puritan clergymen

—Death of James I; accession of Charles I

—Black Death in England

1626—William Bradford and other Pilgrim leaders arrange to purchase control of the enterprise from Weston and the London merchants

—John Robinson dies in the Netherlands

—Roger Conant moves the small outpost of the Dorchester Company from Cape Anne to Naumkeag (Salem)

—Charles I prohibits predestinarian teaching at Cambridge (a similar prohibition is placed on Oxford in 1628)

—Charles I resorts to forced loans to raise revenue

1628—Rev. John White and other members of the Dorchester Company join with London merchants to form the New England Company; New England Company sends John Endecott to assume control of the settlement at Salem

—Parliament passes the Petition of Right

—Plymouth authorities send Myles Standish to break up Thomas Morton's settlement at Merrymount, where Morton provides liquor and guns to the Indians

—William Laud appointed bishop of London

1629—New England Company reorganizes and receives a royal charter as the Massachusetts Bay Company; John Winthrop and other leaders of the company sign the Cambridge Agreement, signifying their willingness to migrate to New England if they can bring the charter and powers of government with them

—Dissolution of Parliament by Charles I

—Bad harvests in England and a renewed slump in the cloth trade

1630—The *Arbella* and her sister ships sail for Massachusetts, beginning the Great Migration of Puritans to the Bay Colony; Winthrop establishes the seat of the new colony at Boston and assumes control from Endecott as governor of Massachusetts

—Peace of Madrid between England and Spain; Puritans angered by Charles I's developing friendship with that Catholic power

—Bad harvests in England

1631—Freemanship expanded in Massachusetts; all male church members eligible for the colony franchise

—Roger Williams arrives in Massachusetts

1632—Massachusetts General Court agrees that henceforth the governor will be elected by vote of the freemen, not just the assistants

1633—John Cotton and Thomas Hooker arrive in Massachusetts

—Dutch establish a trading post at Ft. Good Hope (near the future site of Hartford)

—William Laud raised to archbishop of Canterbury; Feofees for Impropriations disbanded by the courts in case pressed by Laud

1634—Members of Thomas Hooker's Newtown congregation seek permission from the General Court to migrate to the Connecticut River valley but are refused

—William and Anne Hutchinson and their children settle in Boston, having followed John Cotton to the New World

1635—Disputes between Roger Williams and the magistrates of the Bay Colony lead to Williams' banishment

—Anne Hutchinson holds meetings in her home to discuss points raised in the sabbath sermons

—Settlers from Dorchester, Massachusetts, settle at Windsor on the Connecticut River; an advance group from Newtown settles Hartford; John Winthrop, Jr., founds a settlement at Saybrook at the mouth of the Connecticut River

1636—John Davenport and Theophilus Eaton lead a group of London Puritans to New England, stopping first in Boston

—Roger Williams flees Massachusetts, is warned off by Plymouth authorities, and settles at Providence, where he purchases land from the Indians

—Henry Vane, a newcomer to Massachusetts whose father was a member of the royal household, is elected governor

—The Pequot War begins when John Endecott leads a contingent of Massachusetts troops against the Pequots in reprisal for the murder of John Oldham

—The "Great Fundamentals" creates a new governmental structure in Connecticut

—Massachusetts General Court authorizes establishment of Harvard College

1637—Pequots attack settlements along Long Island Sound; Connecticut troops under John Mason attack and destroy the main Pequot village

—Sermon by the Rev. John Wheelwright, a supporter of Anne Hutchinson, brings the controversy between the Hutchinsonians ("Antinomians") and the orthodox to a head; synod at Cambridge defines religious errors and attacks the presumed beliefs of the Hutchinsonians; Henry Vane, a Hutchinsonian, defeated by John Winthrop in his bid for reelection; Anne Hutchinson and her principal followers tried by the General Court and banished

—Davenport, Eaton, and their followers found the town of New Haven

1638—John Wheelwright, banished from Massachusetts, founds the town of Exeter (New Hampshire); William Coddington, William Hutchinson, and other Antinomian exiles found the town of Portsmouth (Rhode Island)

1639—Fundamental Orders approved by the Connecticut General Court

—William Coddington splits with Anne Hutchinson and founds the town of Newport at the other end of Aquidneck Island

—Roger Williams and Ezekial Holiman establish the first Baptist church in America at Providence

—Charles I's efforts to impose Anglican forms of worship on Scotland provoke the first Bishops' War against the rebellious Presbyterians of the northern kingdom

1640—Charles I calls a Parliament to raise funds to conduct his war against the Scots; the "Short Parliament" demands reforms and is dissolved; Second Bishops' War ends with Scots granting a truce after their invasion of northern England

—Charles I forced to call a new Parliament (the "Long Parliament"); Root and Branch Petition presented to Parliament demands reforms of the church; Archbishop Laud imprisoned by order of Parliament

—Portsmouth and Newport colonists reunite under Coddington's leadership

1641—New Haven begins to accept jurisdiction over other towns, adopts Frame of Government for New Haven Colony

—Massachusetts adopts the *Body of Liberties*, a law code drawn up by Nathaniel Ward

—*Bay Psalm Book* published, composed by Richard Mather, John Eliot, and

Thomas Welde

—Massachusetts assumes jurisdiction over Strawberry Bank and Dover settlements

—Parliament debates the Root and Branch Petition; passes Triennial Act, guaranteeing frequent Parliaments; abolishes Court of High Commission; and presents Grand Remonstrance, a list of its grievances, to the king

1642—Charles I raises his standard against Parliament; the English Civil Wars begin; battle of Edgehill

1643—Parliament agrees to the Solemn League and Covenant, an alliance with the Scots against the king and for a reform of the English church; Parliament establishes the Westminster Assembly of Divines to make recommendations to Parliament for religious reform; John Cotton, John Davenport, and Thomas Hooker decline invitations; New Englander John Phillip is among the members of the Assembly

—Samuel Gorton founds Warwick (Rhode Island)

—Exeter accepts Massachusetts' jursidiction

—Massachusetts, Connecticut, New Haven, and Plymouth form the New England Confederation (United Colonies of New England) for mutual defense

1644—Split between Presbyterians and Congregationalists appears in the Westminster Assembly; Congregtionalist minority publishes *An Apologetical Narration*

—Roger Williams' *The Bloody Tenent of Persecution* and John Cotton's *The Keys of the Kingdom of Heaven* are published

—Roger Williams obtains a Parliamentary charter for Rhode Island

—Parliament replaces *Book of Common Prayer* with Presbyterian oriented *Directory of Worship*

—Massachusetts General Court formally divides into two separately seated houses with the Court of Assistants holding veto power over lower house actions

1645—Archbishop Laud executed; Parliament passes ordinances for the establishment of Presbyterianism

—Parliament organizes the New Model Army, which wins a decisive victory at Naseby

1646—Charles I surrenders; end of the first phase of the Civil Wars

—First appearance of the Leveller writings advocating broader based government in England

—George Fox begins his ministry; start of the Quaker movement

—Robert Child and others petition the Massachusetts General Court for a broadening of church membership and of the franchise, threatening to appeal to Parliament if their demands are not met; petition is rejected and leading remonstrants jailed

—First session of Cambridge Assembly in New England to define the colonial church order and faith

1647—Nathaniel Ward's *The Simple Cobbler of Agawam* and John Cotton's *The Bloody Tenent Washed* published

—Key Leveller writings—*Heads of Proposals, The Case of the Army*, and *The Agreement of the People*—published

1648—Charles I escapes confinement and wins support of Scots, who are angered by Parliament's failure to establish Presbyterian church order in England; the second Civil War begins; Charles I and his Scottish allies defeated by the New Model Army

—Pride's Purge drives many of the remaining Presbyterians from Parliament, leaving an Independent coalition of Congregationalists, sectaries, and Erastians in control

—Thomas Hooker's *The Survey of the Summe of Church Discipline* published

—Massachusetts adopts a detailed law code, the *Body of Laws and Liberties*

—*Cambridge Platform* promulgated, defining the New England Way; the platform endorses the Westminster Assembly's Confession of Faith and outlines a Congregational form of church order

1649—Charles I tried and executed by Parliament; Commonwealth of England proclaimed with the government of the realm by Parliament and a Council of State

—John Winthrop dies

—Organization in England of the Society for the Propagation of the Gospel in New England for the advancement of missionary activities among the Indians

1650—Oliver Cromwell promoted to lord general with the resignation of Thomas Fairfax, commander of the New Model Army

—Anne Bradstreet's *The Tenth Muse Lately Sprung Up in America* published

1651—Massachusetts authorities fine and banish three Baptists found in the colony

—John Eliot founds village for Indian converts at Natick, Massachusetts

1653—Cromwell dissolves the Rump of the Long Parliament; establishes the Protectorate with himself as lord protector of England

1654—Cromwell sends military expedition against Jamaica

—Edward Johnson's *Wonder Working Providence* published

—Harvard president Henry Dunster espouses Baptist principles and resigns

1656—First Quakers arrive in Massachusetts; they are arrested and banished

1657—Ministerial assembly with representatives from Massachusetts and Connecticut meets to discuss the question of membership in the churches, recommends what will be known as the Half-Way Covenant

1658—Savoy Conference, gathering of Congregational clergy in England, adopts *Savoy Declaration of Faith and Order*, designed to be the basis of a Congregational establishment

—Death of Oliver Cromwell; Richard Cromwell becomes lord protector, recalls Long Parliament, resigns; struggle for supremacy between Parliament and the generals

—Massachusetts enacts the death penalty for Quakers who return to the colony after banishment

1659—John Eliot's *The Christian Commonwealth* published

—William Robinson and Marmaduke Stevenson hung in Boston under the terms of the 1658 law against Quakers

1660—Convention Parliament invites Charles Stuart (son of Charles I) to assume the throne; restoration of the monarchy with coronation of Charles II; execution of regicides (including New England's Hugh Peter); migration of some English Puritan leaders, especially former colonists, to New England

—Mary Dyer, Quaker and former Antinomian, hung in Boston

1661—Executions of Quakers in Massachusetts halted by order of Charles II

—Massachusetts General Court censures John Eliot for the antimonarchical principles in his *Christian Commonwealth*

—Edward Taylor accepts ministerial post in Westfield, Connecticut

1662—Cavalier Parliament passes Act of Uniformity, issues new Prayer Book in the reestablishment of Anglicanism and imposition of civil disabilities on dissenters

—Michael Wigglesworth's *Day of Doom* published

—John Winthrop, Jr., obtains a royal charter for Connecticut which absorbs New Haven into the jurisdiction of Connecticut

—Synod of 1662 endorses Half-Way Covenant

1663—Rhode Island receives royal charter

1664—Charles II dispatches royal commission to settle boundary disputes and investigate charges against New England governments

1675—Wampanoags under Metacomet (King Philip) attack Swansea, initiating King Philip's War in New England

1676—Losses from Indian attacks continue to be heavy, but Metacomet is killed and the war ends in most of New England; resistance continues in northern New England until 1678

—Great fire destroys much of Boston

—Edward Randolph arrives in Boston as special agent of the crown to report on enforcement of navigation acts; he exploits divisions in the colony to build a faction favorable to the crown

1677—Massachusetts buys out the Gorges heirs and incorporates Maine into its jurisdiction

1678—John Bunyan's *Pilgrim's Progress* published

1679—Reforming Synod in New England adopts Savoy Declaration and urges a thorough reformation of morals in the colonies

1680—New Hampshire separated from Massachusetts and made a royal colony

1681—Persecution of dissenters in England intensified

—Massachusetts General Court gives permission to Boston Baptists to worship in their own meetinghouse

1684—Complaints against Massachusetts from Edward Randolph and others leads to abrogation of the Massachusetts Charter

1685—Joseph Dudley appointed acting governor of Massachusetts, New Hampshire, and Maine

—Charles II dies, succeeded by James II

1686—Sir Edmund Andros appointed governor of the Dominion of New England (Massachusetts, Maine, New Hampshire, Plymouth, and Rhode Island); Dominion eliminates popular base of former governments

1687—Connecticut incorporated into Dominion of New England (New York and New Jersey added to Dominion in 1688); Andros antagonizes colonists by arbitrary rule, challenges to property titles, support of the Church of England, and tax policies; Rev. John Wise imprisoned for opposition to new taxes

 —Solomon Stoddard's *The Safety of Appearing at the Day of Judgement in the Righteousness of Christ* advocates "open communion"

1688—Increase Mather eludes Andros's agents and sails for England to present the colonists' grievances against the Dominion government

 —William of Orange invades England and James II flees abroad in England's Glorious Revolution

1689—Rebellion in Boston topples the Dominion government; Andros imprisoned

 —William and Mary crowned England's monarchs

 —Parliament passes Declaration of Rights insuring greater degree of religious freedom

 —New England expedition under William Phipps captures the French fortress at Port Royal

1690—Connecticut charter restored; Increase Mather lobbies for restoration of Massachusetts charter

 —Association of Boston area clergy formed at Cambridge

1691—William and Mary grant Massachusetts a new charter that restores the popular basis of the General Court but provides for an appointed royal governor; the new charter incorporates Plymouth into Massachusetts; Increase Mather secures the appointment of William Phipps as royal governor

 —Increase Mather aids in securing a temporary alliance of English Congregationalists and Presbyterians signified by the signing of the Heads of Agreement

1692—Witchcraft at Salem

1693—Rhode Island charter restored

 —Cotton Mather's *Wonders of the Invisible World* published

1699—Publication of the Brattle Street Manifesto marks appearance of a new liberal faction in New England Puritanism led by William and Thomas Brattle, John Leverett, and the Rev. Benjamin Coleman of the Brattle Street Church

1700—Solomon Stoddard's *Doctrine of the Instituted Churches* marks another attack on orthodoxy

 —Liberals at Harvard force Increase Mather out of the Harvard presidency

1701—Establishment of Yale by orthodox Connecticut clergy led by Rev. James Pierpont

1702—Cotton Mather's *Magnalia Christi Americana* published

1708—Synod of Connecticut clergy at Saybrook adopt Saybrook Platform, providing for the establishment of clerical consociations to overlook local congregations

1710—Cotton Mather's *Bonifacius: An Essay on the Good* published

1712—John Wise's *Vindication of the Governmnnt of the New England Churches* attacks plans to centralize Massachusetts church government through associations

1721—Smallpox epidemic in Boston; Cotton Mather and Dr. Zabdiel Boylston advocate innoculation and are opposed by most Boston doctors and by the *New England Courant*, edited by James and Benjamin Franklin

1722—Rector Timothy Cutler and six other Connecticut clergy, including Yale tutor Samuel Johnson, proclaim their conversion to Anglicanism at the Yale commencement

1727—Hollis chair in mathematics and natural philosophy established at Harvard

1729—Solomon Stoddard dies, succeeded as Northampton pastor by Jonathan Edwards

1734—Jonathan Edwards stimulates a religious revival at Northampton; the beginning of the Great Awakening in New England

1740—George Whitefield, the most successful of the itinerant revivalists of the Awakening, visits New England and fans the fires of revivalism throughout the region

    —Gilbert Tenent, New Jersey revivalist, follows Whitefield through New England and preaches against "unconverted Teachers"

1742—James Davenport, one of the most extreme itinerants, expelled from Connecticut

1743—Jonathan Edwards's *Some Thoughts Concerning the Recent Revival of Religion* published; Charles Chauncey voices opposition to the revivals in *Seasonable Thoughts on the State of Religion in New England*

1745—George Whitefield visits New England again; region sharply divided over revivals and many churches split over the issues

1750—Jonathan Edwards is dismissed by his Northampton congregation

1754—Jonathan Edwards's *Freedom of the Will* published

1758—Jonathan Edwards's *Original Sin* published; Edwards dies

CONTRIBUTORS

SACVAN BERCOVITCH (BA, Sir George Williams; PhD, Claremont) is in the Department of English and Comparative Literature at Columbia University. He has written widely on the Puritan imagination and its influence on American thought and writing.

TIMOTHY H. BREEN (BA and PhD, Yale) specializes in early American history at Northwestern University. He is the author of *The Character of the Good Ruler: Puritan Political Ideas in New England, 1630-1730* (New Haven, 1970) and numerous articles on seventeenth-century America.

FRANCIS J. BREMER (BA, Fordham; PhD, Columbia) teaches in the history department at Thomas More College. He recently wrote *The Puritan Experiment: New England Society from Bradford to Edwards* (New York, 1976).

B. KATHERINE BROWN (BA, University of Washington; MA, Michigan State) has written several articles on seventeenth-century Massachusetts and, in collaboration with Robert E. Brown, a book on eighteenth-century Virginia.

RICHARD D. BUSHMAN (BA and PhD, Harvard) teaches early American history at Boston University. His publications include *From Puritan to Yankee: Character and the Social Order in Connecticut 1690-1765* (Cambridge, Mass., 1967).

RONALD D. COHEN (BA, University of California; PhD, University of Minnesota) is in the history department at Indiana University, Northwest. His research interests are in Puritan foreign affairs and American education.

JOHN P. DEMOS (BA, Harvard; MA, University of California, Berkeley) teaches early American history at Brandeis University. His writings, including a book and several articles on New England, draw extensively on psychology and other social sciences.

STEPHEN FOSTER (BA, University of Pennsylvania; PhD, Yale) is in the history department at Northern Illinois University. He is the author of *Their Solitary Way: The Puritan Social Ethic in the First Century of Settlement in New England* (New Haven, 1971).

KENNETH A. LOCKRIDGE (BA, Yale; PhD, Princeton) teaches at the University of Michigan, where he specializes in American social history. His latest book is *Literacy in Colonial New England: An Enquiry into the Social Context of Literacy in the Early Modern West* (New York, 1974).

PAUL R. LUCAS (BA, Simpson College; PhD, University of Minnesota) is in the history department at Indiana University, Bloomington. He is the author of *Valley of Discord: Church and Society along the Connecticut River, 1636-1725* (Hanover, N.H., 1976).

JAMES F. MACLEAR (BA and PhD, University of Chicago) specializes in American church history at the University of Minnesota, Duluth. He has written several articles on the evolution of New England Puritanism.

PERRY G. E. MILLER (BA, Chicago; PhD, Harvard) had a distinguished career as a teacher of literature at Harvard and as a scholar of unusual breadth and insight. His writings reshaped the study of American Puritanism.

ROBERT H. MOORE (BA, Davidson; PhD, University of Wisconsin) is in the Department of English at the University of Maryland, where he specializes in the writings of William Faulkner. Moore is also coauthor of *School for Soldiers: West Point and the Profession of Arms* (1974).